KU-710-522

The Women's Movements
in the
United States and Britain
from the 1790s to the 1920s

WITHDRAWN FROM
THE LIBRARY
UNIVERSITY OF
WINCHESTER

KA 0153579 X

The Women's Movements in the United States and Britain from the 1790s to the 1920s

~

Christine Bolt

Professor of American History
University of Kent at Canterbury

HARVESTER
WHEATSHEAF

New York   London   Toronto   Sydney   Tokyo   Singapore

First published 1993 by
Harvester Wheatsheaf
Campus 400, Maylands Avenue
Hemel Hempstead
Hertfordshire, HP2 7EZ
A division of
Simon & Schuster International Group

© 1993 Christine Bolt

All rights reserved. No part of this publication may be
reproduced, stored in a retrieval system, or transmitted,
in any form, or by any means, electronic, mechanical,
photocopying, recording or otherwise, without the prior
permission, in writing, from the publisher.

Typeset in 10/12pt Ehrhardt
by Columns Design & Production Services Ltd., Reading, UK

Printed and bound in Great Britain by
T. J. Press (Padstow) Ltd

British Library Cataloguing in Publication Data

A catalogue record for this book is available from
the British Library

ISBN 0–7108–0780–5 (hbk)
ISBN 0–7108–0785–6 (pbk)

---

1   2   3   4   5   97   96   95   94   93

KING ALFRED'S COLLEGE
WINCHESTER

305.
42
BOL
0153574

To
IAN,
a feminist ally for over thirty years

Contents

Abbreviations

AAS	American Antiquarian Society	NBWTA	National British Women's Temperance Association
AAUW	American Association of University Women	NESWS	North of England Society for Women's Suffrage
AAW	Association for the Advancement of Women	NEWC	New England Women's Club
ACA	Association of Collegiate Alumnae	NFWW	National Federation of Women Workers
AFL	American Federation of Labor	NSWS	National Society for Women's Suffrage
AMSH	Association for Moral and Social Hygiene	NUSEC	National Union of Societies for Equal Citizenship
ASPL	American School Peace League	NUWSS	National Union of Women's Suffrage Societies
AWSA	American Woman Suffrage Association		
BFASS	British and Foreign Anti-Slavery Society	NUWW	National Union of Women Workers
		NWP	National Woman's Party
BWTA	British Women's Temperance Association	NWSA	National Woman Suffrage Association
		SCBC	Society for Constructive Birth Control and Racial Progress
CD Acts	Contagious Disease Acts		
CCW	Conference on the Cause and Cure of War	SL	Schlesinger Library
		SLP	Socialist Labor Party
CNS	Central National Society for Women's Suffrage	SPEW	Society for Promoting the Employment of Women
DAR	Daughters of the American Revolution	SSC	Sophia Smith Collection
ERA	Equal Rights Amendment	TUC	Trades Union Congress
FL	Fawcett Library	WCG	Women's Co-operative Guild
HWS	History of Woman Suffrage	WCTU	Woman's Christian Temperance Union
ICW	International Council of Women	WEIU	Women's Educational and Industrial Union
ILGWU	International Ladies' Garment Workers' Union		
		WEU	Women's Education Union
ILP	Independent Labour Party	WLF	Women's Liberal Federation
IWA	Illinois Women's Alliance	WLGS	Women's Local Government Society
IWSA	International Woman Suffrage Alliance	WLL	Women's Labour League
IWW	Industrial Workers of the World	WPPL	Women's Protective and Provident League
LNA	Ladies' National Association for the Repeal of the Contagious Diseases Acts		
		WPU	Women's Political Union
LWV	League of Women Voters	WSPU	Women's Social and Political Union
NACW	National Association of Colored Women	WTUL	Women's Trade Union League
NAPSS	National Association for the Promotion of Social Science		
		WWCTU	World's Woman's Christian Temperance Union
NAWSA	National American Woman Suffrage Association	YWCA	Young Women's Christian Association

Acknowledgements

It is a pleasure to acknowledge the assistance I have received from many people in the course of this project. I should like to express my sincere appreciation of a generous grant from the Leverhulme Trust, which enabled me to undertake research at a number of libraries in the United States and Britain. My grateful thanks to the many people who have advised me, and granted permissions, at: the Arthur and Elizabeth Schlesinger Library on the History of Women in America, Radcliffe College, Cambridge, MA, especially Patricia King; the Sophia Smith Collection, Smith College, Northampton, MA, especially Margery Sly; the American Antiquarian Society, Worcester, MA, especially Thomas Knowles; the Lamont and Widener Libraries at Harvard University, Cambridge, MA; the Henry E. Huntington Library, San Marino, CA; the British Library; the University of London Library; and the Fawcett Library, London Guildhall University, especially David Doughan. I have benefited from the unfailing helpfulness of the staff of the Templeman Library at the University of Kent, notably Brian Hogben, Stephen Holland, Olive Lindstrand and Margaret Smyth. In the busy Eliot Secretarial Office, the manuscript has been deciphered, typed and retyped with efficiency, cheerfulness and interest by the Secretarial Supervisor, Yvonne Latham, Nicola Cooper, Joan Hill and Suzanne Sherwood. I am particularly indebted to Yvonne, for her hard work and encouragement. My thanks, also, to Jean Gil, of Eliot, and to Di Mayes, of DIMA Consolidates, for their meticulous labours on the endnotes. I have learned much from the diverse and questioning students at Kent who have taken my course on the women's movements in Britain and the United States; and I hope that my students, and others, will find this book useful. My close colleagues at Kent – David Turley, Julian Hurstfield and George Conyne – have made it possible for me to have study leave in which to write, and they understand how much this is valued. The three readers of the typescript for Harvester raised many important points, from which I have greatly profited, and I am extremely grateful to Joyce Berkman for her thorough and constructive reading for the co-publishers, the University of Massachusetts Press. I am indebted to my editor at Harvester Wheatsheaf, Jackie

Jones, for her excellent advice and forbearance, and to the helpful production editor, Alison Stanford. My husband, Ian, knows how much I owe to him.

Grateful acknowledgement is made of permission to cite and quote from the following manuscript collections at the Sophia Smith Collection: to Eleanor Mensel, with regard to the Eastman Papers; David Garrison, with regard to the Garrison Family Papers; James Parton, with regard to the Parton Papers; and Alexander Sanger, with regard to the Sanger Papers. Every effort has been made to trace copyright holders, but, if any have been inadvertently overlooked, the publisher will be pleased to make the necessary arrangement at the first opportunity.

C.B.

Introduction

I have set out to write a history of the British and American women's movements in the nineteenth and early twentieth centuries. My account begins, however, with a brief introduction to the movements' eighteenth-century antecedents, acknowledging that just as women's subordination predated the nineteenth century, so too did challenges to that inferior status. Indeed, historians have recently been active in filling some of the many gaps in our knowledge of American and British women in the eighteenth century;[1] and they have been doing the same for the years between the winning of the vote and the upsurge of feminism during the 1960s.[2] Particular attention has none the less been given to the period of feminism with which I am concerned, and there are a number of reasons for this.

The nineteenth century saw, for the first time, the emergence of organised women's movements which, by the 1920s, had immeasurably strengthened the bonds between women, enlarged their opportunities, and forced the issue of their rights and wrongs into the public arena in a sustained fashion. It witnessed, in addition, developments whose significance for women has been debated – though not disputed – ever since: the growth of urbanisation, industrialisation, a market economy, a powerful class system, and a peculiarly strong emphasis, associated with the middle class, upon separate spheres for the sexes. Industrialising later than its mother country, lacking an aristocracy and frequently uneasy with the overt acceptance of class divisions, the United States offered its female activists a more encouraging ideological climate in which to operate for the first half of the nineteenth century. But women on both sides of the Atlantic were affected by the developments just outlined – most notably, so far as the feminist movement is concerned, by the separate spheres doctrine. Taking account of the era's novel separation of home and production, of private and public life, this doctrine sought to confine women while simultaneously glorifying them and buttressing the family in an era of individualism. In the process, it unintentionally gave feminists a concept they could reconstruct for their own use when they sought a fairer social order.

1

~

The first phase of organised feminism has also attracted attention because it has been deemed to have petered out in the 1920s, its agenda either misconceived or only partially achieved, thus necessitating further battles in the later twentieth century.[3] As a historian, it has been my aim to avoid judging the first feminists by the priorities of a different age. Yet equally, as a feminist, I have been anxious to incorporate the insights of the modern women's movement, and the findings of feminist theory and history, which have expanded markedly since the 1970s. At the theoretical level I have been especially persuaded by two lines of reasoning. The first is sparked by the writings of women anthropologists concerned with tackling the proposition that female oppression is universal. Notable among the universalists are Michelle Zimbalist Rosaldo and Sherry B. Ortner, who have explained women's invariably inferior status with reference to the distinction societies make between the domestic and the public; to the association of the domestic sphere with natural forces, materialistic and particularistic interests, whereas the public domain has been associated with the conquest of the wild, culture and larger social issues. Their argument has taken account of Nancy Chodorow's work on women's mothering role, from which male children, unlike girls, must break away, thereby acquiring more abstract and less personal concerns.[4] Conversely, other anthropologists have emphasised cross-cultural diversity where sexual difference is concerned. And after summarising the entire debate, Linda Nicholson has made a powerful case against seeking a single, cross-cultural explanation for the devaluation of women. Without denying the importance of the domestic–public sphere dichotomy, she persuasively stresses the complex and historically constructed nature of female experience, and maintains that 'feminist theory, to fulfill its potential for radical challenge, must adopt an explicitly historical approach'.[5] In examining the struggles of the British and American women's movements against a historically persistent subordination, I have attempted to bring out their complexities and uniqueness, and thus to contribute to the historical understanding which must infuse all effective social movements.

The second emphasis which I have found particularly helpful is the introduction into women's history of the concept of gender: that is, the social and cultural implications of women's and men's sexuality. One great merit of this concept is that it has offered a social construction of differences that are sometimes seen as immutable because they are rooted in biology.[6] In doing so, it has resembled historians' attempts to show how cultural attributes have been accorded to races and then, like those of women, damagingly generalised about and presented as innate.[7] Gender history has also helped us to encompass the variety of influences on women's lives. It has encouraged us to study women both in relation to their own values and institutions, and in the context of their larger social settings and the key categories through which history has been analysed.[8] And here the work of gender historians parallels that of cultural historians who have sought to historicise the term 'class' and make it more elastic.[9] As late-twentieth-century feminists have endeavoured to confront the differences between women without losing sight of sisterhood,[10] so they have striven to write history which employs a theory of gender and of class, and questions 'natural essences' and traditional distinctions, most importantly between what is private and what is political.[11]

My interest in the Anglo–American connection in reform dates back over thirty years, and I have been teaching a course on the women's movements in the United States and Britain since the early 1980s. But the decision to compare feminism in these two countries stems from a belief that the value of the comparative method is, as Black points out, 'greatly enhanced if the entities compared have enough in common to make the differences significant'.[12] Accordingly, it should be emphasised at the outset that the British and American women's movements had much in common. Although organised feminism developed a little earlier in America than it did across the Atlantic, in each country it was rooted in basically similar and encouraging social conditions. These included a shared heritage of Enlightenment ideas, expanding political rights and political toleration, an economy shifting to industrialisation and urbanisation, an influential middle class and a predominantly Protestant culture.[13] The two movements, over time, pursued roughly the same objectives,[14] which were neither exclusively bourgeois nor always dominated by the vote,[15] and their leaders experienced the same false dawns at the end of the eighteenth century, in the 1860s[16] and in the 1920s. British and American feminists were primarily – though by no means exclusively – middle-class, and were strengthened by their religious activism and feelings of sisterhood as well as by their links with other reform endeavours.[17] In both countries, they grappled with the combined straitjacket and opportunity which Aileen Kraditor has called the cult of domesticity,[18] and found it impossible to transcend their intellectual differences to produce an ideology which was powerfully persuasive to the mass of women.[19]

What is more, I have discovered many instances of a conviction among British and American feminists that they were ahead of activists elsewhere in the world, and that their respective countries held out the best hope of a changed position for women. Fortified by their consciousness of responsibility to an international movement, feminists on each side of the Atlantic were willing to make common cause over issues of mutual interest, notably educational provision, labour rights, peace and suffragism. Yet it is my contention that the undeniably close Anglo–American connection in reform has served to obscure the real sense of distinctiveness that British and American feminists felt, even when they were pursuing a variety of shared concerns. It has also overshadowed their determination not to interfere in the internal affairs of other countries, however closely allied. While I have no desire to use the comparative method simply to confirm American exceptionalism,[20] I feel that it is necessary to stress that American feminists took heart from what they perceived to be the superiority of their social circumstances, and the greater boldness and strength of their movement. This confidence is scarcely surprising. In his interesting study of women in Stuart England and America, Roger Thompson has suggested that the Americans' advantages were a sex ratio favourable to women, superior economic possibilities, the position of women in the Puritan churches and the opportunities available to them on the frontier.[21] Although his findings have not gone unchallenged, and the fate of initial freedoms by the eighteenth century is a complicated question,[22] it was a commonplace among foreign commentators during our period that women in the United States enjoyed unique liberty before marriage, immense respect by their husbands thereafter as wives and mothers, and a happy escape from discrimination on account of class.[23]

British feminists, for their part, were willing to concede that their cause was complicated by class considerations far more than was the case across the Atlantic. This did not mean, however, that the chief difference between feminism in the United States and in Britain was the subordination or inferiority complex of the British crusaders. They were not, I believe, slower to undertake associational activities than their American equivalents:[24] their reformist objectives were simply different, because of their particular national cir- cumstances (just as their style as reformers was different, reflecting British class and educational peculiarities). Hence, if American feminists found a particularly important role to play in anti-slavery, temperance, club and social settlement work, the British established a comparable significance in utopian socialism, the Anti-Corn Law League, promoting female employment, social scientific enquiry, and a host of social purity campaigns.

Nor is it fair to say that Britain, being a more conservative country than the United States, predictably produced a more conservative women's movement.[25] American feminists may have been encouraged by the early enlargement of female educational opportunities in the United States and by their Revolutionary tradition, but the British produced the most influential feminist ideologues of the movements' formative stages. Furthermore, as Frank Thistlethwaite has pointed out,[26] the Anglo–American link was strained and changed in the second half of the nineteenth century when the economic ties between Britain and the United States altered, America acquired many of the problems associated with the Industrial Revolution, and British radicals ceased to regard it as being in the vanguard of social improvement. As a result, American feminists – like other American reformers[27] – looked to Britain for inspiration in such areas as labour organisation, vocational education, industrial legislation and the resolution of urban problems. In addition, though the United States initially produced more sex radicals than Britain,[28] the balance between the two countries had evened up somewhat by the early twentieth century, while the British feminists had become more politically radical than the Americans: more willing to abandon bipartisanship,[29] more tactically inventive and, above all, readier to resort to militant action.

So far as class and political considerations are concerned, advantages and disadvantages were, in fact, rather evenly balanced between the two countries. In the United States, if the Revolutionary legacy was a spur to reformers, agitators were less constrained by rigid party loyalties and the federal political system permitted experiment without dire risk, these factors might equally produce complacency, lack of firm commitment to political programmes and indifference to reform at the national level. The more centralised British political system did undoubtedly limit the options of pressure groups, yet it was also sometimes easier to convert Parliament than to convince the American Congress. Indeed, British opponents of political feminism liked to point out that Parliament had frequently granted the demands of women in the nineteenth century,[30] and Britain's paternalistic governments might seem more helpful to outside protesters than American administrations adamantly committed to the *laissez-faire* doctrines which they had – ironically – imported from across the Atlantic.

Similarly, while American feminists congratulated themselves on their comparative freedom from class restrictions, they were obliged to concede that rich society women in Britain were more likely to be involved in feminism – and public issues generally – than were their American counterparts. Notwithstanding, for example, the radical circle which gathered at the Plymouth home of author Mercy Otis Warren during the Revolution, the influential female salon did not easily transplant to the New World. And though Americans could see that British anti-feminism was especially strongly sustained by privileged individuals of a conservative temperament, who were deeply outraged by the alleged unwomanliness of militant suffragism, they had to acknowledge that in their own country conservative interests were better organised against the cause and quick to publicise British militancy as the unacceptable face of feminism.

Finally, for all the regional variety of Britain, further complicated by class, there were no problems for British feminists to tackle comparable to those posed for Americans by southern slavery and its aftermath, and by the massive numbers of immigrants concentrated in the cities. Southern whites offered resistance to most modernising, non-southern causes, and feminism was no exception. More damningly – since some white southern women were eventually converted – black women remained largely untouched by middle-class feminism, while those who did become involved experienced real difficulties both in relating many of its priorities to their needs and in building up their own variant of the movement. For immigrant women, too, feminism often seemed to be either an irrelevance or a force which was unduly dominated by comfortably off, middle-class elites.

As I see it, then, the story of the British and American women's movements is one of national distinctiveness within an international cause. I have employed the terms feminism and women's movement interchangeably, although feminism was not a word in common usage in either Britain or the United States before the twentieth century, and Victorians spoke variously of the condition and rights of women, the 'woman question' and the woman's rights movement.[31] In using 'feminism' in this anachronistic way, I do not at all deny the distinctiveness of the early-twentieth-century period of women's activism, when the word was actually used; and I have acknowledged that eighteenth-century and nineteenth-century feminism are separate entities which must be understood in the context of their own times. I believe, however, that there is enough common ground between the three periods to justify my practice.

Modern definitions of feminism abound and conflict, while women's rights have sometimes been narrowly interpreted as relating only to the public sphere.[32] Yet though it is true that some nineteenth-century activists were especially anxious to enter the male-dominated public sphere and made political objectives their chief concern, there were many types of feminist from the late eighteenth century to the early twentieth. In trying to do justice to their diversity, I have defined the women's movement and feminism alike as the endeavours of women, together with their male allies, to analyse the nature and implications of womanhood, and to secure a better appreciation of women's wrongs, demands and attainments. They sought both personal autonomy and a collective consciousness. They wanted the right of self-definition, an end to male supremacy, and the creation of a world in which the public and private interacted. And whereas equality between the sexes was a key objective, for feminists who accepted that men and women had contrasting roles to play in society this might mean simply equality of esteem; while there were many activists who emphasised the distinctiveness, and even moral superiority, of their sex.

On the practical level, feminists worked to enlarge their educational, economic, legal and political rights, as well as participating in the other reform movements of the day. Of course the word movement can suggest a 'steady, coherent and consistent continuum of events' from the eighteenth century,[33] whereas the feminist endeavours traced here were seldom tightly co-ordinated and proceeded at an uneven pace. The movements' activists defy neat classification as moderates or radicals, and might embrace one feminist issue while rejecting another;[34] might liaise happily with men or prefer to rely on their own networks. None the less their efforts, considered together, add up to a social movement as modern commentators define it: a crusade aiming at fundamental change in the social order through the articulation of shared beliefs and the taking of action, with or without the aid of organisational backing.[35] Modern women's history largely began as movement history and, as Louise Tilly reminds us, it still retains this orientation, even if there is now a shift away from the initial preoccupation with 'individuals, and unique events' towards concern with 'variation among different groups of women'.[36]

In order to convey a sense of the different pace at which feminism unfolded in the United States and Britain, and to put it in its historical context over time, I have charted the emergence, ideas and campaigns of the women's movements through a series of chronological chapters, each of which is divided into themes. The time periods covered in the various chapters are dictated by the logic of the movements rather than conventional periodisation.[37] The first two chapters consider the position of women in a traditional world, the forces for change and those which shaped the women's movements. Subsequent chapters trace the movements' rise from the 1840s to the 1860s; their consolidation and diversification in the often-neglected 1870s and 1880s; their maturing from the 1890s to 1914; and the challenges of the war and postwar years. Recurring themes in these chapters are politics; work; marriage, sex and morality; protest and reform; ideology and anti-feminism; and women's organisations. The Afterword returns to a general comparison of the movements, and to some of the broader issues raised in the Introduction.

The last such issue to be broached here is the historiographical tradition out of which this work has grown, and to whose architects so many debts are owed. First in the field were the early feminists themselves. Women of their period were exhorted to read history as an improving antidote to novel reading.[38] They managed to write it, too,[39] and made some inroads into the professional societies of the new discipline,[40] despite the general opposition to advanced education for women and their admission to the professions. But their personal struggles to gain acceptance were greatly aggravated by the common assumption that women, living private, repetitive and uneventful lives, had either no history or none worthy of consideration.

The American historian Henry Adams, who – unusually – felt that men should study women of the past, agreed with Jane Austen's Catherine Morland that 'few women have ever been known' to its chroniclers.[41] Hoping to change this state of affairs, feminists of various persuasions played a key role in the development of women's history, and the tract on women's rights by the important eighteenth-century feminist Mary Wollstonecraft begins, appropriately: 'After considering the historic page'. Whatever their disagreements with each other, activists were united by sensitivity to the past circumstances of women and anxiety to have a personal impact on the course of history.[42] And while some pioneer female historians wrote political history featuring few women, or were insecure about their intrusion into a male field,[43] active feminists were defensive but not apologetic. For them, woman was an agent in the past as well as the present, not a passive given or an inevitable victim.

Since the American movement emerged shortly before the British, while Americans in the New England heartland of feminism were especially active in writing history which celebrated the evolution of an allegedly unique national culture,[44] it is not surprising, perhaps, that American feminists initially led the British in the production of feminist histories. Lydia Maria Child, Sarah Hale and Caroline Dall paid special attention to notable women, with Hale, who accepted the doctrine of separate spheres, claiming a moral superiority for her sex and a God- (not man-) given right to assert it that would ultimately be used to good effect by the women's movement.[45] The best-known publication, however, is the six-volume *History of Woman Suffrage* (1881–1922). The first three volumes, which were produced between 1881 and 1886 by the activists Elizabeth Cady Stanton, Susan B. Anthony and Matilda Joslyn Gage, justified 'history written from a subjective point of view',[46] as well as reflecting its compilers' desire to systematise the documents of the movement and hand down to later generations the achievements of American women. It was not an easy venture, because opinions differed about whether the project should be undertaken by one branch of suffragism on behalf of all, before the vote was won. Source material was vast but incomplete, and Miss Anthony discovered that she would ' "rather *make* history than write it" '.[47] Fortunately, Mrs Stanton's drive secured the completion of half the enterprise, which was then carried on by Miss Anthony and a professional writer, Ida Husted Harper, while Stanton prepared her own papers for posterity and published reminiscences which illuminated the feminist cause.[48]

Other American activists did the same. And if they were inevitably open to the charges of exaggeration and self-justification, their memoirs give invaluable insights into the main aspects of the movement.[49] In Britain, the major campaigners have left us comparable accounts,[50] and among the books of suffrage leaders, the history by the moderate Mrs Millicent Garrett Fawcett reveals the feminists' determination to show how the position of women had been better in the past than it was in the Victorian era.[51] Victorian men, for obvious reasons, generally sought to prove that, notwithstanding female subordination in certain aspects of life, women were better off in the nineteenth century than they had ever been. In arguing that some English women 'exercised electoral rights' in 'early times', Mrs Fawcett's study offered a nice point for feminists to use against what she engagingly called 'the "what-I-know-not-is-not-knowledge" pedant'. She also demonstrated that interest in feminism as an international phenomenon which is a feature of the *History of Woman Suffrage*, and which one expects from British and American activists.[52] The history of the women's movement published in 1928 by Ray Strachey, a suffragist, speaker, author, editor and committee woman, remains an excellent reminder of the very varied aims of British feminism, no matter how much came to be written on the vote.[53]

When later historians of the British and American women's movements have added to the activists' accounts, their work has shown similarities and contrasts. Scholars in both countries have given high priority to the suffrage struggle:[54] after all, the vote was the feminist demand most difficult to secure, the campaign for it drew in all kinds of women, and they have left a rich archival and published record. Moreover, since feminists claimed that much would follow from enfranchisement, later commentators have been at pains to see whether their predictions came true. In both countries, too, particular attention has been devoted to the national political scene: after all, it was in the most prestigious field of national politics that opposition to feminine participation was greatest, and in Britain it was only through the national legislature that such participation could be granted.[55] Aware of the danger of the 'New Englandisation' of women's history, however, American historians have turned to studies of the western states, where the first suffrage victories were gained; and – though to a lesser extent – have looked at the South, where the suffragists found it hardest to make headway.[56] Similarly, conscious of the focus on metropolitan activity for the franchise, historians of Britain have recently examined efforts in the provinces and beyond.[57]

Following on from this interest in the vote, there has been a tendency in American writing to equate feminism with suffragism,[58] and to see the women's movement as becoming more conservative over time as women sought enfranchisement not as a right but as a means to do good, in a public sphere that was presented not as the antithesis but as the extension of the home.[59] In their search for political equality, feminists are presented as playing down family and sexual issues, the importance of which has been urged by twentieth-century activists.[60] Recent observers have, additionally, been critical of the concentration, by both the early feminists and historians who first tackled their story, on white women and exceptional women.[61] But while there are obvious pitfalls in the 'women worthies' tradition,[62] the value of biography and group biography cannot be disputed. Some individuals still await 'modern biographical treatment',[63] and it is necessary to study women apart from the family, where modern scholarship first tended to place them. Attention to individuals recognises, furthermore, that the women's movement was concerned with women's right to develop themselves as distinctive individuals: to escape from the group generalisations made about the female sex.

Accordingly, modern writers have continued to salute the prominent activist, even as they have looked at the efforts of groups of women to improve their legal rights and economic prospects;[64] at their involvement in community politics unrelated to suffragism;[65] at the ideas which have shaped their social situation;[66] and at their self-conscious desire to fashion a female culture and address issues of primary interest to women.[67] No more than the pioneer feminists themselves have they agreed about the impact of the domestic sphere concept; the wisdom of instrumental arguments for improving women's position; and the implications of engaging in reform activities which might attract women of all persuasions, but possibly dull the feminists' appetite for a radical reordering of society.[68]

Class issues have been particularly absorbing to historians of the British movement. Commenting on a more overtly class society, they have been aware that organised feminism did not grow out of attempts by activists to introduce the women's rights debate into existing, largely middle-class, reform endeavours. Rather, it drew on a tradition of utopian socialism and took off from feminists' attempts, complicated by class, to improve the economic prospects of their sex.[69] Because of this complication, accounts of British feminist campaigns related to women at work have tended to concentrate on either middle-class or working-class women, with the latter's uneasy relationship with the trade-union and labour movement attracting special attention. The degree to which bourgeois feminism and socialist feminism are separate entities has been a matter of debate and disagreement.[70]

Stimulated by a stronger feminist movement in the 1960s and the subsequent creation of a stronger women's studies discipline in academia, American scholars have been notable for the volume of their output on topics related to the women's movement,[71] leading the way on matters concerning health and sexuality, about which nineteenth-century American feminists were initially

bolder than women in Britain.[72] But British historians have devoted extensive
coverage to the feminists' educational activities, where nineteenth-century
American activists also took the initiative;[73] and they have been equally clear
about the importance of gender, notably as a complicating factor in class
relations.[74] They have increasingly seen feminists as being active on a wide range
of issues; and they have traced the course of women in reform and protest, like
their American counterparts, but without stressing a division in the women's
movement between reformers and feminists.[75] In view of the importance of
networks of influential women in British feminism, they have given appropriate
attention to these activists in group and individual biographies.[76] And in Britain,
as in America, studies of single and lesbian women in the movement have been
slow in coming. None the less, the growing interest in tracing the shift from the
Victorian women's movement to a transitional feminism with new priorities and –
by the 1920s – problems has given an extra emphasis to the issue of sexual
rights.[77]

While there are now several overviews of the women's movement in each
country, and studies which place British and American women activists in the
broader setting of women's history,[78] fewer comparative works have been
produced. The contours of the Anglo–American connection between 1790 and
1850 have been definitively outlined by Frank Thistlethwaite; Jane Rendall has
provided a sensitive thematic analysis of the origins of modern feminism in
Britain, France and the United States; and Richard Evans has illuminated the
context and traced the organisation of feminism in Europe, America and
Australasia. Ross Paulson's similarly wide-ranging account of Prohibition and
suffrage movements sheds light on the meaning of equality and the mechanisms
available for social control in different countries. And William O'Neill's
influential and pioneering work on the British and American movements has
been followed by Olive Banks's interpretation of feminism on both sides of the
Atlantic from the eighteenth century to the twentieth, bringing into strong focus
the intellectual traditions by which it has been shaped.[79]

Building on these earlier studies, and using both primary and secondary
sources, I have sought to provide a fuller examination than currently exists of the
women's movements in Britain and the United States up to the 1920s. I have
tried to remedy the present rather patchy coverage of my chosen period, and
have argued that the two countries produced complex, multicause and changing
movements, which did not neglect the private for the public and cannot be seen
as becoming more conservative over time. I have attempted to do justice to
feminist successes without ignoring their failures; to show the unintended
consequences of some of their efforts and the difficulty of judging those reform
campaigns that were favoured by non-feminists as well as feminists, the state as
well as individuals and pressure groups. While recognising the tensions inherent
in the movements' varied arguments and priorities, and the difficulties involved
in seeking sisterhood among diverse women, I have suggested that female
solidarity was sustained through personal, urban and organisational ties and the

celebration of female values. I have likewise maintained that cross-class alliances were attempted, notably in Britain, despite the difficulties involved. Throughout, I have aimed to bring the British movement out of the shadow of the American, and to point up the distinctive features of each.

Even in such a large undertaking as this, it has not been possible to cover everything, and I am conscious that I have accorded only limited coverage to literary feminism. Moreover, future works will, I believe, be able to give more attention than I have done to Scottish, Irish and Welsh women, and to women of colour in the United States. I consider that the community, benevolent and reform endeavours of American women of colour warrant a separate treatment, in recognition of the equal significance of race and gender for such women. My treatment of black activists has thus largely been designed to highlight the prejudices of white feminists. Finally, my determination to do justice to cross-class feminist ventures does not in any way deny that the white middle-class women who dominate this study were frequently able to forge interesting roles for themselves only by exploiting the labour of other women. Sisterhood did, indeed, have its limits.

1

~

The setting for the women's movements
From the eighteenth century to the 1820s

Perhaps the most important single fact to grasp about modern feminism is that its roots go much deeper than was once supposed. Feminist literature was published in both Britain and America long before the emergence of an organised feminist movement in the 1840s and 1850s. On the assumption that any social protest arises out of a mixture of resentment and sensed opportunity, it will be the purpose of this chapter to establish the historical and immediate context out of which literary feminism and female activism emerged in the late eighteenth century.

I. Women in a traditional world

(i) *The economy*

By the middle of the eighteenth century, on each side of the Atlantic, most women spent their days in a multitude of largely but not exclusively home-based economic activities, the burden of which was eased, for the prosperous few, by servants or slaves.[1] It has been argued that a number of benefits flowed to and from women as a result of this economic system. The differences between married and unmarried women were less marked than they would become in the nineteenth century, even if the situation of the unmarried was frequently unenviable, and in England they appear to have been more numerous than they would be in that century.[2] Female productive capacity was great and – excluding slaves – at the total disposal of the family, while men were more concerned with domestic affairs than they would be in the Victorian period.[3] In the American colonies – where capitalism and industrialisation developed more slowly than in the mother country, prosperity was initially more widespread, class divisions were less pronounced, involvement in the market economy was less common, and female labour was more prized as a scarce resource – feminist tracts did not proliferate as they did in Restoration England.[4] But on both sides of the Atlantic, it is maintained, women enjoyed an economic status which, though it was distinctive from and subordinate to that of men, did not rigidly separate the sexes or stress the undesirability of females working outside the home, when such work was essential to many poor women, especially widows.[5]

The most obvious danger in explaining the position of women primarily with reference to a particular type of economy is that one presents a misleadingly narrow, rather static picture of woman's lot, and may even be in danger of summoning up a mythic golden age of female freedom,[6] as did some nineteenth-century feminists anxious to encourage their friends and shame their foes (see above, p. 8). In fact, the material circumstances of British and American women alike were affected by changes or fluctuations over time in the economy and in the fortunes of individual families, besides being influenced by their geographical, urban or rural location, as one would expect. And in the area of the economy, at least, the colonies, as they matured and diversified, became more similar to the mother country. Hence, if there were no absolute British equivalents of the slave and frontier economies of the New World, in which poor white and black women found themselves working alongside men and facing exceptionally severe physical demands, by the eighteenth century women in Britain and America laboured hard in home manufacture and agriculture; Scottish and Welsh women, particularly, were assumed to be capable of performing 'equally with men'.[7] In both countries, moreover, the position of women was moulded by patriarchal attitudes, the law governing domestic relations, religion, education and politics, as well as by economics.

(ii) *Domesticity*

Patriarchal attitudes were perhaps the most important of these different factors, since they shaped all the others. In Britain, to instruct women how to behave in their supposedly natural sphere, a considerable literature had developed since the sixteenth century which itemised and celebrated a range of 'feminine' attributes: modesty, quietness, passivity, piety, generosity, chastity, domesticity, timidity, vanity and ignorance. And so that her generally superior moral character should work to the advantage of herself and others, while her weaknesses remained unexploited, it was argued that a woman should ideally be attached to a man, children and a home, providing there a refuge from the world's cares and a training ground for the young. The gender construct of domesticity – which we associate with the nineteenth century, and against which Victorian feminists rebelled – was proclaimed in a less urgently elaborated form by both sexes in eighteenth-century England.[8]

In the American colonies, a comparable situation prevailed. Thus, whereas neither men nor women felt it necessary to formulate a 'systematic defense' of the female sphere,[9] they were as ready as their British counterparts to identify the dimensions of femininity, and it is Norton's contention that the traits agreed on gave women a sense of inferiority to men.[10] The colonies' rather more relaxed approach to the 'woman question' may relate to the fact that they had not yet produced a notable feminist literature, whereas in Britain, in the middle years of the eighteenth century, a number of articles appeared arguing against women's alleged inferiority. Bringing to mind the late-seventeenth-century English defences of female capacities, these publications stressed the restrictions on women's education, the oppressive impact upon them of customary expectations, the rationality they shared with men and, contrarily, their moral superiority to men.[11]

The problem with the last point was that it might easily be turned into a defence of the status quo: many men, after all, were willing chivalrously to accept women's moral superiority as long as their virtues were safely exercised in the home. There was, furthermore, a risk that women who refuted men's ideas would be represented as being simply anti-men. Admittedly, suspicion of men was a feature of some feminist writing from the seventeenth century onwards, but the points made by Constance Rover with reference to Victorian feminists seem relevant to their precursors:[12] that they were not generally man-haters, and that no word was coined to express the feminine equivalent of misogyny because it was not needed. Why women should have been less vocal against men than vice versa has not really been explained. However, it seems probable that their moderation sprang from an awareness of their dependence on men to procure change in the public sphere and their more limited experience of acrimonious debate. Perhaps it is also proof of women's desire to exercise the moral strength which they claimed.

It might be supposed that another reason for the absence of feminist tracts in the colonies was the better treatment of women before the law. Unfortunately, the situation in England is clearer than it is in America. There is no dispute that female disabilities sprang from the British common-law doctrine of *coverture*, whereby the married woman's legal existence was absorbed within that of her husband so long as the marriage endured. *Femes coverts* could not control their property or wages, sue or be sued, draft wills, buy or sell property, or make contracts, and although there were some English boroughs which, since medieval times, had permitted wives to trade on their own account, these concessions slowly fell into disuse, while the practice of allowing women whose interests had been protected in pre-nuptial contracts to seek redress in the equity courts was available only to women of means.[13] There is disagreement about how far British legal precedent was modified in the New World.

On the one hand, according to Kerber, Thompson, Richard B. Morris and Mary Beard, the alteration was considerable, and they have paid particular attention to colonial willingness to ignore primogeniture and entail to the benefit of women; to respect for dower rights (widows' portions); to wives' right to be consulted before the sale of real estate that might affect dower provision; and to the greater frequency of ante-nuptial agreements to protect a woman's property rights.[14] According to Marilynn Salmon and Norton, on the other hand, coverture was not substantially amended in practice, since most women were not seriously consulted about real-estate disposal, and the majority did not secure pre-nuptial contracts, whether from optimism, negligence or ignorance.[15] Yet Salmon and others concede that many of the colonies passed *feme sole* trader laws which permitted married women to run businesses in the absence of their husbands, and all the colonies save Connecticut and Massachusetts accepted the possibility of married women having a separate estate.[16] These were significant concessions, but it seems fair to say that they did not make a profound difference to women's self-esteem and patriarchal attitudes in the New World.

Nor was it usually possible, on either side of the Atlantic, to seek a way out of an unsatisfactory marriage through divorce, though the colonies operated in a rather more generous fashion than the mother country. In England, absolute divorce [*a vinculo matrimonii*] was unobtainable in the eighteenth century except by a special Act of Parliament granted on Christian grounds, after which the Church was willing to remarry either of the affected parties. It was, furthermore, so expensive as to remain an aristocratic privilege and so discreditable as to be widely avoided. Divorces *a mensa et thoro* (separation from bed and board) might be granted by the ecclesiastical courts for adultery or cruelty, but such judicial separations were unsatisfactory because they seldom allowed remarriage. Taking the colonies as a whole, absolute divorces and divorce *a mensa et thoro* were also rare, so that couples were driven, as in England, to agreed separations or desertion to remedy a hopeless marriage.[17] In either case, women were left in precarious control of their earnings and might be deprived of any children of the union. But we should note that, as ever, there was considerable variation between colony and colony. Accordingly, South Carolina declined to permit divorce; New York and Virginia seldom granted full divorce, and then as an ecclesiastical matter, even if their legislatures might allow legal separations; whereas in the New England colonies civil divorce was obtainable and statutes governing it were 'part of the legal code', although New Englanders were subject to widely differing laws on the matter.[18] Still more important than New England's departure from English legal practice was the increase in divorce petitions during the eighteenth century: a small indication of women's growing literacy and assertiveness, and of their greater dissatisfaction with their situation when they were deserted (desertion being the main ground on which divorce was requested).[19]

We should not, however, conclude from this survey of the legal difficulties of eighteenth-century women that marriage was, for them, a near-unavoidable oppression. Indeed, a considerable fraction of women in Britain and America never married.[20] Yet as we have already suggested, single women were at a severe disadvantage in societies dominated by the family; while for those who did marry, there were both accepted pleasures and some signs of improving prospects by the last quarter of the century. The early marriage and extraordinary fertility of seventeenth-century colonial women, which bore witness to America's healthy environment, plentiful land and need for an augmented labour force, had then given place to the late marriage pattern of Western Europe and a decline in family size.[21] Since every family was likely to lose children through stillbirth, miscarriage and fatal illness, while the female death rate in childbirth was high, this reduction in fertility lessened the harrowing risks and disappointments of motherhood, which women were expected to bear with resignation.[22]

Women on both sides of the Atlantic might also draw comfort from being attended by other women during pregnancy, childbirth and sickness, and from intimate friendships with women to whom, if they wished, they could complain about domestic routines and expect to find a sympathetic hearing.[23] Moreover, there are clear indications that middle-class men and women were beginning to expect more from marriage than they had in the early modern period. The Puritan emphasis upon marriage as a spiritual and emotional, as well as a material, union had slowly given rise to an appreciation of mutuality and affection in this crucial relationship. As a result, there is the first evidence of a challenge to the right of parents to determine whom and when their children should marry, and to make sure that girl children especially wed in birth order.[24] The extent of such changes outside the middle class should not be exaggerated at this stage: they would become much more pronounced by the nineteenth century, for whatever their aspirations, the poor in England and America were often unable to afford the new ideal of companionable, conjugal marriage, continuing to rely, as they had always done, upon the sustenance of their kin, peer groups and communities.[25] The rich, for their part, were reluctantly influenced by changing concepts of marriage before the nineteenth century, retaining their concern to avert romantic misalliances which might destroy approved ties, contracted with a view to maximising and mobilising wealth and power.[26]

In England, Lord Hardwicke's Marriage Act of 1753 was specifically designed 'for the better preventing [of] Clandestine Marriages', and the expensive licences it required from individuals wishing to wed privately blatantly favoured the affluent: less fortunate couples had to wait for public banns to be called on three successive Sundays in one of the Anglican churches which in future were to be the only valid venues for marriage. (Jews and Quakers managed to get their ceremonies exempted from the Act, and Scotland continued to be governed by an altogether less exacting matrimonial law[27] – hence the popularity of Gretna Green!) It is interesting to find that one of the complaints against the Act was that it unduly increased the power of parents, whose consent to the marriage of children under twenty-one was meticulously to be required after 1753. Upper- and middle-class views about the importance of respectability were also favoured over working-class mores by the legislation's ending of recognition for betrothal rites, which before 1753 had been an important prelude to matrimony, sometimes accompanied by sexual intimacy and pregnancy.[28]

For women in the colonies and Britain alike, children were one of the constant pleasures of matrimony, with strong mother–daughter bonds enduring long after the end of infancy, at which point male children came increasingly under the influence of their fathers.[29] But in England, from the 1740s, formal attention had been paid to women's traditional duties in literature which advised them on how to nurse and rear their children.[30] There were no equivalent publications in America, any more than there were feminist pamphlets circulating – an indication of the cultural lag between England and her colonies. European writing on all manner of topics was keenly debated in eighteenth-century America, but it was not until the next century that the United States attained cultural independence and – in the case of some aspects of the women's movement – leadership. However, the novel opinions about children which found expression in England from the middle of the eighteenth century eventually had a wide circulation in both countries.

The advice manuals for rational mothers indicated, as Schnorrenberg has shown, not only the growing literacy of women but also the increased respect for the work 'that a woman did at home'.[31] And in the writings of the philosophers Jean-Jacques Rousseau and John Locke, the members of the Scottish common-sense school, and the emerging Romantic movement, we find the notion that children were good rather than evil, special beings rather than miniature adults, whose rationality and individuality deserved affectionate consideration. Calvinist teaching on childhood was thereby refuted – a reflection of its diminished power – and though the duty that children owed their parents was not questioned, the means of securing it were. Thus parents were advised to rely less on physical coercion and more on new forms of training – oral, anal and sexual – which, once internalised, would produce a greater degree of independence in young people.[32]

It is impossible to gauge how far parents were influenced by these new ideas. They were out of reach of the illiterate masses, male and female, and poor parents on either side of the Atlantic still expected work from their children at home and could not sustain them in a prolonged period of education.[33] What is more, the role of women was not singled out for special elevation in the early child-rearing literature, as it would be in the nineteenth century.[34] None the less, Norton has argued persuasively that, in practice, the Puritan and Quaker preoccupation with the nurture of children to ensure their formal acceptance of faith 'helped focus attention on adult women in their maternal capacity', while the growing prosperity of the southern colonies gave women there the leisure to devote more time to their children.[35] And at the very least, the prescriptive literature provides us with an important indication of how society was beginning to re-evaluate domesticity and the place of children in the family.[36]

(iii) *Religion*

In the areas of religion, education and even politics, there is similar evidence of the onset of change in social attitudes towards women and female prospects for assertion by the middle of the eighteenth century. Puritanism had placed the community above the individual and men above women, who were expected to be as devout as they were domestic. But from the time of the earliest American settlements there had been women who had used their claims to spiritual equality with men to challenge their practical subordination in religious matters.[37] The Quakers, Pietistic sects and some evangelical churches permitted women a considerable role in their affairs, and the growing numbers of women in New England congregations meant that ministers had to address themselves more directly to the interests of their female constituents.[38] Furthermore, while both men and women were active in the religious revivals of the 1730s and 1740s known as the Great Awakening, Barbara L. Epstein has demonstrated that women 'expressed a particularly sharp pleasure in the sense of community' aroused by these upheavals. Although the Awakening did not provoke women to challenge their roles in society, it was a striking confirmation of that special religiosity which they used to justify their increasing involvement in philanthropy and social reform from the end of the century.[39] For Anglican women in the South, in contrast to New England, religion was more a matter of personal conviction than of state control. Yet what such women gained in greater freedom from church and patriarchal family pressures they lost in terms of their society's lesser concern with training up children in the faith, with the mother's role in the education of children, and hence with the education of women themselves. The attitudes of the small number of American Catholics towards their children were similar to that of the Anglicans, with similar results.[40]

British women, too, from the Reformation onwards, found in religion a means of self-expression and protest. In the judgement of a widely circulated 1774 tract by Dr John Gregory, religion was a peculiar consolation to women which their sensibility made them anxious to acquire.[41] Unfortunately, we have no conclusive way of knowing how many women on either side of the Atlantic responded to religion because it was socially legitimate to do so and because they thought that, as inferior beings, they had more need of it than men, and how many women saw their role in a more positive light. The women who were sufficiently devout to leave records of their views and actions are, for that very reason, atypical. But if motivation remains a vexed question, some broad observations about English women and religion may be offered.

Owing to the importance it attached to the individual's own responsibility for Bible reading, spiritual experience and ultimately salvation, Puritanism gave women who felt that they needed it an excuse for publishing religious works in their lifetime; many such works were also published posthumously.[42] While the prominence of Protestant women as preachers and interpreters of the Bible declined after the turbulent Civil War period,[43] Methodists allowed women to preach in the eighteenth century, and they continued to be welcomed as preachers, missionaries and writers within the Quaker sect.[44] Women likewise played a significant role in sustaining the Catholic faith after the Reformation, refusing to attend the established Church and swear a prescribed oath of allegiance, harbouring priests, securing the celebration of 'the full liturgical cycle', and taking the veil as an alternative to taking a husband.[45] And if the Anglican Church could offer women no comparably heroic role, it produced in Mary Astell, whose anonymous publications appeared primarily between 1694 and 1705, perhaps the best-known English feminist before Mary Wollstonecraft, a century later. A conservative who accepted class distinctions with equanimity and had no sympathy for the religious dissenters of her time, Astell clearly differed from the freethinking, radical Wollstonecraft, yet she displayed a comparable ambition, learning, outspokenness and conviction that female inferiority sprang from educational rather than natural deficiencies.[46] Most women, however, in England as in America, found in religion private satisfactions of one sort or another, and it was not until the end of the eighteenth century that the churches as a whole made a serious attempt to enlist women in their service in an active capacity.[47]

(iv) *Education*

As Mary Astell and other early English feminists had recognised, lack of education was one of the chief obstacles faced by women who aspired to realise their capabilities either in the home or beyond it, in the service of themselves and others. Her proposal for the foundation of a women's seminary came to nothing through lack of support, and for much of the eighteenth century in England, since women's intellectual abilities were held to be as inferior to men's as their needs were different, education was enjoyed by fewer girls than boys, while the female literacy level was below the male. Instruction for poor girls was grudging and designed to fit them for their place. Moreover, when the number of boarding schools for girls increased in the second half of the century, they had low standards and mainly offered training in 'accomplishments'. For this reason they were both opposed for encouraging unsuitable social aspirations in their middle-class pupils, and criticised for inculcating laxity and frivolity in those who should more properly have been instructed in the homely virtues that ultimately made young women into good wives.[48]

There were, however, some signs of progress. Although Georgiana Hill complained that the eighteenth century was one of material rather than intellectual improvement,[49] the object and content of female education were vigorously debated, the educational attainments of women in the middle and upper classes were improved, and by mid-century writing had been accepted as a 'respectable career for women', who published biography and autobiography, novels, plays and poetry, wrote hymns for private and public use, and contributed to women's periodicals. It was also accepted that women were an important sector of the reading public, and their tastes were increasingly considered. As Vivien Jones observes, 'the gendering of mental qualities associated femininity with imagination and creativity' in a helpful way, but publishing was more controversial, exposing 'an essentially private activity to the public gaze, blurring the conduct-book delineation of separate spheres'.[50] In addition, being excluded from the universities and seldom accorded equal education even when they were born into rich households and privately tutored, women only occasionally achieved known scholarly distinction. Elizabeth Elstob, one of the few who did, and a distinguished linguist, was forced to keep school and act as a governess after her attempts to publish her major work had failed.[51] A more promising outlet was the salon, where women might find the stimulation of talented company and combine the traditional part of patroness or audience member with the more controversial role of learned conversationalist or practitioner of the arts.[52]

According to Hill, the emergence of the literary lady may be explained in class terms:

> Great ladies might do anything, and if they chose to patronize literature, even to become writers themselves, they could do so, and were praised and flattered.[53]

Hill's judgement was only partly correct; many of the bluestockings were remarkable neither for their birth nor for their wealth. But her point about the exaggerated response to their accomplishments is a valid one. Praise and flattery unfortunately provided no solid sustenance for aspiring women. Having little opportunity of working together, they did not necessarily feel inspired to support one another,[54] and the applause they received from men was sometimes accorded more for their curiosity value than for their true merit. On the other hand, it must be stressed that a number of the bluestockings were on friendly terms, and that their achievements were as likely to be unjustly dismissed as unduly lauded. The existence of fashionable salons did nothing to dispel society's broad condemnation of learned women as unnecessary and unfeminine, and the term 'bluestocking', applied to members of the intellectual women's gatherings which met in London during the 1770s and 1780s, became a term of disparagement[55] – despite the fact that the subject matter of female publications generally offered no challenge to prevailing assumptions about women's domestic destiny and primary need for moral education, while the bluestockings themselves (unlike a number of women novelists) did not favour alternative lifestyles.[56]

In colonial America, women experienced similar educational disadvantages. Notwithstanding the great importance Puritans attached to the individual's ability to read the Bible, their public schools concentrated on instructing boys; the education of girls was given less attention, whether in the family or in the so-called dame schools run by women.[57] Although Earle maintains that girls did attend public schools in New York in the eighteenth century, she stresses that needlework and reading were about all it was thought necessary for them to know in the first quarter of that century.[58] And Norton points out that if, in affluent southern families, girls might be taught by their brothers' tutors, those in poorer households had to look to members of their own family for education, and females from all backgrounds were even less likely than northerners to acquire any advanced instruction.[59] Accepting these regional variations in educational provision, it is none the less safe to generalise that the gulf between male and female literacy rates showed little sign of closing in the first half of the eighteenth century, even in New England, which had the highest literacy level for both sexes (80 per cent or more for men and over 40 per cent for women).[60] Furthermore, girls were less likely to be taught to write than boys, at a time when reading and writing were taught separately.[61]

Women obtained sufficient education in the elementary schools to obtain work as governesses and teachers, as they did in England. They were particularly valued during the summer months, when male teachers were often engaged in farm labour.[62] However, Dexter was unable to find an instance of a woman teaching in one of the colonial colleges.[63] Like their English counterparts, American women were acutely aware of the disparity between their education and that of men; sensitive about the ridicule or disarming flattery that was likely to meet their efforts at self-improvement.[64] Unlike metropolitan women across the Atlantic, they generally lacked the stimulation to be found in the fashionable salon. Affluent parents might have been happy to see their daughters educated according to English notions of gentility, but rich and privileged colonials were less secure in their class and cultural leadership than were their British equivalents, and American society placed a premium on practical achievements rather than artistic innovation. In consequence, salons of the European type were uncommon. Still more than was the case in the mother country, the talented woman was likely to be rare, uncomfortably dependent on favourable family circumstances, and undermined by the 'absence of literary atmosphere'.[65]

(v) *Politics*

One of the reasons why men looked with disfavour on the prospect of highly educated women was the fear that such women would wish to leave their private realm and enter the public sphere, where male domination was most pronounced. Indeed, by the eighteenth century it was greater than it had been in the past.

During the 1640s and 1650s, English women petitioned Parliament on a number of occasions, claiming a political voice through reference to their Christian rights and duties.[66] Victorian suffragists also liked to remind their opponents that freemen 'in some towns and cities of the medieval and early modern periods' had been able to vote for Members of Parliament, where this entitlement had been part of a freeman's rights. However, actual proof of women voting, either as freemen or as landowners, is hard to come by after the early modern era, and in the eighteenth century women appear to have been excluded from the parliamentary suffrage, albeit on social rather than legal grounds. On the other hand, there is evidence that a few women held local office, serving as 'constables, churchwardens, and reeves of manors', voting 'in the parish vestry', and in one instance acting as an overseer of the poor.[67]

Yet if the study of women and politics in the eighteenth century has been unduly neglected, it remains fair at present to assert that great ladies were interested but generally not active in political matters, especially concerning personalities, while the mass of women were neither interested nor involved.[68] Influence might flatteringly be accorded them, but power was denied them. The eighteenth century was not a period of legal reforms benefiting women; and, as Browne suggests, even proposals that they should have more power in the public sphere were rare.

Individuals like Lady Mary Wortley Montagu, who published a political journal in support of Sir Robert Walpole despite her husband's opposition to him, and Georgiana Duchess of Devonshire, a vigorous backer of Charles James Fox and his friends, are not typical even of the women whose birth or marriage gave them access to the important political circles which were closed to most others. Nor did a political hostess such as the Duchess of Devonshire advance women's cause in any direct sense, since hostesses directed their uncommon abilities and energies into the service of either their own menfolk or chosen favourites in a masculine world.[69] Widows and mothers of minor sons who inherited or looked after political interests are also both exceptional and conventional at the same time, and while female involvement in political electioneering has barely been investigated, it cannot yet be said to have been large.[70]

The eighteenth century may not have been an age of association and combination, yet women were certainly among the Jacobites who supported the risings of 1715 and 1745, and took part in the civil disturbances of the century.[71] But here again, so far as we can judge, women were simply concerned to participate, along with men, in the significant class- or region-based movements that affected them. Thus their prominent role in food riots was understandable, given female responsibility for household management. It is hard to detect signs that protesting women challenged the contemporary view that politics was men's business, or sought to advance the cause of their sex in protecting the immediate needs of their families.[72]

For much of the eighteenth century, American women had a similarly slight political influence. As Linda Kerber observes, they 'were thought to experience politics through husbands, fathers, sons', and so to be less patriotic than men, as well as incapable of making sensible political judgements.'[73] Women, for their part, appeared to accept that decisions and actions in the political arena were appropriately left to men,[74] and their political prospects, like those of their English sisters, were worse in the eighteenth century than they had once been. Hence, if there were a few female political activists in the early years of colonisation – while women enjoyed an indirect political voice in small, developing settlements, when family and community concerns were intertwined – they had soon been excluded from voting and office-holding. Women were thereafter obliged to express any dissatisfaction they might feel over the management of important issues by participating in the violent street protests that were a feature of American and British cities alike. The result of exclusion from formal politics was that British and American women were at the mercy of man-made laws, which were particularly oppressive with regard to females accused of witchcraft or sexual offences in the seventeenth-century colonies, and to the rights of married women on both sides of the Atlantic.[75]

By the time of the American Revolution, then, it would be difficult to argue that women in the colonies were vastly better off than their British counterparts. The economic value they undoubtedly had in a developing region and the absence of rigid class distinctions in the New World did not result in a new division of labour between the sexes which acknowledged female equality, and although the harshness of English common law with regard to women was somewhat modified in America, married women remained subordinate to their husbands and unlikely to obtain a divorce if they were unhappily wed. The lives of colonial women were not shaped by an elaborate home-produced literature of domesticity, but the English works on the subject circulated in America and were influential there. It may be that greater opportunities for women in the colonies account for the dearth of American feminist literature before the Revolution, whereas there was a considerable volume of English publications on the 'woman question'. This output, however, can partly be explained with reference to the cultural maturity of the mother country, which was also reflected in its literary and political salons, whose confident female activists were a product of the class system which the colonists lacked, and which in many respects would prove a hindrance to organised feminism.

In the basic contours of their lives, American and British women were essentially alike: excluded from politics, accorded an inferior education, seen as possessing unique feminine traits, leading domestic lives, uncomfortably placed if single, and taking pleasure in their children, female friends and religion. There was no distant golden age for women in either country, though economic freedoms had been greater and political activities a little less circumscribed in the early modern period than they were in the mid-eighteenth century. Yet, as we have seen, by then there were the first signs of changing attitudes and expectations among women regarding marriage and children, and they had established a position in the churches, especially the Protestant denominations, which indicated both the actual and potential power of female moral energy. New forces of change and reaction in politics, ideas, religion and the economy in the last quarter of the eighteenth century stirred up areas of women's life where there was formerly no flux, accelerated movement in areas where alteration was already under way, and raised expectations which could not always be realised. In so doing, they simultaneously prepared the way for woman as feminist and reformer, and for the Victorian notion of the 'angel in the house'. The experience of the Revolution also helped to implant in American women a sense that they enjoyed special advantages and responsibilities: a belief which, however much nineteenth-century feminists may have exaggerated the blessings of their own past, was to become an important feature of their campaign.

II. Forces for change

(i) *The American Revolution*

The American Revolution, as Kerber, Norton and Countryman point out, had a profoundly politicising effect on the female population of the colonies. Among women and colonial leaders alike, it forced an unusual awareness of women's importance as consumers and potential boycotters of British imports, producers of vital goods and general managers of the household economy. As the conflict with Britain affected their daily lives, took away their husbands and divided their families, women assumed men's jobs, debated political issues and became less apologetic about doing so than they had once been. They participated in crowd actions as a vital part of their communities, petitioned Revolutionary governments and local committees of safety in pursuit of their interests as wives and mothers, and – in Pennsylvania, New Jersey and Maryland – raised money to help the war effort.[76]

These new activities brought women no direct political return. Averting political tyranny and ensuring the survival of the young republic were more important objectives than sexual or racial equality for its male politicians and political theorists. Countryman has shown that only groups which 'had established their political identity in the Revolution' were subsequently 'in a position to struggle for their concerns'; and women, like non-whites, had not effectively done so.[77] Such ventures as boycotts and the homespun production drive unfortunately looked like a mere extension of traditional female undertakings,[78] and women's support was freely given and promptly accepted without apparently provoking any sense that a reward might be appropriate.[79] As a result, women had difficulty in obtaining war widows' pensions after hostilities ended, and they were enfranchised only by New Jersey, which in 1776 gave the vote to all its free adult inhabitants. Although the Revolution was not embarked upon to create a democracy, it did encourage a further democratisation of the suffrage; the meagre consequences of this process for women are therefore particularly disappointing. By 1807, blacks and women had been disenfranchised even in New Jersey, on the grounds that they were the elements most liable to manipulation in the state's corrupt political system.[80]

Since wars frequently provoke extraordinary behaviour which those concerned expect to be only temporary, women's return to their customary exclusion from politics after the Revolution is perhaps to be expected. It becomes the more understandable when we recall that with the exceptions of 'Catharine Macaulay and Mary Wollstonecraft [in England], women are absent even from the second and third ranks of philosophes': notwithstanding their helpful recognition of women's rationality and individual worth, the great writers of the Enlightenment, the members of the British Whig Opposition and the ideologues of the American Revolution were men writing for men. They neither demolished traditional social assumptions about women's lot nor suggested a new function for them in the body politic.[81] 'Indeed, female qualities were commonly made the measure of what a good republican ought to avoid', while the centralisation of politics under the federal constitution and the limited female ownership of land when the franchise rested upon it further disadvantaged women in the United States.

None the less, the Revolution prompted the first serious debate in America about the 'woman question'. In consequence, acknowledging women's wartime contribution and the need to involve all citizens if republicanism were to be viable, the Revolutionary generation was obliged to 'define a public role for American women'.[82] And if some men, such as the author Charles Brockden Brown and the educator Benjamin Rush, contributed to the work of definition, it was mainly in the hands of female writers and controversialists, including Judith Sargent Murray, Susannah Rowson, Hannah Webster Foster, Mercy Otis Warren and Abigail Adams, the wife of the second President of the United States, who exhorted her husband to 'remember the ladies' when the first government was being devised, besides taking a keen interest in politics and the education of women.[83]

Kerber, Norton, Bloch and others have established that what emerged was the concept of republican mothers, who, though they themselves eschewed politics and personal ambition, were accorded the political responsibility of rearing virtuous children to become patriotic citizens, capable of achieving their goals as individuals. With the aid of male and female publicists, women were also made the guardians of social morality, so that the charitable work they had already begun to undertake (generally under church auspices) was regarded with favour as a way of strengthening society rather than a labour which might distract women from their household duties.[84] The image of republican motherhood further enlarged feminine prospects by provoking a debate about the education of women.

While some Americans continued to worry that educated girls would be unfeminine, imbued with European class snobbery and rendered unfit for domesticity, reformers successfully argued that female schooling should be improved in order to create the good mothers, capable homemakers and rational adults that the republic demanded.[85] Between 1790 and 1830 educational provision for women improved dramatically, particularly in the northern states, since a case had been made for schooling them 'beyond basic literacy'.[86] Elementary instruction was provided for girls in the public schools of New England, as it was in the charity schools of the middle states, while better secondary education became available with the founding of new private academies, run by women, which offered girls both the accomplishments long thought suitable for 'ladies' and the academic subjects previously reserved for boys. (Public backing for secondary schools was slight before the Civil War.)[87] Education for men and women alike was justified in terms of its utility, as Cott has established, but given the narrow definition of the female role, the benefits gained by the two sexes were not evenly balanced.[88] However, the literacy gap between men and women closed, and educational opportunities, once provided, had unintended results.

Most obviously, they gave women additional achievements by which to measure themselves and others, increased their sense of sisterhood and enhanced their prospects of obtaining employment outside the home. Although girls still tended to be taken away from school before boys, and large numbers of women applied their education within the domestic sphere, many 'graduates of the republican academies achieved fame in the nineteenth century' as missionaries, reformers, writers and educators.[89] Hence Emma Willard, born into a large and hard-pressed family, began a school at her home in Vermont, improved her education in the process, and in 1814 established at Troy, New York, a seminary which employed women teachers and stressed the importance of the cultivated mother in the republic. In New England, the centre of the most intense educational experimentation, Catharine Beecher, a daughter of the eminent Congregational preacher Lyman Beecher, opened a female seminary during the 1820s at Hartford, Connecticut. At the same time Mary Lyon and Zilpah Grant, recognising that teaching provided women with a respectable source of income, as well as an opportunity of serving the community and continuing their own instruction, ran seminaries at Adams and Ipswich in Massachusetts. While they did not proclaim themselves feminists, and were anxious not to alarm the public whose financial backing they needed, such pioneers urged their pupils to consider themselves as rational beings capable of improvement, and felt that they had begun to dispel the ignorance which had traditionally put women at a disadvantage compared with men. They thus prepared the ground for the nineteenth-century women's movement.[90]

Accepting that the Revolution's main consequence for women was to give a public dimension to their traditional role, we should not expect any profound transformation of the laws and attitudes governing matrimony and children. Indeed, there were some signs of retrogression which women, lacking a formal political voice and a jury presence, were unable to prevent. Coverture still operated in the new republic, with pre-nuptial contracts being narrowly interpreted by equity courts, and dower rights steadily undermined.[91] Yet since family patterns and expectations were already in flux before the Revolution, and the alterations may have influenced Americans' unwillingness to sustain an unsatisfactory imperial relationship which they depicted as a quarrel between an unreasonable parent and wronged children,[92] it comes as no surprise to find a continuation of these changes after the break with Britain. As with many post-Revolution trends, it is impossible to state that they would not have emerged anyway; it would be equally unwise to assert that the upheavals of the late eighteenth century gave them no stimulus.

The most important developments concerning the family would seem to be as follows. After independence, while divorce remained obtainable only by a Bill passed through the legislature in a number of states, it was made a matter for the courts to handle in New England and Pennsylvania. More requests for legal separations and divorces were processed than earlier in the century, and there is evidence from the petitions that women were readier to desert unsatisfactory husbands and less willing than they had formerly been to tolerate adulterers, bad providers, and the loss of property on separation.[93] It appears that women were strengthened in their prewar reluctance to marry prematurely to accommodate others, while both male and female offspring asserted a greater say in their choice of husbands. A rise in the incidence of pre-marital pregnancy also suggests a further growth in the independence of young adults. Within marriage, the tendency towards family limitation continued, particularly in New England, indicating both a high degree of mutual consideration between partners and an enhanced concern for women, who ran the risks of childbirth and subsequently played a key part in raising the children. And if the notion of republican motherhood elevated women's role, it also confirmed the special importance attached to children and child-rearing by the end of the century – an importance which had been heralded by the application of Lockean contractual theories to family relations and the popularisation of his views on the significance of motherly duties.[94]

(ii) *British radicalism*

Although we can be clear that the writing of Locke and a range of more radical eighteenth-century English commentators concerned with political freedom helped American patriots to shape their complaints about British rule,[95] the nature of the Anglo–American intellectual connection and its implications for women are less obvious by the end of the century. British radicals at this time were a very varied group who applauded the French as much as the American Revolution, drew on a long British tradition of utopianism, republicanism and sexual nonconformity, and regarded the world as their stage. Urban in location and especially strong in the metropolis, they consisted of Nonconformists and 'Sceptics in religion, democrats in politics, reformers, visionaries, romantics' who sustained themselves primarily by imaginative and political writing, and by teaching in the dissenting academies. They included the Unitarian ministers Richard Price, Joseph Priestley, Theophilus Lindsay, Andrew Kippis and John Jebb; the poet Percy Bysshe Shelley; the philosopher William Godwin; the political pamphleteer Thomas Spence; and the feminist Mary Wollstonecraft.[96] Pressures for change were not confined simply to intellectual circles but also influenced the organised activism of the late eighteenth century, whether it was the parliamentary campaigns for the repeal of the Test and Corporation Acts, the abolition of the slave trade and parliamentary reform,[97] or the efforts of the artisan radicals who urged these and other causes through 'the well-tried tactics of public meetings, lectures, tracts, networks of correspondents and ... the petition'.[98]

The ideas espoused by the radicals reveal a tension between perfectionist visions on the one hand and reformist programmes on the other, yet they were united in emphasising the importance of individual freedom, and in acknowledging the rationality and basic equality of all human beings. Godwin and Spence envisaged an ideal society composed of small, free producers working in democratically and locally run communities, though unfortunately they did not take sufficient account of the fact that the propertyless proletariat was growing rapidly in Europe, and was by no means negligible even in land-rich America.[99] Their views on sex and marriage were still more problematic. Pledged to the equality of men and women in marriage, the economy, education and politics, with Spence favouring divorce while Shelley and Godwin advocated relationships between the sexes founded exclusively upon feeling rather than convention, dissidents did not adequately allow for conservative responses to their proposals. They were denounced as lewd advocates of 'free love'; the rather conventional preference of many of them for the nuclear family over communal living arrangements was overshadowed, and the high seriousness of their pronouncements on sex was ignored.[100] The sexual views and behaviour of the best-known woman radical, Mary Wollstonecraft, important as they are to an understanding of her life and works, provoked a particularly exaggerated reaction.

Wollstonecraft, born in 1759, grew up in a sizeable family disturbed by frequent moves, declining fortunes and embattled parents. Encouraged to improve her abilities by an accomplished friend, Fanny Blood, she spent her years of young womanhood as a companion to an elderly widow, a governess and schoolteacher, a nurse for her sick mother and a general prop to her family. Throughout this period, Wollstonecraft, like many women of her time, found strength in female company, especially that of her sister Eliza and her friend Fanny. She moved to London in 1787 and, having learned German and Italian there, worked as a translator and continued the writing whose first result had been the publication, in 1786, of her essays, *Thoughts on the Education of Daughters*. Her reply to Burke's *Reflections on the Revolution in France* earned considerable notice and demonstrated Wollstonecraft's skill as a propagandist; in 1792 she proceeded to meet Talleyrand's justification of limited education for girls under the new French constitution with her most famous work, *A Vindication of the Rights of Women*. It attracted immense interest.[101]

Alice Rossi has drawn attention to the fact that far less publicity had been given to Catharine Macaulay's *Letters on Education*, which appeared in 1790. Yet Macaulay was then an established historian and pamphleteer as well as a socially fortunate woman; she, like Wollstonecraft, minimised differences between the sexes in pleading for the equal mental and physical education of boys and girls, and argued that women needed basic rights, not special privileges. (She also wrote, in 1790, a reply to Burke's *Reflections*, which was well received by radicals.)

Rossi's explanation is that Macaulay had fallen from social grace, and hence public interest, by marrying beneath her, and to a much younger man.[102] The *Vindication* was certainly not accorded greater prominence than the *Letters* because it was notably well written; neither Wollstonecraft nor Macaulay was a stylist. However, Wollstonecraft's book was vigorously promoted by her friends (as Macaulay's *History* had been), its appearance in the year the French Republic was declared was auspicious, and it was an altogether weightier treatise than the *Letters*, brilliantly bringing together ideas that had been circulating in Britain for a century and more, while giving further publicity to Macaulay's 'valuable work' in the process.[103]

Although it lacked clear organisation, the *Vindication* offered a compelling indictment of the enemies of women's equality and showed graphically – as did John Stuart Mill and other nineteenth-century feminists – that the subordination of women harmed both sexes and the children who were women's special charge. Accordingly, female emancipation could be seen as procuring the emancipation of the whole of society. Wollstonecraft recognised that feminine women attached too much importance to masculine strength, 'when husbands, as well as their helpmates, are often overgrown children'. She understood the folly of confining girls and women 'in close rooms till their muscles are relaxed, and their powers of digestion destroyed', and deplored the frivolous objects and occupations with which women were forced to fill their minds and hands, particularly in the upper ranks of society. Wollstonecraft's impatience on contemplating women busy at bits of fancy needlework would be echoed in the nineteenth century by the peppery American feminist Elizabeth Cady Stanton.

Denouncing the common obsession with love, 'considered as an animal appetite', deploring 'the lasciviousness of men' and valuing liaisons based on friendship as opposed to lust, Wollstonecraft would seem to have had more in common with her rational moralist predecessors, evangelical contemporaries and later Victorians than with those of her radical allies who celebrated erotic passion. She was as hard on women as on men, believing that the former's 'immoderate fondness for dress, for pleasure, and for sway' put them on a par with savages. Kept in ignorance and encouraged to be foolish, the average woman was frequently jealous of a superior one, indulgent or neglectful of her children, a household tyrant and a threat to her husband's virtue. Flattered into considering themselves angels, the 'slaves of pleasure as they are the slaves of men', women needed sufficient opportunities and rights to stretch themselves and, if necessary, to 'support a single life with dignity'. By the middle of the nineteenth century, when social commentators in Britain deplored the surplus of single women, Wollstonecraft's comment on the single life would seem like simple common sense. In 1792, despite the already large numbers of single women in Britain, it appeared outlandish. Conventional in her condemnation of the boarding schools of her day ('the hot-beds of vice and folly'), she was unsettling in her advocacy of coeducational day schools, her aversion to class distinction and her interest in the civil rights of women. Wollstonecraft's readiness to see rationality, consistency and affection rather than coercion determine the course of child-rearing – though it was not entirely novel, as we have seen – was a further sign of her advanced thinking.[104]

The *Vindication* won applause in Wollstonecraft's own circle, and is the best-known expression of eighteenth-century feminism which, Browne urges, constitutes more than simply a continuation of earlier defences of women or a trailer for the nineteenth-century women's movement.[105] Feminist ideas were encouraged by the growth of (not necessarily feminist) writing for women and by women;[106] and by other wider developments, including arguments about philosophical rationalism, the nature of political authority, and the content and purpose of education.[107] When they were simply defending the feminine qualities men frequently satirised, women offered little challenge to patriarchal attitudes.[108] There was similarly little threat to established ways in the 'mild instrumental feminism' which sought moderate improvements in women's lot to benefit others, rather than because justice demanded them.[109] Furthermore, feminists in the eighteenth century, like their Victorian successors, were motivated both by a belief that women were essentially different from men and by the opposite conviction: they had no unifying premiss from which to work. On the other hand, by the end of the century British feminist writers were managing to combine instrumental feminism with an emphasis upon women's rationality. Sustained by the debates noted above and by a 'new historical and ethnographic sophistication', they were showing a novel interest in women's collective oppression and, at the same time, increasing influence in society.[110]

None the less, the impact of radicalism of every kind during the 1790s was less than its proponents had hoped. Some of its luminaries – including Macaulay, Wollstonecraft and Price – died in the course of the decade. Others lost buoyancy and credibility as the British government, at war with France and fearful of political extremism in that country and at home, moved to curb freedom of speech, publication and assembly, while local conservatives, property-owners and industrialists co-operated to hound suspected supporters of the French Revolution. Popular politics were inhibited for two decades and, as Ditchfield reminds us, had always involved forces opposed to change as well as favouring it. If one result of the French Revolution beneficial to women was the 1792 civil divorce law – well ahead of anything available in Britain or America in the Revolutionary era and far beyond it – and the British were informed about the activism of French women during the upheaval, the revolutionaries as a whole did not pursue a feminist programme any more than their counterparts had done in America. Furthermore, the divorce law was restricted in 1804 and eliminated during the Bourbon Restoration.

Nor were the British radicals concerned in a major way with the 'woman question', however much their critics might have tried to damn them with the charge of sexual immorality. As Dickinson observes, for the vast majority of radicals women were 'dependent creatures, incapable of exercising independent political judgement', while even 'Mary Wollstonecraft ... did not bother to campaign for votes for women', (a campaign hard to envisage in the context of the 1790s). And though the visibility of women writers had undoubtedly increased by the end of the eighteenth century – for the publications of female radicals were augmented by the novels of Mary Hays, Amelia Opie, Eliza Fenwick, Mary Robinson, Charlotte Smith and Helen Williams – moralists mounted a spirited attack on the evils of novel reading and the unwholesomeness of such sexual nonconformists as Macaulay and Wollstonecraft. After her death following childbirth, Wollstonecraft's husband, William Godwin, published in 1797 *Memoirs* of his wife which, though they are moving to the modern reader, repelled many contemporaries by their revelation that the couple had lived together before marriage, that Mary was pregnant when they wed, and that she already had a child by another man, the faithless Gilbert Imlay. The association of political and sexual radicalism damned Wollstonecraft in an age of counter-revolution.[111]

Just as British radicals viewed events across the Atlantic with keen interest, so their American counterparts devoured the intellectual output of British radicals and welcomed their visits. The British liked to proclaim their cultural supremacy, and did so in part by lauding the achievements of their women. Yet while Britons did indeed retain their lead in literary feminism, the British impact on Americans in a period of self-conscious patriotism should not be exaggerated. By the late eighteenth century, we have suggested, America had produced its own reformers and writers concerned with republican motherhood and women's education, and although Wollstonecraft's work was published there, Norton contends that she said little that had not already been expressed by the more forthright republican women. Moreover, in the United States as in Britain, Wollstonecraft's popularity was limited by her unconventional lifestyle.[112] The unsuitably married Mrs Macaulay, who visited America and had powerful American connections including George Washington, Abigail Adams and Mercy Warren, was likewise a poor model for would-be republican mothers; plans for an American edition of her *History of England* had to be abandoned for want of subscriptions, and Mrs Macaulay further tried former friends by her increasing discontent with the post-independence American political and value system.[113]

Republican women might include both Macaulay and Wollstonecraft in their lists of European heroines to be emulated; but they were more likely to admire Abigail Adams and Mercy Warren, who combined intellectual ability with domesticity – albeit with some difficulty in Warren's case, as she strove to reconcile conventional attitudes to womanhood with her roles as active playwright, poet and historian.[114] Their unconventionality undermined the attempt of the British poets Coleridge, Southey and Lovell, influenced by Wollstonecraft and Godwin, to found a new community on the banks of the Susquehanna river in America, where men and women would share in housework and government. The experiment failed as promptly as such utopias were destined to do in the nineteenth century, on both sides of the Atlantic, and it was not imitated in the 1790s.[115] Reform endeavours, and women's participation in them, received more encouragement from religious impulses than from secular rationalism during the next two decades.

(iii) *Religious ferment*

In the United States, the most important religious developments were disestablishment of the churches and a second major wave of revivalism, which together brought about a large growth of Church membership. As a result of the application of Enlightenment thought and the dictates of political prudence, there was no establishment of religion by the Constitution, state establishments were destroyed with a consequent loss of tax revenues, and religious tests for office were ruled out in the new republic. The process of disestablishment in the Anglican South and Congregational New England, though uneven, was complete by the 1830s. Being thus forced to compete for members, funds and power, and obliged to minimise the dogmatic hurdles facing prospective converts, the various Protestant denominations launched recruitment drives which not only restored their fortunes but also elevated the position of women.[116]

Exhorted to contemplate their fragile mortality in the course of pregnancy and childbirth, formally excluded from the public sphere but encouraged to regard themselves as the guardians of the morality of their families and society at large, women in North and South, town and country, responded to the revivalists' appeals with particular fervour. As Barbara Epstein, Susan Juster and others have established, during the Second Great Awakening (1790s–1840s) women were often instrumental in bringing their children and reluctant men into the churches, and recorded more personal, emotional conversion experiences than their menfolk. They seem to have been well aware that religious inspiration, at least, allowed them to challenge male attitudes and authority. With the power of Calvinism further eroded by economic change and sectarian diversity, and with ministers offering a religion which stressed sentiment, feeling and good works rather than learning and theology, spiritual matters were more than ever adjusted towards the traits associated with women. Conversely, men engaged in secular pursuits were slower than they had once been to respond to the appeals of religion, and particularly evangelical religion, because its emotionalism and arbitrariness were at odds with the rationality and calculation required for success in business, and with respect for a government based on the rules of law.[117]

A collection of letters written to each other by New England young women in the early nineteenth century, which survives in the Schlesinger Library, bears witness to their self-conscious spirituality. Offering comfort for the death of loved ones, correspondents presented religion as a support 'which is able to bear us up under any affliction', and trials were accepted, since 'The Captain of our salvation was made perfect through suffering'. Individuals inquired after their friends' responsiveness to a local revival, took pleasure in the power of a woman preacher who had brought many to a sense of their guilt and danger, and contemplated their spiritual state with an almost morbid zeal. After making a public profession of Christianity, and acknowledging the weightiness of 'the duties incumbent on us', converts looked with dread for the signs of weakness, worldliness and retrogression that would bring 'a reproach on the cause'. Their missives served to stiffen the resolve of sender and receiver alike.[118]

Women and clergymen were natural allies in a changing world.[119] Ministers claimed to be the protectors and elevators of women, regarding them less mistrustfully than they had in Puritan times. Their numerous female constituents reciprocated by establishing 'education' societies and sewing circles, designed to finance the education of clerics and raise money for specific congregations. Prompted by religious zeal and displaying great practical skill, from the 1790s onwards – but especially from the 1820s – they went on to found a vast array of benevolent and reform organisations, some of which involved men and some of which had a distinctive feminine orientation. Notable among these were the maternal associations or groups of praying mothers who met 'to secure the conversion and spiritual welfare of their families',[120] and the moral reform societies which tried to help prostitutes and persuade both sexes of the need for 'chastity and marital fidelity'. Women also distributed food, clothes, firewood, sewing and alms to the poor of their neighbourhoods, set up and ran homes for orphans, supported missionary societies, and interested themselves in both schools for the poor and the Sunday School movement, their efforts being formalised in 1816 with the creation of the 'Female Union Society for the Promotion of Sabbath-Schools'. A majority of the movement's teachers were women, and they wrote much of the literature used in its schools, which showed an enterprising willingness to admit adult women unable to attend school during the week. In addition, women formed discussion groups which addressed political and economic, as well as religious, issues.[121]

The pattern of social activism was not uniform throughout the United States. As Sterling has observed, black women facing the consequences of poverty in their communities gave first priority to the formation of mutual benefit societies: organisations for 'mutual improvement in literature and morals' appeared by the 1830s. Moreover, among black and white women alike, such combinations were more characteristic of the northern than the southern states. But Mathews and Lebsock have provided considerable evidence to suggest that some southern women embraced voluntarism with the same enthusiasm as their northern sisters. And Mathews has shown that southern slaves, excluded from the possibility of free associational activities, nevertheless responded positively to an evangelical religion whose conversion experience resembled inherited African rituals and which offered them, as it offered white women, a means of coping with a world they could not control.[122]

The significance of voluntarism for women is no less contentious. Their organisations gave them new work to do at a time when women's work was changing under the impact of industrialisation and urbanisation. They were a way of demonstrating feminine concern for children, the welfare of unfortunate

women, and masculine morality. Through religious benevolence, as through
Church membership, women gave practical expression to their own ideal of self-
sacrificing womanhood, winning the approval of society, an enhanced sense of
individual worth and sisterhood, and an opportunity for moving out of the home
without bringing on themselves the censure of men. It would be foolish, however,
to equate voluntarism with feminism before the 1830s. Indeed, the very fact that
they had found opportunities beyond domesticity may have blunted the need of
many women for more formal 'rights', and thereby strengthened the sexual status
quo. There was no automatic connection between benevolent organisations and
later, more radical female groups. As would subsequently be the case, women
became social activists for the same reasons as men did: to express their religious
convictions and counteract rationalism; to help and improve the poor; to tackle
the urban threat to community; and to redeem the godless West. And orthodox
clergymen, while they generally condoned the public activities involved in female
benevolence, certainly had no desire to see women move out of their customary
sphere in other ways – not least by preaching or leading prayers.[123] None the
less, by the 1830s bolder women were emerging who were unwilling to accept
male controls upon their reform endeavours, religious or otherwise.

In Britain, evangelical religion likewise provided enlarged opportunities for
women within a framework of traditional ideas about the female role. As was the
case in America,[124] the very real competition between the various groups of
evangelicals did not prevent religious women from co-operating in reform; nor
did the contrasting prospects for Church leadership accorded to women by, for
example, the liberal Baptists on the one hand and the conservative Anglicans and
Methodists on the other. In Britain as in America, evangelicalism appealed to
women because it was 'a religion of duty, which placed service above doctrine',
and revered in its converts qualities that seemed 'quintessentially female':
emotion, humility, self-denial and obedience.[125] In Britain as in America,
evangelicals were urged to move from conquest of self to the redemption of the
world, and for women, reform was expected to complement their primary role as
guardians of home, family and sexual morality. In Britain as in America, women
were acknowledged to be particularly sensitive to the claims of religion, and
ministers gave more prominence to the humane and 'feminine' attributes of
Christ than they had formerly allowed. In Britain as in America, the initial
involvement of women as preachers in Methodist revivals, 'when conversion of
the sinner was all-important and order and respectability almost totally
irrelevant', came to be regarded with dismay by male clerics who were, Dews
suggests, determined to defend their authority and impose 'order and structure
on the Methodist church'.[126] And in Britain as in America, revivalism inspired
minority cults which attracted women and produced female leaders, most notably
two working-class prophets: the Mancunian Ann Lee, who in 1774 led a group
of Shakers (of French and Quaker origins) to the United States, there
proclaiming the male and female characteristics of God, sexual abstinence, the
equality of the sexes, and communism; and the Devonian Joanna Southcott, who

in the early nineteenth century attracted some middle-class support, denounced masculine oppression, celebrated woman's divine mission and pledged – unsuccessfully – to give birth to Shiloh, the new Messiah.[127]

Moreover, the links between British and American evangelism were extremely important; the years between 1790 and 1850 witnessed the emergence of what Thistlethwaite has called the Atlantic economy, and with it a set of ideological and personal connections between British and American political radicals, humanitarians, Nonconformists and evangelicals.[128] So far as popular evangelism is concerned, Richard Carwardine has demonstrated that its exponents were united by a sense of joint mission, although revivalism proved strongest in America's 'voluntaristic church system', never achieving 'total respectability' under 'the critical eye of a church establishment' in Britain. As part of the Anglo–American interchange, British Methodists provided the American Church which sprang from them with itinerant preachers, literature and reforming zeal, reinforcing existing pressures towards reform in American society; while the successes of American evangelicals were contemplated with keen interest across the Atlantic and helped to re-energise their British counterparts in the 1830s.[129]

But evangelicalism in Britain, as Hall has shown, had the distinctive function of shaping the ideology of the rising middle class in a transitional period, when old anxieties about lax aristocratic manners were being sharpened by new fears of revolutionary change. In addition, the lead in reform organisation was taken by British evangelicals under the direction of the Clapham Sect, the London evangelical arm of the Church of England. William Wilberforce's Society for the Suppression of Vice, Robert Raikes's Sunday School, the Religious Tract Society inspired by Hannah More, the (interdenominational) London Missionary Society and (Anglican) Church Missionary Society – which operated overseas missions – and the British and Foreign Bible Society were all copied by American evangelicals.[130] And the first American benevolent association to be managed by a woman – the Society for the Relief of Poor Widows with Small Children – was founded in 1797 by Isabella Graham, a recently arrived Scot, who modelled her enterprise on a London poor relief agency. Her society was, she admitted, 'a new thing in this country'.[131]

The part played by women in the organisational activities of British evangelicals was noteworthy; so too was the fact that they were sustained by the poor as well as by members of the middle class, especially in the case of the Sunday School movement. Women helped to found and taught in such schools. They provided some 10,000 workers in 350 female associations for the British and Foreign Bible Society, in which associations they acted as office-holders and proved invaluable at money-raising. As fund collectors they were the mainstay of the Church Missionary Society in its first years.[132] Between 1790 and 1830, Prochaska has established, the proportion of women members in mixed charities was increasing, in parallel with the number of separate female societies.[133] Their role in the campaign against slavery and the British slave trade was particularly interesting – both because it showed that evangelical and non-evangelical women could work together in a shared cause, and because of the varied nature of female involvement in the campaign.

Although women were not active in the radical corresponding societies of the 1790s, and did not generally sign anti-slavery petitions for fear of delegitimising them, they did participate in abolition debates, make financial contributions and support the boycott of slave-grown sugar, which utilised their power within the family and as consumers. They also canvassed in the slave trade election of 1807, and when the anti-slavery movement was reanimated in the 1820s they were prominent in supporting meetings, collecting money, promoting sugar boycotts, getting out publications and gathering names, some of them female, for petitions. They formed their own ladies' associations for these purposes, with the encouragement of men – an indication that political action by individuals without formal political rights could be accepted, by co-workers at least, if the cause was sufficiently worthy and the individuals acted primarily within their own sphere. In other words, the novelty of women seeking to influence Parliament and signing separate petitions was offset by their stress on female concern for slavery's affront to women and the family, as well by their willingness to leave public speaking and policy-making largely under the control of men.

Far less acceptable to male abolitionists was the pressure for immediate emancipation mounted by the radical Quaker pamphleteer and reformer Elizabeth Heyrick, and a number of female anti-slavery societies: most men inclined to gradualism, perhaps being more attuned to the compromises of politics. Heyrick's anonymous publications were so vigorous that they were thought to have been the work of a man. Yet as Corfield attests, she was a believer in feminine mission, not an advocate of women's rights.[134] Anti-slavery activities are correctly seen as impelling American women towards feminism from the 1830s onwards, in advance of their British sisters (see below, p. 63). In Britain, women were a significant force in abolitionism long before the 1830s, but a comparable transition was not made because social conditions were less conducive to substantial changes in their position.

Powerful contributors to this British conservatism were, of course, evangelicals whose determination to preserve the status quo, even when they were engaged in reform, cannot be emphasised too strongly. The fact that Britain produced the best-known woman evangelical in Hannah More is therefore perhaps less to be wondered at than its production of the best-known late-eighteenth-century woman radical in Mary Wollstonecraft. A London poet and playwright who turned her talents to lively and improving tracts for the masses, More, like Wollstonecraft, delivered herself of some well-publicised *Strictures on the Modern System of Female Education* (1799). In this and a 1777 collection of essays on the same subject, More was concerned that girls should be instructed in their spiritual duties so that, as women, they could effectively carry out their responsibilities for educating children and upholding both religion and the family. Reflecting the prevailing conservative alarm about rationalism, democratic excesses and aristocratic dissipation, More's work, which dismissed the contemporary talk of women's rights, sought to strengthen the existing social order by restoring harmony in the family and virtue in all classes of people. It was widely appreciated by conservatives in the United States; More was proud of having numerous correspondents there, and of the 'number of superior Americans who visit me'.

Condemning Wollstonecraft's *Vindication* unread, More accepted that men and women were very different, and destined for different roles in society (although she herself enjoyed the normally masculine status of literary celebrity and notable who must be visited when she retired from London to the Mendip Hills). Yet the two women shared a contempt for novel reading, fashion and frivolity, and an interest in improving female schooling and child-rearing practices – even if More stressed the need for discipline and submission, not love and natural expression, in the parent–child relationship. Like the American proponents of the concept of republican motherhood, More believed that women's education should be functional, designed to fit them for a useful domesticity or other kinds of service. Unlike American educators, however, neither she nor her fellow evangelicals Sarah Trimmer and the Reverend Thomas Gisborne, who similarly addressed themselves to female schooling and duties, envisaged broadening as opposed to improving women intellectually. More's significance as a writer on education lies in her concern for better teaching methods and her ability, as 'a woman of recognised religious and social position', to provide aspiring middle-class readers with a reliable 'guide to female propriety'.

Nor was there any expansion of female academies in Britain comparable to that which took place in America. The charitable day schools and Sunday Schools founded by evangelicals, like the other eighteenth-century charity schools, did provide instruction for girls and an opportunity for women, as teachers, to serve the community. But though they were regarded with suspicion by local ministers and propertied interests who saw no point and much risk in educating the poor, their purpose was more religious and disciplinary than educational. In the day and Sunday Schools she set up in the Mendips with her sisters' help, More acknowledged that she was acting upon a narrow vision of popular education. She favoured the instruction of pupils in reading but not in writing, confining reading to 'the Scriptures and such books as were preparatory to and connected with them'. Anything further was dangerous, and by 1821 More was beseeching political friends interested in education to tread the middle way 'between the Scylla of brutal ignorance and the Charybdis of literary education. The one is cruel, the other preposterous.'[135] The subjects available at the charity schools were predominantly designed to train girls for their future employment as servants and for homemaking, while the fare offered to girls in the elementary schools established by the (Church of England) National Society for Promoting the Education of the Poor (1811) and the (non-denominational) British and Foreign Schools Society (1814) was little better. As a result, the literacy level of women continued to lag behind that of men.[136]

The general enlargement of female opportunities came later in Britain than it did in the United States, despite a continuing debate on women's instruction to which popular novelists as well as pedagogues contributed, and in which the opinions of conservatives were challenged by more radical spirits such as the writer and reformer Harriet Martineau who, in the 1820s, asserted that women could safely be taught a range of subjects without unfitting them for domesticity.[137] This educational lag does much to explain why organised feminism also emerged later in Britain, despite the greater prominence there of female writers on the 'woman question' from the eighteenth century through to the early nineteenth. Schooling expanded more readily in a republic which was anxious to train up women who were the antithesis of frivolous European womanhood than it did in a country divided by class and lacking any 'conception of popular education as the foundation of a common citizenship'.[138]

(iv) *Industrialisation*

The effect on women of the last great development that concerns us in this chapter – the Industrial Revolution – is not easy to gauge. It is certainly difficult to decide whether women and 'the family' lost or gained from industrialisation and the accompanying changes in agriculture. But it does appear that the impact of the industrial transformation was in many ways the same for women on both sides of the Atlantic, although the process was fully under way in the second half of the eighteenth century in Britain, quickening noticeably after 1780; whereas in the United States the move away from home to factory production was only beginning between 1760 and 1808.[139]

For women in both countries, notwithstanding enormous regional variations in each, industrialisation meant that manufacturing they had once done in the home, particularly of textiles, was transferred to factories. None the less, much work continued to be organised by manufacturers on an outwork basis, and this work, though it was generally poorly paid, obviously interfered less with women's family responsibilities than factory labour. For women whose husbands were favourably placed, the loss of home manufacturing responsibilities and the servants made possible by industrial prosperity may have left them with more time to spend on their families, which in turn would bring satisfaction that they were conforming to society's ideal of womanhood. Factory production of goods once made in the home also enhanced the importance of comfortably off women as consumers (just as they had become major consumers of literature by the early nineteenth century). For poor women, however, neither the new role in consumption nor the new dependence on money income was an advantage.

The gains enjoyed by the women who obtained industrial employment were income with which they could help themselves or family members, the company of their peers, emancipation from customary community pressures in the textile towns, and broadened horizons which might lead to improved job or marriage prospects. Yet generalisations are dangerous, and the benefits of the emerging economic order should not be exaggerated. The first stages of industrialisation were generally painful, and in the long term the sexual division of labour and the disparagement of women's work – waged or unwaged – became more marked. Industrialisation added to the divisions between women who, especially in the non-slaveholding sections of America, had previously been divided mainly according to marital status. Now, while working-class women might find employment outside the home, the middle-class woman was barred by her social status from applying for factory work, felt her existing lack of economic opportunities the more keenly, and looked more determinedly for fresh outlets, which she found chiefly in philanthropy. Jobs which had been the preserve of women at home did not necessarily go to women when they were taken over by the factory: spinning, for instance, was shared between the sexes as a result of the transition. Workers dependent on market forces were more likely to experience pronounced fluctuations in their circumstances than labourers in the household economy had been, and women lost one of their means of securing economic independence wherever agriculture was commercialised. Those who were drawn into the factories were made to feel uneasy by contemporary moralists who warned of the dangers of impressionable young women working away from home, married women doing so to the detriment of their families, and females of whatever status being placed in close contact with male strangers. Such warnings were issued despite the fact that women did not automatically labour alongside men in the factories, and were often simply carrying out in industrial plants tasks that had traditionally been theirs in the home.

There were other problems. Women were recruited by employers in part because they felt that they could safely pay them less than men; this did nothing for the female self-image and brought upon women the animosity of male competitors for jobs. Since most women continued to be employed at home, in domestic service, a range of traditional urban occupations or agriculture during the first phase of industrialisation, the female workforce in the factories lacked the numerical strength to challenge economic exploitation or to force male co-workers to consider its interests seriously. Since many women retired from paid employment once they married, or shortly thereafter, and the needs of widowed, deserted and single women were never adequately recognised in family-orientated societies, it is easy to see how industrialisation eventually encouraged the view that women were a temporary element in the waged labour force, and that male wage earners should receive a 'family wage' to enable them to support their womenfolk at home. And since industrialisation imposed strains on all the workers concerned, as they were forced to adjust to strange surroundings, the erosion of old community supports, an unfamiliar stress on timekeeping and decreased independence, it is not surprising that men took out some of their fears and suspicions on women of their own class.[140]

Although female experiences of the Industrial Revolution were similar in Britain and America, there were nevertheless certain differences which were vital for the subsequent development of the women's movement. Having the example of exploitative British industrialisation before them, the first American employers who tried to attract women to the textile mills of the North claimed that they would combine 'doing good and doing well' by taking on Yankee farm girls for better-than-normal pay and providing them with wholesome living conditions.[141] As we shall see (pp. 74–6 below), these appealing terms of employment were not permanent (nor were they offered by all employers who recruited women). They lasted long enough to convince native and foreign commentators that capitalist ventures operated in a more humane fashion in the United States than they did in Britain, and to reinforce the reluctance of contemporary American politicians to recognise the class cleavages which were developing in their own country.

Women were even more important numerically in the early New England textile factories than they were in the British mills, not least because the Americans used frame spinning machinery which could be conveniently managed by women wearing long skirts.[142] But this advantage was offset by their minority status in the workforce as a whole, by the limited development of the American labour movement during the first decades of the nineteenth century, by its leaders' failure to acknowledge the increasing proletarianisation of workers, and by the belief among all sections of the community that 'free' land and political liberty for white men would prevent the social conflicts of the Old World from spreading to the New. Working-class women in Britain and the United States alike tried to improve their circumstances under industrialisation by banding together with both women and men of their own class. As the next chapter will show, the ability of British women to do so was greater than that of their American sisters, just as middle-class feminists in Britain's more advanced industrial society gave greater priority than their American counterparts to employment issues in the formative stages of their campaign. The result would be a feminist movement in Britain which showed a keener awareness of class, and was more divided by it, than the movement which emerged in the United States, where racial and ethnic divisions between women were of larger concern.

2

~

The forces that shaped the women's movements

1820s–1850s

I. Accelerating social change

In Chapter 1 it was argued that by the middle of the eighteenth century there was more evidence of changing social attitudes towards women, and of female opportunities for individual and group assertion, than was once supposed. The quickening pace of change in the last quarter of that century and the first two decades of the next has also been stressed, even though it must be conceded that anti-feminist tracts circulated alongside feminist publications in Britain; that no group base of support for feminism had been established in either country; and that the impact on women's lives of the American Revolution and associated radicalism, of religious ferment and the Industrial Revolution, was complex. We have further noted that if the differences between the experiences of British and American women have sometimes been exaggerated, while the women of both countries most usually entered benevolent and reform activities under the influence of evangelical religion, pioneer feminism took distinctive forms on each side of the Atlantic. Thus, whereas women in Britain produced the earliest feminist literature and anti-slavery crusaders, as well as – in Wollstonecraft and More – the best-known individual exponent and opponent of equal rights feminism, their American counterparts made the first gains in women's education that had clear implications for the nineteenth-century feminist movement. Moreover, the upheavals of the Revolution gave American women a consciousness of possessing special benefits and responsibilities, and an aversion to accepting the intellectual leadership of the British; whereas their prior acquaintance with strict class stratification and the changes induced by industrialisation rendered British women more sensitive to employment and class issues than their American sisters.

Organised feminism in Britain and the United States built upon these foundations, but was further nurtured from the 1820s onwards by economic, political and ideological changes which profoundly altered the prospects of women, not always for the better. The most important among them were urbanisation, the extension of the political rights of white men, and the elaboration and widespread dissemination by an assertive middle class of already circulating ideas about female domesticity.

Urbanisation had many identical features in the Anglo-American world. The dominance of established merchants, clerics, civic leaders, prosperous tradesmen and artisans was challenged as old towns and cities grew and new ones developed under the impact of technological innovation, aspiring capitalists and immigrants from home and abroad. Although industrialisation did not transform all urban areas, it did create industrial towns of an unfamiliar and forbidding character, while the coincidence of urbanisation and industrialisation strengthened contemporary unease about the dimensions of change. As the face of the countryside was transformed by the two processes, and the demands of the marketplace on farmers increased, they added their voices to those critical of the new economic order.

Existing urban facilities and services could not cope with the problems created by rapid expansion and a consequent increase in homelessness, disease, fire hazards, crime and crowd action. The disparity of circumstances between rich and poor was more starkly apparent in the cities than in rural regions, and the affluent feared the aspirations, deplored the actions and disliked the manners of their poorer neighbours. In the midst of city crowds, people were strangers to each other; cut off from their old ties, they were rootless, lonely, and harassed by alien work disciplines and living conditions.[1] Migrants to the town were obliged to forge new social relationships and struggle intensely to secure economic independence. Large numbers failed, sinking into poverty which the combined efforts of municipal relief, charities and – in Britain – the poor law, did not adequately alleviate. Their fate was in sharp contrast to that of the middle class, which grew in size and self-awareness, extolling the work ethic and stressing the importance of professional qualifications. As a result of changes in the class structure and the loosening, for some, of traditional religious and community disciplines, courtship and marriage practices also altered. Yet while middle-class men frequently delayed marriage and reproduction until they could attain the increased standard of living they had come to expect, in the working class the reverse was the case, with men often marrying to secure the economic contributions of their wives and probable children, and illegitimate births increasing when weddings were deferred for economic reasons.[2]

Urban tensions were particularly strong in the United States, whose leaders had hoped to avoid the evils they saw in European cities. The contrast between the intended rural utopia of colonial days and the diverse nation of the early nineteenth century was acutely painful. Adjustment difficulties were further compounded in America by the immigrants from Europe who flooded into its cities in far greater numbers than the Irish migrants who, at the same time, were moving to the west of Scotland and England. And the extension of the franchise to American working men by the 1840s also enhanced their power to alarm the conservative and influential city-dweller, whereas urban working men in Britain were not enfranchised until the second Reform Act of 1867.

The significance of such developments for the emergence of the women's movement is complicated. As one might expect, men competing in a harsh urban environment proved hostile to additional competition in the job market from women, who were in consequence paid less than men and hired specifically for 'women's work'. Moreover, men who spent long periods of time working away from their families might feel less confident of their supremacy at home than they had done in the days of the family economy, and anxious to reassert that authority. In order to do so and – as Barbara Berg points out – to link a cherished past to a worrying present, many male publicists stressed the importance of women remaining in the home as a nurturing force, endowed with supposedly natural virtues and able to humanise an unnatural urban environment. At a time when political institutions were unable to cope with the strains of urbanisation, especially when they were linked with those of industrialisation, the ancient institution of the family was to provide much needed social cement and apply a brake on the careering vehicle of change.[3]

If the family circumstances of women already living in towns and cities might not be greatly altered by urban growth, those who moved there from the country or overseas lost the support of extended kinship and feminine connections. As a result, the very women exhorted to create a companionate haven for their husbands and children might be among the most isolated of urbanites. But just as the city itself was a complex paradox rather than an unmitigated evil, so the experience of urban women was a diverse and contradictory one. Thus, on the one hand, they gained access to better consumer goods, literature, medical services, schools and social amenities of all kinds; yet on the other hand, with the loss of much household manufacture to factories, middle-class women might find themselves with too little to do, while working-class women had too much, and for poor recompense. On the one hand, women might be expected to become the decorative appendages and selfless supporters of their husbands; but on the other hand, in the freer intellectual environment of urban communities and driven by middle-class emphasis on achievement, they might find the stimulation for fresh action on behalf of the lower-class victims of profound economic change, and on their own account.[4]

As far as political change is concerned, following the enfranchisement of white working men in the United States in the period after the War of 1812 through the 1840s, sex and race remained as the two great divisions in American society. Having seen 'aristocracy' overthrown by the Revolution and the subsequent speedy establishment of democracy, it was likely that conservatives of all kinds would rally to defend these last barriers against the creation of a truly equal society. It was equally likely that American women would take heart at the advance of democracy as well as offence at the conservative reaction to it: would seek to advance their own civil rights by pointing out how far the recognition of such rights had proceeded in the New World, and by making a telling analogy between the oppression of women and blacks. But they were cautious in doing so, recognising how unpalatable their claims were to male contemporaries. In Britain, where the franchise was extended in stages during the nineteenth century (1832, 1867 and 1884), and adult male suffrage was not achieved until 1918, women had no Revolutionary or democratic tradition to which they could appeal amid the economic and political turmoil of the 1830s and 1840s: the Reform Bill of 1832 was one element in a complex process of change – albeit one which, as Thomson observes, 'offered a taste of reform and whetted the appetite for more'.[5] They were, none the less, fortunate in not having to cope with the enormous racial, ethnic and regional differences which divided American women and were reflected in American politics with the rise of the second party system from the 1820s.

The ideology of domesticity, which justified separate spheres for the sexes, was, as we have seen, alive in the eighteenth century on both sides of the Atlantic, although its best-known literary exponents were British. In the early nineteenth century, however, it received a tremendous fillip from the expansion of female education, the successes of evangelical religion, the dominance of the more than formerly durable nuclear family, the influence of the middle class, and the tensions generated by industrialisation and urbanisation: developments which left women concerned about their status and ready to make and respond to pronouncements upon the subject. These proliferated in the 1820s and 1830s, in novels and poetry, sermons and tracts, handbooks and magazines. Relying on the scriptural subordination of women and scientific arguments about the weaknesses of feminine physiognomy, theorists of domesticity considered the behaviour appropriate for true women; their social position, education, maternal responsibilities in general and child-rearing duties in particular. And as had been the case in the eighteenth century, feminine characteristics that were constructed to meet specific historical circumstances were sanctioned by being presented as natural.[6]

For women of both countries, the disadvantages that ensued from the veneration of home and matrimony were much the same. Unmarried women were made to feel still more 'redundant' than they had formerly done, while the common law affecting married women, somewhat modified in early America, was rigorously upheld. Driven towards conservatism in all societies and ages because of their physical vulnerability and need to secure a stable environment for their children, women found that their conservatism was now given a formal social function. Yet by providing men with a revered sanctuary away from the workplace and accepting their hostility to female economic competition in the capitalist order, those middle- and working-class women who embraced the cult of domesticity helped to stifle masculine discontent with economic exploitation and made it difficult for radical women to gain social acceptance. Women themselves had no escape from the pressures of their working environment – the home. They were expected to be pure, whereas sexual licence was extended to their menfolk. And if women, because of their alleged identity of interest, were supposed to give stability to societies in flux, the denial of female individuality irked many spirited women and seemed particularly at odds with traditional American veneration for natural rights.[7]

Notions of domesticity accorded women at once too little and too much. Thus they were granted, in moral superiority, a status that did not have to be earned and was not always deserved; while the demand that, in return, women were to be pious, selfless and submissive weighed heavily on the ambitious or the nonconformist. What is more, as Berg and Cott have shown, there were also many contradictions within the doctrine of domesticity to dismay its conscientious supporters. Exhorted to seek solidarity with members of their own sex, women were encouraged to believe themselves incapable of co-operating effectively in the workplace. Expected to control their children, women had little control over their own lives and were in some respects treated as children. They were rebuked when they were frivolous but disliked when they were learned; allowed to nurse the sick, yet celebrated for their delicacy; praised for their creation of compassionate havens for men, but left without masculine company for long periods. Brought up to regard themselves as the antithesis of men, women were urged to consider domestic work, teaching and philanthropy as their professions, modelled on those of men.

The celebration of domesticity none the less brought certain benefits to women. Their roles in housekeeping and child-rearing were elevated, their usefulness was stressed, and their virtues were celebrated. In order to carry out the professional duties of domesticity properly, women had to be educated, and their prospects as writers were further improved by the growing market for literature on domestic issues. If middle- and working-class women alike found it difficult to gain employment beyond the home, once it was pronounced to be their true place, the better-off did find some relief from domestic and social pressures by retreating into sickrooms; while women of both classes might find solace and independence from men in close female friendships and in building on their already established role as reformers, with a special interest in matters which appealed to female sensibilities or affected religion, home and family.[8]

We should not make the mistake of thinking that the concepts of domesticity and separate spheres were static, evenly applied, or an exact description of reality. They were elaborated in a specific historical context, by women as well as men, and although they defined female qualities in relation to those of men, not all men found them appealing, while members of both sexes were involved in modifying (without abandoning) these concepts when social circumstances changed (see below, pp. 126, 182, 214).[9] The cult of domesticity seems to have been more successfully propagated in the United States than in Britain, though it flourished in both countries. In his much-quoted observations on American women, the French commentator Alexis de Tocqueville, writing in the 1830s, noted that 'nowhere are young women surrendered so early or so completely to their own guidance', only for that independence to be 'irrecoverably lost in the bonds of matrimony. If an unmarried woman is less constrained ... [in the United States] than elsewhere, a wife is subjected to stricter obligations.' This paradox was explained by Tocqueville with reference to the Americans' status as a 'puritanical people and a commercial nation', since 'the former consider the regularity of woman's life as the best pledge and most certain sign of the purity of her morals; [and] the latter regard it as the highest security for the order and prosperity of the household'. Tocqueville went on to add that democracy between the sexes was possible without the erroneous supposition that men and women were the same. Women in America voluntarily surrendered their own will to their husbands on marriage, aware of the high regard in which they were held and accepting that the nation had applied 'to the sexes the great principle of political economy which governs the manufacturers of our age, by carefully dividing the duties of man from those of woman in order that the great work of society may be the better carried on'. Tocqueville's judgements were subsequently endorsed by the influential American editor and author Sarah Josepha Hale, who proclaimed her country to be 'the land of modern chivalry, where the moral qualities of women are most highly valued, and her station in society as "the glory of the man" most fully acknowledged'.

Other visitors to the United States during the 1820s and 1830s confirmed the strength of American domesticity but were less convinced than Tocqueville of its benefits. The English writer Harriet Martineau, for example, complained that while her lot was supposedly paradise, the American woman's 'intellect is confined, her morals crushed, her health ruined, her weaknesses encouraged, and her strength punished'. A fellow observer from England, Frances Trollope, deplored the rigid separation of the sexes she found on her western travels. Both she and Martineau criticised the enforced idleness of American women and felt that religion was important to them as an occupation: in Mrs Trollope's words, 'were it not for public worship and private tea drinking, all the ladies in Cincinnati would be in danger of becoming perfect recluses'. The British lecturer and reformer Frances Wright, who passed half her adult life in America, was similarly uneasy about the situation of the country's women, observing the contrast between their free single state and their constricted circumstances on marriage, and mourning their lack of educational opportunities and civic duties. Wright and Martineau were agreed that – as the latter put it – American women were given 'indulgence' as 'a substitute for justice'.[10]

These commentators were inclined to overstate the fixed and universal condition of women in the United States. After all, only the comfortably situated (there and in Britain) could afford to practise the full-blown ideal of domesticity. As radicals who had admired many features of American life from a distance, Martineau and Wright may have overreacted to the sexual inequality they found on arrival. Tocqueville may have exaggerated the prestige accorded to American women because of his jaundiced view of the treatment of their European counterparts, and Mrs Trollope was notoriously hard to please. More importantly, Martineau, Wright and Trollope do not explain what they found, while Tocqueville's explanation is not entirely satisfactory. It is necessary to add that the doctrines of domesticity acquired a more central role in the United States than in Britain – first because of the Revolutionary debate about the importance of motherhood in the republic, and then because in a very rapidly growing and increasingly diverse country they placed women, more respectably than slaves, in a reassuringly stable and subordinate position. Martineau might condemn the generally rudimentary state of American letters, but in the buoyant literature of domesticity we can see one example among many of Americans taking up ideas and organisational forms first envisaged abroad, and applying them with a previously unknown enthusiasm.

It has also been suggested that the elevation of domesticity created the notion of a responsible American 'lady', impervious to class distinctions and so not to be confused with the European, aristocratic variety.[11] Unfortunately, the fashionable American 'lady' all too often displayed the elitism of – and coveted the deference accorded to – the genuine article.[12] Her existence was a barrier to the growth of an individualistic feminism, notably in the southern states, where the desire to create a landowning aristocracy and uphold a patriarchal family structure was firmly entrenched.[13] Furthermore, southerners' enthusiasm for a restrictive ladyhood could increase the sense of difference between the conservative South and the liberal North, as shown in the complaint made to a correspondent by the Boston educator Elizabeth Peabody about the need 'to defend the female sex from the aspersions some of your southern friends are pleased to throw upon it'.[14]

American enthusiasm for the cult of domesticity should not, however, be allowed to obscure its importance in Britain. The domestic ideology was initially associated with the evangelical desire to preserve respectability and social order in the midst of working-class and intellectual unrest; its subsequent popularity owed much to the growing economic, political and moral power of the bourgeoisie in British society from the 1830s onwards. Yet while confident members of the middle class hoped to reform the aristocracy and the working class alike, they were less *anxious* about the existence of class than their American counterparts. Hence their mores, as Jeffrey Weeks points out, were only 'secondarily for export to other classes', and should primarily be seen as a means of self-definition. This was particularly true of the clerics and men of science who, in contributing to the pronouncements on domesticity, confirmed their influence in society and professional status, and might use their knowledge as a weapon against the less well informed. Thus while both feminists and such exponents of separate spheres could agree that the position of its women was the test of any civilisation, patriarchal anthropologists were able to argue that in primitive societies, where women had exercised some power, this was rooted in an unacceptable equality of hard labour with men, besides being accompanied by a promiscuity and lack of polite attentions between the sexes that merely served to demonstrate the superiority of their own domestic arrangements.[15]

II. Educational advances

For all their complexity, the economic, political and social changes of the 1820s and 1830s were sufficient to provoke some women to challenge their prescribed roles and others to enlarge them within the framework of domesticity. Efforts began in education, through which, it was hoped, women's vocational prospects and means of self-development would be increased. These involved both the use of 'informal institutions – reading circles, "conversations", public lectures, the exchange of letters and ideas between friends, acquaintances, and kin' – and the expansion of formal schooling. Self-education, though it was the most accessible form of improvement, was likely to be lonely and unrigorous, unable to provide the confidence and purpose that come from peer-group company and competition. The correspondence of the New England Peabody sisters during the 1820s and 1830s reveals some of the problems, as they sought satisfaction in nature, religion, acquaintances, books and language study, stressing the need for 'some serious pursuit' but reacting uneasily to any woman with 'a tinge of *blue*'.[16] In the United States, however, as we have seen, pioneers also pressed ahead with the creation of private academies and secondary schools for girls. And they were admitted, alongside boys, to the state-funded primary schools set up in the first half of the nineteenth century.

The coeducation of children – initially in elementary schools and, after 1865, in public secondary schools – is seen as a distinctively American development. Why it should have occurred is less obvious. It seems probable, as Woody suggests, that once the states had made their commitment to popular instruction, coeducation was adopted because it offered 'economy of means and forces', and 'convenience to patrons of the school'. A simple American commitment to the equality of the sexes is not the explanation, although the achievements of the academies may have convinced doubters that girls were as educable as boys by the 1860s.[17] After all, coeducation was initially strongly resisted at the college level in both the United States and Britain, and the high schools (of which there were only 44 by 1860) switched to coeducation only once the female academies had proved themselves. While they were doing so, many might have queried the judgement of the American feminist Elizabeth Cady Stanton, based on her own experiences, that it was 'a grave mistake to send boys and girls to separate institutions of learning. ... The stimulus of sex promotes alike a healthy condition of the intellectual and the moral faculties and gives to both a development they never can acquire alone.'[18]

The private academies were easily begun and often ambitious enough in their offerings – writing, spelling, rhetoric, arithmetic, geography, history – to stretch both the pupils and the women teachers they produced and employed. It was pleasant to be able to instruct children previously without an opportunity of learning, and good to feel useful. Yet teaching in either private or public schools did not pay well, the academies were frequently vulnerably small and reliant on affluent patrons, and according to Woody's figures, between 1820 and 1860 boys' schools were incorporated at two and a half times the rate of girls' academies. Moreover, while some women enjoyed the challenge and independence teaching afforded, and found through education a broader vision of their role, others were mainly interested in the money they earned, recorded pupils 'who were backward in learning', or expressed their thankfulness to quit the profession after a while, when anything better offered: 'I think I have done my part of teaching.' In urban schools, they were also subordinated to men.

Race, class and ethnicity were additional complications in the American educational system: the instruction of groups other than women was also discussed in strictly utilitarian terms, and they in turn responded to educational opportunities in varied ways. Whereas educators alarmed about mass immigration and social change commonly saw elementary schooling as a means of assimilating the newcomers and the poor of all kinds, immigrant parents differed in their appreciation of education and found much to alarm them in American public schools, with their emphasis on assimilation and coeducation, and their female authority figures. Only a tiny fraction of the nation's free blacks gained any instruction, and schooling for slaves was frowned on by whites as unnecessary and subversive. Free blacks, unlike Indians, positively desired schools, but were hampered by their own poverty and white prejudice against interracial education, though black women teachers such as the middle-class Philadelphian Sarah Douglass worked hard for the improvement of themselves and their race, and teaching provided them with one of the few alternatives to domestic service. If education for Indian girls was thought to be desirable, so that they might be converted to domesticity on the white pattern and help to 'civilise' Indian males, the instruction of Indian boys and girls alike was at a rudimentary stage before the Civil War (1861–5), notwithstanding the establishment of a government fund for the purpose in 1819. And poor women generally had limited educational opportunities and might find, whatever their acknowledged responsibilities for educating children, that they had 'no time to learn them': as one harassed woman put it,[19] with 'so many little cares, and *big* washings and ironings I cannot get time to do anything else'.

Nor were the influence and character of the new schools uniform throughout the country. Elementary schooling was strongest in the East and in urban areas; the academy's stronghold was in New England and New York. In Pennsylvania, the Quakers 'pioneered in elementary and secondary education for girls and young women'. The female academies of the South (where the first such institution was established) tended to be directed by ministers and staffed by female teachers from the North: educated southern women were expected to put their schooling to use at home.[20] However, the southern states sustained academies longer, being slower to fund public high schools and endorse coeducation than their more interventionist, less conservative northern neighbours.[21] The conditions endured by teachers in the West were distinctly

~

primitive, and the spread of academies in that region, as in the South, was encouraged by northern pioneers, perhaps the best known being Emma Willard and Catharine Beecher.

Already established as a teacher and educator when she moved to Cincinnati from New England in 1832, Beecher hoped to make teaching something it was not at that time: 'a profession dominated by – indeed exclusively belonging to – women'.[22] She subsequently devoted many years to speaking tours designed to raise money for teachers and schools in the West, founding the National Board of Popular Education (1847) and the American Women's Educational Association (1852) to advance her efforts. Like Willard, she was interested in providing teacher training, establishing a department for the purpose at Milwaukee – Downer College (which still survives); such training had been talked of since the 1820s and took off seriously with the founding of state normal (or teachers') schools from 1839.[23]

Beecher's endeavours were helped by the scarcity of teachers in the West, where economic opportunities were burgeoning and men were needed for other jobs.[24] Yet success did not bring complete satisfaction. Although Beecher saw teaching as an excellent preparation for women's care of children in marriage and a respectable alternative to the domestic life she extolled, her own life amply reveals the strains imposed on an ambitious woman by the ideals of domesticity, as her biographer, Kathryn Kish Sklar, has established. The champion of private women in the home, for whom she provided unusually frank and comprehensive advice manuals, Beecher remained an unmarried career woman without a permanent home, and hungry for fame. Envious of men's cultural dominance and determined to define a satisfying role for women as self-denying promoters of religion, class harmony, national unity and social conscience, she was never entirely satisfied with her own circumstances, and aspired to affluence and social position in an anything but selfless fashion. An enthusiast for the teaching profession, she neglected the hard grind of the pedagogue and organiser for the glamour of the travelling celebrity whenever she could, relying on female helpers for a kind of wifely support. Beecher was, Sklar concludes, a feminist and an anti-feminist, a conservative and an innovator.[25] The paradoxes of her life as a public figure who celebrated the joys of the private domain bring to mind the similar tensions in the career of the British evangelical Hannah More.

American women found much greater difficulty in gaining access to higher education, as is borne out by the protest in 1848 of the first ever women's rights convention, held at Seneca Falls, New York, against female exclusion from 'all colleges'.[26] Their advances in elementary and secondary education had not been due entirely to women's own efforts, and certainly not due to overtly feminist pressures. Primary schools had seemed essential to male reformers who felt that the extension of the suffrage and schooling must go together in the interests of a stable republic. These reformers had likewise welcomed the advent of the woman instructor because of her cheapness and their belief that women were 'incomparably better teachers for young children than males'. (As in Europe, though to a much lesser degree, women's suitability to teach older boys was called into question.)[27] Fathers who were fond of their daughters could be persuaded that their schooling would make them still more agreeable companions, or provide them with a respectable living if they remained unmarried; while the contemporary stress upon the need to educate women for their sacred family and church responsibilities might soothe any anxieties among conservatives. Access to college was an altogether more contentious matter.

In the first place, American college education was modelled on that of Europe, and especially England, so that if improvements were to be made, one might expect that they would first be gained for male students. Secondly, whereas advanced instruction was designed to fit men for the professions, for their lives' work, it was harder for conservatives to see what use it would be to women. That it would give them ideas beyond their sphere seemed more than likely; that the women involved would find the work beyond them, damage their health, abandon decorum, and marry late, if at all, was feared. Even so, thanks to the determined efforts of Mary Lyon, Mount Holyoke female seminary opened its doors in 1837 in South Hadley, Massachusetts. With its three-year course and students over the age of sixteen, Mount Holyoke was an institution midway between a school and a college which developed into the latter (in 1893), while Oberlin College in Ohio (established in 1833) was a coeducational foundation which first admitted women on a shortened course and then on the same terms as men. Its example was followed in the 1850s by Antioch College, Ohio, and by several state universities. However, Oberlin expected its female students to prepare themselves 'for intelligent motherhood and a properly subservient wifehood', while Mount Holyoke required its students to undertake domestic tasks.[28] It may be true that the best women's schools offered most of the subjects taught by men's colleges in the first two years of undergraduate life,[29] but it was not until the 1850s, with the creation of four-year female colleges in a number of northern states, that women had institutions of their own – albeit short-lived – which provided fare roughly comparable to that available in the men's establishments.[30]

Although access to higher education was proclaimed as an objective at the Seneca Falls convention, the pioneer feminists were as uneasy about such separate foundations as they were about arguments that there should be a separate female curriculum. They feared that women's colleges and courses could be used to reinforce the notion of separate spheres for the sexes and ease the pressure on the major men's colleges and professional schools to open their doors to women, as proposed in 1848. Like other reformers, feminists accorded priority to those parts of their programme where swift progress looked possible, notably the demand for changes in the law governing the property of married women; the struggle for higher education was given greater support and made greater headway after the Civil War. None the less, just as the early seminaries had produced women who went on to enlarge female employment opportunities, so the first colleges to admit women, including the transitional Mount Holyoke, produced subsequent feminist leaders and pioneers in men's professions, among them the Massachusetts farmer's daughter Lucy Stone, who graduated from Oberlin to become a successful women's rights lecturer; her friend and Oberlin contemporary, Antoinette Brown, whose interest in theology and subsequent career as a cleric owed nothing to the encouragement of the Oberlin authorities; and the first fully qualified American doctor, Elizabeth Blackwell, who began her long struggle to become a practising physician after studying at Geneva College in western New York.[31]

Lacking the impetus provided by the advance of democracy, state intervention and the debate about republican motherhood, education for women in Britain proceeded more slowly than in America at every level, although members of the Dissenting sects, accustomed to providing for themselves in a hostile world, were unusually willing to provide instruction for their daughters. As far as primary schools were concerned, while notions about domestic destiny still flourished and shaped the curriculum for girls, class and religious anxieties continued to play a bigger role in determining educational provision. At a time when the wisdom of educating the masses was still keenly debated and the value of child labour was appreciated by parents and employers alike, it was unrealistic to expect rapid gains. As well as attending Sunday Schools and dame schools (generally run by ill-qualified and unexacting women, desperate for employment) the children of the poor went to institutions established by the National Society and British and Foreign School Society. But since Society schools made a minimal charge, the best hope for children from destitute families was entry to the so-called 'ragged' schools, begun in 1820 and numbering 82 by 1848. One of the most important workers in this field was Mary Carpenter, the daughter of an affluent Unitarian clergyman, whose interest in the ragged children of her home city, Bristol, was aroused by a visiting Unitarian minister and social reformer, Joseph Tuckerman. Following a path common to humanitarians, Carpenter went from concern for one group of the disadvantaged to care for others: the result was a network of individual schools for young vagrants and reform schools for youthful delinquents.[32]

Low standards in the Society schools were somewhat improved once the government granted them support (from 1833) and instituted (in 1839) a Committee of the Privy Council on Education and Her Majesty's Inspectorate of Schools to supervise their activities. Under the leadership of James Kay (later Sir James Kay-Shuttleworth) the Committee emphasised the importance of practical as well as general education, and from 1846 encouraged the training of pupil-teachers to improve on the work of student monitors, who had previously eased the teacher shortage. Teacher training colleges were set up from 1836, and by 1858 the women's establishments were training more students than either their male or mixed counterparts. In 1860, three-quarters of the certificated teachers were women.

Yet if as early as the 1840s there were more female governesses and teachers than male educators, and by the 1860s teaching had emerged as a women's profession in Britain as well as the United States, the women who became primary-school teachers were largely working-class, were paid some 40 per cent less than men, and were encouraged to know their place. They were also regarded with dismay by the mistresses of small private schools, who made a modest living in the nineteenth century, clung tenaciously to their ladylike amateurishness, and felt obliged to defer slavishly to the wishes and opinions of their patrons.[33] The practical training in all elementary schools was poor, the inspectors had too much to do, and sectarian differences continued to hamper the provision of primary education for all. Children of either sex were seldom in school beyond the age of eleven, and Turner estimates that in 1851 only 'about 24 per cent of the male population under twenty and 20 per cent of the girls in the same age-group were enrolled for public or private day schools'. Attendance figures for both sexes were about 4 per cent down on enrolment.[34] Even the Owenite Socialists, who from the 1830s made a serious attempt to involve girls and women at every level of their educational programme, were affected by contemporary arguments that female enlightenment was necessary to enhance that of men; and though Britain was more advanced in working-class adult education than America, they supported women's admission to Mechanics' Institutes partly to embarrass the middle-class advocates of exclusion.[35]

A more determined effort to improve their own educational prospects was made by middle-class women conscious of the limited opportunities offered by teaching and the ample restraints imposed by class. Although the way had been prepared by women writers urging educational improvements since the 1820s, publicity about the poor qualifications and pay of governesses from the 1830s sparked a more profound awareness of the problems of the large number of genteel females who needed to make a living, and a real concern among customers beginning to recognise that the old educational standards would not suffice in an increasingly competitive world.[36] One result was the establishment in London in 1848 of the Queen's College for Women. Owing much to the intellectual commitment of a leading Christian Socialist, the Reverend Frederick Denison Maurice, and other members of staff from King's College London, the new institution was equally fortunate in securing Anglican support and the financial backing of one of Queen Victoria's ladies-in-waiting, Amelia Murray. Like many American colleges of the time, Queen's was actually a secondary school with aspirations, admitting girls from the age of twelve. However, like the early American seminaries, it offered an impressively wide curriculum and attracted a number of students who subsequently achieved public distinction: Sophia Jex-Blake, who pioneered medical education for women; the writer Julia Wedgwood; the poets Jean Ingelow and Adelaide Anne Proctor; and the educators Frances Mary Buss, Dorothea Beale and Frances Martin.[37]

The tone of Queen's College was both adventurous and prudent, as would be the case with other innovative institutions in the field of women's education. On the one hand, its successful lectures were given by reputable male professors, suggesting that women could benefit from higher education even though they were then excluded from the lectures of all but two of the colleges of London

University, and generally barred from the universities. On the other hand, Queen's indicated its caution by the appointment of lady visitors or chaperones, an all-male governing body, the abandonment of teacher training, and an apparent acceptance of women's civilising mission as the chief justification for their education. By contrast, Bedford College in London, which was favoured by Unitarians and founded within six months of Queen's by a rich and philanthropic widow, Mrs Elisabeth Reid, involved women in its governing body, had a headship open to men and women, and aimed at becoming a genuine college, despite admitting girls of twelve and over.[38]

Bedford achieved its objective, but not until the 1870s. The 1850s were years of pioneering in women's education, as in so much else to do with women. Hence the success of two major secondary schools for girls during the decade – the North London Collegiate under the leadership of Frances Buss and Cheltenham Ladies' College guided by Dorothea Beale – owed more to the great skills of their principals than they did to a supportive environment. Parents remained suspicious of lessons which made 'masculine' demands on their daughters, and suitably qualified teachers remained scarce.[39] None the less, these two institutions heralded the arrival in the second half of the nineteenth century of a crop of new girls' schools, comparable in the opportunities they offered to the secondary schools for boys,[40] and Miss Buss, at least, was fortunate in the practical assistance she received from her family. Women also found valuable opportunities to exchange ideas about education and other matters of mutual interest at the meetings of the National Association for the Promotion of Social Science (NAPSS, 1857), which admitted men and women participants, and in the informal context of the so-called Langham Place group.

In Britain, unlike the United States, the most important debates and developments regarding women's education were concentrated in the capital where, from 1855 onwards, a growing number of female activists had come together, with headquarters in Langham Place by 1859. Their endeavours are discussed fully in the next chapter. It is sufficient here to point out that the middle-class ladies of Langham Place, like their American counterparts, saw education in a largely functional light: through it, women would recognise their own worth, obtain better jobs, and be of greater use to their families and society as a whole. The London-based NAPSS provided a forum for these views beyond the feminists' own circle. Education was one of the Association's five departments, issues concerning women were discussed from the first congress, and through the deliberations of this organisation, women reformers, in Fletcher's judgement, 'joined the mainstream of debate on education'.[41] It had been the conviction of some prominent British visitors to America in the 1830s and 1840s that female education there was 'much as with us'. Intellectual women such as Harriet Martineau and George Eliot continued to impress, despite the difficulties they faced in Victorian society; and the initiatives under way during the 1850s were important. But in overall terms Britain still lagged behind the United States educationally. Even allowing for the mixture of pride and insecurity it evinces, the judgement of Sarah Josepha Hale, expressed in her *Woman's Record*, remains a valid one:[42]

> The Old Saxon stock is yet superior to the New in that brilliancy of feminine genius, the artificial state of social life in England now fosters and elicits – surpassing every nation in its lists of learned ladies; yet in all that contributes to popular education . . . the women of America are in advance of all others on the globe. To prove this, we need only examine the list of American female . . . teachers, editors and authors of works instructive and educational, contained in this 'Record.'

III. Religious pressures and outlets

Hale further suggested that American women led the way in their contribution to 'pure religious sentiment among the masses', pointing to the number of female missionaries noted in the *Record*. Although her pronouncement is difficult to assess while we know less about the level of female church membership in Britain than we do about its dimensions in the United States, it has been argued that the religious strain in American proto-feminism was stronger than its counterpart across the Atlantic. This contrast has not been accounted for, but it can be explained in a number of ways. In the first place, we should notice the greater optimism and influence of American evangelical religion, unhindered by a state church and facing a unique opportunity for proselytising in the expanding West. Additional explanatory factors include the urgent concern with social issues generated from the 1830s, as mass immigration, urbanisation and industrialisation transformed a country once proud of escaping European problems; and the growing importance from the same decade of the anti-slavery movement, which drew in many religious women before eventually disrupting the churches. We must also concede, however, that the religious experiences and achievements of women in the two countries continued to be similar, and that in both Britain and the United States the consolidation of a feminine mission in the wider world was more likely to be justified with reference to female duties than female rights. This was especially true in the American South where, by the 1820s, the churches had come to terms with the realities of social inequality, including slavery, and privileged women, if they were active outside their own households, tended to undertake charitable works strictly appropriate to their station and for the benefit of whites.[43]

As we saw in Chapter 1, conversion and the struggle for spiritual purity led many women to accord high priority to their private religious devotions, and to take up reform activities outside the home. These two consequences of religious conviction continued throughout the first half of the nineteenth century, and the piety of evangelical women continued to define not only their femininity but also, for many, their middle-class status. Women seeking self-dependence when it was economically unnecessary, or pursuing self-development through education and other means, were frequently charged with disloyalty to their class or families.[44] Time spent in religious contemplation and study was harder to criticise, and was the focal point of many female lives, as contemporary diaries make plain. Thus Mrs Bardwell of Walpole, Vermont, recording days shaped by sewing, food, gardening, visits, letters, illness, death and the weather, highlights her Sunday School class and church attendance; the Minister's wife, 'truly guided by the spirit of God', addressing a women's meeting; and religion as the only comfort when she contemplated her (not noticeably) misspent hours.[45] For single women particularly, service to God was a respectable way of pursuing personal autonomy. But spiritual labours gave women of all kinds confidence in customary tasks as well as the courage to undertake new ones. In the words of the American Methodist preacher and reformer Phoebe Palmer, who inspired women on both sides of the Atlantic while stopping short of feminism, 'holiness is a gift of power, and . . . nerves [one] for holy achievement'.[46]

Accordingly, while women welcomed the opportunity to be regarded as free moral agents and entered a whole range of denominations as individuals rather than family members,[47] they did not hesitate to urge their relatives to follow them. And if women were traditionally expected to influence their families, religious females had an extra justification for seeking to convert kin to their own seemly ways.[48] Sarah Hale, the supportive wife of a Boston newspaperman, missed him badly when he was away and did not care to go out without him. She none the less confidently advised her husband and son about their social duties, proclaiming herself 'afraid of nothing but sin, and I am horribly fearful of that'.[49] Hale and other devout women were determined to develop conscience in their loved ones, and to see them lead useful lives. The result was sometimes cheerless homes and children who grew up to be anxious, driven adults, although we should acknowledge that in evangelical households fathers were still the dominant figures, and that evangelicals of either sex were by no means so universally opposed to pleasure as was once supposed.[50]

Women were also able to exert their spiritual influence by publishing improving articles, memoirs, hymns, stories, poems and novels. Prochaska's account of feminine philanthropy in nineteenth-century England contains 'about 400 contemporary women's memoirs, autobiographies, etc. in the bibliography', and Margaret Maison's study of the Victorian religious novel reveals that nearly half the most successful authors in this field were women. Similarly lengthy publication lists can be compiled for American women, some of whom, as Hardesty observes, were concerned to question 'traditional biblical definitions of woman's role'.[51] A considerable number of their works were brought out by religious publishers, but many found commercial backers, indicating how profitable the market for women's writing had become. Ann Douglas has pointed out the dangers inherent in the frequently sentimental celebration of the average in feminine productions, and has noted their divorce from the political world of men.[52] Prochaska has likewise conceded the limited scope of much women's literature, which 'dealt largely with the affections, the duties of wives and mothers, and the conventional pattern of women's lives', while Rosman has shown the failure of evangelical novelists of either sex to present a convincing picture of 'vital goodness'.[53] Yet the proliferation of this literature on both sides of the Atlantic, aided by improvements in publishing, the growth of subscription libraries and advancing literacy, is equally a tribute to feminine drive: to its authors' desire to be heard, and their need to earn a living. Despite their frequent discomfort at being accorded professional status in a world which generally opposed the admission of women to the professions, female writers on domesticity strove, in Mary Kelley's words, 'to assess and place a value on women's lives'. Women were doers in the literary sphere, not merely passive consumers of pious publications; and as authors they offered a positive assertion of the importance of women's qualities within and beyond the home, an indirect subversion of patriarchy, and work whose merits have only belatedly been recognised.[54]

Among the role models taken from the Bible by feminine authors were individuals of an 'active benevolence' as well as submissive virtue; and since neither men nor female education encouraged women to embark on theological speculations, they frequently drew the conclusion from their scriptural researches and contemporary preaching that their collective field was practical philanthropy: the equivalent, in society, of their domestic moral influence.[55] Adventurous souls chafed at the round of poor visits and sewing circles which had traditionally been accepted as the proper outlets for charitable women: New Englander Lucretia Hale was serious enough to want to help her brother in his parish duties but sufficiently spirited, when the moonlight was 'very delicious', to prefer the thought of persuading a lover to escort her round the common to yet another trip to what she called 'sewage'. And in urban areas especially new opportunities for doing good presented themselves in abundance for women who, like Sarah Hale, believed that 'WOMAN is God's appointed agent of *morality*'.[56]

While it is difficult to determine the identities of the rank-and-file members of reform groups in either country, it would appear that in Britain evangelical women were the most important female contributors, in keeping with the overall primacy of evangelicals in philanthropy, and that their financial donations rose most at a time when female donations were rising across the whole spectrum of charitable work.[57] As Prochaska observes, no single sect had a monopoly over any single charity, although 'different denominations had different philanthropic emphases': evangelical Quakers, for example, were significant in the peace movement, their Anglican counterparts in religious tract and Bible societies, and Unitarians in educational charities.[58] If these activities might have provided, variously, a distraction from religious introspection, a release for the emotions, and a respectable alternative to frivolity and fashion that itself became fashionable, for the Unitarians in particular reform was a means of gaining the social respectability that their small numbers and early political disabilities would otherwise have denied them. Furthermore, since the sect supported women's rights and admitted women to the ministry, it was natural that Unitarian men would support and join them in philanthropy.[59]

In Britain dissenters as a whole shared many of the disadvantages experienced by the Unitarians, with comparable results. Members of the equivalent sects in the United States, because of their country's post-Revolutionary commitment to religious freedom, did not suffer in like manner, so that while American Quakers remained active in humanitarian endeavours, convinced of the divine sanction for female equality and supportive of a public role for women, American Unitarians, at least, were less concerned to promote social reform than their English counterparts by the 1830s. There were other contrasts. Whereas the establishment of female auxiliaries to reform societies may have been encouraged in Britain by the erosion of clerical opposition, once women proved themselves to be inventive organisers and important fund-raisers,[60] conservative ministers contemplating the social tensions of Jacksonian America (1829–37) were evidently more cautious than they had once been about encouraging feminine activism, despite its similar resourcefulness.[61] In response, some American women became more cautious about involvement in the public sphere.

None the less, clerical opposition to female assistance had largely been eroded by the 1850s, and religion continued to play a vital part in turning (primarily northern) American women to reform, notably anti-slavery, temperance, peace, and assistance to the poor, the sick, the handicapped, the imprisoned, prostitutes and vulnerable children. Moreover, charitable activities were supported by native-born and immigrant women alike, though the two groups tended to organise separately. Historians differ, in fact, about how far such women's organisations 'transcended the loyalties of class', but Hewitt seems to have discovered an unusual situation in Rochester, New York, where a small number of 'ultraist' women tried to 'forge links with their working-class and black sisters not as clients but as coworkers', and has identified three main groups of activists (comprising around 10 per cent of the city's adult women), who 'differed from each other as much as they differed from nonactivists'. It is also important to note that female associations inspired by Christian benevolence, such as the powerful moral reform societies studied by Caroll Smith-Rosenberg, Barbara Berg and Mary P. Ryan, now tended to devise fresh protest tactics, at the same time displaying a new severity towards men and a new dissatisfaction with the position of women in society. And if the participants' embryonic feminism was restrained by their basic respect for domesticity and religious institutions, as Ryan and DuBois have argued, their political activities and their concern for prostitution and the double standard in sexual matters made them more radical than their British counterparts in the 1830s and 1840s. Activists in Britain were aware of the work of the New York moral reformers; but at this point they lacked the boldness that came from political experience. Accordingly it was not until public concern at the level of prostitution and venereal disease rose in the 1850s that British women were personally involved in rescuing prostitutes from the streets and brothels, and providing them with places of refuge.[62]

What is more, Hersh has established that for American women of radical disposition reform 'became the main religion . . . replacing formal church-going as a means of expressing their faith', while their reform experiences drove them 'away from orthodox Protestantism in all its forms . . . and towards more liberal denominations and beliefs'.[63] This process of radicalisation, paralleled in Britain in the later part of the century, took a somewhat different form there during the 1830s and 1840s, when the strength of utopian socialism, unparalleled in the United States, gave women disenchanted with the restrictions on their sex and the constraints of evangelical religion the opportunity to embrace a secular creed. As Taylor maintains, their 'infidelism' tapped the strong vein of working-class anti-clericalism without denoting indifference to religion: on the contrary, it customarily involved recoil from initial spiritual conviction, a constant, defining debate with hostile clerics, and a determined reintepretation of Scripture.[64]

Forging a new role within Church organisation as such proved more problematic, in Britain and America alike. In the Church of England, charitable sisterhoods on the continental European pattern were formed from the 1840s, their members teaching and 'ministering to the poor, the homeless, the ill, the elderly and the unfortunate'. Yet they remained very much a minority outlet for British women, as were nunneries, and for the same reasons. Offensive to Protestant and male sensibilities, both institutions were regarded with disapproval by those who could welcome female self-sacrifice but not feminine autonomy, community, and 'unnatural' withdrawal from the family.[65] In the United States, where Protestantism was equally dominant (though disturbed by large-scale Catholic immigration), there was a similar aversion to harnessing women's religious sensibilities through religious orders.[66] The Anglicans, anxious about the professional status of the clergy, were also reluctant to admit women as deaconesses, notwithstanding the growing awareness by the 1850s of the 'excess' of single women wanting employment, and the invaluable contribution to parish labours, poor visiting and rescue work made by the first recruits from the 1860s onwards.[67] This Anglo-American church opposition to the formal institutionalisation of female benevolence appears to have been instrumental in driving the women of both countries into more wide-ranging reform endeavours than were characteristic of their sisters in Catholic Europe.[68]

Undaunted by male conservatism, women on each side of the Atlantic performed important duties as ministers' wives and volunteered for missionary work in increasing numbers by mid-century, serving not only as aides to male evangelists and their wives but in their own right as teachers, translators, medical assistants and bringers of Christianity.[69] Mission service combined the attractions of adventure, career and calling for single women, although it appealed only to the hardiest. Despite the invariable criticism provoked by such departures from the norm, other unusual women found an outlet in exotic sects, or turned to preaching in numbers that have probably been underestimated. Leaving aside the Quaker meetings, which permitted members of both sexes to become Public Friends, black and white women alike were most active in

Methodist splinter groups (though the redoubtable Antoinette Brown was ordained as the first female Congregational minister in 1853, before eventually becoming a Unitarian). The evangelical stress on female spirituality and empowerment through personal religious experience clashed uncomfortably with continuing male opposition to female ordination in all the principal denominations, including the mainstream Methodists, and was protested by American feminists at Seneca Falls in 1848. However, protest brought few changes before the second half of the nineteenth century in well-established sects with conventional views about authority and procedure. Hence in the short term masculine obduracy produced religious rebels among women, as did a variety of hardships detailed by Taylor: inadequate educational opportunities, unhappy marriages and limited career prospects.[70]

After the death of Joanna Southcott in 1814, control of her movement passed to men before it declined in the 1840s, a decade which saw the appearance of Goodwyn and Catherine Barmby's Communist Church. It is hard to weigh the respective contributions to their church of this middle-class socialist couple, untiring propagandists for most fashionable radical causes and founders of a short-lived utopian community in Middlesex (1843–4). Both despised the polarising Victorian definitions of masculinity and femininity; both embraced Owenite and Chartist demands for better female education, marriage based on affection, division of household labour between the sexes, and women's suffrage. But Catherine's journalism made a pioneering contribution to the case for female enfranchisement, displayed a rare ability to transcend class and gender barriers, and was a considerable addition to the burgeoning contemporary literature critical of women's domestic exploitation and subordination in the labour market. Comparable small religious sects of the same period were the Ham Common Concordium at Richmond, a commune which included Southcottians, published a journal, attracted both middle- and working-class women and advocated celibacy; and the White Quakers, led by Joshua Jacob and Abigail Beale, who professed a desire to return to original Quaker doctrine and practised communism and 'free love'.[71]

In the United States, with the exceptions of Phoebe Palmer and Elizabeth Finney, whose religious work complemented that of their revivalist husbands, no female spiritual leader emerged in the first half of the nineteenth century who exerted the same influence as the Shaker Ann Lee and other women produced by eighteenth-century religious ferment, though mention should be made of the splendidly fraudulent Spiritualist sisters Katie and Maggie Fox, whose rapping spirits were revealed to be their own gifted toe joints,[72] and of the erudite Margaret Fuller, the best-known female Transcendentalist. Transcendentalism, the faith of a cultured handful of New Englanders, was a combination of European philosophy, Romantic mysticism and American individualistic morality for which no one person could claim credit, whereas so many of the religious (and secular) utopias were the creation of a single strong personality.

Fuller, after a period of helping her widowed mother and school-teaching, found liberation in Transcendentalism, conducting informal lectures or Conversations in Boston, co-editing the group's quarterly journal and then moving on to the staff of the New York *Tribune*, her belief in her own intellectual powers enhanced by her association with the leading thinkers of her generation. It is not as a religious guru but as an example of female ability, an indictment of the limited opportunities open to her sex, a successful journalist, and the feminist author of *Woman in the Nineteenth Century* (1845) that Fuller should be remembered. Like Wollstonecraft's *Vindication*, Fuller's major work seems disorganised now, but is equally eloquent in its analysis of the mechanisms of male dominance, its aversion to treating women like children or domestic creatures, and its plea that they should be allowed to develop on whatever lines their talents dictated. Unlike Wollstonecraft, Fuller did not bring herself into disrepute by an unconventional sexual life, though few would now share Harriet Martineau's patronising judgement that Fuller's moral and intellectual eccentricity had ended when she fell in love and married.[73]

None the less, both British and American women joined religious communities in considerable numbers, and although we know too little about most of them, it seems that cult members tended to fall into extreme categories: the affluent and eccentric on the one hand; and the poor and the desperate on the other. The charm of the female-led sects was that they offered an escape, however short-lived, from an unsatisfactory status quo: a positive enhancement of the position of women and a logical outcome to arguments about their moral superiority.[74] The most disappointing feature of all the religious utopias was their inability to bring about the permanent alteration of the family relationship (an objective they shared with the secular utopias). As the American religious perfectionist John Humphrey Noyes saw the communities, when women were prominent, 'Mating on the Spiritual plane . . . becomes the order of the day', whereas 'if the leaders are men, the theocratic impulse takes the opposite direction, and polygamy in some form is the result'.[75] But despite the risks of cohabitation in an era before contraception was widely available, celibacy was a minority preference which doomed its advocates to a limited influence, while 'free love', as female utopian socialists were quick to point out, had more advantages for men than for women.[76]

IV. Opportunities in social reform and protest

We have argued so far that improved education made women more concerned about the other restrictions affecting their lives; and we have maintained that religion, though valued as a personal blessing or one to be acted on immediately in the domestic sphere, helped to enlarge their influence in the wider world. Religion could have this effect because women displayed a selfless benevolence, effectively directed, and because clergymen needed their help. Female activism in secular or broadly humanitarian reform efforts was more controversial, but difficult to oppose once women had proved their moral claims and practical worth in philanthropy. Some participants were thereby embroiled in debates about women's rights, and subsequently went on to campaign for them independently. Yet only a minority of feminine activists were feminists, while women in Britain and the United States came to organised feminism via different concerns: Americans directly through work for anti-slavery, temperance and peace; the British, more circuitously, through an apprenticeship in utopian socialism or the Anti-Corn Law League, and only belatedly through abolitionism and the crusade against drink.

According to O'Neill, the rise of American feminism was facilitated by a tradition of associational activity among women and a 'generalized reform spirit' in the 1830s and 1840s, neither of which was matched in Britain. A typical contemporary expression of pride in this American progressivism might be the claim of the radical Boston abolitionist William Lloyd Garrison, in 1840, that 'Slavery out of the question, our country is a century in advance of England on the score of reform, and of general intelligence and morality.'[77] Without denying the validity of O'Neill's observations about the United States, it now seems clear that the situation in Britain was more complicated than he suggested and Garrison's partiality led him to suppose. Although the different political and social contexts in which they operated did indeed have an impact on the British and American feminist movements, historians have shown that Victorian women were involved in middle-class reforms and working-class protest alike, establishing themselves as writers, speakers and agitators, as well as supportive organisers, just as they did in the United States, and being similarly led on from one good cause to another.[78] And whereas O'Neill maintained that British feminism, emerging in a more conservative climate than the American movement, was more respectable from the outset, the fact is, as Taylor and Malmgreen have established, that it had its roots in a utopian socialism that dismayed the respectable classes by its advocacy of 'a wholesale transformation of private and public life'. Moreover, in Britain there was no section of the country so opposed to modernising reform endeavour generally, and to feminine activism in particular, as the pre-industrial American South, where, Jean Friedman argues, family and church were so powerful that even in urban areas they inhibited the growth of separate women's benevolent associations and prevented those that did exist 'from moving toward organized women's reform'.[79]

This, however, is not to deny that British feminism was stronger in the 1850s than it had been in the 1840s, as middle-class reformism generally intensified after the restoration of economic prosperity and the dispersion of the tensions caused by Chartism. Conversely, American feminism, evolving out of anti-slavery and other reform movements from the 1830s, was struggling to make independent progress in the 1850s; for by then, as Ginzberg maintains, reform increasingly required involvement in electoral politics rather than the moral exhortation and traditional lobbying at which women had excelled.[80] Nor should we underestimate the greater importance of class in shaping the responses of

British women to reform endeavours, including feminism, despite the fact that middle-class crusaders invariably looked for working-class support, and middle-class feminists were not spared the hostility the women's cause aroused just because of their class status.[81] If women reformers in Britain and the United States alike were preponderantly middle-class and inclined to condescend towards their poorer sisters, class pride was more likely to restrain comfortably placed British activists from risky extremes, as Paulson and Thistlethwaite have pointed out with reference to the anti-slavery movement;[82] while reformers were more likely to be denounced as extremists in a hierarchical Britain than in an egalitarian United States, for all the closeness of the Anglo–American reform connection.[83] And that connection, though proudly acknowledged, did not subdue national pride. Direct interference in the affairs of other countries was always liable to provoke complaints about foreign agitators, and to remind those on the receiving end of overseas advice that they themselves aspired to be the moral leaders of the civilised world.[84]

In the United States, the reform movement most significant for women and feminism was abolitionism. Since it was the premier antebellum reform effort, tackling head-on the implications of America's Revolutionary libertarianism, anti-slavery work could be expected to recruit thinking men and women alike. However, there were additional reasons why women should be drawn into the crusade. As had earlier been the case in Britain, anti-slavery attracted women because it appealed to their sense of themselves as the 'more sensitive and sympathetic sex', and because children and 'members of their own sex were in bondage'.[85] Moreover, whereas men denied the analogy, and it had clear limitations, women could effectively compare the slavery of blacks and the slavery of sex. After all, both slaves and women (especially married women) were the victims of generalisations which ignored their individual variations and merits; both were separately socialised and denied the blessings of the natural rights philosophy so conspicuously affirmed during the American Revolution; both were the victims of white male power, clerical conservatism and the tyranny of custom; and both were accorded insulting, compensatory virtues while being assured that their subordination was for their own good.[86]

Building on a largely Quaker foundation, women emerged as a significant force in the American anti-slavery campaign in the 1830s.[87] They were especially attracted to the moral emphasis of Boston's William Lloyd Garrison, who rejected gradualism, argued for immediate, uncompensated emancipation, and made a direct bid for female support. And as DuBois has noted, involvement in Garrisonianism gave women who were already discontented with their position in Jacksonian America 'the ability to perceive and analyze entire institutions; and the assumption of absolute human equality as a first principle of morality and politics'.[88] When they applied these approaches to their own circumstances, some female abolitionists grew irked at being recruited into separate auxiliaries of the American Anti-Slavery Society in Philadelphia, New York, Boston and many New England towns, where they undertook membership drives, organised petitions and raised money for the cause. Their resentments were brought to a head by the 1837 public speaking tour of New England by Sarah and Angelina Grimké. Southern Quakers who had settled in Philadelphia, the sisters had evolved a deep abhorrence of slavery. Following the example of Frances Wright and the devout New England black abolitionist Maria Stewart, the two women proceeded to address 'promiscuous' (male and female) audiences about the need for abolition, provoking much clerical criticism of their boldness in the process. The ensuing debate about women's rights divided abolitionists of both sexes, and contributed to the 1840 schism in the American anti-slavery movement.[89]

It would be a mistake, however, to overemphasise the differences between the various abolitionist factions. Their critics did so to embarrass them, but as Walters has shown, anti-slavery advocates from opposing associations were united in their anxiety about economic change and social flux, and in their determination to 'create a just world'.[90] Nor can the movement's limited success by the time of the Civil War be attributed to the disruptive impact of the 'woman question'. On the contrary, the conspicuous support given by women to abolitionism helped to arouse public opinion, take the issue into the realm of politics and make it the outstanding reform issue of the antebellum era. None the less, once female abolitionists moved on from practical support for male co-workers to become 'anti-slavery agents, lecturers, editors, agitators', they broke new ground in the public sphere for women and challenged conventional notions of proper feminine conduct.[91]

Anti-slavery provided short-term employment for unencumbered women: as Ryan observes, the 'female agents of the American Anti-Slavery Society were, to a woman, unmarried and usually very young'. Yet since a number of leading feminist abolitionists – including Angelina Grimké, Lydia Maria Child, Maria Weston Chapman, Lucretia Mott and Abby Kelley – were married either when they took up the cause or subsequently, their relationships with their husbands were predictably a matter of concern not only to themselves but also to a public which emphasised the primacy of women's domestic duties. As Hersh has established, feminist abolitionists tended to marry late, have fewer children than was customary, and find partners who shared their commitment to religious liberalism, universal reform and female equality, beginning at home. Despite the secure egos of the husbands concerned and the generally supportive attitude of Garrisonian men towards women's rights, these consciously egalitarian marriages suffered from the strain imposed by challenging work, frequent travel, shared child-rearing responsibilities and determined pioneering.[92] The partnership of Stephen Foster and Abby Kelley provides a good case study.

Kelley, a Massachusetts Quaker, began her career as a teacher active in her local anti-slavery association during the 1830s. When, in 1838, she addressed the second Anti-Slavery Convention of American Women, Sarah Grimké congratulated her on speaking in public on behalf of female involvement in the cause: 'what thou has done will do more towards establishing the rights of women on this point than a dozen books'. But once Kelley had become an anti-slavery agent, she found that pursuing both abolition and the controversial 'woman question' was a wearing task. While contemplating matrimony with her fellow-abolitionist Stephen Foster, Kelley confessed that people 'wish me married to get rid of me'; hence, were their relationship known, she would be urged to take care of Foster's *'feeble constitution'*. She had already been reproached and undermined by charges of having neglected her 'dear mother', notwithstanding the presence at home of one – and sometimes two – daughters. Finding the means to marry also caused Kelley anxiety, as neither she nor Stephen was affluent. After marriage, because Abby proved an extremely effective lecturer, whose 'moral organization . . . [was] stronger and far more active' than her 'domestic feelings', she was frequently apart from her fondly regarded husband and daughter, Alla. Stephen accepted these absences, tended the farm, cared for Alla (Abby found her 'such a burden to me at meetings'), and assured his wife that she 'could accomplish more alone than with my aid', since he believed that lecturing and writing were not his forte. Abby replied: 'You need not try to invent excuses for withdrawing from the warfare till victory is won', and generally cheered up her more pessimistic spouse.

Although they were united by mutual interests, uncompromising radicalism, enduring affection, and concern for their own and Alla's health (it 'is of far more importance that she should get a good, strong constitution than a knowledge of books'), their peripatetic lifestyle was feelingly described by Stephen as 'the next thing to being a slave'. And when he was on tour he was conventional enough to inform his wife that he had 'but little confidence in your ability to manage a farm'. Happily, Stephen Foster was a man of sufficient generosity to put cause before self and to take pride in Abby as 'the woman that never says "I can't"': a woman rare enough to move Garrison to declare, at the height of a bruising quarrel between them:

> Of all the women who have appeared upon the historic stage, I have always regarded you as peerless – the moral Joan of Arc of the world . . .[93]

The contribution of British women to abolitionism has been underestimated, partly because it did not lead to a major disruption of the anti-slavery movement and the emergence in the 1840s of a struggle for women's rights. Just the same, the importance of women in bringing about abolition in the British Empire was acknowledged by Garrison when he appealed to American women to take up anti-slavery work in 1833.[94] Building on but greatly expanding the work of the Billingtons, Malmgreen and others,[95] Clare Midgley has provided a much-needed and impressive history of the women's efforts from the late eighteenth century to the 1860s.[96] She has shown that female abolitionists, stressing their moral duty to act, took the lead in pressing the Anti-Slavery Society to campaign for immediate, uncompensated emancipation in the years just before 1833, helping to rally public opinion against slavery, forming new women's organisations in the provinces, and increasing their petitioning activities to the point where they produced nearly a third of all the signatures on anti-slavery petitions in 1833. If anti-slavery subsequently became less important in British politics, female activists did not lose their zeal: indeed, they had the advantage over men in that their work was less concerned with obtaining parliamentary action. Most notably, a combination of middle-class and some working-class crusaders raised money for black education (and particularly the instruction of women and children) in Africa and the West Indies; agitated against the apprenticeship of West Indian freedmen in the 1830s as a perpetuation of slavery under another name; continued to press consumers to use free-grown produce; and gave both moral and material support to American abolitionists and fugitive slaves, while trying to resist involvement in the most destructive minutiae of transatlantic anti-slavery feuds.[97]

Abolitionist women in the two countries had much in common. Convinced that the anti-slavery movement had a special importance for their sex, they were emboldened to step outside the home and engage in essentially political debate. While they left the framing of high national policy to men, women were not merely their faithful supporters, content with a discreetly exerted influence. Rather, they shaped their own priorities, proved invaluable galvanisers of their local communities, became markedly less diffident over time, and did not hesitate to reprove male colleagues, politicians and clergymen when they failed in their duty, rather as devout women had traditionally felt empowered to call their menfolk to religion (see above, p. 32). And on both sides of the Atlantic, their leaders were drawn mostly from reform families. In Britain we find, for example, Eliza and Sophia Sturge of Birmingham, Elizabeth Pease of Darlington, Mary Estlin and Mary Carpenter of Bristol, and Jane Smeal of Glasgow. In the United States, their white equivalents include the New Yorkers Susan B. Anthony, Abby Hopper Gibbons and Matilda Joslyn Gage, Maria Weston Chapman of Massachusetts and Elizabeth Buffam Chase of Rhode Island; and from prominent free black families, Sarah Remond, Sarah Douglass, and the sisters Margaretta, Sarah and Harriet Forten.[98] It was difficult for parents to deny an involvement in reform to children who had grown up in households dominated by its issues and practitioners. It was equally difficult for the children of such households to resist its claims.

Anti-slavery women in Britain and the United States, believing in the possibility of human perfectibility and in their duty to improve themselves and others, took up a variety of reforms, including child-rearing, health and medical improvements, peace and temperance; they tended to belong to sects like the Society of Friends and the Unitarians, both of which, as we have seen, accorded unusually high status to women and admitted them to the ministry. Through visits, correspondence and publications, they kept in touch about the progress of the movement in their respective countries, and shared shortcomings as well as strengths.[99] The most obvious weakness of female (and, indeed, male) anti-slavery campaigners was their unrepresentative nature. Predominantly middle-class and white, they found it difficult to shake off their class and racial prejudices, or to mobilise more than a fraction of the population. Appalled as they were by poverty and social injustice, they commonly failed to offer any suggestions for changing the structure, as opposed to some of the practices, of society.[100] Under such circumstances, and in the contemporary context, the relations between white and black women abolitionists were better than might be expected.

While it is clear that white abolitionists of both sexes welcomed the support of blacks and the emergence of black abolitionists, especially lecturers able to dramatise the slave experience, it is equally clear that they usually judged blacks by middle-class standards, were ambivalent about their qualities and prospects, and expected to guide their activities. Furthermore, black women, like their white sisters, were frequently organised in separate anti-slavery auxiliaries and saw the problem of racism as taking priority over that of patriarchy; while Bell Hooks is right in pointing out that when white women abolitionists compared their lot with that of slaves they were often simply 'drawing attention away from the slave towards themselves'.[101] On the other hand, the female anti-slavery societies of Philadelphia, Rochester, Boston, Salem and Lynn were integrated, while there were some white female abolitionists who established cordial relationships with their black counterparts and rendered them genuine assistance.

Angelina Grimké was well aware that 'the crushing withering influence of Prejudice' existed even among the Quakers, owing to their general aloofness from the black population, and she and her sister Sarah showed themselves sensitive to the feelings on this matter of the black Philadelphia abolitionists Sarah Forten, who deployed her literary talents in the cause, and Sarah Douglass, who had a long and distinguished career as a teacher in New York and Philadelphia. Abby Kelley likewise ignored the colour line, leading Sarah Douglass to rejoice that she had met 'with an Abolitionist who has turned her back on prejudice', and Sarah Remond to acknowledge that Kelley's encouragement had given her the confidence to take up national anti-slavery work. Lucretia Mott was similarly free from prejudice and condescension, regularly entertaining black friends at home. Amy Post and other Rochester abolitionists alarmed their contemporaries by emphasising the equality of blacks and whites. And Lydia Maria Child, whose circle encompassed abolitionists of both races, helped Harriet A. Jacobs to publish her *Incidents in the Life of a Slave Girl*, which courageously recounted a youthful sexual liaison with a white neighbour and sexual harassment by her master, as well as her more acceptable struggles as a slave mother and fugitive.[102]

Women in Britain had less opportunity to meet and work with recent victims of slavery; the native black population was small, long-established and overwhelmingly metropolitan.[103] But between the 1830s and the 1860s a steady stream of black abolitionists visited the British Isles, where they proved adept at informing the public about slavery; interesting the press and publishers in their work; avoiding damaging participation in the factional disputes which beset the movement; and raising money both for white abolitionism and for 'specific Afro-American causes, individuals, organizations, and institutions'.[104] Although the visitors underestimated the degree of race prejudice that existed in Britain, they did receive a warm welcome from their British hosts,[105] and the half-dozen or so black women abolitionists among them, including Ellen Craft and Sarah Remond, were able to tap the strong interest in emancipation of local female anti-slavery groups, and to drive home the message that 'women were the "worst victims" of slavery'.[106]

For all the similarities within Anglo–American female abolitionism, however, the fact remains that in the United States the campaign impelled some women into organised feminism during the 1840s, whereas in Britain it did not, although individual women abolitionists eventually embraced the cause.[107] Despite the important influence exercised by American abolitionism on the British movement after the ending of slavery in a large part of the Empire in 1833 and the longer history of activism by British women in anti-slavery work, which might have been expected to increase their resentment over the unjust treatment of their sex, female campaigners in Britain were less concerned to introduce women's rights into abolitionism in the 1830s. They were also less affronted than American Garrisonians of both sexes at the refusal of the committee of the British and Foreign Anti-Slavery Society to give women abolitionists from the United States delegate status at the 1840 World Anti-Slavery Convention, held in London. While the snub provoked furious debate in the American delegation, determining Lucretia Mott and Elizabeth Cady Stanton to 'hold a convention as soon as we returned home, and form a society to advocate the rights of women' – an objective actually accomplished some eight years later – British female abolitionists of the BFASS and Garrisonian persuasion alike could not be rallied in 1840 to demand a public role contrary to the common usage of their movement and their country.[108]

The radical English Quaker Anne Knight of Chelmsford supported the stand taken by the American feminists in 1840 and sympathised with such outspoken American feminist abolitionists as Abby Kelley, complaining to her about the old 'daddies' of the British anti-slavery movement who spoke but did not act, and noting that some women's society as quick to take initiatives without their direction.[109] Yet though Knight's interest in the rights of her sex was shared by, for example, Harriet Martineau, Elizabeth Pease, Rebecca Moore of the Manchester Ladies' Anti-Slavery Society, Harriet Lupton of the Leeds Anti-Slavery Association, the Irish abolitionist Maria Waring and the Scot Marion Reid, such women were rare in Britain. They may eventually have been radicalised by their connections with American female Garrisonians, but they did not introduce American practices into the British campaign for abolition. It was not until 1853 that the first mixed anti-slavery society was formed in Britain (in Leeds), and not until 1854 that the first two women delegates (from Manchester) were sent to a British anti-slavery conference. Britain produced no national all-women anti-slavery conventions on the American pattern, and female anti-slavery addresses to mixed audiences were extremely rare.[110]

The reasons for this contrast are complex. Since the 'woman question' was plainly divisive in the United States and divided British women, whether they were supporters or opponents of the Garrisonians, prudent patriots in a situation where the ground had not been carefully prepared for a debate could see the case for leaving the issue alone, lest it shatter the more successful British abolitionist movement or set men against women. American observers, with some support from the British, explained their hosts' response in terms of British conservatism,[111] and we have seen that Britain lagged behind the United States in educational provision for women, while their subordination in an overtly class-conscious society was more acceptable than it was in the ostensibly egalitarian American republic. But British organised feminism emerged in the mid–1850s, not very long after its American counterpart, and it seems more probable that the limited short-term impact of anti-slavery on feminism in Britain was due to a combination of alarm at the proved disruptiveness of the link among Americans and the attractions of other reform endeavours for women activists by 1840, when abolitionism in Britain had lost some of the urgency it had generated before 1833. Finally, it seems clear that British women abolitionists, geographic-ally far removed from slavery and secure in both their class position and their sense of worth to the movement (women's societies in fact came to outnumber men's associations during the 1840s), never generally shared their American sisters' insistent equation of sexual and black bondage. Although that equation was differently viewed by black and white female abolitionists in the United States, making sisterhood difficult to realise, it forced a serious reappraisal of how and by whom enslaved women of both races were to be freed; as a result, some American women, at least, came to see self-liberation as a real possibility.[112]

The temperance movement also had more immediate relevance for the feminist movement in the United States than it did in Britain, though in neither country did women make it pre-eminently their concern until the last quarter of the nineteenth century. In both countries there was working-class as well as middle-class involvement, and the 1850s saw the first substantial female activity in a campaign launched nationally two decades earlier with strong Church backing and male direction. In both countries this crusade, rather like abolitionism, came to be seen as having special appeal for women, since they, together with children, were presented as enslaved by the male vice of drinking: as the physically vulnerable and innocent victims of a male institution (the saloon), whose powerlessness forced them to endure the disruption of home and family life and the betrayal of moral principle, thereby making a mockery of the Victorian domestic ideology. Such preoccupations, Thomis and Grimmett remind us, helped to establish the seriousness of British women at a time when they were commonly dismissed as frivolous; the same may, of course, be said of other feminine reform interests. In both countries women were – when they were acceptable as members of temperance organisations – generally confined to separate auxiliaries, directing their efforts to their own sex and youngsters, fund-raising and organising, producing temperance literature and supporting rather than initiating the policies of the movement. And in both countries, despite these restrictions, some prominent women activists emerged. In Britain they included Anne Jane Carlile, co-founder of the youth-orientated Band of Hope, and the temperance writer Clara Lucas Balfour, who was willing to risk obloquy by addressing mixed audiences about alcohol abuse; and in the United States Amelia Bloomer, editor of the *Lily*, and Lydia H. Sigourney, associate editor of *Godey's Lady's Book*, who publicised the cause in the columns of their journals.[113]

Temperance women from the American North were none the less more militant than their British counterparts, partly reflecting the apprenticeship of some of them in anti-slavery and partly mirroring the greater overall drive and radicalism of the American movement: as late as 1840, William Lloyd Garrison declared that 'the temperance cause is somewhat unpopular in England'. In some areas female activists outnumbered male, and through the Martha Washington societies of the 1830s and 1840s they undertook public roles usually reserved for men. They subsequently formed Daughters of Temperance groups and in Albany, New York, in 1852, when their representatives were refused the right to speak at a state convention of temperance societies, a number were sufficiently incensed to withdraw and establish the Women's State Temperance Association later in the year. But by 1853 the Association had been divided over the discussion of women's rights, including whether a husband's drunkenness was a just ground for divorce; and at the 1853 World's Temperance Convention in New York, women were again denied a hearing. In view of what had happened when feminism affected the anti-slavery movement, male unwillingness to debate 'the woman question' in temperance circles was understandable. But the result of refusing women equal rights was to drive many spirited individuals of both sexes out of temperance work and to radicalise further the snubbed women, including Susan B. Anthony and Elizabeth Cady Stanton.[114]

For those whose chief concern was temperance, there was sound sense in the British preference for keeping good causes separate, even while supporting many. Class fragmentation was a damaging feature of Victorian reform, including temperance, as Harrison has observed; other divisions were avoided where possible, though even with the caution shown on gender matters by the abolitionists and Anti-Corn Law League campaigners, opponents grumbled that 'they were encouraging women into public affairs'.[115] However, in the United States, where feminism was organised by the 1850s and temperance societies were a good recruiting ground for supporters, the separation of the two was initially impossible to secure, and thereafter – until the 1870s – brought about on terms helpful to neither movement. The British connection between Chartism and temperance women, though noteworthy, did not have a similarly disruptive impact, since the latter lacked both numbers and militancy in the 1830s and 1840s.[116]

The peace movement, like the temperance and anti-slavery campaigns, was an Anglo–American affair, involving the exchange of ideas, literature and (frequently Quaker) personnel; also like them, it demonstrated that while women were the victims of male power, they could still effectively assert their 'superior moral force'.[117] For the most part, on both sides of the Atlantic, women were happy to play a supporting role in peace efforts, although their extensive international correspondence helped to establish the tradition of cosmopolitanism that would be a feature of feminism in the second half of the nineteenth century.[118] Yet only in the American campaign did any connection with feminism emerge, and that in the familiar context of a debate over the rights of women delegates to speak at a convention: the meeting in question was the 1838 assembly of peace societies which led to the establishment of the New England Non-Resistance Society pledged, among other things, to opposing distinctions based on sex.[119] Once again it would seem that the contrast between the promise of advancing democracy and the actuality of women's lot, of freedom for many and slavery for some (whether actual or comparative), had caused the greatest indignation in the country where that contrast was most marked.

A distinctively British cause involving middle-class women which had a delayed influence on the development of organised British feminism comparable to that exerted by the Anglo-American crusades for abolition, temperance and peace was the Anti-Corn Law League, founded in 1839 and successful by 1846. League women held meetings and bazaars, collected money and signatures, and distributed literature in support of cheap bread and free trade, learning the techniques of modern political protest in the process. But female members did not challenge the dominance of men within the League, or advance claims on behalf of women. Notwithstanding such moderation and their middle-class respectability, they were denounced for unfeminine behaviour, and this censure, together with class conservatism, may explain why League women did not embrace overtly feminist objectives, although a number of them went on to do so later in the century, as Walkowitz has demonstrated.[120] It was even less likely that the working-class women activists of the period would escape ridicule and rebuke, and given their limited leisure and means, it was predictable that they would be less numerous than their middle-class sisters. Yet since the opportunities for action presented themselves, they made an earlier entry into political and economic protest.[121]

As we have already noted (see above, pp. 38–40), the impact of industrialisation on women was mixed, bringing some benefits but also positive harm in terms of family strains, increased class cleavages among women, and tension between competing men and women of the working class. It is none the less clear that working-class women were drawn into the various forms of class action prompted by the new order. In Britain, they were involved in such socioeconomic demonstrations as the early-nineteenth-century food riots; machine-breaking (or Luddism) in 1811–12 and 1826; the labourers' (Swing) riots of 1830–31; opposition to enclosure at different times; and protests against the new Poor Law of 1834, a movement which generated many independent female societies and saw women arranging their own meetings, petitions and speakers, as well as backing male activities directed against the law. They also made an important contribution to the ideological drive behind the last rising of the agricultural labourers in 1838.[122] In the industrial arena, British women found help and entertainment in friendly societies; asserted themselves in unions, especially in the lace, cotton, metal and sweated industries; and supported the drive to recruit unskilled workers into general unions, epitomised by the Grand National Consolidated Trades Union of 1833–4. Moreover, women were associated with the remonstrations against the treatment of the Tolpuddle Martyrs (1834); with the crowd action over 'wages and trade stoppages' known as the Plug Plot riots (1842); and in the efforts made to ensure that both sexes benefited from the Ten Hours Act (1847).[123]

In all these areas, while female activism can now be charted, it is far less easy to establish its connection to feminism. As modern scholars have pointed out,[124] poorly educated and paid women with family responsibilities operating in a male-dominated world were most likely to participate in local, spontaneous demonstrations in response to immediate hardship, rather than in endeavours which required evening commitment, travel, time-consuming organisation and public debate. Many of the working-class movement's female activists – a minority within a minority – inclined to supportive roles either because they thus hoped to avert criticism that their place was in the home or because, from straightforward loyalty, they wanted to help the reform efforts of men of their class. And since they were often unskilled workers at a time when only the skilled were well organised, women were in a weak position in the unionisation campaign, regardless of gender. As they defended their own vulnerable interests in a divisive industrial order, women faced a number of troubling choices, including moving into the masculine political arena; strike-breaking, or accepting low pay and conditions; and opposing the hours reductions of the 1840s in the belief that they would be used to reduce female employment. Small wonder that there was little theoretical discussion of the rights of women in the unions, in protest, or in feminine working-class circles generally.

In utopian socialism, however, which, from the 1820s to the 1840s, attracted a fraction of the working class together with some middle-class intellectuals, a few women found the opportunity to participate in just such a discussion, and to act accordingly. Throughout the nineteenth and early twentieth centuries, some socialists in both countries were unhappy at the prospect of women breaking away from conventional roles and distracting attention from the class struggle. Others, however, transcended contemporary thinking about the female situation. The English utopian socialist movement, although it was influenced by the writings of the French socialist Charles Fourier, owed more to the work and extensive publications of Robert Owen, an immensely successful capitalist first in Manchester and then in New Lanark, near Glasgow, who sought to extend the benevolent principles he had applied to his workforce to humanity at large, and so produce 'a new social order based on classless, co-operative communities'.[125] Owen's ideas caught hold on both sides of the Atlantic, inspiring the foundation in 1824 at New Harmony, Indiana, of a model socialist settlement which, like New Lanark, attracted great remark among his contemporaries.

In Britain, the various co-operative societies, trade unions and communities which attempted to bring about Owen's 'new moral world' displayed an unusual degree of commitment to equal rights between the sexes: a commitment buttressed by debates on marriage and the family, divorce, sexual mores and birth control of a kind which were rare in Victorian society and uncommon in the first phase of organised, middle-class feminism which developed from the 1850s. In the end, Owenite egalitarianism was defeated by working-class divisions, elite opposition, and organisational and financial problems, combined with economic and cultural changes which both strengthened capitalism and softened its worst effects. Long before the end, the weight of established institutions and attitudes had made it intractably difficult to implement genuinely collective family arrangements, fair property relations between men and women, and a new sexual morality which did not work against women. A transclass Practical Moral Union of Great Britain and Ireland formed in London in 1833 – 'the first separatist feminist organization established in Britain' – failed after a few months: as a result, it would seem, of female inexperience and male hostility. And the disadvantage of associating sexual and political radicalism, demonstrated in the 1790s, was once again confirmed. Even so, Owenism left a legacy which subsequent socialists and feminists might ignore but could not permanently suppress. It also produced some memorable feminist leaders from working-class and middle-class backgrounds, whose socialist principles and search for personal development sustained them through economic insecurity and considerable notoriety. Among them were the author-lecturers Eliza Macaulay, Frances Morrison, Anna Wheeler, Emma Martin and Frances Wright, whose repertoire of arguments stressed both women's rights and their special qualities and mission.[126]

Of these women, the best-known is still Frances Wright, her middle-class status making her an especially alarming example of female radicalism. The daughter of a Scottish manufacturer of advanced opinions, orphaned early and brought up in the house of a progressive relative, the philosopher James Milne, Wright was, by the age of twenty-one in 1816, a personally appealing and intellectually confident young woman, determined to make her mark on the world and dismayed by the injustices in British society. Two years later, having crossed the Atlantic to observe conditions in a republic and find material for a book, she discovered a country she could admire, and a reforming mission. Impressed by New Harmony and making a friend of Owen's son, Robert Dale Owen, on whom much of its running had devolved, Wright established her own community at Nashoba, Tennessee, in 1826. She hoped to show blacks and whites how to live in amity, and to aid the anti-slavery cause – not least by the education and emancipation of the slaves who were taken to work out their purchase price there. She also found fame as a journalist, public lecturer, promoter of education and women's rights, and supporter of the New York

Workingmen's Party. Urging the need for 'equality, rationality, tolerance, and peace', Wright elicited far from peaceful audience responses by her short hair and bloomers, and by her advocacy of free love, criticisms of established religion, and habit of pointing out to her hosts the deficiencies of their society.[127]

Like the forty or fifty American utopias established on Fourier's principles in the 1840s, as well as the Christian socialist settlements of Hopedale, Fruitlands and Brook Farm in Massachusetts, New Harmony and Nashoba failed for many reasons, and with their demise foundered a brave effort to welcome women as equals in social affairs. The history of the Indiana and Tennessee ventures in particular demonstrates that whereas European ideas and refugees might find a warm welcome in the United States, visiting radicals who wanted to make over its institutions had a harder job, and frequently misjudged New World conditions. Owen underestimated the power to undermine communitarianism endemic to America's diversity, individualistic creed and abundant land, while his continuing absences in Europe deprived New Harmony of an inspirational director who was also capable of addressing vital practicalities. Fanny Wright, who was never practical, was likewise too often away from Tennessee for the colony's good and too indifferent to the racial and sexual anxieties her experiment aroused, particularly in the conservative South. She could easily be denounced as a dangerous foreign agitator, just as British women abolitionists were when their exhortations to American co-workers were regarded as especially ill-judged.[128] What is more, as a single woman activist operating in a foreign country, Wright lacked the protection of those supportive female networks that made it possible for her more prudent British and American sisters to engage in reform for feminist or non-feminist ends in the first half of the nineteenth century.[129]

It would also have eased Wright's task as an advocate of the rights of labour had the American union movement and the position of women workers been more advanced than they were in Britain. But they were not. While the 1820s and 1830s were years of general unionism and worker militancy in both countries, we saw in Chapter 1 that belief in America's political and economic opportunities, with its corollary of opposition to class-based movements, seriously impeded the growth of unions in the New World. Thus, although women outnumbered men in the textile industry of New England and the South, comprised a quarter of the total population engaged in manufacturing by 1850, and by their cheap labour helped to boost industrialisation in America's high-wage economy,[130] the chief benefit went to the nation and its employers, rather than to women. Even in the early, showplace Massachusetts textile mills, where the wages were better than those offered to female employees elsewhere in the United States,[131] the company boarding-house system was designed as much to supervise as to attract the labour force. None the less, as Dublin and Eisler have observed, the educational facilities, clubs and boarding houses of the mill towns broadened the horizons of the Yankee farmgirls who flocked there, with communal living especially breeding 'new values, solidarity, and political activism' once conditions deteriorated in the houses and mills alike during the 1830s and 1840s: the result was walkouts at Lowell, Massachusetts, in 1834 and 1836, and subsequent pressure for a ten-hour day.[132]

The Lowell strikes were unsuccessful, as were similar actions by women textile operatives at Pawtucket, Rhode Island, in 1824; at Patterson, New Jersey, in 1828; at Dover, New Hampshire, in 1828 and 1834; in New Jersey in the 1830s; and in Pennsylvania in the 1830s and 1840s. In her study of women in antebellum New York, Christine Stansell presents a similar picture of unsuccessful – though not unvarying – female struggles in the city's labour movement; she concludes that 'no explicit feminist politics emerged from the changed circumstances of working-class women'. These setbacks may be accounted for in various ways. Women in America, as in Britain, inclined to spontaneous protest because they lacked 'organization, leadership, financial support, and techniques to make use of their numbers'. Male unionists, fearing or resenting their female counterparts, gave priority to men's struggles, and the public at large – including, of course, unpaid women in the home – were not impressed by unfamiliar appeals to America's radical political tradition to justify feminine activism. By the late 1830s, employers could use depression conditions to justify harsh terms, and replace native women by Irish and other immigrants who were glad of the work and were less likely to invoke that tradition. Any strong direction of women's interests in the mills was difficult because workers stayed an average of only four years, and the fact that – by their own account – women often entered employment to help their families suggested that the feminine tradition of service had simply been transferred from the home to the factory: something which blocked much assertion there of women's rights.[133] The conflict in the *Lowell Offering*, the famous magazine produced by the Lowell female operatives, between seeking a literary outlet and urging the workers' cause reveals its supporters' reluctance to face up to the increasingly harsh realities of their class position, while the patronising praise bestowed on their efforts by comfortably placed observers 'did not bode well for the hardening of class lines'. Even more vulnerable were women doing industrial outwork at home.[134]

The campaign for the ten-hour day had succeeded by the late 1840s, and by that decade women workers were clearly aware of the need for sustained action beyond plant level. In Lowell, for instance, not only did a more militant journal appear to publicise the ten-hour movement but a Female Labor Reform Association was formed which testified before the state legislature's investigatory commission and obtained publicity for its aims through the New England Workingmen's Association. Comparable associations followed in Massachusetts, New Hampshire and New York. Admitting women from outside as well as within the textile industry, these associations avoided strike action for less risky forms of persuasion, but the hours restrictions eventually achieved were the work of both men and women, and were far from satisfactory in application. Moreover, by the 1840s the well-organised British textile workers had won better conditions than the Americans enjoyed, despite continuing American resentment of comments on 'the condition of the factory population of England, and the station which the operatives hold in society there', as though it were 'descriptive of *our* condition'.[135]

If, however, acceptance of the existence of a permanent working class and the growth of working-class solidarity were delayed in the United States by a widespread belief in American exceptionalism and some genuinely exceptional circumstances, there was enough hardening of class lines in both countries to make co-operation between women of different classes in reform increasingly difficult to achieve after the 1840s.[136] And in both countries the 1840s witnessed the consolidation of capitalism, a decline in hopes of establishing an alternative, co-operative and communal order, and a growing celebration of the feminine sphere of domesticity – which, in the face of the limited economic prospects before them, had understandable charms for women.[137] The impact on female activism of a more conservative social climate during the 1840s is seen in American women's lower profile in the anti-slavery movement,[138] and in the nature of the feminine involvement in the British Chartist demands for political and social reform.

Building on the precedent of female participation after 1815 – especially in the North of England – in associations concerned to reform Parliament, women throughout Britain played a prominent part in the campaign, establishing some eighty 'Political Unions and Chartist Associations between 1837 and 1844'. What is more, some male spokesmen believed that women had a right to 'interfere in political affairs', and that ' "The agency of the Women sent the Missionary on his Christian pilgrimage; it redeemed the slavery of the Negroes! It has ever triumphed, and it shall now secure the most glorious and perfect of its victories".' But while the Chartist agitation aroused much contemporary debate on the position of women, they had long received flattering tributes to their usefulness in reform. Votes for women, though favoured by some Chartists of both sexes, did not become an official aim of the movement, and Chartist women, who seldom exercised executive authority outside their own associations, were found in the customary supportive and often spontaneous roles of female reformers. Specifically, this meant swelling crowds and audiences; holding meetings, raising money, making needed items, signing petitions and distributing literature; asserting their power as consumers in dealing with pro-Chartist shopkeepers; educating children into the cause; invoking a moral sanction for public actions; and backing up male demands for wages that would support a family. As in the Anti-Corn Law League agitation, extraordinary conditions were used to justify extraordinary class actions by women, not actions on their own account. Male and female Chartists alike subscribed to the doctrine of separate spheres for the sexes in a way that the more radical and wide-ranging Owenites had not; and as Schwarzkopf has established, their stance had a lasting impact on working-class gender relations. Furthermore, whereas utopian socialism had attracted the support of middle-class women reformers, they generally recoiled from the clear class consciousness, radical political demands and violent actions of Chartism. The veteran Anne Knight was unusual in her contempt for the 'shoals of charitable societies' that would be unnecessary if Chartists concentrated on and achieved political rights.[139]

In the course of this chapter it has been argued that many of the forces that shaped feminism in Britain and the United States were identical. During the first half of the nineteenth century, women in both countries were affected and impelled to action by industrial and urban growth, political change, the task of class definition, and the fashioning of an elaborate ideology of domesticity which allegedly defined their qualities and mission. In both countries a minority of women, responding to these factors and the promptings of religion, expanded their activities outside the home, working through a complex network of church causes and secular reform movements in which they established their worth and priorities, supported their male and transatlantic counterparts, and laboured for class as well as broader social objectives. In both countries, involvement in the church, in moral issues, or in the newly feminised career of teaching was generally sufficient satisfaction for activist women: the majority did not campaign for gains specifically intended to benefit their own sex. But on each side of the Atlantic, involvement in one form of activism could lead to involvement in others and could be a radicalising process, drawing women into non-electoral politics and economic endeavours at variance with the doctrine of separate spheres.[140]

There were, however, some significant differences between the experiences of British and American women. In the realm of education – and especially advanced instruction – the United States sustained its early lead, and it is undeniable that the gap between the expectations created by the country's natural abundance, popular politics and libertarian ethos on the one hand, and its particularly oppressive cult of domesticity on the other, prompted middle-class American women reformers to take political action and to make feminist claims sooner and more often than their British sisters. In doing so, they shared the view – common among their countrymen – that the United States represented the vanguard of reform, often sidestepping the growing class differences between women and ignoring the fact that in the South they faced a formidable obstacle to change. None the less, British feminism took an organised form only marginally later than its American equivalent, while the strength of the British reform tradition and the pride British women took in its achievements must not be underestimated. Without the spur provided by the rapid advance of democracy, such activists were less politicised than those across the Atlantic; but they were more secure in their class position, and less discomfited than American women were in the 1850s by that decade's focus on electoral, state and national politics.

Feminist claims did not disrupt the anti-slavery, peace and temperance movements in Britain as they did in the United States; nor did they divide and radicalise the British Anti-Corn Law League or Chartism. Yet these movements did provide a training school for women who subsequently campaigned as feminists and, in the multifaceted and class-riven world of Victorian reform, served to strengthen the distinctively British emphasis on keeping contentious causes apart. The radicalism of British women was shown in utopian socialism, which had less significance for their American sisters, although women in both countries were interested in the efforts of secular and religious utopians to create a fairer sexual code and family structure. And although hard-pressed, working-class women on both sides of the Atlantic played a smaller part in reform and protest than middle-class women, those in the United States struggled with the double burden of lacking an overtly acknowledged class framework in which to campaign and having to meet the problems posed by mass immigration.

It will be the work of the next chapter to trace further the similarities and differences between American and British women as some of them went on from reform and proto-feminism to organising on their own account.

3

~

The women's movements take off
1840s–1860s

In Chapter 2 we saw how social change and faith in female values impelled British and American women into a range of benevolent associations, reform movements and economic protests, sometimes independently of men but often in co-operation with them and invariably within the confines of their own class. Yet while it was acknowledged that 'In moral revolutions women have ever signalised themselves',[1] such endeavours occasioned masculine anxiety as well as backing, and for many women activists they were a sufficient outlet for their talents beyond the home. When a few bolder spirits went on to work specifically for the rights of women, it is perhaps not surprising that they organised themselves in the accepted manner for pressure groups in their respective countries, and initially concentrated on discussing the 'woman question'. In these discussions they squarely challenged the notion that men ruled the public sphere, women the private, recognising that male power prevailed and had to be challenged in both. And they raised without resolving two dilemmas which have always troubled feminists: whether to play gender differences up or down, and how far to seek improvements in women's position as of right.

Once they did venture into campaigning, British and American feminists alike first took up the reform of the married women's property law, a cause which had already attracted masculine support. But such support did not guarantee this cause a straightforward passage in either country, and the accompanying questioning of the divorce and child custody laws raised further unease as well as dividing feminists themselves. The fears of conservatives could only intensify as women on each side of the Atlantic also attempted to change fashionable dress and health practices, end the male monopoly of the medical profession, enlarge female economic (and related educational) opportunities, and secure the enfranchisement of their sex. In Britain, the feminist argument was generally made in connection with the campaigns women sought to advance, though in both countries it had been evolving for years before the 1850s. And in the United States, at meetings under way from 1848, feminists caused alarm by publicly debating the broad rationale for women's rights as well as laying down a large number of goals for which they intended to labour.[2] Priority was not immediately given to winning the vote; but its usefulness was becoming increasingly apparent to British and American feminists during the 1850s. It is for this reason that the present chapter ends with the political developments of the 1860s. There was, of course, no equivalent for British women of the trauma of the American Civil War (1861–5), which forced southern as well as northern women into new roles, while further bureaucratising and politicising the work of reform. But on either side of the Atlantic, during the 1860s, feminism underwent a 'premature radicalisation',[3] as debates on extending the suffrage to excluded categories of men galvanised some women to seek their own enfranchisement with a new urgency, in new associations.

I. Early organisation, ideas and objectives

An organised women's movement emerged first in the United States, beginning with the convention at Seneca Falls, New York, in July 1848. This was followed by other gatherings at Rochester, New York, in August, and at Salem, Ohio, in 1850, during which year the first national women's rights convention was held at Worcester, Massachusetts. Similar national assemblies met annually until 1860 (with the exception of 1857), supplemented by state meetings; but there was no national organisation beyond a changing Central Committee which, after 1850, co-ordinated annual activities through a few 'representative men and women of the several States'.[4] Women's rights meetings were concentrated in New England, New York, New Jersey, Pennsylvania, Ohio, Indiana, Wisconsin and Kansas. These gatherings and the national conventions reached only a small part of the female population, as did such newspapers as Amelia Bloomer's *Lily*, Paulina Wright Davis's *Una*, Jane Swisshelm's *Saturday Visitor*, and Anna McDowell's *Women's Advocate*, whatever their importance in demonstrating that women were not entirely dependent for sympathetic publicity on the journals of the anti-slavery and temperance campaigns. Fairs, lectures, speaking tours, pamphlets and petitions to legislatures supplemented the meetings and conventions but did not fundamentally strengthen the organisation of the women's rights campaign.

It is hard to see how a better beginning could have been made, though it went against reform developments of the time: as Ginzberg has established, by the 1850s the move was towards institution-building and organisational entrenchment. Feminists, however, inclined towards the methods of earlier years. Conventions had been used by abolitionists, free blacks and other radicals to secure solidarity among themselves and notice from the uncommitted or hostile.

~

Large bureaucracies were not a feature of the pioneering antebe
crusades, and great faith had been placed in the efficacy of the higr
individual. Although some of the women who attended feminist
middle-class, they were not well-off. Those who were constrained by home ties,
the lack of independent funds and inexperience of reform might easily have been
intimidated by an elaborately structured and hierarchical movement: we have
already noted the preference for local and spontaneous action among their
discontented working-class sisters (see above, p. 72). Hewitt has established
that the association of 'ultraist' (feminist) women she studied in Rochester were
'characterized by fluid forms of authority, event-orientated selections of leaders,
and decentralized decision making, with only small differences in tasks'
developing 'between leaders and members'. This libertarian style was a feature of
early feminism as a whole and suited women who lacked numbers, challenged
established institutions and gave priority to spreading their unpopular message.
Regular meetings with the like-minded raised confidence among individuals,
helped to create the sense of sisterhood which was vital to the women's efforts,
clarified and publicised feminist ideas, and provided enjoyable as well as testing
social occasions at a time when the secular activities available to respectable
women outside the home were few and their male connections were increasingly
absent on business or pleasure.[5]

The feminist meetings and conventions were the more valuable in the 1850s,
as radical women encountered opposition to their claims for equality in the
temperance and peace movements, and found their opportunities limited by
causes like temperance and abolitionism turning to 'electoral means and goals'.[6]
Susan B. Anthony is one of the best examples of a determined woman reformer
who moved from temperance and teachers' conventions to the rights of her sex,
convinced that the ballot others were increasingly using to further their reforms
would best enable women to tackle alcohol abuse and similar social evils.[7]
However, there are numerous lesser-known instances of women experiencing the
gradual nurturing of their abilities through these feminist gatherings. A case in
point is Martha Coffin Wright, sister of Lucretia Mott, who signed the Seneca
Falls Declaration of Sentiments but confessed:

> to being very stupid & dispirited at Seneca Falls [,] the prospect of having more
> Wrights than I wanted tending materially to subdue the ardor & energy that would
> doubtless have characterized me 'at another time' . . .

A year later, writing about 'our cause', she envied Mrs Stanton 'the ability to
clothe her thoughts in words that burn! I can only stand at a humble distance
responding (mentally) most heartily to the sentiments of others, without the
power to say anything myself.'

As the mother of seven, like Stanton, Wright was often kept at home by 'my
boys'; there she took an affectionate pleasure in the activities of the 'sterner sex',

detailing the inadequate efforts of her male children, whom she had instructed in knitting and sewing; noting the desperate, gossiping idleness of men 'when business flags a little'; and enjoying the unconscious foolishness of a male visitor who, while she fussed around him, warned her that 'when women gets the rights they're talking about, they won't find men wait on 'em as they have done'. Once she found time to attend the conventions, Wright was grateful to escape from 'speakers [who] dwell longer than was wise, on uninteresting or egotistic schemes', and concerned that vital details like heating in meeting halls should be efficiently arranged. Eventually, she went on to play a full part in the women's movement, both in New York and nationally, advising Stanton and Anthony, and bringing to correspondence and meetings an attractive blend of judgement, humour and practicality.[8]

Moderate as the conventions appear to have been, they encountered much initial audience and press criticism,[9] and seemed quite radical enough to those who were unaccustomed to public speaking, or speaking out at all on controversial issues.[10] In conducting them effectively, women demonstrated that though they were intellectually alarming, they were both personally decorous and able to handle their business in a manner familiar to men. The 'rallies, demonstrations, and parades' employed by 'ultraist' female abolitionists in Rochester would probably have been unwisely attempted by the majority of feminists, since Rochesterians were apparently more accustomed to hearing radical demands 'than the citizens of other Northern communities'.[11] But feminists did consider the question of organisation seriously, and although DuBois has rightly pointed out that they were unduly reliant on the personnel, presses and methods of abolitionism,[12] the danger involved in this alliance was not fully apparent until the 1860s (see below, pp. 119–20).

Confident leaders thus believed that their meetings had 'done much towards disseminating the great principles of equality between the sexes' and arousing 'a spirit of earnest inquiry' about women's rights. It was deemed a positive advantage that 'women in Ohio, Indiana, Pennsylvania, and Massachusetts' had met 'without the least concert of action', and displayed a 'striking uniformity in their appeals, petitions, resolutions, and speeches'. Their activities, and those of their counterparts in Europe, showed that 'new liberty for woman was one of the marked ideas of the century, and that . . . the time had come for her to take her appropriate place'.[13] Sanguine that 'a well-digested plan of operation whereby these social rights, for which our fathers fought, bled, and died, may be secured by us',[14] feminists none the less drew back from creating a national society. Since many rejoiced in having escaped from the 'thumb-screws and soul screws' of 'permanent organizations', they were determined to preserve the liberty of individual supporters and, despite their concern for the national and international progress of feminism, inclined to put faith in state and local associations, if associations were necessary.[15]

The women's faith is understandable. In a country the size of the United States, there was always a danger that a national society without genuine state and local support would narrow or wither, and this was especially threatening while American nationalism remained comparatively weak. It is also understandable that the women's movement took off in areas that had been strongly canvassed by the abolitionists, were 'most distinguished for intellectual and moral culture', or were 'young States', because it 'was a thousand times more difficult to procure the repeal of unjust laws in an old State, than the adoption of just laws in the organization of a new State'. And anxious as the feminists were about organisational constraints, from 1850 the Central Committee set up committees on education, industrial avocations, social relations, civil and political functions, and publications, whose members were to call conventions as they saw fit and to 'correspond with each other and with the Central Committee, hold meetings in their respective neighborhoods, gather statistics, facts, and incidents to illustrate, [and] raise funds for the movement'. Through 'the press, tracts, books, and the living agent', they were to 'guide public opinion upward and onward in the grand social reform of establishing woman's co-sovereignty with man'.[16] If men were allowed to participate in the proceedings, they were not permitted to dominate them, while some areas produced female organisers of great ability – Elizabeth Jones of Ohio; Clarina Nichols of Vermont and Kansas; Mary Ferrin of Massachusetts; the Reverend Amanda Way of Indiana; Amy Post and Susan Anthony of New York. Of these, Anthony was perhaps the most notable, systematising the work in New York once the State Committee had appointed her its General Agent, and arranging speaking tours; conventions 'at the fashionable watering places in the summer, and at the center of legislative assemblies in the winter'; the production of petitions to secure 'the civil rights of married women'; the sale of literature and other forms of fund-raising; and the establishment of societies.[17]

Yet though there may have been no obvious or palatable alternatives to the organisation adopted by the first American feminists, its deficiences remained considerable. The women's rights endeavours never rivalled the anti-slavery movement and recruited only a handful of blacks – for example Margaretta Forten in Philadephia; Sarah Remond of Massachusetts; Sojourner Truth of New York. Feminists also failed to make headway in the South. As Elizabeth Fox-Genovese has stressed, southern slaveholding women did not advocate 'equality among the women in their society', and black slave women 'increasingly focused on the violent repudiation of the system and on the assertion of their own wills and personal worth'. In other words, 'Class and racial struggles assumed priority over the gender struggle', and women's protests against men in the South 'did not assume the forms or use the language developed by the early northern feminists'.[18] Meetings between the committed and the interested gave the feminists involved a false idea of the difficulties facing them,[19] while to the extent that they tried to draw in all kinds of recruits and avoid 'ultraisms',[20] they risked undermining the radical planks of the women's programme and alienating their radical agitators. And whereas some feminists recognised the need to help labouring women to organise themselves,[21] the premium that their own associations put upon the leisure for debate and the ability to communicate from the platform and in print disadvantaged working-class women.

What is more, local groups created in response to a visiting lecturer found it hard to sustain the interest thus aroused, and women themselves recognised the danger of drowning in 'interminable' resolutions, reacting defensively to the prediction of abolitionist Gerrit Smith, in 1855:

> The next 'Woman's Rights Convention' will, I take it for granted, differ but little from its predecessors. It will abound in righteous demands and noble sentiments, but not in the evidence that they who enunciate these demands and sentiments are prepared to put themselves in harmony with what they conceive and demand.[22]

After five years of labour, Anthony confessed: 'I can not get up a particle of enthusiasm or faith in the success, either financial or spiritual, of another series of conventions. ... There has been such a surfeit of lecturing, the people are tired of it.' Even when they were not weary of the women's message, their ability to support it was bound to diminish during the depression of the late 1850s. Before receiving funding from two Boston philanthropists in 1858 and 1859, the feminists were in real financial difficulties; they had not had time to build up substantial coffers from the legacies of supporters, and had failed to attract contributions from rich women.[23] By the Civil War, whatever the practical results of the women's movement of the 1850s – and the petition campaigns for a married women's property law enjoyed some success (see below, pp. 95–101) – its organisation was not strong enough to sustain feminism in a crisis.

Women in Britain coalesced a few years after their American sisters, and in a different fashion. As we have seen (pp. 66, 69 above), their role in anti-slavery grew rather than diminished after the 1840s: they were not embarrassed, as women in America were, by the politicisation of abolitionism. But many, as a result, moved on to women's rights only in the 1860s and 1870s, after the conclusion of fund-raising efforts for the American freedmen. British feminists were thus obliged to organise independently of the anti-slavery movement; from the first they favoured single-issue campaigns tackled by specialised committees. However, it is hard to see that they gained from this independence, since their efforts were consequently on an even smaller scale than those of their American counterparts. If the early women's movement in the United States was a northern phenomenon, in Britain before the 1860s it was primarily metropolitan, which was certainly not true of abolitionism. From 1854 onwards a growing number of feminists came together in London – first in a committee to plan reforms to the married women's property laws by means of collecting proof of hardship and petitioning, and then to establish the *English Woman's Journal* (1858) and the Society for Promoting the Employment of Women (SPEW, 1859). They also found sympathy for their views among members of the Law Amendment Society (1844) and the National Association for the Promotion of Social Science (NAPSS, 1857), which in that year appointed, as its assistant secretary, Isa Craig, a Scottish newcomer to London feminism. Both the journal and the SPEW were located at a house in Langham Place in the West End, sufficiently large to include, in addition, a dining-room, a library and an employment bureau. It quickly became a meeting place for women interested in or already involved in the incipient movement for women's rights.[24]

At this serious club women debated their priorities, acquired experience in fact-finding, organisation and campaign planning, and took pleasure in the stimulating friendship of like-minded pioneers. Among the prominent individuals who visited, worked and discovered inspiration there, several names stand out. Perhaps the best-known and boldest was the financially independent and artistically talented Barbara Leigh-Smith (later Bodichon).[25] The illegitimate daughter of a radical MP of Unitarian persuasion, she attended lectures at Bedford College, ran a progressive school in Paddington with her sisters, wrote an influential pamphlet on *Women and Work* (1857), campaigned for women's suffrage and higher education, and sustained much feminist endeavour from her own funds. Then there was her friend, Bessie Rayner Parkes (later Belloc),[26] another radical MP's daughter from a Unitarian background, the author both of poetry and of a critical book on girls' education (1854), and editor of the *English Woman's Journal*. Vitally involved with these two allies was Jessie Boucherett.[27] Boucherett, a Lincolnshire landowner's daughter who founded a school in Charlotte Street, London, designed to help older women as well as young girls, also set up the SPEW with help from the poet Adelaide Proctor and the reformer Maria Susan Rye, whose interests were soon to centre on female emigration. And in time their circle was joined by the restless clergyman's daughter and eventual educationalist Emily Davies, who, before moving to London in 1861 after the death of her father, was kept going in provincial society by awareness of Langham Place developments and establishing a Northumberland and Durham branch of the SPEW, for which she acted as treasurer.[28]

In organisational terms, the British feminist movement resembled its American precursor: directed by a number of middle-class women rather than a single leader, it attached importance to the spoken and written word; to recruiting the frustrated and disenchanted for materially unrewarding but personally challenging work; to mounting campaigns on a number of fronts; and to lobbying liberal and influential men in a manner designed to be acceptable to them. Like their American sisters, British feminists did not immediately fashion a strong organisation, though there is no evidence that this was the deliberate decision it had been in the United States. But the country that had produced Mary Wollstonecraft and Frances Wright did not find their equivalent in the prosperous and sentimental 1850s. However striking Barbara Leigh-Smith may have been for her vision, self-confidence, simplicity of dress and tolerant affection for 'the cracked [people of the world] . . . such as queer Americans, democrats, socialists, artists, poor devils or angels',[29] her unconventionality and that of her co-workers were limited. There was not, at this point, a notorious agitator among them with the range of interests of Abby Kelley, Ernestine Rose,

Lucy Stone or Elizabeth Cady Stanton, although a brave campaign by the unhappily wed hostess and writer Caroline Norton to improve the rights of married women to their children and property brought her prominence in Britain and America alike.

In fact there was little to distinguish the methods of the first British feminists from those favoured by women in other kinds of reform and in philanthropy, and the *English Woman's Journal*, welcoming the inauguration of the NAPSS, reassured its readers:

> There is no fear of English women flinging themselves recklessly into the arena of public speaking, even if public opinion were to give way so far as to enable them to do so with as little trial to modesty or timidity as is incurred by men.

As Leigh-Smith's biographer, Sheila Herstein, has pointed out, as late as 1856 'public speaking was out of the question' for British women, and when they did eventually speak at NAPSS meetings they were ridiculed as 'unladylike'. Bodichon's name on the 1856 married women's property petition was not mentioned for fear that it would be a liability, and a year after the SPEW affiliated with the NAPSS in 1859, thereby losing 'its exclusively female leadership', papers produced by the society's feminist founders were read out by their male allies at an Association meeting.[30]

The advocates of women's rights during the 1850s were probably wise to concentrate on influencing metropolitan opinion-formers, given their valuable London connections; but the city also had the attraction, for marginalised women, of being obviously the nation's cultural capital, a role disputed in the United States between Boston and New York. Emily Davies, for instance, chafed at her life as a dutiful spinster in a Gateshead rectory, despite her efforts there to secure press interest in female employment and enlist activists to promote that cause. On settling in London she found both a more stimulating social life and the personal challenge she had long been seeking: an opportunity to press for the admission of women to university degrees, on the occasion of the University of London seeking a new charter. From the outset, it proved necessary to organise sustained campaigns – for reform of the married women's property law, enfranchisement, and the repeal of the Contagious Diseases legislation – and the necessary workers were found regionally, while NAPSS annual congresses were held at cities throughout the country. Yet involvement of the provinces, drawing on well-established urban and Nonconformist family reform networks, came about without that initial phase of itinerant public lecturing to identify and encourage the feminist constituency which gave the American movement a head start; and until recently, partly as a result of its origins, British feminism has been discussed too much in terms of the exploits of London-based leaders.[31]

As far as the ideas of feminism are concerned, the American women – through their regular meetings, as well as in lectures and journals – found ample opportunity to debate the case for women's rights. And even by the time of the first feminist assembly at Seneca Falls, given the long history of feminist arguments and their recent promotion by Garrisonian abolitionists, they should have been in a position to present it confidently. The task none the less proved daunting once the 1848 convention had been called, after a gathering of New York's Hicksite Quakers brought Lucretia Mott into Elizabeth Cady Stanton's neighbourhood and prompted the two women to act on their 1840 pledge to arrange such a meeting (see above, p. 68). But if the timing and location of the New York convention were fortuitous, they were also fortunate, since the town of Seneca Falls was situated in a region experiencing economic change and regularly swept by religious and reform enthusiasms; the state legislature was so advanced that in March it had enacted a Married Women's Property Bill; and local interest in national anti-slavery politics was running high. Some three hundred people from this restless region responded to the *Seneca County Courier*'s advertisement of 14 July for a convention on 19–20 July, 'to discuss the social, civil, and religious condition and rights of women'; when it assembled, Mott and Stanton, aided by three other women of liberal sympathies and 'several well-disposed men', had agreed a declaration and series of resolutions.[32]

Following a 'faithful perusal of various masculine productions' from the peace, temperance and anti-slavery movements, all of which seemed 'too tame and pacific for the inauguration of a rebellion such as the world had never seen before', the planners took as their inspiration the Declaration of Independence. They were right to do so, despite having to hunt through 'statute books, church usages, and the customs of society' to find the same number of grievances as the colonists, prompting one male observer to remark: 'Your grievances must be grievous indeed, when you are obliged to go to books in order to find them out.'[33] Although most of the sixty-eight women and thirty-two men who eventually signed the Declaration of Sentiments appear to have been comfortably off and middle-class,[34] the reworked language of the Declaration of Independence gave the women's manifesto an aura of legitimacy and radicalism; while countless reformers over the ages have toiled indignantly against evils from which they suffered only in part, if at all.[35] Stanton had been radicalised by exchanging her privileged life in Boston for the lot of most married women in small-town America – that is to say, she had become overworked, consumed by the cares of the moment, intellectually starved, socially isolated. And Stanton, like other early American feminists, was able to empathise with women in general, regardless of race or class, and to express forcibly their common hardships at the hands of men.[36]

The Seneca Falls documents were infused with a belief in natural rights and natural law, buttressed by the individualistic emphasis of romantic reform and evangelical religion.[37] As rational individuals endowed with natural rights, women were the equals of men 'in capabilities and responsibilities', entitled to pursue happiness and develop themselves as actively as they could, and as their Creator intended. The 'highest good of the race' demanded the recognition of female equality, and legislation that oppressed women, contrary to the 'higher law' of nature, was deemed 'of no validity'. Men's refusal of natural rights to women involved confining them to a distinct 'sphere of action' and, in consequence, inflicting on them many specific 'injuries and usurpations'. Having been denied the vote, woman had been forced to submit to taxation without representation and to laws 'in the formation of which she has no voice'. Her economic, religious and educational opportunities had been restricted; she had been deprived of 'all rights', if married; and the double standard of morality for the two sexes, approved by men, required at once too little and too much of her. The purpose of these restrictions was to destroy woman's 'confidence in her own powers, to lessen her self-respect, and to make her willing to lead a dependent and abject life'.[38]

In positively invoking the authority of natural law and all the 'rights and privileges' which belonged to women 'as citizens of the United States', feminists sought to demolish the power of 'corrupt customs' and misinterpreted Scripture. They were clear and bold in recognising the importance of psychological and social forms of oppression, and in marking the link between economic and political dependence. They were less clear about the proper role of man in their endeavours. At the convention's last session, Mott successfully presented a resolution which stated that the success of the cause would depend 'upon the zealous and untiring efforts of both men and women', but this might be hard to secure in view of the references to man's oppressions; to the 'ignorant and degraded' men who enjoyed rights withheld from women; and to the hypocrisy of men who objected to a public role for woman while encouraging 'by their attendance, her appearance on the stage, in the concert, or in feats of the circus'.[39] Moreover, if Stanton was determined to stress women's political aims, her plea for the ninth resolution – that it was 'the duty of the women of this country to secure themselves their sacred rights to the elective franchise' – was only just successful. While Ginzberg has suggested that the demand for the ballot indicated women's recognition, in a changing political climate, that voting was 'an essential tool' of reformers, such women were not numerous at Seneca Falls. According to the *History of Woman Suffrage*, those 'who took part in the debate feared a demand for the vote would defeat others they deemed more rational'. They may also, as Paulson suggests, have been reluctant to alienate their male allies and alarmed by the support this resolution received from the radical black abolitionist Frederick Douglass, dreading the consequences of equating black and female rights in the public mind.[40]

None the less, the activists of 1848 had highlighted one of the best intellectual bases for feminist claims and outlined the major objectives for which the nineteenth-century women's rights movement would campaign:

> such as equal rights in the universities, in the trades and professions; the right to vote; to share in all political offices, honors and emoluments; to complete equality in marriage, to personal freedom, property, wages, children; to make contracts; to sue and be sued; and to testify in courts of justice.[41]

And whereas self-culture had long been possible for determined and exceptional individual women, the commitment made at Seneca Falls recognised both the importance of female individuality *and* the need to emphasise what women had in common if changes from which all would benefit were to be effected.

Although the analogy was not stressed at the New York convention, many feminists before and after 1848 further illuminated their plight by comparing it – and especially matrimony – with the institution of slavery. They, like blacks, could complain of the inconsistency of their treatment in a country tempered by its struggle for liberty and proud that its 'far-famed' freedom continued to attract immigrants from the Old World. Women, like blacks, could complain that they were reduced to dependence: denied individuality, control of their bodies, their names, their property, their development. But there were drawbacks to such an argument. The analogy between slaves and women was hardly likely to recruit women infected with contemporary racial and class prejudices; and since it was most telling in the case of married women, there was a temptation to give priority to their concerns (as in the campaign for married women's property legislation), which could alienate single women. Men could also point out that women, unlike slaves, willingly embraced their bondage and, if the limited response to the feminists was any guide, were reluctant to leave it.[42]

In replying that the alternatives to matrimony for women were few, ill-paid and lacking in status, activists were generally careful to recognise the attractions for many of their sisters of the publicly venerated goals of marriage, children and domesticity. Nor were they anxious to disown the special feminine moral qualities that had already legitimised female claims to an expanded role in religion, benevolence and reform. (Some, in fact, were happy to claim that women were morally superior to men.) Accordingly, what was proposed was not the destruction but the reform of the family relationship, so that a woman no longer married because men had 'the means to get money which she can not have', and there was no longer 'assumed superiority on the part of the husband, and admitted inferiority with a promise of obedience on the part of the wife'. However, few feminists before the Civil War were bold enough to propose easier divorce as part of this reform (see below, pp. 101–4), and none advocated free love and liberal abortion legislation – which was, perhaps, as well in view of the concern expressed by the press and the medical profession during the 1850s (against the background of a declining birth rate) about the rising number of allegedly selfish bourgeois women who resorted to abortion.[43]

Contrary to the historic presentation of feminists as sexual radicals, the first American feminists agreed with their contemporaries that if women were capable of passion, they were frequently critical of its indulgence and saw themselves as more capable than men of exercising restraint. These pioneers did not favour the contraceptive devices which were marketed by the 1850s, which gave power to the men who used them while possibly encouraging promiscuity. Instead, taking account of feminine sensibilities, the known risks involved in childbirth and the middle-class conviction that fewer children meant better children, feminists urged women to use their influence to bring about mutual sexual restraint within marriage. In questioning whether men's unchecked pursuit of their sexual inclinations was either natural or desirable, women had the support of some members of the medical profession, but in general their relations with that male monopoly were strained. As we shall see (pp. 104–12, below), feminists did advocate medical careers for women, talking about sexuality and taking an interest in everything that affected female health. They were not, at this stage, in a position to refute the doctors who drew upon supposedly scientific evidence to show that women, unlike men, were prisoners of their biological processes and – for some of the time, at least – incapable of rationality and self-control.[44]

Still more difficult to refute were arguments against women's rights which had a religious sanction, and these had emerged well before Seneca Falls, most notably in the 1837 'Pastoral Letter' sent to all New England clergymen by the Council of the General Association of Orthodox Churches of Massachusetts, produced in response to the Grimké sisters' public speaking. Prizing the 'modesty and delicacy' of women, 'which is the charm of domestic life and which constitutes the influence of woman in society', the letter denounced as unnatural women who assumed 'the place and tone of man as a public reformer'. The 'unobtrusive and private' duties designed for woman were stated in the New Testament, and her power was 'her dependence, flowing from the consciousness of that weakness which God has given her for her protection'. Feminists seeking to rebut such assertions, and claim for their sex a greater role in the churches' pulpits and assemblies, were divided on their best course.

On the one hand, there were individuals like Sarah Grimké, Lucy Stone, Antoinette Brown, Abby Price and Elizabeth Wilson, who sought to reinterpret and question the binding nature of Old and New Testament texts which appeared to endorse female subordination. In the process, they stressed passages with a democratic tenor; the blending of 'the masculine and feminine elements of humanity' in Christ; and the 'independent, self-reliant characteristics sanctioned in woman, by the examples of the sex given in the Bible'. On the other hand, there was a smaller element, including Stanton, Anthony and Rose, who felt that since conflicting interpretations were clearly possible, the Bible was an authority feminists might be wiser to avoid. A more productive alternative would be to examine the ways in which 'the religious element in woman' had been abused by those who were anxious to use their fund-raising abilities and direct their attention to the manifestations, rather than the principles, of religion.[45] Better still – lest attacks on the clergy or churches should alarm upholders of traditional authority – reference could be made to the great secular text upon which the republic was founded, and which women now made their own.[46]

In putting the case for change, women may have concentrated on their grievances regarding home and religion,[47] but the economic and political aspects of their case were also made from the beginning, with the same stress on the functional as well as the theoretical basis for female advancement: 'The question of Woman's Rights is a practical one.'[48] The essence of the economic argument was that as long as women were crowded into a few lines of employment and paid less than men in the same work, they were likely to experience either poverty or dependence, regardless of background; to be tempted by vice or marriage for pecuniary motives; forced into empty and frivolous lives; and embittered by the injustice of their treatment. Male anxiety about female competition was recognised, but dismissed as groundless. Instead, women stressed the failure of men to protect them in marriage, and their willingness to exploit them in the marketplace.[49] The argument for political rights consolidated the points advanced at Seneca Falls: that the American system was founded, theoretically, on consent and a belief in no taxation without representation, whereas in practice it unjustly extended its benefits to men who were less qualified than many women.

Various additional points were then made. Since men and women were different, feminists maintained, men could not adequately represent women's interests. And since might was no longer the crucial factor in public life, it was unnecessary for them to do so. Women should be able to speak for themselves, because male legislators could always take back favourable legislation they had granted. Like men, women could combine political activities with family life, and would not disrupt the family circle with their views. On the contrary, shrewd spouses seeking to influence each other politically would employ tact, not shrillness, for the purpose. If women were, indeed, the moral sex, and politics was a dirty business, then it was more logical to involve women than to exclude them. It was certainly illogical to conclude that if politics would degrade women, it would not degrade men. Women, it was hoped, would attack many of the evils and errors that resulted from the male political monopoly and would, through the franchise, be able to protect their interests and effect the redress of their various wrongs: 'the right to vote ... includes all other rights'.[50] It is notable that in shaping their economic, political and other claims, the feminists tried at the same time to rebut male objections, and that those objections were much the same by the 1850s as they would be later in the century.

Ideologues must seek to be persuasive even at the expense of consistency, and the early American feminists were not consistent. They disagreed with each other, were agitators before they were theorists, and produced no single spokeswoman or unifying text. They also had to struggle with the fact that 'most women are more readily enlisted in the suppression of evils in the concrete, than in advocating the principles that underlie them in the abstract, and thus ultimately doing the broader and more lasting work.' Confronting male assumptions that women's circumstances were ahistorical and the same the world over, while the facts of social life indicated that inequality, not equality, between the sexes was the 'self-evident' truth, feminists underlined the consequences for women of cultural conditioning and discrimination, but remained divided about what would – what should – result from abandoning them. After all, pride in being women, which produced the sense of sisterhood essential to feminism, was grounded in satisfaction with what made women different from men, not in what women might become. Moreover, given male accusations that feminists were masculine in their characteristics, disappointed old maids, childless and invariably unattractive individuals, it was prudent to stress the recognisably female attributes of women's rights advocates.[51] It was equally important to strike the right balance between a celebration of the values of voluntary domesticity and a paean for the advantages of change.

Yet feminists argued both that most women would not want to forsake their customary occupations, although individuals able and willing to do so should have the chance;[52] and that certain consequences of biology aside, men and women were – or could be – equal in their interests and abilities, as well as their 'natural wants and emotions'.[53] A popular proposition was that each sex would profit from embracing some of the characteristics of the other, but neither would profit from the degradation of women: the interests of the sexes being 'one, we rise or fall together'.[54] The question as to whether men and women were intellectually equal was a difficult one and would become still more problematical later in the century, as the medical profession appeared to provide scientific evidence unhelpful to feminism. While existing inequalities could be explained with reference to women's restricted opportunities and expectations, feminists generally avoided this subject. Few were bold enough to state, as did Ernestine Rose, that 'where her mind has been called out at all, [woman's] . . . intellect is as bright, as capacious, and as powerful' as man's.[55]

The most common outcome of adapting the domestic ideology to the needs of feminism was proposals for overlapping spheres for men and women, and equality of esteem for the sexes, regardless of their differences. The risks involved in such a compromise were twofold. In the first place, it was probable that the spheres would not overlap substantially, and implementation of the doctrine of separate spheres had shown that separate was no more equal in sexual than it was in racial matters. Secondly, it was probable that the activities traditionally – and still – dominated by men would continue to generate greater esteem than women's roles – hence the need to recruit masculine supporters for the cause. Unfortunately, it remained unclear how this could be done, with some feminists tactfully reassuring men that they had no wish to dominate them and blaming 'society' for female subordination, while others bluntly slated men. All recognised that, as the proposer of reform, 'Woman must act for herself'.[56]

The main arguments used by feminists in Britain and the United States were very similar; and since the American women's rights conventions were followed with interest by British activists,[57] this is to be expected. In both countries, women could draw on a long history of debate about woman's characteristics and destiny, and in both countries they articulated the dismay of middle-class women especially at their lack of independence, individuality, opportunities and legal rights. Like their American sisters, British feminists generally accepted sex difference, though some saw the usefulness of claiming moral superiority while others urged that the two sexes were 'of equal value in the moral world'. They,

~

too, reformulated the ideology of domesticity to meet their needs, and acknowledged that women would have to emancipate themselves. Just as American feminists stated their commitment to reform on a wide front in 1848, British activists were convinced that 'all the various movements for improving the condition of women help one another', and should 'go on simultaneously if we are to hope to see any considerable effect produced in our time'. And, like their American counterparts, they were positive, practical individuals who, despite their diverse views, took pride in sisterhood, used whatever arguments seemed appropriate to advance their belief in overlapping spheres for men and women, and produced no definitive summary of their ideology.[58]

None the less, there were real differences of style and emphasis between British and American feminists. The heavy American stress on the slavery of sex and natural rights philosophy was not paralleled in Britain, though both themes are present in the British debate. *The Times* advised in 1867 that British women should make their case for the suffrage with reference to expediency, not right; but feminists could see the importance of arguing that the 'liberal principles of freedom and equality' applied as much to the private as to the public sphere. Hence from the first they varied their arguments, emphasising woman's *duty* to educate herself, for example, while often claiming her *right* to work. There was nothing in the British movement to match the American discussion of Scripture and conflict with clerics over the proper female role, though in the second half of the nineteenth century clergymen would play their part in opposing higher education for women, and throughout the nineteenth century approved no change in women's position in the power structure of the established church (see below, p. 179). This difference possibly results from the greater strengths of the cult of domesticity in the United States, and American clergymen's greater vulnerability to social change (see above, pp. 45, 56).

Halévy described the British women's movement as intellectual in origin, 'not economic, bourgeois not proletarian'; but his judgement must now be modified. We have already noted the importance of such intellectual pioneers as Wollstonecraft, Wright and Martineau, the significance of British literary feminism, and the forum provided for feminist ideas in the *English Woman's Journal* and the NAPSS. However, since British women produced no convention system through which their ideas might publicly be refined, and lacked the theoretical possibilities provided by republicanism and the affront of black slavery in the land of the free, they tended by mid-century to shape their arguments very closely to the gains they wished to achieve in, for example, further education, employment and the reform of the married women's property law. And if the leading activists of the 1850s were middle-class and offered no indictment of the industrial capitalism that was transforming the female role, they were more outspoken in their recognition of the difficulties class posed for women than were the American pioneers, although the *History of Woman Suffrage* ventured an occasional frank acknowledgement of the class divide and a genuine concern for the problems of poor women, while American feminists such as Jane Swisshelm,

Lucretia Mott and Susan Anthony believed that 'all the agitation about woman's rights, is to secure the toiling millions of her own sex a just reward for their labor'. As Anthony expressed it:

> I should like a particular effort to call out the teachers, seamstresses and wage-earning women generally. It is for them rather than for the wives and daughters of the rich that I labor.[59]

Awareness of the need to respect class differences permeates the writing of the Langham Place group, as does appreciation of the economic injustices suffered by all women, and ruefulness that their lack of unity rendered members of the female sex 'weak and helpless'.[60] Conscious that women already worked hard, both inside and beyond the home, these reformers had no desire to add 'to the severity of their toil',[61] or, in the case of ladies, to urge upon them work involving 'the forfeiture of social position'.[62] The fear of declining in class and respectability was a spectre for members of the newly powerful bourgeoisie, and prudent British feminists were also aware that 'no class are more sensitively alive to the influence of public opinion, than the parents of daughters'.[63] Their usual solution to the problems of working-class women was the provision of 'instruction in household and domestic matters, to enable them to become good servants and useful wives for working men'.[64] Such a proposal was understandable, if unadventurous. As women's employment opportunities had shrunk in agriculture, the handicraft trades, apprenticeship and the family economy following the onset of industrialisation, the number of female domestic servants had grown. And even in America, where opposition to servitude was great and equality of opportunity proclaimed, middle-class feminists saw domestic service as good for working women and a matter over which they might have influence. There was no open consideration, at this point, of how poorer women might hope to advance by working through their own class-based organisations; British utopian socialism had, after all, shown that middle-class and working-class leaders could act together.

Victorian feminists nevertheless acknowledged that women's need to act in the economic area was paramount, since their inability to make a decent living brought '*dependence on marriage for the means of subsistence*' and was a recent difference between the sexes. What rendered it so acute in Britain was the female 'overplus' created by male emigration to the colonies and aggravated by the *laissez-aller* of political and social life, which allegedly allowed the poor to suffer more acutely than they did in any other country.[65] (The fact that American free-market policies were equally unfortunate for the poor was, in the context of this debate, immaterial.) All practical efforts to improve women's prospects were to be welcomed, provided that 'the arguments upon which they are based are not strained too far, so as to become narrow and doctrinaire'.[66] And the arguments most commonly used were that there was no fixed number of jobs in the economy, so that working women would not crowd out men; that women as individuals had as much right to work as men; and that the skills they acquired by doing so would raise the standard of household management and contribute to the improvement of society as a whole.[67]

II. The campaigns

(i) *Reforming the marriage laws*

Appropriately, given the importance in both countries of the domestic ideology and women's attack on matrimonial injustice, the first organised feminist campaigns in the United States and Britain were designed to change the laws of marriage as they affected women. American efforts for the amendment of these laws got under way even before the feminists had launched their regular conventions, and were by no means exclusively dependent on women's efforts. Nor was work in this cause the sole radicalising experience which bred British and American activists for the women's rights movement: as we have seen (p. 62 above), the anti-slavery, temperance and peace campaigns, utopian socialism and the Anti-Corn Law League were alternative routes to feminism. The question of how far the situation of women improved in the nineteenth century through the intervention of feminists, and how far by other means, was as interesting to anti-feminists as it is to historians and feminists today.[68] And while such a question is difficult to answer, it is clear that in this particular instance – as in the case of women's education – much was owed to reformist men acting without feminist objectives in mind. It is also clear that the legislators' lack of genuinely egalitarian objectives limited the impact of the laws they achieved on the quality of women's lives.

The dependence of married women on their husbands under English common law, which was only marginally liberalised in the New World, has already been noted (pp. 14–15 above).[69] It is easy to see how feminists would be affronted at a society which theoretically elevated woman's role as wife and mother even as her husband controlled her personal property and real estate, services and wages. The teacher of his children and the guardian of the nation's morals owned nothing, could neither carry out transactions nor transact for others. A husband's obligation to meet any debts brought to the union or incurred thereafter by his partner, and to support his wife and children, merely confirmed that married women had no more independence than their offspring. There was some dignity in the widows' dower rights acknowledged by common law and through the equity courts, which recognised the right of married women to acquire a separate estate, over which the husband's customary common-law rights did not extend. Separate estates, however, were the safeguard of the affluent few, and dower rights were eroded early in the nineteenth century.

When – between the late 1830s and the 1870s, and often after memorials from feminists – legislatures moved to reform married women's property laws, they acted in North, West and conservative South alike: indeed, the breakthrough came in Mississippi. And as Basch and Rabkin have shown, they frequently did so less from egalitarianism than from a desire to simplify the law, adjust it to the needs of a changing economy, undermine the power of judge-made rulings (in equity courts), and safeguard married women's property against seizure by their husbands' creditors during periods of adversity. The consequences of the rash of married women's property laws were also mixed: lawmakers faced frequent and complicated litigation arising from the Acts, and the courts limited their application, not least by continuing to uphold the old common-law doctrine of marital unity. And as Leach points out, although 'the laws permitted married women to earn their own living and keep their own earnings during marriage, they did little or nothing to alter the sexual division of labor within marriage.'[70]

For women in several northern states, however, the issue of women's property rights filled a void left by the waning of female involvement in anti-slavery. The hardships produced by the common law were of concern to middle- and working-class women alike, especially as growing numbers of them chose or were obliged to work outside the home. By focusing attention on the importance of legislative action, they led women to fret at their own political impotence, and the interest they aroused helped the setting up of local feminist associations. In Vermont, Kansas, Ohio, Pennsylvania and Massachusetts, much was owed to a few prominent women who wrote articles, spoke and gathered signatures for female property rights.[71] But the most significant area of activism was New York where, in 1836–7, Ernestine Rose began her campaign for a woman's right to 'hold real estate in her own name' by dispatching to the state legislature a supporting petition containing five signatures, obtained 'after a good deal of trouble'. It failed, owing to insufficient public interest. During the eleven years which elapsed before success in 1848, Rose continued to send petitions, and addressed the New York legislature five times.[72] Having arrived in America only in 1836, after several years of travel away from her Polish homeland and marriage to an English follower of Robert Owen, Rose's enterprise may seem surprising. Yet before she left Poland, she had successfully gone to court at sixteen to overturn a marriage contract made for her by her father, and her determination, born of personal experience, was strengthened by the support of three other feminists: Paulina Wright Davis, a New Yorker married from 1833 to 1845 to a wealthy merchant who shared her wide reform interests; Lydia Mott, Lucretia's sister-in-law; and Elizabeth Cady Stanton, who lobbied members of the legislature and helped with the petitions.

Progress in New York, as elsewhere, depended on a range of factors. Proponents of the codification and simplification of the law saw it as becoming more available in the process, and some welcomed the prospect of thereby easing married women's common-law disadvantages. As the rights of Americans were debated and manhood suffrage was extended, while female economic and political opportunities failed to keep pace, women found some male sym-pathisers. Such men could appreciate the value of protecting the wives of bankrupts, and preventing the property of daughters from falling into the hands of 'dissipated, impecunious husbands, reducing them and their children to poverty and dependence'. Despite the emergence of these sentiments, Basch has established that change came in stages, with conservatives opposing the creation of 'advantages for potential new wealth' and fearing 'a sexual revolution set off by changes in the laws of marriage'.[73] The law eventually passed in New York in 1848 was the most liberal of its kind.[74] Women were given control of the property (plus earnings) that they owned on and after marriage; a husband could not use it to meet his debts, and all 'contracts made between persons in contemplation of marriage' were to 'remain in full force after such marriage takes place'.[75] As some critics had dreaded, this legislation encouraged American feminists to tackle the remaining legal restrictions affecting married women, to debate female subordination generally, and to attach growing importance to the vote as a means of improving their condition. It also brought new recruits to the fledgling women's rights movement, in and beyond New York.[76]

The 1848 statute was first amended a year later, giving women the contractual power enjoyed by their single sisters, and permitting a 'married woman who was the beneficiary of a trust to petition a justice of the Supreme Court for personal control of her property'.[77] But much remained to be done, and the unsettled business in this whole area was discussed by the feminist conventions of the 1850s. In 1854, Susan Anthony organised a petition with 6,000 signatures for the right of married women 'to the wages they earned and to the equal guardianship of their children'. A two-week women's rights convention held in February of that year at the New York state capital guaranteed her publicity when she presented the petition to the legislature, together with another for the suffrage. Both petitions were thereafter referred to a select committee of the Senate and Assembly, before which Miss Anthony spoke. Mrs Stanton, for her part, outlined the civil rights women still wanted in a comprehensive address to the legislators.

Although the women's hopes were disappointed, there was enough male support in the legislature to foster persistence, notwithstanding an impassioned protest against 'unsexed women' seeking to 'overthrow the most sacred of our institutions, to set at defiance the divine law which declares man and wife to be one, and establish on its ruins what will be in fact as in principle but a species of legalised adultery'.[78] The next breakthrough did not come until 1860, with the passage of a Bill which allowed a woman independent ownership and control of her property; to trade or perform any services on her own account; to control her earnings; to 'buy, sell, make contracts, etc.,' with her husband's consent (unnecessary if the spouse was a habitual drunkard, deserter, insane or a convict); to sue and be sued; to be the joint guardian of her children; and at the decease of her husband to 'have the same property rights as the husband would have at her death'.[79]

The 1860 victory was notable for two fine speeches by Mrs Stanton, before the Assembly and the Judiciary Committee of the legislature; intensive lobbying of politicians by Miss Anthony; and the backing of liberal male allies in the Senate, Assembly, Judiciary Committee, and press.[80] While these friends played a crucial part, Ida Husted Harper's verdict is fairer than the judgements of partisans normally are:

> This remarkable action, which might be termed almost a legal revolution, was the result of nearly ten years of laborious and persistent effort on the part of a little handful of women who, by constant agitation through conventions, meetings and petitions, had created a public sentiment which stood back of the legislature and gave it sanction to do this act of justice.

Anthony's work 'practically every month of every year' during 'the entire period' was especially commended by Harper.[81] And it was Anthony who felt most keenly the vulnerability of voteless reformers when in 1862 a newly elected, conservative New York legislature, taking advantage of the feminists' absorption in war work, amended the 1860 Act. (In consequence women forfeited, for example, the right to equal guardianship of their children and the rights they had secured in cases of intestacy.) As she exclaimed bitterly to a co-worker, 'The echoes of our words of gratitude in the Capitol scarcely died away, and now all is lost!'[82]

Anthony exaggerated in her vexation: all was not lost. The New York women's property Acts had stirred up American feminists, influenced their British counterparts, and provided a model for the developing western states.[83] Nor did the 1862 statute undo everything the 1848 law had achieved. Even so, the New York courts were as cautious in interpreting the property legislation as courts elsewhere. They were aided in their conservatism by the male monopoly of the legal profession as well as by the resilience of the common law. And while middle-class women benefited considerably from the property rights campaign, their working-class sisters, for whom they showed genuine concern, were not assisted until the 1860 Act. If much had been achieved initially without feminist pressure, the results of removing such pressure after 1860 were indeed damaging to women's interests, and revealed the weakness of feminism when it was confronted by entrenched masculine power in both the legal and political arenas. Women in the post-Civil War era became more concerned with securing the suffrage, and it was not until 1884 that another married women's property law was passed in New York (guaranteeing them equality with men and single women in the matter of contracting, a status implied in 1860). The campaign for legal equality, which stimulated the broader women's rights movement in parts of America, was left incomplete; and the concept of the domestic unity of men and women before the law survived into the twentieth century.[84]

During the 1850s British efforts to change the married women's property law, like those of their American counterparts, gathered pace due to both feminist and non-feminist protests. As in America, amendment of the legal system was urged to bring it into line with a more democratic, industrial era, which recognised the growing importance of movable property.[85] As in America, British women worked with the law reformers and found in the injustices of the common law a foundation upon which to build the feminist movement. Like their American sisters, they accepted the conventional division of labour in the home, objected to coverture for its denial of female individuality and responsibility, and recognised that middle-class and working-class women unable to command marriage settlements in equity were equally disadvantaged. Moreover, British feminists learned – as had their co-workers across the Atlantic – that there was no substitute for a direct political voice in the nation's affairs, however effectively they were able to bring pressure to bear on sympathetic men in the long run.[86]

By the time the first Victorian feminists took up this issue, it was apparent that earlier attempts at reform had achieved little, and the hardships women might suffer under the common law were already in the public eye. This was as a result of Caroline Norton's activities and the government's establishment in 1850 of a Royal Commission on divorce, responding to 'half a century's demand for the reform and cheapening of law and the persistent attack by middle-class people on the privileges of aristocracy'.[87] None the less, once they were involved, feminists became the driving force behind efforts for change. In 1854, aware of the injustice of the marriage laws both in the abstract and as they affected such prominent writer friends as Anna Jameson and George Eliot, Barbara Leigh-Smith published *A Brief Summary, in Plain Language, of the Most Important Laws of England Concerning Women, Together With a Few Observations Thereon.* Her pamphlet aroused fierce debate and was studied with interest by the Law Amendment Society, which set up a committee to study the question. In due course this body reported in favour of reform, and by 1855 a group of feminists, led by Barbara Leigh-Smith, Bessie Rayner Parkes and Maria Susan Rye, had come together to work for it.[88] Recognising the need to intensify sympathy for women's sufferings, the organisers set about gathering as much evidence on this point as they could. They also worked to produce 3,000 signatures on a London petition to Parliament and, through mobilising (enduring) contacts in the provinces, to secure similar petitions with upwards of 26,000 signatories, men and women, from the country at large. Lord Brougham presented the women's petition in the Lords in 1856, Sir Thomas Erskine Perry in the Commons; and these two friends of the cause were gratified by a serious reception.[89]

The following year, a Married Women's Property Bill drawing on the proposals of the Law Amendment Society's committee was introduced, only to collide with the Matrimonial Causes Act. That Act contained clauses allowing married women 'who obtained either a judicial separation or a divorce ... to have all the rights of an unmarried woman with respect to property', and permitting an unjustly deserted woman to 'apply to a court for an order protecting against her husband and his creditors all property she acquired after desertion', over which property she might exercise all the rights of a single woman.[90] The clauses were designed to remove the need for the more comprehensive Married Women's Property Bill, which proposed placing single and married women on equal terms in the acquisition, holding and disposing of property; and allowing the latter to make contracts; sue or be sued; assume responsibility for debts accumulated and torts committed before and after marriage; and dispose of their property by will. The ruse was successful: the Bill was lost, the London committee was disbanded (though its feminist members remained in touch), and the matter languished for a decade.[91]

Despite the considerable sympathy for women's grievances displayed in Parliament, there was evidence, too, of the fears expressed in the United States about undermining marriage and producing strong-minded, independent women, interested in public life. Such fears flourished despite the care taken by the married women's property committee to 'have an eye to the moral status of the persons supporting this movement', and to gain the backing of 'eminent women whom the public held in high regard'.[92] Yet there were some distinctive British emphases. The American movement, emerging earlier in the century, operated without benefit of encouraging precedent, albeit in a country with long experience of amending its British common-law heritage and the ability to do so piecemeal at the state level. The British petitioners of 1856, by contrast, publicised and took heart from the progress of American female property rights. Their opponents subsequently used the charge of 'Americanisation' to try and discredit feminists, on property rights and other contentious issues.[93] In making their case, Victorian women faced the daunting task of directly tackling the national legislature, and received less assistance than their transatlantic sisters from economic pressures for common-law reform. Nor do they themselves appear to have stressed the need to secure family property in turbulent times. Both parties to the debate in Britain, operating in an economic order more secure than that of the United States, fashioned their arguments accordingly; as a result it took rather longer to achieve progress, with more depending on the feminists and less on other concerned groups.

Progress was nevertheless made from the 1860s onwards, as women involved in the question polished their organisational techniques and effectively liaised with the NAPSS and other feminist campaigns, including the burgeoning suffrage movement. During the discussion of the 1867 Reform Bill, the political philosopher and MP for Westminister John Stuart Mill introduced an (ultimately unsuccessful) amendment to give the vote to women on the same terms as men, and argued that the law governing married women's property was one of the ills that enfranchised women would be able to remedy.[94] In these hopeful circumstances, a new married women's property committee was established in Manchester, by then a centre of activity for the suffrage. It involved both such new leaders as Ursula Mellor Bright, the activist Quaker wife of the radical MP for Manchester, and Elizabeth Wolstenholme (later Elmy), the Cheshire campaigner for improved education for women, and a faithful cohort of metropolitan feminists, including Frances Power Cobbe, Clementia Taylor and Frances Buss.[95] Gains were hard won; the first was secured under a Liberal government in 1870, when a Bill mangled by the Lords gave women, as their separate estate, any earnings and property acquired after the act, 'money invested in several specified ways', and, 'with qualifications, property coming to them from the estates of persons deceased'.[96] Excluding minor gains in 1874 and 1877, the next step forward was not made until 1882, again during a Liberal administration. Then a Married Women's Property Act (added to in 1884, 1891 and 1893; more limited measures were applied to Scotland in 1877 and 1881) extended to married women not *feme sole* status, but control of their 'separate property', limited contractual and testimentary capacity, and freedom from responsibility for their torts.[97]

In working for this legislation, British feminists had stressed the equal right of men and women to control their own property, the benefit of reform to vulnerable poor women, and the improved marital relations that would result. They also maintained that 'all reform originates with the people, and that the sustained and organised expression of public opinion can alone lead to a successful issue'.[98] In the hope of assuaging popular fears, much time was accordingly devoted to showing that the women involved wanted only to change outmoded laws which, by casting husbands in the role of all-powerful protectors and reducing women to irresponsible dependants, oppressed both sexes: they did not seek to repudiate marriage or threaten the established fabric of society. Unfortunately for them, the public support feminists aroused through meetings, articles in their own and the general press, petitioning Parliament and mobilising influential male connections (notably husbands in politics) was offset by the stubborn conservatism of opponents who feared that change would subvert male authority in the family and strengthen the suffragist cause. Such men, Shanley has shown, were willing to give women protection, but not equality. And the long campaign revealed the futility of relying on Private Members' Bills that were easily defeated by government opposition or a logjam of business – something which the suffragists were simultaneously discovering.[99]

The interest that a minority of the first British and American feminists showed in child custody and divorce did nothing to reassure traditionalists predicting the worst from married women's property laws. Although women's involvement in the American temperance campaign was in certain ways conventional before the Civil War, there were activists who advocated separation or divorce from drunken husbands and custody of children by women, 'if they were qualified'.[100] We have seen (p. 70 above) that the divorce issue damagingly divided temperance workers in New York during the early 1850s; it also produced dissension in the young feminist movement. For Amelia Bloomer, divorce was an interim measure until intemperance had been eradicated;[101] but for Lucy Stone, Paulina Davis, Anthony, Stanton and Rose, interest in the marriage question was an integral part of their feminism. They did not, however, agree about the best method of pursuing the matter, knowing the hostile reaction that was likely to meet any public discussion of women's right to control their own bodies, and escape from sexual or other exploitation within marriage. When a frank letter on this subject from Stanton to the 1856 national women's rights convention alarmed the audience, Stone, who had requested the letter, decided that in future divorce and related topics should be kept clear of the conventions, ostensibly on the grounds that they were of concern to men as well as women. Her view was unacceptable to Stanton and Anthony.[102]

The spirited drive at the state level for married women's property legislation nevertheless encouraged experimentation with the divorce laws, which the states likewise controlled. The resulting variation was most marked in regional terms, with the areas where the women's movement gained ground – New England and the West – generally permitting divorce for a wider range of causes than the more conservative southern states. Thus, for example, in the 1850s Iowa 'allowed women to sue for divorce on grounds other than adultery'; in 1859 Indiana passed a liberal law 'adding desertion, habitual drunkenness, and cruelty to adultery as grounds for divorce by wives'; while after heated debate a similar Bill was narrowly defeated in New York in 1860.[103] Cruelty, especially, had become 'the ground of choice in mid-nineteenth-century America'. Furthermore, though the subject was still an alarming one in polite society, complacency in such circles had been shattered by 'several very aggravated cases among leading families, both in America and England'.[104]

These developments fortified Mrs Stanton who, in 1860, made ten resolutions in favour of divorce the focus for her speech on that subject to the tenth national women's rights convention. Having dwelt upon female powerlessness and frequent wretchedness within marriage, Stanton favoured making it a compact harder to enter and easier to leave for a variety of causes, including simple incompatibility. Since she was opposed by Wendell Phillips and William Lloyd Garrison as well as many women, though aided by Rose and Anthony, Stanton was only able to secure a wide-ranging debate, followed by the tabling of her proposals. She was none the less denounced for her boldness by the press.[105] Her subsequent support for individual women caught up in well-publicised struggles to end unhappy marriages only served to strengthen Stanton's convictions,[106] and in her reminiscences she maintained:

> I had no thought of the persecution I was drawing down on myself for thus attacking so venerable an institution. I was always courageous in saying what I saw to be true, for the simple reason that I never dreamed of opposition. What seemed to me to be right I thought must be equally plain to all other rational beings.[107]

Mrs Stanton's priorities, confidence and love of combat were not shared by her fellow-feminists. While she continued to concern herself with the marriage question, they turned to less disruptive topics, and the divisions that question had caused during the 1850s between Stone on the one hand and Anthony and Stanton on the other were destined to harden further in the years that followed (see below, p. 120). As Anthony later recalled, the divorce debate of 1860 'produced the first unpleasantness in the ranks of those who had stood together for the past decade'. Moreover, it failed to produce any concerted feminist campaign to improve women's child custody rights, though changing attitudes to children and parental responsibility for them had caused courts to repudiate the notion of automatic custody for fathers by mid-century. Aware of the threat to the family posed by mass immigration and increasing urbanisation, and influenced by such British reformers as Mary Carpenter, Americans in the antebellum period had provided Sunday Schools, houses of refuge, industrial schools and reformatories for poor and wayward children. But custody rights were extended only as divorce laws were liberalised, and as we have seen, this was a complicated and controversial business.[108]

The nearest British equivalent to Elizabeth Stanton on marital issues was Caroline Norton. Like Stanton she was a well-connected loner, fearlessly determined to make herself heard despite public odium. Both women gloried in the abilities that rescued them from the common lot of women. Yet there the similarities ended. Norton had to endure the notoriety of separation from her husband and a destructive battle over child custody and property rights, whereas Stanton, for all the tensions in her own marriage, relied on her motherly demeanour and known family responsibilities to soften the impact of her intellectual iconoclasm. What is more, Mrs Norton, though she was driven through hard personal experience to question marital law and bring injustice in the private sphere firmly into the public arena, declared herself in favour of the indissolubility of marriage and asserted that she did not believe in the equality of the sexes, thereby adding feminist censure to the other kinds she encountered.[109]

Nevertheless, Norton enjoyed more practical influence on the marriage question than the radical Stanton ever did. Her two widely circulated pamphlets about infant custody helped the sympathetic Whig MP and sergeant-at-law Thomas Telfourd to secure an Act in 1839 granting an estranged wife access to her children under sixteen, and even permitting infants under seven to live with her if she was of good character and the Lord Chancellor consented. (For later developments in child custody rights, see below, pp. 136–8.) Norton's efforts in the 1850s, together with those of Leigh-Smith and her circle, also had an impact on the clauses of the 1857 Matrimonial Causes Bill, which recognised the property rights of certain married women.[110] The 1857 legislation, besides being designed to block a thorough overhaul of such rights, reflected middle-class dissatisfaction with divorce by private Act of Parliament, a procedure which blatantly favoured the rich, and lawyers' dissatisfaction with the conflict between English and Scottish divorce laws. Its passage was assisted by a lessening of the power of Church teachings on people's lives, and a consequent questioning of the part played in matrimonial matters by the ecclesiastical courts. And Stone points out that leading lawyers and politicians had come to see the virtual exclusion of women from parliamentary divorce as antiquated and unjust, without agreeing about the case for equal access.[111]

Neither the 1839 law nor that of 1857, reported very circumspectly by the *English Woman's Journal*, changed the lives of the majority of women. (For later efforts at divorce law reform in both countries, see below, pp. 136, 231, 273.) It remained difficult for them to gain custody of their children in cases of marital breakdown, though the interests of children were given greater consideration: custody was left to the judges' discretion, which was strengthened by legislation in 1859 (extended to Scotland in 1861). The new court for divorce and matrimonial causes established in 1857 cheapened and 'altered the procedure for obtaining divorce', but the Act 'introduced no new principles'. The double standard of morality was upheld by allowing men to divorce on grounds of adultery, women for adultery plus 'the additional aggravation of desertion, cruelty, incest, rape, sodomy, or bestiality'.[112] While the divorce rate increased after 1857 and there were more female petitioners, the cheaper procedure, being concentrated in a single London court, still did not put divorce within the reach of working-class women, and was not intended to do so; consequently they were driven, as Gillis has established, to 'self-divorce' according to well-understood rules.[113] Finally, some women feared that easier divorce would disadvantage ageing females, and the stigma attached to divorce for women remained. It was no wonder that feminists concentrated on reform of married women's property laws at this stage, rather than the liberalisation of divorce. The forces of respectability were stronger than the forces of feminism on both sides of the Atlantic at mid-century.[114]

(ii) *Dress and health reform*

Less controversial than their questioning of contemporary marriage practices was the early feminists' concern with health reform. If the mothers of marriageable daughters, artists ready to pay tribute to feminine beauty, as well as those who supplied the wants of the fashionable, encouraged women to cultivate their appearance, not all commentators were happy with the consequences by the first half of the nineteenth century. Middle-class women and male doctors on each side of the Atlantic recorded their conviction that the female population was less healthy than in the past as a result of the unnerving pressures, debilitating comforts and frivolous entertainments of modern urban life.[115] But neither the growing number of doctors in Britain and America nor the considerable advances they made in obstetrics and gynaecology provided any quick remedy for perceived ills. Although women conscious of living in a progressive age might be disinclined to accept 'pain and early death as uncontrollable aspects of existence',[116] and eager to visit doctors rather than largely untrained midwives when finances allowed, consultations remained an infrequent luxury for the majority. Given the unhealthiness of lying-in wards, and the painfulness and common fatality of early surgery to treat women's ailments, this was perhaps no bad thing. However, the problem of female anxiety remained.[117]

One way forward for women, under these circumstances, was to seek reassurance from the health advice contained in doctors' manuals and popular magazines, or relief in the patent medicines that confidently promised remedies for every known affliction. Another alternative was to embrace homeopathy, with its emphasis on the body's ability to heal itself, and to sample some of the water cures and diets that were meant to purify and invigorate the system.[118] In sickrooms and health resorts women might enjoy peace and female companion-ship, and through stressing their ill-health they had 'a means of getting attention, of obtaining psychological and emotional power even while apparently acknowledging the biological correlatives of their social and political unimportance'.[119]

To pioneering British and American feminists, this female frailty was both unnecessary and unacceptable: the wretched consequence of women's ignorance, restricted lives and new reliance on male doctors and nostrums.[120] Accordingly, in journals, female physiological societies and middle-class drawing-rooms, they preached the moral and practical importance of preventive medicine, purity and self-control: of knowledge about female physiognomy, and the benefits of hygiene, informed childbirth and care, unrestrictive clothes, a simple diet, water, the avoidance of sedatives and stimulants, fresh air and exercise.[121] For the women of both countries, these activities followed on from and strengthened their established concern for sick and poor visiting, through which self-help and 'domestic management' were to be promoted among the unfortunate – a concern which, from the late 1850s onwards in Britain, was being fostered by the NAPSS. With the blessing of the Association, the Workhouse Visiting Society and the Ladies' Sanitary Association were formed; the latter popularised the writings of medical men, distributed literature about dress, child care, health and household economy, produced its own lecturers and influenced those who worked in schools and among the poor.[122]

More boldly, some American health reformers campaigned for the limitation of male sexual demands in deference to women's lesser appetites and to reduce the frequency of childbirth, with its attendant risks.[123] Such arguments might endorse a view of female sexuality entertained by observers as various as utopian socialists and practising physicians. Such restraint might be attainable in the companionate marriages revered in middle-class circles, or could be expected to appeal to those who feared the debilitating effects on men of the loss of sperm more than they worried about falling birth rates. However, women enjoyed most headway when the reforms they urged depended primarily on feminine responses. And as a result, in part, of following their own sensible advice, many early feminists found the energy for extraordinarily varied lives and survived longer than was usual for nineteenth-century middle-class women.[124]

None the less, even women's independent action could stir up controversy, as the general reaction to the 'bloomer' outfit in the 1850s makes plain. Introduced first in the United States by Elizabeth Smith Miller, a staunch women's rights supporter, and publicised by Amelia Bloomer in the *Lily* in 1852, the costume of long full trousers worn under a short dress was adopted delightedly by a handful of feminists, 'farmers' wives ... skaters, gymnasts, tourists' and patients in sanatoriums. But as one of its advocates recalled, with irritation, 'while all agreed that some change [in their fashionable attire] was absolutely necessary for the health of women, the press stoutly ridiculed those who were ready to make the experiment.' The public followed suit. By common consent the bloomer dress was not especially attractive, and neither this nor the immodest showing of ankles could have helped its progress. More damning might have been the association of the new dress with alarming new ideas that played down the differences between the sexes: the two things had gone together before, as when the women of New Harmony donned a trouser costume in the 1820s and that notorious 'Red Harlot of Infidelity', Fanny Wright, took to the public platform with cropped hair and unconventional clothes. Despite the stoical backing of some sympathetic men and the establishment of a National Dress Association (1856–63), which claimed several hundred supporters, even feminists as intrepid as Elizabeth Stanton and Susan Anthony came to feel that an increase in comfort and freedom was being bought at too high a price for the cause. As Leach has shown, the Americans who feared that aristocratic European fashions might undermine their country's republicanism, Puritan heritage and early commitment to nature were too few to stem the tide of economic change, which by the 1850s had given rise to an increasingly influential fashion industry. And as time passed, some feminists were themselves prepared to condone fashionable dress, minus corsets and irrational excess.

In Britain – where organised feminism was just stirring, health reform was therefore less vigorous, and conservative opposition to American imports was strong – the bloomers never caught on, notwithstanding support for sensible dress in the *English Woman's Journal* towards the end of the decade. By then the costume had been abandoned in America. And in both countries, what women wore was also bound up with class to a high degree; for once the mass production of cheap clothes by the fourth decade of the nineteenth century had put fashionable attire within the reach of the clothes-conscious working girl, the latter aspired to be in vogue. Neither she nor the average bourgeois matron aspired to dress reform; for though the female textile or department store worker might have little in common with the leisured-class women who found independent diversion in such stores, they all accepted the alliance between femininity and fashion. Hence the *English Woman's Journal* deplored the fact that 'no sumptuary laws can now be made to restrain the extravagance of the rich, or the unwise imitation of the poor'.[125] Yet if tyrannical custom had triumphed over feminist invention, there were to be many more skirmishes between the two: the effort to rationalise women's dress continued for the rest of the century, producing campaigners on each side of the Atlantic (see below, p. 173).

Feminists in both countries also argued that women would find it easier to discuss their ailments with female doctors and nurses, and would receive more sympathetic treatment from them. It was hoped that women physicians would specialise in the illnesses of women, which either failed to bring prestige for masculine practitioners or brought them into positive disrepute, besides encouraging reckless experimentation in the nineteeth century.[126] From the first, the desire of women to become doctors met with fierce opposition from male educators and physicians, whose experience of female patients gave authority to their pronouncements. The arguments deployed by the opposition were much the same in Britain and the United States and, while reference was made to women's natural unsuitability for medicine, culturally constructed gender concepts plainly shaped the pronouncements of medical men on women's bodies and ailments.

Women, it was maintained, being burdened with menstruation and child-bearing, and equipped with weaker bodies and smaller, lighter and less complex brains than men, were mentally and physically unsuited for the strains and challenges of the medical profession. The training itself was felt to be too taxing for women, who would not only unsex themselves by studying indelicate subjects but cause grave embarrassment to any men instructed alongside them. Those who stayed the course would make themselves unhappy, fail to marry, or marry late and bear few children (the first two generations of women doctors did indeed tend to remain single), thereby leaving the future of the race to the prolific 'lower orders' and 'lesser breeds'. They were also likely to be unemployable, since women patients allegedly preferred to consult men; but if they did manage to succeed, they would offer unwelcome competition to men in a profession which, in the nineteenth century, was raising its standards and anxiously comparing itself with other professions. In Britain, this self-scrutiny resulted in the creation of a Medical Register in 1858, which 'withdrew legal protection from any practitioner not on the Register' and required, for registration, 'the possession of a degree in Medicine awarded by any British university' or a foreign degree utilised in 1858 within an English practice. In America, the licensing of doctors during the first half of the nineteenth century was designed to augment the prestige of practitioners who had been through an apprenticeship or medical college.[127]

Generalisations about the consequences of the professionalisation process for women are dangerous. While it is true that the growing emphasis on scientific knowledge, instruments and qualifications helped to undermine the position of untrained women midwives, neither licensing nor the Medical Register was devised specifically to bar women from the practice of medicine. (Such *was* the intention when, as the result of efforts by English women to qualify abroad as doctors, individuals with foreign medical degrees were excluded from the Register in 1860, and the British Society of Apothecaries ruled in 1865 that 'candidates for their diploma must have worked in a recognized medical school'.) Furthermore, many women continued to use the services of cheap female midwives throughout the century, while many male doctors continued to prosper because of their money, connections and social status rather than any formal qualifications. Feminists, as we saw in Chapter 2, were inclined to glorify the past in order to challenge the notion that the Victorian age represented the apogee of human progress, and so justify their attacks on the status quo. Yet there were few female doctors before the nineteenth century, despite the fact that women were traditionally expected to oversee the health of their families. And as Walsh has stressed, the new professional qualifications gave women, 'already suspect because of their sex', a useful 'corroboration of their expertise to meet a disbelieving public' and a precise target at which to aim, albeit one determined by men. It is in this context that we can understand the caution displayed by some of the first female doctors towards the 'amateurs' of that alternative medicine which their feminist sisters frequently applauded; and appreciate the support Elizabeth Garrett gave, as a sober professional, to the controversial inspection and treatment of prostitutes for venereal disease under the Contagious Diseases Acts of the 1860s.[128] (The significance of these Acts is discussed below, pp. 127–31.)

In medicine, midwifery and nursing alike, British and American women struggled to improve their standard of training, hampered by the opposition noted above but assisted by certain sympathetic medical men and politicians, as well as by customers who were happier to accept their ministrations in these professions than they were in any others (teaching excepted) to which the feminists laid siege. Gains in the medical profession came first in America, reflecting in part the more liberal educational climate in that country. As early as the 1830s the Bostonian Harriot Hunt, blessed with supportive parents and unflinching dedication, had proceeded through private study to private practice. But whereas Hunt's efforts to enter Harvard and obtain a medical degree were thwarted, forcing her to embrace unorthodox medicine and build her career as best she could, Elizabeth Blackwell, whose family emigrated to the United States from England when she was eleven, became the first woman to begin training at a formally established medical institution, entering the obscure Geneva College Medical School in 1847 and graduating at the head of her class in 1849. Her example was followed in the 1850s and 1860s by Hannah Longshore, Mary Frame Thomas, Clemence Lozier, Lucy Sewall and Hannah Tracy Cutler; they, like Hunt, received family backing for their ambitions and worked for and were sustained by the emerging women's movement. Blackwell, married to her career in the same way as Hunt, was at best a cautious feminist, emphasising women's maternal role and their need to choose between career and matrimony even as she urged the case for a fairer relationship between the sexes.[129]

As the first professionally qualified woman doctor, Blackwell attained celebrity status and an especially warm welcome from the leading metropolitan feminists when she visited London on the way to and from postgraduate study in Paris in 1849–50, and during another trip in 1858–9. What she experienced, in part, was that exhilarating sense of being at the centre of things which eluded American reformers, notwithstanding the claims to cultural leadership of Boston and New York and the strength of the British reforming tradition in the provinces. However, if celebrity did not ensure success in either country, Blackwell was convinced that she must settle in America; in 1851 she wrote:

> I believe it is here that women will be first recognised as the equal half of humanity. . . . In England, where the idea can be intellectually comprehended, there is a deep-rooted antagonism to its practical admission which it may take generations to modify. [Feminism has not] . . . yet found in England a single earnest advocate; and, as far as I can judge, I should say that the time for woman to be acknowledged as the free fellow-worker and necessary complement of man is still in the invisible future. In America, this subject has already been recognised as one whose practical

elucidation cannot be much longer delayed; and many of the best thinkers in the country are prepared to give it their earnest and attention and sympathy.

Such convictions must have been comforting to Blackwell as she endured isolation, street abuse and anonymous letters before she could launch a dispensary (later an infirmary) for women and children in New York City, aided by her sister Emily and a redoubtable German–American, Marie Zakrzewska.[130] Sharing with her Prussian mentor a romantic belief that 'only in a republic can it be proved that science has no sex', Zakrzewska, like many immigrants to America, discovered the limits of republicanism too late. Nevertheless, she managed to establish the New England Hospital for Women and Children; to extend a growing range of services to its patrons; to provide within it opportunities and training for women physicians; and to secure for her institution the support of the feminist movement.[131]

Medical pioneering proved still more difficult in Britain, despite the help and inspiration British women received from their American sisters, and the Victorian feminists' conviction that women were capable of becoming doctors and would find the profession mentally, physically and socially satisfactory. As we have seen (pp. 52–5 above), Britain lagged behind the United States in educational provision, and between 1860 and 1876 – when a parliamentary Bill was secured by the Recorder of London, Russell Gurney, allowing universities in the United Kingdom and Ireland to grant women degrees – it was impossible for women to obtain an English MD. Until Dublin and London agreed to admit women to medical degrees in 1877–8 they endured a period of almost total frustration, with only Elizabeth Garrett (Anderson) qualifying for the Medical Register via the Society of Apothecaries, and managing to obtain her MD in France after the University of Paris accepted women for medical degrees in 1868. The less diplomatic Sophia Jex-Blake, though she was backed by a group of fellow female students, indefatigable in her canvassing, and furnished with money as well as brains, could convert neither the male medical students nor the establishment of Edinburgh University to the women's cause. She was obliged to qualify in Berne before Dublin opened its doors, whereupon she and three other women from Edinburgh were successfully examined in Ireland. Both Garrett and Jex-Blake gained national prominence through their labours, and in time also enjoyed interesting careers: the latter as founder of the London School of Medicine for Women and the driving force behind a less successful school in Edinburgh; the former as the originator of St Mary's Dispensary for Women (subsequently the New Hospital for Women and Children), and then as the Dean of the London School. Garrett was also an active suffragist in the 1860s, and while subsequently – being 'responsible for the medical women's movement' – she 'had to be very cautious about working for the suffrage', she had resumed her activities by 1908.[132]

There were mixed results from so much effort. British and American women had shown that they wanted training for work in the health field, but the crusade to become doctors did not smooth their path in midwifery or nursing. Midwives in each country faced opposition to their attempts to obtain instruction and status from doctors unwilling to encourage or upgrade competition. When improvements came in Britain, they followed from the creation of a Ladies' Medical College on the initiative of the Female Medical Society. Women's suitability for the nursing profession could not be denied, since both feminists and anti-feminists were agreed that 'If anything in the whole world is women's work, it is the nursing of the sick.' Yet whereas British and American doctors were concerned to keep nurses properly subordinate and cheap, women argued the need for a powerful base in the health field, and for proper training in nursing schools to 'professionalize what had previously been a part of untrained domestic service'. They were, however, undermined by the low value attached in both countries to caring, despite its frequent sentimentalisation, and by the class and race differences between nurses themselves, once their numbers grew.[133]

In Britain the well-born Florence Nightingale, seeking emancipation from boredom and family pressures, trained as a nurse in Germany and used her excellent contacts to get permission to take a nursing team to the Crimean War (1854–6), where she demonstrated immense organisational skills in the face of army and medical suspicion. After two years Nightingale returned to England a heroine, respected enough to advise politicians on a whole range of health matters and, in 1861, to establish a training school for nurses, attached to St Thomas' Hospital, from the money collected in honour of her Crimean work. It proved difficult, however, to attract and retain a large number of high-calibre recruits for the Nightingale school, and determining the academic component of the training was a problem. The other training schools that followed encountered similar difficulties, and varied greatly in quality. One of the many achievements of Florence Nightingale was to make nursing deserving of adequate pay and a respectable calling for all classes of women, to the discomfort of male doctors accustomed to directing nurses drawn from the lower orders. (As late as 1862, Emily Davies noted that nursing could not be 'looked upon as a profession for a lady. The salary of a hospital nurse is less than the wages of a butler or a groom', and a nurse's position was 'in every way . . . allied to that of an upper servant'.) None the less, Nightingale herself opposed the registration of trained nurses in the 1880s. It was not achieved until 1919, and in 1906 anxiety was still being expressed that registration 'would stereotype existing evils'. Nightingale certainly feared that a routine listing of professionals might eliminate the careful screening of individual nurses – not least for those moral qualities she thought they should possess. Whereas Barbara Bodichon regarded nursing as a welcome female occupation, Nightingale saw it as 'an Art. And till it is considered as such,' she wrote, 'little or no progress will be made in it.'[134]

American women likewise found the opportunity to improve the status of nursing during a national crisis. The Civil War of 1861–5 prompted them to undertake traditional supplies provision for the troops, elevating an old service to a new sophistication in the North through the approximately 7,000 societies of the Sanitary Commission, which had raised and disbursed $50,000,000 by the end of the conflict. Elizabeth Blackwell, who was personally familiar with Nightingale's exploits, was prominent in the establishment of the Commission. Women were also inspired, in both North and South, to volunteer as nurses on the front line and in established hospitals. The sixty-year-old Dorothea Dix, who had already made her name in the reform of prisons and asylums, was appointed to manage the nursing service in northern military hospitals (an operation epitomising the shift from individualistic to highly organised, 'masculinised' philanthropy which was a feature of the war, and with which members of her generation might feel distinctly uncomfortable). Many obscure women, among them Clara Barton, similarly welcomed the excitement, exertion and responsibility which emergency nursing afforded, frequently encouraged by the example of Florence Nightingale and encountering the kind of male opposition she had faced.[135] It was still thought remarkable that formerly idle women could efficiently undertake testing work, and desirable that they should support rather than lead. In the judgement of the Reverend Henry Bellows, president of the American Association for the Relief of the Misery of Battle Fields, 'Detailed men are the appropriate nurses in military hospitals. Women are rarely in place at the front, or even at the base of the armies.' In his experience, only a handful out of the few hundred women involved in nursing were very useful, although he did acknowledge that the war had 'proved not only the admirable capacity for business which usually slumbers in women, but the steadiness of principle, to which their admirable impulses may be trained, and their capacity for comprehending and cooperating in the largest and most impersonal plans'.[136]

Small wonder that once the fighting was over, the struggle to organise and upgrade American nursing was a long one.[137] Clara Barton, like Florence Nightingale, was intermittently affected by bad health after her initial taste of a thoroughly useful and demanding life, and she too steered clear of the alarming women's suffrage movement in order to concentrate on her own work and lobby for it without alienating men of power. Similarly, neither woman allowed herself to be seriously incapacitated by the recurring bouts of illness which afflicted a number of British and American feminists as they attempted to find permanently satisfying roles to play. Nightingale took to bed or sofa to find time for her writing; while Barton, whose papers abound in doctors' files and who apparently suffered from 'a scrofulous diathesis', constipation, piles, a dyspeptic stomach and bladder irritation, palpitations, neuralgia, and a 'lack of *vital magnetism*' requiring the treatment of a blood invigorator, founded the Red Cross and lived until 1912, resigned to suffering but rejecting 'dolorous reports of me'. 'I have', she declared, 'never lost my activity.'[138]

By the second half of the nineteenth century, women in Britain and America had gone backwards in midwifery; feminised nursing but without improving their academic status or position *vis-à-vis* doctors; and secured only a token presence in the medical profession – even in the United States where, in 1900, the

Table 3.1 Women doctors in the USA and Britain, 1850–1911

	USA			England and Wales	
Date	Number of women doctors	% of total	Date	Number of women doctors	% of total
1850	–	–			
1860	200*	0.4			
1870	544	0.8			
1880	2,432	2.8	1881	25	0.17
1900	7,387	5.6			
1910	9,015	6.0	1911	495	1.98

* Estimated

Sources: Walsh, *Doctors Wanted*, p. 186; Harrison, 'Women's health and the women's movement', p. 51.

number of female physicians 'was double that in France, England and Germany combined'. Coeducational establishments in which women were a discouraged minority did not help women to advance in medicine in either country. Of most assistance were their own separate establishments, yet whereas these provided a supportive environment and valuable opportunities for women, they suffered from inferior resources and, sometimes, personnel. Despite enjoying the backing of feminists, female doctors as a whole had an ambivalent relationship with the women's movement. Their small numbers made it impossible for them to challenge male dominance of gynaecology and obstetrics, while as Harrison has shown, the improvement in women's health from the 1840s cannot be attributed in any major way to the increased involvement of women in health care.[139] However, feminists' efforts to help themselves in this area led them on to other campaigns concerned with sexuality and liberty (see below, pp. 127–38, 225–34, 258, 275), and their first achievements were at least as impressive as those attained in the broad field of employment.

(iii) *Self-help in work and education*

In the area of economic feminism, British women were – for once in these early years – ahead of their American sisters. On both sides of the Atlantic, the first feminists stressed the need to open up new employment opportunities for women, and to improve educational facilities to make this possible. But in Britain, by mid-century, there was a particular urgency to act because it was clear that a large number of women no longer depended on men for their support, even if that was their wish. In a widely circulated article in the *Edinburgh Review* in 1859, Harriet Martineau pointed out that more than two million out of six million British women over the age of twenty were 'independent and self-supporting like men', and that there were 'over half a million more women than men in Britain'.[140] Although a considerable number of independent and self-supporting women might eventually marry and leave this paid workforce, and such women were not necessarily working away from home, the two million made an arresting statistic. What is more, while middle-class women constituted only approximately 7 per cent of all working or financially independent women in 1851, the imbalance between the sexes was most marked in the middle class: the class whose male members were most opposed to respectable women working for money, and whose own late marriages, to support dependent wives as well as a high standard of living, contributed directly to the 'surplus' women problem. It was also, of course, the class from which most feminists were drawn.[141]

As Helsinger, Sheets and Veeder have observed, Victorians had been uneasily debating the problems of working women since the depressed and restless 1840s, and had focused on 'the needlewoman, the governess and the factory girl' as representative figures: equally the victims of the new industrial order. On behalf of these female victims, male reformers were willing to act, in the same way as they were, with caution, prepared to enlarge married women's property, child custody and divorce rights. Accordingly, the pressure for the ten-hour day, which had succeeded by 1847, was in part designed to protect vulnerable women and children, and sprang from a strong conviction that their proper place was in the home, not competing with men in the paid job market. The fact that most married women were and remained working at home (paid and unpaid) throughout the nineteenth century was beside the point. So, too, was the reluctance of most feminists who claimed the right to work (and they included Martineau, Jameson, Boucherett, Parkes and Leigh-Smith, speakers at NAPSS meetings and contributors to the *English Woman's Journal*) to abandon the notion of work for which each sex was specifically suited – which, in the case of women, included social work, whether remunerated or not. Just as the vote was seen by alarmists as the wedge that would prise open the door to political office for women, so growing numbers of women in the paid workforce were seen as a vanguard that immediately depressed men's wages, and could in time undermine the family and launch a new social order in which such labour was seen as 'a psychological necessity' for both sexes. Whereas middle-class men might accept that some working-class women were driven to waged work from necessity, they shrank from the assertion that 'frivolity is not harmless' and that respectable women should be helped 'to exchange a condition of labour without profit, and leisure without ease, for a life of wholesome activity, and the repose that comes with fruitful toil'.[142]

The feminists – as a result of public anxiety about married women working and because this group had been the focus of their property law campaign – may have deliberately concentrated their economic effort on single women, although Leigh-Smith Bodichon, for instance, urged the claims of the married even as she stressed that to 'be a noble woman is better than being mother to a noble man'.[143] But for all their concern about the single 'distressed gentlewoman',[144] feminists did not abandon their stated concern for middle-class and working-class women alike, though it was by no means obvious how they could help both;

or how middle-class activists, in encouraging female co-operation, could become better acquainted with their working-class sisters and shake off the assumption that such women needed their 'superintending activity'. Clearly, without better secondary and higher education – which was not to be achieved swiftly – any long-term improvement in middle-class female prospects was unlikely. In particular, activists could not hope to transform the overcrowded governessing and teaching profession, where the well-qualified were threatening the merely genteel, and the classes competed uncomfortably.[145] None the less, inquiries from desperate women had convinced feminists of the need for action in the short term to open up new lines of work, and those whom they primarily assisted were aspiring women from the working class and lower middle class.[146]

The SPEW was formed to promote the training and placement of women in 'industrial pursuits': manual occupations from which, as Hammerton notes, 'many Victorian young ladies would shrink'. The Society kept a register of women seeking employment, and of agencies that might help them; established branches in Dublin, Edinburgh, Gateshead, Nottingham and other cities; and, while it welcomed male members, was dominated by its female supporters. The main openings were found in nursing, shopwork, hairdressing, photography, house decoration, proofreading, telegraphy, printing, lithography and the administration of charitable bodies. Classes were provided (for nearly forty years) in bookkeeping and other skills useful for aspirants to shop and clerical work; the SPEW fostered an all-female law-copying office; and Emily Faithfull established the Victoria Press. With calculation and optimism, it was named for 'the Sovereign to whose influence English women owe so large a debt of gratitude, and in the hope also that the name would prove a happy augury of victory'; while Queen Victoria's reactionary views on gender questions were in sharp contrast to her liberal views on race, the sovereign's power and public role provided Victorian feminists with valuable ammunition. By 1860 the Press was employing nineteen female compositors as apprentices, and publishing Faithfull's journals (the *Alexandra Magazine* and the *Victoria Magazine*), together with many additional feminist periodicals and pamphlets.[147]

The Victorian press won considerable notice, not only for its unusual emphases and success but also because it continued to hire men for tasks requiring real strength.[148] In a country where protective legislation for women had already been established, this is understandable. Attitudes about what were appropriate jobs for men and women proved hard to change among working women, employers and the male labour force, as well as among feminists themselves. The positions secured by the SPEW might have been dismayingly ungenteel in the eyes of ladies, but they were not overtly unfeminine in the way that most heavy manual work would have been. Nor were they numerous: with an income of a few hundred pounds a year, the Society could directly help only a few hundred women.[149]

Recognising the financial and other difficulties they faced, SPEW members and feminist publications acted prudently; the *English Woman's Journal* rejoiced that it did not have to offer 'the complete *rationale* of every question' to which it opened its columns.[150] Women workers and would-be workers were expected to help themselves – Boucherett had been directly influenced by Samuel Smiles, whose bestselling *Self-Help* appeared in 1859.[151] They were to look after their health, learn to endure small discomforts, avoid grumbling, cultivate good manners, sound principles and public-spiritedness, suppress all 'desires for worldly glory' and 'inordinate *individual* enrichment', and rest content 'with moderate success'. In urging her sex's duty to work, a correspondent of the *Journal* could conclude: 'I have in these few lines carefully avoided the subject of woman's rights; our duties are more interesting to us at present.'[152] And the feminists' frequently expressed concern about the shortage of good servants, the need to train them and the need to confine them to the working class, brought them very close to anti-feminists like the liberal manufacturer and writer W.R. Greg.[153] Such pronouncements could only serve to limit the emancipating effect of the activists' practical assistance for working women, and to win acceptance for them in employment on a disadvantageous basis. Moreover, as Davidoff has suggested, the desire of working women to advance through domestic service may have helped to make them politically conservative. While there was little alternative to the line followed, the fact is that the feminists raised important questions which they could not resolve. An expanding economy's need for cheap labour and its creation of new jobs ultimately provided more employment chances for women than the first feminists – though by no means on better terms.[154]

The results of attempts to resolve the 'surplus' of women by sponsoring emigration to the colonies were equally disappointing, notwithstanding the admirable enterprise of those involved. Emigration was seen by a number of the Langham Place circle as offering an immediate answer to the problems of distressed gentlewomen who were not reached by the SPEW. Unfortunately for the feminists, there were fewer colonial openings for middle-class women than for domestic servants, and a number of male backers of emigration plainly favoured it as a means of improving female marriage rather than job prospects, or of reducing the number of discontented women at home. The colonisation of women – like the colonisation of American blacks – thus turned out to be a controversial and difficult matter, even after the establishment in 1862 of the Female Middle-Class Emigration Society. Under the direction of its first honorary secretary, Maria Rye, women from the middle class and working class were helped to emigrate, although Rye felt that only the highly motivated should make the journey: those 'Who dislike work, or who are not very steady in their principles' were 'a thousand-fold better off at home'. But after 1865 Rye's successor, Jane Lewin, concentrated on the middle class, and especially upon placing governesses abroad. As a result – given the nature of colonial labour needs – only a few hundred women were assisted, and Hammerton concludes that feminism 'failed to capitalise on the potential of female emigration'.[155]

In the United States, as we argued above, feminists at their antebellum conventions stressed the right of women to paid work. They, like their British counterparts, feared that desperate women might fall back on prostitution to earn a living.[156] In New England and the mid-Atlantic states, as in Britain, there was a 'surplus' of single women, and the same male outmigration and economic change to dismay the middle-class women who, while they constituted only a fraction of the paid labour force, dominated the feminist ranks.[157] In America, too, when middle-class reformers concerned themselves with the problems of working women, they tended to present them as victims outside their true place (the home); to accept that men and women were suited to different jobs; and to see domestic service or the migration of women (westward) as one solution to their difficulties. They were, however, more inclined than British feminists to avoid a rigorous analysis of class in preference for a broad emphasis on the unifying bonds of womanhood.[158] Immigrants from the Old World, accustomed to 'family-based labour', were in the United States an additional element which proved unresponsive to demands for women's rights in the economic arena and contributed to the peculiar strength of the American domestic ideology.[159] Government power was less in the United States, while aversion to class legislation was greater. Hence no protective laws specifically designed to help women were produced during the 1840s (although both sexes benefited from shorter hours acts). Furthermore, since the 'surplus' of American women was a phenomenon only in part of the country, it produced no national debate, and the lack of any viable national feminist organisation would have made it hard to sustain a body comparable to the SPEW, had one been launched. It was not. The committee on industrial avocations set up by the Central Committee was not its equivalent, and the Civil War presented women with more job opportunities than the first American feminists had been able to provide.[160]

The War also expanded school-teaching opportunities for American women: among the freedmen of the South as well as in the immigrant-swollen cities and the expanding West. For British women, the employment debate rather than a national crisis led to a renewed interest in educational issues. An array of commentators debated the purpose of women's education, fearing that it might break down class barriers, change men's instruction and endanger the family. They pondered, too, the likelihood of highly educated women finding appropriate jobs or even completing their courses when marriage beckoned.[161] The most important developments of the 1860s were the drive to obtain medical training (already noted); the forging of links between girls' schools and the universities; the inclusion of 'the education of girls and the means of improving it' in the brief of the government's Taunton Commission, established in 1864 to investigate boys' secondary schools;[162] and the beginning of a sustained campaign for college education for women.

Having cut her teeth as an educational reformer in 1862, with Leigh-Smith Bodichon, in a fruitless effort to persuade London University to admit women to its degrees, Emily Davies had learned how to mobilise religious and family friends, lobby influential people, and not give up. The following year she formed a committee to obtain entry for girls to the local examinations started in 1857 and 1858 by Oxford and Cambridge to test secondary-school leavers. The middle-class schools involved were thereby connected to the leading universities, and standards were established for which pupils and teachers alike might aim. After a period of 'incessant and un-remitting talking and pushing',[163] by October 1863 Cambridge had agreed to test girls as an experiment. A scramble then ensued to secure a respectable tally of examinees by the next examinations in December. Eighty-three candidates, over half of whom were from Queen's College and North London Collegiate, were tested, and performed with overall credit, though markedly well in English and badly in arithmetic. Girls' ability to take competitive examinations had been confirmed, despite contemporary allegations about their intellectual limitations and physical frailty,[164] and testing on a permanent basis was agreed to by Cambridge in 1865 and Oxford in 1870. However, a divisive note was introduced at a special meeting of the NAPSS, held to publicise the breakthrough, when it was proposed that in future the arithmetic tests for girls should be made less exacting. Davies rejected such an argument at once, but the meeting had produced one of those clashes – which were an enduring feature of the women's movement – between feminists who believed that differences between men and women were considerable, and should be accepted, and activists who made the achievement of equality between the sexes their goal.[165]

Davies and Bodichon again used their persuasive skills and valuable contacts to broaden the scope of the Taunton Commission, before which they and a number of other women testified. The Commission's report (1868) helped the feminists, but they were not alone in working to improve girls' secondary education. Also concerned were 'reform-minded women teachers, male academics, and some parents', who were aware that the erratic girls' schooling highlighted by the investigation was inappropriate in 'an urban industrial culture' which valued systematic organisation, academic achievement and advancement on merit.[166] The commissioners deplored the poor quality of teaching in girls' schools, blessed the local examinations and higher education for women, and concluded that the learning abilities of the sexes were essentially the same. And even while they had been deliberating, Davies had formed the London Association of Schoolmistresses (1866), which brought together teachers anxious to raise standards and grateful to discuss problems with fellow professionals. When that step seemed inadequate, she formed a committee to raise £30,000 for the establishment of a women's college.[167]

In addition to the usual strains involved in fund-raising from already well-worked public figures, Davies once more had to struggle with an opposing element in the women's movement, epitomised by Anne J. Clough and Josephine Butler, the leaders of the North of England Council for Promoting the Higher Education of Women, which was based in Liverpool between 1867 and 1875. As a way of moving cautiously towards female participation in university life by focusing on the needs of schools and their staff, the Council co-ordinated the provision of lectures to instruct teachers on both school subjects and teaching methods, and in 1869 it was happy to accept lecture courses from Cambridge for women preparing for the local examinations. Whereas Clough was ready to co-operate with such male curriculum reformers at Cambridge as Dr Henry Sidgwick, who believed that women should not pursue the outmoded and taxing courses followed by men, Davies avoided such alliances, insisting that doubts about female abilities would never be dispelled until women showed that they could study the same subjects as men, and graduate in the same period. And she predictably disliked the separate local examinations for women, pitched at a level below honours degree standard, offered by London from 1868 and Cambridge from 1869. This division led in time to the creation by Davies and her allies of Hitchin College in 1869 (it subsequently moved to Girton, near Cambridge, opening there in 1873); and by Clough's group of Newnham College, at Cambridge, in 1871.[168]

The working out of the campaign for better education for women will be considered in the next chapter. In the formative years of British feminism it was not apparent what the outcome would be, although the activists had been assisted as well as constrained by the complexity of contemporary prejudices. If feminists were not united about either tactics or the purpose of education, then neither were their opponents.[169] Furthermore, the clashing views of Davies and Clough galvanised each into action as well as tart exchanges, while representatives from a varied group of reformers could be recruited to the different feminist factions. Even the most radical women, such as Davies, felt obliged to campaign with circumspection: during the work for Girton she deliberately kept Leigh-Smith Bodichon's support in the background, lest her name alarm prospective supporters, and she avoided 'masculine looking' women as a liability to the cause.[170] The price of educational progress was behavioural conformity,[171] as it had been for the founders of American academies for girls many years before: but the gains were greater. It was not the least of the achievements of this period that – in addition to the established functional arguments for education – considerable support was generated for the proposition that education was a duty for individuals of both sexes, just as some observers believed work had become.[172] In the words of the *English Woman's Journal*:

> The first duty of women is to themselves, and that duty is to fulfil the will of God, by developing their nature to its highest, and then progressing in the scale of spiritual intelligences; this only is the result which shall survive alike the sorrows of this world or its joy.[173]

(iv) *The suffrage fight begins*

Although the women's movement assumed an organised form in America earlier than it did in Britain, suffragism took off at the same time in both countries and evolved in a similar fashion for several years. During the Civil War, despite differences about the wisdom of this course, American women undertook war work and formed a Loyal League (1863–4) which collected petitions against slavery and thereby helped to secure, in 1865, the passage of the Thirteenth Amendment emancipating the slaves. Like other reformers at the time, and during twentieth-century wars, the feminists hoped to be rewarded for subordinating their own concerns to the national interest. They were to be disappointed. Continued subordination was expected once the war was over, as Republican politicians worked to secure black voting rights by first the Fourteenth (1868) and then the Fifteenth (1870) Amendments.

The agitation against slavery had predated the women's rights campaign; so, too, had the demands of the free blacks for their enfranchisement. Blacks had fought for their freedom in a war which was centrally concerned with the future of slavery. Moreover, the minority Republican Party might hope to gain from loyal black voters, and needed to take account of an increasingly politicised and optimistic abolitionist leadership. Women's work for black emancipation was appreciated by abolitionists and Republicans alike, but neither group could accept that an embryonic, largely white and bourgeois women's movement had established claims for parity of treatment with the freedmen. Enfranchised women would constitute a larger and possibly less predictable political voting bloc than blacks; and given that the radicalism of the Republican coalition was limited, the safest course was to declare the postwar situation to be 'the Negro's hour'.[174]

To some American feminists, the situation looked very different. Having increasingly come to realise the value of a political voice as they struggled to change the married women's property laws, and having supported the American Equal Rights Association founded at the end of the war jointly to further black and female interests, radical women were appalled when abolitionists of both races endorsed the Fourteenth Amendment. They recoiled because the Amendment introduced the word 'male' into the Constitution for the first time, equating citizenship and voting rights (formerly considered a state matter), defining each in terms of masculinity, and presenting feminists with the prospect of having to seek a constitutional amendment to secure their enfranchisement. A petition drive mounted by Stanton and Anthony to prevent 'The states from disenfranchising any of their citizens on the grounds of sex' produced a fraction of the signatures women had secured for the Thirteenth Amendment, and failed to secure Republican backing. Similarly disconcerting were the array of masculine arguments mustered against women's suffrage when it was debated for the first time in the Senate in 1866, during discussion of a Bill to extend the vote to blacks in the District of Columbia. The opposition – as it had done since the 1840s and would continue to do until the twentieth century – focused on feminine weakness and, paradoxically, on the threat enfranchised women would pose to the family, the division of labour, and harmonious relations between the sexes. Most women, it was suggested, were uninterested in the vote and would be unwise to sacrifice the influence and respect they enjoyed within the domestic sphere.[175]

In 1867, there were two further disappointments. Appearances by Mrs Stanton before the New York Judiciary Committee and a convention to revise the state constitution, backed up by petitions collected throughout the state, failed to win acceptance for women's suffrage and alienated the influential editor of the *New York Tribune*, Horace Greeley. And a referendum prompted by the Kansas legislature on whether to add 'negro' and take 'male' out of the state's voting requirements resulted in a defeat for both propositions, although black suffrage had been favoured by Republicans, reformers and some eastern newspapers, while a broad spectrum of feminists had canvassed the state for female enfranchisement. Turning in desperation to the unconverted but mischievously opportunistic Democrats for support, Stanton and Anthony accepted help in Kansas from a notable railroad promoter with presidential aspirations, George Train: rich, radical and a racist. His money enabled them to launch (but not secure the future of) the *Revolution* (1868–70), the most advanced and wide-ranging feminist publication of its day.[176]

There were, however, less happy consequences of this alliance. Train's racial prejudice alienated feminist-abolitionists and encouraged Stanton's existing elitism: her pronouncements on an educated franchise which would recognise the superiority of women and the unfitness, as voters, of ignorant immigrants and emancipated 'Sambos' were soon shocking her fellow-campaigners. The divorce question having first divided moderate and radical feminists, the aftermath of slavery deepened the rift between them. Stanton and Anthony further exasperated abolitionists by fighting to extend the provisions of the Fifteenth Amendment to women as well as blacks. After acrimonious exchanges during the 1868–9 annual meetings of the American Equal Rights Association, and after failing to win endorsement for women's suffrage from either of the national political party conventions, Stanton was convinced of the need for an independent feminist organisation to push for the suffrage and other vital goals. By May 1869 she and her friends had launched the National Woman Suffrage Association (NWSA) in New York. By November of that year her opponents, centred in Boston and led by Lucy Stone, had countered with an alternative organisation, the American Woman Suffrage Association (AWSA); and from January 1870 they were publishing, in the *Woman's Journal*, a well-financed, conservative and enduring answer to the *Revolution*.[177] Each national society was able to draw on the numerous state suffrage societies which had come into being as women were radicalised by their Civil War experiences and reached out to by the American Equal Rights Association, and it is significant that the women involved were invariably white. In a struggle between white women reformers and black male abolitionists, black women experienced divided loyalties and few opportunities for feminist advancement.[178]

In Britain also, from the mid–1860s onwards, female suffrage came swiftly to the fore during a period of political change, and was confronted by obdurate political realities. There, too, women were affected by a serious debate about the concept of citizenship, and became active after experiencing the frustrations attendant on votelessness in the married women's property campaign. Occasional demands for their enfranchisement from the 1820s had received little notice, notwithstanding the belief expressed in the *Westminster Review* in 1851 by Harriet Taylor, wife of John Stuart Mill, that women's civil rights had an 'irresistible appeal' for 'Radicals and Chartists in the British islands'.[179] But two developments during the 1860s gave particular encouragement: Mill's election as an MP, despite receiving feminist support and urging the extension of the franchise to women in his election address; and consideration by Parliament of a new Reform Bill, designed to enfranchise urban ratepayers. (The 1832 Reform Act gave the vote to the middle classes; the 1867 Act to the urban working classes, in the main; the 1884 Act to the agricultural labourers; the 1918 Act to adult males and women over thirty who – or whose husbands – were local government electors.)

The suffrage issue was debated in London by the Kensington Society – a group with origins in the drive to open local examinations to women – and Leigh-Smith Bodichon formed a committee there to raise a petition for the vote. It was unsuccessfully presented in the Commons by Mill in 1866. The petition's 1,499 signatories included prominent women of diverse opinions, and Bodichon was sufficiently heartened by its reception to publish a careful case for enfranchising women freeholders and householders, in which she maintained that the measure transcended party, interfered with no special interests, would assist taxed but unprotected spinsters and widows, and would encourage all women to take national affairs seriously. Some women, she contended, were clearly fit to vote, and 'any class which is not represented is likely to be neglected'. Bodichon's arguments were summarised in a 1866 paper to the NAPSS in Manchester, where they inspired a highly educated local single woman, Lydia Becker, to take up the suffrage cause, for which she would labour relentlessly until her death in 1890.[180]

In 1866–7 a new committee organised three new suffrage petitions. These were presented to Parliament in the spring of 1867, and on 20 May 1867 Mill moved an amendment to the Representation of the People Bill 'to leave out the word "men" in order to insert the word "person" instead'. A year after the first Senate discussion on the subject of female suffrage, it was debated in Parliament. The amendment, which would have enfranchised women on the same terms as men, was defeated by 196 votes to 73; but it necessitated a serious response and, as in the United States, members concentrated on the threat women's suffrage posed to domestic relations. By 1867 a London society for women's suffrage had grown out of Bodichon's petition committees (though it was not under her control), and suffrage associations had been formed in Manchester and Edinburgh. In 1868, groups were established in Birmingham and Bristol. During that year, while retaining their independence of action, they became the National Society for Women's Suffrage, and from 1870 a *Women's Suffrage Journal*, edited by Becker, detailed their aims and activities.[181]

Throughout these struggles, British and American women generally employed techniques they had already tested: petitions, meetings, speeches, pamphlets, and the lobbying of sympathetic politicians. They none the less added a bold new form of direct action, seeking as citizens to test their political rights under existing law. In the United States, women tried to register and vote from 1869 until such efforts were deemed invalid by the Supreme Court in 1874; a similar attempt was made in Britain in 1868, only to be defeated by decisions of the Court of Common Pleas and the Scottish courts.[182] Women on both sides of the Atlantic were dismayed at the insertion of the word 'male' into legislation covering political rights – during the 1830s and 1860s in Britain, during the 1860s in the United States. Once this had happened – and disregarding various predictions about the early attainment of the vote – some suffragists in both countries were unhappily aware how long their struggle would last.[183] This being the case, it was fortunate that in both countries the cause was able to attract women of all types from within the middle class, and secure enough backing to keep them going from the contemporary parties of reform: the Liberals in Britain, the Republicans in the United States.[184]

Even so, there were considerable differences between British and American suffragism. British women, though determined to steer clear of party politics, were much less able to do so than radical American activists, who distanced themselves from the Republicans after the conflict about black suffrage. (Members of the American Woman Suffrage Association continued to court Republican support.)[185] The British women did not divide over tactics during the 1860s (for later splits, see below, pp. 131, 145–6), whereas the American feminists' divisions over politics, personalities, the wisdom of campaigning on a broad front, and freedmen's rights harmed their campaign in the eyes of the public. That they gained organisations independent of anti-slavery for the first time was a benefit dearly bought, and feminists recognised this privately. As Martha Wright put it: 'In *union* there is strength', and 'in a cause so momentous, petty or personal differences should have no place'. The existence of two national associations made it clear 'to the world that "those Christians" do *not* "love one another"'; yet she herself was unable to accept the criticisms made of the National or bless the reasoning of the American Association, and concluded firmly that 'no attempt to narrow our platform can possibly succeed'.[186]

The radical American feminists were also distinguished from the British suffragists by a bold – albeit brief – attempt to strike a political alliance between suffragism and labour reform, and to mobilise working-class women behind the suffrage. This effort involved Anthony in forming a Working Women's Association, primarily of newspaper typesetters, and putting the case for the vote at the 1868 National Labor Union congress. While both Stanton and Anthony were genuinely and lastingly concerned, in speeches and writing, with the problems of working-class women, the attempt to organise feminism across class lines was premature. The women involved agreed about the injustice of the prevailing sexual division of labour but disagreed about the importance of the suffrage; while male unionists believed that women's place was in the home, and were suspicious of demands for the suffrage 'because of its implications for real feminist power'. And whereas the female typesetters had craft skills which they could make men in the printing industry take account of for a brief period, with the aid of feminist pressure, most women wage earners were not so fortunately placed.[187]

Although the suffrage movements in Britain and America both debated the proper role of men in their organisations and contained some women who contemplated with pleasure the entirely independent management of their own affairs, this element was stronger in the United States, where hostility to male membership was a notable feature of the National Woman Suffrage Association. Since British women had not experienced the degree of independence in earlier reform movements (notably anti-slavery and temperance) that their American sisters had enjoyed, the contrast is hardly surprising. But British activists were far-sighted in recognising the degree to which success depended on the sexes working together, and realising that women-only associations might suit men very well.[188] Conversely, if American suffragists argued over the desirability of an educated or partial suffrage for women, they were never as occupied by this issue as the British. To many Victorian feminists, conscious that not all the men of their country were enfranchised, partial suffrage seemed the only practical proposition, albeit one which stood to benefit property-holders and spinsters at the expense of married women affected by coverture.[189]

The most striking development in British and American suffragism during the 1860s, however, was the deference American activists were, for the first time, prepared to pay to their British counterparts. The British press might continue to warn of the disagreeable antics of American feminists,[190] but the *Revolution* found it useful to publish the works of Mary Wollstonecraft and Frances Wright; Stanton and Anthony to use 'ten thousand copies of John Stuart Mill's speech to Parliament advocating woman suffrage' during the New York campaign; and suffrage workers in Kansas to circulate 'reprints of Harriet Taylor's *Westminster Review* article of 1851, and copies of Mill's speeches on women's suffrage'.[191]

The intellectual leadership of international feminism was also recovered by the British following the publication of Mill's *The Subjection of Women* in 1869. Drafted in 1861 but published when he thought it could do most good, Mill's study avoided controversial issues like divorce and may be further criticised for dwelling too long on female mental capacities, accepting the existing division of labour in the family and ignoring the concerns of working-class women. By no means the sort of enthusiast for women's rights that British conservatives instinctively disliked and opponents ridiculed him for being,[192] Mill had nevertheless been influenced by his more radical wife and daughter. With feeling still unsurpassed, he presented female subordination as 'one of the chief hindrances to human improvement' in a world no longer ruled by physical force. The denial to women of educational, economic, political and legal opportunities and rights robbed them, he maintained, of the power of individual self-development, rendered mutuality and harmony in marriage unlikely, corrupted men and impoverished society as a whole. Mill did not enjoy totally harmonious relations with the leading British activists, but he gave feminists on each side of the Atlantic a formidable answer to emerging anti-feminism: the best demolition a reformer could desire of the proposition that what was customary must equally be right.[193]

By the end of the 1860s, the main ideas and agenda of the nineteenth-century women's movement had been discussed and pursued in Britain and the United States. Not surprisingly, in these formative years feminists had proved better at evolving an argument,[194] producing able leaders and seeing the need for supporters than they had at mobilising their constituency and achieving their programme. They had made considerable progress in the area of education and married women's property rights, where male backing had been forthcoming; less headway in the economic and political arenas, where men most feared competition. More than enough had been accomplished to demolish the contemporary charge that feminists were chiefly interested in spouting about their imaginary wrongs. But the very skills they had shown in dissecting the injustices of the domestic and public spheres, applying prevailing political ideas to their predicament, and organising to take their concerns into the public domain, had brought them male and female opposition in both countries.[195]

What is overwhelmingly apparent is that early Victorian feminism, despite emerging a little later than the American movement, quickly developed equal strength, and in some areas took the lead. It was British feminists who first recognised that sisterhood – based on women's moral mission and shared oppressions, and encouraged by faith in social progress – could not be assumed. Acknowledging the importance of class and not seeking to dismantle its barriers, they reached out to working women through the SPEW and thereafter continued to set the pace in such cross-class endeavours. By contrast, American activists, for all their radicalising experience in abolitionism and hopes of transcending class, failed at the outset to confront the threat to female solidarity posed by race, and were not to find the alliance with labour women attempted by Anthony a useful model for the future.

British feminists were also fortunate in building their networks in what were expansive years for their country, and experiencing few qualms about political endeavour; whereas American feminists, beginning dramatically and placing considerable initial faith in moral exhortation, had to struggle with the tensions of sectionalism and Civil War, which put a premium on masculine and party political action. Both countries produced activists who liked to focus on single issues as well as women who were comfortable only with many: Davies and Bodichon in Britain and Stone and Stanton in the United States are good examples of these opposing styles. On the whole, however, British women continued to prefer one cause over umbrella organisations, and were more adept than their American sisters at keeping their numerous differences of opinion from becoming damagingly public. Thus, for example, they were able to turn

Mill's work and position to their advantage without advertising radical criticisms of them, and to present a tolerably acceptable image to a conservative public.

While the contrasts between the two movements should not be exaggerated, the feminists concerned were very conscious of them. Rather like members of a large family – for the transatlantic reform community was united by ties of kin and sentiment – British and American feminists were interested in corresponding, meeting and publicising each other's activities, but determined to defend their individuality.[196] Accordingly, American activists celebrated their 'plastic and fusible' country, where progress of all kinds was possible, and noted the 'inexorable prejudices' blocking change in Britain.[197] Victorian feminists, for their part, accepted the more complex inequalities of their own society, yet congratulated themselves on being more practical and gradualist than their American sisters,[198] whom they regarded as competitors in doing good. As the *Englishwoman's Review* declared in 1867, the failure of women's suffrage in Kansas was to be regretted, 'yet we cannot help feeling that it would be a glorious thing for this country if it should be the *first* to revive the good customs of other days, and to restore to women the political rights they formerly possessed'.[199] Whether their contemporaries regarded British feminists as sensible gradualists once they turned their attention to prostitution and the double standard, the next chapter will seek to establish.

4

~

The women's movements, 1870s–1880s

Consolidation and diversification

The 1870s and 1880s were transitional years for feminists in Britain and America. This was a period in which activists continued to try to bond the private and public spheres, and to negotiate their way into public roles. In the process, they responded to their changing environment, improved their organisations, pressed forward on issues already raised (such as work and education), promoted new priorities (such as social purity, temperance and the vote), and struggled to sustain the excitement and interest – in themselves and in those to be converted – of the movements' first phase. As ever, the coherence suggested by the term movement should not be exaggerated. The feminist cause did not evolve smoothly and continuously. Campaigners in each country were encouraged by success: the British in the leadership of the newly emerging social purity movement, the Americans in creating a club movement which built on women's increased associational activities during the Civil War and was sometimes prudently reformist, sometimes fully feminist. Equally, British and American women met with disappointments, notably on the suffrage front, and were conditioned by distinctive as well as shared developments.

Thus, while activists in both countries had to take account of the consequences of urbanisation and industrialisation, and of demands for new forms of organisation appropriate to the new economic order, American feminists faced peculiar challenges in westward expansion, the divisive aftermath of Civil War and the country's uneasily increasing class consciousness. For their British sisters, a key challenge was the state's growing tendency to interfere in the lives of individuals, to concern itself with regulating public and private spheres alike. Since the 1850s they had aimed to secure equal legal rights for women, giving priority to reform of the marriage laws and revealing, in the course of their agitation, the immensity of male power in both spheres. When Parliament proceeded in the second half of the nineteenth century to 'incorporate assumptions about women's sexuality and maternal capacity' into intrusive new laws covering prostitution and female employment, unparalleled in America, Victorian feminists renewed their drive for legal equality with a fresh vigour, but not without internal divisions.[1]

I. Sex and morality, divorce and singlehood

In no area was the anxiety of Victorian feminists over the proper balance between state intervention and individual liberty more pronounced than in the debate about prostitution which erupted during the 1860s and 1870s. The prominence of British feminists in the debate is noteworthy, since Victorian women had hitherto lagged behind their American sisters in considering this evil and its remedy (see above, p. 58). But in the 1860s, as politicians, law enforcement officers and doctors in both countries expressed concern about the growth of prostitution and venereal disease, and saw regular physical inspection of prostitutes as a means of controlling an ancient evil that could not be eradicated, the British Parliament acted, passing the Contagious Diseases Acts of 1864, 1866 and 1869.

The first two Acts, approved by men with the health of military men in mind, provided for the periodic genital examination of garrison town prostitutes, to establish whether they were infected with a sexually transmitted disease. Although attempts to subject armed services personnel to such examinations had encountered strong resistance, it was not suggested that men should seek to control their sexuality; instead it was assumed that provision should be made for the safe indulgence of male 'needs'. Police were empowered to arrest and register individuals suspected of being 'common prostitutes' on evidence such as soliciting, and women found to be infected could be detained for treatment for up to six (later nine) months. Noncooperation could result in imprisonment. In 1869, an additional Act extended the geographical scope of these measures. A determined campaign against this legislation, spearheaded by a male organisation and a Ladies' National Association for the Repeal of the Contagious Diseases Acts (LNA, 1869), brought about their suspension in 1883 and their repeal in 1886.

If its complex causes and changing nature have interested scholars rather than contemporaries, prostitution plainly epitomised women's subordination to men and raised questions about class exploitation and gender ideology that politicised Victorian feminists were keen to exploit. American feminists applauded their zeal but found in regulation no comparable trials or opportunities. In the disgusted judgement of Mrs Stanton at a women's rights meeting in 1870, whereas the 'recent acts in the British Parliament licensing houses of prostitution roused the indignation of the entire womanhood of England, . . . similar propositions in this country scarce create the ripple on the surface'. Actually, when regulation was debated in a number of American cities, it encountered assorted difficulties that proved fatal to the proposal. While police surveillance of prostitutes flourished in the United States, there was no strong military lobby with good political connections in favour of new laws. Other political questions seemed more urgent, and American puritanism was revolted at the prospect of importing a system supported by continental cynics. Knowledge of British objections to the

CD laws increasingly stiffened the determination of American social purists, who included feminists, to prevent regulation. And in the end it was implemented only in St Louis, for a four-year period from 1870 to 1874. Accordingly, while prostitution continued to be a major concern of moral reformers, it did not take centre stage for American feminists.[2]

As Judith Walkowitz has shown, the LNA leadership included veterans of the Anti-Corn Law and abolitionist campaigns,[3] in which women had forged for themselves an important role that stopped short of feminism (see above, p. 71). The British movement to aid the American freedmen had drawn in many women who were now free to take up fresh tasks,[4] and some of the LNA leaders had also been involved in NAPSS gatherings and the campaigns for married women's property legislation, improved education and the suffrage.[5] The timing of the CD Acts was, in fact, as important for British feminism as the rise of Garrisonian abolitionism had been for the American movement. Victorian feminists' campaign against the legislation absorbed women who might otherwise have been attracted to temperance, with its comparable stress on women victimised by male vice and power; but their critique of male-dominated society was far more radical. In contrast to the feminist organisations of the 1850s and 1860s, the repealers' association (like the suffrage movement of the 1870s) was national in scope rather than largely London-based, claiming ninety-two local associations by 1882. The LNA was especially strong in big cities, where prostitution was conspicuous, and in middle-class Nonconformist circles. Reforming families – notably the Brights and the Estlins – were engaged in the cause, as they had been in anti-slavery, and both single and married women spoke out against the legislation. Once again, in Britain, a tension emerged between married and single women that caused more of a problem than it did in female endeavours across the Atlantic. In each country, married women had received priority in the agitation for property law revision, single women in the push for employment and educational gains; but the divisive British emphasis on a limited suffrage that would disproportionately benefit single women may have stengthened the determination of married women in the LNA to take the lead on matters where their sexually inexperienced sisters were at a disadvantage.[6]

Josephine Butler embodied the background and preoccupations of the LNA leadership.[7] The daughter of a Northumberland agricultural reformer and abolitionist, married to a supportive Anglican clergyman and educator established in Liverpool, she could speak for the middle-class provincial activist, proudly independent of the London elite. Single-minded in her pursuit of repeal, she had none the less established her reform credentials in the North of England Council for Promoting the Higher Education of Women and in practical rescue work among Liverpool prostitutes, besides sustaining – while no longer highlighting – her opinion that women needed the protection of the vote.[8] Like many other women who undertook moral reform – in the first and second halves of the nineteenth century alike – Mrs Butler was driven by religious conviction and faith in human perfectibility, strengthened in her case by a youthful crisis of conscience and the tragic loss of a child. It was her belief that 'all things are possible with God; that nothing can resist the progressive force of a pure principle, and the aroused conscience of a great nation': 'God has the power and we have access to God.' Elizabeth Cady Stanton, no friend of organised religion, commented that Butler's speaking style was 'not unlike that we hear in Methodist class-meetings from the best cultivated of that sect; her power grows out of her deeply religious enthusiasm'.[9]

Mrs Butler also alluded frequently to the inspiring example of American opponents of slavery, who had similarly faced the assertion that the institution they denounced had always existed, and always would.[10] Whereas she herself had not been an abolitionist, Butler shared with anti-slavery activists empathy with powerless fellow-women debased by circumstances. She rejoiced that the 'Anglo-Saxon women have been the first to rise up in rebellion against this most degrading bondage',[11] and in her glorification of the Anglo-Saxon race she introduced a theme that would be used by members of the American women's movement later in the century (see below, pp. 171, 198). And like other major feminists Butler, though afflicted with intermittent ill health, summoned immense willpower, physical courage and the ability to endure disappointments that would have finished the faint-hearted.[12]

The LNA attracted some working-class women to its meetings, and Mrs Butler, together with its other middle-class leaders, stressed that repeal was essentially a women's cause and a cause for all women.[13] Their male colleagues agreed, although they had begun – and were crucial in completing – the organised fight for repeal; and both male and female activists employed medical, moral and constitutional arguments against the CD Acts. These stressed that they were passed in an underhand fashion; failed to detect and check venereal disease; unfairly penalised the working-class woman prostitute while ignoring her better-off male client; infringed women's civil liberties; and sought to condone, sanitise and regulate sin, the physical consequences of which might be visited on innocent married women. All in all, the Acts made a mockery of formal Victorian veneration of womanhood. Furthermore, repealers from each sex thought it was women's function 'to form public opinion by their moral influence. It is their peculiar duty to make manifest and uphold purity.'[14]

But women campaigners were especially concerned to 'abhor the sin and yet be gentle to the sinner',[15] crossing the class divide and acknowledging what God might do 'for this country if he could but find among the more favoured classes of society the humility of some of "the poor of this world, rich in faith"'.[16] Whereas middle-class evangelicals had worked for the poor as clients since the early part of the century, striving to stamp out the alleged immorality of the working class under the impact of industrialisation and urbanisation, leading repealers believed in the power of united womanhood and openly laboured with, as well as for, the objects of their concern. Thus they sought out registered prostitutes, gave them practical help and moral support in opposing the legislation, and took considerable personal risks in the process.[17] To dramatise their case, female repealers spoke in public, before mixed audiences, to a degree hitherto unprecedented among British women reformers. They also added by-election protests (resulting in mob harassment) and paid agents to the tried tactics of a newspaper, letters, pamphlets, lobbying, testifying to Parliament and arranged meetings.[18]

In addition to showing, for the first time, women's willingness to undertake risky direct action, feminists of the LNA supported the contemporary campaign for female doctors, and challenged male doctors, politicians and army men with a number of telling points. In the first place, they denied the naturalness of male lust and the double standard of morality for the sexes. Feminists rejected the commonplace, directed at middle-class women, that prostitutes in the public realm protected virtuous females in the private sphere against unreasonable sexual demands. It was their contention that all women were vulnerable to sexual exploitation within their profession of marriage and that men should raise themselves to women's level of sexual self-control. In a reformed army, soldiers might be able to do so. Secondly, activitists condemned MPs' prurient interest in the sordid matters raised by the repeal effort, and criticised physicians' cruel insistence upon internally examining arrested prostitutes with a speculum: the steel rape. The support for the CD Acts of Elizabeth Garrett who, like male doctors, put checking disease before defending liberty, was an embarrassment to the LNA, which was not concerned with the control of venereal disease. Thirdly, feminists declared that a Parliament of rich men was unfit to legislate for poor women on such matters, contrary to politicians' proud claim that they looked after the interests of disenfranchised females. Indeed, while Mrs Butler enjoyed the ever exceptional marriage of equals extolled by feminists, and saw her struggle as being in the interest of both sexes, the rhetoric of women repealers occasionally foreshadowed the anti-man strain detectable in certain pronouncements by militant suffragettes, and frequently charged against feminists with damaging effect. Feminists rightly resented the way in which women were defined only in relation to men and motherhood. Men predictably objected to changing a state of affairs from which they greatly benefited.[19]

There were further difficulties. Female repealers reached out to working-class women, prostitutes and otherwise, and some explained prostitution in terms of women's exclusion, by men, from most rewarding and reliable work. Others, however, emphasised the institution's immorality and, in presenting the prostitute as a helpless victim of male lust, drew attention away from her social context and attitudes to the institution, thereby reducing the woman at the centre of their fight to an abstraction. Black slaves had often suffered a comparable fate at the hands of abolitionists. The LNA leadership and rank and file also had different priorities: the former stressed the importance of political agitation while local workers, outside exceptional branches such as Bristol, highlighted religious objections to regulation. Preferring to concentrate on the less controversial and well-established work of providing refuges for prostitutes, they subsequently proved susceptible to 'the more repressive purity crusades of the 1880s'.[20]

Moreover, middle-class members of the LNA were sometimes condescending towards their working-class supporters,[21] and gave more time to mobilising recently enfranchised and therefore politically useful working-class men, whom they could direct.[22] Such assertiveness was regarded with dismay by male repealers of their own class, who were accustomed to women playing supporting parts in joint endeavours; they 'viewed this alliance as a threat to their leadership and a breach of class solidarity'.[23] The connection was not a politically comfortable one for the women, however, since they did not see eye to eye with working-class activists on issues like protective legislation.[24]

The women's crusade against the CD Acts did not destroy the double standard of morality for the sexes any more than it materially improved the lot of the prostitute.[25] Politicians may have become disenchanted with the CD legislation and tired of the struggle it had provoked, but they had not been persuaded that Parliament should abandon other attempts to regulate vice. Women were divided on this question, and London suffragists split over the desirability of associating their own contentious cause with another. Rescue work attracted both feminists and non-feminists, members of the LNA and women outside the Association. It reinforced those notions about feminine mission and moral superiority that had encouraged female community and justified women's involvement in reform earlier in the century, without substantially affecting their economic or political disabilities. And during the 1870s and 1880s it led some of them, mobilised in a host of social purity groups like the National Vigilance Association (1885), to believe that legislation could be used to 'force people to be moral'.[26]

Josephine Butler, by contrast, believed that 'evil could not be reached by legislation alone, "the law must be aided by moral influences acting upon both men and women" ';[27] and speaking at the fourth annual meeting of the Vigilance Association for the Defence of Personal Rights, she urged the need for curbing 'a busy but not over-wise philanthropy'. In her judgement, 'There is probably more prying, laborious benevolence in this country than in any other', too ready to intervene without system or large vision.[28] After touring Europe for the LNA in 1874–5, Mrs Butler established the first international organisation for moral reform, with equally libertarian goals: the British, Continental and General Federation for the Abolition of Government Regulation of Prostitution.[29] The Federation owed much to Butler, its general secretary, and gave British feminists a leadership role in transnational humanitarianism that had been occupied in the antebellum period by their American sisters (for example in anti-slavery, temperance and peace), and would be held by them again in the drive to bring about international co-operation among suffragists and temperance workers in the 1880s.

However, in converting the LNA into a broad social purity alliance, Mrs Butler and her co-workers showed themselves willing to accept parliamentary action to raise the age of consent for sexual activity by girls to sixteen in 1885 (it had already been raised from twelve to thirteen in 1876), as well as to punish 'seducers and third parties who traded in vice'.[30] At this point, the gulf was not great between them and 'moral repressionists' who, affected by religious revivalism and affronted by revelations about prostitution, the white slave traffic and corruption in high places, backed legislation to commit the children of prostitutes to industrial schools (1880); to deter procurers and suppress brothels (1885); to penalise male homosexuality (1885); and to prohibit indecent advertising (1889).[31] These novel measures were often inadequately enforced[32] – a possible indication of the government's uneasiness about its new role, just as the moral reformers were uneasy about whether the best way to secure equality between the sexes was to insist on special protection for women.

The overall benefits to the British women's movement of female participation in social purity campaigns were clearly mixed. On the one hand, activists had secured the abandonment of regulation, raised their profile, diversified their tactics, endorsed a wide range of reforms, appealed for female cross-class co-operation and forced an unprecedentedly frank public discussion of sexual matters, designed to purify family life and promote one standard of morality for men and women. Influential reformers such as Frances Power Cobbe, Ellice Hopkins, Catherine Booth and Margaret Bright Lucas were also led to endorse women's suffrage in the hope that it would advance their primary causes, while the LNA trained activists who went on to serve other organisations and train other women. On the other hand, the emphasis of some of the campaigns was on women's duties, not their rights; on desexualising and restricting women, not freeing them to work out an independent vision of female sexuality. They associated feminists with puritanism while making them some powerful male enemies.[33]

The American feminists' experience of social purity was very similar, and strongly influenced by the example of the movement in Britain. They, like their British counterparts, publicly argued in the 1870s and 1880s for a single standard of morality, stressed the role of female poverty and male exploitation in prostitution, expressed sympathy with prostitutes, and successfully opposed their regulation. They, too, devised new organisations – the moral education societies – through which to instruct themselves and others about the need to reform the marriage laws and sexual relations. They, too, were hampered by objections – most strongly expressed by the country press – to women 'lecturing upon subjects that no modest woman ought, in respect of her sex, to acknowledge that she is so familiar with'. Unmarried speakers like Susan Anthony and Anna Dickinson were particularly offensive, and were advised:

> The best lecture a woman can give the community 'on moral purity' is the eloquent one of a spotless life. The best discourse she can furnish us on the ['social evil'] . . . is the sincerity of her profound ignorance of the subject.[34]

American activists, including feminists, followed the British lead in agitating to raise the age of consent for girls; success came in Maine in the 1880s, and most states set a minimum age of at least fourteen during the following decade. A key role in this campaign was played from 1883 onwards by the active social purity department of the Woman's Christian Temperance Union (WCTU), which drew inspiration from British social purity developments and, under the leadership of Frances Willard, moved from concentration on the alcohol question to become a 'do-everything' reform movement. Although such British temperance workers as Margaret Bright Lucas and Lady Henry Somerset supported social purity, there was no equivalent of the broad-ranging WCTU in Britain; in the 1880s the British Women's Temperance Association preferred to focus its primary energies on the drink issue.[35] (For developments in the 1890s, see below, pp. 226–7.) But leading suffragists in the United States, with no high-profile campaign against the regulation of prostitution to complicate their tactics, could be more outspoken than their Victorian sisters in linking the case for social purity to an argument for the full emancipation of women. Susan Anthony used a speech on the subject written in 1875 and delivered 'to crowded houses' in Wisconsin, Illinois, Iowa, Kansas and Missouri to stress the economic causes of vice in women, and went on from that point to claim that:

> girls, like boys, must be educated to some lucrative employment; women, like men, must have equal chances to earn a living. . . . Women, like men, must not only have 'fair play' in the world of work and self-support, but, like men, must be eligible to all the honors and emoluments of society and government. Marriage, to women as to men, must be a luxury, not a necessity; an incident of life, not all of it. And the only possible way to accomplish this great change is to accord to women equal power in the making, shaping and controlling of the circumstances of life. That equality of rights and privileges is vested in the ballot, the symbol of power in a republic. Hence, our first and most urgent demand – that women shall be protected in the exercise of their inherent, personal, citizen's right to a voice in the government, municipal, state, national.[36]

Activists in each country were equally affected by the assumptions about sexuality bound up in social purity when they turned their attention to the profoundly testing questions of birth control and abortion. The case for equality before the law that feminists had made to their advantage when tackling women's property or the CD Acts could not be similarly used here, even though the law shaped both practices. In the case of birth control, so much depended on private negotiations between men and women; in the case of abortion, it was impossible to give equal rights to men, women and unborn children. Hence feminists were obliged to work out a position that accommodated rather than affronted male and conventional female opinion about sexuality, population size and women's role in the family.[37]

While the view of women as passionless propounded in mid-century by doctors and other contemporary observers was disputed by a number of medical experts and feminists, and there was no simple repression of unacceptable sexual behaviour in the Victorian period,[38] it was both more prudent and more likely to achieve results for women to argue that contemporary social problems related to the unchecked indulgence of male sexuality, rather than to offer a view of female sexuality which claimed greater licence for women and was shaped without reference to reproduction or male sexuality. Feminists did not deny female sexuality but maintained that in the interests of women's health, the wellbeing of their children, and marital harmony, men should exercise restraint within as well as beyond the family, so that women could achieve the goal of voluntary motherhood.[39] Birth control, or woman's right to contain her fertility by natural means, was accepted, but this was not to be confused with the artificial methods of contraception, which the church condemned as unnatural, most doctors criticised as unhealthy and disreputable, and feminists generally opposed as likely to encourage sexual excess within marriage and promiscuity beyond the home.[40]

Feminists on both sides of the Atlantic were equally critical of abortion as a degrading and risky means of family limitation: they were right to be so, since it was made a statutory offence during the nineteenth century (starting in 1803 in Britain and 1821 in America). The movement to tighten up the laws against abortion began in Britain as a reaction to the liberalisation of criminal law, thereafter reflecting medical men's dislike of abortionists, new understanding of when life began, and rejection of women's equation of life with foetal movement. It had culminated there in 1861, before Victorian feminism was very strong. American legislators moved more cautiously until the 1860s, when they were prompted to act by the coincidence of feminism, doctors seeking to assert their knowledge, morality, and prestige, and awareness of an increased abortion rate in all classes, but notably among bourgeois married women. The new laws outlawed abortion at any time, not just after quickening, and punished mother and abortionist alike.[41]

The overt desire of legislators also to control the advertising of abortifacients was given its most effective expression in the 1873 Comstock law, enacted by Congress. This extraordinary legislation brings to mind the efforts of antebellum pro-slavery activists to prevent the circulation of abolitionist propaganda. Besides excluding from the mails all literature, pictures and other materials deemed obscene by the specially appointed United States Post Office agent Anthony Comstock, it banned the mailing of any 'drug, medicine, or article for abortion or contraceptive purposes, forbade the advertisement of such items through the United States mails, and outlawed their manufacture or sale in the District of Columbia and the federal territories'.[42] It was followed by a series of similar state laws. In Britain, where medical concern had shifted to the regulation of prostitution, there was no equivalent measure. Divided over Comstockery, unable to counter the medical lobby and unwilling to condone abortion, American feminists contented themselves with blaming male sensualists for its high incidence and took the opportunity, as they did when discussing prostitution, of urging the full emancipation of women as a means of tackling this social problem.[43]

It is impossible to estimate how far the feminists' campaign for voluntary motherhood succeeded: the birth rate in Britain and the United States was declining by the last quarter of the century, and they were blamed for this by their enemies,[44] but other factors such as the advance of education, delayed marriage, abortion, birth control and contraception may have played just as important a part as agreed limits on the frequency of intercourse. The difficulty is compounded by fragmentary data about the use of contraception. Condoms, syringes, sponges, diaphragms, spermicides and information on contraceptive techniques were all available by mid-century; their employment apparently varied by class in both countries, and in America by nativity too.[45] Candour on the subject is understandably less common than the historian would like, and was certainly discouraged by the Comstock law, whose zealous author, backed by his New York Society for the Suppression of Vice, hunted down abortionists, supervised the confiscation of offensive literature, and enlisted the backing of social purity groups, including the WCTU.[46]

In 1877, events seemed to be moving in a similar direction in Britain when the radical publicists Charles Bradlaugh and Annie Besant were tried for reissuing a birth control pamphlet originally published in the first half of the century. However, the drift towards Comstockery did not continue in a country whose earlier experience of industrialisation and class formation had stimulated an earlier debate about population and birth control among conservatives and radicals alike. The trial did not lead to further legal action to restrict birth control propaganda, and Besant went on, after her 'conversion' to Socialism in 1885, to try (with little success) to recruit fellow-Socialists to the cause of family limitation.[47] It did give 'the birth-control movement wide publicity', prompted a 'demand for more information' – which was promptly met – and led 'to the setting up of the first organisation to campaign on birth control, the Malthusian League'.[48] While it endorsed feminist aims and issued a vast array of pamphlets, the League was hampered by its primary commitment to a conservative economic theory.[49]

Abortion and contraception were not issues that publicly brought women together across the class divide, although they were of interest to women of every kind. This is scarcely surprising, considering the superior access of affluent women to both practices; the pronouncements of conservatives on the desirability of inducing the 'fittest' to breed and the lower classes to refrain; and the belief of the poor (and many supporting Socialists) that population limitation would not cure, and might in some cases compound, their difficulties.[50] Feminists and other women reformers might sometimes discuss sexual matters with working-class contacts;[51] they certainly did so among themselves and in 'sexual and marital advice books addressed exclusively to bourgeois women readers'.[52] Yet when the middle-class Bessie Parkes asked 'To whom will the woman of the working-class come to tell a thousand petty troubles except to a woman?',[53] it is unlikely that she envisaged exchanges on fertility control. The major contribution to the birth control movement by British and American working-class women did not come until the twentieth century.

Bearing in mind the risks attending sexual activity, women's social disabilities and the hostility encountered by advocates of free love, feminists were wise in striving for greater self-control by men and greater freedom for women within the family, avoiding a direct attack on that institution. Their zeal in doing so does not suggest that this was regarded in any way as a defeatist or second-best course. Just as the unconventional private lives of Mary Wollstonecraft and Frances Wright had helped to discredit their ideas with conservative comment-ators, so the criticisms of marriage offered by the sisters Victoria Woodhull and Tennessee Claflin during the 1870s detracted from their achievement in opening, in New York, the first female stockbroking office; overshadowed their energetic advocacy of women's advancement; and embarrassed the more conventional American feminists with whom they associated. Mrs Stanton deplored the fact that women had traditionally 'crucified' sexually iconoclastic women, and that men had used 'sentimental, hypocritical prating about purity' to divide and subjugate the opposite sex.[54] As on so many matters in this area, she was in advance of most of her co-workers, and she could risk speaking out just because she was a respectable matron: advocates of a new woman in sexual matters did not appear in any numbers until the 1890s, although the first free-love feminists did influence more conservative activists to reconsider their views on birth control (see below, pp. 229–30). And while O'Neill may correctly have concluded that when feminists' efforts to reform the family ran into obstacles they thereafter attached too much importance to political emancipation, he fails to show how they could have acted differently.[55]

Progress for women of all classes was comparably difficult to achieve in the area of married women's property legislation (considered above, pp. 95–101); in child custody and divorce law reform; and in popularising the option of remaining single. In the United States, fear that the number of divorces was rising unduly prompted a study by a federal government agency. Its report in 1889 revealed that 'between 1870 and 1880 the number of divorces had grown one and a half times as fast as the population and that in 1886 the annual number of divorces was over 25,000.' Women gained approximately two-thirds of the divorces granted between 1867 and 1886.[56] Feminists were less concerned about such statistics than they were about the varied nature of state laws affecting women, including those governing divorce, child custody and family violence; they highlighted this diversity in their 1876 Declaration of Rights for Women, produced as part of NWSA's contribution to the celebration of the one hundredth anniversary of American independence.[57] The result, activists alleged, was 'dodging from one State to another, . . . to secure freedom', contempt 'for all law', and a society which condoned mistresses, bigamists and polygamists.[58] But while a feminist as brave as Mrs Stanton might favour the western states with liberal laws offering to women what Canada did to 'the fugitive in the old days of slavery',[59] her colleagues were divided in their responses to conservatives who, alarmed by the divorce figures, plural marriage and shopping around, pressed for a uniform national law to make divorce more difficult and campaigned for stiffer laws in offending states.

A national government that had retreated from the interventionism of Reconstruction and states ever jealous of their powers none the less tested the conservatives' persuasive abilities to the utmost. Leading churchmen and other moralists organised themselves into the National Divorce Reform League from 1885. Legislative changes making divorce harder to obtain were passed during the 1880s in Maine, Vermont, Massachusetts, New York and Michigan, and a stern resistance to liberalisation was sustained in the South, the region most opposed to feminism. Congress, however, did not respond to requests to legislate in this area, and state co-operation to promote uniformity proved elusive. Meanwhile, the total number of divorces continued to mount, and women of all kinds benefited in the matter of child custody from the variety and independence of American courts, which used their discretion over custody with a growing determination.[60]

In England and Wales the numbers of divorces lagged far behind those granted in the United States, not least because of the greater expense involved and the concentration of court business in London. The escalating American divorce rate, like other American social trends, was regarded with gloom by British conservatives. British courts, in the conservative reaction that followed the French Revolution, were also slower to use their discretion over child custody than American courts. Only the Divorce Court, after 1857, had broad discretion. Conversely, the British ability to obtain matrimonial legislation at the national level proved an advantage, as it had earlier in the century; while the keen interest in moral questions and in the connection between private and public powerlessness aroused by the social purity movement created a promising climate for further debate. From the 1870s onwards, evidence drawn from working-class districts had raised anxiety about violence against women and this added to the long-felt feminist concern over masculine abuse of sexual rights within marriage. Two women active in a range of feminist campaigns – Frances Power Cobbe and Elizabeth Wolstenholme Elmy – did much to publicise the fears and insecurities of wives, and contributed – by lectures, articles, petitions and lobbying politicians – to the passage of reformist laws.

The 1878 Matrimonial Causes Act permitted women to obtain separation orders through a magistrate's court and empowered the courts to grant maintenance to a women 'whose husband had been convicted of an aggravated assault upon her. An aggrieved wife also became entitled to the custody of any children of the marriage under ten years of age.' In 1884, a further Matrimonial Causes Act outlawed the imprisonment by a husband of a wife who refused conjugal rights, and two years later the Maintenance of Wives (Desertion) Act authorised magistrates to grant maintenance orders, not exceeding £2 a week, to neglected or deserted wives. By 1873, the 1839 Child Custody Act had been altered to permit innocent mothers to have the care of their children until they were sixteen years old, and the 1886 Guardianship of Infants Act gave parents 'an equal right to name testamentary guardians or to have a court award custody after a legal separation'. Meanwhile, the 1872 Bastardy Amendment Act had given mothers legal redress against the fathers of children born after the Act and gone some way towards softening the harshness of the poor law which, since 1834, had discouraged illegitimate births by the punitive treatment of unmarried mothers.

Like previous amendments in this area, the new laws continued to favour the affluent and disappoint the feminists. Although their provisions were welcome as far as they went, they could only stiffen the activists' resolve to obtain the vote and so increase their political leverage. Working-class women were glad to take advantage of separation orders but still could not afford divorce, which could not be obtained on the grounds of a husband's aggravated assault; and the courts proved ineffective at extracting money from recalcitrant husbands. Deserted wives had no redress against fathers of illegitimate children born before 1872. Despite changes in child custody, the feminists' desire for spousal equality was thwarted by a patriarchal Parliament. The father remained the sole guardian at law, and as Annie Besant discovered, the law continued to favour men and convention. In 1878, her 'Atheism and Malthusianism' were used as grounds to deprive Mrs Besant of custody of her daughter, granted five years before; rather than distress her child, she reluctantly abandoned her drive to enforce access. Since absconding working-class husbands generally left their children behind, the child custody legislation was not a major concern for their partners, and nothing the feminists had been able to do by this point had substantially achieved the enhancement of the economic prospects of working-class women by which desertion might have been rendered less problematic.

While feminists express dismay at further evidence of the injustice of a double standard in morality, and men legislating for disfranchised women, they did not seriously take up the issue of marriage to a deceased wife's sister, recognising that it had some support among certain women and a number of their male allies. Accordingly the measure, which was held up as another baneful American practice by its opponents, was debated by Parliament between 1882 and 1907, when it was approved without reference to the possibility of a widow's marriage to her deceased husband's brother. And, as had been the case during their campaign for married women's property laws, they did not tackle the prevailing division of labour within the home, or wives' continuing economic dependence upon husbands. Justice could not be achieved in this area – or, indeed, in many others of concern to feminists – simply by legal changes.[61] Given the opposition women encountered even to such changes, it is hard to see how a wider-ranging programme could have succeeded.

The decision of women activists to emphasise the abuse of women in marriage, men's immorality and the female moral mission beyond the home also had unintended consequences for the single woman. During the first part of the nineteenth century, strong female friendships had flourished unquestioned within the reassuring context of a cult of domesticity, and it had been possible to emphasise the blessings of singlehood – the unfettered 'search for self, truth, achievement, and independence' – without seeming to threaten the family, to whose members single women remained securely linked. After mid-century, however, when feminists in Britain especially had made much of the need for more educational and economic opportunities for 'surplus' women, singlehood seemed more threatening to conservatives. As women took up the educational openings they had struggled for, cemented intense friendships with other women at college, continued to seek job openings, found company and an outlet in a host of new clubs and organisations, and embraced such controversial reform movements as social purity, they strengthened existing fears that feminism would foster female independence, jeopardise the concept of separate spheres for the sexes, foolishly encourage women to deny their biological destiny, undermine the family, and contribute to the decline of the middle-class birth rate. Although the sexualisation of spinsterhood is a phenomenon associated with the rise of the 'new woman' and a new school of sexual researchers from the 1890s onwards (see below, pp. 229–31), it is clearly foreshadowed in the debates and developments of the previous two decades.[62]

The fact that the leaders of the women's movement on each side of the Atlantic were still both married and single, did not propose that married women should go out to paid jobs, and were able to work amicably together as well as with male relatives, husbands and contacts, was insufficient reassurance in a period of disturbing social change. Hence, in addition to the normal difficulties encountered by women activists, unmarried feminists like Helen Taylor, Lydia Becker, Louisa Twining, Frances Power Cobbe and Caroline Ashurst Biggs in Britain, and Susan Anthony, Frances Willard, M. Carey Thomas, Harriot Hunt and Anna Howard Shaw in the United States, had to anticipate critical observations on their appearance, mannishness and spinster state, despite their customary respectability, feminine demeanour and positive choice of singlehood. This is not to say that they were therefore made wretched. Mrs Stanton, visiting Britain in the 1880s, described the appealing lives of two devoted single friends – Frances Lord, a poor law guardian and translator, and Henrietta Muller, a reformer and member of the London School Board – and noted that Muller's essay on 'the dignity and office of single women' had 'been printed in tract form and circulated extensively in England and America'.[63] Means, ability, and the company and interest of other reformers at home and abroad made life rewarding for such women: but their formidable qualities and flouting of convention did not help to popularise – even while they helped to forward – the feminist cause.[64]

II. The women's movements and politics

No less divisive than the moral crusades thus far examined, the suffrage movement in Britain and America during the 1870s and 1880s is a story of organisational and ideological inventiveness; of valuable independence but little help from the political parties, and few practical gains. Such gains as there were came at the end of feminism's takeoff period in the 1860s, and in the United States they owed nothing to the targeted suffrage campaigns by women which would be a feature of the ensuing decades. By the 1860s, as the *History of Woman Suffrage* records:

> To reach the goal of self-government the women of England and America seemed to be vieing with each other in the race, now one holding the advance position, now the other. . . . At last we reached the goal, the women of England in 1869 and those of Wyoming in 1870. But what the former gained in time the latter far surpassed in privilege. While to the English woman only a limited suffrage was accorded, in the vast territory of Wyoming, larger than all great Britain, all the rights of citizenship were fully and freely conferred by one act of the legislature – the right to vote at all elections on all questions and to hold any office in the gift of the people.[65]

In fact, British women were able, at the local level, to make political gains beneficial to women that were not paralleled – and were unjustly slighted – by their American sisters. The pragmatism and gradualism on which feminists in Britain prided themselves seem to have paid real dividends here.

When British feminists failed to obtain the vote either during the suffrage extension struggles of the 1860s or by direct action and turning to the courts, they accepted the need for a long political campaign to gain their point. Although, as one pioneer recollected, they began with great intensity and unity, the campaign proved daunting. For two decades after 1870, Private Members' Bills advocating women's enfranchisement were regularly introduced in Parliament and disposed of by majorities of fluctuating sizes; only two (in 1870 and 1886) passed a second reading. The value of major debates on the subject in the House of Commons and the creation, in 1887, of a committee of over seventy sympathetic MPs to liaise with the suffrage societies was offset by the MPs' initial determination to decide the form any suffrage Bill might take; by the creation in 1875 of a parliamentary committee, dominated by conservatives, for 'Maintaining the Integrity of the Franchise' as a masculine prerogative; and by the women's failure to secure the vote when the agricultural labourers were enfranchised in 1884. From this point onwards parliamentary interest in suffrage reform declined, and feminist optimism faltered. Contemplating the passage of the 1884 Reform Act, British activists felt – much as many American suffragists had done after the passage of the Fifteenth Amendment – that:

> the position of the women will be sharply accentuated and made infinitely worse than before; the residuum of the unrepresented will have been so diminished that practically every family will have its voice recognized except the many thousands of families of every grade who own women at their heads.

The 'bright hopefulness of the earlier times was gone out of the movement'.[66]

The women were not defeated because of organisational incompetence or undue reliance on metropolitan direction. Local committees of the National

Society for Women's Suffrage (NSWS) were autonomous, and attracted vigorous workers as well as figurehead dignitaries, including MPs. Female suffragists were especially prominent in cities which had produced women activists for the Anti-Corn Law League, anti-slavery societies and other reform movements. In Manchester, important work was done by Mrs Jacob Bright and Miss Lydia Becker, who initiated the monthly *Women's Suffrage Journal* (1870) and was the parliamentary secretary for the Central Committee of the NSWS, acting as a link between the suffrage societies and the pro-suffrage MPs. In London, key figures included the writer and reformer Mrs Millicent Garrett Fawcett, younger sister of Dr Elizabeth Garrett Anderson and wife of Professor Henry Fawcett, the Liberal MP for Brighton, and Miss Caroline Ashurst Biggs, editor of the *Englishwoman's Review*. Invaluable activity was undertaken in Leeds by Mrs Alice Scatcherd, the wife of a wealthy manufacturer; in Bristol and the West of England by Miss Lilias Ashworth, niece of Jacob Bright, the Priestman sisters and Miss Estlin; in Birmingham by Miss Eliza Sturge. Valiant efforts in Edinburgh came from the Wighams, Mrs Priscilla McLaren, sister of John Bright and wife of the city's MP, and Miss Agnes McLaren, a pioneer doctor and the local committee's first secretary. In Belfast, an indispensable campaigner was the reformer Miss Isabella Tod.

The tactics favoured were those of other pressure groups of the day. Parlour meetings were arranged to persuade the indifferent or hostile in affluent circles, while ward and district meetings were held among the working class. More excitingly, nine demonstrations were organised between February 1880 and March 1884 in Manchester, London, Bristol, Birmingham, Bradford, Nottingham, Sheffield, Glasgow and Edinburgh. They involved women 'of all ranks and occupations', with working women attending 'in very large proportions. Men were only present as spectators, and that in the galleries by payment of half-a-crown.' Letters and articles were sent to the press, pamphlets were published, and the newspapers as well as the faithful were informed of progress through the *Women's Suffrage Journal*, which also brought in needed funds. Itinerant speakers were deployed who reached the small towns, stirred up suffragist activity there, and still had novelty value on the public platform.

Notable in this capacity was Miss Mary Beedy, an American who, in the 1870s, visited Bangor, Shrewsbury, Denbigh, Wrexham, Mold, Welshpool and Newtown for the Manchester committee, toured the West Country for Bristol, and as a graduate of Vassar College puzzled audiences with the letters MA after her name: the degree was not then obtainable by British women. An example of the long tradition of Anglo–American co-operation in reform, Miss Beedy charmed by 'her amiability and practical good sense'. Drawing on the public interest they had aroused, suffragists were able to send a steady flow of petitions to Parliament. During the first session of the 1874–80 Parliament alone, 1,273 were produced; and the local committees, in recording the growing number of petitions and signatures they were able to muster, noted the willingness of municipal corporations to forward them under their corporate seal – a reflection, suffragists believed, of women's possession of the municipal franchise (see below, pp. 147–8). The fact that, in time, these petitions were 'silently and indifferently dropped into the bag under the table of the House of Commons' was ruefully acknowledged.

Men and women were active in the suffrage societies (Bristol recorded 45 male and 54 female contributors in 1871); and after years of separate female auxiliaries in reform endeavours, this collaboration was regarded as a sensible step forward in a campaign which required men to achieve the desired objective. Some American feminists – both before and after the split in 1869 – were more inclined to take pride in separate female organisations and would not have sympathised with the comment, in the *Englishwoman's Review* in 1878, that since English feminists were determined not to imply antagonism towards men, 'far from beginning [their movement] with a Woman's Conference, we have never yet held one, nor, apparently, are likely to do so'. Female enfranchisement, declared another article in the *Review*, was not about 'Women's Rights – an unlucky phrase fostering bitterness. It is a question of men's and women's rights, the rights of both to the fullest good that our social and political system can yield.'

Given the priority accorded to achieving a limited suffrage which would have disadvantaged married women, it is worth noting that the suffrage societies were supported by married and single women alike (in 1871 the Bristol committee recorded subscriptions and donations from twenty-seven of each); and given the degree of clerical opposition to feminism, they were pleased to report meetings at which ministers of religion expressed their support for the cause, and to recruit them as branch members. Fund-raising was an essential part of the societies' work, despite the fact that they used largely voluntary labour, with only the most successful employing paid secretaries. Operations were generally sustained by small annual subscriptions, though most branches relied on a few well-to-do or committed individuals for large sums. Committee records reveal that subscriptions, like members and activities, increased at a steady rather than exciting pace, and that givers were various: in Manchester in the 1870s they included 'a Father of seven daughters', 'a White Slave', a 'Lover of Pluck', and a 'Well-robbed, Well-crushed, and Effectually Suppressed Wife'.[67]

The British suffragists, like their American counterparts, attempted to influence legislators directly and monitor their activities with care. They circulated prospective parliamentary candidates to establish their views on women's suffrage, and supported those who were in favour. From election returns and House of Commons division lists a tally of 'known friends' was produced, and the Central Committee – comprising delegates from the local committees, and supporting a full-time secretary and parliamentary secretary – worked with MPs to keep the cause alive in Parliament. Suffragists throughout the country tried to bring 'the question under the notice of Members of Parliament whenever they appear before their constituents'.[68] As aware as their American sisters of their need to rebut the objection that 'political representation for women is only desired by women who have failed to find another field for their energies', British activists made their case wherever and whenever they could. It is well summarised in a pamphlet published by the Central Committee in 1879, containing the opinions of about one hundred women 'engaged in such non-political work as makes them more or less known to the public'.

Among those quoted were members of school boards; poor law guardians; women engaged in literature and art; individuals following scientific and professional careers; promoters of the higher and technical education of women; principals of colleges and heads of high schools; and activists in philanthropic and temperance work. Taxation without representation aroused particular resentment and was regarded as contrary to British political principles; but the range of arguments was considerable, and not much augmented with the passage of time. Women, it was suggested, were 'more free from party politics and party bias than men are, and consequently, more likely to take measures on their own merits'. The pamphlet contended that existing female abilities and moral qualities would be useful in public life; that women voters would be able to get their opinions across to legislators on matters of which men were ignorant, or on the domestic issues with which Parliament was becoming increasingly concerned; and that through having the vote, women would gain 'a fair field of justice'. Suffrage was seen as a protection, a privilege, and a natural right that was not invalidated if some did not exercise it when they could. Since it was opposed only by women occupying 'well-feathered nests', it was extraordinary to refuse suffrage 'in a land where a woman rules' and at a time when mental and moral force were as important as the physical force deployed by men to uphold the law. Granting the vote to women would, it was believed, increase their interest and knowledge of political subjects, reduce disaffection, and acknowledge that the female role had changed and expanded in other aspects of life.[69] Although conservative and functional points were made – for instance, that most enfranchised women would not want to become political agitators and candidates for political honours, or that the vote would help women to protect their children – the pamphlet noted working-class women's need for the franchise to increase their powers of self-help, and stressed the right to vote as much as the good things it would make possible.[70]

Unfortunately for the suffragists, their critics were busily engaged in elaborating a case against women voting; and it did not matter that – as the educator, reformer and local political activist Emily Shirreff complained – they frequently contradicted facts, flew from argument to prophecy, or appealed repeatedly to custom, association, predilection, and the sentiments of the ancients.[71] Anti-suffragism – which, feminists felt, was much the same on both sides of the Atlantic – spoke to a potent combination of conservative supporters of separate spheres and radicals who envisaged women voters as priest-ridden and reactionary. The suffragists' assertion that the world was changing and should change further understandably alarmed sentimental male traditionalists of all kinds, while their official indifference to party politics, though customary for a pressure group and in line with the two main parties' designation of women's suffrage as a non-party subject, was unpersuasive in this instance. Women's suffrage drew most support from Liberal and Radical politicians, and most of the leading suffragists who declared a political interest – with the notable exception of the Tories Frances Power Cobbe and Jessie Boucherett – were Liberals.

Such a pronounced Liberal connection alienated Conservatives without being effective, since Liberal leaders opposed female enfranchisement. Gladstone, with a government mandate to enfranchise the agricultural labourers, publicly feared to risk the 1884 Reform Bill by adding on this still controversial measure, for which he had no mandate, and privately subscribed to the usual anti-suffragist sentiments about women's indifference to the suffrage and the need to preserve their special qualities within the home. As a result, over one hundred Liberal MPs voted against female enfranchisement in 1884. Conservative leaders who favoured women's suffrage (notably Disraeli, from 1848) were thus under no real pressure to act on their views, and offered the feminists no help when they were in power (Disraeli in 1867 being a case in point), while members of the normally hostile Tory rank and file could enjoy the experience of voting for a women's suffrage measure if by so doing they embarrassed the Liberals (as in 1884).[72]

The suffragists' request for the vote on the same terms as men was seen as a realistic aim, and a means of disarming those who feared an unpredictable, female majority electorate.[73] It was also, of course, an indication of how much more class considerations complicated the disposition of the franchise in Britain than they did in America. But it created as well as responded to a political difficulty when it was first made in the 1860s. Because unpropertied women were thereby excluded, together with married women under the doctrine of coverture, this approach allowed opponents to say that the suffrage movement was concerned simply with the well-to-do, and that female enfranchisement as proposed was an unfair measure which would chiefly benefit the Conservatives. The leader of the Social Democratic Federation (1884), H.M. Hyndman, an affluent London businessman who despised the diversionary reform movements that had grown up within capitalism, accordingly declined involvement in the suffragists' cause, though he was aware of what his group owed to such female activists as Eleanor Marx (Karl Marx's daughter) and Annie Besant, and fully admitted 'the justice of giving suffrage to all women'.[74]

Suffragists themselves were uneasy about the limited nature of their claim. Hence a number were glad to rally – successfully – against a proposal in 1874 to add to the Women's Suffrage Bill a clause excluding married women from voting in parliamentary elections, thus adding a statutory to a common-law disability; and after the passage of married women's property legislation (1870–82), Mrs Fawcett led an attempt by suffragists in 1884 to include married women with the necessary property qualifications in the proposed amendment to the Reform Bill.[75] None the less, the priority given to spinsters and widows divided British suffragists, occasioned unhelpful public comment, and in Mrs Stanton's view showed that the single sisters were not to be trusted. She felt that in America, where suffragists were still advocating the vote for all women (for later arguments about an educated suffrage, see below, p. 198), and aired their differences in protracted conferences, the whole matter would have been thrashed out at a convention 'if it had taken us until midnight, or . . . [necessitated adjournment] over until next day, "the spinsters and widows" having been the target for all our barbed arrows until completely annihilated'.[76]

This was not the only matter that disturbed the suffragists, for in 1888, after the division about the CD Acts in the 1870s, came a split over whether political groups should be allowed to affiliate to the NSWS. The result was a smaller Central Committee led by Becker and Fawcett, which adhered to the original policy of non-partisanship and declined to accept such groups; and a breakaway element calling itself the Central National Society for Women's Suffrage (CNS), which agreed to accept political affiliates. It was hoped that such affiliates would be Liberal women's organisations; in the years that followed, this overwhelmingly proved to be the case. Of the two new bodies – both based in London – the CNS received the largest amount in donations, but both were financially viable. Local committees joined one or the other, or neither.[77]

The events of 1888 came about because of the increasing involvement of British women in party politics, encouraged by the parties' need for unpaid workers once the Corrupt Practices Act 1883 had outlawed paid canvassers. Those of Liberal leanings, attracted by Gladstonian policies, recruited through increasingly effective party machinery, and alarmed by the activism of Tory women, had already formed local women's Liberal associations by the time the Women's Liberal Federation was established in 1886. The Federation, Hollis observes, aimed to foster the principles of liberalism, engage in electoral work, and promote political education and protective legislation for women; the involvement of female reformers and professional women was particularly desired. The Conservatives' Primrose League, created in 1883 as a response to the Liberals' more efficient organisation during the 1880 election, was originally intended to mobilise only male party workers, but soon recruited women in mixed or (less commonly) separate branches. Notwithstanding some League interest in women's suffrage in the second half of the decade, its members were exhorted to confine their efforts to the objects of the League; for women this meant striving 'to build popular conservatism between elections, and return fathers, husbands and brothers at elections'. The politicisation of British women through these formal, major party associations, which had no parallel in the United States and often took them canvassing in rough districts, made a nonsense of the anti-suffragists' argument that women were too delicate to be exposed to the rough world of politics. For Mrs Stanton, however, the prospect of English women working without charge for those who denied their enfranchisement was simply 'an insult to women'.[78]

The split in British suffragist ranks in 1888 is comparable to the split in the American women's rights movement in 1869, though it has not attracted the same degree of notice from historians, perhaps because it lasted for only twelve years compared with the twenty-year NWSA–AWSA estrangement, and did not occur at the more closely studied outset of the British suffrage campaign. Division came in Britain, as in America, when the suffragists were suffering the depression that follows a major defeat: the failure of the amendment to the 1884 Reform Bill in the British case; the passage of the Fourteenth Amendment in the American. Like the 1869 schism, it primarily represented national leadership differences, both personal and ideological, although some local resentment of the prominent Central Committee activists had surfaced. As with the 1869 divide, there was a conflict between those who favoured bipartisanship and embracing causes besides women's suffrage, and those who wanted to strengthen their relationship with the most sympathetic political party.

Yet there the similarities end. Given the unitary British political system, suffragists did not have to choose between alternative political strategies for winning the vote, as American feminists, contemplating national or state-by-state campaigns, felt that they did. And since the Liberal leadership had destroyed the suffragists' chances of success in 1884, it seems clear that the women should not have hoped to capture the Party for their cause, despite the high suffragist profile of Liberal women, the large number of sympathetic Liberal MPs, and the willingness of a National Liberal Federation and National Reform Union conference to endorse female enfranchisement in 1883 (the Conservative conference did so in 1887; the annual conference of the Conservative Association of Scotland did so in the same year).[79] The 1888 split therefore seems less justifiable than its American predecessor, though the abandonment of a bipartisanship that had failed to impress the Conservatives can be applauded as a bold move when suffragist tactics – in Britain as in the United States – were becoming stale through familiarity. The press were quick to make 'the most of what savoured of a quarrel', but Miss Becker stressed that both organisations were vigorously at work in a common concern;[80] and the greater prudence of the parties to the British quarrel, as well as the low level of general interest in women's suffrage when the conflict erupted, limited the damage it did to the movement.

More threatening for the future was the emergence of concerted female anti-suffragism by the end of the decade, however much activists might seek to explain it as 'a tribute to the growing strength of the cause'.[81] In 1889 *The Nineteenth Century* printed 'An Appeal Against Female Suffrage', signed by 104 prominent women who thought it distasteful, mischievous and unnecessary. Although the feminists claimed to have all 'the *intellect* among women' on their side, and mustered far more signatures for their reply by Mrs Fawcett in the *Fortnightly Review*, while Miss Becker won a hearing in the *Manchester Examiner and Times*, Mrs Humphrey Ward organised additional distinguished 'antis' behind her 'Rejoinder' and it, together with the original manifesto, made a greater impact than the sporadic anti-suffragist statements published by individual women since the 1860s.[82] The most important female anti-suffragist was the often unwell but always intrepid Mrs Ward, an established novelist, advocate of woman's education at Oxford and supporter of female participation in local government: just the kind of successful, reformist and articulate woman the suffragists hoped to find in their camp.[83] Too often for comfort, in fact, feminism and anti-suffragism could combine, as they did for a while in Beatrice Potter (later Webb), who signed the 1889 appeal and did not publicly recant until 1906, initially seeing no contradiction between her commitment to a life of public service and denying women the formal entry to the public sphere that the vote would bestow.[84]

Amid these many disappointments and frustrations, British suffragists, like their American sisters, enjoyed not only organisational progress but also the gain of partial suffrage. Unlike the American feminists, they energetically seized it as a blessing. In 1869 Jacob Bright, advised by Lydia Becker, managed to secure an amendment in the Commons, late at night and without discussion, giving English women ratepayers the municipal franchise – from which they had been excluded in 1835 – on the same terms as men. (The Married Women's Property Act 1870 notwithstanding, the courts had ruled by 1872 that this vote should be confined to unmarried women.) Bright's argument that the proposal was not innovatory and was much desired by a wide range of women appears to have carried the day, though one statesman remarked at the time: 'This is a revolution; this vote means still another, and there never was so great a revolution so speedily accomplished.'

Women ratepayers in England were also allowed to vote for members of the school boards, established by the government in 1870, in emulation of American practice, to oversee schools set up to supplement existing voluntary institutions in the evolving national system of elementary education. And 'with or without property, husband, or home', they could stand for election to the boards: around seventy were serving in 1879. Although it was not clear whether women were eligible for election to the poor law boards instituted by the Poor Law Act of 1834, and both the electors and the board guardians were required to possess property, the first woman successfully stood for office in 1875: by 1895 over eight hundred were serving. From 1872 onwards Scottish women were allowed to vote for and stand as members of school boards, but it was not until 1882, following feminist pressure and the representations of Glasgow's Member of Parliament, that they enjoyed the municipal franchise and the right to vote in police burgh elections, whereupon they voted in satisfactory – though varying – numbers.[85]

The activities of women on these bodies in England (and in other branches of English local government to which they were later admitted) has been the subject of an excellent recent study by Patricia Hollis. Coming into the work from philanthropy, moral reform, suffragism and party politics, the elected women, she argues, shared 'a feminist perspective which they deployed, quite explicitly, on behalf of women and children, the old and the sick, the morally, mentally, and physically deformed. They spoke to the moral community', while personally enjoying the power that came from their new roles. They also determinedly linked the local and parliamentary franchises, maintaining that the one led logically to the other. It was therefore necessary to establish that women took advantage of what they had gained, and – encouraged by the suffragists – it seems that they voted 'in much the same proportion as men', though London, with its great size and variety, presented feminists (and reformers generally) with problems.

The metropolitan and provincial school boards, operating in diverse circumstances, drew in many able women – including Lydia Becker, Emily Davies and Elizabeth Garrett – who gave a larger commitment to their tasks than more variously employed male colleagues. They learned how to play politics, build support networks (which included family allies), make policy and administer it, cope with demanding workloads, adapt middle-class mores to the working-class communities they frequently served, and persuade the working class to accept features of the educational system (such as compulsory attendance) that they viewed with dismay. It was harder for women to secure election as poor law guardians – partly because of the property qualification required (until 1894) but also because the small farmers, shopkeepers and businessmen who dominated the boards, and put pecuniary considerations first, feared that women would combine inexperience with extravagance. None the less, women gradually came forward, and while they usually held conventional views about poverty, they brought a more humane approach to the management of the institutions, the care of children, the training of girls, the rescue of unmarried mothers, nursing the sick, guarding the feeble-minded, and helping the elderly.[86]

Such was the often approving publicity given to these efforts – greater than it was in the United States – that anti-suffragists were persuaded to accept women's involvement in local politics as being concerned with domestic and social affairs, and to argue that it need go no further. American anti-suffragists, by contrast, opposed all kinds of female enfranchisement, and felt entitled to do so because of women's mixed response to partial suffrage.[87] The enfranchisement of women in the Isle of Man (1880), which owed something to suffragist lecturing there, does not appear to have impressed mainland commentators in the same way as the local government developments. Although Mrs Fawcett described the island as a British Wyoming, asserted that its women had gone to the polls enthusiastically and saw the gain in a place 'rigidly conservative of its ancient institutions' as even more valuable than when it was given in a fluid young territory, victory in these two unusual areas, far from the centres of national power, proved less inspiring and exportable than she hoped.[88]

The breakthrough in Wyoming was indeed welcome to American suffragists, but it came before opposition could organise, and without concerted pressure from the women in the territory or assistance from eastern leaders of the women's movement. It was achieved by a Bill quickly put through a very small legislature in 1869 by key male politicians, and – according to recent scholarship – was neither a feminist victory nor a tribute to frontier egalitarianism but a conservative move to help build and stabilise a raw community by attracting and empowering that element in the population which symbolised 'home and civilization'.[89] In Utah, women's suffrage was secured in February 1870; the legislature passed the statute to unify the territory's Mormon population in the face of Congressional hostility to polygamy and Mormon power. In so far as the measure was enacted to 'improve the image and reinforce Mormon control of the community',[90] it was only partially successful. Mormonism continued to excite outsider hostility, resulting in 1887 in the disfranchisement of women in Utah because the vote was 'thought to be exercised by the Mormon wives at the bidding of their polygamous husbands, and thus to strengthen the polygamous party' (although Utah was admitted to the Union in 1896 with women's suffrage, according to the wishes of its people).[91] It was also difficult for feminists beyond the territory to praise women's enfranchisement in Utah for fear of implying approval for polygamy,[92] whereas the female political role in Wyoming could be welcomed, as the territory's governor welcomed it, for bringing to bear women's 'better conscience, . . . exalted sense of justice, and . . . abiding love of order'.[93]

Yet when the *History of Woman Suffrage* hailed the Wyoming governor's judgement, its authors were endorsing a case for the vote which focused on women's distinctive qualities rather than those they shared with men, and moved away from the feminists' antebellum emphasis on suffrage as a right: a political tactic of some shrewdness, given the manifest self-interest of male voters, but of considerable risk if breaking down separate spheres for the sexes was to remain a primary objective. Despite such arguments, at this early stage the association of women's suffrage with the vagaries of frontier society may have done the cause no good in the East.[94] Nor did the extraordinary conditions prevailing in these two western territories, and helpful to suffragism, ensure that it would make progress throughout the West. While women were granted the vote by the legislature in Washington territory in November 1883 – following agitation by Abigail Scott Duniway, Mary Olney Brown and other local feminists – the law was invalidated by the territorial Supreme Court after women voters had been seen to give their support to advancing the cause of temperance. Moreover, it was alleged that few women voted in Washington when they were able to do so, while women's suffrage was proposed and rejected in popular referenda in Colorado in 1877, Oregon in 1884, Washington in 1889 and South Dakota in 1890. Of the eleven states in which the seventeen referenda on this issue were held between 1870 and 1910, eight were west of the Mississippi, suggesting that 'we can find in frontier democracy a greater willingness to submit the question to the voters'; but there were clear limits to the radicalism of the electorate when expediency did not dictate a change.[95]

The best way for suffragists to proceed was unclear once the women's efforts to claim the vote as citizens whose rights were protected by the Fourteenth Amendment had been defeated by court denials of any automatic link between citizenship and the suffrage (see above, p. 122), and a hasty attempt by some activists to create a new political alliance of suffragist and labour reformers during the fluid political conditions of the 1872 presidential election had failed.[96]

Unwilling to abandon hopes of a national solution to their dilemma, members of NWSA attached particular importance to securing a 'Sixteenth Amendment to the constitution, which would protect them as the Fifteenth protected the negroes'.[97] Its wording would ultimately be used in the successful Nineteenth Amendment (1920): 'That the right of citizens of the United States to vote shall not be denied or abridged by the United States or by any state on account of sex.' A proposal for enfranchising women by constitutional amendment had been introduced in Congress in 1868, and debates on women's suffrage had occurred there in 1866 and 1874 (on the creation of Pembina Territory, in time a part of North Dakota).[98] In 1878 the proposed Sixteenth Amendment, drafted by Susan Anthony, was unsuccessfully brought forward in Congress by the sympathetic Republican Senator A.A. Sargent of California, and it was regularly reintroduced during the 1880s, helped by the creation of Select Committees on Woman Suffrage by both Houses in 1882, as well as by a steady flow of petitions asking for the vote.[99] Besides organising these, the suffragists of NWSA made their annual conventions in Washington an opportunity to lobby legislators, attend hearings on suffrage Bills, rally the faithful and contact the press.[100]

Yet by the end of the 1880s Congressional support for women's suffrage was not much greater than it had been during the 1860s: though it was no longer novel, it continued to be seen as a radical measure, and opponents continued to argue that its passage would 'tear down all the blessed traditions, . . . desolate our homes and firesides, . . . unsex our mothers, wives and sisters, and turn our blessed temples of domestic peace into ward political assembly rooms'.[101] Those voting yes (16) at the first vote in Congress on the Sixteenth Amendment in 1887 were all Republicans, while the noes (34) included many southern Democrats. Such an alignment complicated NWSA's attempts to present their cause as being above party, thereby hoping to attract support from as many quarters as possible and avoid the absolute reliance on the Republicans that had served feminists ill in the 1860s.[102] The Anthony amendment, in fact, caused offence to state rights southerners by proposing to give Congress power to enforce its provisions, and she herself was convinced of the need to stay on terms with the Republican Party because it had 'thus far furnished nearly every vote' in favour of the Sixteenth Amendment.[103] Unperturbed by the implications of a close alliance with Republicanism, the women of AWSA none the less shared the frustrations of this period, since their preferred option of mounting local campaigns to obtain female suffrage amendments from state legislatures, enfranchisement through changes in state constitutions, or statewide reference on women's suffrage, secured the vote nowhere during the 1870s and 1880s – even with backing from NWSA activists in addition to their own, and their practice of holding annual conventions outside Washington to encourage local workers. Neither NWSA nor AWSA ever had a budget commensurate with its ambitions.[104]

Moreover, suffragists of every persuasion were dismayed by the emergence of female anti-suffragism: a phenomenon no other group seeking the franchise had had to contend with. During the 1870s an Anti-Woman Suffrage Society (1871) memorialised the Senate against the Sixteenth Amendment. Its leaders were women of social prominence; they included the wives of General Sherman and Admiral Dahlgren, and the distinguished educator Mrs Almira Lincoln Phelps. They did not wish to be put 'on an equality with the rabble at the "hustings"', valued women's privileges and the 'quiet of domestic life' (although Mrs Phelps had ventured beyond it), respected the differences between the sexes, and feared that the cause had attracted women 'with loose morals'. In Boston, similarly prosperous women with comparable opinions were organised in a Committee of Remonstrants by the 1880s, opposing first the campaign for municipal suffrage in Massachusetts and then suffrage efforts in other states. They were aided from 1889 onwards by an alliance of like-minded men. Yet in producing hostile literature, hiring male counsel to act for them at legislative hearings and soliciting names for their remonstrances, they were undertaking essentially political work. In the words of one Boston newspaper:

> The anti-women suffrage women get deeper and deeper into politics year by year in their determination to keep out of politics. By the time they triumph they will be the most accomplished politicians of the sex, and unable to stop writing to the papers, holding meetings, circulating remonstrances, any more than the suffrage sisterhood.[105]

There were some gains to offset these disappointments. Having formerly been strong only in the North-East and, to a lesser extent, the Midwest, the suffrage arm of the women's movement now consolidated its organisation in these areas, moved into the West and even tried to foster activity in the South, notwithstanding the acknowledgement of southern women that their region resisted 'new and progressive ideas'.[106] Lacking aid from the kind of national crisis that had made the 1860s 'the Negro's hour', women needed to convince sceptics not only that they were fit to vote but also that they wanted to do so. The campaigns of state groups, encouraged by the national leaders, were intended to demonstrate female interest. They taught the suffragists concerned how to spot promising circumstances for action, persist in the face of setbacks, co-operate with a variety of women's associations, produce petitions, organise conventions and canvassing, raise money, secure press coverage, and argue their case with all who needed wooing, from the voter to the men of power in state capitals.

Along the way, able leaders emerged, including Elizabeth Boynton Harbert in Illinois; Julia Ward Howe in Massachusetts; Lillie Devereux Blake in New York; Rachel Foster Avery in Pennsylvania; Isabella Beecher Hooker in Connecticut; Laura M. Johns in Kansas; and Ellen Clark Sargent in California and Washington, DC. The first three volumes of the *History of Woman Suffrage* – published in 1881, 1882 and 1886, and generally well received – set out to present a comprehensive picture of these feminist struggles while the records remained and the pioneers 'lived to see it properly done'. Its authors, having tried to show 'the dignity, self-reliance and independence' of women, and to cheer them in their 'struggle for liberty', made every possible use of HWS 'for missionary work'.[107] In particular, they and their allies were able to point to suffrage gains in addition to those in the West, and to leadership by American women of the international suffrage movement.

In 1875, Michigan and Minnesota followed the earlier example of Kentucky (1838) and Kansas (1861) in giving women school suffrage: the right to vote for members of school committees. Nineteen states had done so by 1890, when three also permitted tax and bond suffrage: the right to vote on questions submitted to taxpayers.[108] In addition, Kansas women, with the aid of the WCTU, had won the municipal suffrage in 1887.[109] Furthermore, women were elected to the school district boards, as well as voting for their members. Yet though the prominence of women as teachers and public interest in educating their children made the school franchise easier to achieve than full voting rights, partial suffrage was regarded with mixed feelings by watchful American feminists.

In Kansas, for instance, it was believed that women's active participation in school elections, and their membership of school boards, was 'resulting in a steady growth of sentiment in favor of woman suffrage'.[110] In Massachusetts, by contrast – where the school suffrage came in response to pressure from the New England Women's Club and not from the organised suffragists, who 'opposed any scheme for securing the ballot on a class or a restricted basis, holding that the true ground of principle is equality of rights with man' – it was seen as a disappointment. Little regarded by either sex and variously interpreted throughout the state, it was underused by women and so unable to forward the general suffrage cause.[111] The evidence from other school suffrage areas is similarly conflicting;[112] and in Kansas, where municipal suffrage resulted in 1887 in an 'all-female town council' and 'the first female mayor in the country', no tradition of female office-holding was established: the pioneers, having made their point – using egalitarian and home protection arguments – 'retired and were not replaced'.[113]

Partial suffrage was bound to excite attention from suffragist and anti-suffragist alike, and Ginzberg has emphasised its attraction for moderates and socially prominent women interested in immediate ends. While they recognised the danger in half a loaf, the more pragmatic British feminists, having been presented with a great opportunity when they acquired partial suffrage, were right to seize it and use it as an argument for the parliamentary vote. This is not to deny the complications that partial suffrage brought. As Flexner has observed, opponents seized on any evidence that women were slow to vote when they could, while the enfranchised women found themselves caught up in divisive party politics, like men, or subjected to continuing harassment from those who were hostile to their emancipation.[114] The fact that suffragists anxious for a school franchise amendment in Minnesota deliberately omitted 'to agitate the question', for fear of alerting 'the combined forces of ignorance and vice' customarily ranged against them,[115] is a good indication of the problems women faced over even the most modest of their political objectives. Small wonder that they sought encouragement in the company of the converted, abroad as well as at home, with Stanton and Anthony taking the initiative, after a trip to Britain in 1883, in establishing a committee of correspondence to promote the formation of:

> an International Suffrage Association for purposes of mutual helpfulness and the strength of co-operation. ... After a time it was judged expedient to enlarge its scope and make it an International Council, which should represent every department of women's work.

The Council, arranged by NWSA, met for eight days and evenings in Washington in 1888, in time to celebrate the fortieth anniversary of the Seneca Falls convention. Fifty-three national women's organisations were represented by 'eight speakers and forty-nine delegates from England, France, Norway, Denmark, Finland, India, Canada and the United States', and sessions were held on such topics as 'Education, Philanthropy, Temperance, Industries, Professions, Organizations, Legal Conditions, Social Purity, [and] Political Conditions'. The gathering, which brought to the fore a new generation of feminist leaders, demonstrated once again the feminists' organisational powers; and in order to sustain the strengthened international contacts, it was agreed to form national councils of women which would meet once in three years, with the international council meeting once in five. Moreover, according to Anthony's biographer, the Council took place despite the initial doubts of British activists: 'The most radical of English women were conservative compared to those of America', and 'the suffrage women of England and Scotland were not themselves in thorough unison as to plans and purposes.'[116] Although there were indeed divisions among Britain's suffragists – with the Scottish women conscious that they were strong enough in suffragism, as in many other reform endeavours, to pursue an independent national course – the radicalism and international leadership of British social purity activists has already been noted. This comment, in fact, suggests nothing more than that friendly rivalry and conviction of their own superiority which was intermittently displayed by British and American feminists.

It is partly in the light of their drive to demonstrate women's desire for the vote, and generally to disarm their opponents, that we can understand the American suffragists' considered stance on questions relating to marriage and morality in the 1870s and 1880s. Hoping to enlist the backing of the WCTU (given from 1881 as part of its 'do everything' policy), and of the other women's organisations and clubs that proliferated during these years, prudent feminists tried to show such groups how the vote would advance causes dear to them, and to seek it in a manner unlikely to alienate their more circumspect supporters. While NWSA's presentation of the Declaration of Rights at the 1876 centennial showed that its leaders were capable of bold tactics, whereas AWSA's polite publicity-seeking achieved nothing, it is notable that the Declaration gave greater prominence to political rights than to the social and cultural dimensions of women's oppression outlined in 1848.[117] The vote no longer alarmed women as it had done then; though it was not slighted, the rest of the Seneca Falls programme did not loom as large to activists who were confident that they could forward their cause by building upon traditional feminine qualities and roles. And by the end of the 1880s, Flexner suggests, the women's movement as a whole had become more respectable and self-consciously middle-class than it had formerly been: less actively in touch with working women and their concerns than it had been in the 1860s.[118]

A comparable picture of growing conservatism at the state level is painted in Buechler's study of the Illinois suffrage movement. Giving welcome attention to the period from 1870 to 1890, he traces the transformation of a wide-ranging early suffragism into a narrow endeavour as activists battled unsuccessfully to win the vote, lost ground to temperance campaigners, and struggled with mixed success to establish local suffrage organisations throughout the state. In Buechler's analysis, the Illinois suffragists' ideology and practice reflected the changing world from which they were drawn. Fearful of immigrants and the consequences of industrialisation, they were respectably reformist and coercive rather than radical and emancipatory. Averse to class conflict but aware of growing class differences between women, they were determined to recruit their followers more widely, if necessary by playing down women's rights and equality with men. They also recognised the risk of diluting 'their distinctively political focus'.[119]

Despite the links between suffragism and other women's associations in Illinois, Buechler has found 'no significant organizational connection between the suffrage movement and working-class women in this period', though such women were mobilised on their own account through the Illinois Woman's Alliance (1888–94), whose work was 'informed by left, labor, socialist, and feminist perspectives'.[120] Buechler's negative finding here strengthens his contention that there were different brands of feminism in the 1870s and 1880s promoted by different groups of women – domestic (advanced by women's clubs), moral (by reformers) and professional (by professional associations), as well as political (by suffrage organisations). All these, he argues, had been present in the 'early and broad phase of the suffrage movement'.[121] However, without denying that there are differences between feminist endeavour in 1850–70 and in 1870–90, there is a danger of exaggerating the radicalism of feminism's first phase; while defining it as a suffrage movement, even in the 1860s, would seem inappropriate. The women's movement up to 1870 had little organisation or concerted action, and its ideology, though wide-ranging, did not elevate the vote. When, after 1870, American feminism developed into a movement containing several movements – something its British counterpart had always been – diversity allowed for a broader level of support, and there were more achievements than there had been in the formative years, in suffragism as in other areas.

Thus if the suffragists of Illinois did not seek out working women, urban working women there and elsewhere sought to defend their right to labour and improve their conditions of employment not only through unions such as the

Knights of Labor and political groups such as the Socialist Labor Party, but also in co-operation with middle-class allies, including the WCTU and women's clubs. Many of the women involved in these community activities accepted that they had a wide political dimension, and some advocated female suffrage. Rural women, too, were politicised and converted to the merits of female enfranchisement through protest groups like the Patrons of Husbandry (the Granges, 1867), the Farmers' Alliances (1877 and 1880) and the Populists (by the 1890s; see below, p. 212). Yet while the Populist, Prohibition and Socialist Labor parties were willing to endorse women's suffrage,[122] no political party was reliable in its support, and all parties opposed women voting when they felt that their 'political power would be threatened' as a consequence.[123]

In defining a distinctive women's culture in the years between 1870 and 1890 – one which recognised the importance of organisation and saw women as playing an expanded role in the world using the investigative methods of social science and the redemptive power of feminine values – American feminists should not simply be seen as conservatives.[124] They, like the pioneers of the 1840s and 1850s, shaped an ideology and a programme that suited their times. During an era of political reaction – when the Republican Party retreated from egalitanarianism and reform, and southern opponents of the black vote sought to discredit it as one way of advancing their campaign to reassert Democratic control of the region – feminists were wise to accompany their radical claims for political rights with an updated version of women's traditional moral mission. As they did so, they were able to question the corruption and materialism of the Gilded Age, and the selfish power of the men who had produced its excesses.[125]

III. Education

In the area of women's education, the feminist activists of the 1870s produced less to shock than the social purity campaigners, and had more precedents to build on than the suffragists. On each side of the Atlantic, they worked with women who were not associated with the larger cause as well as with male philanthropists and men prominent in business and the professions. Yet while both countries faced similar challenges – the extension of secondary schooling to the children of all classes, and of college instruction to women – the United States was less openly committed to class solutions to problems, more sympathetic to coeducation, and able to sustain the lead in educational provision which it had acquired in the early nineteenth century. In 1872 Thomas Wentworth Higginson, an American writer and friend of the women's cause, reporting to AWSA's *Woman's Journal* about British education, found something to envy only in the specialist instruction of the Queen's Institute at Dublin. As he saw it, Europeans

can generally teach us nothing in regard to literary or even scientific education; our

High and Grammar Schools being far in advance of what they offer. But in systematic industrial training, they have much to teach; and, in artistic education, they are very far beyond us.[126]

During these decades American educators, politicians and parents fiercely debated the appropriate education for the children of racial and ethnic minorities,[127] and revisionist historians have subsequently exposed the recurring gap between public rhetoric and actual programmes.[128] Female secondary education also prompted keen discussion. The public high schools which grew in number between 1860 and 1880 from over 40 to around 800 quickly became coeducational, and parents' faith that girls would succeed in such schools had undoubtedly been strengthened by the proof of their educability offered by the female seminaries from the late eighteenth century (see above, pp. 25–6). None the less, their admission owed at least as much to the successful mingling of the sexes at primary-school level, and the economy and convenience of coeducation, as it did to America's egalitarian tradition.[129] Feminists supported this development with enthusiasm though, as Woody points out, both advocates and opponents of coeducation relied on 'almost nothing but personal views and experiences, to support the favored contention'.[130] But he adds that the high school 'came to have an even larger enrollment of girls than boys. In time, its general course became so diversified as to offer vocational preparation, enabling thousands of girls to at once take up some occupation.'[131] Thus, if high-school expansion did not occur in response to feminist demands for better job opportunities for women, the eager feminine response to this expansion helped to secure a key objective of the women's movement.[132]

As the ex-slaves adjusted to freedom, Americans moved westward, immigration accelerated, and the country's economy and political organisation became more complex, commentators of every kind could see the value of increasing the school attainments of girls and boys alike. Yet, as in the antebellum period, women were obliged to campaign for college instruction, while the feminists' argument for coeducation as natural, healthy and just was only slowly accepted outside the West, which acted from pecuniary motives rather than on the promptings of democracy or feminism. Mixed facilities were the only sort the region could afford. Just the same, the proportion of coeducational institutions out of the total number of colleges (excluding technical schools and women's colleges) rose from 30.7 per cent in 1870 to 65.5 per cent in 1890. The main reasons for opposing the admission of women to established male institutions were the apprehended '"loss of reputation and caste among universities, the decline of scholarship, and the corruption of morals".' For their part, women sought entry because the better-endowed male colleges had higher standards and were more numerous. They were encouraged to apply and to petition their opponents by a number of helpful factors, including the confidence that stemmed from women's work during the Civil War and Reconstruction; the support of all the leading women's organisations, and of sympathetic men; the growing demand for teachers; and the boost administered to college building by the Morrill Land Act of 1862. This Act had given public lands to endow colleges to teach agriculture and the mechanical arts, and had not excluded women from attending them.[133]

There was no shortage of college types confronting the aspiring. As Solomon observes, these comprised 'the private women's college, the religiously oriented coeducational college, the private coordinate women's college, the secular coeducational institution, both public and private, and the public single-sex vocational institution'.[134] The separate women's colleges, whatever their prewar struggles, appealed equally to conservatives who favoured separate education for the sexes and women who appreciated a friendly environment in which sisterly relationships flourished and women staff obtained more – and more important – posts than they were able to secure elsewhere in the college system. Existing female seminaries upgraded themselves in the 1880s, and four new foundations – Vassar, established in 1865 in New York State; Wellesley and Smith, begun in 1875 in Massachusetts, and Bryn Mawr, created in 1884 in Pennsylvania – attained national prominence. All but Smith were endowed by men, and each college owed its existence to religiously motivated individuals with clear views about the need to educate women to be better teachers, mothers and members of society: scarcely novel objectives, but ones which gave them broad acceptability.

Once in existence, their objectives were shaped both by the larger educational environment and by the women who studied and taught in them. Hence, though female educators, like their British sisters, struggled both to take the still inadequately prepared applicants who wanted to learn and to demonstrate that women could attain the same standards as the men's colleges, in the end they emulated Smith's tough decision to set masculine admission requirements. Similarly, there were divisions over whether to relax the compulsory classical curriculum that had for so long been the test of excellence – and denied to women – in favour of elective courses. And, once again, differences surfaced about the purpose of educating women, with the advocates of female professionalism accepting (from the 1880s) the legitimacy of domestic science courses, while the eastern women's colleges resisted what they saw as a 'step backward into the kitchen'.[135]

There were many other matters during these years to discomfit the advocates of female tertiary education. Women's desire for coeducation, especially at the best male institutions, was thwarted by the creation of the degree-awarding co-ordinate college, notably at Harvard, Massachusetts (Radcliffe, originating in 1879 although not chartered and so named until 1894) and Columbia, New York (Barnard, 1889). Lesser-known co-ordinate arrangements were worked out at Western Reserve, Brown, Tufts, Rochester and Tulane. Harvard and Columbia were openly influenced by the example of such British universities as London and Cambridge in making examinations available to women with a view to averting further demands. Co-ordinate colleges were an advance on former times and brought together interesting reform combinations –

particularly in Boston, where the agitation made a public figure of Elizabeth Cary Agassiz, the once diffidently supportive wife of a Harvard scientist, Louis Agassiz, who had died in 1870. But they did not satisfy American women, given their acceptance as full collegians elsewhere in the country.[136]

The South presented women seeking instruction with special difficulties. Reconstruction had transformed the educational prospects of poor whites and blacks, and the poverty of the region had meant that black boys and girls were often educated together in the expanding public-school sector and the first black colleges. With the restoration of home rule in the southern states, however, expenditure on black education fell, while postwar economic difficulties and the conservatism of the former Confederates also constituted real obstacles to progress for whites. Yet since the new public schools required teachers, and women were acceptable in this role, male and female educators successfully agitated for the establishment of normal (teacher training) schools. Offering shorter and cheaper courses than colleges, normal schools understandably prospered. Unfortunately, in the South, they did so at the expense of female colleges and coeducation, and the few women's colleges that there were – such as Goucher in Baltimore, begun under Methodist auspices in 1884 – were poor by northern standards. For black women, generally unwelcome at northern colleges and handicapped by parental poverty, prospects were bleak: there were perhaps only thirty black college women in 1891.[137]

During the 1870s and 1880s, college women still remained a vulnerable – if rapidly growing – minority of the college population and female population of the nation: 21 per cent of collegians in 1870, 35.9 per cent in 1890; a mere 0.7 per cent of women 18 to 21 years old in 1870, 2.2 per cent in 1890. And just as they were demonstrating their ability to tackle the intellectual challenges of rigorous higher education, their critics, influenced by Darwinian pessimism, stirred up a considerable storm about their physical ability to do so. At the centre of the furore was former Harvard medical school professor Dr Edward Clarke, whose treatment of *Sex in Education* (1873) contended, after a limited case study of Vassar students, that women who studied damaged their health in the process and stored up future health problems for themselves. Most particularly, they risked masculinisation and endangered their reproductive capacity. For the good of society, female education should therefore be reconsidered.

In the short term, Clarke's findings, which epitomised contemporary scientific thinking about sexual diversity and fears of undermining the native-born strain in the population, were unhelpful to the women who were then seeking medical training (see above, pp. 106–7, 109) and generally worrying to female students and reformers. In the longer term, women educators were able to reply to them effectively without denying female distinctiveness and evolutionary teaching, not least through a graduate survey produced in 1885 by the Association of Collegiate Alumnae (ACA, 1882), in co-operation with the Massachusetts Bureau of Statistics. None the less, there was enough evidence of ill-health among women students to strengthen the determination of their instructors, especially at female colleges, to extend the provision for physical exercise that had been introduced from the 1880s. For those who feared the masculinisation of women through education, the spectacle of college girls bicycling was, of course, the confirmation of their worst fears, as were further indications that a considerable percentage of the first generation of college women either failed to marry or married late.[138] Nay-sayers also began to complain of the feminisation of certain (arts) subjects once the number of female college students grew, while feminists were well aware that women were less likely than men to obtain funding for their studies, or to go on to graduate work.[139]

The ACA brought together alumnae of Vassar, Wellesley, Smith, Oberlin, Michigan, Cornell, Boston and Wisconsin. It encouraged women to apply to college, seeking to enlarge their prospects on leaving it and to sustain for its members the female companionship they had enjoyed as undergraduates. Associations were formed in the West in the 1880s and eventually (1903) in the South, but the western group (part of ACA from 1899 onwards) spoke for all, in remarking: 'No question is more constantly asked than, "What shall I do? How shall I make the best use of my life?"' And if pleasure could be found in investigations, contacting European – and especially English – activists, or setting up fellowships for study and research, it was difficult to ignore the slowness of women's entry into business corporations and professions other than those already breached (teaching, librarianship, journalism, social work and nursing). American women who wished to become doctors remained heavily dependent on female colleges and institutions practising 'alternative medicine', and the first woman obtained a law degree only in 1870. A protracted struggle to obtain admission to university law schools ensued, with a familiar pattern of male resistance emerging. Addressing a meeting of the western alumnae in 1887, a Michigan graduate, Miss Lucy Andrews, proclaimed: 'The age of woman has come because the world is ready for her special gifts. Her self-sacrifice and devotion to others are essentially altruistic. Our civilization is upon the threshold of an altruistic movement.' Yet she was forced to concede – Darwinist critics would have put it more bluntly – that women needed to throw themselves 'with enthusiasm into the practical affairs of life' before they could claim man's state of development.[140]

Some brave individuals could already do so, and the life of Mary Putnam Jacobi indicates the difficulties involved. Born in England of American parents, the eldest of ten children, she returned with the family to the United States at the age of six and, after being taught both at home and at an enlightened public school, she attended the New York College of Pharmacy, graduating in 1863. Having obtained an MD from the Female Medical College of Pennsylvania, she was, in 1868, the first woman to secure entry to the École de Médécine in Paris, graduating with honours in 1871 after taking her turn, with the other women in the household where she lived in 1870–71, to secure their 'rations of horse flesh, cats meat or rats meat from the sewers'. A tough eldest child, Jacobi appreciated her mother's abilities and enjoyed her father's confidence. But financial difficulties caused him to urge his daughter to delay medical studies, and he once advised her:

> My dear, you know very well that I am proud of your abilities and am willing that you should apply them to the repulsive pursuit of Medical Science. But *don't* let yourself be absorbed and gobbled up in the branch of the animal kingdom ordinarily called strong-minded women! . . . All I want to say here is that I do hope and trust you will preserve your feminine character, and with all your other studies, study a little the proprieties of life. Be a *lady* from the dotting of your i's to the color of your ribbons – and if you must be a doctor, be an attractive and agreeable one.

Mary Jacobi did retain her femininity, though because of the demands of her profession she gave up her literary work, to her family's regret. She was not obliged to sacrifice marriage and children for medicine, however, as many pioneers chose to do; she was lucky enough to find a husband who shared her medical and reform interests, and fitted the description of a possible partner she mused about in Paris:

> if at home I should ever find a physician, intelligent, refined, more enthusiastic for his science than me, and for whom I would entertain about the same feeling that I have for Haven [her brother] I think I would marry him if he asked me, and would leave me full liberty to exercise my profession.

Abraham Jacobi did just that, though he occasionally found his wife's strong sense of self trying. Impatient with women who lacked intellectual and physical ambition, Mary Jacobi recalled an early yearning to 'be great'. Not for her the belief which, she held, was much more prevalent in America than in Europe: that 'a woman is always destined to be supported by some man – either father, brother, or husband, – without equivalent, either in dowry or household labor.' She indignantly rejected women's subordination, arguing for better economic opportunities and treatment, the suffrage and exacting education, and entertaining no hankerings for the country of her birth, 'where there is so much that is dismal and tedious'.

In Jacobi's judgement, American higher education began to improve when women were admitted to colleges, and she could not believe that the opposite sex would be weakened if women learned the things that were said to make men strong. Accepting present differences in intellectual capacity between men and women, she none the less repudiated Clarke's strictures about female health in a study awarded a prize by Harvard. And as an advocate of women's admission to that institution, she would have rejected the private defence of it she received from Alexander Agassiz – not least that it placed them:

> on a very low level to take it for granted that their own sex does not supply them with the needed mental pabulum and that they can get this only in their intercourse with the other sex.

It is fitting that when Jacobi's own excellent health eventually failed – she had lived 'in an equable golden calm' – she kept a careful diary about the brain tumour that killed her, to provide information for those who were treating this disease.[141]

In Britain the 1870s and 1880 saw, as a result of Forster's Education Act, the establishment of that universal primary-school provision which had long existed in America's northern states, and the open acknowledgement of class considerations which were looming larger in the United States but still clashed awkwardly with its national ethos. The feminists did not affect the 1870 Act, or the subsequent commitment in state schools to increasing the domestic training for working-class girls. (See above, p. 52, for the introduction of such training in the first half of the nineteenth century.)[142] In the area of secondary education, by contrast, women activists did play a part, alongside government, concerned public servants and a variety of other liberal male supporters.

After the passage of the Endowed Schools Act (1869) to reform the grammar schools, commissioners were appointed to administer it and empowered to reorganise endowments to benefit girls. They were in harness until 1874, when their work was taken over by the less sympathetic Charity Commissioners. The shift of management made a difference: 47 girls' schools were launched by the Endowed Schools Commission, whereas by 1903 only another 47 had been set up through the Charity Commission. As Sheila Fletcher has demonstrated, both groups of administrators were opposed by entrenched interests, and feminists acknowledged ' "the apathetic, if not the adverse state of public opinion" '. Notwithstanding these difficulties, the first commissioners instituted school schemes with a comparable curriculum for both sexes and routinely incorporated examinations. They avoided social exclusiveness by fixing low fees, gave headmistresses great authority while paying them well, and provided for female governors. Their efforts were viewed gratefully by co-operating feminists such as Emily Shirreff and her sister Maria Grey, Emily Davies, Frances Buss and Anne Clough. But the women allowed themselves to be discouraged once the Charity Commissioners showed less interest in establishing girls' schools and appointing female governors, and failed to evolve an adequate programme for enforcing their schemes. While the new schools were a success, the endless small struggles over endowment were dispiriting and hard to prepare for, particularly when the London feminists decided it would be more productive to seek other ways of advancing girls' secondary education.[143]

One important way was through the activities of the National Union for the Improvement of the Education of Women of All Classes (1871), soon known as the Women's Education Union (WEU). Formed by Maria Grey, Emily Shirreff, Mary Gurney and the Dowager Lady Stanley of Alderley, the Union was encouraged by the NAPSS and the Endowment Commissioners. It reciprocated by supporting their efforts and eventually putting pressure on the Charity Commissioners. It held public and drawing-room meetings, gathered information and published a journal, working to improve the qualifications and standards of women teachers, to help women students with loans and scholarships, and to improve the prospects of pupils and teachers alike through founding new schools.

With this last aim in mind, the Girls' Public Day School Company (from 1905, Trust) was also founded. Offering £5 shares, the Company used the money received from their sale to start the non-denominational schools: 17 in the course of its first ten years, sustaining over 2,800 pupils. They offered an academic curriculum and physical instruction from qualified teachers for moderate fees. From its inception the Company 'was self-supporting and has remained without endowment; schools were established in response to initiatives from local people who became shareholders'. Although the fund-raising went slowly at first, the eventual response bore witness to the erosion of that public hostility feminists had deplored and the advantage of appealing directly for funds, thereby avoiding the resentment of entrenched local interests which had impeded the Endowed Schools Commissioners. (These years might have seen the growth of 'central authority and responsibility' in Britain but, as Emily Shirreff noted, the 'English jealousy of centralization and love of local independence' survived to bedevil education, just as the same spirit did across the Atlantic.) Company schools, like the endowed schools, demonstrated the pool of female ability waiting to be tapped at pupil and teacher level, and by 1895 they had won '271 external scholarships to university colleges . . ., 587 students had been provided for university colleges, 245 diplomas had been obtained, and 141 students had gone on to training colleges'. In secondary education, women were at last emulating the progress their American sisters had made by the early part of the nineteenth century.[144]

In tertiary education, British women lacked the advantage enjoyed by American feminists of social support for a vast expansion in the number of colleges and college students (from 52,000 in 1870 to 157,000 in 1890). Yet there was some university growth and reform in Britain, and women gained from both. As we have seen (above, pp. 117–18), women's struggle to qualify as doctors, for which they required university degrees, had raised the broader question of college entry, and this had been taken up by feminists with clashing views about how to proceed, resulting in the creation, with different emphases, of Girton and Newnham women's colleges at Cambridge. Thanks to Dr Henry Sidgwick and Anne Clough, Newnham had grown from the 1871 experiment of providing residential accommodation in Cambridge for women attending its special lectures. The first two Newnham students were entered for a tripos by 1875, the college appointed a female lecturer a year later, and such was the demand for places that its students also had to be lodged in the town. The experiment drew support from sympathetic dons and their wives, as had educational reform at Harvard, but Newnham's willingness to allow its students to bypass the male examination route to the triposes and to pursue studies of their own choosing, as well as to prepare short-term residents simply for the new, subdegree, higher local examinations, kept alive the animosity with Girton. There Emily Davies insisted on her students following exactly the same academic paths as men, and resented Newnham's happier relations with the Cambridge power structure.

Newnham's Cambridge-located management (Girton's was based in

London) and Sidgwick's careful diplomacy may have brought the college advantages, while its members were more appreciative than their Girton sisters of the university's 1881 decision, in response to memorials organised inside and beyond Cambridge, formally to admit women to tripos examinations, post their classified results, and award them certificates. But members of both colleges, encouraged by evidence that women could perform as well as men, increasingly wanted the right to take degrees, and after 1881 they were still denied this right, as well as entitlement to attend lectures and university membership. Memorials in 1887 requesting admission to degrees failed, not because of the continuing differences between Davies, Sidgwick and their respective followers – indeed, these were compromised so that an approach could be made to the university in that year – but because of the Cambridge authorities' opposition to anything more than a cautiously managed element of change. They and their colleagues at Oxford feared that women would lower standards, disturb the male pattern of college life, and gain an access to university government inappropriate for a politically disfranchised group.

Predictably, the campaign for female education at Oxford took a similar course to the campaign at Cambridge, except that there was no equivalent to the radical Girton and its outside feminist support. Lectures were established for women at Oxford in 1873, and two colleges were founded for them in 1879. The non-denominational Somerville and the Anglican Lady Margaret Hall initially trained students for special examinations; teaching was provided by friendly dons, and broad backing came from these fellows, their daughters and sisters, and other local reformers. From 1884 onwards, Oxford women were allowed to take the degree examinations, and in 1886 another female college, St Hugh's, was begun; but, like their Cambridge counterparts, they were denied degrees. By 1890, Newnham, Girton, Somerville and Lady Margaret Hall had 328 students between them.[145]

Given the importance of Oxford and Cambridge in British intellectual and public life, and the feminists' own class background and connections, their focus on these institutions was understandable. Their American sisters' efforts to gain entry to such elite establishments as Harvard were not of comparable national significance. But there was greater progress in other parts of Britain. In Scotland, the universities opened their doors to women in the 1880s amd 1890s because they wanted to extend their appeal and had discovered the attraction of lecture courses mounted for them in Edinburgh and Glasgow from the 1860s. The contest at Edinburgh over admitting women to medical school was not repeated elsewhere in the system, though when Scottish institutions did accept women students, considerable social distance between the sexes was preserved. In London – which was developing, not defending, its traditions, and was unembarrassed by the residence requirements of Oxford and Cambridge – University College was providing classes and certified examinations for women by 1874, while the university moved from laying on special examinations to opening its degrees to women in 1878, and its government in 1882.

This is not to say, however, that uneasiness about coeducation failed to surface in London. The upgrading of Bedford and the creation of King's College for Ladies in 1878, Westfield College in 1882 and Royal Holloway College in 1886 testified to the strength of contemporary feeling that women would be most safely educated in their own separate facilities. The same feeling also prompted suggestions in the 1880s that a women's university might usefully be created. The new universities and university colleges that grew up in Wales and the provinces none the less admitted both men and women to degrees, prompted by a modest version of the factors that caused new institutions in America to embrace coeducation: increased educational provision was considered to be in the national interest, some women had shown that they could benefit from it, and old ways did not have to be changed.[146]

The students produced by these colleges, like their American sisters, overwhelmingly chose teaching as their subsequent profession, believing in its suitability and glad to be accepted. Their attainments then helped the new private girls' schools to produce pupils able to pass the university examinations and enter college, though women's colleges such as Bedford, Westfield and Royal Holloway – like Vassar and Wellesley across the Atlantic – were willing to offer their early students preparatory work to bring them up to the necessary standard where the schools failed. In addition, graduates introduced pupils to the competitive sports they had encountered at college. The WEU started a Teachers' Training and Registration Society in 1876 to foster further gains in this area, and by 1879 it had launched its first foundation, the Maria Grey Teachers' Training College. By 1885, prompted by Miss Buss, Cambridge women had established a training college, primarily to benefit Newnham and Girton graduates intending to teach. And public-school teachers, proud of their large, outward-looking, intellectually testing and objectively regulated institutions, strove to enhance their own status, raise standards further and discuss matters of mutual interest through the Association of Headmistresses, begun by Miss Buss in 1874; the Teachers' Guild, set up in 1873; and the Association of Assistant Headmistresses, founded in 1884. No comparable efforts were made to upgrade the training of the state schools' working-class teachers, whose numbers had been expanded as a result of the 1870 Education Act.[147]

Members of the middle class were generally the chief beneficiaries of the improvements in secondary and college education, though feminists did support the creation in London of a College for Working Women in 1874 and, 'like male radicals, were frequently involved in teaching in evening classes for working people'.[148] Women educational reformers, drawn from the middle class, understandably concentrated on the group they knew best, and were inclined to confine themselves to educational crusades and public service connected with education rather than risk controversy and distraction by simultaneous involvement in an array of causes.[149] Such prudence may seem both selfish and occasionally unwise: the failure of the Association of Headmistresses to help the endowed schools system to expand is a case in point.[150] But we should acknowledge that it was difficult to sustain educational pressure groups after the first victories had been achieved: the North of England Council was disbanded in 1876, the WEU in 1882, claiming – rather unconvincingly – that its work was complete. Equally clearly, women's lay and clerical opponents were never finally won over by female educational efforts and successes.[151]

When, in 1874, Henry Maudsley, Professor of Medical Jurisprudence at University College London, initiated a controversy in Britain about the damaging effects of education on female health, influenced by Clarke's work in America the previous year, women at Oxford and Cambridge took up the challenge, heartened by the response of the ACA. Their survey of women students and their sisters at these two universities reported even more encouraging findings: for while the young women in both categories had a low marriage rate, there was little difference in their age of marriage; and the students had a lower proportion of childless marriages and a higher average number of children per year of marriage, those children apparently being healthier than their sisters' offspring. Yet as Burstyn has shown, 'conventional wisdom in medical matters was hard to override', and the pioneering women students on both sides of the Atlantic were consequently subjected to monitoring and restrictions on their behaviour that male students escaped. These measures may have ensured self-discipline and seriousness, academic achievement and respectability: they did not necessarily promote the intellectual and personal adventuring that are an integral part of advanced education.[152] As late as 1884, Maria Grey felt it prudent to argue that most women, in using the educational privileges they had won, needed to show 'that the most cultivated women can be, and is, the most womanly in all the essential attributes and offices of womanliness'.[153]

IV. Clubs and reform

Just as many of the women who laboured for and benefited from educational changes were careful not to seem otherwise atypical, so many women who came together in clubs during the later part of the nineteenth century did so without declared feminist intent. Some of the best-known were none the less feminists, and women with varied motives working together enhanced female self-awareness and solidarity, broadened the horizons of members, assisted the communities in which they were located, and through their activities advanced the interests of both middle-class and working-class women. They were an integral part of the women's movement – and they were primarily the product of American society.

As Flexner observes, the clubs were remarkable for their breadth of interests and their national distribution. They developed from the 1860s and 1870s onwards in the East and West; from the 1880s in the South. By 1890, there were enough to warrant the formation of a General Federation of Women's Clubs.[154] In the South, women commonly moved to club membership from involvement in missionary and temperance societies. Nellie Nugent Somerville in Mississippi, for example, engaged in all these activities, and the section of her papers dealing with the organised efforts of local Methodist Episcopal Church women in clothes-making, parsonage aid, and home and foreign mission support noted unhappily the superior attractions of fashionable literary clubs in the larger cities. In a region deficient in educational facilities for women, the clubs provided opportunities for cultural enrichment in a supportive context. In a region with depleted resources and an aversion to interventionist government, club women found acceptance when they undertook civic projects of all kinds, even though these brought them into contact with legislators and the masculine world of politics. In a region isolated by defeat, southern women were energised by visits from and to club activists in other parts of the country, and found in their alliances 'one of the few available roads to anything approaching real power'.[155] Throughout the West, clubs for women came quickly after organisations involving members of both sexes had set up schools and churches. There, too, they were social, study and civic improvement groups, providing participants with the opportunity 'to gain a good deal of organisational leadership and experience'. Sometimes, by the end of the 1880s, they were turning to women's rights issues, including the suffrage.[156] For black women in all parts of the country, clubs fulfilled these functions and, additionally, were a forum through which race objectives could be formulated and pressed. The fact that black women were, at this time, invariably obliged to organise separately because of the prejudices of whites is another indication of how much the women's movement reflected, as well as challenged, the prevalent mores of its day.[157]

For numerous middle-aged, middle-class white women in the urban centres of the North, club membership was made possible by increased leisure, which sprang both from the greater availability of labour-saving devices and (immigrant) servants, and from earlier marriages which produced fewer children. Better-educated and professional women were also eagerly looking for appropriate networks and outlets for their abilities. Prompted by religious conviction and their belief in the moral mission of their sex, women had long involved themselves in voluntary philanthropic and reform associations, but the clubs of the second half of the nineteenth century brought to the fore a more confident, secular-minded and class-conscious woman, determined to cement existing links between the home and the world, and to challenge men's domination of the public sphere, especially in economic matters. Three of the best-known of these clubs were Sorosis in New York (1868), the New England Women's Club (NEWC, 1868) in Boston, and the Chicago Women's Club (1876): each was committed to the members' self-improvement and community service.

As Mari Jo Buhle has shown, the club activists' sense of sisterhood meant reaching out to working-class women. The Women's Educational and Industrial

Union (WEIU), launched by the NEWC in 1877 and imitated by female reformers in 'at least thirteen other cities, including Buffalo, Providence, San Francisco, and Cleveland', set up a centre in downtown Boston where women could talk, lunch, read, and attend entertainments and courses on useful subjects. In addition, the Union investigated working conditions for female employees, advised those who were seeking employment, published details of respectable lodgings, assisted women robbed of their wages or anxious to learn how to secure binding wage contracts, and provided a market for goods made by home-based women. However, class frequently remained a dividing factor and, Buhle concludes, sympathetic club women 'lacked the financial and political power to alter significantly the condition of wage-earning women'.[158] Under these circumstances – and bearing in mind the stiff membership dues charged by some of the leading middle-class clubs – we should not be surprised to find working women forming their own clubs in northern cities and towns from 1884 onwards. Nor is it surprising to find that these clubs, which sustained premises, educational programmes and (from 1885) a national association, were usually short-lived and had no more success than affluent bodies like the NEWC in enhancing the bargaining power of women in an exploitative job market.[159]

Despite the personal achievements and social standing of many club members, their organisations moved with understandable caution, taking account of the varied motives that drew women to them. We have already noted the clubs' conventional stand on race, and this was matched by a similar reluctance openly to endorse women's suffrage. The Chicago club might have been 'the mature woman's college', but like the women's colleges, it began circumspectly,[160] as did even the prominent NEWC. For the Bostonians, their club provided 'individual pleasure and convenience' and the possibility of doing 'good work' if 'there should occur need of cooperation', as 'there was during the war'. While it was not a substitute for home life, it gave women valuable social facilities and varied contacts in 'a larger sort of home'. The club encouraged women to be 'more just and generous' to their own sex; and while it offered hospitality 'to all new thought', it was acknowledged that the NEWC had not intended 'to start as a great movement, but to grow gradually'. There was, in fact, ambivalence about how to present the record of an association whose motto was 'Nothing which concerns humanity is foreign to us', so that by the mid–1880s the secretary was claiming on the one hand that 'many good and important movements have received their first impulse here – and have grown within our limits and then beyond them into matters of public interest'; on the other hand that the club, 'like most Associations of women', was 'rather a conservative body: conservative in the best sense, that is, it has never shown any inclination to adopt radical, and sweeping alterations simply for the sake of having something new.'

Committees were established and regularly reported on such matters as hospitality, the home, work, health, art, and home and foreign correspondence. The club sought funds to assist women's education, worked for the founding of a female horticultural school and the improvement of children's homes, and backed the creation of the Girls' Latin School to prepare applicants for liberal arts colleges. It endorsed the admission of Massachusetts women to the school suffrage, and took an interest in discipline and moral training in public schools, co-operative kitchens, and the condition of Boston needlewomen. The study of needlewomen, completed in 1869, was well received (Sorosis was likewise involved in surveying actual working-class conditions). Such social investigation was then a bold undertaking for women, and the recommendation that boarding houses, cooking schools, industrial schools and emigration aid should be provided for those who were investigated anticipated the practical efforts of the WEIU. The records of the club also reveal other successes, including raising educational monies, a brief launch for the horticultural school, and sending help to the New England Hospital for Women and Children.

Equally, there are signs of frustration and insecurity, and of the middle-class outlook that the club was concerned to transcend. The report on co-operative kitchens regretted that the native-born scorned domestic work, leaving 'our kitchen service in the hands of inexperienced and ignorant foreigners', and noted anxiously the 'spirit of combination' among servant girls, as well as their desire to do as little as possible for as much as possible. What was needed was better education, in industrial schools, to persuade people that 'labor when done scientifically and in the spirit of art, is the basis of all dignity'. A talk on rich women and poor women envisaged a fairly conventional exchange between the two: 'give us your services and we will give you our money'. Though they were keenly interested in the subject of dress reform, club members clearly found it hard to decide how to achieve it, beyond promoting, in a limited way, the making of 'approved' clothes. They were ready to hear speakers on such controversial subjects as the treatment of the Indians and Chinese in America, but when Lucy Stone addressed the NEWC in 1871 she was asked to confine herself to women's legal position, 'without considering the question of suffrage'. And despite a steady flow of varied lecturers, a subject was sometimes 'left pretty much where it started', with many attenders failing to participate in discussion:[161]

> We lose and must lose much of what ought to be our gain in this way by our reluctance, our timidity in the simple expression of our thought and experience.

For all its teething troubles, however, the American club movement gave women a collective outlet that was not matched in Britain. Female alliances for specific purposes were plentiful there, and purely social clubs could, of course, be found. But the 1870s and 1880s produced no proliferation of high-profile female clubs, combining cultural, social and civic purposes with a distinctive conception of the role of women. American clubs kept in touch with British activists, and events across the Atlantic were reported with interest by English feminists, who thought clubs were needed, especially for working-class women, and drew attention to the few that did exist. London was better endowed than most places, in this as in other respects, so that when Mrs Stanton and Miss Anthony visited in the early 1880s, they were able to report engagements at women's clubs. Miss Anthony also called at the mixed Albemarle Club, 'the only one of the kind in London'; while Mrs Stanton attended a mixed club in Bristol, of a type then being organised 'for the discussion of all political questions'. And from 1883, first in southern England and later in the north, the branches of the Women's Co-operative Guild (see also below, pp. 177, 207–8) offered working-class women some of the mental stimulus and social diversion provided by American clubs, albeit in the context of a movement begun by men.

Yet on the whole the growth of women's clubs, like women's education, proceeded more slowly in the Old World than in the New, and there are several reasons for this difference. In the first place, men's clubs were so strong in Britain, and their members were so hostile to feminism, that it took very bold pioneers to create similar enclaves for women. More positively, British women had a far stronger tradition of participation in influential salons than their American sisters, and a clear preference – stated at the time of the 1840 World Anti-Slavery Convention and subsequently reiterated – of co-operating with men rather than organising entirely separately from them in reform endeavours. They did not see this as a sign of weakness: from the 1860s onwards, when the eyes of British feminists were so strongly fixed on the national legislature, such a strategy made particularly good sense. In a country as vast as the United States, with a federal political system, concentration on female institution-building made better sense.[162]

Whatever their difficulty with the suffrage, club women had no qualms about supporting temperance efforts during the 1870s and 1880s: indeed, the campaign against drink then finally realised its potential to mobilise women, and – unlike social purity and educational campaigns, but like the club movement – it was capable of attracting conservatives, moderates and radicals alike. Like the club movement, temperance also achieved its greatest successes and chief connection with feminism among American women, although from the first, in both countries, it was seen as a cross-class women's issue, and female members were welcome in temperance organisations. (See above, pp. 69–70, on female involvement in the early movement.)

The organising agency in the United States was the Woman's Christian Temperance Union (WCTU). It was begun in 1874 in Cleveland, Ohio, to take further the initiative seized by Midwestern women who – invoking the sanction of evangelical religion, and in the context of an unsettling economic depression – had picketed, occupied and closed (usually temporarily) saloons in 1873–4.[163] And while the spark that ignited this fiery women's crusade had been a lecture by the male health and dress reformer Dio Lewis, the WCTU was a female initiative, recruiting and led by women: president Annie Wittenmyer until 1879, president Frances Willard until her death in 1898, and a host of capable state activists.

Mrs Wittenmyer favoured a top–down campaign strictly directed against alcohol, using genteel tactics and avoiding politics: the women's crusade had prompted the creation of new temperance societies but there was to be no repetition of its extraordinary tactics, and the emphasis had shifted from what men should not do to what women could, acting disinterestedly.[164] Miss Willard – already an experienced Illinois educator, and soon to prove herself a fine orator and the ablest female organiser of her generation – envisaged a national cause which exalted women's powers and brought them out of the home, on which governments now impinged, to defend their interests and 'make the whole world HOMELIKE'. This stance, she felt, would lead women into a cornucopia of reforms designed gradually to realise God's Kingdom on earth; and a goal of such magnitude would necessitate an innovative organisation which chivvied its supporters for action and money, while none the less giving local groups much programmatic leeway.

In manoeuvring for control of the WCTU, Willard secured her state base, worked full-time, saved and then used the Union journal to project her opinions, and skilfully strengthened links with the rural and small-town communities of the Midwest and the West, where the movement's strength initially lay. Recognising the pro-suffrage sentiment in these areas, she proposed WCTU support for the 'home protection ballot' – that is, the opening to women of 'local elections [under 'local option' laws] on questions of the licensing of saloons and the enforcement of prohibition'. Her agitation of the matter drew favourable notice in Illinois, and by the 1880s, through Willard's direction, the Union was supporting suffrage of all kinds for women, as local circumstances dictated.

To facilitate the 'do everything' policy, departments were set up in the various states, each overseen by a national administrator, ultimately numbering nearly forty and grouped under the general headings of temperance, women, welfare and labour. Contacts were made with the Republican and Prohibition parties, the Patrons of Husbandry and the Knights of Labor, and the WCTU was an active presence at the polls on election days. By co-operating with women's clubs and other women's organisations, the Union built up a strong base in the cities. In 1884 the World's WCTU was founded on Willard's initiative, dedicated to banning opium and alcohol worldwide; within four years branches had been created in China, Japan, Australia, New Zealand and Hawaii. Parlour meetings, well-staged conventions and promotional literature were further ways of rousing the faithful and attracting public attention. Paid organisers were employed at every level of the Union, and juvenile groups attended to the rising generation. Between 1879 and 1883, the number of WTCU locals rose from just over 1,000 to just over 2,000; the number of states in which it operated from 24 to 42; and the membership from 27,000 to 73,000. By 1892, there were 10,000 locals with 200,000 members.[165]

Judgements on the WCTU in this period are mixed, and likely to remain so. The size of the movement demonstrated that Willard and her allies had both good timing and an accurate awareness of the yearning of many types of mainly white, middle-class American women to assert an independent influence in the world. However, Epstein has pointed out that the Union, though it aimed to extend the influence of the home, urged men not to shirk their family responsibilities, and campaigned with some success for better job opportunities for women, took as given the patriarchal family and social structure, upholding conventional morality and opposing the liberalisation of divorce laws.[166] In addition, Buechler has suggested that the strength of anti-suffragism in the WCTU should not be underestimated, and that temperance provided women with an alternative movement to suffragism at a time when the latter was vulnerable: single-cause feminists like Susan Anthony recognised this, and remained sceptical about the connection.[167]

Because of the similarity between WCTU goals and those of other contemporary reform movements, it is impossible to measure the Union's achievements precisely. For some women it brought friendships, occupation, interest, a sense of worth and organisational experience that mattered more than any measurable achievements, although the high turnover of members may indicate that there were those for whom success – and swift success – was important. Some of the departments had objectives that could be realised easily without fanfare: the provision of flowers for the sick and unfortunate; cooking classes for young women; materials about temperance for schools; education for women about health, diet and exercise. The programmes to establish evening, industrial and reform schools for working girls and kindergartens for working mothers offered a practical way of lowering class barriers while emphasising traditional female concerns. The department which targeted 'negroes and foreigners' for temperance work would have appealed to native-born whites and underlined the importance of Anglo-Saxon attitudes in the Union. Yet some departments had objectives which were both contentious and difficult to realise: notably social purity, prison reform, peace and arbitration, and labour organisation.[168]

Involvement with political parties stirred controversy in the Union without securing any important concessions from the parties concerned; it is easy to see why radicals felt that only the vote would make politicians pay them serious attention. The backing for Knights of Labor efforts to achieve better pay and shorter hours for working people was bold for the time, enhancing the WCTU's appeal beyond the middle class; but when it led Willard towards a Socialist vision of society and acceptance of industrial action from the late 1880s (see below, p. 225), she left many of her members behind.[169] And the central campaign for state anti-liquor laws and amendments, undertaken with male allies, though it made headway in the first half of the 1880s, was thereafter contained by an expanding and hostile brewing industry.[170] The WCTU none the less drew on female abilities and boosted female confidence in a refashioned domestic culture with a panache demonstrated by British social purity women but never shown by women in British temperance circles.

The British Women's Temperance Association (BWTA), launched in 1876, aimed to unite existing female temperance groups and found new ones. As Shiman has demonstrated, it came into being after a period of renewed organisational activity, which followed the spread to Britain of American 'gospel temperance' missions. These presented the signing of a teetotal pledge as a way to religious salvation. 'Armies' saving souls from drink and for Christianity also sprang up in many parts of the country, inspired by the heroic exploits of British armies abroad and welcoming female recruits from the middle and upper classes. So, too, did the Order of Good Templars, copied from the United States in the 1860s. The 1873–4 women's crusade in the American Midwest likewise made an impact across the Atlantic, and this was reinforced by visits from such leading American campaigners as Eliza Stewart and James Gough. All-female temperance organisations were formed in different parts of Britain, and the Church of England Temperance Society was established in 1876.

With female interest and American influences so strong, the BWTA looked set to become the British equivalent of the WCTU. Instead, Shiman argues, it was a disappointment. The Association did grow under the presidency of Margaret Bright Lucas, a woman with wide reform interests. Yet by 1892, when it claimed 510 branches with 50,000 members, over half the branches 'were affiliates with primary loyalty to their regional union[s]' in, for example, Scotland, Belfast and Yorkshire. Unlike the WCTU, it allowed men to chair its meetings and play a public role in its affairs, did not train women to lead and expand its operations, and failed to make its journal an independent mouthpiece. Furthermore, it built a major part of its programme (which included pressing for Sunday closing and temperance instruction in schools) on 'projects started by other temperance or reform organisations'. When Mrs M.C. Leavitt visited from America in 1889, representing the World's WCTU, she expressed her disappointment and put forward specific suggestion for improvement. But with the President ill and BWTA affairs managed by Mary Dowcra, a conservative in the Wittenmyer mould, little altered until the setting up of a dual presidency in 1890 pushed into the limelight Lady Henry Somerset (see below, pp. 226–7), a friend and supporter of Frances Willard.[171]

During the 1880s, even the determined effort of the Anglo-Saxonist Willard to 'enlist our British cousins to the utmost' as the 'active friends' of international temperance came to nothing. Bright's three-year presidency of the WWCTU, engineered by Willard, brought neither dividends for that body nor American inventiveness to the BWTA; it ended with Willard in charge both of her home movement and of its dynamic offshoot.[172] While the reasons for the lacklustre performance of the BWTA are not altogether clear, it must be remembered that British temperance women had always been less radical than their American counterparts. Fully in touch with developments in the United States, in the 1870s and 1880s they emulated only those which fitted in with their own traditions of moral mission and conciliatory relations with men. In the view of a contributor to the *Englishwoman's Review*, temperance was not a question that belonged exclusively to women. They might have a special interest in it, but they were advised to work with men 'in any movement to repress a vice which is as reprehensible in men as in women, and injurious equally to both'. With no equivalent of Frances Willard to transform the organisation and enlarge the vision of Victorian temperance women, their engagement with feminism would not come until the end of the century.[173]

The importance of such a catalyst in the pioneering stage of a movement cannot be ignored, despite twentieth-century suspicion of elevating the exceptional woman. In its absence, a movement like dress reform never realised its considerable potential. The wearing of bloomers by prominent individuals had taken the issue a little way in the 1850s (see above, pp. 105–6). Later in the century it was periodically exhumed, evoked interest, and was talked to death. Thus, just as the Boston club women, lacking an inspired champion to give a lead, had failed to advance their interest in rational dress, and its discussion in other women's clubs, social science groups, a short-lived American Dress Reform League and local societies had led nowhere, so attempts to form a British women's dress association petered out in the 1870s. Its fate caused one observer to predict that change in this area would be a 'gradual outgrowth of progressive civilization': not a recommendation likely to appeal to women of an activist bent. Neither the discussions of the Women's Co-operative Guild and the Ladies' Sanitary Association, nor the exertions of the Rational Dress Association initiated in 1881, moved the matter forward in Britain. Progress against the forces of fashion was made slowly in connection with the physical education for women that educational reformers recommended on both sides of the Atlantic; but so slowly as to suggest that, far from being a minor matter, it was a major one that defeated those who took it up.[174]

In the areas of reform where women were most successful in seeking an outlet for their talents during the 1870s and 1880s – such as social purity, urban mission work, the care and protection of children and girls, workhouse visiting, and the relief of poverty – advances were secured with the aid of exceptional individuals, superior organisation, or a combination of both. Two good examples of the former are Mrs Catherine Booth in the Salvation Army (1877), who was moved by the egalitarian implications of Christ's message to encourage the recruitment and promotion of women in the movement she ran with her husband; and the well-educated and well-connected Miss Louisa Twining, whose Workhouse Visiting Society (1858–78) owed much to her ability to win support from prominent male and female reformers, to recruit and train volunteers from diverse backgrounds for specialist duties, and to liaise with the poor law guardians. Hers was a powerful voice raised in favour of women guardians, and she was eventually elected to that office in Kensington. The Charity Organization Society (1869), which drew on the administrative enterprise of another well-connected Victorian spinster, Octavia Hill, was similarly able, despite growing doubts about the adequacy of its austere attitude to the poor, to secure respect and impact by the thorough training it gave its voluntary workers, and the close links it forged with local government professionals.[175]

~

V. Economic issues

We have already seen that feminists, first in Britain and then in the United States, were concerned to give an economic dimension to the women's movement, although to do this across class lines proved immensely difficult. American reformers, after all, were becoming more class-conscious, British feminists had always been so, and in both countries the problems faced by paid working-class women remained daunting. Concentrated in exploitative home work or in domestic service, agriculture and factory work, they frequently lacked bargaining skills and, though more numerous and economically important to their families than was once supposed, they constituted a minority of the paid workforce. They proved themselves capable of workplace resistance, but were held back by youthful inexperience and low expectations of jobs they were supposed to leave on marriage. They had limited money for union dues payments, and encountered hostility, paternalism or indifference from men in a century when governments made no pretence of being able to secure full employment. And like their bourgeois sisters, they were constrained by prevailing notions of domesticity (albeit differentially: 15 per cent of native-born white American women were gainfully employed in 1890, compared with 20 per cent of the foreign-born and 40 per cent of black women).[176] Yet though the unions neglected women's concerns, and though working-class women at this time responded to the ties of class before they acknowledged the bonds of womanhood, some middle-class feminists did try to assert the primacy of sisterhood.

This was an area in which British feminists gave a clear lead, because as usual they were more willing than their American counterparts to accept the divisions in society brought about by economic change. In order to effect cross-class co-operation, two organisations were formed in 1874: the Women's Protective and Provident League (WPPL) and the National Union of Women Workers (NUWW). And the women received a major spur to action not only from the resurgence of male unionism – which assisted female unionisation in America too – but also from the question of legislative protection for workers, which had first emerged in Britain in the 1830s and 1840s and did not become an issue across the Atlantic until the end of the century. The NUWW had a somewhat uncertain career as a privileged and apolitical holder of conferences and producer of literature for diverse groups of women interested in female trade unionism, protective legislation, and a wide array of issues concerning women's welfare. But it attracted some feminist support, helped to keep interest in the movement alive in the provincial cities where it met, and survived to become the National Council of Women in 1895.[177] The WPPL, though it was equally insecure and shared the NUWW's educational function by publishing its own journal, was more directly involved in the organisation of working women.

In the course of a honeymoon trip to the United States, Emma Paterson, a

Bristol bookbinder, unionist and suffragist, who had married a cabinet maker, had the chance to observe female unions in New York, and was impressed by what they were doing.[178] Returning to settle in London, she was determined to stir her countrywomen to seek 'the protection afforded by combination', thereby avoiding exploitation by employers and the hostility of working men who, fearful 'that the employment of women . . . [would] lower their wages', were 'forbidding their members to work with women' and agitating 'to limit the hours of women's work in factories and workshops'. To Paterson, such legislation was offensive because it both reduced female earning power and put women on a par with children, for whom protection was also sought.[179] With the backing of middle-class male and female reformers, including Mrs Mark Pattison (subsequently Lady Dilke), the WPPL was launched. Based in London, where it originally concentrated on signing up members from the bookbinding and dressmaking trades, the League later sent its personnel further afield to organise 'women's unions among Leicester hosiery workers, Glasgow tailoresses, jam and pickle makers, shop assistants, cigar makers'. By the time of Mrs Paterson's premature death from diabetes in 1886, the League had thirty affiliated unions; but their combined membership of 3,000 compared poorly with the 30,000 female members of textile unions.[180]

Recognising the importance of breaking down traditional attitudes among men as well as women, in 1875 Mrs Paterson had secured the right to go to the all-male Trades Union Congress. She subsequently attended each year, together with representatives from WPPL unions, winning support for the organisation of women yet abandoning none of her egalitarian views in that suspicious assembly.[181] Her successor, Lady Emilia Dilke, continued to attend and cultivate good relations with the TUC, establishing a meeting for women in conjunction with Congress. She was able to contribute generously to the WPPL's inadequate funds, and by the 1880s the League no longer had to reassure its middle-class allies by combining its unionising activities with offering members a range of uncontroversial social benefits, including a loan society, a holiday house and entertainments. More attention could therefore be paid to union work and fund-raising, as a result of which, for a small fee, affiliated unions were accepted that were not all-female but simply admitted women members. In return, they received the services of paid organisers. The need for strike action was conceded and Paterson's opposition to protective legislation was abandoned. Underlining its new image and the greater acceptability of unions, the WPPL changed its name – first to the Women's Trade Union and Provident League (1889) and then to the Women's Trade Union League (1891).[182]

After the success of the Match Girls' Strike in 1888, the League's reappraisal of striking seemed sensible: Annie Besant had published articles about the inadequate pay and hazardous conditions of the women employed at Bryant and May's match factory; they refused to repudiate her charges and struck when their leaders were victimised. Assistance from Besant, her Socialist and feminist friends (not least Clementina Black of the WPPL) and the London Trades

Council resulted in a beneficial settlement for the strikers. The Matchmakers' Union formed with Besant's aid did not survive, however, and her intervention was resented in trade-union circles when she deplored the neglect that had brought it about.[183] There was similar resentment of what was thought to be the inability of middle-class women to appreciate the case for protective legislation, and the League's change of heart on the matter could not still the controversy.

As Levine has pointed out, protection was in fact a complicated question which saw different groups of feminists opposing each other, and working-class women (so far as their opinions are known) comparably divided. The split between humanitarians of libertarian and coercive disposition, which affected the Victorian reform community as a whole by the second half of the nineteenth century – and notably in the matter of social purity – emerged here. Hence protective laws were opposed either as an infringement of liberty or as class legislation if they affected only women; or welcomed as the product of a properly paternalistic and progressive government. Just as feminists like Josephine Butler had upheld women's individual rights in the face of the CD Acts and objected to Parliament legislating for unrepresented women on moral matters that affected them, so feminist contemporaries like Jessie Boucherett and Lydia Becker denounced it for doing so on economic issues, fearing reduced job earnings, lost jobs and an increase in domestic dependence for women, whose maternal role was unduly emphasised by protectionists.

Of course protesting middle-class feminists, distant from the lives of working women, might be charged with a similarly inappropriate interventionism; but their serious inquiries into working-class conditions undermined such a charge, as did their co-operation with working women in agitating for female factory inspectors (this aim was achieved in the 1890s). It is tempting to see the backing for protection given by middle-class women associated with the unionisation drive as an indication that they were better acquainted than other feminists with the world of working-class women. Yet it is necessary to acknowledge that their conversion may have been in part a capitulation to the thinking of male unionists, whose motives regarding protection were certainly mixed. What is more, while some women workers, such as miners, opposed regulation, some (shop workers, for instance) may have welcomed it, accepting that women were particularly vulnerable to exploitation, or that men and women had different needs, capacities and responsibilities. In the end, while workshops and laundries were exempted from the full rigours of factory regulation and the government concentrated on areas of employment involving both sexes – to the relief of certain feminists and the dismay of others – legislators consulted their own wishes, as Levine concludes, rather than those of either women or unions.[184]

The tensions produced by the debate over protection were not experienced in America, where *laissez-faire* politics were at this point less effectively challenged by interventionist reformers. But they should not distract attention from the fact that during the 1870s and 1880s in Britain, middle-class and working-class women worked effectively together for the benefit of the latter, even though they did so most effectively when no major male vested interests were jeopardised. A good case in point is the Women's Co-operative Guild, a spin-off from the main co-operative movement. Started by Alice Acland, the prosperous wife of an Oxford don, led from 1889 by Margaret Llewelyn Davies, the niece of Emily Davies, and supported by other middle-class reformers, the Guild recruited thousands of respectable working-class women to its branches. Like the American clubs and the WPPL, it offered an acceptable combination of stress upon women's domestic role (as housewives and supporters of the co-operative store) and acknowledgement of their larger interests. Hence the Guild fostered – by cautious degrees, and without threatening male direction of the overall co-operative campaign – social events, mutual assistance projects, lectures and wide-ranging discussion sessions. Then, from the 1890s onwards, it approved investigations into working women's conditions and backing for female unionisation, suffrage and service in local government. The Guild – like the WPPL in its various guises – also offered working-class women the opportunity for leadership roles which the men of their class were generally unwilling to concede. In the United States, where women were considered too individualistic, uninterested in saving money and determined to shop in light, pleasant stores, the co-operative movement did not take off.[185]

Neither did cross-class feminist endeavours. The Illinois Women's Alliance, founded in 1888, did win support from women's clubs, the WCTU and other associations of reformist women in Chicago, in its fight for a programme which included shorter hours and better educational facilities. But Buhle concludes that though 'elements of the I.W.A. experiment' were present in other communities, 'they remained incompletely assembled'.[186] The alternative way forward was for women of the middle and working classes to act separately for their own advancement, and it is important here to consider the prospects held out to American women by the Socialist movement. These were initially discouraging. German-American Socialists in the 1870s, struggling to establish their credentials in the New World and 'entertaining romantic conceptions of womanhood', had 'no qualms about attacking the woman's rights campaign as a danger to woman's destiny as well as a major distraction from the class struggle'. While Socialism welcomed women in supporting social, cultural and charitable roles, their political mobilisation was neglected and their wage-earning opposed.

At the end of the decade, the few separate institutions Socialist women had established crumbled in the wake of setbacks to the Socialist Labor Party (SLP), as the movement named itself in 1877. From the 1880s, however, under the pressure of fresh thinking on the 'woman question' and the demand for unskilled labour which drew more women (including German-Americans) into the job market, the SLP encouraged women to form new associations and support male struggles more directly. These associations in turn pressed for more say within the Party, and equal pay for equal work.[187] By the end of the decade, particularly in New England and California, women's sections were making their mark, and at the same time women of Socialist bent were drawn to the Nationalist Clubs which sprang up to forward the collectivist vision and commitment to women's emancipation contained in Edward Bellamy's best-selling utopian novel *Looking Backward* (1888).[188]

Although women unionists, like men, suffered great setbacks after the panic of 1873, throughout America they joined the Knights of Labor (1869) during the 1880s. Female assemblies were formed from 1881, their delegates attended the General Assembly from 1883, and largely through the efforts of women themselves, in 1886 a Department of Woman's Work was established, led for four years by a hosiery mill machine hand, Mrs Leonora Barry, who was employed to investigate conditions, organise and agitate for improvements. Unfortunately for such activists, the Knights were divided over tactics and hampered by the diversity of their members, while Mrs Barry and her colleagues had too much to do, felt it prudent to avoid radical tactics, and failed to make much impact on the largely negative female perception of unions. The American Federation of Labor (AFL), founded in 1881 and concentrating on recruiting skilled workers, had less to gain than the Knights from organising women, and resisted doing so until the 1890s.[189] And while in rural regions the Patrons of Husbandry celebrated family unity and welcomed women as voters, officials and lecturers, as well as providers of social amenities, women tended to play a more active part in the Midwestern Granges, where the movement supported temperance and female suffrage, than in the South, where a lower female profile was encouraged. None the less, women from North and South alike were driven by the hardship of the late 1880s to support a more determinedly political agrarian uprising – Populism (see below, p. 212) – in the following decade.[190]

For middle-class American women in the 1870s and 1880s, the concern for better job prospects, sounded as early as 1848, gave rise to no single feminist campaign. Rather it found expression in such multipurpose organisations as the WCTU, women's clubs, the ACA, and the Association for the Advancement of Women (1873), whose congresses brought middle- and upper-class women together to discuss professional careers. It was also illustrated in the struggles of individual women to gain access to the medical, legal and other professions, and in their shouldering of all kinds of reform and community labours. These included, from the end of the 1880s, a very distinctive form of practical social work, which began as a masculine initiative in Britain but was subsequently feminised on both sides of the Atlantic: the urban settlement house (considered below, pp. 216–19). The struggle for the right to preach intensified and though the Protestant churches denied their ordination, women in these denominations formed home and foreign missionary societies and deaconess Orders through which women greatly increased their organisational base and work opportunities, both paid and unpaid.

British middle-class women were similarly placed. Although the Society for Promoting the Employment of Women was still active, and feminist pressure for better education had enhanced female prospects, most gains for women continued to come because new openings in business, government and the professions required cheap labour. Like their American sisters, they found that sales and clerical jobs brought only respectability, not prestige or good pay, while the disapproval of married women working had not abated. Female professions lacked the organised clout and prestige of the older professions, despite the efforts of bodies like the teachers' associations and the Royal British Nurses' Association (1893). An encouraging breakthrough had been made in local government and a female presence had been established in medicine, with twenty-six women on the medical register in 1882 and three dispensaries run by women in 1884.[191] Susan Anthony, however, happily recording her visit in 1883 with 'England's first and only women lawyer', was obliged to add: 'or as nearly one as she can be and not have passed the Queen's bench' – women were not admitted to the legal profession until 1922.

In Britain as in America, the deaconess (and sisterhood) movement flourished during the second half of the century, justified with reference to women's moral mission and need for employment, and leading them to varied social work among the poor. In Britain as in America, male clergy were ready to bless these labours but not to reassess women's position in church government and ministry.[192] Following the earlier lead of the SPEW, feminists helpfully published details of job possibilities in their journals.[193] Yet whereas opportunities for philanthropic women to labour for nothing except satisfaction abounded, Jessie Boucherett reported gloomily in the mid–1880s that the situation for women of the 'higher classes' who needed paid work had got worse, not better.[194] Given their limited success in launching new initiatives to advance their own economic position, the willingness of British middle-class women to try to help working-class women improve theirs is all the more remarkable.

If feminism is equated with suffragism, the 1870s and 1880s can be seen as years of organisational growth but substantial failure, sandwiched between the movement's heady origins and its successful climax. They can be presented as years in which the American women's movement began to move towards the conservatism that was its alleged hallmark from the 1890s onwards, playing down the marriage question and claims to equal rights with men, and seeking to enlarge woman's sphere by emphasising with new urgency that her special moral qualities, long appreciated in the home, could usefully be applied to many of the problems of the wider world. American feminism, thus regarded, might be thought to be growing closer to its British counterpart, which has been seen as a more conservative movement in a more conservative country. To some extent this contrast was encouraged by the activists themselves. Thus Stanton and Anthony rejoiced in American freedom and radicalism when they visited Britain, and disparaged the 'hesitating, apologetic way' that 'seems to be the national idea for an exordium on all questions': none of the reformers they met 'can touch Wendell Phillips'. English feminists, for their part, celebrated their prudent national style. Mrs Fawcett noted that 'practical moderation and rather humdrum common sense' had stamped the women's campaign in England, preventing 'a good deal of what strikes one as rather comic about the movement in other countries', while a writer in the *Englishwoman's Review* believed that English feminists had always tried to increase 'their power effectively with men', to establish 'their joint, but not antagonistic rights, on the ground that the exclusion of either sex from common fields of action or intellect tends not only to the disadvantage of the excluded sex, but to the deterioration of both'.[195]

It has been argued here, however, that the case for the growing conservatism of American feminists depends on a false definition of feminism, and that criticism of such conservatism offers no indication as to how the family structure could, at this time, have been reformed, once changes in the married women's property law had been achieved. It has been stressed that the American women's movement during the 1870s and 1880s became more diverse than it had been in its first phase, better able to mobilise women and – appropriately, in a country historically pledged to avoid European class conflicts – to produce middle-class activists who were anxious to engage in reform efforts with, rather than for, working women. Although there were undoubtedly differences of style and emphasis, and a certain rivalry between the British and American feminist crusaders, it is not helpful to label either as radical or conservative, and on the whole the reformers concerned genuinely welcomed contact with each other: rejoiced that friends of the women's movement were 'coming into closer sympathy in the different countries. ... Nothing can conduce more to the successful guidance of this movement than familiarity with the progress and methods used in different countries.'[196]

American feminists conceded that the British had taken the lead in social purity and technical education; they themselves were clearly ahead in other branches of education, temperance and international feminist endeavours (although the British spearheaded the social purity drive abroad as well as at home). Conscious that the public was said 'never to pay attention to more than one political question at a time',[197] British feminists generally continued to avoid umbrella organisations. Yet their movement was multifaceted from the start, with feminists urged to insert the thin end of the wedge wherever they could, and convinced that by 'broadening the basis of the work' from suffragism alone, 'by asking simultaneously for better laws, better education, better employments and wider fields of usefulness, the sympathies of more women were engaged'.[198] And by the 1880s, some of their associations – notably the Women's Co-operative Guild and the WPPL – did carefully embrace a range of issues and sustain a remarkable degree of cross-class support. There was a radical strain in British feminism which first enlivened the activities of the utopian Socialists and subsequently reappeared in the periodic protests of activists who put principle before British pragmatism: in Mrs Butler's campaign against the CD Acts; and in the activities of Elizabeth Wolstenholme Elmy and her allies, who formed the Women's Franchise League in 1889 to protest suffragist willingness to accept partial suffrage. When the 1890s began, feminism had produced complex movements which were not in the doldrums on either side of the Atlantic, but had rather – as Leach urges with respect to the American campaigners – accepted both the tenets of reforming liberalism and a modified version of Comtian positivism; which were therefore committed to 'a truly altruistic, symmetrical, and rational society', where individualism was effectively combined with 'a more structured, ... centralized, and harmonious social system'.[199]

5

~

The women's movements in maturity
The 1890s to 1914

In the years between 1890 and World War One, American and British feminists experienced more success and sharper disappointments than at any period since Seneca Falls. American women achieved their biggest gains as reformers by preparing the ground for and shaping the movement known as Progressivism, which was dominated by the concerns that women had been seeking to make their own since the Civil War: greater democracy, better educational provision, the protection of women and children, and the alleviation of urban problems with a view to bridging the class divide. Women's claims to a public role in reform were fully recognised for the first time, and their ability to act was increased from the 1890s onwards by creating new separatist organisations and expanding old ones. Working-class women, though willing to co-operate with their middle-class sisters in union formation, were playing a more independent part in cross-class and working-class associations. Even the women's suffrage campaigners made real gains, broadening their base of support, adopting bold new techniques and winning the vote in additional states.

Yet the franchise still eluded American feminists nationally, and their opponents had become more vocal, though not the organisational equals of the suffragists. There was also a danger that as Progressive reformers women would become indistinguishable from other Progressives, or at least unduly shaped by the pressures of non-feminist colleagues. As Hart reminds us, some effective women bureaucrats did emerge, and were linked to an outside network of feminists; but the passage of reformist laws was often hailed without sufficient attention to the bureaucracies that would administer them. Moreover, anticipating the open divisions in the women's cause after 1920, there were signs of a challenge to the broad consensus about women's distinctive characteristics that feminists had turned from a liability, confining them within a subordinate sphere, to a building block for their movement. The first challenge was offered by the 'new woman' of the 1890s, whose independent lifestyle and (in some cases) views on moral issues minimised the differences between the sexes, and were taken up by feminists who now gave themselves that label, in the 1910s. The second came from scholars, women among them, who questioned the Victorian elevation of biology over culture and 'the Victorian conception of sexual polarity', and whose views slowly influenced the country's college population.[1]

British feminists were similarly involved in adapting liberal ideals to the needs of a mature industrial economy, helping to fashion the legislation of the early welfare state and grappling with the challenges posed by an increasingly complicated state bureaucracy. They, like their American sisters, fought more determinedly for the rights of working-class women, and were disconcerted as well as encouraged by the growing assertiveness of such women. While sustaining their efforts for moral reform, they too found their moral claims and reform mission threatened by the new woman and fresh theories about female attributes. If they have not always attracted the notice they deserve, they were part of a coalition of reformers and politicians that was better able to achieve liberal social welfare legislation than its American counterpart, unduly preoccupied with fighting inefficiency and corruption. They had already faced up to the divisive implications of protective legislation for women and children, and their example influenced the American feminists in this area, in settlement work and suffragist methods. With larger and longer experience of party and local government politics than American activists, and affected by working-class and Irish protest tactics, Victorian feminists mounted a campaign for the parliamentary franchise that both exhilarated women at home and inspired observers throughout the world. When the war came, however, the greater boldness of British suffragists still had not won them the vote, and the willingness of British feminists to work through such male-dominated institutions as labour unions and political parties carried with it the real risk that they would fail to develop independent political leverage.

I. Politics

During the 1890s, no one could have envisaged that Britain was destined to become the storm centre of the suffrage movement. Since neither of the two major parties had changed its position on the enfranchisement of women, they found themselves favoured by kind words from their political friends, but received no useful assistance. What is worse, they saw the continuing defeat – in 1892 and 1897 – of Private Members' Bills that carried their hopes.[2] Like their American sisters, leaders of the British campaign tried to strike a proper balance between giving national direction and encouraging local effort. They endeavoured to sustain the enthusiasm of the often disappointed, stir up the apathetic, and prevent frustration from venting itself in family quarrels. Like suffragists across the Atlantic, they enjoyed mixed success on all fronts, though the British took comfort from the fact that they, unlike American activists, did not have to seek both the approval of the national legislature and the votes of a majority of men, including the foreign-born, for their enfranchisement. Suffragist quarrels also took a distinctively British form: over whether to seek enfranchisement on the same terms as men or press for full enfranchisement, the latter course being urged by the Women's Franchise League; and over the relationship with the parties.

Mary Jacobi noted in 1894:

> We are unshackled by the English tradition of partisanship, because we have no ancestral tradition, working in our blood and brains, of party devotion to Whig or Tory. I believe that, unless under some special personal influence of a near fanatic friend, women find it very difficult to get up lively enthusiasm for purely party issues.

As we shall see (pp. 198, 202, 242–5 below), the traditional non-partisanship of American suffragists, already affected by accommodating the multipartisanship of women who could actually vote in several states, was dramatically strained from 1914.[3] In Britain for much of the 1890s, even without the vote, women did give their support to the Liberals and Tories; and this presented the leadership with problems. The Liberal Party was most sympathetic to women's suffrage, but the Women's Liberal Federation split over the issue in 1892, with a breakaway Women's National Liberal Association distancing itself from female enfranchisement and a ginger group within the WLF – the Union of Practical Suffragists – agitating for more radical tactics to achieve the vote. Then from the mid–1890s the Parliamentary Committee for Women's Suffrage, led by Mary Cozens, made it plain that it looked to the Conservative Party to act; and Cozens's blatant partisanship brought her into conflict with the well-established – predominantly Liberal, but officially non-partisan – suffrage societies.[4]

None the less, Rubinstein has established that the suffrage movement enjoyed increased support in the 1890s, as indicated by the good showing of the two suffrage Bills; the size of the petition for enfranchisement produced in 1896; and the growing interest of working-class women, notably in the Women's Co-operative Guild. Moreover, women's capacity in political affairs, first shown modestly, in family or community activities, but now formally demonstrated by the efforts of the WLF and the Primrose League 'during the three general elections held between 1892 and 1900', may have impressed the general public. Though it brought them no direct political reward, it was certainly put to good use once the suffrage campaign moved up a gear from the end of the century.[5] Women's involvement in local government also continued to provide them with a political education and confidence-boosting experience: continued to reveal women's political ability to those who were willing to consider their performance without partiality. At this level of politics, the major gain of the 1890s was the 1894 Local Government Act, pressed for by women's groups. It created secular parish councils and rural and urban district councils, 'based on the old poor law union', for both of which women ratepayers and married women who owned property separately from their husbands could vote. District councillors automatically became members of boards of guardians, while the Act abolished the £5 property qualification for guardians and ruled that any adult who satisfied a residence requirement could be elected. As a result, the number of women guardians greatly increased: it had been 136 out of a total of 28,000 in 1892; by 1895 it was between 800 and 900.[6]

The number of women elected to the new councils was modest. Approximately 200 served on the nearly 8,000 parish councils of England and Wales in 1896, and at the end of century there were around 150 rural and 10 urban district councillors.[7] But apparently they 'worked hard, they worked constructively, and they worked quietly', and 'far more than most men, they fought resolutely to repair the cottages and improve the lives of country women.'[8] Among the many women's associations active in encouraging female participation in local government, the Women's Local Government Society (WLGS) stands out; it was, in Hollis's words:

> an upper-middle-class, Liberal and London group, which functioned through family, social, philanthropic, and Liberal connections. It was also stoutly feminist, supporting the claims of all women to elected local office, whatever their policies and their views on suffrage, while refusing to support men, however sympathetic, to anything at all.[9]

Notwithstanding the skill of WLGS members, the support they gave to developments outside London so far as finances permitted, and their valuable efforts on behalf of the 1894 legislation, there were disappointments in this area as well as on the national political scene. Women could not serve as borough councillors or as members of the county and county borough councils created in 1888 (the election of two women as county councillors was contested in the courts, and legal clarification in 1889 and 1891 confirmed their exclusion). Married women were still not qualified to vote in county, county borough and municipal elections. After 1894 there were women on the vestries that helped to govern London, paying special attention to the needs of women and the poor, and appreciating the importance of improvements in 'the built environment'.[10] Yet in 1899, when the London Government Act swept away the vestries and replaced them with metropolitan boroughs, women (without a property requirement) were granted only the right to vote for, not to serve as, councillors, despite lobbying by feminists.

As Rubinstein maintains, their 'failure owed much to the fact that since ... 1894, ... advances in local government had come increasingly to be regarded as a means of furthering the campaign for the parliamentary vote.'[11] Suffragists had always made the connection, their enemies had always denied it, and when the anti-suffragist Mrs Humphrey Ward launched her Local Government Advancement Committee in 1911, she underscored the point.[12] However, with national government's role expanding in social welfare, where women's interest was acknowledged, it was growing harder to deny them the national suffrage, while the belief that one thing leads to another may have been strengthened by the way in which pressure from feminist groups and the election of women to local political office had 'encouraged an increase in the number of women sanitary, school and factory inspectors and other local and national officials, including members of royal commissions and other government bodies, whose appointment was a notable innovation of the period'.[13]

Further problems had to be confronted. In 1902 the Education Act abolished school boards, so that women who wished to sit on local education authorities had to be co-opted with the approval of all-male councils, losing the right to take their chances with the electorate.[14] And when, after 1907, legislation (again requested by the WLGS and opposed by anti-suffragists thinking of the parliamentary vote) allowed women, regardless of marital status, to seek election to borough and county councils, they were hesitant in coming forward, sparingly elected, and slow to make an impact once in post: by 1915 some 50 women were serving, along with a few on the Welsh councils. Since women (until an Act of 1914) had to be ratepaying electors before they could become councillors (from that point residents as well as ratepayers might stand), and since the seats were fiercely contested along political lines, being seen as 'dry runs for general elections', the small number of female incumbents is understandable. In addition, the wide-ranging nature of council work and its bureaucratic organisation left less scope for the individual pioneering and close attention to detail that had been the hallmark of women on school and poor law boards.[15]

Yet, Hollis concludes, local government has in time afforded women accessible and politically important jobs, services and public advancement, while the pioneers, with calculation and conviction, advanced by using the language of separate spheres. In the process, they gave it:

> a radical cutting edge. Standing for election, selling one's virtues, seeking votes, was itself a profound challenge to ladylike notions of propriety. . . . At their bravest, women were well aware that they were refusing to accept male definitions of what was central and what was marginal, that they were asserting that women's needs counted for as much as men's.[16]

They did so, moreover, with greater vision and enthusiasm than American feminists could muster about the benefits of local suffrage until the late Progressive period; though of course the British had the inestimable advantage of being able to obtain national legislation on the matter, instead of needing to secure action from innumerable separate localities.

From the end of the nineteenth century, when 37 per cent of men as well as all women lacked the parliamentary suffrage, the fruitless struggle for that vote was resumed. The two primary actors on the feminist side were the moderate or constitutional National Union of Women's Suffrage Societies (NUWSS), which in 1897 brought together all associations 'then existing [a total of 16] which were devoted exclusively to women's suffrage'; and the militant Women's Social and

Political Union (WSPU), formed in Manchester in 1903. They were supplemented by the Women's Freedom League, the East London Federation of Suffragettes, various organisations representing occupational groups, suffrage associations within the WLF and Primrose League, and a Men's League for Women's Suffrage (1907). The demand of both major groups was for the franchise ' "as it is or may be granted to men" '.[17]

At the parliamentary level, no bills or resolutions to advance that end were introduced in Parliament between 1897 and 1904. Since there was no alternative, Private Members' Bills then continued to be presented, but they continued to fail. In addition efforts were made to amend government bills: three regarding plural voting (1906, 1913 and 1914); one touching Irish Home Rule (1912); and the Franchise and Registration Bill of 1913, which was withdrawn when the Speaker ruled against the validity of such an amendment. When the political parties persisted in dividing over the terms on which women's suffrage could safely be introduced, an all-party Conciliation Committee was set up to try to reconcile their differences, and in 1910 a Conciliation Bill was produced, only to be stopped as too narrow by Liberal suffragists in the government: the Liberal fear of enfranchising ideologically conservative women of property was a real one. A second such Bill received a majority of 167 on its second reading in 1911, before being defeated by government unwillingness to provide time for it to continue; and a third in 1912 narrowly failed on its second reading, principally due to the defection of Irish Nationalist supporters who feared that if the Bill succeeded the Prime Minister might resign, and Irish Home Rule would be jeopardised. The government's indication of its intention to introduce its own Reform Bill, able to be amended in favour of women, also undermined the last conciliation measure.[18]

The tactics employed by moderate and militant suffrage societies alike to produce this level of parliamentary action imparted fresh zest and drama to the cause. It is now apparent that the differences between the two groups should not be exaggerated, and that a vital role was played in both factions by democratic suffragists who, Holton has established, saw 'women's suffrage as part of a more general democratisation of British society', requiring 'an alliance with the new force in radical politics in this period, the Labour Party'. It is equally clear that the NUWSS, despite its halting progress between 1897 and 1906, deserves the notice it has recently received from scholars.[19] By 1914, it 'had over 50,000 adherents, [and] was the single largest organization for the promotion of women's suffrage in Britain'.[20]

As Hume, Holton and Garner have pointed out, the Union's ideas and political goals broadened over time. It first tried to strengthen pro-suffrage sentiment in the Liberal Party, which it regarded as the women's best hope; and, with that in mind, to concentrate more on the constituencies than on Parliament, and to sponsor women suffrage candidates at by-elections.[21] It aimed to recruit more members and publicise its efforts through attention to visual imagery, mass demonstrations and marches, banquets and pageants, tours of the country, memorials, meetings in drawing-rooms and with Church groups, women's organisations and political associations. It sought to run a professional operation by maintaining offices, an administrative staff, a team of organisers, a literature section and a newspaper, *The Common Cause*. Recognising its strength in England, it paid close attention to forwarding the cause in Wales, Scotland and Ireland, accommodating the independent spirit of the Scottish and Irish workers. And its executive committee of well-connected, able, reformist, frequently Liberal women, headed by the then non-partisan Mrs Fawcett, was a major asset.[22]

The Union was impressed by the initiatives of its North of England Society for Women's Suffrage (NESWS), and guided by the democratic suffragists. It was anxious to bring pressure to bear on the party in power, find new allies and broaden its social base. Accordingly, from 1912 it turned to the Labour Party, rather as American suffragists had turned to Populists, Progressives and other third parties. The shift entailed cultivating Labour leaders, employing working-class organisers, promoting the formation of suffrage clubs for working men and women in industrial communities, setting up suffrage committees in poor urban areas, and reaching out to the unions. It involved extending associate membership to working-class women who could not afford to join its societies (by 1914 there were 46,000 such Friends of Women Suffrage) and establishing an Election Fighting Fund to support 'individual candidates standing in the interests of Labour in any constituency where the N.U. [WSS] thinks it advisable to oppose a Liberal Antisuffragist'.

The Union also canvassed in the constituencies of the Liberal government's anti-suffrage ministers and approached Tory leaders to try to get them to promise that they would introduce a Women's Suffrage Bill when next in government: after all, it was believed that women had conducted themselves in a conservative fashion in local government.[23] Furthermore, Hume has shown, in adopting new tactics the NUWSS played down Liberal arguments for the vote grounded in individual right, acknowledging instead the differences between the sexes and the value of the ballot in protecting women's interests as wives, mothers and workers. Yet we have seen (p. 143 above) that British suffragists had, from the first, employed both equal rights and moral mission arguments. And while Holton and Garner stress the importance of the latter, the emphasis on women's distinctive qualities and aims does not seem to have been as pronounced as it was in the United States, reminding us once again of the danger of characterising the British women's movement as more conservative than the American.[24]

For its part, the WSPU committed itself to achieving women's suffrage through action by the party in power. The Union was founded by Mrs Emmeline Pankhurst, the widow of 'another John Stuart Mill': a Manchester barrister and reformer whose interests had included women's suffrage. She came to the cause, bringing with her three daughters (Christabel, Sylvia and Adela) via experience in Labour politics, as a poor law guardian, a member of the Manchester school board, and a registrar of births and deaths. Her strength was as an agitator, just as Fawcett's was as an organiser, and she was aptly described as the John Brown of the suffrage movement. Both she and Christabel were influenced by the work of the NESWS, in which Christabel was active, and Mrs Pankhurst was convinced that a new organisation was necessary to 'fight for the interests of working-class women'. Like the NUWSS, the WSPU made a slow start, and immediately found itself at odds with the Labour leadership's preference for a measure securing universal suffrage. But it drew valuable lessons from the robust style of Socialist meetings and labour protests, and its early supporters had the working-class perspective that the NUWSS members initially lacked, outside the NESWS.[25]

Militant suffragism, as Evans has observed, involved the use of 'modern propaganda techniques', and ranged from 'an *active* form of non-violent defiance of government and the law' to acts of violence and destruction. These methods have been most commonly associated with the WSPU. They began in 1905, when Christabel Pankhurst and a fellow-activist, Annie Kenney, an Oldham millhand, were gaoled after protesting the suppression of their attempt to make two prospective Cabinet ministers, speaking in Manchester, indicate whether their government would enfranchise women. The incident attracted considerable notice, admittedly hostile; and from this point militancy escalated as the suffragettes of the WSPU, relocated in London in order to focus their protests on Parliament, mounted mass gatherings and marches, disrupted political meetings and clashed with police. In the process they endured often harsh treatment, got arrested, began a programme of window-smashing in London from 1909, intensified it in 1911–12, and drew attention by hunger-strikes and noncooperation with prison officials when they were imprisoned (over 1,000 were), a stance which resulted in force-feeding. By 1913 the suffragettes were engaged in a major programme of property damage and arson, and militancy did not cease until the outbreak of World War One.[26]

Such behaviour by women was news. Their exciting tactics presented a new image of women to the public. They brought the WSPU notice it did not command before 1905, attracted new members, increased funds, galvanised the NUWSS into bolder initiatives, and won sympathy at first when women were brutally handled by the authorities, who declined to recognise gaoled activists as political prisoners. Militancy proved that suffragettes felt as strongly about their cause as male rebels, past and present. Like them, they could deploy physical force and were prepared to suffer for their beliefs: Emmeline Pankhurst cited the example of the Irish Nationalists. Yet unlike many radicals, they were determined that 'women will suffer violence only to themselves'. This rule was very seldom breached, and the sole fatality was in the suffragette ranks. In 1910 and 1911 the WSPU switched to peaceful pressures, in order not to endanger the campaign for conciliation bills, resuming the militancy they had begun because of politicians' intransigence only when it seemed clear, by the time of the third measure, that the government opposed such bills.

In view of the fact that women had been moderately seeking the ballot without success since the 1860s, it is not surprising that Union members thought militancy long overdue. And though the WSPU appealed particularly to the young and unmarried, and was buoyed up by the class confidence of its leaders, it attracted men as well as women 'of all political sympathies and social classes', established regional offices, and for some years enjoyed the benefit of organisers with experience in other reform movements.[27] Nor, though dedicated to 'Deeds not Words', did it neglect conventional methods or the normal means of pressure-group communication. From 1907 the Union published a monthly, *Votes For Women*, which was supplemented from 1912 by the *Suffragette*, and a wide range of arguments for the ballot were employed in its publications, ranging from 'taxation without representation is tyranny' and 'so long as woman has no political status she will be the "bottom dog" as a wage-earner' to 'Politics have invaded the home, and women must therefore enter politics' and 'Whenever women have become voters, reform has proceeded more rapidly than before.' None of these arguments, of course, was either very novel or very radical.[28]

However, if the militant and constitutionalist campaigns initially stimulated one another, each had its drawbacks. For the 'antis', suffragette behaviour was the antithesis of femininity and confirmed what they alleged: that women, being irresponsible and irrational, were unfit for the vote. As the fashionable doctor Sir Almroth E. Wright put it in *The Times* in 1912, militancy was a 'hysterical revolt'; there was 'mixed up with the woman's movement much mental disorder'. Militant tactics, once embarked upon, had to become progressively more radical to retain their newsworthiness, and might bring notoriety rather than lasting support or influence. Governments are always loath to yield to violence, and can invariably defeat violent protesters with the superior force of the state. Britain's Liberal premier from 1908, Herbert Asquith, no friend to suffragism and repelled by suffragette tactics, was certainly determined not to give way before militancy, despite the outcry caused by force-feeding. The Americans to whom WSPU leaders appealed for financial and moral support did give it and might have enjoyed the flattery; Mrs Pankhurst declared: 'All my life I have looked to America with admiration as the home of liberty', and predicted that American suffragists would not have to fight as hard as British women, and would have the franchise sooner. But the general American reactions to militancy were mixed, as we shall see. Furthermore, though Mrs Pankhurst's assertion that out of women's voteless condition had 'grown the most appalling slavery, compared with which negro slavery falls into insignificance', was the kind of hyperbole that might have pandered to the openly prejudiced views on race of some American suffragists, it revealed an extremism in ideas as well as actions that brought the WSPU critics in its own time, and has done so ever since.[29]

WSPU literature contained the claim that women were not fighting against men but were militant because they were 'determined to sweep away those barriers which are perpetuating a condition of deadly severance between those who must be one. . . . Joint-heirs are we with man himself in all that evolution has to unfold.'[30] This statement was called into question, fairly or not, with the launching of a moral crusade by Christabel and Emmeline Pankhurst in 1913 – 'votes for women and chastity for men' – following Christabel's public denunciation of the high level of prostitution and venereal disease in Britain, and the consequent risks for women contemplating matrimony. While her statistics appear to have been faulty, the crusade linked suffragettes to well-established concerns of the social purity campaigners, concerns that were shared by suffragists; and given the setting up of a Royal Commission on Venereal Disease in 1912, it was timely. Yet as Mrs Pankhurst acknowledged, the opponents of women's suffrage hated it 'more than the vote & now realise that votes for women means less moral license for men'; she believed that nothing but militancy could 'break down the barrier in England [,] which is such a stronghold for selfish and vicious interests'. Such views were unlikely to win over leading – and usually married – male politicians, ever sensitive to the possibilities of a sex war breaking out of feminism.[31]

The WSPU tactics also presented problems for moderate MPs and members of the NUWSS who had initially accepted that 'quiet and respectable' tactics were played out and 'more aggressive methods of work' called for. Having sympathised with the physical courage of suffragettes badly treated for non-violent protests, they drew the line at violence which, they felt, made the militants criminals rather than innocent victims. The constitutionalists and democratic suffragists believed that their political manoeuvres were being undermined by the WSPU, whose Irish analogy was false, since the suffragettes 'did not have any political hold on Parliament'. In their judgement, the Union's political strategy favoured the Tories, and its fighters made 'a sort of inverted appeal to the privileges of sex. On the one hand they challenged physical violence, as if they were real fighters, and yet they refused any real contest because they were women.'[32]

Equally seriously, male working-class leaders were disheartened by the WSPU's increasingly middle-class composition, neglect of class analysis, persistent support for a limited franchise, and failure to help their candidates at by-elections (from 1906 onwards the Union opposed all Liberal candidates and was impartial towards all others). And radical suffragists in the North of England – restored to their proper place in the movement by Liddington and Norris – feared that their attempts to build up a mass-based campaign, involving factory workers, trade unions and the WCG and focused on objectives like equal pay and child allowances as well as the vote, were being jeopardised by increasingly narrow and self-indulgent leisured women.[33] The growing autocracy of the Pankhursts divided their followers in 1907, when perhaps a fifth of WSPU members left to form the militant but democratic and pro-working-class Women's Freedom League; thereafter splits in the Union occurred almost annually until war broke out. The expulsion of long-time comrades and capable organisers Emmeline and Frederick Pethick Lawrence in 1912 and the alienation of Sylvia Pankhurst's East London Federation of the WSPU in 1913 were particularly unfortunate. These conflicts weakened suffragism and were exploited by its opponents. As Harrison has concluded, 'Encouraging leader-worship was no preparation for democratic politics.'[34]

It should not, therefore, be supposed that NUWSS tactics could quickly carry the day. The WSPU rightly regarded it as being too committed to the Liberal Party and establishment, but the links it eventually formed with the Conservatives and young Labour Party had their limits. This was because the Conservative Party contained too many opponents of female enfranchisement, while Labour was itself anxious for Liberal goodwill, and fearful of risking its independence or aggravating existing divisions within its ranks on women's suffrage by too close an alliance with the NUWSS. If the Liberals were uneasy about NUWSS strategy, the most the Labour Party conceded was a promise in 1912 to oppose any franchise Bill that failed to include women; while for all the con-stitutionalists' efforts to reach labour women and persuade them of the vote's class value, as late as 1911 a settlement worker could write about the leading figure in the NUWSS: 'Mrs. Fawcett is unknown to the working woman'. And neither of the national suffrage societies, any more than the specialist and splinter groups in the field, with perhaps 300,000 members between them by 1908, was able to demolish the objections to the female ballot, despite having several advantages over their American counterparts, according to the anti-suffragist Lord Bryce.[35]

The 'antis' were certainly vocal sooner in the United States than in Britain, sporadically mobilising liquor and textile interests that were not activated against female suffrage across the Atlantic. American suffragists had to combat the 'respectful deference' shown to women in their country and the strong aversion to politics of 'refined Americans', who did not want to see their women politically embroiled. There was opposition to 'doubling constituencies which are already enormous', while the leaders of the two great American political parties were 'unfriendly'. Conversely, 'a section of the Liberal party' and – in time – many Tories favoured granting women the vote.[36]

Yet Bryce underestimated the obstacles confronting British activists. None of the parties was willing to make women's suffrage a party issue. Even the Liberals, for all the encouraging noises from Cabinet ministers and MPs, had too many more pressing issues on the agenda when they returned to power in 1906 after ten years in opposition. The Party also faced hostility to female voting from the Lords (until neutralised by the Parliament Act of 1911) and the self-interested Irish Nationalists (described by Morgan as 'the equivalent of the American sectional vote', and holding the balance of power in the House of Commons from 1910). And it was led by a Prime Minister hostile to the women's cause, whom various interests wanted to retain in office. Militancy did not delay the coming of the vote: the circumstances conducive to political action would not be created until the war.[37] The 'antis' could not then delay it, although their existing 'tightness of association' had been translated into formal organisation in the Women's National Anti-Suffrage League (1908), which accepted male affiliates;

the Men's League for Opposing Women's Suffrage (1910); and the Scottish Women's National Anti-Suffrage League (1910). Despite sounding 'complacent, privileged and self-serving', and organising only when suffragism was receiving the serious attention of politicians, they helped to strengthen contemporary beliefs that women who demanded the ballot were an unrepresentative minority. Furthermore, with great skill – if some inconsistency – they constructed a case against female voting that was 'political, medical, psychological, sociological, imperialist, military and philanthropic'; one which employed 'the disabilities resulting from women's existing deprivation for the purpose of perpetuating it'.[38]

In a political climate more conducive to reform than for many years, new militant tactics had been encouraged on both sides of the Atlantic by 1914, although in the United States they stopped short of violence. They were, Evans suggests, born of frustration with making some, but not enough, progress; justified in terms of the Revolutionary tradition in America and the Irish precedent in Britain; and monitored in each country by police forces less draconian in their methods than those of continental Europe.[39] Mrs Stanton's sixth child, the suffragist Harriot Blatch, after paying tribute to her Revolutionary inheritance and the 'picturesque forms of propaganda' borrowed from 'the militants of England', concluded that 'American women had not won the vote through violence. To suggest [violent] militancy in the United States is singularly inept. In our country the final appeal is to the body of voters.' Relatively unembarrassed by the argument used by British 'antis' that partial suffrage having been granted, there was no need for the full suffrage, American activists, unlike their British counterparts, could by 1914 appeal to fully enfranchised women voters. And those voters were concentrated in the West, the region most hotly contested by the two major parties. This encouraging factor is the major reason why militancy on the suffragette pattern made a late and limited appearance in the United States.[40]

The gains made by American women in the suffrage movement were neither evenly spaced over time nor spread throughout the country as a whole. In 1890, a merger was achieved between NWSA and AWSA after three years of discussions, and the creation of the National American Woman Suffrage Association (NAWSA, or the National) officially closed the breach in suffragist ranks opened in 1869: the great days of the individual suffrage agitator were over. Wyoming was admitted to statehood in 1890 with its commitment to women's suffrage upheld, as was Utah in 1896; while the vote was won through referenda in Colorado in 1893 and Idaho in 1896. In these two victories, good organisation and fortunate political circumstances were of prime importance. The Colorado suffragists, short of money and workers and anxious to dispel charges that the vote was wanted by only a minority of women, gladly co-operated with women's clubs, the WCTU, Socialist groups and the Knights of Labor, all of whom had come to support votes for women, though they differed from each other in 'motivations and priorities'. The endorsement of female suffrage by the Populist government encouraged activists and the public alike, especially when the other parties, unwilling to yield any advantage to the politicians in power, likewise gave it their backing.[41] In Idaho, struggles for power between Republicans and Populists caused both to favour female enfranchisement, whereupon the Democrats and Silver Republicans came round. The state organisers were also fortunate that the temperance issue was in abeyance, and in commanding the services of several capable NAWSA representatives with whom they could get on, including Carrie Chapman Catt. Catt's skills and strengths as a self-confident and highly educated woman, with first-hand knowledge of the West, a most supportive husband, an awareness of what tactics had failed in the past, and the imagination to mobilise her volunteers on a precinct system which paralleled that of the political parties had already been enhanced by involvement in the Colorado campaign.[42]

These happy circumstances did not come together generally. Hence the good news of victories, spread by NAWSA and the *Woman's Journal*, was soured by tales of defeat in South Dakota, Kansas, Washington, California and Oregon, where Mrs Duniway was regarded as a domineering maverick, at odds with other western suffragists and hostile to the National.[43] The *Journal* observed that anti-suffragists were rarer in the West than the East.[44] But eastern anti-suffrage alliances were happy to send their envoys westward during the 1890s, and in California – where a large number of the inhabitants were foreign-born, wine production was an important industry, and there were more saloons in proportion to population than in any other state – home-grown 'antis' were active, galvanised by the liquor interests. Organised opposition – not present in Colorado and Utah – was sufficient to offset a fluid political situation, initial support from the Populists and Republicans, endorsement by the Prohibitionist, Socialist Labor and Single Tax parties, and efforts by the women themselves that were said to be 'the most thorough, the most systematic and the best organized' yet mounted for a suffrage amendment. It was enough to nullify the creation of a coalition for the vote similar to that formed in Colorado and comprising the suffragist associations, the WCTU, the 'colleges, the churches, the teachers' conventions, the philanthropic societies, the women's clubs, the educated and respectable people generally'.[45] California women, though disappointed, were not prepared to give up. But their emphasis on the opposition of the ignorant, and occasional expressions of sympathy during the campaign for an 'educated suffrage' (limited to those who were able to write their names and read the United States Constitution in English), indicate a strain of conservatism in the Californians' thinking that was curiously at odds with their sincere bid for support from the black community and the foreign-born.[46]

After the clamorous protest movements of the first half of the decade receded and the two-party system stabilised once more, a barren period set in for the feminists. It ended when a suffrage referendum was finally successful in Washington in 1910. Other victories followed in California in 1911, in Arizona, Kansas and Oregon in 1912, in Alaska in 1913, and in the same year in Illinois, where a law was enacted permitting 'women to vote for all national offices and virtually all municipal, county, town, and village offices', thus adding it for 'all practical purposes ... to the ranks of suffrage states'.[47] Suffrage legislation was also passed in Montana and Nevada in 1914. These gains were achieved partly because of local conditions and exertions. The development of Progressivism brought a renewed period of party political competition from which women could benefit, as in California, Washington and Oregon.[48] Suffragists in Washington, California and Illinois set out to activate sectors of the public known to favour the suffrage, ranging from labour to women's clubs. Socialist women emerged as key agitators in Kansas, Montana and Nevada.[49] And new tactics paid dividends – notably in California, where the prominence of temperance women once more assured vigorous opposition from the liquor industry.

In addition to renewing their efforts to promote suffrage sympathy and activities among targeted groups, the state suffragists got their message across to the voters generally by automobile tours, billboard advertisements, school projects, temporary offices in prominent locations to attract the passer-by, and mass meetings.[50] The breakthrough in California was particularly welcome because of its size and the known difficulty of carrying states with large populations and urban centres; that in Illinois for the same reasons, and because it was the first state captured east of the Mississippi. However, the 1912 defeats experienced by suffragists in Ohio, Michigan and Wisconsin, where the opposition was well orchestrated, suggested that there was still no winning state strategy outside the West; and as Myres concludes, the reasons for success there remain disputed, although much seems to have depended on the innovatory character of its politics, especially in the youngest states, and western men's willingness to act.[51]

Throughout its first fifteen years, the relationship between NAWSA and the state activists was an ambivalent one, and its record was mixed. The merger of the National and American associations was thought desirable in the interests of economy and image. It was made possible because it was felt that the National had become more conservative and narrower in its interests, and the International Council had apparently shown that the two factions could work together.[52] Yet even when the practical and vastly experienced Anthony became president of the new organisation in 1892, remaining a force in its deliberations until her death in 1906, NAWSA leaders disagreed about the way forward, state campaigns were simply helped as and when they came up, and no effective programme was mounted in Washington for a federal suffrage amendment once the association met there biennially instead of annually.[53] And although NAWSA aid was needed by hard-pressed state activists, they sometimes resented outside interference in their affairs.[54] Matters did improve after 1895 when Mrs Catt, running NAWSA's Organization Committee, fostered training, planning and the setting up of headquarters for state workers, and endeavoured to systematise the association's membership and financial arrangements. Unfortunately, having served as NAWSA president for four rather difficult years (1900–4), Catt took temporary leave from national suffrage endeavours for personal reasons, as well as to further the international movement which Americans had launched in 1888 and which, after additional International Councils in 1893 and 1902, had led in 1904 to the creation of the International Woman Suffrage Alliance (IWSA), whose affiliates included Great Britain. Her aim was 'to encourage existing foreign women's groups and to found others', and she attracted wide notice wherever she went.

Catt's rival and successor from 1904 to 1915, Dr Anna Shaw, was a woman of warm sympathies who, in the course of an inspired lecturing career, had made contact with suffragists throughout the country: 'during her tenure membership rose from 17,000 to 200,000'. But these assets were outweighed by her inability to secure NAWSA a permanent base before 1910, and her failure to expedite business, clarify strategy, or prevent embarrassingly public defections from the Association. To make matters worse, opposition elements were more in evidence than they had been, spreading from Massachusetts to New York in the 1890s and thereafter intermittently apparent in Alabama, Connecticut, Delaware, Georgia, Illinois, Iowa, Maine, Maryland, Michigan, Minnesota, New Hampshire, Nebraska, New Jersey, North Dakota, Ohio, Pennsylvania, Vermont, Virginia, Washington, DC, and Wisconsin. A National Association opposed to Woman Suffrage was not organised until 1911, in New York. It was flattering, but no real comfort to the suffragists, that their opponents were finally taking them seriously, since they had to expend a good deal of energy in rebutting their voluminous objections to women voting (one suffragist list contained 100 of those deployed), while trying to avoid giving them free publicity. They were also obliged to combat appearances by 'antis' during state campaigns, as well as before Congress and state legislatures.[55] And by 1914 it was obvious that even with a single national organisation, there was no one and no quick way to win the national suffrage in a federal political system.

Three more difficulties confronted NAWSA. First, it had to decide what to do about the South: the section which, if it voted *en bloc*, would need very little assistance to veto a women's suffrage amendment. Secondly, it needed to consider how best to publicise the consequences of women voting. And thirdly, the Association had to determine the most effective way of making the case for female enfranchisement. As Scott has pointed out, whereas suffrage efforts in the South before the 1890s were sustained largely by a few dedicated individuals, by 1896 there was 'some degree of suffrage organization . . . in every southern state', and every state could claim a few prominent male supporters. After 1910 new suffrage associations appeared, more recruits were won, greater headway was made in the press, and the activists were taking their case to the political centres of power. Much of this transformation had come about as a result of the labours of southern women in 'church societies, the WCTU, and the clubs', and because growing numbers of working women, as in other parts of America, had come 'to feel the vulnerability of their voteless state'.[56] But though the national suffrage convention was held in the South in 1895 and an organiser was sent to Mississippi in 1897, while southern suffragists followed national developments with interest and were represented on NAWSA's Official Board, the Association evolved no programme for the South. Rather, from 1903 it formally left each state to determine its own membership and policies.[57]

Given the uneasiness about outside activists shown elsewhere, NAWSA's position was wise in the short term for the region of the United States most jealous of its independence. (As it was, by 1913 a Southern States Woman Suffrage Conference had been established to oppose NAWSA's national suffrage amendment policy, and by 1914 the Shafroth–Palmer Amendment had been put to Congress, with backing from some members of the Association, in an attempt to meet objections to the national amendment by encouraging state referenda on women's suffrage.) None the less, the Association's stance could serve only to strengthen the tactical caution of southern women, who ran no campaigns to equal those of the West and East. That noted, it must be acknowledged that the southern suffragists were as broad in their objectives as feminists elsewhere in America. Thus the Mississippi Woman Suffrage Association, founded at Meridian in 1897, aimed 'to advance the industrial, education and legal rights of women, and to secure suffrage by appropriate State and National legislation'. It stressed that the franchise was claimed as a constitutional right; and even while it avowed that its members had 'no political ax to grind, and are simply working for the good of our homes, town and state', it pressed for child labour laws (very unpopular with southern employers), protective legislation for women, the raising of the age of consent, female involvement in school management, and institutional representation for women.[58]

The Mississippi Association was circumspect in reporting the relevance to women's suffrage of 'the Negro question', which was the major reason for northern reluctance to intervene in the South. While conservative southern politicians generally feared that female enfranchisement would make unwelcome voters of black women and reopen the question of black male voting rights, which were being drastically curtailed during this period, some thought that women's suffrage might act as 'one more bulwark of the maintenance of white supremacy'.[59] In Scott's judgement, this bulwark argument was only a minor part of the case made by southern suffragists,[60] which suggests that the Mississippians' circumspection was not unusual. But they did, just the same, interest themselves in obtaining *white* woman suffrage, while the fact that NAWSA could produce its formulation and that southern women could advance such an argument at all, in a movement with origins in abolitionism, is an indication of how far 'the Southern white viewpoint on the Negro question' had 'spread throughout the rest of the country'.[61]

Perhaps the best excuse for NAWSA's position was offered by Illinois suffragist Catharine Waugh McCulloch, in a 1907 letter to a Kentucky co-worker, Laura Clay. Seeing white women's suffrage in the South as being rather like other forms of partial suffrage, she felt that if Mississippi women obtained it, the gain would be 'helpful to all women and assist our earlier enfranchisement'. McCulloch was clear that to 'use the hatred of the black race to secure justice for white women, and to ... keep the whites dominant' was 'a poor motive for a noble deed. However, it is a war strategem', and if it was persisted in, she would not oppose it publicly but defend it as 'the entering of the thin end of the wedge'. The '"National officers of the North"' should not be expected to help this matter', McCulloch added, since they did not sympathise 'with the Southern man's prejudices'. Under the circumstances, it is easy to see why mainstream suffragism still failed to galvanise black women, now organising vigorously on their own account (see below, pp. 222–3). At the same time, the growing popularity of the demand for an educational qualification for the suffrage among white northern women proud of their 'Anglo-Saxon' heritage and fearful of the 'new immigrants' was hardly helpful to the efforts of some urban activists to recruit more vigorously among working people.[62]

On contemplating publicising the consequences of female voting, suffragists faced a quandary of a different moral and political order to that posed by race and state rights, but one that was none the less severe. We saw in Chapter 4 (p. 152 above) that some American feminists were ambivalent about partial suffrage, which they did not value as highly as the national suffrage and thought would probably complicate the case for it. Their fears proved to be well founded after 1890, when the number of women eligible to vote in municipal elections and on school, tax and bond questions continued to grow, while female voters continued to show very variable degrees of interest in going to the polls.

Anna Shaw had predicted in 1896 that the greatest political influence of her sex 'would be in local affairs'.[63] But events in the years that followed did not show women's influence mounting as she would have wished, and certainly did not suggest to sceptics the need for a further extension of female voting rights. Lucy Stone's husband, Henry Blackwell, was not alone in concluding: 'We have worse than wasted our strength in obtaining school suffrage and municipal suffrage which have become *obstacles* by arousing local jealousies and enmities.'[64] Shaw's view that the women's ballot would 'take all local and municipal affairs out of politics' was also unlikely to endear itself to the major parties, although anti-partisanship sentiment did gain ground as part of the Progressive era campaign to clean up the cities. Nor was political partisanship a matter on which suffragists agreed. Blackwell, for example, felt that for women's suffrage to succeed it needed 'a party behind it', and awareness of the importance of political action to secure both the vote and women's urban reform objectives led some activists to back the Progressives, Socialists and Prohibitionists, agitate for municipal suffrage, and form women's suffrage parties in New York and other key cities during the early twentieth century.[65]

Furthermore, whereas suffragists were happy to invite Congress to make 'an investigation of conditions in the equal suffrage States', and regularly quoted their own findings on the matter, anti-suffragists liked to argue that nothing much had changed in the states where women enjoyed full suffrage, and that politics were certainly not 'substantially purer'. Historians have subsequently suggested that the ballot was secured partly because this became apparent to calculating politicians, who ceased to fear the consequences.[66] Other factors are just as important in the eventual granting of votes to women, however, and if suffragists sometimes exaggerated what would follow from the suffrage, then so did their opponents. Of the two, the women had the better excuse, since they could hardly hope to mobilise supporters for an unpopular cause by arguing that victory would yield little, or that no newly enfranchised group had ever achieved much. Feminists, unlike other such groups, had to undertake a protracted fight for the vote; and they did at least try to show that their enfranchisement would not harm the family either abroad[67] or at home.

A report was commissioned by the Collegiate Equal Suffrage League of New York on conditions in Colorado in 1906, after twelve years of complete women's suffrage. Published in 1909, it concluded, following a detailed review of conditions in the state, that women were the chief gainers from the measure. While few were active in public life, thousands voted, and for them the ballot 'means a little broadening in the outlook'. The cultivation of intelligent public spirit had been achieved without loss of womanly qualities: indeed, families generally went to the polls together. Men and women were thought to differ, and most of their characteristics were allegedly too strongly marked to be subverted by the franchise, but comradeship between the sexes had increased since women obtained the vote. In California, suffragists claimed, 'women voters had supported good laws, and refrained from infringing masculine rights'; they 'had neither neglected their homes and families nor "become frenzied for office".'[68]

The problem involved in presenting the results of female enfranchisement parallel the difficulties activists experienced in expounding their case for the ballot. It has been argued that from the last decade of the nineteenth century, as America's Revolutionary heritage became more distant, while the egalitarianism of the young Republican Party faded and was discredited, the suffrage movement failed to find an ideology that adequately encompassed all features of female subordination.[69] Inasmuch as it found new arguments for changed times, it is seen as bowing to the affluent upper-class women who were finally entering the suffragist ranks.[70] And after 1900 it allegedly subordinated idealistic and individualistic claims for the vote to functional and socially conservative claims that had first gained ground, as we have noted, between 1870 and 1890. Thus female enfranchisement was sought not because political equality was just but because it was expedient: because it would enable women to extend their reforming mission on behalf of social purity, education, labour organisation, equal pay for equal work, children – even white supremacy.[71] In reappraising these judgements – primarily associated with O'Neill and Kraditor – Buechler usefully reminds us that the early movement 'advanced all manner of prosuffrage arguments', and concludes that more important than the shift to expediency arguments was the fact that all of the later suffragists' 'prosuffrage argumentation was motivated by an expediency principle and an instrumental orientation whose goal was to maintain support for the suffrage'. The danger of such a strategy, though it ultimately developed the 'cross-class, multiconstituency alliance' that was necessary for victory, was that the different elements of the coalition were united by their commitment to the vote rather than any 'larger feminist program'.[72]

What should also be stressed is that despite its careful references to 'government as housekeeping' and to the world as a larger home, in the eyes of considerable numbers of women, as well as men, suffragism still seemed a radical threat to the social order, particularly home and family: one that they found seriously unacceptable, though they themselves claimed an interest in female advancement. Janet Giele, explaining the greater attractiveness of temperance for many women in terms of its stress on personal issues and service to others, found that '31 per cent of the articles of the *Woman's Journal* between 1885 and 1915 dealt with the intellectual and civic equality of women; only 3 per cent of the pieces in the [WCTU's] *Union Signal* did.'[73] While some of the choices that leading suffragists made – notably over the race question – were a betrayal of old ideals, the women's movement in its first phase was likewise an elitist one, and there is some evidence to suggest that NAWSA's eastern leaders, whose ideas have been most closely scrutinised, were more prejudiced and conservative than activists (especially Socialists) in the Midwest and West, where immigrant and racial issues were somewhat less pressing.[74] Suffragists remained divided as to whether the sexes were more similar than different, and the best proposition they could advance was Wendell Phillips's formulation:

> Either woman is like a man, in which case she is inevitably entitled to all the rights and privileges that a man has; or she is unlike a man, in which case it is impossible that any man should speak for her.[75]

They were similarly divided about the best way to claim the vote.

Mary Putnam Jacobi held firmly to the view that the case for woman suffrage should not be based 'upon the capacity of women for missionary work', asking 'when before, in the history of the world, was a right to citizenship made to depend on readiness to reform the vices of other people?' The Tennessee lawyer and suffragist Sue Shelton White advocated female enfranchisement because she wanted the 'legal equality of women with men . . . she did not seek to remake or "purify" the man's world into a feminist image'. By contrast, her fellow-lawyer Catharine McCulloch asserted that the vote for women would bring 'new purity and justice to our government', that it would 'educate the ignorant, protect the poor, raise the fallen and defend the helpless'. McCulloch declared: 'No suffragist wants any part of man's kingdom. She only wants the whole of her own. She only wants to be free and enfranchised.' The Consumers' League president, Maud Nathan, declared: 'I believe in suffrage because it is just and because it is expedient.' Carrie Catt was convinced that women could 'simultaneously be rights-oriented individuals concerned with their self-development *and* devoted to the service of the larger community': she did not explain how.[76]

Until these differences were resolved, and at the risk of drawing close to the anti-suffragist position, many feminists by the beginning of the twentieth century probably chose to emphasise female distinctiveness: what the reformer and political activist Mary Dewson called women's 'more truly practical and idealistic nature'.[77] But since their individualistic concerns have been criticised as an irrelevance to working-class, non-white women, feminists should be given considerable credit for celebrating at this point, like contemporary Socialists, a feminine culture based on sorority, articulating the special needs of their sex and epitomised by service to others, which won the support of a large cross-section of contemporary women, including some black and working-class activists.[78]

Credit must similarly be given to the willingness of American suffragists, in the years before 1914, to see what they could learn from the tactics of their militant sisters in Britain. The eyes of the 'antis' were likewise often turned across the Atlantic. Feminist borrowings began in New York in 1907, when Harriot Blatch launched the Equality League of Self-Supporting Women (from 1910 the Women's Political Union). After twenty years in England, Mrs Blatch brought to the languishing suffrage activities of New York a knowledge of that country's 'orthodox and unorthodox suffrage societies', as well as insights drawn from Fabianism and her investigation of the condition of British working women. Determined to appeal to 'industrial women', make 'suffrage propaganda more dramatic' and render suffrage workers 'politically minded', the League committed itself to parades, open-air meetings, the use of working-class speakers at suffrage hearings before the state legislature, pickets, campaigns against hostile politicians, and a high-profile presence at elections. Its visiting speakers at big meetings included English suffragettes: the social worker Mrs Cobden-Sanderson, daughter of Richard Cobden, in 1907; two years later the WSPU leader, Mrs Emmeline Pankhurst, who was an old friend of Mrs Blatch; one of her daughters, Sylvia Pankhurst, in 1911; and Mrs Pankhurst again in 1913. As in Britain, such activities caused the press to take 'notice as if the few were a multitude', for which Mrs Blatch gave thanks, and the British suffragist Ray Strachey believed that the militant movement did 'nothing but good in other parts of the world', where 'the courage stood out undimmed by undignified incidents or political unwisdom'.[79] In fact, as militancy and American contacts with it grew, a rather complicated interaction became apparent.

Mrs Catt, during her travels for the IWSA, also became convinced from observing the British scene that new tactics were warranted in the United States. By 1908 she was clear that 'The English campaign stands out as the most remarkable ever conducted for woman suffrage', and she was to bear in mind 'the fight and spunk' she had observed on returning to New York suffragism in 1909, and to the NAWSA presidency in 1915. Prompted by the NUWSS, a charter member of the IWSA, the Alliance none the less declined to admit WSPU militants as full members of its 1906 congress, on the grounds that their methods were 'too unpredictable'. Opponents of the Pankhursts attended IWSA meetings in 1908 and 1909, while WSPU representatives stayed away. Hence it is not altogether surprising that in 1913 IWSA declined requests to support militancy on the grounds that it was neutral 'on all questions concerning national policy or tactics'.[80] Accounts of British militancy were given at the NAWSA conferences of 1908, 1910 and 1911, and initially excited some sympathy.[81] But the most important example of British militants' influence was the drive for a federal suffrage amendment undertaken from 1912 by NAWSA's Congressional Committee, which quickly spawned an independent body with this objective: the Congressional Union (1913).[82]

Central to its existence were two highly educated women: Alice Paul, a New Jersey Quaker who had worked in the settlement movement and with the English suffragettes between 1907 and 1910, and had experienced the rigours of gaol, a hunger-strike and force-feeding; and Lucy Burns, a New Yorker who had become a WSPU organiser in Edinburgh after she too had been 'caught in the maelstrom of the "militant" suffrage movement' while 'studying and doing social welfare work' in England.[83] Both women were committed to applying the lessons learned in 'the Pankhurst school of direct dramatic action', and Paul had soon spoken to various American suffrage groups 'on the lessons of the British movement', winning support from such influential feminists as the social reformer Jane Addams and the journalist and lawyer Crystal Eastman. The New Jersey activist was, however, 'coldly received by the suffrage leaders', except for Anna Shaw, who encouraged a grand suffrage parade in Washington as an alternative to a campaign of militancy, and because she 'had seen and taken part in such parades in London'.[84] The poorly policed parade, timed to coincide with Woodrow Wilson's inauguration as President, gave Paul and her cause welcome publicity and sympathy. It did not convert more conservative women to the merits of militancy; to the wisdom of an all-out campaign for the amendment; to the need for a competing national organisation; or to the Union's policy of holding the party in power responsible for failing to enact women's suffrage. This policy, copied from the British suffragettes, was held by NAWSA to be inapplicable to the American political system, 'since one party may conduct the national administration and the other control the Congress; one may control the entire national business, executive and legislative, and the other many State Legislatures'.[85]

While relations between like-minded and similarly organised British and American constitutional suffragists remained cordial, American ambivalence about adopting suffragette tactics is understandable. In the first place, they were associated with insurgents. For that reason alone militancy was regarded with suspicion by older leaders. In the second place, they were foreign. American moderates feared that when suffragettes visited the United States they raised funds that would otherwise have gone to native suffragists, and distracted attention 'from our issues and our methods'. And outside agitators, especially from the mother country, had always been suspect to those Americans who had not courted their presence. Even the suffragists who borrowed from the British and actually found that they made money when the militants came to speak did not make a major point of their debt outside suffrage circles. Indeed, they denied that Americans had adopted the organisation or violence of the suffragettes, while taking care to point out that militants across the Atlantic were provoked by a vacillating and false government which was 'extremely lenient to men who incite to violence'. It was further stressed that they had not taken human life, and that property had been destroyed during the American Revolution.[86] Since militancy drew hostile comment from American 'antis' in politics and the press, sympathisers understandably might not feel able to 'sanction openly such proceedings'.[87] In the third place, activists who deplored the British treatment of the suffragettes liked to think that their menfolk were less barbarous and might yield the vote without resorting to extremes. As one commentator put it, 'under no circumstances' would they 'treat women with the lack of consideration which, being carried even to extreme brutality, has characterized the conduct of Englishmen towards English women in this struggle for the vote'.[88] A similar reaction was recorded by the American sculptor and reformer Alice Morgan Wright, who worked with the English militants, served two months in Holloway prison in 1912, and was bombarded by the American press with requests to relate her experiences. She asserted that the suffragettes were harshly treated as common criminals, in spite of the moderate amount of property they had destroyed, with honourable motives, and that this situation was 'found to be so nearly unbelievable in the States'. (Miss Wright could not help adding that she knew of no attempt by the United States Embassy in London to secure her release, and had been led to believe 'that it pays its sole attention to the protection of Americans who enjoy the vote'.)[89]

A fourth and vital reason – already touched on – for Anglo–American differences with regard to militancy was that because of western success, militancy was thought to be unnecessary. And we have already seen that western suffragists were proud of managing their own affairs free from eastern, let alone foreign, influences. During the winning 1911 campaign in California, suffragists showed 'new energy and political awareness'[90] but disliked, as the local press did, 'the militant attitude of the suffragettes', aspiring instead to 'teach men better ways and not to follow their methods'. This attitude can be found among suffragists in other parts of America, and is predictable in the light of the contemporary stress on women's superior morality.[91] There was a feeling (shared by British moderates) that the militancy of British activists somehow belittled the struggle:

> the women of America should stand for bigger things ... in a different sort of campaign than one strictly for OUR RIGHTS. ... We, the women of America should stand for the WHOLE PEOPLE ... HAVE A MOTHERLY CARE FOR ALL.[92]

At this point suffragists and 'antis' coincide, for feminism's opponents – predictably – saw militancy as a negation of everything they revered in women. Equally predictably, the historian's careful distinctions between degrees of militancy were not mentioned. It was simply equated with violence, lawlessness and radicalism, and presented as elitist: taken up as a fad by 'a set of women who

~

are always looking for "some new thing", especially anything approved by English social leaders'. It was dismissed as counterproductive. The defeat of women's suffrage in Michigan in 1912 was accordingly explained as a reaction by men against 'the continual spectacle of British Sabotage', although opponents did not fear that Michigan women 'would become rioters and arsonists and vengeful public nuisances in imitation of their misguided, law-breaking sisters across the ocean'.[93] And it was also offensive to anti-suffragists who recoiled from enthusiasm and were suspicious of those who would go to the stake for the vote, having in mind a martyr's crown. 'I wish I could feel so about any political measure', was the cool judgement of the prominent journalist Ida Tarbell.[94]

In sum, it is apparent that their stronger cult of domesticity and greater confidence in their country's democratic polity inclined American suffragists to cling to ladylike tactics for longer than their British sisters. In economic matters, by contrast, they were more willing than they had been to learn from Victorian activists. After all, the British had sustained the lead in this aspect of feminism since the 1850s, and by the later nineteenth century American reformers were ready to recognise the challenges posed by their country's increased acquaintance with industrial, urban and class problems.

II. Economic issues

In certain respects, of course, the difficulties facing women who were active in labour affairs were identical on each side of the Atlantic. In Britain and America alike, notions about gender had played a central role in the industrialisation process and class formation, to the detriment of women. The politicisation of the labour movement in both countries was of recent date. Its strength was not evenly spread geographically for either men or women (the textile industries of the North of England were the main strongholds of British female unionism). And it was dominated by men who put the class struggle before the sex struggle, despite evidence that women unionists were capable of solidarity. British labour men, like their American brothers, had no intention of altering their priorities at a time when Socialism was making serious gains; although on both sides of the Atlantic – and unlike the major parties – Socialists committed themselves to the civic and political equality of women. Yet within the more deeply rooted British labour movement, women were able to sustain a greater variety of cross-class groups dedicated to advancing their interests. Moreover, the period of co-operative ventures between middle- and working-class women, begun sooner than in the United States, came to an end sooner, as British labour women found the confidence and means to stand alone. Their associations included the Women's Labour League (WLL, 1906; the first Scottish branch was established in 1908), the Women's Co-operative Guild (WCG), the Women's Trade Union League (WTUL), the National Federation of Women Workers (NFWW,

1906–20), and the Women's Industrial Council (1894). For middle-class activists, they provided the opportunity to relieve and right the oppressions endured by less fortunate 'sister women'; for those of the working class, there was the opportunity to become 'a fighter'.[95]

The WLL, founded two years before the Woman's National Committee of the Socialist Party of America, was headed by Margaret MacDonald, the middle-class wife of a leading Labour politician, Ramsay MacDonald, and by Mrs Mary Macpherson. A London journalist and honorary secretary of the Railway Women's Guild, Macpherson was soon to be replaced as the League's secretary by Mrs Mary Middleton, a miner's daughter who had been in domestic service before her marriage. The League's aim was to 'work for Independent Labour Representation in connection with the Labour Party and to obtain direct Labour representation of women in Parliament and on all local bodies'. It welcomed the poor and the prosperous, wage earners and professional women, the wives and daughters of Socialists and trade unionists, and women 'whose chief work is the care of their homes and families'. Liaising with the female trade unions and admitted to membership of the Labour Party in 1909, the League had 70 branches by 1910, and was active internationally.[96]

In seeking to educate its members 'on political and social questions, awaken the interests of working women in their own neighbourhood, and ... improve their social and industrial conditions',[97] the WLL, as Hollis remarks, interlocked with the WCG and the WTUL, operating through 'meetings, discussions, leafleting, petitioning, canvassing, and lobbying'. Its activities included protesting against sweated labour, agitating for universal higher education, pressing local authorities to implement permissive government social welfare legislation, opening a baby clinic in London, and successfully working for Treasury funds to be made available for such clinics. Campaigning for women jurors, magistrates and local government members was another area of interest, though in a period of growing Tory strength, few Labour women gained political office.[98] League members also worked hard for women's enfranchisement, keeping the issue before the Labour Party, organising meetings, resolutions, deputations, letters and suffrage literature, and co-operating with the WCG, the WTUL and the constitutional suffragists. The question of militancy disturbed the League, and its commitment to adult suffrage and aversion to suffragette tactics meant that it lost to the WSPU individuals who gave priority to women's enfranchisement. The militant suffragist Charlotte Despard of the Women's Freedom League, whose reform interests included child welfare and the founding of workingmen's clubs, meanwhile stayed on as a provoking presence within the WLL.[99] But if this split was an irritant, it was harmless compared with the splits which rent the WSPU.

The Women's Trade Union League, which had been consolidated under the leadership of Lady Dilke, was encouraged from the 1890s by the existence of the ILP and the 'new unionism', aimed at unskilled and low-paid workers. It none the less had to grapple with the suspicion of male unionists, the apathy of poor women workers, the hostility of employers, the high number of female home workers and the low number of female unionists. Women comprised only 7.69 per cent of all union members in 1900, though 'the percentage growth of women unionists was considerably greater than that of men' between 1900 and 1914.[100] The WTUL was dominated after 1903 by its Scottish secretary, Mary MacArthur. Middle-class in origin, Miss MacArthur was an inspirational figure who had embraced unionism and Socialism, and whose pride in what the League had already achieved did not prevent her from re-evaluating its work. After three years of travelling the country, encouraging unions with women members, fostering the formation of new women's societies, and attracting 12,000 new recruits for the WTUL, she concluded that a more rigorously managed national organisation was necessary if gains made during crises were to be sustained, and real progress was to be made. The result was the formation of the National Federation of Women Workers, which was active in England and Scotland, and modelled on 'the new general unions of unskilled workers', with 'central funds and local branches fully under central control'. Open to all women who were in unorganised trades or excluded from their relevant unions, the Federation had recruited 2,000 members in 17 branches in six months.[101]

In the years that followed, the American WTUL (1903) several times contemplated the establishment of a similar federation, but concluded that such an association would probably not be granted a charter by the AFL, and that the leagues could do the work mapped out for the Federation. The AFL opposed the possible alternative – to grant women federal union charters giving them direct affiliation to the organisation – on the grounds that this would infringe the jurisdiction of its member internationals. As a result of the AFL's attitude, the American WTUL continued in existence for nearly thirty years longer than its British counterpart, which ceased to exist in 1921.[102] Before winding up, the WTUL, together with the NFWW, continued to campaign for protective legislation; to support the pressure against sweated labour that resulted in the setting of statutory minimum wages through Trade Boards (1909); to employ salaried working-class organisers; to assist strikes by women for better conditions (as in 1911); and to secure consideration for women's interests in the National Insurance Act 1911. The League also worked with other women's groups which had comparable objectives – a policy which brought it into contact and conflict with radical northern suffragists, who 'opposed all legislation that put any restrictions upon women's right to work', favoured women's rather than adult suffrage, and were more staunchly in favour of women-only unions than the WTUL had come to be by the 1890s.[103]

Speaking at the second biennial conference of the American WTUL in 1909, and aware of how that body had looked to Britain for precedents when seeking to devise benefits for its members,[104] MacArthur expressed her pride in its leading position in the legislative protection of workers:

> I don't think I would say this in my own country, but I feel free to say here that I do believe England has led the way in industrial legislation. . . . I don't think England

quite realizes what has been done. It is simply a revolution. It means revolution in our industries.[105]

That may have been true, but the gains had been resisted all the way by women activists of a different disposition. The Factory Acts of 1891, 1895 and 1901 had been weakened as a result of their representations, so Rubinstein observes, with the same broad and unfortunate division that we have already noted (see above, p. 176) persisting between protectionists associated with organised labour and equal rights feminists. The latter either opposed all restrictions or repudiated laws which affected only women, thereby reducing them to the level of children and lowering the market value of their labour in the employment field, where men were already dominant and machines encroaching. Yet as the example of the northern suffragists makes plain, this line-up of forces was not immutable.[106]

The Women's Industrial Council managed to avoid damaging engagement with the controversies of its time. It stayed aloof from the actual organisation of unions, maintained a bipartisan stance and, while endorsing the case for legal change, concentrated on gathering and disseminating information about the conditions of working women and children that might be valuable to others.[107] Less comfortably placed, the Women's Co-operative Guild, like the WTUL, had to consider the sensibilities of men within its parent movement, but became less inhibited by them than the League was once it decided to work through unions with women members, and not just through women-only unions. Both bodies, Liddington and Norris observe, were 'essentially practical organizations without an official line on political questions', so that they 'could accommodate the competing claims of feminism and socialism more easily than could the I.L.P. or Labour Representation Committee'.

By the 1890s the Guild was increasingly concerned with social reform, and by the opening years of the twentieth century it had a membership of around 14,000 to represent.[108] In advocating female suffrage, it stressed what women could do with the suffrage 'for the good of the community, as well as in the name of the individual'. It aided women willing to stand for local government office, supported suffrage lectures, statements and petitions, pushed the Labour Party to take a firmer stand on the matter, and skirted disruptive fights over the respective merits of adult and female suffrage. The WCG also pressed for – and won by 1912 – a minimum wage scale for women employed by the Co-operative Wholesale Society. It successfully agitated for the mother's control of maternity benefits, instituted by the National Insurance Act of 1911. And it contributed to the 1909–12 inquiry into divorce law reform; arguing for equality before the law and cheaper divorce, but combining agreement 'on the basic issues of divorce law reform ... with a commitment to family stability'. Divorce reform, a question long played down by prudent feminists, divided the Guild. Notwithstanding its balanced policy, protests against change were strongly expressed by Catholic members, and conflict ensued with the more cautious Co-operative Union, which gave the Guild a grant. However, the WCG stood firm, and the quarrel was contained. Meanwhile, its counterpart north of the border, the Scottish Co-operative Women's Guild (1892), underwent a similar process of radicalisation and allied itself firmly with the Labour Party.[109]

The Guild and comparable groups encountered real difficulties with their middle-class allies, and within the broader labour movement. They might consequently be tempted to deny their attachment to the women's rights that male Socialists, particularly, feared as bourgeois reformism. But British organisations like the Guild, the WTUL, the WLL and the NFWW demonstrated more convincingly than the American WTUL and Woman's National Committee that there was no inevitable conflict between Socialism and the women's movement: between affluent and working women.[110]

In the United States, women from every background were adversely affected by the great depression of 1893–7, which undermined businesses and labour organisations alike. Happily it was followed by an expansion of the female wage-earning population in every sector of the economy, with especially significant gains being made in 'steam laundries, retail sales, food processing, and almost all areas of light manufacturing'.[111] Trade-union membership also began to climb again, but women's union prospects remained poor. As Kessler-Harris maintains, this was not simply because women lacked interest in collective action. Whereas some were deterred by the time involved and the nature of union meetings, other women, notably in the International Ladies' Garment Workers' Union (ILGWU), 'were devoted and successful union members'. Unlike their English sisters, who were thought to decline work 'which is arbitrarily called men's work', American women were said to be willing to 'work at whatever trade they can, and at any part of a given trade where they can obtain a foothold'.

A familiar host of barriers to female involvement nevertheless remained, fortified by the organisational challenges attendant on mass immigration. Employers continued to profit from low-paid women workers, to resist and penalise their unionisation, and to agree with labouring men that woman's primary role was as a homemaker. While resenting the job competition and threat to male pay levels posed by women, unionists alternately fought to exclude them from paid work, and to minimise their threat by organising female wage earners to suit male interests. The AFL remained suspicious of unskilled workers generally and women in particular; having appointed its first woman organiser for a period of five months in 1892, it did not replace her until 1908. The number of female organisers then gradually increased, but they were scarcely in a position to realise the Federation's official policy of equal pay for equal work.[112]

In this dispiriting context, the founding of the Women's Trade Union League (WTUL) in Boston in 1903 offered the hope of change. Open to wage and non-wage earners, Socialists and middle-class reformers, the League aimed to train women as labour leaders, help them in existing unions, and promote the formation of new ones. As far as the last objective is concerned, success proved elusive. Fortunately, the League was able to make a real impact during strikes, involving itself in organising and picketing, publicity, fund-raising and support for the striking workers: and being repaid in turn by increased support. By 1911, the WTUL's branches had grown in number from 3 to 11; it had gradually strengthened its own organisation, investigated working conditions, issued guides for local leagues battling for equal pay for equal work, the eight-hour day and a living wage, and put out a monthly journal. It endeavoured to establish good relations with the AFL, and enjoyed at least a degree of success. By the autumn of 1909 the WTUL was directly affiliated with labour associations in eight different states, and visiting unionists, notably those from Britain, were made welcome. And the direct model for the organisation was the British Women's Trade Union League.[113]

Able working-class unionists and Socialists such as Pauline Newman, Leonora O'Reilly and Rose Schneiderman achieved prominence through the American League, but the presidency did not go to a working-class woman until 1921. The involvement of women from very different backgrounds in a joint movement created problems for all concerned, as such ventures generally had in the past and as the co-operation of men and women – for example, in the suffrage campaign – often did. These problems were only latent during the strike of shirtwaist makers which started at the Leiserson and Triangle Waist Companies in September 1909, spread to other garment shops by November, lasted until February 1910, and was felt by participants to be 'probably the greatest struggle for unionism among women the world has ever seen'. Although the strike secured mixed results according to shop, it boosted the ILGWU and fostered a spirit of solidarity among the workers, with single strikers helping those who had families and all proving willing to take on leadership roles when necessary. In the process, middle- and upper-class women learned how their words and money could help – Wellesley College students sent $1,000 to aid the strike – and when college-educated League members arrested for picketing were discharged in a sycophantic way, such treatment, 'far from conciliating the ladies ... redoubled their efforts on behalf of their humbler sisters and had the effect of bringing to the attention of the newspapers the conditions that obtained in the strike and also influencing many more girls to join the union'. As the language of this League pamphlet suggests, however, if privileged women scorned unfair class advantage, they found it difficult to jettison feelings of class superiority.[114]

League women were active once more in the 1910–11 strike of Chicago male and female garment workers, which, like the struggle in Philadelphia and New York, ended in a disappointing settlement; indeed, with concessions in only a single shop. WTUL contributions included the drawing up of a careful plan of action, welding together a vary varied labour force, investigating worker grievances (sexual harassment was mentioned in addition to overwork, underpayment and unfair exactions), explaining them to the city's women and the larger public, raising money for food, and administering relief. Prominent local women again tried to use their social influence on behalf of the strikers, while members of the women's and suffrage clubs endorsed the strike and sent assistance. Yet in doing so they confirmed the view of women's primary home role that was employed, to their disadvantage, against female unionists:

> This was indeed a new voice, the woman's voice, in industrial disputes. These women knew practically nothing of what the strike was about; many came from small towns and rural communities. They were sheltered women, home women, unacquainted with the actual conditions of the working world, but they said: 'Simply because we are mothers, because we are home folks, because we are women, we wish to protest against conditions which seem to make motherhood a sorrow, childhood bitter, and the maintenance of a decent home a growing impossibility. For centuries we have been silent about these matters, but we are finding ourselves. You men, who have so long run the world and made its laws without us, you are going to listen in the future to what we, the mothers of the race, have to say about the world in which we and our children live.'

After the strikes had failed to yield the hoped-for results, the League concentrated on organising 'American' (that is, primarily English-speaking and skilled) workers, a policy which aggravated its internal divisions.[115]

The letters of Pauline Newman, the first woman organiser for the ILGWU, bring out remarkably vividly the tensions encountered by an intelligent and ambitious working-class woman in union activities and in a mixed organisation like the WTUL. She arrived in the United States from Lithuania in 1901, and joined members of her family already settled in the Lower East Side of New York. Having acquired some education through attending her father's Talmud class, reading, and membership of the Socialist Literary Society, Newman was employed by brush and cigarette factories as well as by the Triangle Shirtwaist Company (1901–9). She then left the company to work for the ILGWU, travelling between 1911 and 1918 primarily in the Midwest, talking to labour and women's groups, organising and raising money for strikers, while at the same time involving herself in the New York branch of the WTUL and in the Socialist Party, for which she spoke and stood as a candidate in 1908.[116] Like early-nineteenth-century itinerant women agitators – and unlike the later well-supported lecturers for women's suffrage – Newman lacked strong support networks when she was in the field. As a result, she led a *'very interesting'* but 'at the same time a very lonely life. Always alone. Except when you are out doing your work. . . . I am just thrown about like a wave. From one city to another. When will it end?' Like all travellers, Newman got tired and wished she had a place 'where I could rest and do things I desire most'. The exacting nature of her main tasks made it hard for her to improve her English and cultural life, branch out into writing, sustain warm personal relationships, and help the girls she encountered with leisure outings. In fact her 'enormous [*sic*] amount of energy and ambition to rise in this "wonderful" world of ours – is all that keeps me going as I do'. But Newman's chief problems stemmed from the nature of the American labour scene; from being a woman in a man's world; and from being proudly working-class in a cross-class endeavour: as she acknowledged, 'to be the fighter, is more natural to me than to be the diplomat, after all'.[117]

Striving to show female operatives 'the importance of being within the organization', Newman recognised the need to retain their loyalty by constant innovation and agitation. If pioneering was hard, it had to be persisted in 'whether you get results or not', and she struggled with Jewish–Gentile differences, reactionary employers and inadequate local leaders. As a case in point, when she was helping to direct the corsetmakers' strike in Kalamazoo, Michigan, during 1912, Newman criticised the leadership for trying to conduct a strike with a mere fraction of the workforce out, omitting the question of wages, and condemning the company and its morals. In the face of an employer who was a hundred years behind the times and would respond only to being hurt financially, immoral conditions were a side issue, she felt, which 'can be done away with by educating the girls, instead of attacking the company'. It helped her cause that unionists now realised 'that women can do more effective work, than men, especially where girls are involved'. It irked her that the AFL disparaged the Socialist Party, and that the middle-class activists frequently would not give their working-class sisters enough freedom of action. The St Louis branch of the WTUL won Newman's warm praise for its 'good and wonderful' efforts as 'a strictly working class organization; in spirit as well as in action'. Conversely, she felt strongly that Mrs Margaret Dreier Robins, the League's wealthy national president from 1907 to 1921, could dominate it unduly:

> because one person is giving the money. Mrs. Robins means well I am sure, but in the end it is bound to suffer. She does not give a chance [to] the girls to use their brains, she does not want them to think, but wants them to agree with everything she does. And unfortunately they do; they have to, she pays their salaries. And to work for the Chicago League is a sinche, you do not have to know any thing and your work is appreciated. A good many organizations here look at them as on a philontrophic [sic] bunch. They do mingle too much with the other side. The girls here are not imbred with the spirit of Unionism - but philontrophy [sic].

Newman's objection to 'the "cultured" ladies' in the women's movement was that however sincere they might be, 'their views are narrow, and their knowledge of social conditions limited'. In view of her feelings, it is not surprising to find the exclamation 'My work is horrible! The keeping sweet all the time and pleading for aid from the "dear ladies" and the ministers is simply sickening.'[118]

Strictures like Newman's are understandable, and bear witness to the existence of a working women's consciousness, charted by Eisenstein, that accepted part of the Victorian definition of womanhood and the feminists' demand for the suffrage, but found in the comradeship of union organisation the confidence to question that definition in terms of their own experience. Understandably, such grumbles were damaging when they surfaced publicly. If women did not work together regardless of class, then the women's movement could be condemned as bourgeois, and divisions among reformers were always seized upon with pleasure by their opponents, who demanded from them a unity they did not require from themselves.

Even with the well-publicised collaboration of women from all classes in the WTUL, and its espousal of policies ostensibly favoured by the AFL, female union membership grew very slowly: from 3.3 per cent of the women employed in industry in 1900 to 6.6 per cent in 1920, with a fall to as low as 1.5 per cent in 1910, largely reversed by the activities among female garment workers just outlined.[119] Yet this very collaboration with the AFL by middle-class WTUL women, their prominence in the League, and their alleged failure to give due acknowledgement to Socialist allies during the strikes of 1909, alienated a Socialist Party dismayed that the strikes brought no sustained increase in party members. The result was the denunciation of bourgeois WTUL campaigners in a fictionalised *Diary of a Shirtwaist Striker*, published in 1910, and criticisms in the Socialist press.[120] To the extent that the WTUL was grudging, it was foolish, for as Buhle points out, Socialists had played a vital part in the garment workers' strikes: enrolling union members, raising money, addressing meetings, publicising events, rallying the local community and helping with relief. What is more, female activists like Newman, Schneiderman and O'Reilly were particularly important to the Party's effort during the strikes, because though it no longer opposed women's wage labour, it had 'neither altered its political priorities nor directed its energies towards this newly recognised sector'.[121]

While the events of 1909–11 'prompted Socialists to reaffirm their faith in working women', they made less headway in the textile strikes of 1912–13, in communities where the Party was not securely rooted, the unions were less strong, the AFL was unhelpful, and the Industrial Workers of the World assumed a leadership role. Hostilities developed between the Socialists and the IWW, and the subsequent thrust of female unionism was blunted by the quarrel, in which women activists took sides, as well as by worsening economic conditions in 1913.[122] The sensitivity of the Socialist Party has to be understood in the context of the history of the movement, and of American radicalism generally since the 1890s.

When the Socialist Party of America was created in 1901, few women were present and women's 'equal civil and political rights', though included in its platform, were not debated. For some time, therefore, Socialist women in small towns and the industrial cities organised independent clubs, with those in the small communities of the Midwest, Plains states and far West preaching the power of womanhood and a brand of Christian Socialism reminiscent of Populism. Populism, the political movement that had grown out of the Farmers' Alliances, gave women opportunities to speak, write and serve as local officials, and they seized the chance to make the case for equal pay, enfranchisement and the regenerative power of female qualities beyond the home, while cementing contacts with other women reformers, including temperance advocates and suffragists. But the higher levels of policy in this political endeavour were controlled by men, and when the Socialist clubs emerged in the early twentieth century – doing well in former Populist strongholds and attracting some ex-Populists – it is understandable that many of their older members, as Buhle has shown, preferred to operate outside the Socialist Party itself, being wary of the consequences 'of weak commitments to women's emancipation'.[123]

The city clubs, attracting more diverse supporters and younger women than their small-town counterparts, were more committed to working within the Party; and theirs was the way of the future. In 1908, responding in part to the example of German female Socialists and direction from the Second International, the Party set out to enhance its appeal to women and established a Woman's National Committee to 'care for and manage the work of organization' among them.[124] It attracted an able staff, and conducted a recruitment and educational programme that proved highly successful. By 1912 an estimated 10 to 15 per cent of party members were women, and they 'served as secretaries of six state organizations and 158 locals'; in addition, 'sixteen states had appointed special correspondents to coordinate women's activities'.[125] However, if those opposed to organisational autonomy for female Socialists had formally prevailed, disputes about the role of gender continued within the Party as women activists pursued their interest in unionisation, suffrage and other reforms which concerned women regardless of class.[126] The creation in 1912 of the Progressive Party, which attracted a few Socialist defectors and might, it was feared, draw in women voters, provided another reason for Socialist suspicion of bourgeois reformers.[127] For all their valiant suffrage, union and recruitment efforts in the name of Socialism, Pauline Newman painted a dispiriting picture of her fellow-comrades in 1912, and her judgement may show why the political mobilisation of Progressives was regarded with dismay:

> As to the women of the Socialist movement, ... with the exception of New York, some in Chicago, and one or two, in other cities, they are all still timid, and have no idea of how to do work. This you know, is my fourteenth State, and I can speak from personal observation. I am really discouraged about the women Comrades. Of course we can easily find a reason for their ignorance, but at the same time, I expected to find them more alive in the west, but they are not.[128]

Just as the Socialists' differences with the WTUL were one factor in their troubled effort to integrate sex questions into a class movement, so the WTUL, as it attempted to do the same, struggled to fashion a harmonious relationship with suffragists, settlement house workers and other women reformers, as well as with the Socialists. The question of how to pursue women's enfranchisement (to which AFL was pledged from 1890 and the League from 1907) was resolved by the formation of affiliated suffrage leagues of working women. The question of protective legislation was fraught with more difficulties, since there was fiercer disagreement in the United States than in Britain about how far the state was entitled to interfere with the rights of the individual.

Since the late nineteenth century, pressured by women and other reformers, states had been using their 'police power' to pass protective labour legislation. By 1908, note Sachs and Wilson, there were nineteen laws either fixing maximum hours or prohibiting night work for women. But the variable impact of protective laws became a matter for debate. Anti-sweating laws, for example, benefited women factory workers and children released for schooling, but not the displaced female home and sweatshop workers. And opinion varied about whether protection should be gender-specific. In 1905, in Lochner v. New York, an uneasy Supreme Court rejected a ten-hour law for bakery workers because it violated their 'liberty of contract' to accept the terms they chose 'in regard to their means of livelihood'. However, in 1908, in Muller v. Oregon, the Court approved a ten-hour law, accepting that states could infringe woman's individual rights because her 'physical structure', 'maternal function' and responsibility for the 'well-being of the race' put her 'in a class by herself'. After the 1908 decision, the WTUL and its branches made clear their support for protective labour legislation, giving it priority from 1912; by 1914, 27 states had adopted such legislation in some form. Progress was none the less uneven as a result of hostile economic and judicial interests, and the American lack of experience in this area; and by 1914 three dangers were emerging. First, there was a risk that legal protection might be used by the unions to restrict female prospects. Secondly, there was a possibility that it could be regarded as an alternative to union protection, which was still harder to realise. And thirdly, there was a likelihood that some feminists, despite their emphasis upon the special needs of women and children, would see legislative protection as an unacceptable form of paternalism.[129].

III. Female reform and the challenge to its ideology

If the concept of separate spheres was under strong challenge in the later nineteenth century from women's efforts to enter the supposedly masculine world of industry, so the boundaries between public and private life were increasingly blurred not only by suffragists but by women determined to shape as well as be shaped by state policies. Throughout the nineteenth century women had sought to assert their own influence and interests by involvement in mainstream reform movements, and it seems entirely proper to include these activities in a study of the women's movements. Suffragists based their case for the vote in part upon the reforms they could achieve with it, while female reform endeavours frequently benefited all women and certainly emancipated the participating women in a variety of ways. In the United States, from the late nineteenth century, female reformers were especially important in two national protest movements. During the early 1890s they participated in the alliance of temperance advocates, Populists, Socialists, Nationalists and suffragists which tried to moderate the excesses of the Gilded Age and bring about a co-operative commonwealth. After Depression struck and Populism disintegrated, the next grand coalition of reformers did not emerge until the Progressive era of 1900–17, when concerned citizens, drawn primarily from the middle class, reappraised the practical problems created by the unchecked growth of industry, railroads and banking; large-scale immigration; rapid urban growth; and the failure of political institutions to keep pace with economic change. Coming together in a movement which was no more coherent or regionally uniform than Populism but certainly more respectable and optimistic, intellectuals, journalists, educators, exponents of the social gospel, professionals, businessmen, farmers, labourers, social workers, and women of all kinds aimed, like the Populists, to rejuvenate democracy and rectify economic injustice. Yet in the process they placed a distinctive emphasis upon the importance of honest, efficient and responsive government, the control of natural resources, the regulation of business, and the humanising of the industrial environment in order to achieve social justice for the masses.

American women were consolidating and adding to their own vehicles and programmes for reform during the 1890s: active in settlement houses, clubs and consumer leagues, in the WCTU and social purity groups. Accordingly, when reform again became a national concern around 1900, they were able to supply experienced personnel for its campaigns and 'much of its ideological direction': Progressivism is now acknowledged as having applied to 'society moral issues matured in women's domain'. Through these organisations, and influenced by the first university-trained female social scientists, women reformers whom O'Neill has termed social feminists worked for their economic emancipation, better education and social services generally, the legal protection of all workers (but particularly women and children), and government that was more responsive to the needs of ordinary people (particularly at the local level).[130] Determined to assert women's influence in the world, they often endorsed the suffrage, even as suffrage societies endorsed reformist goals. Female cross-class alliances on both sides of the Atlantic, considered separately in this chapter, were an integral part of the women's reform coalition which, like Progressivism, was at once both forward-looking and conservative.

In Britain, where the 1890s saw no divisive climax of nineteenth-century reform comparable to that focused on Populism, women also continued to work for economic, educational, moral and political gains, strengthening their already marked commitment to community service and responding to changing views of poverty. And during the years before 1914, as politicians evolved social policies in response to the challenges posed by the rise of Labour, imperial tensions and the threat of powerful economic competitors abroad, feminists of various political persuasions contributed vitally to the adoption of measures concerned with the welfare of women and children. These measures, though they did not meet all their demands, drew upon the greater willingness of British governments to regulate the lives of their citizens, and were an important part of the foundations of the welfare state. Yet because British women were mobilised through the political parties in a way that had no parallel in America, their independent input into legislative reform is sometimes harder to isolate than the contributions of separately organised Progressive women.[131]

(i) *Settlement houses and clubs*

The settlement house movement began in England with the setting up of Toynbee Hall in London's East End in 1884. It represented a long-established Christian commitment to the achievement of economic change and social justice, and an immediate dissatisfaction with the existing machinery for doing good.[132] Located in the working-class districts of London and other cities, settlements attracted as residents well-educated and idealistic members of the middle class who believed that personal service, not the giving of money, was the only real charity.[133] They aimed, theoretically, to 'make friends with the neighbourhood – to become part of its common life; to associate with the people on equal terms, without either patronage on the one side or subserviency on the other'.[134] Although the movement was initiated by men, it quickly attracted primarily single women who were anxious to prove their fitness for the vote, and to put their education to good use. Such women craved an exciting challenge, congenial company and social freedom. They were accustomed to regard social service as their special preserve, and were needed in ever greater numbers with the 'increasing bureaucratization of the social services'. The first female settlement was inaugurated in 1887 in Southwark by college women from Oxford and Cambridge, subsequently aided by members of London University. Other communities for women in and outside London soon followed,[135] sometimes with a religious connection: after all, the Anglican sisterhoods formed from the 1840s onwards were a successful precedent for the new houses,[136] and city missions run by the churches were well established on both sides of the Atlantic.

Innovative in form, the settlement houses were in some ways conservative in practice, upholding middle-class values and giving local help 'to existing organisations, whether the parish or the special society'. Nor did they vary greatly between themselves:

> Nearly all take part in school management, in boys' and girls' clubs, in the Children's Country Holiday Fund, in the case of invalid children; most help the Charity Organisation Committee of their district, and provide for district nursing: perhaps all make some endeavour to encourage thrift, and to advance education.[137]

Permanent staff were – not without friction – supplemented by interested visitors, and a number of the settlements recognised their 'secondary value . . . as a training place for workers elsewhere'. A stint in a settlement house came to be regarded as a good preparation for social and local government work, and settlement women co-operated with the many different bodies engaged in that work. Despite their links with the Charity Organization Society, the settlements were less censorious of the poor and less closely linked to government policy. They were more appealing to working people, more in tune with academic debate on social problems and more akin to the Guilds of Help: civic groups operating from 1904 onwards to foster official and voluntary neighbourhood efforts for the promotion of social welfare. As Vicinus notes, the women's settlements nevertheless made much of women's instinctive and practical bent for the undertaking, which confirmed rather than extended contemporary thinking about them, and pushed them towards practical social work rather than policy management once their activities were taken over by the state.[138]

The settlement house idea was taken to America in 1886 by Stanton Coit, who spent a few months at Toynbee Hall after postgraduate work in Berlin. His University Settlement in New York was supplemented by a second in the city, the College Settlement,[139] and in 1889 Hull House was begun in Chicago by Jane Addams and her old school friend, Ellen Starr. Additional houses were set up in these two centres as well as in Boston, Cambridge, Buffalo and other parts of the country: by 1898 there were over seventy.[140] Like its British prototype, the movement appealed particularly to single, educated women in search of work and companionship. Addams, the highly educated and comfortably circumstanced daughter of an Illinois state senator, saw the settlement house as a place 'in which young women who had been given over too exclusively to study might restore a balance of activity along traditional lines and learn of life from life itself'. It was a centre where 'they might try out some of the things they had been taught and put truth to "the ultimate test of the conduct it dictates or inspires"'.[141] Her two visits to London before the founding of Hull House had impressed her with the wretched suffering of the poor, and she thought it was 'easy to see why the Settlement movement originated in England, where the years of education are more constrained and definite than they are here, where class distinctions are more rigid. The necessity of it was greater there.'[142]

But the British were similarly prone to take comfort in the conditions of their own society. They reflected that the urban problem was 'rendered more complex in the United States by the racial question, and the difference in politics and religion resulting therefrom'.[143] They supported the proposition that America had a more powerful aristocracy than England, an equally cruel – if less clear – class system, and greater difficulty in organising its diverse workforce. They reproached Americans for the lack of 'well-considered legislation' and 'political machinery adapted to modern city life', the dearth of 'blue books and governmental reports' on urban affairs, the little attention 'paid to experiments and methods of amelioration', and the absence of knowledge even among leading citizens about 'the conditions of the poor'. Addams, though she was anxious that American settlements should not become 'mere echoes and imitations of the English movement', acknowledged that the settlements were the result of 'theories of social reform, which in their full enthusiasm reached America by way of England', was herself influenced by the English Fabians, set out to learn all she could from Toynbee Hall, and was impressed by the evidence of 'research, of scholarship, of organized public spirit' that she found in England during a stay in 1896. Addams was driven to explain America's hesitancy to tackle urban difficulties in terms of the youth of its cities, and with the statement that 'our very democracy so long presupposed that each citizen could care for himself that we are slow to develop a sense of social obligation'.[144]

Once Americans were involved in the settlement movement, women swiftly assumed a prominence they did not enjoy in Britain, where they had come into a movement initiated by men and dominated, in its political ramifications, by men. According to a contemporary, American women were able to take the lead because 'The men are so much engaged in commercial pursuits, and the aggregation of huge fortunes, that they have no time for altruistic effort or philanthropic endeavour.'[145] A somewhat similar criticism can be found in *The Education of Henry Adams*,[146] and certainly women made the most of their claims to a distinctive sensibility when they were pursuing cultural activities in their clubs[147] and reform endeavours generally. The success of these clubs, not paralleled in Britain, may also explain the prominence of women in the settlements, as may the earlier push of American women into higher education, and their longer search for suitable ways of applying it.

American men and women alike seem to have had a still greater faith than their British models in what the settlements could achieve, since they were less willing to accept the division of society into classes.[148] But the programmes of the American settlements do not appear to have varied according to the sex of their personnel; they generally included kindergartens, children's clubs, social and cultural activities, classes of various kinds, meetings or conferences on urban problems, direct action where it was feasible, and the mounting of pressure on city, state or federal politicians to resolve difficulties where it was not. Settlement workers co-operated with other urban reformers and lent their backing to the labour movement, assisting unionisation, strikes and the WTUL. It was said that Hull House 'supported every judicious attempt on the part of the workers to better their position', and on top of the usual facilities it sustained 'a day-nursery . . . a children's playground, a children's dining-room, . . . a co-operative association, a gymnasium, a coffee-house and restaurant, a New England kitchen, with a mid-day delivery of food at the factories, a temporary lodging-house, a labour bureau, and a public dispensary, with a resident physician'. At Henry House on New York's Lower East Side, Lillian Wald applied her own training as a nurse to give the settlement a unique emphasis on health care.[149]

In settlement houses on both sides of the Atlantic, residents devoted special consideration to the needs of women and – as theorists urged their unique qualities and social importance – to the interests of children. But the American women activists were particularly well connected and aware politically, successfully campaigning with various interested parties to secure a federal children's bureau (1912), and state laws covering child labour, compulsory school attendance, maximum hours and minimum wages, mothers' pensions, factory inspection, and the creation of juvenile courts. Anticipating the eventual family duties of working girls, they provided classes for them in cooking, sewing and housekeeping. And though their work was often taken over by city authorities – just as Victorian female charitable workers, acting individually or through voluntary groups, had been gradually superseded by state-employed professionals – their efforts were seen as necessary, and won respect: *Independent Magazine* readers in 1913 voted Jane Addams the second most useful American, after Thomas Edison.[150]

The extended family of the settlement afforded a peculiarly suitable outlet for women's educational skills and concern for the promotion of culture. It gave equal scope for their qualities of sensibility and practicality, and for their interest in the family and community matters that shaped women's lives more closely than those of men. They may frequently have begun their work as amateurs, but they turned themselves into experts as their settlements grew, in the process necessarily broadening their horizons, making valued contacts with fellow-women, and gaining small financial reward but great personal and career satisfaction.[151] Settlement houses were always in danger of being no more than what O'Neill has called 'first-aid stations in the urban wilderness',[152] ameliorating rather than fundamentally changing the divisive and exploitative economic system they deplored. Similarly, residents risked losing 'themselves in the cave of their own companionship',[153] opposing working-class pleasures and giving off an odour of *noblesse oblige* that not all the needy could relish. Yet at their best, imbued by a sympathetic environmentalism,[154] they improved the quality of life in their neighbourhoods and demonstrated that the ideal of cross-class fellowship, intermittently pursued by middle-class feminists, was, though elusive, not unattainable.

As the women's club movement strengthened and acquired a national dimension in America during these years, it finally made its appearance in Britain. Although a few clubs had been founded since the 1870s, most appeared during the 1890s, and by 1899 'there were twenty-four in London, two in Edinburgh and Glasgow, and one in Dublin, Bath, Leeds, Liverpool and Manchester'.[155] As in the United States, they were a reflection of the emancipation of women, catering for those who had money, leisure and cultural interests they wished to pursue; for those who had jobs and wanted somewhere to stay where they would find a social centre and congenial companionship. But the British clubs did not, Rubinstein suggests, aim 'consciously to advance the cause of women's emancipation'. They did not move into reform and cross-class ventures, like their American counterparts, since British women activists preferred to work either directly with men or through their home, family, political and specific reform associations. None the less, some of their foundations did resemble the bolder clubs of the United States – notably the Pioneer Club in London, which was patronised by 'advanced' women, tried to recruit a mixed class membership, and organised debates on serious topics; and the Grosvenor Crescent Club, also in London, which provided 'a general employment service for members and various social and educational features . . . for women engaged in professional, social and related work'.[156] And while they may have experienced the internal difficulties that beset most fledgling organisations,[157] the clubs were yet another reply to sceptics who felt that women did not enjoy each other's company and direction, and could never replicate the networks through which men conducted so much of their business.

The creation of the General Federation of Women's Clubs in the United States in 1890, and of state federations in 1894, indicates how far American club creation had proceeded since the 1860s, and how far American women had drawn ahead of their British sisters in this aspect of the women's movement. The Federation, which boasted over a million members by 1912, built on the work of the Association for the Advancement of Women (AAW, 1873–97; see also p. 178), a national alliance of women launched by the New York club Sorosis and promoting debate about reform as well as encouraging clubs to be more socially active.[158] In the same way, the Federation stressed the need for club women to be useful, a focus which led to an upgrading of practical reform projects and a downgrading of debate and purely cultural endeavours – although, as Blair observes, the transition was not automatically an easy one.[159]

The *Federation Bulletin and Club Woman* detailed club aims, complaining about inadequate funds and data and warning against the variety of local needs leading to a dissipation of energy, but generally maintaining an optimistic outlook and praising women's 'philanthropic altruism'. Stress was placed on the benefits of club operations for women of all kinds; on the necessity of women who had leisure and means helping those who had not; and on the value of club women from different backgrounds co-operating to overcome 'that class misunderstanding and prejudice which democratic forms are no longer able to conceal even in this republic of America'. Importance was attached to and progress made on consumer and conservation issues, educational projects, the improvement of home economics, settlement work, municipal and civil service reform, the eradication of sweatshops, the 'stamping-out of injustice and cruelty in eleemosynary institutions', and the securing of legislative protection for women and children. And it was acknowledged that club women, though they did not aim at political power, had been driven to acquire it to achieve their reformist ends. Encouraging note was taken of the ground gained by southern clubs which, if less active in legislative efforts and less affluent than those elsewhere, were said to be democratic and forward-looking, keenly committed to 'education, philanthropy, literature, library extension, civics and village improvement', and supplementing the work done by the South's home mission societies. In these groups, acting 'as . . . elsewhere . . . as *man's help meet*', women raised money for the Church, helped the needy, visited strangers and the sick, assisted black schools, reached out to 'fallen women' and aided educational ventures overseas.

The *Bulletin* took pride in the strong position of American women, which was 'absolutely without parallel in any other age or any other country'; but it was obliged to admit that Britain, with worse urban problems springing from the fact that the majority of the population lived in urban communities, had 'gone far beyond us' in making a success of city life. Indeed, the United States lagged so far behind the rest of the world that even good men regarded 'all efforts for betterment as dangerous experiments, if not horrible inventions, of the socialists'. A fitting – if provoking – tribute to the club women's reforming zeal came in 1905 from ex-President Grover Cleveland who, though an admirer of female

~

religious and charitable efforts, failed to appreciate the Federation's labours for domesticity in a larger context, and therefore condemned it as a threat to the home, wifehood and motherhood.[160]

There was a less progressive side to the Federation. Aware that local clubs feared loss of identity inside the Federation and the confusion of state and national objectives,[161] its leaders adopted several policies to reassure conservatives, which have damaged the club movement with modern commentators. The Federation tended to stress the services women might perform rather than their rights. When controversy erupted over the admission of a black club in 1900, it sidestepped an opportunity to promote the solidarity of women regardless of colour, and engineered a compromise – reminiscent of the suffragists' compromise of 'the Negro question' – which ruled:

> Clubs containing colored women shall be eligible to the General Federation in those states and territories in which they are eligible to membership in their state or territorial federation, and that where these organizations do not exist, race eligibility shall be declared by a three-fifths vote of the clubs.

Nativist sentiments likewise found expression within the Federation, and it resisted pressure publicly to endorse the suffragist sentiment many of its members entertained from 1906 until 1914, when the risk – particularly of alienating southern club women – no longer seemed grave.[162]

Whereas the Federation's stance demonstrated that neither the organisation nor its members rose above contemporary prejudices, it facilitated the growth of the club movement and accurately reflected grass-roots views that did not necessarily become more liberal as club objectives changed. The New England Women's Club did develop a more positive attitude to the suffrage over time, and by 1900 Julia Ward Howe felt able to claim that in states where it was granted the result had been the 'raising of the age of protection for girls to eighteen years; the providing of seats for saleswomen and enforcing that ordinance; ... the increasing of property rights of married women; the making of father and mother joint guardian of children; the forbidding of child labor; and the causing of equal pay for equal labor'. The NEWC also continued to interest itself in practical projects – for example, giving money for children's vacation schools and the education of deserving individuals. Moreover, it welcomed speakers who stressed the broadening influence of women's clubs, believed that immigrants could be successfully assimilated, and spoke on such topics as Socialism and Christian Socialism; settlements; the Consumers' League; race; divorce; the English suffragettes; municipal and civil service reform; college, mixed-sex and vocational education; the need to give schools 'closer contact with the people at large'; the welcome appearance of 'stronger, self-reliant and older' heroines in fiction writing; women in social service and the industrial world; and the desirability of unions, since 'organization is necessary to secure necessary reforms'. Members were indignant at the suggestion that their club – like, perhaps, all clubs – was 'composed of society women who knew & cared nothing for any of the great interests of the day – & had no hand in bringing about any reform'. The truth of the matter was that members in Massachusetts were urged to embrace a vast array of causes devoted to 'social, civic, intellectual and moral uplift', and 'If the question is unpopular, it is all the more essential that you should take hold of it and help to make it popular.'[163]

On the other hand, the club records indicate that it was sometimes a struggle to find suitable speakers and engage audience attention: easier for women to listen than to do. As the 'rush of women's life increased, the members, more and more . . . "wanted to absorb like a sponge, but not be squeezed out!" ' All 'these puzzling questions about children, races and peoples, had left some of us in a state of depression. So many difficult problems in State and Nation and we poor women powerless to set them right.' Speakers were entertained who were hostile to foreigners, economic radicalism and female suffrage, and although the Massachusetts Federation favoured the admission of the black club that had forced the General Federation to consider the race question, while the NEWC hoped that in future its 'votes may be thrown against a color line', women of Garrison's home city were not radical on the matter. It was felt that it took more courage to be quiet than to criticise the national leadership when the future of the General Federation was at stake:

> It seemed very necessary that the southern clubs should not withdraw because they are the ones who need the aid and are now showing the progress gained by the connection with the national organization.[164]

As a result of white women's prejudice, and because they had been accustomed to organise separately for their racial and sexual advancement, black women consolidated their own club activities. They were encouraged by the experiences of the few black participants in the AAW, and by such leaders as the southern journalist and anti-lynching crusader Ida B. Wells, who was driven North by the hostility to her message, and the New England editor and suffragist Josephine Ruffin. Other important role models were the Maryland author and reformer Frances Harper; the Virginia community, race and feminist activist, Maggie Lena Walker; and the teacher, lecturer and suffragist from Tennessee Mary Church Terrell. In 1896, Terrell established and became the first president of the National Association of Colored Women (NACW). Building on preliminary work done by the National Federation of Afro-American Women (1895), the NACW brought together 'two generations of women' and existing clubs throughout the country; its aim was 'to secure harmony of action and co-operation among all women in raising to the highest plane, home[,] moral and civil life'. In addition to the normal problems attendant on such a venture, the circumstances of its members guaranteed the association extra financial difficulties and a closer scrutiny of its performance. Its projects none the less resembled those of other women's groups of its time, and included the establishment of kindergartens, school visiting, rescue and reform work among women and children, and assistance to old people and the poor.

The NACW also tried to give a distinctively female dimension to the concern of black spokesmen with racial advancement: from the outset it addressed itself to improving public sentiment, protesting lynching, exposing white bigotry and encouraging self-help. Thus while complaints that black labourers were 'neither reliable nor skilled in their work' were condemned as stemming largely from prejudice, the Association hoped to establish 'schools of domestic science in which our women and girls may be trained to be skilled in their work'. And as part of her contribution to racial betterment, Mrs Terrell both wrote articles and took to the lecture circuit, confiding to her much-missed husband, who was taking care of their daughter:

> I really feel that I am putting the colored woman in a favorable light every time I address an audience of white people, and every little helps. . . . It grows harder and harder every time I leave. . . . Only a sense of duty to my race and thrift for myself could reduce me to sally forth as a lecturer.[165]

Despite their struggles, black clubs – like their white counterparts – offered women the opportunity to strengthen their ties with other women: provided a stepping stone or base for female activists who took up various campaigns on behalf of their sex, including suffragism and urban political reform.[166]

(ii) *The consumers' leagues*

Another important way in which American women responded to the growing conviction that industrial evils were not immutable was through the creation of consumers' leagues. The first was founded in New York in 1890, they spread to twenty states, and by 1899 a National Consumers' League had been established; both men and women participated. In 'accord with the modern emphasis upon social well-being as contrasted with individual prosperity', their objective was to mobilise comfortably placed consumers to protest the unsatisfactory wages, hours and conditions of employment of vulnerable workers in the retail stores, and to support with their custom fair employers, whose names were published in a League 'white list'. Concern with the stores led to interest in the employees of public utilities; clothing manufacture and food preparation; sweatshops and child labour.

The consumers' leagues prepared the way for independent investigations of working conditions; the labelling of approved goods; an early Christmas shopping movement; and efforts to secure and monitor various kinds of protective legislation.[167] Like the club and settlement movements, they capitalised on the belief that 'men could not investigate the private affairs of women', and that women had a special affinity for matters requiring sensitivity to suffering and affecting social welfare.[168] Like them, the leagues drew in women of energy and distinction. These included the early-widowed Josephine Shaw Lowell, who had served a reform apprenticeship on the Sanitary Commission and the New York State Board of Charities, and her friend Maud Nathan, who – supported by her husband, a fellow-suffragist – became an able publicist for the National Consumers' League. Another key activist was the Quaker Florence Kelley, daughter of Radical Republican 'Pig Iron' Kelley. A divorcée who had resided at Hull House, done research for the US Commissioner of Labor and served as the first Chief Factory Inspector in Illinois, Kelley had monitored, between 1893 and 1895, the operation of the state's new – albeit short–lived – law curbing women's hours and prohibiting child labour.[169]

There was no exact equivalent of the leagues in Britain, though they were launched in continental Europe, and international conferences were held in 1908 and 1913. However, the British WTUL shared their interest in protective legislation, the Women's Co-operative Guild 'stood for the organized purchasing or consuming power of the working-class community of the country',[170] and in holding up the example of European countries, American consumer activists particularly praised developments in England.

The consumers' leagues of Connecticut, campaigning against the employment of children who were 'under the legal age for wage-earning', were very conscious of the educational deficiencies as well as the economic pressures that contributed to child labour. Sharing the Progressive belief that schooling must train head and hands alike, and aware that many children left school early 'because of their indifference to book learning', they worked with some success for the provision of vocational instruction for boys and girls in grade and special trade schools. While doing so, they studied European trade schools, offering special tribute to those in England, whose main motive was not to enhance national performance but the 'humanitarian . . . desire to give the boy the best possible chance in life'. They similarly recommended the common English practice of vocational guidance: giving personal attention to the needs of 'every child who leaves school at fourteen'. Yet if good British precedents were lauded, attention was also paid to grim British tendencies, and league members heard with gloom of:

> the 'factory type' which has arisen in England and which has been found distinctly below the standards of the army, and when admitted to the army have been the earliest victims of disease. Such an inferior type is discerned rising in our Southern factory towns.

Since the consumers' leagues initially relied so much on education and persuasion – working 'through the aroused conscience of the . . . employer to his employee' – it behoved them to stay on terms with employers and labour, factory inspectors, boards of education, the Bureau of Labor Statistics, and allied women's groups, whatever their differences of emphasis. Courted by suffrage and anti-suffrage associations, the Connecticut League determinedly preserved its neutrality, pointing out that 'both parties are represented among our officers and directors, that our membership is made up from both parties and even more from those who have not joined either organization'. But the league stance on industrial education brought difficulties with labour, which opposed trade schools as threatening its control of the workforce, disliked their focus, and did not necessarily wish to see children go into the trades. The debate about industrial education, gathering pace since the 1880s, was a vexed one, with black and white working-class leaders holding out for quality, rather than differentiated, schooling. The more entrenched nature of the British class system explains why its educators had an easier passage on this issue.[171] Nor was it clear what kind of vocational assistance could be offered to girls, given their anomalous position in the labour market. The danger was, as in Britain, that instruction in the household arts invariably received priority; although training in the artistic trades and sales techniques were supported too, and in America there was a certain coyness about programmes to resolve 'the servant problem'.

Resisting the temptation to take on too much which beset all the female reform associations and reformers, the Connecticut League, like the National Consumers' League, centred its efforts on several related campaigns. Accordingly, in attacking 'the causes of the unrest of our laboring people', it concentrated on 'child labor, lack of training, unsanitary conditions of employment, and the overwork and underpay of our wage-earning women', pointing out that whereas the child labour legislation had attracted the most attention, it had experienced harder legislative fights and found 'overwork and the underpay of wage-earning women ... the most perplexing [subject] with which we have to deal'.[172]

(iii) *Moral crusades and intellectual challenges*

If the interacting personnel of clubs, settlement houses and consumers' leagues – linked to the suffrage societies and cross-class economic alliances – provided the major support for the multicause women's movements of Britain and America by the 1890s, a significant role within those movements was also played by female social purists. By this time the issues which they raised – and which were once regulated by individual conscience and religious precepts[173] – were increasingly tackled by secular agencies and the state, though religious bodies continued to involve themselves in social purity. What is more, while the objectives of social purists were comfortably at one with nineteenth-century women's culture, the issue of sexuality, to which they gave prominence, was to prove dangerously divisive for feminists during the first decades of the twentieth century.

In the years immediately after 1890, the Woman's Christian Temperance Union under Willard's leadership, while appealing to women's special moral qualities and mission as it had always done, placed a new stress on the environmental causes of intemperance, and strengthened its support for the labour movement, Nationalism, Socialism and third-party politics. Although this strategy drew some support in the Midwest and West, Willard had moved too far to the left and the public sphere for many of her members, and she herself was disillusioned by the Populists' failure to endorse temperance and women's suffrage in 1892. Approaches to third parties were discredited with the defeat of Populism in 1896. In that year the national WCTU convention questioned the

Union's established endorsement of the Prohibition Party, and in 1899 it was withdrawn. By then Willard, who had failed to secure unanimous re-election in 1897, was dead.[174] The established lines of work were sustained after her death: the social purity department, for instance, campaigned successfully for state laws raising the age of consent and for town curfews for young people, seeking the removal of material it considered offensive from public libraries and protesting the immodest liberalisation of women's dress.[175] But the WCTU lost its high political profile in the Progressive era, since many Progressives did not favour Prohibition, as the Union did, while for those who were uncomfortable with the wide ambitions of the WCTU the single-issue Anti-Saloon League (1893) provided an alternative association, whose tactics of 'local option' contests (see above, p. 170) followed by state prohibition drives were enjoying considerable success.[176]

At the time when one aspect of the WCTU's operation was shrinking, the ambitions of the British Women's Temperance Association were at last expanding. This change relates directly to the election of Lady Henry Somerset, a feminist with wide reform interests, to the presidency of the BWTA in 1890. Her determination to commit the organisation to a 'do everything' policy and active involvement in the World's WCTU (WWCTU) put Somerset at odds with her Executive Committee chairman, Mary Dowcra, who favoured concentrating on temperance and national priorities. The two women also had different attitudes to the general principle of borrowing from America, though British temperance activists had always done so. Thus while Dowcra disapproved of imports, Somerset visited the United States, where she was well received, learned organisational techniques, and cultivated a close personal friendship with Willard, whom she introduced to Fabianism and the merits of British Liberalism. Willard in turn stayed in England for extended periods and converted her to the value of the WCTU's departmental structure, political activism and internationalism.

When Somerset's viewpoint prevailed at the BWTA's annual meeting in 1893, Dowcra and her allies withdrew, going on to establish the temperance-only Women's Total Abstinence Union, while the majority of the Association's members remained with Somerset in the now renamed National British Women's Temperance Association (NBWTA).[177] Under Somerset's direction, temperance women grew in numbers; they agitated for the vote, worked to get women elected to local government offices, backed suffragist candidates for Parliament, and asked men running for office whether they 'would allow pub licences to lapse, would ban drinking from public halls and institutions, would support labour legislation, better housing, and municipal water-supplies for the urban poor'.[178]

British women were thus politicised through the NBWTA, as their American sisters had been through the WCTU, and the process continued after Somerset's retirement in 1903: her successor was the feminist Rosalind Howard, Countess of Carlisle. However, diehards were never reconciled to Somerset's activism, while Willard was criticised for interfering in British temperance affairs and neglecting her American duties. As Shiman concludes, the late-developing British association did not operate on the scale of the WCTU, and while temperance societies 'were to be found in all the churches, ... in all political arenas and parties', the temperance campaign as a whole was conservative and male-dominated, offering no threat to the established order and less important to the women's movement than it was in the United States.[179]

Moreover, their experiences during the 1890s made the NBWTA and Josephine Butler's Ladies' National Association uneasy about the practicality of multicause and international movements. Both groups, together with the WWCTU, were interested in efforts to end state regulation of prostitution in India, but to different degrees. Nevertheless, Somerset felt able to plunge into the debate with a letter to *The Times* in 1897 favouring regulation, thereby discomfiting Willard, who privately agreed with her, and alienating Butler, who resigned from the WWCTU and produced a vigorous rebuttal of the views of Somerset and her supporters. Even as they extended their activities, this embarrassing controversy could only stir up sympathy in British temperance and purity circles for Mrs Butler's belief that 'our cause has not gained, but is suffering sadly from the union with it of the WWCTU', and that in the struggle for the purification of society, 'I do not myself greatly desire uniformity. ... I had rather see the genius of each nation develop itself freely in its organised methods.'[180]

Social purity activities besides temperance continued to absorb British and American feminists from the 1890s onwards, as old evils such as prostitution took new forms, while new challenges such as the 'white slave' traffic stirred reformers and, through them, the public conscience.[181] In both countries, social anxieties prompted agitation. Against the background of mounting immigration, urban and industrial expansion and municipal corruption, conservatives fretted about the declining birth rate and stressed the importance of maintaining a healthy racial stock in the face of imperial challenges and the alleged overbreeding of the unfit poor. There was, in addition, a related unease over the 'surplus' of single women in Britain and their growing number in the United States; and in America the rising divorce rate caused dismay.[182]

In both countries, voluntary associations performed 'moral surveillance' duties, invoked available laws, sought new ones, and promoted educational programmes designed to eliminate vice.[183] Within the two countries' coalition of social purity organisations, religious, medical, eugenical and women's associations, there was ample room for feminists to pursue their special mission to persuade men to control their sexuality and curb their violence for the benefit of women and children.[184] But in both countries, feminists ran the risk that their broad-ranging desire to protect women and children would be submerged by their allies' interest in legislation to coerce and control them; by reforms which promised too much, and 'defined women's social roles quite conservatively'. In both countries, not all women were comfortable with the purists' growing concern with social

~

hygiene, a philosophy which emphasised nationality rather than religion, social efficiency rather than purity, and the educated affirmation rather than control of sexual expression.[185]

Just the same, there were achievements. Although in Britain after 1913 the Ladies' National Association merged with the men's association to form the Association for Social and Moral Hygiene, it was directed by a woman, the suffragette Alison Neilans. And British social purists, aided by Britain's unitary political system, proved more successful at securing legislation than the Americans did, with women contributing to the pressures which produced the 1904 Children Act, allowing a longer period of time during which prosecutions of offences against children might be brought; the 1913 Children Act, permitting children to give evidence without taking the oath, such evidence to be used at the discretion of the jury; and the 1908 Punishment of Incest Act, which 'made incest (by men) punishable by imprisonment for up to seven years and not less than three'. The 1908 measure, long proposed and officially linked to worry about conditions in working-class homes, fell short of feminist hopes of securing a higher age limit for victims and punishment for 'all abuse of authority which the law vests with the father', and may have owed as much to 'middle-class anxieties and tensions concerning the sanctity of the family' as to fear for the poor or condemnation of the sexual abuse of girls.[186] The alliance of feminists and other interested groups also secured the passage of a Criminal Law Amendment Act in 1912, principally designed to combat the 'white slave' traffic and tighten up the law against procurers and brothel-keepers.[187]

Women in Britain and the United States were important to the educational part of the purity crusade, capitalising on their role as teachers and mothers to assist the production and distribution of improving literature.[188] American women – concerned about the health of wives and children as well as prostitutes, and inspired by British revelations and activities – joined in new efforts to eradicate 'red-light districts' and 'white slavery'. As Harriet Laidlaw and many others saw it, 'The greatest single element in the whole problem is the economic struggle that denies a living wage to girls', and it was vital to take abolitionist action, not to waste time endlessly investigating the social evil. These efforts became an essential part of Progressivism's campaign for good government and resulted in the Mann Act 1910, prohibiting the transportation of women across state lines for immoral purposes; the creation of municipal vice commissions; and the widespread enactment by major cities of red-light abatement laws.[189] America's female social purists additionally advocated dress reform, the employment of matrons at police stations, the establishment of clubs to counteract dangerous social influences, censorship and municipal reform. To improve social hygiene, they also pressed for the 'development of parents–teachers associations, sex education, age of consent legislation, institutions for the protection of young women, ... improved industrial conditions, and new techniques for helping the criminal and delinquent': programmes which 'touched upon the vital social reforms of the Progressive era'.

On one level, the efforts of middle-class feminists and their allies to protect children can be presented as an unattractive form of social control, made possible by the declining need for children in the economy and designed to project middle-class views about parental duties and the special nature of childhood on to a recalcitrant working class. But as Linda Gordon persuasively maintains, child protection agencies and legislation – including the mothers' pension laws passed by the states between 1910 and 1920 – were valued and used by women, however much middle-class strictures about the behaviour of the poor might have been resented. They were, in fact, feminist measures in their concern that the conditions of motherhood, still women's central concern, had been made more difficult in industrial society and should be improved by a lessening of male power, specifically as neglectful fathers and abusive partners. And in its early adoption of mothers' pension laws, in part as a result of the strength of American social feminists and the cult of domesticity, the United States was ahead of Britain, where the welfare state generally developed sooner.[190]

Feminists on both sides of the Atlantic, led by those in Britain, made through social purity a major and a radical contribution to reform concerned with women and children; though neither they nor other activists in this area respected the sensitivities of those who would be the recipients of their exhortations, investigations and legislation. Through social purity activities they were able to raise formerly taboo subjects like male and female sexuality and woman's right to control her body; could challenge the efforts of the medical profession to dominate debate on sexual matters, and help to transform an ancient preoccupation with prostitution into a broad crusade to purify society.[191] Once debate was joined, however, it moved in directions unforeseen by social purists, and often unwelcome to them.

In the first place, the 1880s and 1890s in Britain and the United States saw the emergence of an intense fear of sexual anarchy: a fear which, as Showalter has shown, affected relations between and within the sexes and was allegedly marked by the emergence of a 'new woman'. Educated and fit, she rode a bicycle and played games, might wear the rational dress recommended by various reform groups, and even smoked. She expected to exercise free speech – on sexual as on other matters – to shake off close supervision, and to work outside the home as well as marry, though marriage was not taken for granted: in short, 'to belong to the human race, not to the ladies' aid society to the human race'.[192] The problems of such emancipated women were an important theme for British and American women novelists of the 1890s.[193] While to younger feminists and even some non-feminists the 'new woman' was an admirable figure, to many commentators – social purists among them – she represented a threat to marriage, home and family: someone to be ridiculed as unnatural and masculine, as strong-minded women traditionally had been.

The critics' vehemence has to be understood in the context of the social anxieties we have just noted. But though it is understandable, these commentators' reaction to the 'new woman' both obscured how far feminists were from realising their economic and educational objectives, and made their goals harder to attain. For working women, there remained the problems of social disapproval, sex-typing, low pay, lack of suitable accommodation, and their own ambivalence about the world of jobs.[194] Equally disadvantaged were women seeking higher education, who discovered that the larger number of female students – and, belatedly, the appearance of female faculty – had strengthened the determination of Oxford (1895) and Cambridge (1896–7) not to admit women to the BA degree, and provoked a reaction against coeducation and college-educated women in the United States.[195] Under these circumstances, it is not surprising that the colleges of the American South found it hard to raise their academic standards, and to achieve their aim of 'the organic union of industrial with intellectual education'. As late as 1913, the Southern Association of College Women felt that the colleges of their region trained young women how to get a man and keep a home.[196]

In a period of social tension, the consideration of female sexuality sparked by social purists and fanned by the 'new woman' controversy had also fostered a school of sexologists who asserted that female sexual desires equalled those of men, and that abstinence benefited neither.[197] Equally, it had encouraged eugenicists who wished to see a reversal of the birth-rate decline, primarily by exhorting the best to breed.[198] The intellectual lead in sexology and eugenics, as in social purity, was taken by Britain. The eugenicists' willingness to entertain intervention to secure the health of mothers and children was acceptable to social purists and feminists, and from the late nineteenth century onwards in Britain and America all three groups favoured the proliferation of voluntary associations dedicated to maternal and child welfare, the enforcement of compulsory school attendance, the inclusion of domestic economy in the education curriculum for girls, and the passage of welfare legislation. The measures enacted in America – mostly at the state level – have already been touched on (see above, pp. 228–9). Those passed in Britain, and interpreted by Davin and Lewis, include school meals (1906); medical inspection in schools (1907); the requirement that births be notified within six weeks (1907), to expedite visits by health visitors; the Children Act 1908; and the provision for maternity insurance in the Health Insurance Act 1911. However, since the aim of the new laws was to strengthen the family, uphold the father's role within it, and foster population growth, as Jane Lewis points out, policy-makers resisted women's pressures (from the 1920s) for 'free access to birth control information', and ignored their requests for 'direct economic assistance for mothers'.[199]

Even less pleasing to social purists and moderate feminists were the consequences of sexology. Whereas one effect of their writings was to strengthen the maternalists' arguments, to the delight of radical feminists they were equally capable of legitimising the sexually emancipated woman, thus rekindling the fears of free love which had so long embarrassed Socialists and feminists, despite the small numbers of either who were its practitioners.[200] Furthermore, whereas sexologists were sympathetic to male homosexuality as a 'congenital inversion', the female variety was frequently regarded as a 'pseudo', 'artificial or substitute' inversion, resulting from the repression of sexuality enjoined particularly upon women. The consequence of such reasoning – to which feminists contributed, and by which they were divided – was the sexualisation of spinsterhood and the stigmatising of lesbianism (although, unlike homosexuality, it was not subjected to regulation by law).[201]

At a time when more unmarried women than ever were working outside the home, speaking up on the benefits of independence,[202] and being drawn into the women's movement, an increase in hostility to singlehood was damaging. Women had always found it difficult to embrace radical lifestyles at odds with the family, but households shared by women had seemed to offer love and the benefits of a home without loss of respectability. Small wonder, with attitudes to such liaisons changing, that there was little support among women at large for the proposals for reforming the home advanced by a number of radical feminists in Britain and by their American counterparts, including the best-known feminist intellectual of the early twentieth century, the American Socialist writer and lecturer Charlotte Perkins Gilman.

A twice-married woman who believed women should be economically independent, and whose only daughter was eventually taken care of by her first husband and his second wife as she pursued her career, Gilman represented in her own life the kind of unconventionality that affronted anti-feminists. Yet her acceptance of sexual difference and her essentially nineteenth-century views about sexual expression should have offset the alarm caused by her personal history and repudiation of undue sexual divergence. For Gilman, like her equally influential South African contemporary, Olive Schreiner, work was 'an exercise of faculty, without which we should cease to be human'. Unfortunately, women were inadequately trained for the domestic tasks they made their own, and the results of that neglect were woeful. She candidly acknowledged the invaluable role played not only by the mother but also by the school in teaching children 'of fairness, of justice, of comradeship, of collective interest and action'. She was eloquent about the need of everyone, not just married people, for a home. As Gilman and other feminists recognised, unless they made an attempt to transform the home through such innovations as professionalised, co-operative or paid housework, their frequent acceptance of women's domestic aptitudes and aims could be used to confirm rather than improve their traditional role. But reform attempts were generally defeated by cost, class and convention.[203]

The debate on sexuality fostered by social purity had similarly mixed consequences for thinking and action on divorce, abortion and birth control. Although some purists – for instance, in the WCTU – opposed any liberalisation of divorce as an irreligious subversion of the family,[204] by the 1890s women's leaders had come to accept it, without campaigning for it, as part of their commitment to defending women's rights within the family.[205] Their hand had been forced both by the social and intellectual shifts outlined above, and by the actions of a great many individual women, for the incidence of divorce rose rapidly in the United States – far more rapidly than in Britain – from the end of the nineteenth century. It was also being resorted to by more women than in the past, and by women of the middle class and working class alike. This upsurge has been explained by O'Neill in terms of women's high expectations in conjugal marriage; and Degler has noted the greater assertiveness of women seeking divorce, and their unwillingness to tolerate the betrayal of their high moral standards. Even so, as he indicates, the number of American single women fell in the early twentieth century, perhaps as the greater availability of divorce made marriage more attractive to the kind of woman who might once have shunned it as a restriction.[206]

The growth in divorce did not come about because of great changes in the law. The drive for constitutional amendments empowering Congress to standardise the terms of marriage and divorce was strengthened during the Progressive era but remained unsuccessful, so that liberal and conservative state divorce laws remained on the books, and it was still harder to obtain a divorce in the conservative South than in the rest of the country.[207] And since some of the factors that produced the American divorce increase – such as better employment prospects for women and the growing secularisation of society – existed in Britain without producing the same result, one must conclude that there were special factors at work in the United States. These would seem to be the diversity of its state laws and the strength of its domestic ethos, individualism and bourgeoisie. Having no aristocracy, Reed observes, America lacked 'a hedonistic tradition that sanctioned frivolous relations between the sexes'.[208]

In England during the 1890s, a very different situation faced the minority of feminists who translated their support for liberalising the divorce law into action. In so doing they were spurred on by the decade's stimulating intellectual climate; by the 1891 Court of Appeal confirmation that conjugal rights could not be exacted through imprisonment of a spouse; and by awareness of the equal grounds for divorce that existed between the sexes in Scotland. In England, more men than women still benefited from divorce which, due to its cost, was still available only to the prosperous. The reformers made no progress until 1909, despite the production of literature and petitions in favour of easier divorce by Elizabeth Wolstenholme Elmy and the Women's Emancipation Union (1892–9), the airing of the question in the press, and the intensification of efforts for change in the early twentieth century. A Royal Commission on Divorce and Matrimonial Causes was then established, with two female members. It reported in 1912. War intervened before the government's objections to change could be overcome and the Commission's recommendations acted upon, but not before it had taken evidence from individual feminists and received proposals from concerned women's groups. Their testimony indicated that women from all classes wanted the equalisation of the divorce law and additional grounds for divorce, including cruelty and refusal to maintain.[209]

As far as birth control and abortion are concerned, we argued in chapter 4 (see pp. 134–5 above) that British and American feminists and purity crusaders in the 1870s and 1880s were critical of contraception and pregnancy termination but convinced of women's right to control their fertility. So they remained in the 1890s, even if by then the growing stress on the importance of motherhood was prompting condemnation of population limitation by some commentators, including eugenicists (although they accepted the need for control of the 'unfit'). In Britain, none the less, a handful of Socialists and feminists, such as John Robertson and J.W. Stella Browne, continued to follow Annie Besant's example in publicly advocating birth control – indeed, artificial contraception. Their efforts were aided by the increased availability of 'commercial literature . . . which publicised sex manuals, contraceptives, and abortifacients', and by the willingness of some working-class women to discuss the matter at meetings and in print. The persistent reluctance of British doctors to consider abortion, and the failure of the unpopular Malthusian League to provide practical birth control advice until 1913, may have encouraged the considerable take-up rate on abortifacients, which were primarily a working-class resort, because members of the middle class were more likely to be able to employ birth control or obtain professional help if it failed.[210]

In the United States – where, as we have seen (p. 134 above), doctors had mounted a spirited campaign against abortion – medical practitioners were comparatively quiet on the subject after 1890. Mohr has established that there are several reasons why this was so. The incidence of abortion, he points out, had declined, and the laws against it had been tightened up across America. Additionally, the drive to professionalise medicine in the face of competition from 'irregulars' had been successful, and the married middle-class women whose abortions had once caused so much concern were no longer resorting to it as a major means of birth control. Comstockery and intolerance of abortion notwithstanding, American advocates of birth control took over the lead from the British, following Annie Besant's retirement from the fray. Supplementing the debate on birth control by a few physicians and some New York neo-Malthusians, trained nurse and Socialist Margaret Sanger tapped real interest when she addressed working-class meetings on hygiene and sex education, and published her views in the *New York Call*. Unfortunately, Sanger's support among Socialists was undermined by the Party's divisions after the failure of the 1912–13 strikes, and from 1914 (see below, pp. 250–1) Sanger was pursuing an insecure existence as a radical journalist and researcher in exile, before deciding to focus single-mindedly on birth control.[211] A similar attempt to spread knowledge about birth control in the context of an integrated Socialist–feminism was made by Sanger's inspiration, Emma Goldman, a nurse and leading anarchist, who was aided by her doctor lover, the many-sided radical Ben Reitman. Goldman lectured widely on that subject and on a range of topics of interest to feminists, besides distributing birth control literature.[212]

But while the response to them and other radical activists was strong, the fact that Goldman and Reitman were 'often arrested and harassed by the police as radical agitators', and were concerned with birth control only as one pressing subject among many, did not help the numerous Americans for whom Socialism was anathema. Fee and Wallace, like Gordon, rightly emphasise the conservative consequences of a narrow preoccupation with birth control. Equally, the unusual wartime radicalism which had encouraged outspoken working-class interest in the issue was not destined to survive the conflict. Even before the postwar conservative reaction, Gordon has noted, a deep-seated set of fears about the consequences of sexual change prevented 'birth control from becoming an official program of either the Socialist party or any national women's rights organization'.[213]

We must note one other side-effect of the debate about women's sexuality associated with social purity: the rise of intellectual inquiry which modernised Victorian views on the distinctiveness of female mental and physical character- istics. And here the most significant studies done by women were carried out in the United States. In Britain, as Love has shown, the findings of researcher Alice Lee, at University College London, helped to demolish the contention that there were intellectual differences between the sexes which related to differences in cranial capacity.[214] However, women scholars were more numerous in America, and in a few institutions they enjoyed conditions which encouraged their questioning of old intellectual assumptions.[215] And although their influence was limited to university circles before World War One, American female social scientists – hoping, in the process, to prove themselves, and working in the fields of psychology, sociology and anthropology – rebutted Victorian notions of feminine physical weakness. At the same time they repudiated contrasting male and female mental and psychological traits and separate social roles for the sexes, necessitated by cultural evolution. As Rosenberg has argued, while some of the new female researchers sympathised with the women's movement, their findings did not help women activists who had accepted Victorian ideas and turned them to their own advantage. When they did become more influential, their divisive impact on feminism was considerable.[216]

By the outbreak of World War One, the women's movements in the United States and Britain had both reached maturity as optimistic, large-scale alliances dedicated to improving the position of women through a multitude of reforms. Both deployed a modified version of the separate spheres concept to further their claims, without abandoning equal rights arguments. Both had managed to 'domesticate' politics,[217] persuading politicians to take up issues of vital concern to women, while at the same time leaving ample room for eminent and lesser- known individual reformers, who worked 'for the good of our people and humanity' and not specifically for their own sex.[218] And both movements operated through single-issue organisations (as in the case of suffrage), cross- class bodies (for example, the WTULs) and 'do everything' associations (such as the WCTU, the NBWTA and other social purity groups). Since female enfranchisement provoked the most opposition in both countries, the most elaborate organisation and arguments were mobilised in the suffrage campaign, but social purity, which addressed concerns vital to the emancipation of women, could also command national and cross-class backing on both sides of the Atlantic, whereas sexual radicalism in its various manifestations, though it was a growing feature of the feminism of the 1910s, could command least support. In both countries, the cross-class organisations were dominated by the middle-class women within them, notwithstanding their efforts to develop working-class leadership. This state of affairs followed naturally from the contrasting experience, education, and economic circumstances of the two elements rather than from major personal failings on the part of the middle-class activists, though failings they naturally displayed.

As had been the case in earlier periods, there were substantial differences as well as similarities between British and American feminists. Given the greater strength of the labour movement in Britain by 1914, working women in cross-class alliances like the WCG, the North of England Society and the WTUL were more confident of their ability to stand alone than were their American counterparts, even though they shared their disabilities. Women in America still tended to see themselves as being more radical than British activists, and to regard the condition of American women as more advanced and less class-ridden than that of women in the old country; they were encouraged in this tendency by the comments of sometimes envious British observers.[219] They were certainly more willing to join multi-issue associations (notably the clubs, settlement houses and consumers' leagues). For their part, the British still worked alongside men whenever they could,[220] congratulated themselves on their effective pragmatism, and steered clear of the multi-issue alliance – a prejudice which was strengthened in some feminists by the experience of the NBWTA and Ladies' National Association with wide-ranging endeavours, and shown to be misplaced as far as social purity is concerned.

In fact, each approach had its problems, and the British suffragists, for all their single-mindedness, felt obliged to seek the collaboration of other reform groups with other priorities in the later stages of their campaign, just as the American activists were obliged to do. If the basic perceptions feminists in Britain and the United States held of themselves had some validity, they do not tell the whole story, for each movement continued to have its special strengths. The British led their American sisters in – for instance – social purity, practical remedies for urban difficulties, involvement in politics,[221] and devising radical tactics to revitalise suffragism. But the American women's clubs, settlement houses, consumers' leagues and intellectuals in the early twentieth century were more dynamic than their British equivalents. There was, indeed, diversity within a common cause.

6

The War, the vote and after
Doldrums and new departures

The advent of World War One was helpful to the winning of the vote in both Britain and the United States. In 1918, British women of thirty or over who were – or were married to – local government electors had been enfranchised; women in general had to wait until 1928. By 1920 their American sisters had also received the vote. Women's suffrage never became a party measure in either country, and politicians acted because changed wartime conditions made it seem both possible and necessary. Nor were votes for women secured in either country because the anti-suffragists generally changed their views, though the conversion of Wilson and Asquith was important, and the British and American suffragists played a crucial part in bringing that about and keeping pressure on other politicians, as well as on the public at large, for their desired end. After 1914, however, suffragists were less active in Britain than in America, where the war and female involvement in war work did not come until 1917. In the United States – having resisted the adoption of the more extreme forms of suffragette protest, not least because they hoped such tactics would be unnecessary – women finally resorted to militancy on the British pattern, though they stopped short of violence. Their tactics offended the moderate suffragists as bitterly as suffragette activities eventually alienated the constitutionalists in Britain. To the mortification of American activists, the vote was gained first in the allegedly more conservative country. Yet as in the earlier phases of suffragism, campaigners on both sides of the Atlantic also drew pleasure and inspiration from one another's progress.

The war gave women the opportunity to serve their country, and by doing so they gained gratitude and found personal satisfaction. They did not necessarily seek to change society's attitudes to women and other disadvantaged groups in the process. War work, like reform, attracted feminist and non-feminist alike, and the conflict divided women just as it did men. When it ended, while many female reformers continued their labours with customary zeal and found satisfying new objectives, few feminists were prepared for the social changes and reactionary pressures that shaped the postwar world. And without the discipline imposed by the highly organised forces of suffragism, without the excitement of its final phase, the women's movement in each country eventually suffered from anticlimax and the disunity that had plagued them in the years just before the vote was won. Although they certainly did not disintegrate, they became more specialised, less overtly woman-centred, and harder to characterise.

I. Winning the vote

By the time Britain declared war on Germany on 4 August 1914, the tactics of suffragists and suffragettes alike had failed to achieve a breakthrough for their cause. The Liberals continued to put other issues higher on their political agenda, and their leader, Asquith, was determined not to yield to militant pressure. Conservatives, like Liberals, feared the possible consequences of female enfranchisement, and while each Party was apprehensive that the other might act, neither, Hume asserts, was 'concerned enough . . . to take pre-emptive action on the suffrage question'. None the less, the suffragist mood was not despondent. There were clear indications of sympathy for the women among MPs, the Labour Party, the TUC and the wider public. Whereas the suffragettes were feeling the strain of internal divisions and public odium, Holton has shown that suffragists were making headway with their strategy of keeping pressure on Liberal ministers, encouraging 'prosuffrage opinion within the Conservative Party', and stressing that women's enfranchisement was 'an essential component of democratic government', much desired by the working class. It is no accident that when the Liberal government chose to enter into talks about female suffrage in 1914, it did so with members of Sylvia Pankhurst's East London Federation of Suffragettes (1913) and of the United Suffragists (1914): independent militants with Socialist connections, who could usefully be cultivated both to undermine the WSPU and, together with the constitutionalists and the pro-suffrage women Liberals, to weaken 'the position of the anti-suffragists in the cabinet'.[1]

And then the war came. On 6 August, following intensive deliberations, the NUWSS executive committee decided to keep its organisation in being but to recommend the suspension of suffrage agitation in favour of war work. Mrs Fawcett's exhortation was that women should show themselves 'worthy of citizenship whether our claim to it be recognized or not'. By 1914, the NUWSS had an estimated membership of over 100,000 in more than 500 societies to release for new labours.[2] The stance of the slower-moving WSPU became clear on 13 August, when Mrs Pankhurst declared 'a temporary suspension of activities', to give union finances a chance to recover and members a chance to recuperate; she added:

> with that patriotism which has nerved women to endure endless torture in prison cells for the national good, we ardently desire that our country shall be victorious –

this because we hold that the existence of all small nationalities is at stake and that the status of France and Great Britain is involved.

The release of the imprisoned suffragettes, without strings, had been agreed by the government prior to her announcement.[3]

Not all the rank and file of the WSPU were happy with this decision; some wished to maintain the suffrage campaign, worried that the union's funds would be misappropriated, and objected to its renaming as the Women's Party (1917–19). However, the resulting splinter groups of ex-WSPU adherents – 'The Suffragettes of the WSPU' and the 'Independent Women's Social and Political Union' – appear to have attracted few supporters and little notice.[4] The WSPU dissidents were also unhappy about the wartime activities of the Pankhursts and their allies, who were notably vehement in denouncing Germany and advocating 'military conscription for men, industrial conscription for women, the internment of all people of enemy race of whatever age, and the more ruthless enforcement of the blockade against enemy and neutral nations'. The WSPU journal, *The Suffragette*, was appropriately rechristened *Britannia* (1915). Shirkers, strikers and pacifists were sternly denounced. And Mrs Pankhurst toured America once more; only now her object was to secure backing for the British war effort. Christabel Pankhurst did the same. When the WSPU arranged a march in 1915 asserting women's 'right to serve' in the munitions industries, opposing union attempts to sustain the benefits they had won for male workers in those industries, it received government money and a blessing from Winston Churchill and Lloyd George. Though they were a far cry from the WSPU's early links with working men and its condemnation of the 'selfish and vicious interests' of British society, the wartime activities of the Pankhurst group suited its members' taste for wholehearted crusading.[5]

The NUWSS, the Women's Freedom League and the East London Federation of Suffragettes responded more moderately and without jettisoning suffragism completely. All three bodies undertook war work, even if there were serious divisions within the NUWSS over this issue, as well as over the need to sustain the suffragists' backing for Labour and the wisdom of campaigning for full adult suffrage, described by one supporter as 'trying to snatch two legs of mutton at once like Aesop's dog'.[6] The suffragists' war efforts were diverse, and included supporting workrooms for women thrown out of employment by the conflict; helping refugees; providing clubs, canteens and other services for soldiers and sailors, and assisting their wives; maternity and child welfare work, especially among the poor; and fruit picking and preserving to augment national food supplies. In addition, they were involved in relief, medical aid and nursing schemes; the activities of the Scottish Women's Hospitals for Foreign Service were especially notable. As Mrs Fawcett reflected, the fact that the suffragists were already mobilised and used to working together was a great asset to them during the war.

Meanwhile, Sylvia Pankhurst continued her efforts for adult suffrage and equal pay for equal work, helped the women of the East End, and expressed hostility to conscription. The Pethick Lawrences took part in wartime peace efforts: he as the losing peace candidate at the Aberdeen by-election of March 1917; she speaking in America on the need for a negotiated peace; and both in sympathy with the Women's International League for Peace and Freedom, founded in 1915, the British section of which subsequently attracted many democratic suffragists who were looking for an organisation of their own.[7] The Women's Interests Committee of the NUWSS pressed the government 'on behalf of both job opportunity and equal pay', and the Union united with over twenty other suffrage associations to form a consultative committee which kept the government informed, by 'repeated communications, letters, memorials and deputations', of their agreed views on any developments concerning the franchise.[8]

Mrs Fawcett reassured Mrs Catt in 1915 that 'we see no signs of disruption in our suffrage organisations', that income had kept up, and that the cause was 'stronger in this country than it was'. But she was aware that some observers – for example, Lord Northcliffe – believed that the suffrage movement was dead, and she was determined to prove them wrong. Encouraged by two prominent political allies, Mrs Fawcett wrote to Asquith in May 1916, asking for women to be included in any suffrage Bill, prompting him to acknowledge women's 'magnificent contribution to the war effort' and promise that when such a Bill was considered, their claims would be 'fully and impartially weighed, without any prejudgment from the controversies of the past'. Then in August, following suffragist deputations to Asquith, Bonar Law and Lord Robert Cecil, she sent a collaborative letter to the Prime Minister stressing that suffragists would appeal to Parliament and the country if 'the Government determined to proceed by creating a new basis for the franchise, or changing the law in any way which would result in the addition of a large number of men to the register, without doing anything for women'. During the same month, Mrs Pankhurst indicated that she favoured soldiers and sailors being given the vote without reference to female enfranchisement – an intervention which, happily, did not undermine the moderate suffragists' message to the politicians.[9]

By 1916 the government was considering electoral reform – not because of these suffragist overtures but because, as Mrs Fawcett conceded, a new Parliament had to be elected after 1915 and, at a time when eligible householders needed a residence qualification to vote, many men had disfranchised themselves by moving to serve in the armed forces or to take up war work. It was also prompted to act by a desire to tackle plural voting and consider the possibility of proportional representation.

Although Asquith had not lost his personal aversion to women's suffrage he had, by 1914, acknowledged the force of feminist requests for a democratic suffrage. He recognised the strength of suffragist arguments that women's war work had enhanced their case for the vote, and that postwar reconstruction would raise important questions 'directly affecting their interests, and possibly meaning for them large displacements of labour'. As a result of the suspension of militancy, any government accommodation of the women could not be presented as a weak capitulation to violence. There was, however, some fear that the 'detestable campaign' would be resumed at the end of the war, if women's political emancipation was still denied. Following the report of an all-party Speaker's Conference on Electoral Reform, established in October 1916, a Reform Bill which gave the vote to all adult males and proposed a measure of female suffrage was recommended by the converted Asquith to the House of Commons, debated, and accepted by a large majority in March 1917. It became law on 6 February 1918. The women to be enfranchised were householders on the local government register, together with wives of men on the register, occupiers of property of £5 annual value, and university graduates. And an 'age limit of thirty was imposed upon women, not because it was in any way logical or reasonable', Mrs Fawcett observed, 'but simply and solely in order to produce a constituency in which the men were not outnumbered by the women'. In November 1918, there was further pleasure in the suffragist camp when women were given the right to be parliamentary candidates. The wives of householders had secured the municipal suffrage a year earlier.[10]

Progress at the last was aided by the creation in May 1915 of the coalition government, which elevated a number of suffragists, dispensed with the services of several 'antis', replaced Asquith by Lloyd George in December 1916, and involved all parties except the Irish Nationalists, who refused to join. Having adhered to Asquith's line on women's suffrage for their own ends, they could no longer block electoral reform. With the coming of the coalition, it at last proved possible to harness female suffrage to a government Franchise Bill.[11] The suffragists were understandably unhappy about the unequal treatment of men and women, proposed with their foreknowledge, and accepted it only as a considerable step in the right direction: the revised electoral register in 1919 recorded 12,913,166 men and 8,479,156 women, the limited Suffrage Bill having given votes 'to approximately six times the number of women whose enfranchisement had been attempted under the pre-War Conciliation Bills'.[12]

They were right to do so. On the one hand, suffragists and suffragettes had prepared the ground for victory. Female anti-suffragists had abandoned their embarrassing activities during the war, and women had won gratitude and admiration as they undertook jobs once thought beyond them, their number in employment in Britain rising by 1,345,000 between July 1914 and July 1918.[13] The war, like all wars, helped to create a 'mood favourable to change', as Marwick argues, and when the Prime Minister received a 'great deputation of women war workers' in March 1917, he found that they wanted the vote, and that their delegation had the 'support of between thirty and forty women's organizations, including nearly all the existing suffrage societies, besides such well-known bodies as the British Women's Temperance Association, the National Union of Women Workers, the National Organization of Girls' Clubs, and the Women's Co-operative Guild, etc.'.[14] On the other hand, Mrs Fawcett herself, though convinced that the conflict 'had revolutionized the industrial position of women',[15] conceded that they would not have obtained the vote when they did if it had not been necessary to act to prevent the disfranchisement of men,[16] and Pugh has shown convincingly that old attitudes to women had not substantially changed.

Thus, whereas the press found the new workers interesting and politicians hesitated to deny woman 'the civil right which she has earned by her hard work',[17] the government was initially reluctant to recruit women workers,[18] while the unions were reluctant either to admit that women with little or no training could do jobs they designated as skilled, or to organise them as long-term labour and accept their case for equal pay. By a Treasury agreement of March 1915, unions were persuaded to suspend the operation of their rules excluding the employment of female workers as long as the war lasted. In fact, although women gained regular employment and better pay than formerly, they did not receive equal pay, and the unions for the most part 'kept membership closed to women'.[19] Many of the women who took jobs in munitions-making, manufacturing industry of all kinds, farming, and hospitals were not feminists seizing long-sought opportunities, and these largely young women were not the ones who were rewarded with the ballot in 1918. Rather, they were responding to the national emergency and expecting, like many men, that life would return to what it had been once the fighting ceased. The contemporary veneration of motherhood was certainly heightened during the war: in Pugh's words, the struggle 'emphasized as nothing else could that a woman's most important function was to rear the fighting men of the future'.[20]

Hostile MPs were not converted by women's wartime efforts. The already-persuaded majority of the House was simply freed to act by changed political circumstances. Even so Labour declined to help the Workers' Suffrage Federation continue the struggle for adult suffrage; while in the Lords, prominent 'antis' remained unhappy about female voting, predicting that it would change little and declaring that 'the suffrage movement had made no progress in America'.[21] As Mrs Fawcett acknowledged, 'We had an anxious time almost up to the end.'[22]

In the United States, the last stages of the struggle for the vote were harder and the final victory came two years later, after a campaign in which militancy gained ground.[23] The outbreak of world war did not immediately affect the American suffrage movement as it did the British, since the United States was not involved as a combatant until 1917. Yet American activists viewed with sorrow the disruption of the international work they had dominated. Feminists attending the 1914 IWSA board meeting in London appealed to Lord Grey and the European ambassadors based there 'to leave untried no method of conciliation or arbitration which may avert deluging half the civilized world in blood'; but they were bitterly aware of their 'political nonentity' during the world crisis.[24] The best that could be hoped for was to keep the organisation going, with the aid of American money, and look forward to a time when the women of the warring nations could be brought together again: 'We Americans', wrote Mrs Catt, 'have a mission to perform when the right time comes.'

In the short term, if the IWSA headquarters secretary might rely on American women for news of 'the more hopeful side of the movement', those who tried to sustain an interest in pacificism, even before 1917, were fiercely accused of being unhelpful to the American effort to prepare for possible involvement in the conflict, and of disloyalty to the national interest in Allied victory. When Jane Addams founded the Women's Peace Party to press for neutral mediation in the war, arms limitation, a world organisation which would work for international understanding, open diplomacy, the 'removal of the economic causes of war' and female suffrage, she was unprepared for the censure she and other opponents of militarism encountered.[25] For Mrs Catt, returning to national suffrage labours, the women's peace movement was a minefield she was unwilling to abandon entirely, but in which she trod with understandable calculation. Accordingly she kept her support for Addams and the Peace Party low key, and while urging neutrality upon President Wilson and Secretary of State Bryan in 1914, she later helped to publicise the news of women's war work that came in from abroad. No Congressman or other legislator was allowed to remain ignorant of it by NAWSA, whose members proselytised politicians 'in conversation, at dinners, and on tennis courts'; got their message across through the mails and in the corridors of power.[26]

There were few other positive developments for NAWSA activists to extol between 1914 and 1916. Operating separately from the Congressional Union for Woman Suffrage after February 1914, but adversely affected by its existence, they were divided by the Shafroth–Palmer Amendment which, to gratify supporters of state rights and promote state referenda on women's suffrage, committed the National during those years to persisting in the daunting state-by-state route to enfranchisement. When seven state campaigns were undertaken in 1914 and only two (Montana and Nevada) succeeded, the doubters seemed to be vindicated and the NAWSA leadership spent much of 1915 in disarray.[27]

The efforts of the Congressional Union, controversial though they were, gave the languishing movement a needed boost, rather as WSPU militancy had once galvanised suffragism in Britain. In its first major initiative in 1914, it dispatched organisers to the nine western states where women had full suffrage, hoping to unseat Democratic candidates there – though some were suffragists – and so make the ruling Party fear the power of the female vote. Small in size but directed by a highly professional staff and appealing to rich and poor women alike, the Union had by 1915 extended its activities to other states and maintained a high profile in the capital, holding meetings and demonstrations, producing suffrage petitions and sending deputations to Wilson, both to keep the issue on his mind and to indicate the wish for the vote that existed among women of all kinds. It had also forced a Congressional vote on the female suffrage amendment, although both Houses had voted the measure down. Whereas members of Congress did 'take notice' of the Union's party strategy, it naturally produced resentment in Democratic circles. While the women claimed to have contributed to the defeat of 23 out of 43 western Democrats in 1914, 'the campaign of the Union did not suffice to put the party in power out. Instead of the eighteen Democrats from the suffrage States in the 1913–1914 Congress, there were nineteen in the 1915–1916 Congress.'[28] In casting his vote for women's suffrage in a New Jersey referendum on the issue in 1915, Wilson was at pains to stress that he acted 'as a private citizen, "not as the leader of my party in the nation" ', and that he believed it 'should not be made a party question'.[29] And despite spirited efforts by local activists, the New Jersey referendum went against them, as did women's suffrage referenda in New York, Massachusetts and Pennsylvania in 1915.

If New Yorkers lost by the largest majority, they were the least disheartened. Undeterred by the state's size, large population, ethnic diversity and hostile politicians, or by the inability of Mrs Blatch's Women's Political Union (WPU) to combine with Mrs Catt's Empire State Campaign Committee, workers and energy were found for further demonstrations, 'stunts' and lobbying of every imaginable group. When the WPU turned to agitating for the national amendment after 1915, amalgamating with the Congressional Union, other suffrage associations in the state steeled themselves for another referendum drive. Mrs Catt, who had been preparing to join them, was drafted away from her dismayed state admirers, on the retirement of Anna Shaw, to resume the presidency of NAWSA and manage its push for the suffrage amendment. She did so magnificently, and was persuaded to accept the job by a happy combination of circumstances. Catt's international tasks had diminished, and it was apparent that the National's finances could be stabilised by injections from a large bequest. The organisation was willing to drop the Shafroth–Palmer Amendment and give her a free hand, while she herself wondered whether 'the state approach alone could ever work. Its chances in many states were nearly hopeless. State election laws and constitutional provisions often made state constitutional revision almost impossible. Even worse, Catt doubted whether there was a majority of men in many states who would soon vote for women's enfranchisement if they got the chance.'[30]

The focus of the Congressional Union and the NAWSA was thus the same from 1916, but they continued to employ different methods and to regard each other with anxiety, just as the WSPU and the NUWSS had done in Britain. In June 1916 the Union founded the National Woman's Party (NWP) to campaign in the twelve equal suffrage states for the defeat of Wilson and the Democratic Congressional candidates standing there. In fact, the President carried all except Oregon and Illinois out of the twelve, although the number of his electoral votes was reduced; and his Party's strength was not undermined, even while the importance of the women's vote in securing Wilson's victory had been demonstrated. Despite his swing towards the Progressives in the summer of 1916, on subsequently seeing a deputation from the Woman's Party the re-elected President declined to say more than he had said 'on previous occasions of this sort', beyond expressing his conviction that 'the Democratic Party is more inclined than the opposition to assist in this great cause'. The pro-suffrage planks secured in 1916 from the Republican and Democratic parties, after pressure from both groups of suffragists, had not proved helpful, since 'they ruled out conferring the vote by Federal amendment'.[31]

The response of the disappointed Woman's Party was increased militancy, beginning in January 1917 with pickets outside the White House: 'sentinels of liberty, sentinels of self-government – silent sentinels'. A tactic which initially attracted curiosity, some sympathy and invaluable publicity brought violence from bystanders once the United States had been drawn into the war and the pickets' banners carried provoking suggestions that democracy should begin at home. By June, the women were being arrested, though obstructing the traffic on the sidewalk was their only offence. In time they were imprisoned under grim circumstances in the district jail or government workhouse, and as had been the case with the British suffragettes, those (including police) who committed violence against them were allowed to go free. Like the suffragettes, many of the activists in the Woman's Party (united with the Congressional Union from 1917) came from highly respectable backgrounds, and their allegedly unwomanly and unpatriotic behaviour embarrassed an administration dominated by suffragists. Once the militants resorted to hunger-strikes to protest their treatment, it none the less employed force-feeding, as the British had done. The women's retort – to which no similarly telling reply could be found – was that they were being arrested not for obstructing traffic, but for offending politically; and that their sentences exceeded those meted out to British suffragettes, though Americans observing the British scene had said that ' "never would such things happen in the United States. The men told us they would not endure such frightfulness." '[32]

Woman's Party workers were undeterred by the government's attempts to intimidate them and suppress news of their frequently brutal treatment. They were undefeated by their failure to secure political status from those who feared having to extend it 'to conscientious objectors and to all prisoners now confined for political opinions'. They scornfully rejected accusations that Woman's Party activists were 'pro-German, disloyal, and un-American'. And they persisted with militancy. The Woman's Party picketed the Capitol, burning the President's 'past and present speeches or books concerning "liberty", "freedom" and "democracy" ', and eventually torching his effigy in a series of watchfires for freedom outside the White House. It protested when Wilson docked at Boston on his brief return from peace discussions at Versailles, and staged a demonstration in New York before the President went back to Europe. Arrests and imprisonments again resulted from the women's activities, and they publicised their experiences on release by touring the country in a hired railroad car, dubbed the 'prison special'. A further campaign against Democrats standing in the suffrage states was also undertaken during the 1918 elections, primarily to induce Wilson to give public support to the Democratic candidates for the Senate in New Jersey and New

Hampshire, whose votes might secure the passage of the suffrage amendment through that body. While the President gave the desired endorsement, Republicans won in New Jersey and New Hampshire.[33]

It is difficult to gauge the overall importance of the militants' tactics. They took pride in belonging to the only organisation that was putting all its efforts into the suffrage movement.[34] They were undoubtedly newsworthy, and though they exaggerated their role they at least believed that 'parades and soap-boxing and publicity demonstrations' had secured the vote in six years, when 'humble petitions and polite resolutions' had failed to stir stubborn and conservative men for sixty. They at least believed that their pressure had moved Wilson from anti-suffragism to support for the once hopeless-looking women's cause: from insincere words to necessary actions.[35] Such a conviction, as well as an unshakable belief in the righteousness of their endeavour, kept the militants going through many harrowing experiences. After all, in the course of their agitation the chairman of the Senate Suffrage Committee had visited the imprisoned women and recommended action on the suffrage amendment. A House Committee on Woman Suffrage had been appointed and the House had set a date to vote on the amendment, doing so in the affirmative in January 1918. Only the Senate had remained as a stubborn stumbling block during the life of the sixty-fifth Congress (1917–19). Some prominent men had protested the treatment of the pickets and Dudley Field Malone, the Democratic Collector of Customs for the Port of New York, had resigned his post to underline his disgust over the imprisonment and his Party's failure to act on women's enfranchisement.[36]

It was an astute move to relate votes for women in America to the world war for democracy, since the link discomfited Wilson and took note of the Democrats' decision in 1917 that 'only "war measures" should be included in the legislative program, and ... that no subjects would be considered by them, unless the President urged them as war measures'. Wilson finally backed female suffrage in the September 1918 debate on the amendment as 'a vitally necessary war measure'.[37] Furthermore, the administration plainly did not relish imprisoning women from the influential classes – as witness its unconditional release of women prisoners in November 1917.[38] And equally plainly the American militants, unlike their British counterparts, were prepared to continue their efforts until the vote was won – not a prospect that the Democrats could relish.[39]

But if supporters of the Woman's Party accepted the charge of militancy 'rather cheerfully, and even proudly', while suggesting that the term 'can hardly be applied to any of the acts of American suffragists',[40] the Party's avoidance of property destruction and violence on the British pattern did not stop its radical members and tactics from alarming a diverse people inclined to intolerance at times of national tension. In addition, though American suffragists tried to conceal from the press the bitter dissension among British activists,[41] they found themselves engaged in similar disputes, evasions and cover-up tactics. As Mrs

Catt saw it, Woman's Party members, by adopting a confrontational, anti-Democratic stance, had 'alienated many democratic sympathizers and it has been very difficult to win them back. We have found that they have been untrustworthy and extremely disloyal to the old association [NAWSA] which made conditions possible for their work.'[42] Sorry that 'all suffragists cannot unite in tactics and follow the same plan', yet determined to be 'distinctly separate' from the militants, since unity was impossible,[43] Catt and her allies sought to avoid sharing their bad press and alienating influential men by privately and publicly distancing themselves from the pickets' 'obtrusive, noisy, and irritating methods'.[44] They thereby ignored the 'injustice being done' to the protesting women.[45]

Some suffragists believed that 'Because war will interrupt the regular suffrage work, as war has for long done in other cases, is no reason why we should turn aside from our chosen work and take up other work.'[46] Recognising this feeling, the Woman's Party left participation in the war effort to individual members, declining any organisational involvement. Yet Catt, like the equally pragmatic Mrs Fawcett, was right in recognising that war was changing the status of women and that 'woman's hour has struck', as it had struck for American slaves during the Civil War. With the example of European women before them, American women stepped into men's shoes from 1917, in city and country alike, their endeavours monitored by the United States Department of Labor through a Division of Women's Work, with branches in every state.[47] They were employed in making armaments and explosives, tools and machinery, by foundries, refineries and chemical plants, in transport and agriculture, as well as traditional activities such as nursing, kitchen gardening, food-canning, knitting, sewing and fund-raising, nursing and assisting the Red Cross. On occasions doing work 'as efficiently as it could have been done by any American business man',[48] women earned the President's gratitude. Thus, when he eventually urged adoption of the suffrage amendment, he did so in the light of their war services: 'services rendered in every sphere, – not only in the fields of effort in which we have been accustomed to see them work, but wherever men have worked and upon the very skirts and edges of the battle itself'.[49]

None the less, feminists continued to find the war work question trying. Despite encouraging women's mobilisation, sustaining a hospital in France and themselves undertaking valuable labours, the moderates' leaders, Shaw and Catt, were patronised on the Women's Committee of the Council of National Defence, where the partnership with women to which Wilson alluded in 1918 was one in which they were very much the juniors.[50] Since NAWSA's reputation was enhanced by the connection, however, Catt sustained and publicised it, bearing with fortitude the anti-suffragists' persistent questioning of her patriotism. With an eye to public respectability, she also played down the suffragists' former Socialist connection, since that Party's anti-war stance was deemed a liability.[51]

Just as women's war work was an important element, alongside the militancy of the Woman's Party, in converting the President to active support for women's suffrage, so the tactics of the NAWSA suffragists played a vital part in the final victory; although they, like the militants, were inclined to overvalue their own contribution,[52] even as both suffragettes and suffragists in Britain claimed the credit for winning the vote. By 1916 Mrs Catt had devised a careful plan to secure the franchise. In pursuit of her national strategy, which secured the backing of thirty-six state associations, Wilson was to be cultivated – rather than harassed – to persuade him into action. But the states were not be neglected during the struggle to obtain a favourable vote from Congress on the amendment. The suffrage states and the states where suffragism was strong were instructed to keep up the pressure on Washington legislators, and assistance was pledged to 'the "fighting states" above and beyond all else', so that full or partial suffrage could be won in additional designated states, some progress achieved in the hostile East and South, and the 'ratification sentiment throughout the nation' strengthened. The plan's details were to be kept secret, and NAWSA's national board was given supreme power in its implementation. It was felt necessary, at this vital stage of the campaign, to 'take a big view', and Mrs Catt stressed that:

> The littleness of the view which our American states rights' plan has stimulated for a hundred years, is the greatest enemy of woman suffrage, of successful war activities and of everything else we wish to do as a nation.[53]

Mrs Catt's strategy enjoyed a large measure of success, and under her leadership NAWSA grew into 'the largest voluntary organization in the country'. President Wilson, who had expressed sympathy with suffragists at the 1916 NAWSA convention, continued to see its representatives and, notwithstanding Woman's Party provocations, told a deputation received in June 1918 that he hoped the Senate would pass the franchise amendment.[54] The Association's state drive – aided by Woman's Party workers – bore fruit in 1917, with presidential suffrage being granted in North Dakota, Ohio (where it was cancelled by referendum), Indiana (where it was cancelled by court action), Rhode Island, Nebraska and Michigan, the primary vote in Arkansas and full suffrage in New York. Pressure from the country at large, therefore, was strong when NAWSA and the Woman's Party lobbied members of the House to pass the suffrage amendment on 10 January 1918. It duly did so. The struggle for Senate assent was more protracted, despite presidential encouragement and progress in the states. Mrs Fawcett, who had rejoiced when the House of Lords and the House of Representatives approved female enfranchisement on the same day, wrote to Mrs Catt after the first defeat: 'Truly the task of the United States is gigantic. If we had your conditions, we should have failed in the House of Lords. British authorities have always said your constitution is the most conservative on earth.'[55]

This was not the kind of sympathy that American suffragists, convinced of British conservatism, could altogether relish. Impelled to fresh action and influenced in part by the tactics of the Woman's Party, NAWSA swiftly set about implementing its 1917 decision to try to unseat senators opposed to the amendment who were up for re-election in 1918: two of them were defeated in November.[56] The winning of suffrage referenda in South Dakota, Michigan and Oklahoma in 1918 helped to keep tension high in Washington, as did the granting of presidential suffrage in Iowa, Minnesota, Missouri, Ohio, Wisconsin and Maine.[57] And in 1919 the amendment was at last passed by both Houses, with men from the states where women were enfranchised carrying the day.[58] Ratification by the necessary two-thirds (thirty-six) of the states took from 4 June 1919 until 26 August 1920, with NAWSA, according to a pre-formulated design, frantically working all the while to prevent the premature disbanding of the state organisations, to rally the faithful, and to secure the necessary votes from regular or special sessions of the legislatures.[59]

Women's enfranchisement did not come in America, any more than it had come in Britain, because conservatives' prejudices had been overcome. During the debates on the amendment in the House and the Senate, and on ratification in the states, anti-suffragists predicted that 'the deterioration of manhood', the breakdown of family life, and the loss of woman's position as 'the uncrowned queen in the hearts of all right-thinking American men' would follow from female voting.[60] Women 'antis' 'pressed the sharp point of Negro woman suffrage into Southern traditions' which denied blacks the vote; and in the hard-fought Tennessee ratification campaign, opponents included 'the former "whisky lobby" in full force, the one-time railroad lobby which was alleged to have directed Tennessee politics for years, and a newer manufacturer's lobby'.[61]

Such corporate interests, well organised in American politics generally, played a more important part in the antis' activities in the United States than they did in Britain, and this is not surprising. American women were more influential in the 'do everything' temperance crusade than their British sisters, and the political consequences of their moralism, and that of women Progressives, were feared. In the words of one opponent: 'As to your cause, ladies, it is opposed to freedom. Wherever you vote, you pass laws against liberty. We shall oppose you to the last.' With the passage of the Prohibition amendment in December 1917, the opposition to women's suffrage may have abated among the more practical members of the liquor lobby; but we cannot be certain.[62] In the wartime context, moreover, antis liked to suggest that suffragism depended on 'German, pro-German, pacifist and Socialist votes, each class being at that time anathema'.[63] As the suffrage amendment went through a ratification process that British suffragists thought they were fortunate to avoid,[64] last-ditch opposition to the measure grew, with governors refusing to call or delaying calling special legislation sessions, and antis trying to secure referenda on its ratification. To suffragist relief, these were invalidated by the Supreme Court in June 1920; in 1922 the Court 'handed down the second of two decisions upholding the Nineteenth Amendment against further challenge'.[65]

After seventy-two years of striving, the vote had been won. But the South had not been reconstructed: Virginia, Maryland, North Carolina, South Carolina, Georgia, Alabama, Louisiana, Mississippi and Florida failed to ratify.[66] After decades of mutual exhortation and information exchange, the friendly competitors of American and British suffragism were at last able to rejoice in their mutual good fortune, while Americans might privately give thanks that they, at least, had no further suffrage hurdles to surmount.

II. From wartime to postwar challenges

(i) *The United States*

When the war came, it was easier for organised women's groups whose main concern was not the suffrage to adjust their normal programmes. Accordingly, bodies like the WCTU, the YWCA, the consumers' leagues and the women's clubs worked among soldiers and sailors, informed themselves about conditions in Europe, supported the efforts of the Red Cross, and turned women's traditional skills to good effect in – for example – food conservation, while continuing on a reduced scale with their customary fund-raising, educational, social purity, legislative and community activities.[67] Awareness that the world was in a turmoil did not, however, alter entrenched opinions and behaviour with regard to race.

At the eleventh biennial convention of the National Association of Colored Women in 1918, reports of war work were delivered and it was confirmed that the Association had supported every 'means used by our Government to finance and win the war'. It was hoped that war service and closer contacts between the races would reduce white prejudice. Yet the signs were not entirely hopeful, and resolutions were recorded against mob violence and in favour of an anti-lynching law; endorsing bodies working to ease the situation of blacks moving North; and opposing the election of those who were not pledged to eliminate race discrimination.[68] The NAWSA leadership continued to avoid accepting black organisations for fear of undermining its efforts to capture southern states. Disliking the views of anti-black, states rights women such as Laura Clay and Kate Gordon, it none the less acknowledged the need 'to leave state work absolutely to the direction and control of each state'. Nor was the conduct of the NWP on race issues any more admirable.[69] Not surprisingly, black suffragists were still difficult to find outside black associations.[70]

On contemplating the difficulties facing the war-torn world in 1915, Mrs Robins of the Women's Trade Union League felt that whatever was done by England and France:

> the challenge is ... thrown out to American men and women to safeguard the hard won liberty of the people, the great constructive social work of the last one hundred years and all the finer expressions of civilization, to guard these liberties and to further develop them.

Her concluding query – 'Can we answer?' – brought no clear response from the women whom she thought were one of the two great exploited groups in the United States. (Immigrants were the other: black Americans went unmentioned.) Female reformers continued to work for women, children and society as a whole, but feminists did not, in any concentrated way, debate what the priorities for a new era should be. Contemporary observers of womanhood, however, were in agreement about the salient feature of the 1920s: the emergence of the 'flapper'. Member of a young generation captivated by the writings of Freud and the dictates of a highly commercialised fashion and beauty business, she was a sexually emancipated creature who put personal enjoyment before service to society. The 'new woman', who was said to have emerged in the 1890s in Britain and America, allegedly came into her own in both countries during the 1920s.

Given the upheavals of war, and the growing number of women in the workforce and public endeavours, it was inevitable that the Victorian female culture would be further eroded, and not just among unusual groups like the Greenwich Village feminists. Bourgeois women were now drawn to the urban amusements long sought by their independent working-class sisters, and many kinds of new women were perceived. However, there was continuity as well as change. The divorce rate might have soared after the war, but most women continued to marry and raise families. The winning of the vote and involvement in new wartime roles clearly did not launch women on a path of new freedom unhampered by male disapproval, economic or legal barriers, educational or media conditioning, biological factors or inherited stereotypes about appropriate female behaviour. We have also seen (pp. 134–8, 229–34 above) that substantial changes in the Victorian moral code in Britain and America alike had been accomplished, long before the roaring twenties, by nineteenth- and early-twentieth-century purity reformers, social scientists, advocates of voluntary motherhood, and proponents of liberal divorce and child custody legislation.[71]

None the less, reform in the area of women's sexual rights was the most significant advance that affected them during the 1920s. As always, changing social circumstances paved the way. More women, including married women, were working outside the home. American industry, which had long recognised women's power as consumers, was more willing to produce intimate goods for them, including maternity wear and sanitary towels. There was a growing tendency among members of both sexes to accept women's changed role in the nuclear family; and the increasing prosperity and secularisation of American society encouraged its citizens to come to terms with the fact that 'young men and women in the early twentieth century sought the pleasure of companionship before marrige in the world outside the home'.[72] The outstanding birth control advocate in the United States was Margaret Sanger (see above, p. 233), whose stridently anti-bourgeois journal, *The Woman Rebel*, fell foul of 'the federal law against mailing obscene material', leading her to flee to England in 1914. There she was soon at home in neo-Malthusian, feminist and intellectual circles, formed a close attachment to the sexologist Havelock Ellis, and 'found a new style of reform aimed at educating social leaders rather than appealing to the silent masses', as yet unaroused in England to the possibility of obtaining birth control advice, or to the benefits it would yield.[73]

Like other American feminists who had visited Britain, Sanger patently enjoyed the swiftness with which a newcomer with the right credentials could enter into the heart of the protest networks. In the tradition of cosmopolitan Garrisonian abolitionism, she confessed: 'I know I have never had a country'. Rather less nobly, she enjoyed the attention she received as a 'lone woman', appreciated the aristocratic English style, and could hardly fail to relish the respectful reference of English allies to their 'slow little country' and the 'sleepy air of Europe'.[74] But flattery is an insubstantial food, and in 1915 Sanger returned to the United States, where she set about legalising birth control education, sticking to her task with an impressive single-mindedness. Describing the stages of her work in 1928, she recollected that the first step had been:

> to awaken the consciousness of the American public to the idea and the necessity of contraception; the second was to bring the discussion of Birth Control out of the abyss of prurient silence to which it had been condemned by prejudice and convention – to bring the doctrine out into the sunlight of frank and open discussion; the third necessary step was to awaken the interest and effect the alliance of scientists and doctors which would eventuate in the perfecting of a practical and hygienic technique; while the fourth and large step would aim at the establishement of clinics and the creation of a research department.

She felt that she was closer to realising these aims than 'anyone ten years ago could have believed possible', and that the cause had little to fear from fanaticism, much from 'Apathy and languid convictions'.[75]

The struggle had not been an easy one, and Sanger had been put on her mettle in the course of it by the existence of rival forces to her own in America: the National Birth Control League (1915) and the Voluntary Parenthood League (1919). Set up by the reformer Mary Ware Dennett, with the backing of liberal New York women, these bodies were dedicated to repealing rather than breaking the laws which, since the federal Comstock Act of 1873, had prohibited the dissemination of contraceptive information by defining it as obscenity. A further inducement to action had come in 1921, when a birth control clinic had been opened in England by Marie Stopes (see below, pp. 268–70), a palaeobotanist who had turned her considerable energies to sex education. Sanger's youthful radicalism persisted into middle age, showing in her willingness to state her message boldly on the public platform and, when necessary, to go to court or jail for her beliefs. But as Reed has shown, she was complex figure who, in maturity, was ready to cultivate influential allies from the bourgeoisie she had once lambasted and to recognise that the medical profession, ever jealous of its standing, must be won over.

Accordingly, though the first short-lived birth control clinic Sanger opened in 1916 in New York operated without the services of a doctor, her Birth Control Clinical Research Bureau, launched in 1923, did employ one; and she was prepared to campaign for legislation giving doctors the right to disseminate contraceptive advice, rather than seeking outright repeal of anti-contraception legislation. Her approach secured the grudging interest and involvement of medical practitioners, and allowed her to emerge by 1925 as the dominant figure in the American birth control movement: the author of two bestsellers, a conference promoter, and the initiator not only of the Bureau but also of the *Birth Control Review* (1917) and the American Birth Control League (1921). Accepting the need to organise, though she had 'an uncanny dread of social organizations', Sanger triumphed through her distinctive combination of personal flamboyance and fearlessness with practicality and political acumen. The times demanded no less, for despite the alleged sexual emancipation of the 1920s, legislators who limited the size of their own families did not feel able to act publicly to benefit others, fearing the Roman Catholic lobby and anxious to avoid the charge either of encouraging immorality or of fostering what the eugenicists feared: a further decline of the birth rate among affluent Americans. The poor, they believed, could not be helped.[76] Though she was increasingly willing to deploy eugenic arguments, Sanger thought otherwise, responding to requests for help both from members of the middle class and from the ' "always ailing, never failing" sort of mother' in the working class, who wanted a better standard of living for herself and her family.[77]

Sanger did not abandon her opposition to Comstockery, however, just because she acknowledged that 'our Congressmen are timid about this subject'. Who, after all, was better placed to see the absurdity of the situation prevailing in 1929, when there were 'twenty-five Birth Control Clinics legally operating throughout the U.S.A. and yet the federal law makes it a five-year prison sentence for any one of us to write to another person and tell him where these clinics are!'[78] She resigned as president of the American Birth Control League in 1928 partly to devote more time to fighting for a change in the law, and by the 1930s, through her National Committee on Federal Legislation for Birth Control, she was engaged in numerous court actions to help the cause. As Sanger explained:

> The clinics now need Federal legislation in order to get supplies via parcel post. We also need Federal legislation so that doctors can get data and material from one clinic to the other and from Europe.[79]

Partial success was achieved in 1936, when a legal judgement 'opened the mails to contraceptive materials intended for physicians. The right of individual citizens to bring such devices into the country for personal use was not established until 1971.'[80]

All the while, Sanger continued to keep in touch with the international campaign for birth control, and to retain staunch friends even as her dominating style made her enemies. In addition, she kept up the fight to raise adequate funds for her many ventures: one of the reasons the Clinical Research Bureau and the clinic she began in Harlem attracted critism from doctors was that they were subsidised.[81] It was a happy day for Sanger's fortunes in every sense when she met a rich and enterprising manufacturer, J. Noah Slee. Since she was by then (like Slee) contentedly divorced, and had no intention of retiring to the unsatisfying domesticity from which she had escaped at considerable personal cost, her marriage to Slee in 1922 was solemnised only after he had agreed to respect her independence and help the birth control movement. That he did magnificently, in the style of Frederick Pethick Lawrence in the British suffragette crusade – in other words, he used his existing expertise tactfully in a new fashion. Specifically, this meant importing needed diaphragms by way of Canada, manufacturing contraceptive jelly at his New Jersey plant, and financing a company to take over the work, headed by another capitalist admirer of Sanger, Herbert R. Simonds. During the 1920s, the Clinical Research Bureau also inspired the setting up of other birth control clinics, instructed patients and doctors in contraceptive techniques, and kept careful records that proved the utility of contraception while trying to determine why some patients used it only for a short time or irregularly, or gave it up altogether.[82]

Yet if many women in the 1920s were able to pursue personal autonomy and companionate marriage thanks to the birth control research, literature and clinics fostered by Sanger, it was not only doctors and legislators who expressed misgivings. Some women reformers, having long condemned the sexual indulgence of men, were uncomfortable at the prospect of greater sexual activity and less sexual distinctiveness for women. The best they could believe was that Sanger had made possible, by modern means, the nineteenth-century feminist objective of voluntary motherhood. Sanger's expectation was that women, once they were freed from unwanted pregnancies and harrowing abortions, could do more for their children, themselves and the world: a view at one with that held by Victorian activists. But she overestimated, as they did, the social consequences of a single reform. Accordingly, as Reed points out, though she denounced America's high infant mortality rate and criticised her country's inequitable health-care system, Sanger 'drew back from radical criticism of American capitalism'. Since the United States was the dominant capitalist power in the world during the 1920s, providing extraordinary material benefits for the majority of its citizens who were able to find work, we can hardly suppose that she would have achieved much by adopting a different course. Yet Gordon rightly concludes that when the birth control issue lost its ties to Socialism and working-class activism in the period of postwar political reaction, it became increasingly shaped by doctors and eugenicists who shifted the focus from women's individual freedom to 'planned parenthood' in the interests of race health. As they did so they, like Sanger, isolated birth control from the broader context of feminism.[83]

American women remained active in other areas of reform after World War

One, their leaders experiencing no immediate consciousness of fatigue or disappointment with the results of their protracted labours. Indeed, like their British counterparts, they often enjoyed great energy and long lives.[84] Having failed either to prevent American entry into the war or to play a formal part in the peacemaking process – 'The fighting male sat alone in the Peace Conference', complained Mrs Blatch – feminists in nearly all the major women's associations were none the less determined to take up peace ventures and internationalism. They believed that as 'the commanding cause of the last generation was the war against slavery, the commanding cause of ours is the war against war'.[85]

A good illustrative case would be that of Fannie Fern Andrews, a pro-suffrage Radcliffe graduate with an encouraging husband, who became an authority on international law and the international aspects of education. In 1908, a year after a meeting of the National Peace Congress in New York, she founded the American School Peace League (ASPL). With the aid of members and patrons (comprising educators, students and the generally interested) it organised the distribution of literature to the press and libraries, arranged talks and peace days, and devised courses for instructors. Working closely with women's clubs and state associations, the League aimed to persuade teachers to study the international peace movement and apply their learning in schools: to use education to foster international understanding as well as patriotism. By 1913 it could report thirty-five state branches, and recognised that 'in the future our country is destined to play a larger part than ever before in the councils of world affairs.' But from the first the ASPL had a programme for world organisation, which included a regularly convened world congress; arbitration treaties between nations; gradual, proportionate disarmament; an international police force; and the funding of educational work and exchanges.

When war came, Mrs Andrews believed it would be folly for the League 'to place itself in a wrong attitude before the country'. She therefore urged the desirability of America acting as a world mediator in 1915, accepted the need for America's entry into the conflict in 1917, and was ready to 'co-operate with the President in his desire to make the world safe for democracy'. In order to 'assist the nation in winning the war for permanent peace', the ASPL devised a special wartime programme, while still stressing 'the value of arbitration, conciliation, and judicial settlement' and drawing the line at compulsory military training in public high schools. As a result of this prudence Andrews found herself assisting the US Commissioner of Education in educational war work, especially the promotion of the League of Nations; and going as the Commissioner's representative to the peace conference, reporting back on the educational needs of the new era that was dawning. Undaunted by the ease with which the United States had embraced the martial spirit, even while she acknowledged that the war had affected funds and retarded her work, Mrs Andrews resumed her school activities in the 1920s. Then the League – rechristened the American School Citizenship League – linked up with the citizenship and international committees of many national and local associations, particularly those sustained by women.

As before, the aim was to 'promote co-operation among the nations' – not least through contacts with campaigners in other countries, notably Britain. And having attended the 1915 International Congress of Women, which protested against the war and attempted to lay down the principles on which a permanent peace might be built, Andrews predictably took part in the women's international gatherings of the postwar period, through which British and American activists kept in close touch.[86]

When, in 1925, she recalled the presence at Versailles of a Conference of Women Delegates organised by the International Council of Women (ICW) and the International Woman Suffrage Alliance, Andrews proudly claimed that it had inspired 'several of the provisions in Article 23 of the Treaty of Versailles, as well as some of the great humanitarian and educational efforts now being put forward on a world scale'.[87] But she and other feminists had shouldered an impossible task in trying 'to rouse America to join other nations of like mind in putting an end to world disorder, and establishing world peace'.[88] Even achieving co-operation among women at home and abroad continued to prove difficult, and the link between feminism and pacificism had always been a complicated one, in America and Europe alike.

The sixth quinquennial of the ICW, for instance, was held in Washington in 1925, with delegates attending from forty-two countries, and it eventually produced an impressive number of resolutions, which endorsed the ideals of the League, the Court of International Justice and the Geneva Protocol; 'simultaneous international disarmament'; destruction of the 'economic barriers' between nations; European reconstruction schemes; and careful study of 'the problem of national minorities'.[89] However, the press commented that the meeting was 'one of the most criticized and least understood conventions in the history of the feminist movement', pointing to contemporary condemnation of the participants for their alleged Communism and pacifism, and to internal dissension among the women, financial difficulties, poor organisation, the segregation of black visitors from whites, and a peace programme on which American and German delegates refrained from voting.[90] A Conference on the Cause and Cure of War (CCW), put on by nine of the major women's groups in the country earlier in the year and the first of many, had likewise been condemned – not least by women's patriotic societies – as a propaganda vehicle for the League of Nations, a magnet for Communist sympathisers and a feminist threat to national virility and preparedness.[91]

American women might have prided themselves that their 'instinct to shelter humanity' could be 'used in building for peace':[92] that 'the history of the International Council of Women shows a constant development of world co-operation among women which has proved to be a potent factor in World Friendship and World Peace.'[93] In fact, the United States in the 1920s was a mass of contradictions, and women divided over the significant developments of their time, just as men did. On the one hand the United States was the world's major creditor nation, an active trading power which took a keen interest in the parts of the globe where it had established connections, supported the non-political work of the League of Nations, and participated in the disarmament conferences that began in 1921. On the other hand, it rejected formal participation in the League and the World Court, pursued high-tariff policies unhelpful to the international economy and, in a reaction against Wilsonian reformism and internationalism, endorsed reactionary Republican administrations in Washington, the persecution of those suspected of Communist sympathies, immigration restriction, lynching, child labour, the revival of the Ku Klux Klan, and an exaggerated nationalism.

In this climate, women's patriotic groups such as the Daughters of the American Revolution (DAR) flourished along with bodies like the ICW and CCW, and they did not share the feminist commitment to 'full and free discussion'.[94] The Women's International League for Peace and Freedom, the National Consumers' League, the League of Women Voters, the General Federation of Women's Clubs, the Young Women's Christian Association and the Woman's Christian Temperance Union were all attacked by the DAR as pro-Communist, though they had merely 'expressed the hope that peace will one day supplant war; that children will be taken from factories and sent to school; that mothers and babies will not die of preventable causes; [and] that this country may at least have as high as percentage of literacy as Japan'. Despite the heroic speaking, organising and educational efforts of long-term female peace campaigners of the calibre of Andrews, Carrie Catt, Jane Addams, Catharine McCulloch and Harriet Laidlaw, they – like their 'super-patriot' opponents – remained minorities among American women. Despite efficient lobbying in Washington and such occasional satisfactions as the part they played in the ratification of the Kellogg–Briand anti-war treaty of 1928, women mobilised for peace and internationalism were frequently reduced to the production of futile paper. And by the 1930s they were obliged to recognise that 'all proposals for disarmament had proved illusory'.[95]

For the established women's associations, less distracted than suffrage or peace groups by the upheavals of war, the 1920s saw a familiar focus on the concerns of women and children, including education and social purity. But there were also new organisations, such as the parent–teacher associations, and new emphases to suit the new era. This blend of customary and fresh concerns is evident in the postwar history of the Southern Association of College Women and the American Association of University Women (AAUW), of which it became a part in 1921. The southern organisation continued to try to persuade women to attend college, to improve standards and conditions among students and staff, and to raise money for scholarships and fellowships, loans and gifts. At the same time it gave more encouragement than formerly to the provision of home economics courses, the direction of women into vocations other than teaching, and the fostering of student and faculty exchanges. These were facilitated through the International Federation of University Women, set up in London in 1920, following a British educational mission to the United States two years earlier. The AAUW had begun in 1881 with sixty-six members; by 1931 it claimed 36,800 in 521 branches, and sustained a successful journal.

Yet, as always, the economic opportunities facing educated women lagged far behind those awaiting men, while the problems of combining career and family persisted: facts of life which the Association was powerless to change. And while the new stress on home economics training must be seen in the context of a broader effort to improve vocational training for the masses during the 1920s, it scarcely challenged conventional notions of female destiny, even when a successful career woman, reformer and political activist like Mary Dewson, who taught the subject at the Boston School of Housekeeping, supported the school's view that it was 'a Profession demanding scientific training', useful to housewife and settlement worker alike. Equally disturbing was the growing practice of women working 'to help husbands secure degrees', instead of enrolling in college themselves. Making the best of this unpromising situation, the AAUW was pleased to offer information to individual university women, and to provide a stimulus for its many college graduate members who had become homemakers.[96]

For the National Association of Colored Women, the 1920s involved a similar renewal of old struggles and beginning of new ones. Activists concerned themselves with the building of old folks' homes, the opening of day nurseries, kindergartens, orphan asylums and reformatories, the maintenance of social settlements and community centres, child welfare work of all kinds, and scholarship fund-raising. And they took note of Mrs Terrell's view that since the vote 'means more to us than it does to any of our sisters in the other racial groups', it would 'be a terrible reflection upon us, if we do not use our ballots to promote the welfare of our race'. The result was the creation of special departments to take an interest in all Bills affecting the black population, and to educate black women in their citizenship duties. Cautious support was also given to organised attempts to achieve interracial co-operation in the South, despite awareness that many of the blacks' difficulties arose from white discrimination, and perhaps because it was conceded that the work of the Association was hampered by meagre finances. These had not, however, prevented the black woman from plunging in 'penniless and without experience to attack poverty problems as they presented themselves in every locality'.[97] But Terrell's own struggle to make a living in 'prejudice-ridden' Washington, notwithstanding 'the training, the experience and the success that I have', indicated just how little entrenched racial attitudes were affected by the valiant self-help of Association women. Small wonder that by the end of the decade NACW membership had dwindled and black women were seeking advancement through the better-financed, male-led black associations, as well as their own.[98]

White southern women, as Scott has shown, were not neglectful either of the challenge posed by racism or of the opportunity to prove that they could, as they had predicted, put the vote to good use. In consequence, after 1920 they turned old suffrage societies into leagues of women voters which, in conjunction with other female organisations, instructed the new citizens, made sure they voted, and campaigned for legislation to protect children and improve the wages and conditions of women workers. They supported bodies like the Commission on Inter-racial Cooperation in efforts to improve black schools, libraries, housing, health and railroad accommodations, speaking out at last against lynching, as black women such as Terrell and Ida Wells had long been doing. In addition they attempted, with some success, to reform state and local government, engage in party politics and secure public office.[99] But if Progressive reform was strong in the postwar South, thanks in part to its women, the still substantial female purity alliance was, like the peace activists, in difficulties there and elsewhere during the 1920s. As an itinerant purity lecturer, Mrs Terrell may have been spurred on by the knowledge that white morality left much to be desired.[100] But she and her co-workers could find little cause for satisfaction as they contemplated the relaxation of public standards with regard to dancing and smoking, the unabated threat caused by the white slave traffic and venereal disease, and the inadequate enforcement of the Prohibition amendment.

Nevertheless, though the creation of the Women's Organization for Repeal of National Prohibition and the Women's Organization for National Prohibition Reform bore witness to the decline of the women's temperance endeavour, social feminists generally were active on many fronts, agitating effectively for the passage of new marriage and divorce laws, state welfare codes, and maternity and infancy protection acts. Despite their general retreat from politics, individual women's clubs of all kinds still attracted those who felt comfortable with active community work, allying with helpful professionals and lobbying for selected legislation, but who did not aspire to prominence in political life. And the WCTU still pursued its 'do everything' policy, working for racial betterment, Sabbath observance, the enforcement of the Eighteenth Amendment and social purity, as well as for newer concerns, among them the election of women to public office, the prevention of narcotics use and the Americanisation of immigrants.[101]

Nor did winning the vote dissipate the entire array of female political expertise that had been assembled for the final phase of the suffrage campaign. At the 1919 convention of NAWSA, Mrs Catt proposed the inauguration of a League of Women Voters (LWV) to strive for the ratification of the Nineteenth Amendment, the removal of remaining limitations on American women's equal rights, and the extension of such rights to women in other countries.[102] The League was formally established in 1920 – attracting around one-tenth of former NAWSA members, headed by Maud Park Wood, one of NAWSA's most acute lobbyists and organisers, and strongly influenced by Catt, who was honorary chairwoman of the LWV until her death in 1947.[103] The creation of the League had no strict parallel in Britain (though Women Citizens' Associations had been formed in Britain from 1913 to instruct women in public affairs); and the British produced no precise equivalent to the National Woman's Party (NWP), which redefined its objectives in 1921 and adopted a narrow but self-consciously feminist stance. In addition to sustaining these two bodies, American feminists with political interests supported a Women's Joint Congressional Committee during the 1920s.[104] Through its various subcommittees, the Committee brought what Florence Kelley called 'a very substantial power' to bear on Washington legislators for bills of interest to women, including measures dealing with child labour and to secure a uniform marriage and divorce amendment. Each of the women's organisations that backed the Committee 'retained its autonomy and participated only in the subcommittees that it approved of'.[105]

Launched for a trial five-year period, the LWV was an enduring success in the face of criticisms from anti-suffragists who thought it too radical, politicians who feared it might mobilise women voters into a formidable bloc, social feminists who preferred to concentrate on less politically orientated reform, and Woman's Party activists who wished it to use its influence to promote politicians sympathetic to feminism and make women's concerns its exclusive focus. In fact, after a few early forays into partisan politics by branch leagues, the LWV adhered to Catt's ideal of a non-partisan association in the Progressive mould, committed to 'carry on education in citizenship', to support reform legislation and to co-operate with existing organisations for social welfare. Accordingly it worked at rooting out political corruption, improving state and city government, and procuring such measures as the child labour amendment (put through Congress by 1924 but never ratified), minimum wage and protective legislation for women, and the Sheppard–Towner Act of 1921, giving federal funds to states which would operate programmes for the benefit of pregnant women and to reduce infant mortality.[106] The state leagues promoted the policies of the National League through a range of standing committees, while they themselves organised local leagues and provided them with policies, educational material, speakers, assistance in legislative activities, and state and National literature. They also liaised with groups pursuing similar aims, and introduced, supported and publicised desired legislation.[107] Careful study of issues was a characteristic of the LWV,[108] and members were unwilling either to support bills on which they had not been active, or automatically to endorse general principles that might be drawn from their backing for specific acts.[109] Northern leagues were as active as those in the South and, following National prompting, interested themselves, with some success, in civil service and political reform; in protective labour legislation; and in laws extending school requirements and opportunities, admitting women to jury service, giving the sexes equal infant guardianship rights, and providing more money for child and maternity hygiene.[110]

A number of criticisms can be made of the LWV. Its cautious, deliberative style limited what it could achieve, and branches did not always follow the centre's lead. It signally failed to persuade women to vote in the expected large numbers, and its concentration on educating women voters delayed the emergence of women politicians. Their emergence was never going to be easy, given the historic opposition even to women voting and the reassurances of some suffragists before 1920 that the majority of women wanted the franchise, not office. None the less, by the end of the decade there were signs of defensiveness in the League. Thus if the road embarked on was felt to be the right one, it was acknowledged that:

> results in political education must . . . come slowly for women as they have for men. We have learned that to reach the results we are aiming at in legislation we must go back to educating the electorate rather than spend our time trying to persuade persistently antagonistic legislators.

It was rightly pointed out that those who had claimed that women would never 'develop a capacity to understand the intricacies of government' were inconsistent in marvelling 'that we are not all crowding the great game of politics'. But the point rankled, made sharper by the realisation that women in England had made greater strides 'in holding public office' and leading to the rueful acknowledgement:

> The criticism that American women are too soft is not without justification. We are too comfortable and well fed to do the best work with our newly acquired weapon, the ballot.[111]

The two major organisations concerned with advancing women's economic rights – the Women's Trade Union League and the Consumers' League – remained active in the 1920s, though both were adversely affected by the economic and political climate of the period. After a few unhappy years of postwar readjustment – marked by business failures, falling prices, unemployment and labour violence – the United States entered a period of remarkable industrial development in which Progressive economic regulations were moderated and the businessman again took centre stage. While union membership had risen during World War One, and the War Labor Board's guiding principles had included the eight-hour day, equal pay for equal work by women, and the right of collective bargaining, labour failed to sustain its gains in the 1920s. Although the child labour deplored by female reformers declined, in part because of their efforts, class consciousness and union membership also declined. Furthermore, worker solidarity was eroded in the face of hostile courts, renewed open-shop drives by the National Association of Manufacturers, the benefits offered to their employees by big companies, the better social amenities provided for American citizens, and the poor showing of the Socialist and Communist parties. As far as women were concerned, if the unions looked to see them removed from men's jobs and benefits, employers were not opposed to their remaining in the workforce in larger numbers. All they opposed was the continuation of wartime benefits.[112]

For the Consumers' League, American entry into World War One distracted attention from measures that the League had pending, and it was subsequently obliged, as Florence Kelley put it, to resume its struggle 'to do against tremendous opposition some things that England did seventy-five years ago'. Critics continued to 'cry that our work is all dictated from Moscow', as the underfunded leagues investigated and publicised industrial conditions, furnished standards by which desirable conditions in industry might be determined, campaigned against child labour, sweatshops and night work, and agitated for the organisation of workers and minimum wage legislation for women (against which the Supreme Court ruled in 1923).[113]

The Women's Trade Union League, though similarly dismayed by the wartime pressure to lift labour laws in order to increase productivity, likewise accepted the need for women to do war work, cultivated old allies, and went on with its efforts for protective labour laws, industrial education, civil service reform (achieved in 1923) and the establishment of a women's division in the Department of Labor to lay down standards and policies to foster the welfare of female wage earners. (Success came in 1918, and the Women's Bureau was made permanent in 1920.) Like other women's groups at the time, the WTUL strengthened its international links, committed itself to the outlawry of war, and was denounced for its policies by conservatives. It supported the Sheppard–Towner Act and agitated for its extension in 1926 (it expired in 1929); backed the Cable Act giving women independent citizenship (it was passed in 1922); pressed for adequate appropriations for the Children's and Women's Bureaux; and 'worked for a bill to establish a department of education with a secretary in the President's Cabinet'.

Between 1913 and 1926, the League also ran a training school for activists in the labour movement. Unfortunately, it proved difficult to interest Americans who were prospering in giving to the WTUL. It also proved as hard as ever to organise unskilled, badly paid female workers, and to sustain fruitful relations with the American Federation of Labor. Hence if the Federation appointed a woman organiser, answerable to both the Federation and the League, individual unions still excluded women. In consequence, the League was often confined to educational activities – as when it tried to turn the women's auxiliaries to unions into 'active agents for trade unionism rather than merely social clubs', and launched a campaign to foster the idea of women's unions in the South. Whereas the female workforce increased by 26 per cent during the decade – largely because of growth in the economy and the American population as a whole – membership of the WTUL declined, and the number of women it trained remained small. But the original aim of promoting class co-operation between women was never abandoned, despite continuing criticism of the middle-class women in the League, and by the 1920s there were more working-class leaders than there had once been.

Nor did the example of England in organising the unskilled fail to inspire, even though there was doubt whether 'the political labor party idea' would work in the United States as it had in Europe, where working-class and middle-class women were allegedly unwilling to work together politically.[114] Equally, women like Pauline Newman and Leonora O'Reilly did not lose their dislike of 'the learned sometimes speaking for and ruling the mass', and their proud belief that the American labour movement was more labour-led than its English counterpart. Inured to personal and systemic difficulties alike, they retained their conviction that it was necessary to feed the spirit as well as sustain the body, and kept their faith in the importance of the work they were doing.[115]

However, the 1920s are – unfairly – best remembered for a division in the ranks of women's associations, which should not be allowed to blot out the sustained achievements of social feminists. The rift paralleled that of the late 1860s, another period when feminists were entering a new phase of activity; and it kept alive some of the personal hostility that had existed over militancy between members of NAWSA and the National Woman's Party. It came about because from 1923 the single-issue NWP pressed for an Equal Rights Amendment (ERA) to the Constitution; this read:

> Men and women shall have equal rights throughout the United States and every place subject to its jurisdiction. Congress shall have the power to enforce this article by appropriate legislation.[116]

The Party launched its amendment so soon after the exhausting campaign for the Nineteenth Amendment because it believed that 'Women today, although enfranchised, are still in every way subordinate to men before the law, in government, in educational opportunities, in the professions, in the church, in industry and in the home.' In making its pitch, the NWP was careful to appeal to women in familiar language. The outstanding result of female enfranchisement – declared its journal, *Equal Rights* – was 'an augmented interest in education, equal rights and social and moral work'. But, it went on:

> we are wasting the mother love, the maternal instinct of the world, by not hitching it up to our social machinery. If you want better schools, if you want a single standard of morals, if you desire to place human life beyond the reach of greed and its inevitable counterpart in war, don't spend time reasoning with the unreasonable, go straight to the point, emancipate women.[117]

The NWP was right about the obstacles to female equality, especially economic equality, that remained; and in the years after 1923 it managed to secure the passage of hundreds of state and local legislative bills covering such matters as equal rights in the labour force, eligibility for office, the guardianship of children, inheritance and jury service. It was right in believing that 'power is the best protection' and that women could be 'encumbered with too much serving'.[118] It was unappealing in its neglect of the needs of wives and mothers, its deliberate detachment from former Socialist allies, and its shunning of such radical feminist concerns as birth control; and it was cavalier in its attitude to the opinions of women reformers when it proposed that sex should be removed in protective industrial legislation. While the National Federation of Business and Professional Women's Clubs (1919) eventually came to share the NWP's uneasiness about protective legislation for women, the Party was subjected to an avalanche of criticism from the main women's organisations during the 1920s.[119] Understandably, they could not accept the jettisoning of laws obtained over a considerable period with much effort. In the pro-business atmosphere of the 1920s, it was not surprising that some successful women might have become 'weary of being treated as social problems' and that labour legislation might be acceptable only for 'the correction of abuses' rather than 'the regulation of industry'.[120] But it certainly did not help the NWP's relations with social feminists that its chief ally was the National Association of Manufacturers, and they could field a variety of arguments against their adversary.

The ERA was opposed because it offered a 'blanket cure' to a complicated set of ills; and since it would 'never be adopted', the time spent on it was seen as wasted time. Protective legislation was defended as guarding women and children against the hardship and injustices of modern industrial life, without affecting their civil rights. State and federal laws, it was maintained, could achieve anything desired by the amendment, which might affect women beyond the workplace: the right to alimony, penalties for rape, and mothers' pension laws might also be put in jeopardy. Working women and all the significant women's associations – other than the prosperous elite of the NWP – were said to oppose the ERA. As union members, women were 'an ever-changing, shifting group' who looked to the state to provide them with benefits men had won through their unions. Men did not need or want protective laws, as the NWP alleged. Even if they did, new legislation would take a long time to obtain, while standards for women went backwards. Women's employment, critics of the Party claimed, had improved in states operating protective legislation, and women who had worked knew that they could not do heavy labour as well or as long as men. It was hoped that British union women would lend their support, although middle-class feminists had divided on the question long before their American sisters (see above, pp. 176, 207). Some did, but the British continued to differ on the matter, which was also contentious in the International Woman Suffrage Alliance during the 1920s. And it was conceded that the debate over labour laws revealed ideological differences between women, since:

> For . . . millions of women, group conditions must be treated by group action, and the labor woman therefore has a collective ideal, with a program which may sometimes restrict individual liberty in the interests of the group. The non-wage-earning feminist, on the other hand, or the professional woman in her individualized, creative job, is more often an individualist, asserting the laissez-faire philosophy and her own personal liberty without realizing the hardships it imposes upon women in modern industry.[121]

In a country with such a strong veneration for individual rights, and in a decade when old *laissez-faire* notions were again fashionable in Washington, the line pursued by the NWP is understandable. Given their recent habit of justifying the extension of women's power beyond the home in terms of their need to protect women and children, so is the fury of its opponents. But the bitter personalities involved in the quarrel – between old adversaries like Alice Paul and Mrs Catt – tended to obscure the fact that the combatants had much in common. Like the embattled feminists of the 1860s, they sought shared goals (notably economic independence) by different means, and part of the bitterness expressed by critics of the NWP sprang from their sense that the Party was unfairly claiming a monopoly on work for equal rights.[122] NAWSA, while stressing female distinctiveness, had never abandoned the equal rights arguments of the first feminists; and by 1925, Catt declared:

> the League of Women Voters has secured the passage of more than four hundred bills in the various legislatures, and little by little the old discriminations which made the civil status of women so unjust are being removed. No other organisation agrees with the National Woman's Party amendment. . . . We all believe in equal rights, but we think we are getting it by a much faster process.[123]

Unconvinced – and with some working-class backing – supporters of the NWP replied that protective legislation made it harder for women to earn a living, was supported by male trade unionists for that very reason, and did not assure 'the rights of motherhood'. These would be upheld 'more intelligently' by 'Family allowances, the State endowment of motherhood, widows' and old-age pensions'. The Party maintained that the unmarried female needed 'few industrial strings tied to her'; and that if women were not treated as minors, actual minors might win a better deal. As the NWP saw it, the ERA was general, not vague, because the national Constitution dealt with the general principles upon which government rested, not with specific details. The amendment would not jeopardise existing labour legislation, mothers' pension laws, or provisions against rape, but would either make benefits available to both sexes or make penalties apply to the person committing the offence, regardless of sex. The protective laws desired for working-class women by their middle-class patrons were no substitute for union protection, not least because such laws were often undermined by their interpretation and administration. And it did not matter that only the NWP favoured the ERA: after all, few women had supported the suffrage amendment when it was introduced in 1878.[124]

In campaigning for the ERA, the Party employed methods which were very similar to those of other women's associations. It sought to educate the public through meetings, speeches and the production of literature, including a journal. It lobbied politicians. And it pursued the formation of councils for the various professions to investigate discrimination against women, press for its removal, and work for equal rights legislation wherever necessary. Unfortunately, as Cott has shown, the NWP's emphasis on legal equality polarised feminists who had long struggled to resolve the tension within their movement resulting from both seeking equal rights and celebrating women's differences from men. What is more, the NWP did not fight for labour legislation for both sexes; nor did it acknowledge that in the female-dominated industries protective class legislation had served a useful purpose, even as it restricted women's present and long-term prospects elsewhere in the economy.[125]

None of the women's organisations of the 1920s aimed at transforming the position of their sex in party politics; this was a mistake, since there was keen public interest in the consequences of female suffrage, and the more optimistic feminists had predicted that they would be great. While some women had involved themselves with the parties during the Progressive era (see above, pp. 198, 215), most female pressure groups had favoured bipartisanship, and it was hard to throw off old habits. Male politicians were suspicious of the female variety, whom they had long resisted: certainly of veteran suffragists with considerable political skills. Such veterans, for their part, felt that women were too varied to form a strictly feminine bloc, found it difficult to mobilise their sex for sustained rather than sporadic political campaigns, and had learned the hard way to expect a struggle.

Struggle certainly presented itself from the middle of the decade, when the parties, having found that they need not fear women, proved far less responsive to their reform demands.[126] The 'feminine' role in politics favoured by the reformer and political adviser to Al Smith, Belle Moskowitz, was rooted in power in women's organisations and behind-the-scenes influence on men of politics. But it was a vulnerable one, even when played with Moskowitz's skill, as her biographer, Elizabeth Perry, has established. The career of Sue Shelton White, who helped to draft the ERA in 1923 and by the 1930s had become executive secretary of the Women's Division of the Democratic Party's National Committee, illustrates similar difficulties entailed in combining feminist and conventional politics.

In 1924, White found herself torn between her Democratic sympathies and the NWP's decision to support women candidates for Congress regardless of party. The best she thought she could hope for in this situation was not to act in a way that would harm any woman. Four years later, White could still declare: 'I expect nothing from the Democratic party for myself and little from it in this generation for the cause of woman', and she could not see that 'an organization that professes to be truly and solely a feminist organization has anything to choose or any favors to grant'. By 1930 she had committed herself to the Democrats and, aware of their anxiety about her former endorsement of the NWP and ERA, had backed away from both. Despite all the vigorous efforts of the South's women throughout the 1920s for legislative and other reforms, White believed that women remained in a parlous state in southern politics.[127]

Mary Dewson, who was likewise active in the Women's Division of the Democratic National Committee during the 1930s, did not have White's embarrassing antecedents. She arrived in national politics via work for the Women's Educational and Industrial Union in Boston; the Massachusetts Industrial School for Girls, where she was a probation officer; the Red Cross in France (1917–18); the National Consumers' League, where she was concerned with minimum wage issues; and the Women's City Club of New York, through which she fortuitously met Eleanor Roosevelt in 1924. Nevertheless, Dewson did not escape the normal problems encountered by postwar feminist politicians. Having long wished to see women involved in government, because they possessed different qualities from men, she also wanted them to be 'an official, working part of our Party', not 'relegated to supplying refreshments and to the domestic ends of meetings, or the Democratic Women's Clubs'. But clearly, when she turned to Roosevelt 'to show his confidence in the ability of women' who had helped him to victory, he was so absorbed with recovery plans that he could not give the matter as much attention as she would have liked, and of the sixty-five women who were considered, only some wanted positions for themselves. Others, in traditional fashion, 'preferred to have their husbands placed and be free to go on with their own political work'. Dewson concluded:

> Although having husbands appointed would not have satisfied most women and certainly not the feminists, from the party point of view it was very practical.[128]

Women were generally reluctant to urge women for public office just because they were women.[129] They thought they should enter politics from the bottom, as men did, and could take pleasure, by the mid-1920s, in 'picking up after the men, just as women have always done': that is, in undertaking exactly the kind of unpaid party political labours about which Mrs Stanton had once chided British women (see above, p. 145). For those, like Ida Tarbell, who were content to expect no significant consequences from women's suffrage before fifty years had elapsed, such an approach to political opportunities in the 1920s was understandable.[130] For those who feared that women's magnanimity was more likely to make politicians consider them to be 'a negligible quantity in politics'[131] it was a miscalculation, and they could only look with gloom at the small number of female office-holders, a fair proportion of whom had simply succeeded dead husbands. By 1925, the Women's Research Foundation reported, of 'the aggregate membership of 7,542 in the [legislatures of the] 48 states, 139 (1.84%) are women'.[132]

The women's movement in the United States clearly had not failed by the 1920s, but it was passing through a turbulent, transitional period. Experienced feminists continued to work for old causes and pursue fresh ones; to labour in established organisations and found new associations. Indeed, the inability of women to sustain their overrated wartime gains in the labour market and improve their position in professions traditionally dominated by men made organisational employment more necessary than ever for educated, middle-class women. The feminist movement could still find room for these practical women and for ideologues, though the poor showing of the Communist and Socialist parties during the decade made it hard for radical feminists to draw strength from a radical political base as they had formerly done.[133] And in the conservative atmosphere of the 1920s, when the existence of class conflict in American life was again played down, self-consciously cross-class alliances – notably the consumers' leagues and WTUL – were unable to keep going with the strength of their early days.

In the eyes of older feminists, the younger generation of women seemed especially susceptible to the pursuit of individual rather than group goals after the war; black leaders were similarly worried in the 1920s about the propensity of their bright young people to put self before race betterment.[134] One can see why this might have been so. The vote had been won, prosperity had many attractions, and boredom with old debates had set in. Moreover, it could not be said that the huge array of women's groups developing since the nineteenth century had cured the social ills they had been attacking, and they were not helped by the postwar decline of Progressivism as a national political force. Even a widely revered campaigner such as Jane Addams felt that she had not accomplished 'a drop in the bucket'.[135] However, just as there had always been women like Ida Tarbell, who questioned the importance of conventions, 'conferences, elections, resolutions, legislation',[136] so there were always activists like the southern-born sculptor Nancy Cox-McCormack Cushman, who enjoyed working in the Chicago reform network and believed it was the trying that counted;[137] and crusaders like Carrie Catt and Nellie Nugent Somerville, the first woman in the Mississippi legislature, who were able to retain their faith that women could lead the struggle against the destructive power of 'disease, drugs, liquor, poverty, lawlessness and war'.[138] These were the feminists who, if they had reinforced conventional attitudes about womanly qualities and failed to conquer intractable social evils, did not by any means exaggerate the benefits that would flow from the Nineteenth Amendment. These were the campaigners who had made a substantial contribution to the improvement of social welfare, especially that of women and children, and would play a vital part in the reforms and decision-making bodies of the New Deal. They were not women who could resolve the difficult, continuing debate about the nature of womanhood and the meaning and priorities of feminism.[139]

(ii) *Britain*

The impact of World War One was greater on British than on American activists, since it directly affected them for four years rather than one. However, though the militants of the WSPU abandoned suffrage entirely, a range of more moderate women's societies co-operated throughout the conflict in both war and suffrage work, so that by the time the vote was won, British feminists were more united than their American counterparts, who were rent at the last by an upsurge of militancy. Some would have shared Helena Swanwick's faith that her countrywomen were 'going still to be among the world's pioneers', and all would have agreed with the Prime Minister's message to women in 1918, in which he stressed that it was essential for female opinion to be brought to bear on 'education, public health, housing and the manifold problems connected with the welfare of women and children'. But opportunities and difficulties arose so fast that there was no time for a grand debate on future priorities, and in the short term British activists were disturbed by the requirement of government and unions alike, when peace came, that female war workers should yield their well-paid jobs to men. The distress of these workers, whom the feminists had helped to place in employment, kept pressure on the latter to hold their groups

~

together;[140] and in 1919 the National Union of Women's Suffrage Societies, which had been discussing its future since 1917,[141] became the National Union of Societies for Equal Citizenship (NUSEC).

None the less, as in the United States, the most significant reform encouraged by the war – and under way by the 1920s – was the dissemination of birth control advice. And on this issue, in Britain as in America, progress initially owed more to the efforts of a single exceptional feminist prepared to accept medical and eugenic assistance than to campaigning by cautious women's organisations trying to see their way forward. The result, in Britain as in America, was the transformation of birth control into family planning and its detachment from a feminist context, to the detriment of the women's movement and birth control alike.

Although the Malthusian League had begun distributing a practical pamphlet on family limitation before the war, and was by then directing its efforts at the working-class poor, its effectiveness was hindered by the brevity of its pamphlet; by its prudent determination to prevent the document from falling into the hands of the young and unmarried (many still regarded such material as obscene); and by the continuing unpopularity of its economic doctrines and association with freethinking. Nevertheless, its central concern had been helped during the war by the government's issuing of contraceptives to the troops, to protect them against venereal disease (one-fifth still managed to contract it). Still more important was the nation's growing appreciation of the health risks attendant on repeated pregnancies, and women's heightened awareness of the value of family limitation as more of them worked outside the home. The League's plan to open a birth control clinic had to be postponed because of the conflict, but was put into practice in the autumn of 1921.[142] However, the League lost the honour of opening the first such clinic in the British Empire, which went to Marie Stopes in March 1921.

Like Margaret Sanger, Stopes had the disadvantage of not being a doctor, but like Sanger she had the great advantages of energy, self-confidence, ability and a supportive, rich husband, the manufacturer and flier Humphrey Verdon Roe, who made her venture practically possible and whose interest in the subject had been aroused before they met. Like Sanger, Stopes came to her life's work with the aid of a 'moment of vision', possibly exaggerated with hindsight. Like Sanger, she survived an eventually unhappy first marriage. But unlike Sanger, who was a trained nurse and a mother by the time she took up birth control, Stopes had not acquired, from her successful career in science and unconsummated first marriage, a practical knowledge of birth control, or of the contraceptive needs of poor women. Rather, her understanding of the subject had been enhanced by a meeting with Sanger in 1915.[143] Prompted by her own experience and steeped in the writings of the sexologists, Stopes was then at work on *Married Love*, the famous marriage manual she published three years later. Her interest in birth control thus followed from a prior concern to improve sex education.[144]

Marie Stopes is generally acknowledged to have made birth control acceptable to a wide array of groups whose motives for supporting her varied: 'women, doctors, health officials and MPs'.[145] This she did by her focus on its positive aspects; by 'emphasizing the value of a harmonious sex life to married couples, the right of women to happy motherhood, and the right of children to be wanted and loved'.[146] After *Married Love* was published, and she herself was remarried and a public figure with much at stake, Stopes did not dwell upon her early fear that woman's sexual fulfilment, realisable through both partners being educated to her distinctive physiological needs, might be achieved at the expense of her intellectual growth. Nor did she continue to fret that single women were denied 'sex joy or relief' because of society's view that 'a woman once having given herself in love has nothing left'.[147] Stopes's respectability was further increased by her Christianity and her sympathy with the basic aim – though not the secularism – of the eugenics movement. Some signs of conventionality were perhaps just as well, since her first tract was considered outspoken in giving independent value to the sexual act, while her *Wise Parenthood* (1918) was bold in providing a practical (if sometimes inaccurate) guide to contraceptive methods, thereby offending the sensibilities of Catholics and qualified medical personnel.[148]

Nevertheless, the overall reaction to the two books would have encouraged anyone, and Marie Stopes was not a woman to be daunted by either apathy or enmity. As well as opening her birth control clinic, where advice was free, Stopes founded, in 1921, a Society for Constructive Birth Control and Racial Progress (SCBC), to promote the clinic and spread the views she had been expounding since 1918 in press articles and public lectures. She also addressed her efforts more pointedly to the working class, highlighting her interest in relieving suffering and hardship among its individual members. Believing that this tactic would be successful, British eugenicists supported her campaign. In 1928, in fact, the SCBC had come so close to the eugenicists' position that it suggested sterilisation for women in the medical problem category, and an NUSEC deputation to the government in 1932 similarly recommended the extension of birth control and sterilisation 'on behalf of the social problem group', by which they meant the unemployed. Stopes nevertheless kept the needs of the individual to the forefront, and was able to use the statistics that she, like Sanger, carefully collected from her patients to show much morbidity due to childbirth that birth control might help to avert. In 1924 and in 1936 the WCG and NUSEC asked for abortion to be legalised because of the high maternal death rate: birth controllers hoped that they offered a better way forward.[149]

Like Sanger, Marie Stopes preferred to work alone, but her work – extended to Leeds, Aberdeen and Belfast in the 1930s – was supplemented by the Society for the Provision of Birth Control Clinics, set up to run the Malthusian League's clinic in 1923. By 1928 'it had twelve clinics in operation, three in London, seven in the provinces, and two in Scotland'. Moreover, 'other groups and even private individuals ... began to open centers and dispense contraceptive advice by the mid twenties.' In 1930, when an estimated 36,000 women, primarily from the working class, had been assisted, many of the activists came together as the National Birth Control Council (Association from 1931), attracting backing from the WCG and the Women's Institutes, which had been launched during World War One, with suffragist approval, to help with women's war work.[150] Yet if attitudes to birth control were changing by the 1920s, and most women's organisations at last felt able to give it public support, there are signs in Britain of those value conflicts that were a feature of America during the decade, as economic change sped ahead of cultural and political adjustment. Stopes herself admitted in 1931 that she had not dispelled the popular conviction that her crusade was anti-baby.[151] Feminists might welcome greater sexual freedom and birth control for women, while opposing any lowering of moral standards or undermining of the family. And politicians, as Jane Lewis has shown, remained more concerned about the declining birth rate than feminist demands that all women had a right to birth control information, making that information available only to special cases at maternal and child welfare centres in 1930 and 1934. (Pressure for it to be given had come from the WCG and labour women, NUSEC, the Women's National Liberal Federation, birth control associations and public health authorities.) Birth control was officially encouraged only in 1949, when a Royal Commission on Population recognised that the market needed an expansion of married women's work. Only in 1967, following the passage of the National Health Service (Family Planning) Act, were local health authorities empowered to 'give birth control advice without regard to marital status and on social as well as medical grounds'.[152]

As the discussion of the work of the British birth controllers will have made plain, the debate on sexuality during the 1920s centred upon the married woman, the heterosexual woman, and the link between sexuality and reproduction. A comparable situation prevailed in the United States. The decade which permitted a freer discussion of sexual matters than any before it did indeed afford greater opportunities for lesbian women to meet and assert their identity, and novels dealing with lesbianism and androgyny continued to appear.[153] As an indication of the increased awareness of lesbianism in Britain after the war, an attempt was made in 1921 to bring it under the scope of the criminal law, emulating the 1885 Labouchère Amendment criminalising 'acts of gross indecency' between men. The bid failed, because legislators, on reflection, did not wish to publicise what they hoped most women had 'never even heard a whisper of', as happened when Radclyffe Hall's novel about lesbianism, *The Well of Loneliness* (1928), was banned.[154] That it was made at all is simply evidence of contemporary unease over sexual change – not least when World War One had left many women without husbands or the prospect of them, and intensified fears about a declining middle-class birth rate. Under these circumstances, 'deviant' sexual behaviour by women, of whatever kind, remained unacceptable on both sides of the Atlantic.

The debate in 1921 also illustrates the common concern with the physical aspects of lesbianism, whereas a number of historians have pointed out the inappropriatness of exploring 'female homosexuality in terms of categories derived from male experience', and have tried to present female friendships – the cement of the Anglo–American women's movement – in all their complexity.[155] But one can understand why, in the 1920s, older feminists, who had already witnessed the denigration of the spinster before the war (see above, pp. 230–1), and now saw the invention of the frigid woman and attacks on the sexual abnormality of the independent 'new woman', preferred to address themselves to the rights and problems of married women and children, because here they might expect some sympathy from conventional men and women. The indictment of men's sexual licence, which had been central to the social purity wing of the nineteenth-century women's movement, was muted under the impact of 'sexology and . . . a changing sexual ideology'.[156]

The women's movement in Britain during the 1920s has been most commonly presented, since the appearance of Jane Lewis's pioneering study of 1975,[157] as being gripped by a conflict between the old, equal rights feminism and a new feminism which acknowledged and sought to meet women's distinctive needs and interests. However, this conflict, though it was apparent from the end of the main struggle for the vote, did not come to a head until the mid-1920s. After 1918 British feminists, like their American counterparts, were at first energised by victory. Undeterred by a resurgence of public hostility towards feminism and the frequent indifference of younger women, they were determined to press on for measures which seemed more attainable in the aftermath of the political breakthrough. Unlike their American sisters, they had failed to gain the suffrage on the same terms as men, and were especially determined to win voting rights for all women before too much time had elapsed. With this and other ends in mind, the Women's Freedom League remained in being, working alongside NUSEC; the National Council of Women; the equality-orientated Six Point Group (1921); the London and National Society for Women's Service, which concentrated on the fight for economic equality; and an array of small organisations which lobbied in Westminster on single issues. They included the Equal Pay Campaign Committee, the National Association of Women Civil Servants, Women for Westminster, the Married Women's Association and the Association for Moral and Social Hygiene, and their efforts have been examined in David Doughan's valuable essay on British feminism from the 1920s to the 1960s. More cautious middle-class women might be drawn towards one of these feminist groups by an initial involvement in the National Women Citizens' Association, which stirred individuals in 'many quiet little towns to hold meetings and take community action'.[158]

In 1917, Emmeline and Christabel Pankhurst had formed a Women's Party out of the WSPU, but it lasted only until 1919 and bore no resemblance to the NWP in the United States, since it took an immediate interest in foreign affairs (the subjugation of Germany) and favoured a combination of equality and special treatment for women. Specifically, this meant demanding equal pay for equal work, equal employment opportunities and marriage laws, a higher age of consent, the endowment of motherhood and the provision of co-operative housekeeping facilities. After standing unsuccessfully for Parliament in 1918, Christabel Pankhurst, together with her mother, turned away from feminist politics, so there is no means of knowing how the Party's ambitious programme might have been pursued. The militant wing of British feminism continued to decline in the 1920s, its tactics undermined by the winning of the vote and the ageing of its activists; and British feminists made no attempt to launch a women's party that would challenge the existing political parties. British awareness of the political potential of the League of Women Voters has been noted by Pugh. Yet as we have seen (pp. 259–60 above), that potential was not sustained, while in Britain, where women's organisations were similarly diverse and their party political loyalties were far stronger, an independent party for women was a non-starter.[159]

The NUSEC, which commanded the support of some two hundred societies formerly affiliated to the NUWSS, set out 'To obtain all such reforms as are necessary to secure a real equality of liberties, status and opportunities between men and women'. It also declared an interest in achieving 'such reforms as are necessary to make it possible for women adequately to discharge their functions as citizens'. The president of the Union from 1919 to 1928 was Eleanor Rathbone, a Liverpool councillor and suffragist, who was interested in the conditions of the poor and belonged to an eminent Liberal and philanthropic family. Like the NUWSS, the new body was composed of confident, well-connected women who were quick to deploy their parliamentary links (some of its members were, in time, MPs) and to use the customary array of non-partisan, pressure-group tactics to achieve goals which included the equal franchise, equal pay, the opening of the professions and civil service to women, the right of married women to employment and separate taxation, and the application of equal moral standards regarding divorce, solicitation and prostitution.[160] These were ambitious objectives, but veteran feminists such as Dame Millicent Fawcett were happy to report Parliament's responsiveness to the new voters and the speedy securing of numerous long-sought measures.

The 1918 Sex Disqualification Removal Act, for instance, while it was less comprehensive than Labour had hoped, allowed women to sit on juries, serve as JPs and police officers, enter the legal profession, and receive membership of and degrees from Oxford and Cambridge on equal terms with men (Cambridge declined to give equal treatment, in fact, until 1948). Following the passage of the Act, women were admitted to various professional bodies. In 1919 the first woman took her place in the House of Commons, and there were eight women MPs by 1923. The political parties prudently recognised the wisdom of courting women and integrating them into their organisations, and British women played a full part in the postwar movement to promote peace and internationalism. In 1921, women were admitted to all grades of the home civil service (though they did not enjoy equal pay for equal work, and were denied entry to the consular and foreign service until 1946). In 1922 'husbands and wives, mothers and fathers, sons and daughters' were made equal in intestacy cases, and in 1923 an increase was granted in fathers' maximum contribution towards the support of their illegitimate children. By the Matrimonial Causes Act of the same year, divorce was permitted on equal terms for men and women; and in 1925 the Guardianship of Infants Act put the sexes on an equal footing with regard to their offspring, while the Widows' Pensions Act gave widows with dependent children a pension similar to the old age pension. The Criminal Justice Act 1926 abolished the presumption that a married woman was coerced by her husband when she committed a crime in his presence, and several laws between 1925 and 1926 improved matters in the area of separation and maintenance orders, adoption, the legitimation of children, and the conditions of childbirth. Finally, in 1928, all women received the vote, and the Prime Minister declared hopefully – if inaccurately:

> The subjection of women, if there be such a thing, will not now depend on any creation of the law, nor can it be remedied by any action of the laws.[161]

Such a spate of legislation confirmed the occasional advantage British feminists derived from their country's unitary political system. At the same time in America, activists were engaged in a slow, state-by-state drive to obtain equality. But Pugh's work makes it plain that politicians in Britain – as in America – became less responsive as the decade progressed. They also supported pro-women measures for non-feminist reasons and resisted the feminists' more radical demands. Although NUSEC was determined to promote the return of women as MPs, candidates were as hard to find in Britain as they were in America, and women voters were particularly effectively wooed by the Conservatives, the Party least sympathetic to feminism. Activists found that they made most headway on social welfare issues and in local government. It was hard to make much impact on the political parties, which looked for loyalty, not sectional demands, from the new voters. The Liberal Party's decline in the 1920s was also unhelpful to feminists, who had so often supported it. So, too, was the weakness of Labour and the strength of the Conservatives during that decade. And as Strachey observed in 1928, there were aspects of the women's movement:

> not susceptible to victory by law; there are changes of thought and outlook which even yet have not arrived. There are consequences, too, of the victories already won which have not as yet fully emerged; and, above all, economic equality is still a distant dream.[162]

Furthermore, if middle-class women could feel cautiously pleased with their gains during the 1920s, there were those in NUSEC, led by Rathbone, who felt that the interests of working-class women were inadequately served by 'me too' feminism, which had sought rights prized by men and desired by 'unmarried career women'. These self-proclaimed 'new feminists' advocated family allowances (not achieved until 1945) to secure the endowment of motherhood, together with birth control advice (achieved from 1930 onwards) to help poorer women and mothers. In so doing, they acknowledged that the majority of domesticated women had distinctive needs and interests, which were equal in value to those of men. As Harrison observes, the 'long-term programme of "new feminists" was obscure'.[163]

The conflict between old and new feminists inside NUSEC was less publicised and damaging than that between the NWP and its enemies in the United States, but no less heartfelt. Yet it is difficult to see what was new about the 'new feminism'. British feminists (notably the social purists) had concerned themselves before and during the war with the rights of mothers and children, and, as Jeffreys notes, the proposal that feminism should adjust its focus away from men and towards motherhood was made as early as 1913 by the sexologist Havelock Ellis, in his book *The Task of Social Hygiene*.[164] Nor is there anything new about the new feminism in the wider context: the endowment of motherhood had been urged in Germany in the early twentieth century, and the needs of women and children had been elevated in the American women's movement since the late nineteenth century. The British new feminism of the 1920s was simply a complex variant of prewar democratic suffragism, with its emphasis on the special needs of different groups of women, and American social feminism.

However, NUSEC differed from the LWV, its nearest equivalent – not just because of its shorter life (renamed, it wound up its operation in 1945) but also because it encompassed within itself the dispute which, in America, divided the NWP from the LWV and other major women's associations. In both countries, there was a hope that equality and special help, jobs within and beyond the home, could be properly balanced. As Mrs Blatch of the NWP expressed it, motherhood should be:

> revalued, not over-emphasized, not sentimentalized and surrounded with an aura of glory, but viewed in an intelligent, sensible light. To this end, I recommend motherhood endowment. Through motherhood endowment, the mother of tomorrow will escape from perpetual tutelage. ... In addition to this, all discriminations in the law ... should be repealed, and also all laws forbidding to women information on questions of child-bearing and contraception.[165]

But in Britain as in America, the danger was that special treatment for women would be secured because it appealed to supporters of separate spheres for the sexes: the line between new feminism and anti-feminism could easily be blurred.

In the face of economic recession and revived prejudice against women working, especially if they were married, NUSEC had achieved no progress towards its 1919 goal of equal pay for equal work. The Union therefore hoped that family allowances, by making children (to a degree) the responsibility of the state rather than the male wage earner, would undermine the need for a family wage and so prepare the way for equal pay. New feminists believed that mothers, by being paid for their services, would be able to improve their health and that of their families, and be able to fulfil their roles adequately. It was this part of the women's argument that brought them backing from the eugenicists, who were mainly anxious to see healthy, middle-class women having more children. The new feminists did not wish to undermine the family, did not envisage that the women to be assisted from economic subjugation would become economically independent, whatever old feminists and more hostile critics suggested. Indeed, Rathbone, like many labour women, may have been chiefly interested in motherhood endowment for what it would do for children, not for women. And the feminist case for family allowances was not the preoccupation of the Socialists who endorsed the proposal: for them, it was a means of redistributing wealth by taxing the rich to pay allowances to poor families. Amid these assorted difficulties, NUSEC opted for prudence and left much of the work for motherhood endowment to the frequently Socialist activists of the Family Endowment Committee (later Society, 1917), just as it largely left the still contentious birth control campaign to other groups.[166]

The question of motherhood endowment came to a climax in NUSEC in 1925. It was thus poorly placed, two years later, to resolve another debate – this time about protective legislation, an issue which had long disturbed British feminist circles and tended to separate middle-class feminists from labour women. A compromise measure was approved in 1927, agreeing to consider each case of protective legislation individually, accepting those favoured by and benefiting the workers. Half the NUSEC executive, at odds over protection and the meaning of equality, was thereupon moved to resign. The disagreement did not reach American proportions, though it attracted American interest; but it prompted the formation of the Open Door Council, specifically to fight against protective legislation, and the Council's outlook was shared by the Six Point Group and the Women's Freedom League. What is more, by the late 1920s British feminists, like their American allies, had discovered frustration and disunity, as well as satisfaction, within the international peace movement.[167]

Under the circumstances, it is perhaps not surprising that the prewar feminist ideal of ending the double standard of morality between the sexes – supported by the Women's Freedom League as well as NUSEC – continued to prove elusive. The Association for Moral and Social Hygiene (AMSH) was active during the 1920s. But while the reform of the divorce law in 1923 was a real achievement, after 1922, when the age of consent was raised in response to feminist pressure, there were no extensions of the criminal code on sexual matters, and equitable treatment of men and women involved in prostitution was not realised.[168] The purity movement, long challenged by the tenets of social hygiene, was in decline by the 1920s in the face of the new emphasis on female sexuality and fulfilment within marriage.[169] Yet it would be unreasonable to regret the leaving of purity issues mainly to AMSH. The proliferation of special-interest women's pressure groups did indeed increase the risk that feminist issues would be pursued out of context – we have seen how this happened with birth control – and that attempts to shape feminism to a new era would be neglected. However, umbrella organisations had never been much favoured by British feminists, and the difficulties in deciding priorities and reconciling their assorted members encountered by NUSEC, the Six Point Group and the other co-ordinating groups of the decade were unlikely to make more converts. Even in the United States there were activists, like Florence Kelley, who strongly favoured single-issue campaigns. Feminism in Britain and America alike had always taken many organisational forms, and both countries had made the greatest gains by working with, not against, the political grain.[170] The most striking, and perhaps genuinely unfortunate, development in British postwar feminism would rather seem to be the demise of such genuine cross-class endeavours as the WTUL and NFWW, and the clearer delineation of middle-class and working-class endeavours within feminism, as labour women increasingly, though uncomfortably, operated through the women's section of the TUC, the WCG, the Fabian Women's Group, the Independent Labour Party and the Labour Party, the established trade unions and the international labour organisations. However, the history of the American WTUL in the 1920s is not an inspiring one, while at least in Britain the labour movement was gaining strength and, despite its conservatism on family matters, showed more sympathy towards its women activists and their goals than did labour in America.[171]

By the early 1930s, NUSEC was divided into 'Educative and reformist' wings: the former consisting of Townswomen's Guilds, the latter of the National Council for Equal Citizenship, which continued NUSEC's lobbying for egalitarian reforms. The debate between old and new feminism had abated by then, and in any event the National Council, like NUSEC, with its old-fashioned methods and primarily middle-class membership, was not well placed to take new feminism further. But it is difficult to imagine that interwar feminists would have gained by abandoning the 'political prudence' Harrison sees as their hallmark. It is similarly difficult to disagree with Lewis's judgement that new feminism, far from constituting a betrayal of founding ideals, had represented 'a vital opportunity for the women's movement ... to work not just for an equal society, but for a better society', as well as offering 'the beginnings of an ideological base for the future'.[172]

In both Britain and America, feminism had prospered in times of liberal reform and intellectual questioning, and neither the intellectual nor the political circumstances of the 1920s were conducive to further growth of a spectacular kind. Equally, one can talk about the decline of feminism in both countries during the 1920s only if one focuses upon the absence on either side of the Atlantic of any single feminist group with the numbers, confidence and unifying power commanded by the suffrage associations in the final phase of their campaign. Quarrels are a sign of life, and in the 1920s, as in the 1860s and 1880s, those of the feminists dismayed the participants and pleased their enemies, but did not destroy the cause.

Afterword

From the eighteenth century to the early twentieth century feminists in Britain and the United States read each other's works, watched each other's progress, exchanged visits and even laboured in each other's campaigns, but took pride in their own successes, their own ways of doing things. If overt attempts were made in either country to import feminist methods, they aroused fierce controversy among activists: as when the British Women's Temperance Association embraced their American temperance sisters' 'do everything' policy, and the National Woman's Party copied the British suffragettes' militancy. British and American anti-feminists were also prone to scrutinise women's activities across the Atlantic with disfavour. Accordingly Americans denounced suffragette tactics while commentators in Britain warned about the dangers of Americanisation when married women's property legislation, divorce law reform and women's enfranchisement were being considered.[1]

Yet despite their conscious independence, the British and American women's movements experienced a similar chronology. On both sides of the Atlantic, organised feminism appeared after a period of literary feminism and social change which encouraged a new emphasis on separate spheres for the sexes. On each side of the Atlantic, the 1860s were a forcing period for feminism, when claims for the suffrage came to the fore; whereas social or welfare[2] feminists made their greatest strides from the late nineteenth century onwards. On both sides of the Atlantic, the women's culture created during that century came under intellectual challenge from the 1910s; while during the 1920s the cause lost some of its coherence and organisational strength, notwithstanding continuing successes. But in Britain, of course, there was no Civil War to accelerate the bureaucratisation of benevolence, and intensify existing class and racial divisions. Although the American women's movement was largely white and middle-class from the start, these developments altered the radical image it first derived from its anti-slavery connection, adaptation of the Revolutionary tradition, perfectionist rhetoric, and occasional boldness on religious, labour and marriage questions. Conversely, the American movement was not so affected as

277

the British by a pulling apart of labour and middle-class women during the 1920s.

The content of the American and British women's movements likewise reveals both their similarity and their distinctiveness. Taking points of similarity first: we have seen that feminists were not simply concerned with the concerns of single women any more than they were preoccupied with the suffrage, though the need for the vote was recognised before the 1860s, just as women were politicised and politics was domesticated long before politicians in the 1920s were obliged overtly to change the agenda of politics to take account of women voters. It is equally clear that if an engagement with sexual, family and marriage matters was central to the two movements, it was difficult to proceed rapidly in these areas because of the strength of opponents and the unease of many women, including some feminists. Indeed, in political and sexual matters alike, attitudes did not begin to shift in the feminists' favour until the early twentieth century, reflecting the impact of their own activities, women's changing role in the economy, and governments' growing determination to act regarding threatening social problems. As late as 1910, an NUWSS correspondent admitted to living in a part of England 'where a suffragist is regarded as a dangerous lunatic'.

British and American feminists also saw educational advancement as a key to their emancipation, and stressed the need for new employment opportunities for women as a right, an alternative to marriage, and a means of alleviating hardship among women who lacked male support. Even so, it is plain that whereas the right to paid work beyond the home was especially important to middle-class feminists, working-class women had their own priorities and might be more sceptical about its intrinsic value, though they were less ideologically opposed to married women working. It is likewise apparent that they engaged in more complicated struggles to combine varied home tasks and outside work, and were eventually confronted by competing claims on their loyalties from unionists and Socialists who were often unsympathetic to bourgeois feminists. What is more, their workplace experiences cannot be understood simply through the part they played in union organisations, despite the interest of both male unionists and sympathetic feminists in labouring women's potential for organisation.[3]

American and British activists of all kinds, aware that male power affected them in the private as well as the public realm, sought justice in both and the creation of interlocking spheres. In doing so, they appealed for equal treatment as rational human beings and citizens, *and* for consideration of their special needs and qualities as women. The social feminists who tended to stress sexual difference rather than equality, were initially nervous about such radical planks of feminism as birth control and the vote, and urged goals that might be embraced by non-feminist reformers, have been presented in this study as an integral part of feminism. These campaigners were uncomfortable with the title 'feminist', once it was in use in the early twentieth century, and they failed to secure female autonomy. They did, however, improve the confidence, organisational range, status and practical circumstances of women. They, like bolder feminists, may have held views about the control middle-class women were entitled to exercise over their poor sisters that do not appeal to us now. But I have maintained that working women derived some material advantages from feminists' attempts to cross the class divide; even if the latter were increasingly – and not evidently rightly – inclined to see protective legislation rather than unionisation as the labour woman's best hope.

This study, while accepting these shared emphases, has told a story of two women's movements of equal significance and particular strengths. It has rejected the view that American feminists became unwisely conservative after radical beginnings, whereas the respectable British only briefly threw caution to the winds in the years before World War One. Instead it has argued that each movement was progressive and took the lead in some ways and at some times. And radicalism, I believe, can be measured by looking at the scope and tactics, as well as the ideas, of the movements. Thus pragmatic British feminists, having seen the disruptive impact of early American feminism on the anti-slavery, peace and temperance movements, and observed the jaundiced reactions of many of their countrymen to American traits, from the outset showed a preference for single-issue committees and campaigns, carefully involving men where appropriate. Yet this prudence did not prevent them from sustaining intricate connecting networks, profiting from their country's intellectual leadership, showing the way in cross-class and social purity movements, and employing methods in the crusade against the CD Acts that political feminists would later emulate. It did not prevent them from entering more wholeheartedly than American feminists into local and party politics, or from devising exciting tactics that would give British suffragists world attention in the twentieth century. Nor, as already indicated, did it incline them to rely upon instrumental in preference to egalitarian feminism. In addition, until the 1920s middle-class British feminists were more successful than Americans in their dealings with working women, being more willing to acknowledge the existence and problems of class and relatively unaffected by race considerations, given Britain's overwhelmingly white home population.[4]

Some leading American feminists, for their part, may have expressed more elitism and less anti-clericalism with the passage of time,[5] but they enjoyed the benefit of a more democratic educational system and generally remained radical in terms of their support for feminist separatism and for a wide range of causes. They were also innovative enough to transform women's temperance efforts, to launch an immensely important club movement, and to help shape the objectives of Progressivism. And they were confident enough frequently to reject the half-loaf of partial suffrage, to mobilise a huge constituency for the vote, to seek the international leadership of feminism, and to defend the non-partisanship which, though it was favoured by many reformers, was cherished as part of a distinctively feminine approach to politics.

The performance of the two movements may be judged in various ways, and, as one would expect, there were victories and disappointments. In comparison with their small and tentative beginnings, by World War One they could command considerable support and attention. Having demonstrated that women were more than victims, they had survived the reordering of priorities that followed as a new generation of women came into the cause during the second part of the nineteenth century. Equally, they were strong enough to survive organisational and generational strains during the interwar years of the twentieth century. The 'antis' had never been able to match the feminists organisationally, although they had been vocal in the 1840s and 1850s, and remained vocal in the 1920s: a tribute to the importance of the feminist cause.

On the one hand, the structures and personnel of *formal* politics remained largely masculine after 1920, and the gendered system of economic inequality between the sexes, a feminist target from the first, proved too useful to men in general and employers in particular to be surrendered. Feminists' class divisions, the weakness of Socialism and organised labour until near the end of our period, and the many market and technological factors influencing employers, all made headway in this area especially hard to achieve. On the other hand, the demarcation line between the public and private spheres had been eroded, and the agenda of politics had been changed by the feminists. Largely by concentrating on the practically possible and intellectually acceptable, they had helped to secure the passage of many laws favourable to women.

Proportionately to the size of their political system, British feminists were more successful in gaining legislation than their American counterparts, and were politically orientated from the beginning. However, they had the advantage of focusing their energies on a single legislature, while the Americans had the advantage of varied courts which took varied views on matters of concern to women, notably divorce and child custody. They were also less divided over protective labour laws than the British before the 1920s, and this legislation is a good example of the danger of depending on rule changes to achieve justice. Too much depended on the goodwill and good judgement of those who had to implement reform legislation, which had often already suffered at the hands of hostile politicians.[6]

It is hard to know what more the movements could have done to improve their position. Both made their greatest progress on issues with which men sympathised: educational improvement, legal revision, social purity, welfare provision. But we have seen that purity was an arena in which groups with very different aims achieved at best an uneasy coexistence; and even with masculine support, feminist gains might be meagre because of the fiscal or political problems involved. The early welfare state legislation, for example, benefited women less than other social groups,[7] besides having coercive intentions and enshrining views of the female role that were not always appealing to the women affected. If the geographical strength of feminism varied in Britain and the United States alike, and only the suffrage campaigns, among the exclusively feminist endeavours, produced national organisations, women devised small-scale networks, congenial to their sex, which were a source of strength, not weakness. Large national bureaucracies are often slow to respond to new challenges, but the fluid feminist groups were not. While unionists, suffragists, educators and temperance workers all felt the force of localism, they were not defeated by it. Indeed, Frances Willard's willingness to encourage local variety played no small part in the success of the Woman's Christian Temperance Union in the United States.

Historians have usually applauded the constitutional and traditional pressure-group methods favoured by British and American feminists, who themselves found such methods appealing and hoped that they would be acceptable to cautious and bold women alike. The demerits of British militancy should not be exaggerated in consequence, and I have tried to show why 'the emergence of the Pankhursts' was seen by some activists as 'a miracle' of great moment for what they thought of as 'the mildly meandering' British movement.[8] Naturally feminists in both countries had their periodic quarrels, with those of American feminists being unfairly well known. I have recorded but not dwelt upon these conflicts, since they seem in no way greater than the divisions which have beset other social movements grappling with major problems over a long period. But there was a danger that the nineteenth century's productive tension between those who stressed sexual equality and those who highlighted female distinctiveness could degenerate into a polarising barrier between feminists, as it did in the controversy over protective legislation.

Though they devoted much attention to fashioning an interpretation of womanhood that would help them to amend the doctrine of spheres, feminists did not, for the most part, seek to revise the middle-class construct of masculinity. There were dangers, too, in the fact that social feminist groups came to outnumber the more exclusively feminist associations, and that practical, single-issue groups in the women's movements came to outnumber co-ordinating organisations. Since means undoubtedly affect ends, we should not be surprised to find that overall direction and attention to broader ideological questions suffered. None the less, we should not mourn unduly what cannot be remedied. Followers of any movement want some short-term gains, which in the twentieth century are generally best sought through specialist organisations. And the different emphases within feminism had not been reconciled by the 1920s because they were – and are – irreconcilable; yet they could normally be accommodated, just as the current debates over the implications of deconstructionist feminism and gender studies can be accommodated.[9]

It cannot be claimed that American activists devised wiser tactics than the British, or that the British were more astute than the Americans. Neither separatist nor integrationist approaches were guaranteed success in the face of unpromising social or political circumstances,[10] on matters where women were reluctant to flout custom, and when followers were tired or complacent. In developing their distinctive tactics and priorities, British and American activists built up movements that suited their respective environments, and they were right to do so. The supreme irony was that their combined efforts brought them enhanced influence, something women had always been told they possessed, but not the power they needed to carry through the whole of their programmes.

Notes

Introduction

1. See, for instance, Bridget Hill, *Eighteenth-Century Women: An anthology* (London and Winchester, MA, Unwin Hyman, 1987); Bridget Hill, *Women, Work, and Sexual Politics in Eighteenth-Century England* (Oxford, Blackwell, 1989); Alice Browne, *The Eighteenth Century Feminist Mind* (Hemel Hempstead, Harvester Wheatsheaf, 1990); Mary Beth Norton, *Liberty's Daughters: The Revolutionary experience of American women, 1750-1800* (Boston, MA and Toronto, Little, Brown, 1980); Linda K. Kerber, *Women of the Republic: Intellect and ideology in Revolutionary America* (Chapel Hill, University of North Carolina Press, 1980).
2. See, for instance, Nancy Cott, *The Grounding of Modern Feminism* (New Haven, CT and London, Yale University Press, 1987); Susan D. Becker, *The Origins of the Equal Rights Amendment: American feminism between the wars* (Westport, CT, Greenwood Press, 1981); Susan Ware, *Beyond Suffrage: Women in the New Deal* (Cambridge, MA, Harvard University Press, 1981); David Doughan, *Lobbying for Liberation: British feminism, 1918-1968* (City of London Polytechnic, 1980); Martin Pugh, *Women and the Women's Movement in Britain, 1914-1959* (London, Macmillan, 1992); Brian Harrison, *Prudent Revolutionaries: Portraits of British feminists between the wars* (Oxford, Clarendon Press, 1987); and Dale Spender, *There's Always Been a Women's Movement This Century* (London, Pandora, 1983).
3. For an example of this kind of judgement, see Marlene Dixon, 'Why Women's Liberation', in T.R. Frazier (ed.), *The Underside of American History: Other readings* (New York, Harcourt, Brace, Jovanovich, 1971, 2 vols), vol. 2, pp. 320, 325–6.
4. Michelle Zimbalist Rosaldo, 'Woman, culture and society: a theoretical overview', in Michelle Zimbalist Rosaldo and Louise Lamphere (eds), *Woman, Culture and Society* (Stanford, CA, Stanford University Press, 1974), pp. 67–87; Nancy Chodorow, 'Family structure and feminine personality', in *Woman, Culture and Society*, pp. 43–66; Chodorow, 'Being and doing: a cross-cultural examination of the socialization of males and females', in Vivian Gornick and Barbara K. Moran (eds), *Women in Sexist Society: Studies in power and powerlessness* (New York, Basic Books, 1971), pp. 173–97; Carol P. MacCormack and Marilyn Strathern, *Nature, Culture and Gender* (Cambridge, Cambridge University Press, 1980). But see also Rosaldo,

'The use and abuse of anthropology: reflections on feminism and cross-cultural understanding', *Signs*, vol. 5, no. 3, Spring 1980, pp. 389–417; and Susan C. Rogers, 'Woman's place: a critical review of anthropological theory', *Comparative Studies in Society and History*, vol. XX, 1978, pp. 123–62.

5. Linda J. Nicholson, *Gender and History: The limits of social theory in the age of the family* (New York, Columbia University Press, 1986), p. 6, ch. 3 and *passim*.

6. Nicholson, *Gender and History*, pp. 71–2, 78. See also Michael Rose, 'Love without the sex object', *Times Higher Education Supplement*, 25 December 1992, pp. 15–16, for some critical reflections on sexual identity as a construction of society.

7. See, for instance, Christine Bolt, *Victorian Attitudes to Race* (London, Routledge & Kegan Paul, 1971) and 'Race and the Victorians', in C.C. Eldridge (ed.), *British Imperialism in the Nineteenth Century* (London, Macmillan, 1984), p. 131; G.W. Stocking, *Race, Culture and Evolution: Essays in the history of anthropology* (New York, Free Press, 1968); M. Harris, *The Rise of Anthropological Theory: A history of theories of culture* (London, Routledge & Kegan Paul, 1968).

8. 'Editors' introduction', in Judith L. Newton, Mary P. Ryan and Judith R. Walkowitz (eds), *Sex and Class in Women's History* (London, Routledge & Kegan Paul, 1983, History Workshop Series), pp. 4–5.

9. Kathleeen Canning, 'Gender and the politics of class formation: rethinking German labor history', *American Historical Review*, vol. 97, no. 3, June 1992, p. 737.

10. See Robin Morgan, *Sisterhood is Global* (New York, Anchor Press, Doubleday, 1984); and for some of the responses to this proposition, which recognise the differences between non-white and white, non-Western and Western women, see Ellen C. DuBois and Vicki L. Ruiz (eds), *Unequal Sisters: A multicultural reader in U.S. women's history* (New York, Routledge, 1990); Nancy A. Hewitt, 'Beyond the search for sisterhood: American women's history in the 1980s', *Social History*, vol. 10, October 1985, pp. 299–321.

11. 'Editors' introduction', Newton, Ryan and Walkowitz (eds), *Sex and Class*, pp. 5–6. Other influential articles relating to these issues include Joan Kelly, 'The doubled vision of feminist theory', in *ibid.*, pp. 259–70, who suggested how 'the sexual/ reproductive and the economic productive/reproductive orders operate together'; Catharine A. MacKinnnon, 'Feminism, Marxism, method and the state: an agenda for theory', in Nannerl O. Keohane, Michelle Z. Rosaldo and Barbara C. Gelpi (eds), *Feminist Theory: A critique of ideology* (Brighton, Harvester, 1982), pp. 15–16; Joan Scott, 'Gender: a useful category of historical analysis', *American Historical Review*, vol. 91, December 1986, pp. 1053–75; Gayle Rubin, 'The traffic in women: notes on the "political economy" of sex', in Rayna R. Reiter (ed.), *Toward an Anthropology of Women* (New York, Monthly Review Press, 1975), pp. 157–210, on 'the mutual interdependence of sexuality, economics, and politics' and the arrangements 'by which a society transforms biological sexuality into products of human activity'; Sally Alexander, 'Woman, class and sexual differences in the 1830s and 1840s: some reflexions on the writing of feminist history', *History Workshop Journal*, vol. 17, Spring 1984, pp. 133–49; Leonore Davidoff, 'Class and gender in Victorian England', in Newton, Ryan and Walkowitz (eds), *Sex and Class*, pp. 17–71. And see Leonore Davidoff and Catherine Hall, *Family Fortunes: Men and women of the English middle class, 1780–1850* (Chicago, University of Chicago Press, 1987), for an important study of how gender and class interacted to fashion middle-class identity; Sherry B. Ortner and Harriet Whitehead (eds) *Sexual Meaning: The cultural*

construction of gender and sexuality (Cambridge, Cambridge University Press, 1981) and Jeffrey Weeks, *Sexuality and Its Discontents: Meanings, myths and modern sexualities* (London, Routledge & Kegan Paul, 1985) on the social construction of sexuality; Joan Scott, *Gender and the Politics of History* (New York, Columbia University Press, 1988); Karen Offen, Ruth Roach and Jane Rendall, *Writing Women's History* (London, Macmillan, 1991); Gerda Lerner, *The Majority Finds Its Past: Placing women in history* (New York, Oxford University Press, 1981; originally published 1979); Carole Pateman and Elizabeth Gross (eds), *Feminist Challenges: Social and political theory* (London, Allen & Unwin, 1986).

12. See, however, Jane Rendall's excellent study *The Origins of Modern Feminism: Women in Britain, France and the United States, 1780–1860* (Basingstoke and London, Macmillan, 1985); and the wide-ranging comparative studies by Erna Olafson Hellerstein, Leslie Parker Hume, and Karen M. Offen (eds), *Victorian Women: A documentary account of women's lives in nineteenth century England, France and the United States* (Brighton, Harvester 1981); Richard J. Evans, *The Feminists: Women's emancipation movements in Europe, America and Australasia, 1840–1920* (London, Croom Helm and Totowa, NJ, Barnes & Noble, 1984 edn); and Ross E. Paulson, *Women's Suffrage and Prohibition: A comparative study of equality and social control* (Glenview, IL, Scott, Foresman, 1973). Also C.E. Black, *The Dynamics of Modernization: A study of comparative history* (New York, Harper Torchbooks, 1966), especially ch. 2, p. 40 (source of quotation).

13. See Evans, *The Feminists*, ch. 1; Paulson, *Women's Suffrage and Prohibition*, ch. 1; William O'Neill, *The Woman Movement: Feminism in the United States and England* (London, Allen & Unwin, New York, Barnes & Noble, 1969), pp. 16–17.

14. Evans, *The Feminists*, p. 34.

15. Olive Banks, *Faces of Feminism: A study of feminism as a social movement* (Oxford, Blackwell, 1986), chs 2–7, p. 118; Philippa Levine, *Victorian Feminism, 1850–1900* (London, Hutchinson, 1987), pp. 16–17.

16. Evans, *The Feminists*, pp. 57–8, 66, on the 'premature radicalization' of the British and American movements in the 1860s.

17. Banks, *Faces of Feminism*, ch. 2; Rendall, *The Origins of Modern Feminism*, ch. 3; Nancy F. Cott, *The Bonds of Womanhood: 'Woman's sphere' in New England, 1780–1835* (New Haven, CT and London, Yale University Press, 1978 edn), ch. 5; Evans, *The Feminists*, p. 33; Levine, *Victorian Feminism*, 'Introduction'.

18. Aileen S. Kraditor's 'Introduction' to her anthology *Up From the Pedestal: Selected writings in the history of American feminism* (Chicago, Quadrangle Books, 1968); Mary P. Ryan, 'American society and the cult of domesticity, 1830–1860', PhD dissertation, University of California, Santa Barbara, 1971; Cott, *The Bonds of Womanhood*, ch. 2 and 'Conclusion'; Rendall, *The Origins of Modern Feminism*, ch. 6; Catherine Hall, 'The early formation of Victorian domestic ideology', in S. Burman (ed.), *Fit Work for Women* (London, Croom Helm, 1979), pp. 15–32.

19. For an introduction to some of the problems involved in defining and shaping feminism, see Sarah Slavin Schramm, *Plow Women Rather Than Reapers: An intellectual history of feminism in the United States* (Metuchen, NJ and London, Scarecrow Press, 1979).

20. See C. Vann Woodward (ed.), *The Comparative Approach to American History* (New York, Basic Books, 1968), ch. 24, especially pp. 347–8, on America's move away from the tendency to assert 'the *in*comparability of her history'.

21. Roger Thompson, *Women in Stuart England and America*: *A comparative study* (London, Routledge & Kegan Paul, 1974), especially Part II and 'Epilogue'.
22. See, for instance, Norton, *Liberty's Daughters*, pp. xiv, 315; and 'The evolution of white women's experience in early America', *American Historical Review*, vol. 89, no. 3, June 1984, pp. 593–619.
23. See Page Smith, *Daughters of the Promised Land*: *Women in American history* (Boston, MA and Toronto, Little, Brown, 1970), ch. 5.
24. O'Neill, *The Woman Movement*, p. 18, stresses Tocqueville's point about Americans' tendency towards association.
25. In *The Woman Movement*, pp. 29–30, William O'Neill suggests that the British movement, emerging in a more conservative era than its American counterpart, was respectable from the start.
26. Thistlethwaite, *America and the Atlantic Community*: *Anglo-American aspects, 1790–1850* (New York, Harper & Row, 1963 edn), pp. 174 f.
27. Arthur Mann, 'British social thought and American reformers of the Progressive era', *Mississippi Valley Historical Review*, vol. 42, 1955–6, pp. 672–92; Mann also points out the British developments which were criticised by American liberals.
28. This argument is made in Constance Rover's *Love, Morals and the Feminists* (London, Routledge & Kegan Paul, 1970), pp. 55–60.
29. A point noted by O'Neill, *The Woman Movement*, pp. 31–2.
30. See Martin Pugh, *Women's Suffrage in Britain, 1867–1928* (London, Historical Association, 1980), p. 8.
31. The word feminism was accorded dictionary recognition in England in the 1890s; it seems not to have been in common usage until the early 1900s. The term was first used in France in the 1880s.
32. The *Shorter Oxford English Dictionary* defines feminism as 'advocacy of the claims and rights of women'; on definitions, see also Schramm, *Plow Women*, p. 5; Rendall, *The Origins of Modern Feminism*, p. 1; also Cott, *The Grounding of Modern Feminism*, pp. 3 f; and Levine, *Feminist Lives*, ch. 1.
33. S. Barbara Kanner, 'The women of England in a century of social change, 1815–1914', in Martha Vicinus (ed.), *Suffer and Be Still*: *Women in the Victorian age* (London, Methuen, 1980 edn), pp. 174–5 (quotation from p. 175) on difficulties with early movement history.
34. Barbara Caine, *Victorian Feminists* (Oxford, Oxford University Press, 1992), effectively brings out these tensions.
35. On social movements see Rudolph Heberle, *Social Movements*: *An introduction to political sociology* (New York, Appleton-Century-Crofts, 1951), p. 9; R. Ash, *Social Movements in America* (Chicago, Markham, 1972), p. 1.
36. Louise A. Tilly, 'Women's history and family history: fruitful collaboration or missed connection?', *Journal of Family History*, vol. 12, nos. 1–3, 1987, pp. 304, 313.
37. On the need to 'reexamine conventional periodization', see Linda K. Kerber and Jane DeHart Mathews, 'Introduction', in Kerber and Mathews (eds), *Women's America*: *Refocusing the past* (New York and Oxford, Oxford University Press, 1982), p. 5. See also, on the need to shift from calendar time to sequences, Charles Tilly, 'Family, social history, and social change', *Journal of Family History*, vol. 12, nos 1–3, 1987, pp. 327–8.
38. Linda K. Kerber, 'Daughters of Columbia: educating women for the republic, 1787–1805', in Kerber and Mathews (eds), *Women's America*, p. 86; and Barbara

Welter, 'The cult of true womanhood, 1820–1860', in H. Gordon (ed.), *The Family in Social-Historical Perspective* (New York, St Martin's Press, 1978), p. 322.

39. See Bonnie G. Smith, 'The contribution of women to modern historiography in Great Britain, France, and the United States, 1750–1940', *American Historical Review*, vol. 89, no. 3, June 1984, pp. 709–32; Kathryn Kish Sklar, 'American female historians in context, 1770–1930', *Feminist Studies*, vol. 3, nos 1–2, 1975–6, pp. 171–84; Natalie Zemon Davis, 'Gender and genre: women as historical writers, 1400–1820', in Patricia Labalme (ed.), *Beyond Their Sex: Learned women of the European past* (New York, New York University Press, 1980); and Christine Bolt, 'The emergence of women historians and women's history', unpublished paper for the Canterbury branch of the Historical Association, 1989.

40. Bolt, 'The emergence of women historians', pp. 4–5; Pauline W. Davis, *A History of the National Woman's Rights Movement For Twenty Years ... From 1850 to 1870*, etc. (New York, Journeymen Printers' Co-operative Association, 1831; New York, Kraus Reprint Co., 1971), p. 44; George H. Callcott, *History in the United States, 1800–1860* (Baltimore, MD and London, Johns Hopkins University Press, 1970), p. 35; Doris S. Goldstein, 'The organizational development of the British historical profession, 1884–1921', *Bulletin of the Institute of Historical Research*, vol. LV, no. 132, November 1982, pp. 180–93; *The Historical Association, 1906–1956* (London, The Historical Association, 1957), pp. 7 f., 143–4; R.A. Humphreys, *The Royal Historical Society* (London, Office of the Royal Historical Society, University College London, 1969), pp. 3, 11–12, 68–71. Women's progress was slower in the RHS than in the HA, with its broader-based membership, and women did not rise high in either organisation. On the problems of American women, see Jacqueline Goggin, 'Challenging discrimination in the historical profession: women historians and the American historical profession, 1890–1940', *American Historical Review*, vol. 97, no. 3, June 1992, pp. 769–802.

41. Adams quoted in Page Smith, *Daughters of the Promised Land: Women in American history* (Boston, MA and Toronto, Little, Brown, 1970), p. ix; Jane Austen, *Northanger Abbey* (Harmondsworth, Penguin, 1981; originally published 1818), p. 123; Alice Clark, *Working Life of Women in the Seventeenth Century* (London, Routledge & Kegan Paul, 1982; originally published 1919), p. 1, complaining of historians' neglect of women because they were 'regarded as a static factor in social developments'; and Berenice Carroll (ed.), *Liberating Women's History: Theoretical and critical essays* (Urbana, University of Illinois Press, 1976), p. xi; Christina Crosby, *The Ends of History: Victorians and the 'woman question'* (London, Routledge, 1990).

42. See George E.G. Catlin (intro.), *The Rights of Woman ... The Subjection of Women ...* (London, J.M. Dent, New York, E.P. Dutton, 1929), pp. 3, 39; Margaret Fuller, *Woman in the Nineteenth Century* (Columbia, University of South Carolina Press, 1980; originally published 1845), pp. 35–7, 39–49, 79, 126, 152, 159, on 'the idea of woman in the past'.

43. Mercy Warren, *History of the ... American Revolution*, etc. (Boston, MA, Manning & Loring for E. Larkin, 1805, 3 vols), vol. I, pp. iii–iv; Lawrence J. Friedman and Arthur H. Shaffer, 'Mercy Otis Warren and the politics of historical nationalism', *New England Quarterly*, vol. XLVIII, 1975, pp. 208–10; Mary Ann Everett Green, *Lives of the Princesses of England* (London, Henry Colburn, 1846–55, 6 vols), vol. I, p. vi; vol. III, p. iii; vol. IV, 'Advertisement'; vol. V, pp. iii–iv, for evidence of this apologetic or humble spirit.

44. Callcott, *History in the United States*, on the social utility and rapid institutionalisation of history: pp. 72–82, 177, and chs II, III and IX.

45. Caroline H. Dall, *Historical Pictures Retouched: A volume of miscellanies* (London, Edward S. Whitfield, 1860); Lydia Maria Child, *The History of the Condition of Women*, etc. (Boston, MA, J. Allen & Co., 1835, 2 vols); Sarah Hale, *Woman's Record*, etc. (New York, Harper & Brothers, 1853), pp. x, 902 and *passim*, stressed the moral superiority of women. Hale, of course, was not a feminist to those who see the movement as being concerned with sexual equality and the repudiation of separate spheres: as I see it, she combined feminism with anti-feminism. See Sherbrooke Rogers, *Sarah Josepha Hale: A New England pioneer, 1788–1879* (Grantham, NH, Thompson & Rutter, 1985); Nina Baym, 'Onward Christian women: Sarah J. Hale's history of the world', *New England Quarterly*, vol. LXIII, 1990, pp. 249–70. Child's history stresses the wrongs women have endured.

46. Elizabeth Cady Stanton, Susan B. Anthony and Matilda Joslyn Gage (eds), *History of Woman Suffrage* (New York, Fowler & Wells, 1881–6, 3 vols) (hereafter HWS), vol. I, p. 8.

47. See Ellen C. DuBois, *Feminism and Suffrage: The emergence of an independent women's movement in America, 1848–1869* (Ithaca, NY, Cornell University Press, 1985 edn), p. 15; Elizabeth Cady Stanton, *Eighty Years and More: Reminiscences, 1815–1897* (New York, Schocken Books, 1971 edn, introduction by Gail Parker; originally published 1898), p. 327; Elizabeth Griffith, *In Her Own Right: The life of Elizabeth Cady Stanton* (New York and Oxford, Oxford University Press, 1984), pp. 176–7 (Anthony quotation from p. 177).

48. Griffith, *In Her Own Right*, pp. 235–6.

49. See, for instance, Carrie Chapman Catt and Nettie Rogers Shuler, *Woman Suffrage and Politics: The inner story of the suffrage movement* (New York, Charles Scribner's Sons, 1923); Harriet Stanton Blatch and Alma Lutz, *Challenging Years: The memoirs of Harriet Stanton Blatch* (New York, G.P. Putnam's Sons, 1940); Doris Stevens, *Jailed For Freedom* (Freeport, NY, Books for Libraries Press, 1971 edn, originally published 1920); Mary A. Livermore, *The Story of My Life* (Hartford, CT, A.D. Worthington, 1899); Pauline W. Davis, *A History of the National Woman's Rights Movement*; Julia Ward Howe, *Reminiscences, 1819–1899* (Boston, MA, Houghton Mifflin, 1899); Jane Grey Swisshelm, *Half a Century* (Chicago, Jansen, McClurg, 1880, second edn); Jane Addams, *Twenty Years at Hull House* (New York and Scarborough, ON, Signet Classic, New American Library, 1981 edn of 1910 original); Maud Nathan, *The Story of an Epoch-Making Movement* (Garden City, NY, Doubleday Page, 1926); Alfreda M. Duster (ed.), *Crusade for Justice: The autobiography of Ida B. Wells* (Chicago, University of Chicago Press, 1970); Mary Church Terrell, *A Colored Woman in a White World* (Washington, DC, Ransdell, 1940); Jane C. Croly, *History of the Woman's Club Movement in America* (New York, Henry G. Allen, 1898).

50. See, for instance, Helen Blackburn, *Women's Suffrage: A record of the women's suffrage movement in the British Isles* (London and Oxford, Williams & Norgate, 1902); Sylvia Pankhurst, *The Suffragette Movement* (London, Virago, 1977, originally published 1931); Emmeline Pankhurst, *My Own Story* (London, Eveleigh Nash, 1914); Christabel Pankhurst, *Unshackled* (London, Hutchinson, 1959); Emmeline Pethick Lawrence, *My Part in a Changing World* (London, Victor Gollancz, 1938); Elizabeth Blackwell, *Pioneer Work in Opening the Medical Profession to Women* (London,

~

Longmans & Co., 1895); Josephine Butler, *Personal Reminiscences of a Great Crusade* (London, H. Marshall & Son, 1896); Louisa Twining, *Recollection of Life and Work* (London, E. Arnold, 1904); Annie M.A.H. Rogers, *Degrees by Degrees: The story of the admission of Oxford women to membership of the university* (London, Oxford University Press, 1938); H.M. Swanwick, *I Have Been Young* (London, Victor Gollancz, 1935); A. Kenney, *Memories of a Militant* (London, Edward Arnold, 1924); M. Bondfield, *A Life's Work* (London, Hutchinson, 1949); *Life of Frances Power Cobbe: By herself* (London, R. Bentley, 2 vols, 1904).

51. For American examples of this tendency, see *Proceedings of the Women's Rights Conventions, Held at Seneca Falls and Rochester, New York, July and August, 1848* (New York, Robert J. Johnston 1870; reprinted by Arno and the *New York Times*, 1967), Seneca Falls Convention, pp. 6, 9; and William Leach, *True Love and Perfect Union: The feminist reform of sex and society* (Middletown, CT, Wesleyan University Press, 1989 edn), pp. 160–3.

52. Millicent Garrett Fawcett, *Women's Suffrage: A short history of a great movement* (London, Jack, 1912), pp. 8–9, ch. IV and *passim*. Even John Stuart Mill, one of the outstanding intellectual proponents of women's rights, was influenced by his generally optimistic view of his own time to argue against inequality as a no longer necessary consequence of women's muscular inferiority to men, which had originated in the 'very earliest twilight of human society': see his *The Subjection of Women* (1869), in Catlin, *The Rights of Woman*, pp. 22–3. By contrast, Mrs Stanton believed in the past existence of 'The Matriarchate': see *Eighty Years and More*, pp. 430–1.

53. Ray Strachey, *The Cause: A short history of the women's movement in Great Britain* (London, Virago, 1989 edn, first published 1928).

54. See, for instance, Aileen Kraditor, *The Ideas of the Woman Suffrage Movement, 1890–1920* (New York, Columbia University Press, 1965; 1981 Norton edn); Alan Grimes, *The Puritan Ethic and Woman Suffrage* (New York, Oxford University Press, 1972); David Morgan, *Suffragists and Democrats: The politics of woman suffrage in America* (East Lansing, Michigan State University Press, 1972); Anne F. Scott and Andrew M. Scott, *One Half the People: The fight for woman suffrage* (Philadelphia, PA, B. Lippincott, 1975); Paulson, *Women's Suffrage and Prohibition*; Ellen C. DuBois, *Feminism and Suffrage: The emergence of an independent women's movement in America, 1848–1869* (Ithaca, NY and London, Cornell University Press, 1978–1985 edn); David Morgan, *Suffragists and Liberals: The politics of woman suffrage in Britain* (Oxford, Blackwell, 1975); Andrew Rosen, *Rise Up Women! The militant campaign of the women's social and political union, 1903–1914* (London, Routledge & Kegan Paul, 1974); Constance Rover, *Women's Suffrage and Party Politics in Britain, 1866–1914* (London, Routledge & Kegan Paul, 1967); Les Garner, *Stepping Stones to Women's Liberty: Feminist ideas in the women's suffrage movement, 1900–1919* (London, Heinemann, 1984); Leslie Hume, *The National Union of Women's Suffrage Societies, 1897–1914* (New York and London, Garland Publishing Inc., 1982); Sandra Holton, *Feminism and Democracy: Women's suffrage and reform politics in Britain, 1900–1918* (Cambridge, Cambridge University Press, 1986); Pugh, *Women's Suffrage in Britain*.

55. See books cited in Note 54, with the exception of Grimes, *The Puritan Ethic*, and Paulson, *Women's Suffrage and Prohibition*, for this national focus; and on New Englandisation, Elizabeth Fox-Genovese, *Within the Plantation Household: Black and*

white women of the Old South (Chapel Hill and London, University of North Carolina Press, 1988), p. 40.

56. See Grimes; Paulson; 'Suffering for suffrage: Western women and the struggle for political, legal, and economic rights', ch. 8 in Sandra L. Myres, *Westering Women and the Frontier Experience, 1800–1915* (Albuquerque, University of New Mexico Press, 1982), and the sources she cites, especially in Note 66; Christine Bolt, 'The less privileged half: women's suffrage, temperance and the women's movement – and the case of California', ch. 5 in Alec Barbrook and Christine Bolt, *Power and Protest in American Life* (Oxford, Martin Robertson and New York, St Martin's Press, 1980); Anne Firor Scott, *The Southern Lady: From pedestal to politics, 1830–1930* (Chicago and London, University of Chicago Press, 1970); Helen Deiss Irvin, *Women in Kentucky*, (Lexington, University Press of Kentucky, 1979), ch. 6; James P. Louis, 'Sue Shelton White and the woman suffrage movement', *Tennessee Historical Quarterly*, vol. xxii, no. 2, June 1963, pp. 170–90; Elizabeth Taylor, *Woman Suffrage Movement in Tennessee* (New York, Bookman Associates, 1959), and 'Women suffrage movement in North Carolina', *North Carolina Historical Review*, vol. 38, April 1961, pp. 173–89; Kraditor, *Ideas of the Woman Suffrage Movement*, ch. 7, and the sources she cites.

57. See Jill Liddington and Jill Norris, *One Hand Tied Behind Us: The rise of the women's suffrage movement*, (London, Virago, 1984 edn, originally published 1978); Cliona Murphy, *The Women's Suffrage Movement and Irish Society in the Early Twentieth Century* (Hemel Hempstead, Harvester Wheatsheaf, 1989).

58. See, for instance, DuBois, *Feminism and Suffrage*, p. 15.

59. See, for instance, Kraditor, *Ideas of the Woman Suffrage Movement*, ch. 3.

60. William O'Neill, *Everyone Was Brave: A history of feminism in America* (New York, Quadrangle, 1971, originally published 1969), pp. 22–33; Tilly, 'Women's history and family history', p. 309.

61. See, for instance, Barbara Hilkert Andolsen, *Daughters of Jefferson, Daughters of Bootblacks: Racism and American feminism* (Macon, GA, Mercer University Press, 1986); 'Introduction' by DuBois and Ruiz to DuBois and Ruiz, *Unequal Sisters*; Tilly, 'Women's history and family history', p. 313.

62. The term is used dismissively by Barbara Kanner, 'Introduction, old and new women's history', in Kanner (ed.), *The Women of England*, p. 15; positively by Natalie Z. Davis in 'Women's history in transition: the European case', *Feminist Studies*, vol. 3, nos. 3–4, 1975–6, pp. 83–103.

63. Gerda Lerner, 'Priorities and challenges in women's history research', *Perspectives* (American Historical Association Newsletter), vol. 26, no. 4, April 1988, p. 19.

64. See, for instance, Peggy A. Rabkin, *Fathers to Daughters: The legal foundation of female emancipation* (Westport, CT, Greenwood Press, 1980); Norma Basch, *In the Eyes of the Law: Women, marriage and property in nineteenth century New York* (Ithaca, NY, Cornell University Press, 1982); Glenda Riley, *Divorce: An American tradition* (New York, Oxford University Press, 1991); Mary Roth Walsh, *Doctors Wanted, No Women Need Apply: Sexual barriers in the medical profession, 1835–1975* (New Haven, CT and London, Yale University Press, 1977); William Leach, *True Love and Perfect Union: The feminist reform of sex and society* (Middletown, CT, Wesleyan University Press, 1989 edn); Mario Jo Buhle, *Women and American Socialism, 1870–1920* (Urbana, University of Illinois Press, 1981); Nancy Schrom Dye, *As Equals and as Sisters: Feminism, the Labour movement and the Women's Trade Union League of New York* (Columbia, University of Missouri Press, 1980); Barbara Wertheimer, *We Were There* (New York, Pantheon, 1977).

65. See Paula Baker, '"The domestication of politics'": women and American political society, 1780–1920', *American Historical Review*, vol. 89, no. 3, June 1984, pp. 620–47.
66. See, for instance, Barbara Welter, 'The cult of true womanhood', *American Quarterly*, vol. 18, Summer 1966, pp. 151–75; Glenda Riley, 'From chattel to challenger: the changing image of the American woman, 1828–1848', PhD dissertation, Ohio State University, 1967; Kraditor, *The Ideas of the Woman Suffrage Movement*; Sheila M. Rothman, *Woman's Proper Place: A history of changing ideals and practices, 1870 to the present* (New York, Basic Books, 1978); Leach, *True Love and Perfect Union*.
67. See, for instance, Cott, *Bonds of Womanhood*; Caroll Smith-Rosenberg, 'The female world of love and ritual: relations between women in nineteenth century America', *Signs*, vol. 1, 1975, pp. 1–30.
68. See, O'Neill, *Everyone Was Brave*, pp. 47–8, for example.
69. 'Editors' introduction', Newton, Ryan and Walkowitz (eds), *Sex and Class*, pp. 2–5; Barbara Taylor, *Eve and the New Jerusalem: Socialism and feminism in the nineteenth century* (London, Virago, 1983; 1984 edn); Gail Malmgreen, *Neither Bread nor Roses: Utopian feminism and the English working class, 1800–1850* (Brighton, Harvester, 1978); Lee Holcombe, *Victorian Ladies at Work: Middle class working women in England and Wales, 1850–1914* (Newton Abbot, David & Charles, 1973); A. James Hammerton, *Emigrant Gentlewomen: Genteel poverty and female emigration, 1830–1914* (London and Totowa, NJ, Croom Helm, 1979); Malcolm I. Thomis and Jennifer Grimmett, *Women in Protest, 1800–1850* (London, Croom Helm, 1982); Jane Rendall (ed.), *Women and Politics, 1800–1914* (Oxford, Blackwell, 1987).
70. Holcombe, *Victorian Ladies at Work*; Levine, *Victorian Feminism*, pp. 16–17, chs 4–5; Banks, *Faces of Feminism*; Evans, *The Feminists*; Shelia Rowbotham, *Hidden from History* (London, Pluto Press, 1973); Philippa Levine, *Feminist Lives in Victorian England: Private roles and public commitment* (Oxford, Blackwell, 1990), chs 7 and 8.
71. 'Editors' introduction', Newton, Ryan and Walkowitz (eds), *Sex and Class*, p. 4; Lerner, *Teaching Women's History*, pp. 1–5.
72. See, for a complaint about the shortage of studies of British women's health compared to those about American women, Martha Vicinus (ed.), *A Widening Sphere: Changing roles of Victorian women* (London, Methuen, 1980 edn, originally published 1977), p. 232; by the 1980s the output of work on marriage, sex and morality relevant to the British movement had increased. American scholars have also been more active in charting the link between religion and female activism: see references in chs 1 and 2.
73. See, for instance, Margaret Bryant, *The Unexpected Revolution: A study of the history of the education of women and girls in the nineteenth century* (NFER Publishing Company, University of London, Institute of Education, 1979); Barry Turner, *Equality for Some: The story of girls' education* (London, Ward Lock Educational, 1974); Josephine Kamm, *Hope Deferred: Girls' education in English history* (London, Methuen, 1965); Carol Dyhouse, *Girls Growing Up in Late Victorian and Edwardian England* (London, Routledge & Kegan Paul, 1981); Joan Burstyn, *Victorian Education and the Ideal of Womanhood* (London, Croom Helm, 1980); Edward W. Ellsworth, *Liberators of the Female Mind: The Shirreff sisters, educational reform and the women's movement* (Westport, CT, Greenwood Press, 1979); Sheila Fletcher, *Feminists and Bureaucrats: A study in the development of girls' education in the nineteenth century* (Cambridge, Cambridge University Press, 1980); Rendall (ed.), *Women and Politics*.

74. See, for instance, Davidoff, 'Class and gender'; Davidoff and Hall, *Family Fortunes*.
75. See, for example, Levine, *Victorian Feminism*; Thomis and Grimmett, *Women in Protest*; Frank Prochaska, *Women and Philanthropy in Nineteenth-Century England* (Oxford, Clarendon Press, 1980); Susan Kingsley Kent, *Sex and Suffrage in Britain, 1860–1914* (London, Routledge, 1990; originally published 1987), p. 227: Kent stresses – rightly in my view – the significance of sexual issues in the women's movement.
76. These are cited throughout the text: three important group biographies are Caine, *Victorian Feminists*; Brian Harrison, *Prudent Revolutionaries: Portraits of British feminists between the wars* (Oxford, Clarendon Press, 1987); and Jane Lewis, *Women and Social Action in Victorian and Edwardian England* (Aldershot, Edward Elgar, 1991).
77. See Cott, *The Grounding of Modern Feminism*; Sheila Jeffreys, *The Spinster and Her Enemies: Feminism and sexuality, 1880–1930* (London, Pandora, 1985); Jeffrey Weeks, *Sex, Politics and Society: The regulation of sexuality since 1800* (London, Longman, 1986; originally published 1981); Cate Haste, *Rules of Desire: Sex in Britain, World War I to the present* (London, Chatto & Windus, 1992); Doughan, *Lobbying for Liberation*; Pugh, *Women and the Women's Movement*; Johanna Alberti, *Beyond Suffrage: Feminists in war and peace, 1914–1928* (London, Macmillan, 1989); Lee Virginia Chambers-Schiller, *Liberty, A Better Husband. Single Women in America: The generations of 1780–1840* (New Haven, CT and London, Yale University Press, 1984); Caroll Smith-Rosenberg, *Disorderly Conduct: Visions of gender in Victorian America* (New York, Oxford University Press, 1985); Martha Vicinus, *Independent Women: Work and community for single women, 1850–1920* (London, Virago, 1985).
78. These include Kent, *Sex and Suffrage*; Levine, *Victorian Feminism*; Josephine Kamm, *Rapiers and Battleaxes: The women's movement and its aftermath* (London, George Allen & Unwin, 1966); Marian Ramelson, *The Petticoat Rebellion: A century of struggle for women's rights* (London, Lawrence & Wishart, 1967); Eleanor Flexner, *Century of Struggle: The women's rights movement in the United States* (Cambridge, MA, Belknap Press of Harvard University Press, 1982 edn; originally published 1959); O'Neill, *Everyone Was Brave*; Lois W. Banner, *Women in Modern America: A brief history* (New York, Harcourt, Brace, Jovanovich, 1974); William H. Chafe, *The American Woman: Her changing social, economic and political roles, 1920–1970* (New York, Oxford University Press, 1978 edn; originally published 1972); Mary P. Ryan, *Womanhood in America: From colonial times to the present* (New York, New Viewpoints/Franklin Watts, 1979 edn; originally published 1975); Jane Lewis, *Women in England, 1870–1950* (Sussex, Wheatsheaf and Bloomington, Indiana University Press, 1984); Sara M. Evans, *Born for Liberty* (New York, The Free Press, 1989).
79. Thistlethwaite, *America and the Atlantic Community*; Rendall, *The Origins of Modern Feminism*; Evans, *The Feminists*; Paulson, *Women's Suffrage and Prohibition*; O'Neill, *The Woman Movement*; Banks, *Faces of Feminism*.

Chapter 1   The setting for the women's movements

1. Cott, *The Bonds of Womanhood*, pp. 20–2; Mary Beth Norton, 'The evolution of white women's experience in early America', *American Historical Review*, vol. 89, no. 3, June 1984, p. 601, stresses the importance of household work for American

women but sees English women as being less confined; Norton, *Liberty's Daughters*, ch. 1; Julia Cherry Spruill, *Women's Life and Work in the Southern Colonies* (Chapel Hill, University of North Carolina Press, 1938), ch. 4; Bridget Hill, *Women, Work, and Sexual Politics*, chs 2, 3 and 5 especially; and Hill (ed.), *Eighteenth Century Women*, Parts 10–12 and pp. 8–9.

2. Mary P. Ryan, *Womanhood in America*, p. 40; Hill (ed.), *Eighteenth Century Women*, pp. 11–12, Part 7; Hill, *Women, Work, and Sexual Politics*, ch. 12, especially p. 221, on numbers; Mary Prior, 'Women and the urban economy: Oxford, 1500–1800', in Prior (ed.), *Women in English Society, 1500–1800* (London and New York, Methuen, 1985), pp. 96, 110, 112, 114; Norton, *Liberty's Daughters*, ch. 2.

3. Clark, *Working Life*, 'Introductory'; Clark, p. 5, maintains that men 'were much more occupied with domestic affairs than they are now', but does not develop the point elsewhere: Prior, 'Women and the urban economy', p. 96, suggests otherwise; and see Norton, *Liberty's Daughters*, p. 8.

4. Thompson, *Women in Stuart England and America*, chs 2, 3, and p. 77 especially; Norton, 'Evolution', pp. 600–1, 605.

5. On the need for poor women to work outside the home, see Norton, 'Evolution', p. 605; Barbara B. Schnorrenberg with Jean E. Hunter, 'The eighteenth-century Englishwoman', in Barbara Kanner (ed.), *The Women of England: From Anglo-Saxon times to the present: Interpretive bibliographical essays* (London, Mansell, 1980), pp. 184–5.

6. Mary Beth Norton has been most notable in attacking the concept of a golden age: see, for instance, 'Evolution', pp. 593–4.

7. See Norton, *Liberty's Daughters*, ch. 1, on the variation in women's economic activities in colonial America; Norton 'Evolution', pp. 604–5, on the development of home manufacture in the colonies; Thomis and Grimmett, *Women in Protest*, p. 20.; Hill, *Women, Work, and Sexual Politics*, p. 259 and *passim*; Hill (ed.), *Eighteenth Century Women*, pp. 156–244.

8. See Patricia Crawford, 'Women's published writings 1600–1700', in Prior (ed.), *Women in English Society*, pp. 211–22; Schnorrenberg, 'The eighteenth-century Englishwoman', pp. 185–6.; Hill (ed.), *Eighteenth Century Women*, Part 1: Vivien Jones (ed.), *Women in the Eighteenth Century*, Section 1, 'Conduct', especially p. 15; Browne, *The Eighteenth Century Feminist Mind*, Part One.

9. Norton, *Liberty's Daughters*, p. 110.

10. *Ibid.*, ch. 4.

11. See Patricia Crawford, 'Women's published writings', pp. 228–30; Schnorrenberg, 'The eighteenth century Englishwoman', pp. 202–3; Jones (ed.), *Women in the Eighteenth Century*, Section 5, 'Feminisms'; Hill (ed.), *Eighteenth Century Women*, pp. 12, 247–54; Katharine Rogers, *Feminism in Eighteenth Century England* (Brighton, Harvester, 1982).

12. Rover, *Love, Morals and the Feminists*, pp. 146–50; Mary Astell, the late-seventeenth- and early-eighteenth-century writer on marriage and female education, has been seen in this light: see Bridget Hill (ed. and intro.), *The First English Feminist: Upon marriage and other writings by Mary Astell* (London, Gower/Maurice Temple Smith, 1986), pp. 2, 53–4 and *passim*.

13. Schnorrenberg, 'The eighteenth-century Englishwoman', pp. 193–4; Janelle Greenberg, 'The legal status of English women in early eighteenth century common law and equity', *Studies in Eighteenth Century Culture*, vol. 4, 1975, pp. 171–81; Prior,

'Women and the urban economy', p. 103; Browne, *The Eighteenth Century Feminist Mind*, p. 17; Hill (ed.), *Eighteenth Century Women*, Part 6, and *Women, Work and Sexual Politics*, ch. 11.

14. Thompson, *Women in Stuart England and America*, pp. 161–9; Richard B. Morris, *Studies in the History of American Law* (Philadelphia, PA, 1959, 2nd edn) ch. 3; Mary R. Beard, *Woman as Force in History* (New York, Macmillan, 1946), pp. 114–15; Kerber, *Women of the Republic*, pp. 139–40.

15. Marilynn Salmon, 'Equality or submersion? Feme covert status in early Pennsylvania', in Carol Berkin and Mary Beth Norton (eds), *Women of America* (Boston, MA, Houghton Mifflin, 1979), pp. 92–113; Norton, *Liberty's Daughters*, pp. 45–7.

16. Norton, 'Evolution', pp. 605–6; Marilynn Salmon, 'Women and property in South Carolina: The evidence from marriage settlements, 1730 to 1830', *William and Mary Quarterly*, vol. 39, 1982, pp. 654–85; Salmon, 'Equality or submersion?', pp. 93–113.

17. Oliver Ross McGregor, *Divorce in England: A centenary study*, (London, Heinemann, 1957), pp. 17–18; Norton, *Liberty's Daughters*, pp. 46–51; Thompson, *Women in Stuart England and America*, pp. 169–72; Hill (ed.), *Eighteenth Century Women*, pp. 108–9; Lawrence Stone, *Road to Divorce, 1530–1987* (Oxford, Oxford University Press, 1990), Part I, Sections II–IV, and Part II.

18. Kerber, *Women of the Republic*, pp. 159–60.

19. Thompson, *Women in Stuart England and America*, pp. 174–80; Kerber, *Women of the Republic*, pp. 162 ff.; Nancy F. Cott, 'Eighteenth-century family and social life revealed in Massachusetts divorce records', *Journal of Social History*, vol. 10, Fall 1976, pp. 20–43; Cott, 'Divorce and the changing status of woman in eighteenth-century Massachusetts', *William and Mary Quarterly*, 3rd series, vol. 33, 1976, pp. 586–614.

20. Accurate figures are hard to come by, but see Hill, *Women, Work, and Sexual Politics*, pp. 222–6; John R. Gillis, *For Better, For Worse: British marriages, 1600 to the present* (New York and Oxford, Oxford University Press, 1985), p. 15; Carl N. Degler, *At Odds: Women and the family in America from the Revolution to the present* (New York and Oxford, Oxford University Press, 1981 edn) p. 8; see also, however, the suggestion that in pre-nineteenth-century America, marriage was 'near universal', in Daniel Scott Smith '"Early" fertility decline in America: a problem in family history', *Journal of Family History*, vol. 12, nos 1–3, 1987, p. 76.

21. Degler, *At Odds*, pp. 7–8, 179; Scott Smith, '"Early" fertility decline', p. 76.

22. Norton, *Liberty's Daughters*, pp. 72–7; Schnorrenberg, 'The eighteenth-century Englishwoman', p. 196.

23. Norton, *Liberty's Daughters*, pp. 78–80, 105–9; Kerber, *Women of the Republic*, p. 7; Catherine M. Scholten, '"On the importance of the obstetrick art": changing cultures of childbirth in America, 1760 to 1825', reprinted in Kerber and Matthews (eds), *Women's America*, pp. 51–5; Browne, *The Eighteenth Century Feminist Mind*, pp. 18–19, 43–5: as Browne points out, however, male interest in childbirth and the care of infants was growing.

24. Schnorrenberg, 'The eighteenth-century Englishwoman', pp. 191–3; Norton, *Liberty's Daughters*, pp. 51–60; Degler, *At Odds*, pp. 10–11, 14–18; Alan MacFarlane, *Marriage and Love in England, 1300–1840* (Oxford, Blackwell, 1985); Lawrence Stone, *The Family, Sex and Marriage in England, 1500–1800* (New York, Harper & Row, 1977).

25. See, for instance, Gillis, *For Better, For Worse*, pp. 4–5, 12, 116–17; Jacqueline Jones,

Labor of Love, Labor of Sorrow: Black women, work, and the family from slavery to the present (New York, Basic Books, 1985), pp. 31–2 and *passim*, emphasises that though 'the two-parent, nuclear family was the typical form of slave cohabitation', kin and community ties were also immensely important.

26. Gillis, *For Better, For Worse*, pp. 135–40; Ada Wallas, *Before the Bluestockings* (London, George Allen & Unwin, 1929), pp. 118–19, 216–17; Stone, *Road to Divorce*, pp. 60–1, notes that 'the concept of affective individualism' had, however, penetrated even 'elevated circles'.

27. J. Campbell Smith, 'The marriage law of Scotland', in *Transactions of the National Association for the Promotion of Social Science* (London, John W Parker & Son, 1861), pp. 217 f., notes that the law in Scotland recognised irregular marriages (that is, contract and private marriages entered into without a clergyman present) if they were capable of proof; see also Stone, *Road to Divorce*, pp. 130–1.

28. Gillis, *For Better, For Worse*, pp. 84–5, 114, 140–1; Stone, *Road to Divorce*, pp. 121–30: the conduct of clandestine marriages was already a penal offence in Ireland.

29. Norton, *Liberty's Daughters*, pp. 71, 102–5; Browne, *The Eighteenth Century Feminist Mind*, pp. 18–19.

30. Schnorrenberg, 'The eighteenth-century Englishwoman', pp. 195–6; Hill (ed.), *Eighteenth Century Women*, pp. 104–7; Jones (ed.), *Women in the Eighteenth Century*, p. 59; Browne, *The Eighteenth Century Feminist Mind*, pp. 51–4.

31. Schnorrenberg, 'The eighteenth-century Englishwoman', pp. 196–7; Brown, *The Eighteenth Century Feminist Mind*, p. 18.

32. Schnorrenberg, 'The eighteenth-century Englishwoman', pp. 195–6; Degler, *At Odds*, pp. 66–7; Nancy Cott, 'Notes toward an interpretation of antebellum childrearing', *The Psychohistory Review*, vol. 6, no. 4, 1978, pp. 4–5; J.H. Plumb, 'The new world of children in eighteenth-century England', *Past and Present*, no. 67, May 1975, pp. 64–95; Philip J. Greven, *The Protestant Temperament: Patterns of child-rearing, religious experience, and the self in early America* (New York, Knopf, 1977); Ivy Pinchbeck and Margaret Hewett, *Children in English Society* (London, Routledge & Kegan Paul, 1969–73, 2 vols); Hugh Cunningham, *The Children of the Poor: Representations of childhood since the seventeenth century* (Oxford, Blackwell, 1991).

33. See, for instance, Gillis, *For Better, For Worse*, pp. 116–17; Degler, *At Odds*, pp. 69–71, 82–3, 140–2.

34. Norton, *Liberty's Daughters*, pp. 95, 100; Browne, *The Eighteenth Century Feminist Mind*, pp. 18–19, 51–2; Ruth H. Bloch, 'American feminine ideals in transition: the rise of the moral mother, 1785–1815', *Feminist Studies*, vol. 4, no. 2, June 1978, pp. 102–8, notes that before the late eighteenth century, American literature did not emphasise motherhood.

35. Norton, 'Evolution', pp. 606–7.

36. See Jay Mechling, 'Advice to historians on advice to mothers', *Journal of Social History*, vol. 9, Fall 1975, pp. 44–63 on the danger of assuming that advice was translated into action. See also Rudolph Trumbach, *The Rise of the Egalitarian Family* (New York and London, Academic Press, 1978).

37. See, for instance, Lyle Koehler, 'The case of the American Jezebels: Anne Hutchinson and female agitation during the years of antinomian turmoil, 1636–1640', *William and Mary Quarterly*, 3rd series, vol. 31, 1974, pp. 55–78; Norton, 'Evolution', p. 599.

38. Norton 'Evolution', pp. 608–9; Mary Maples Dunn, 'Saints and sisters', *American Quarterly*, vol. 70, no. 5, Winter 1978, pp. 583–601; Norton, *Liberty's Daughters*, pp. 127–32; Richard D. Shiels, 'The feminization of American Congregationalism, 1730–1835', *American Quarterly*, vol. 33, no. 5, Winter 1981, pp. 46–62: the reasons for this phenomenon relates to women's interest in supporting missionary work in the West and men's growing distraction by other organisations and ties; Linda Grant DePauw, *Remember the Ladies: Women in America, 1750–1850* (New York, Viking Press, 1976), pp. 75–6.

39. Barbara Leslie Epstein, *The Politics of Domesticity: Women, evangelism and temperance in nineteenth-century America* (Middletown, CT, Wesleyan University Press, 1981), ch. 1, especially pp. 43–4; Norton, *Liberty's Daughters*, p. 132.

40. See Norton, 'Evolution', pp. 606–7.

41. John Gregory, *A Father's Legacy to His Daughters* (London, 1774); and see Browne, *The Eighteenth Century Feminist Mind*, p. 24; Hill (ed.), *Eighteenth Century Women*, pp. 18, 21–5; Jones (ed.), *Women in the Eighteenth Century, passim*.

42. Crawford, 'Women's published writings', pp. 221, 222–3; and Lilian Lewis Shiman, *Women and Leadership in Nineteenth-Century England* (London, Macmillan, 1992), ch. 1.

43. See Phyllis Mack, 'Women as prophets during the English Civil War', *Feminist Studies*, vol. 8, 1982, pp. 19–45; Keith Thomas, 'Women and the Civil War sects', *Past and Present*, no. 13, April 1958, pp. 42–62.

44. R.T. Vann, *The Social Development of English Quakerism, 1655–1755* (Cambridge, MA, Harvard University Press, 1969); Judith Jones Hurwich, 'The social origins of the early Quakers', *Past and Present*, no. 48, 1970, pp. 156–64; Browne, *The Eighteenth Century Feminist Mind*, p. 14.

45. Marie B. Rowlands, 'Recusant women, 1560–1640', in Prior (ed.), *Women in English Society*, pp. 149–80; quotation from p. 163.

46. See Ruth Perry, 'The veil of chastity: Mary Astell's feminism', in Roseann Runte (ed.), *Studies in Eighteenth-Century Culture* (Wisconsin, Colleagues Press Inc., 1979), pp. 25–43; Perry, *The Celebrated Mary Astell: An early English feminist* (Chicago, University of Chicago Press, 1986); Joan Kinnaird, 'Mary Astell and the Conservative contribution to English feminism', *Journal of British Studies*, vol. 19–20, 1979, pp. 53–75; Wallas, *Before the Bluestockings*, ch. IV; Hill (ed. and intro.), *The First English Feminist*, pp. 1–2, 13, 16–17, 52–3; Jones (ed.), *Women in the Eighteenth Century*, pp.194–5.

47. This point is made by Georgiana Hill, *Women in English Life from Medieval to Modern Times* (London, Richard Bentley, 1896, 2 vols), vol. II, p. 83.

48. Wallas, *Before the Bluestockings*, pp. 111, 211, 213–14; Schnorrenberg, 'The eighteenth-century Englishwoman', pp. 186–7; Josephine Kamm, *Hope Deferred: Girls' education in English history* (London, Methuen, 1965), pp. 78–81, 136–41; Dorothy Gardiner, *English Girlhood at School: A study of women's education through twelve centuries* (London, Oxford University Press, 1929), pp. 222, 426–69; Hill (ed.), *Eighteenth Century Women*, pp. 44–8.

49. Hill, *Women in English Life*, vol. I, p. 309.

50. Schnorrenberg, 'The eighteenth-century Englishwoman', pp. 187–90 (source of first quotation); Margaret Maison, ' "Thine, only thine!" Women hymn writers in Britain', in Gail Malmgreen (ed.), *Religion in the Lives of English Women, 1760–1930* (London and Sydney, Croom Helm, 1986), pp. 11–40; Browne, *The Eighteenth*

Century Feminist Mind, pp. 8, 26–8, 103; Jones (ed.), *Women in the Eighteenth Century*, pp. 11, 140 (source of second quotation), and Section 3, especially p. 98.

51. Wallas, *Before the Bluestockings*, pp. 145 ff.

52. Chauncey Brewster Tinker, *The Salon and English Letters: Chapters on the interrelations of literature and society in the age of Johnson* (New York, Macmillan, 1915); Walter Sidney Scott, *The Bluestocking Ladies* (London, John Green & Co., 1947); Edith Rolt Wheeler, *Famous Bluestockings* (London, Methuen, 1910); Gardiner, *English Girlhood*, pp. 413–26, 453–4; Sylvia Harcstark Myers, *The Bluestocking Circle: Women, friendship, and the life of the mind in eighteenth-century England* (Oxford, Clarendon Press, 1990).

53. Hill, *Women in English Life*, vol. II, p. 44.

54. Crawford, 'Women's Published Writings', p. 220.

55. See Scott, *The Bluestocking Ladies*, and Hill (ed.), *Eighteenth Century Women*, p. 48. Kamm, *Hope Deferred*, ch. VII, p. 110, notes Hannah More's denial of any 'desire to make scholastic ladies or female dialecticians'; the term bluestocking allegedly originated from the blue stockings worn by a male attender at the ladies' gatherings, one Benjamin Stillingfleet. For sympathetic accounts of the bluestockings, stressing their friendly relations, see Dale Spender, *Women of Ideas* (London, Routledge & Kegan Paul, 1982) pp. 75–83; Myers, *The Bluestocking Circle*.

56. Schnorrenberg, 'The eighteenth-century Englishwoman', pp. 188–90; Barbara Miller Solomon, *In the Company of Educated Women*, p. 6; Kamm, *Hope Deferred*, pp. 110–11; D. Tyack and E. Hansot, *Learning Together* (Yale, 1990), ch. 1.

57. Cott, *The Bonds of Womanhood*, pp. 101–2; Lawrence Cremin, *American Education: The colonial experience* (New York, Harper Torchbooks, 1970).

58. Alice Morse Earle, *Colonial Days in Old New York* (London, David Nutt, 1896), pp. 35, 39.

59. Norton, *Liberty's Daughters*, pp. 260–1.

60. Kenneth A. Lockridge, *Literacy in Colonial New England* (New York, Norton, 1974), pp. 38–42, 57–8.

61. Norton, 'Evolution', pp. 607–8.

62. Dexter, *Colonial Women of Affairs: A study of women in business and the professions in America before 1776* (Boston, MA and New York, Houghton Mifflin, 1924), pp. 78–82, 88, 97.

63. *Ibid.*, p. 97.

64. Kerber, *Women of the Republic*, pp. 190 ff.

65. Earle, *Colonial Days in Old New York*, p. 168 (source of quotation); Solomon, *In the Company of Educated Women*, pp. 5–6, on talented women and their problems, and the desire of affluent parents to foster gentility in their daughters; see also Linda Grant DePauw's chapters on 'Accomplished Women' and 'Creative Women' in *Remember the Ladies*.

66. Crawford, 'Women's published writings', pp. 223–4.

67. *Woman's Suffrage Journal*, vol. xv, no. 170, 1 February 1884, p. 34, 'The relation of women to the state in former times'; Fawcett, *Women's Suffrage*, pp. 8–9; Ray Strachey, *The Cause* (London, Virago, 1978, first published 1928), pp. 113–14; Mary Prior, 'Women and the urban economy' p. 93 (source of first quotation); Karl Von Den Steinen, 'The discovery of women in eighteenth-century English political life', in Kanner (ed.), *The Women of England*, pp. 240–1 (p. 241 source of second quotation); Shiman, *Women and Leadership*, pp. 38, 40, 59.

68. Hill, *Women in English Life*, vol. I, pp. 330, 336, 339, makes these points; see, however, Von Den Steinen's more recent work.
69. See Browne, *The Eighteenth Century Feminist Mind*, pp. 130–6; Von Den Steinen, 'The discovery of women', pp. 233–8.
70. Von Den Steinen 'The discovery of women', pp. 242–4.
71. *Ibid.*, pp. 244–5.
72. Thomis and Grimmett, *Women in Protest*, pp. 10–11; E.P. Thompson, 'The moral economy of the English crowd in the eighteenth century', *Past and Present*, no. 50, February 1971, pp. 76–136; Hill (ed.), *Eighteenth Century Women*, pp. 247, 254–7.
73. Kerber, *Women of the Republic*, pp. 35–6.
74. Norton, *Liberty's Daughters*, p. 170.
75. Ryan, *Womanhood in America*, pp. 29 ff., 71–2; Norton, 'Evolution', pp. 610–12; Paula Baker, 'The domestication of politics: women and American political society, 1780–1920', *American Historical Review*, vol. 89, no. 3, June 1984, p. 622.
76. Kerber, *Women of the Republic*, pp. 36–104; Norton, *Liberty's Daughters*, pp. 155 ff.; Edward Countryman, *A People in Revolution: The American Revolution and political society in New York, 1760–1790* (Baltimore, MD and London, Johns Hopkins University Press, 1981), pp. 182–3.
77. Countryman, pp. 288–9, quotations from pp. 289, 371.
78. Norton, *Liberty's Daughters*, p. 163.
79. Kerber, *Women of the Republic*, p. 119.
80. Norton, *Liberty's Daughters*, pp. 191–3.
81. Kerber, *Women of the Republic*, pp. 8, 15–32, quotations from pp. 15, 31; Baker, 'The domestication of politics', p. 624; Ryan, *Womanhood in America*, p. 42.
82. Norton, 'Evolution', p. 616.
83. Kerber, *Women of the Republic*, pp. 11, 82–3, 191 and *passim*.
84. See Norton, *Liberty's Daughters*, pp. 238 ff.; Kerber, *Women of the Republic*, ch. 9; Ruth H. Bloch, 'American feminine ideals in transition', pp. 101–26.
85. Norton, *Liberty's Daughters*, pp. 263–9, 272; Kerber, *Women of the Republic*, ch. 7; Solomon, *In the Company of Educated Women*, pp. 7–13; Cott, *The Bonds of Womanhood*, pp. 110–11; Linda K. Kerber, 'Daughters of Columbia: educating women for the Republic, 1787–1805', in Stanley Elkins and Eric McKitrick (eds), *The Hofstadter Aegis: A memorial* (New York, Knopf, 1974), pp. 36–59.
86. Cott, *The Bonds of Womanhood*, p. 101; Kerber, *Women of the Republic*, p. 199.
87. Solomon, *In the Company of Educated Women*, pp. 14–15, 22–3; Eleanor Flexner, *Century of Struggle: The woman's rights movement in the United States* (Cambridge, MA and London, Belknap Press of Harvard University Press, 1982 edn; originally published 1959), p. 28; Norton, *Liberty's Daughters*, p. 273; Kerber, *Women of the Republic*, pp. 201 ff.; Cott, *The Bonds of Womanhood*, pp. 112–17; Thomas Woody, *A History of Women's Education in the United States* (New York, Octagon Books, 1966), vol. I, pp. 544–5.
88. Cott, *The Bonds of Womanhood*, p. 109.
89. Norton, *Liberty's Daughters*, p. 288; also pp. 280–1 and 287; Epstein, *The Politics of Domesticity*, p. 72; Cott, *The Bonds of Womanhood*, p. 125.
90. Solomon, *In the Company of Educated Women*, pp. 18–20, 25–6; Willystine Goodsell, *Women's Education in the United States: Emma Willard, Catharine Beecher, Mary Lyon* (New York, McGraw-Hill, 1931).
91. Kerber, *Women of the Republic*, pp. 141–2, 146–7, 153–6.

92. Edward Burrows and Michael Wallace, 'The American Revolution: the ideology and psychology of national liberation', *Perspectives in American History*, vol. 6, 1972, pp. 167–306.

93. Kerber, *Women of the Republic*, ch. 6.

94. Norton, *Liberty's Daughters*, pp. 228 ff.; Norton, 'Evolution', pp. 614–5; Burrows and Wallace, 'The American Revolution'; Cott, 'Notes toward an interpretation of antebellum childrearing', p. 17; Kerber, *Women of the Republic*, pp. 17–18; Robert V. Wells, *Revolutions in Americans' Lives: A demographic perspective on the history of Americans, their families, and their society* (Westport, CT, Greenwood Press, 1982), pp. 65–6. The anti-patriarchal strain in Locke (and Hobbes) is examined in Elizabeth Fox-Genovese, 'Property and patriarchy in classical bourgeois political theory', *Radical History Review*, vol. 4, nos 2–3, 1977, pp. 36–59; Bloch, 'Feminine ideals in transition', pp. 109 f.; Jay Fliegelman, *Prodigals and Pilgrims: The American Revolution against patriarchal authority, 1750-1800* (Cambridge, Cambridge University Press, 1982).

95. See, for instance, Bernard Bailyn, *The Ideological Origins of the American Revolution* (Cambridge, MA, Harvard University Press, 1965); Gordon Wood, *The Creation of the American Republic, 1776–1787* (Chapel Hill, University of North Carolina Press, 1969), ch. 1.

96. Barbara Taylor, *Eve and the New Jerusalem: Socialism and feminism in the nineteenth century* (London, Virago, 1984 edn), pp. 1–3, 8; Gillis, *For Better, For Worse*, pp. 102–4; J.F.C. Harrison, *The Second Coming: Popular millenarianism, 1780–1850* (London, Fontana, 1979); Lynne E. Withey, 'Catharine Macaulay and the uses of history: ancient rights, perfectionism, and propaganda', *Journal of British Studies*, vol. XVI, no. 1, Fall 1976, pp. 60–1.

97. See G.M. Ditchfield, 'Repeal, abolition, and reform: a study in the interaction of reforming movements in the Parliament of 1790–6', in Christine Bolt and Seymour Drescher (eds), *Anti-Slavery, Religion and Reform: Essays in memory of Roger Anstey* (Folkestone and Hamden, CT, Dawson & Archon, 1980), pp. 101–18.

98. James Walvin, 'The rise of British popular sentiment for abolition, 1787–1832', in *ibid.*, pp. 152–3.

99. Taylor, *Eve and the New Jerusalem*, pp. 7–8; Gillis, *For Better, For Worse*, p. 223.

100. Taylor, *Eve and the New Jerusalem*, pp. 8–9, 43–5; Gillis, *For Better, For Worse*, pp. 222–3; and see H.N. Brailsford, *Shelley, Godwin and their Circle* (London, Williams & Norgate, 1913).

101. Alice S. Rossi (ed.), *The Feminist Papers: from Adams to de Beauvoir* (New York and London, Columbia University Press, 1973), pp. 25–9; Caine, *Victorian Feminists*, pp. 22–7, on Wollstonecraft's nineteenth-century influence.

102. Rossi, *The Feminist Papers*, pp. 29–30. There are many studies of Wollstonecraft: see, for instance, Eleanor Flexner, *Mary Wollstonecraft: A biography* (New York, Coward, McCann & Geoghegan, 1972); Margaret George, *One Woman's 'Situation': A study of Mary Wollstonecraft* (Illinois, University of Northern Illinois Press, 1970); Claire Tomalin, *The Life and Death of Mary Wollstonecraft* (Harmondsworth, Penguin, 1977); Virginia Sapiro, *A Vindication of Political Virtue: The political theory of Mary Wollstonecraft* (Chicago, University of Chicago Press, 1992).

103. See Wollstonecraft, *Rights of Women* (ed. Catlin), p. 115, for a tribute by Wollstonecraft to Macaulay's 'valuable work'; on Macaulay see Bridget and Christopher Hill, 'Catharine Macaulay and the seventeenth century', *Welsh History*

Review, vol. III, no. 4, 1967, pp. 381–402; Lucy Martin Donnelly, 'The celebrated Mrs. Macaulay', *William and Mary Quarterly*, third series, vol. VI, April 1979, pp. 173–207; Withey, 'Catharine Macaulay and the uses of history', pp. 59–83; Claire Gilbride Fox, 'Catharine Macaulay, an eighteenth century Clio', *Winterthur Portfolio*, vol. 4, 1968, pp. 129–42 – Donnelly is critical of Macaulay as a historian; the remaining articles are more sympathetic, as is Bridget Hill's impressive biography *The Republican Virago: The life and times of Catharine Macaulay* (Oxford, Clarendon Press, 1992).

104. For these points, see the Catlin edition of the *Rights of Women*; quotation from (in order) pp. 26, 69, 80, 195, 207–8, 192, 37, 175; Browne, *The Eighteenth Century Feminist Mind*, pp. 42–3, on contemporary fears about girls' boarding schools: also pp. 157–9 on Wollstonecraft.

105. Browne, *The Eighteenth Century Feminist Mind*, p. 10; see also Jones (ed.), *Women in the Eighteenth Century*, p. 192.

106. Browne, *The Eighteenth Century Feminist Mind*, pp. 7–8.

107. Jones (ed.), *Women in the Eighteenth Century*, pp. 192–3 and Section 3; Browne, *The Eighteenth Century Feminist Mind*, ch. 5.

108. Jones (ed.), *Women in the Eighteenth Century*, p. 196.

109. Browne, *The Eighteenth Century Feminist Mind*, pp. 5–8 (quotation from p. 6); see also Rogers, *Feminism in Eighteenth-Century England*.

110. Browne, *The Eighteenth Century Feminist Mind*, pp. 2–5, 21, 178, ch. 6 and *passim* (quotation from p. 21); Jones (ed.), *Women in the Eighteenth Century*, pp. 193–4.

111. Rossi (ed.), *The Feminist Papers*, pp. 32–40; Withey, 'Catharine Macaulay and the uses of history', p. 83; Taylor, *Eve and the New Jerusalem*, pp. 9–11; Schnorrenberg, 'The eighteenth-century Englishwoman', pp. 203–4; Ditchfield, 'Repeal, abolition, and reform', p. 102; C.B. Cone, *The English Jacobins* (New York, Charles Scribner's Sons, 1968); Walvin, 'British popular sentiment for abolition', pp. 152–3; Harry T. Dickinson, *British Radicalism and the French Revolution, 1789–1815* (Oxford, Blackwell, 1988 edn), p. 15, for quotation on Wollstonecraft, and see ch. 4 on the aspects of radicalism which still survived in the early nineteenth century; Wollstonecraft, of course, was interested in the possibility of an enlarged political role for women and, writing at a time when there was neither a radical nor a bourgeois movement to support her, was not really in a position to 'campaign' for the vote: see Sheila Rowbotham, *Women, Resistance and Revolution* (Harmondsworth, Pelican, 1982 edn; originally published 1972), p. 45; Jane Abray, 'Feminism in the French Revolution', *American Historical Review*, vol. 80, 1975, pp. 43–62; George, *One Woman's 'Situation'*, chs 8 and 11, pp. 169–70; Browne, *The Eighteenth Century Feminist Mind*, ch. 8.

112. Norton, *Liberty's Daughters*, p. 251; Kerber, *Women of the Republic*, pp. 159–60, 222–5; Jones (ed.), *Women in the Eighteenth Century*, p. 99.

113. Donnelly, 'The Celebrated Mrs. Macaulay', pp. 193–8; Kerber, *Women of the Republic*, pp. 82, 226–7, 279, 281; Fox, 'Catharine Macaulay', p. 141.

114. Kerber, *Women of the Republic*, pp. 206, 226–7, 259; Lawrence J. Friedman and Arthur H. Shaffer, 'Mercy Otis Warren and the politics of historical nationalism', *New England Quarterly*, vol. XLVIII, 1975, pp. 206 f.; see also Judith Markowitz, 'Radical and feminist: Mercy Otis Warren and the historiographers', *Peace and Change*, vol. 4, 1977, pp. 10–21; Joan Hoff Wilson and Sharon Bollinger, 'Mercy Otis Warren: playwright, poet, and historian of the American Revolution', in J.R.

Brink (ed.), *Female Scholars: A tradition of learned women before 1800* (Montreal, Eden's Press Women's Publications, 1980), pp. 161–82.

115. See W.H.G. Armytage, *Heavens Below: Utopian experiments in England 1560–1960* (London, Routledge & Kegan Paul, 1961), pp. 62–8; Brailsford, *Shelley, Godwin and their Circle*, pp. 51–5.

116. Ann Douglas, *The Feminization of American Culture* (New York, Avon, 1978), ch. 1.

117. Epstein, *The Politics of Domesticity*, chs 2, 3, pp. 67–76; Susan Juster, '"In a different voice": male and female narratives of religious conversion in post-revolutionary America', *American Quarterly*, vol. 41, no. 1, March 1989, pp. 34–62. Donald G. Mathews, *Religion in the Old South* (Chicago, University of Chicago Press, 1977), ch. 3; Degler, *At Odds*, pp. 299–300; and Cott, *The Bonds of Womanhood*, pp. 128–32: Juster helpfully reminds us that after the conversion experience, gender distinctions were blurred (pp. 37, 56–7), with men and women possessed of 'moral agency and spiritual potency'.

118. See the following letters in the Hooker Collection, the Arthur and Elizabeth Schlesinger Library on the History of Women in America, Radcliffe College, Cambridge, Massachusetts (hereafter SL): in correspondence of Case family of Connecticut, Pluma Merrell to Melissa Case, 3 June 1815 (Folder 3); letters to Weltha Brown of Connecticut from Almira Eaton of Nov. 1812, 31 Jan. 1815, 1 May 1815, 7 April 1816, 19 Jan. 1822, 23 Aug. [?], 1 Sept. [?1815], 30 Sept. [?] (Folder 6); letters to Weltha Brown from Harriet Whiting of 2 May 1815, 20 Dec. 1815 and 22 May [?] (Folder 7); letters of Rebecca Root to Weltha Brown (Folder 8); undated letter from Eliza Perkins to Weltha Brown (Folder 10); letter to Weltha Brown from E.S. Gunnell, 9 March 1821 (Folder 15); letters about the preacher Rachel Baker to Weltha Brown (Folder 22).

119. Douglas, *The Feminization of American Culture*, ch. 3; Barbara Welter, 'The feminization of American religion, 1800–1860', in Mary Hartman and Lois Banner (eds), *Clio's Consciousness Raised* (New York, Harper Torchbooks, 1973), pp. 137–55.

120. Richard Carwardine, *Transatlantic Revivalism in Britain and America, 1790–1865* (Westport, CT, and London, Greenwood Press, 1978), p. 71 (source of first quotation); Cott, *The Bonds of Womanhood*, pp. 149–53 (source of second quotation: p. 152).

121. Cott, *The Bonds of Womanhood*, pp. 132–5, 146–8; Anne M. Boylan, 'Evangelical womanhood in the nineteenth century: the role of women in Sunday Schools', *Feminist Studies*, vol. 4, no. 3, Oct. 1978, pp. 62–80; Degler, *At Odds*, pp. 300–1; Richard D. Brown, 'The emergence of voluntary associations in Massachusetts, 1760–1830', *Journal of Voluntary Action Research*, vol. 2, 1973, pp. 64–73; Keith Melder, 'The beginnings of the women's rights movement in the United States, 1800–1840', PhD dissertation, Yale University, 1964; Berg, *The Remembered Gate*, pp. 145 f.; Mary P. Ryan, *Cradle of the Middle Class: The family in Oneida County, New York, 1790–1865* (Cambridge, MA, Cambridge University Press, 1981); Carwardine, *Transatlantic Revivalism*, p. 19; Anne M. Boylan, 'Women in groups: an analysis of women's benevolent organizations in New York and Boston, 1797–1840', *Journal of American History*, vol. 7, no. 3, December 1984, pp. 497–523.

122. See Dorothy Sterling (ed.), *We Are Your Sisters: Black women in the nineteenth century* (New York and London, W.W. Norton, 1984), pp. 104 f. (quotation from p. 110); Suzanne Lebsock, *The Free Women of Petersburg: Status and culture in a southern town, 1784–1860* (New York, Norton, 1984), ch. 7; Donald G. Mathews, *Religion in the*

Old South, ch. 4; Mathews, 'The Second Great Awakening as an organizing process', *American Quarterly*, vol. 21, 1969, pp. 23–43; and Mathews, 'Religion and slavery – the case of the American South'; in Bolt and Drescher (eds), *Anti-Slavery, Religion and Reform*, pp. 220 f.; Catharine Clinton, *The Plantation Mistress: Woman's world in the Old South* (New York, Pantheon, 1982), pp. 6–15, suggests that northern benevolence found no parallel in the plantation South.

123. Cott, *The Bonds of Womanhood*, pp. 135–59; Boylan, 'Women in groups' and 'Evangelical womanhood'; Ryan, *Cradle of the Middle Class*, pp. 71–5; Degler, *At Odds*, pp. 301–2; Berg, *The Remembered Gate*, pp. 154 f.: both Melder (see Note 121) and Berg see these voluntary societies as preparing the ground for feminism; Cott presents a more complicated account of them; while Boylan maintains that there was no clear progression from benevolence to reform and feminism, and that evangelical women carved out their own distinctive view of feminine nature, and created institutions through which their ideals could be expressed.

124. Cott, *The Bonds of Womanhood*, pp. 144–5.

125. F.K. Prochaska, *Women and Philanthropy in Nineteenth-Century England* (Oxford, Clarendon Press, 1980), pp. 9–10 (first quotation from p. 9); and see his 'Women in English philanthropy, 1790–1830', *International Review of Social History*, vol. 19, 1974, pp. 426–45; Rendall, *The Origins of Modern Feminism*, p. 73 (source of second quotation).

126. Rendall, *The Origins of Modern Feminism*, pp. 74–7, 87–93; D. Colin Dews, 'Ann Carr and the female revivalists of Leeds', in Malmgreen (ed.), *Religion in the Lives of English Women*, pp. 68–87 (quotations from pp. 71, 84); in her 'Introduction', Malmgreen points out that while women were a majority of the membership in most American denominations from the mid-seventeenth century to the first quarter of the nineteenth, equivalent figures are not available from Britain – but that preliminary figures show a similar picture: pp. 2, 9–10; Catherine Hall, 'The early formation of Victorian domestic ideology', in Sandra Burman (ed.), *Fit Work for Women* (London, Croom Helm, 1979), pp. 21 f.; Ian Bradley, *The Call to Seriousness: The Evangelical impact on the Victorians* (London, Jonathan Cape, 1976) ch. I; Louis Billington, 'Female labourers in the Church: women preachers in the Northeastern United States, 1790–1840', *Journals of American Studies*, vol. XIX, 1985, pp. 369–94, points out that the Freewill Baptists of New Hampshire and the Christians of Vermont were especially supportive of women's mission – even after the Methodists became more conservative; Shiman, *Women and Leadership*, ch. 2.

127. See Thompson, *The Making of the English Working Class*, pp. 420–6; Taylor, *Eve and the New Jerusalem*, pp. 161–7; Alice Felt Tyler, *Freedom's Ferment: Phases of American social history from the colonial period to the outbreak of Civil War* (New York, Harper & Row, 1962 edn), chs 6, 7; and J.K. Hopkins, *A Woman to Deliver Her People: Joanna Southcott and English millenarianism in an era of revolution* (Austin, University of Texas Press, 1982).

128. Thistlethwaite, *America and the Atlantic Community*, chs 1–3.

129. Carwardine, *Transatlantic Revivalism*, pp. xii–xiv, 29, 32, 42–4, 56, 71.

130. Hall, 'The early formation of Victorian domestic ideology', pp. 29–31; Thistlethwaite, *America and the Atlantic Community*, pp. 87–8.

131. Berg, *The Remembered Gate*, pp. 158–9; Cott, *The Bonds of Womanhood*, p. 134: Cott gives the founding date of the society as 1796.

132. Bradley, *The Call to Seriousness*, pp. 48–9; Rendall, *The Origins of Modern Feminism*,

pp. 93–5; Boylan, 'Women in groups', pp. 510–11, suggests that there was little cross-class involvement in pre–1830s American benevolent organisations.

133. Prochaska, 'Women in English philanthropy'; Bradley, *The Call to Seriousness*, especially pp. 123 f.

134. See Seymour Drescher, *Capitalism and Antislavery: British mobilization in comparative perspective* (London, Macmillan, 1986), pp. 78–9, 85, 215–16; Drescher points out (p. 221) that in 1792 in Belford, women signed a petition, and that 'In Scotland several female petitions were drawn up in 1814.' See also James Walvin, 'The propaganda of anti-slavery', in James Walvin (ed.), *Slavery and British Society, 1776–1846* (London, Macmillan, 1982), pp. 61–3; and Kenneth Corfield, 'Elizabeth Heyrick: radical Quaker', in Malmgreen (ed.), *Religion in the Lives of English Women*, pp. 41–67; and Shiman, *Women and Leadership*, pp. 46–7.

135. Rendall, *The Origins of Modern Feminism*, pp. 88–9, 91; Bradley, *The Call to Seriousness*, pp. 45, 111–16, 147–9, 151; Smith, *Daughters of the Promised Land*, pp. 100–1; Kerber, *Women of the Republic*, p. 242; Norton, *Liberty's Daughters*, pp. 271–2; Hannah More, *Strictures on the Modern System of Female Education* (London, T. Cadell and W. Davies, 1799); Gardiner, *English Girlhood*, ch. xiv; M.G. Jones, *Hannah More* (Cambridge, Cambridge University Press, 1952), chs V, VI, VII and *passim*, quotations from pp. 193, 212, 217; M.G. Jones, *The Charity School Movement: A study of eighteenth century Puritanism in action* (Cambridge, Cambridge University Press, 1938), pp. 4–6, 13–14, 74, 158–60, 345 and *passim*; Shiman, *Women and Leadership*, pp. 44–5.

136. Rendall, *The Origins of Modern Feminism*, pp. 140–2; Gardiner, *English Girlhood*, pp. 313–14; Kamm, *Hope Deferred*; ch. VI, pp. 154–5; Jones, *The Charity School Movement*, pp. 77, 81, 94–5. See also Doreen M. Rosman, *Evangelicals and Culture* (London, Croom Helm, 1984), pp. 217–19, on evangelical interest in education, including female instruction: Rosman suggests that there was some support for teaching girls severe or scientific subjects.

137. Rendall, *The Origins of Modern Feminism*, pp. 108–115; Thistlethwaite, *America and the Atlantic Community*, pp. 134–6.

138. Jones, *The Charity School Movement*, p. 13; see also Kerber, *Women of the Republic*, pp. 203–9; Cott, *The Bonds of Womanhood*, pp. 104–9, 115–18.

139. On the period of transition in America, see Abbott, *Women in Industry*, ch. III.

140. On the impact of industrialisation on women, I am indebted to the following: Hill, *Women, Work, and Sexual Politics*, chs 4–14; Abbott, *Women in Industry*; Cott, *The Bonds of Womanhood*, ch. 1; Thomis and Grimmett, *Women in Protest*, ch. 1; Louise A. Tilly and Joan W. Scott, *Women, Work and Family* (New York, Holt, Rinehart & Winston, 1978), Part II; Ryan, *Womanhood in America*, ch. 2; E.P. Thompson, *The Making of the English Working Class* (Harmondsworth, Penguin, 1972 edn); Ivy Pinchbeck, *Woman Workers and the Industrial Revolution, 1750–1850* (London, Routledge, 1930) pp. 1–2, 4, 307 f. and *passim*; Julie A. Matthaei, *An Economic History of Women in America* (Brighton, Harvester, 1982), Part II; Susan E. Kennedy, *If All We Did Was to Weep at Home: A history of white working-class women in America* (Bloomington, Indiana University Press, 1979), ch. 1; Richard J. Evans, *The Feminists* (London and Totowa, NJ, Croom Helm and Barnes & Noble, 1977), pp. 23–5; L.C.A. Knowles, *The Industrial and Commercial Revolutions in Great Britain During the Nineteenth Century* (London, Routledge, New York, E.P. Dutton, 1921), pp. 86, 95–8 and *passim*; Hans Medick, 'The proto-industrial family

economy: the structural function of household and family during the transition from peasant society to industrial capitalism', *Social History*, vol. III, 1976, pp. 291–316; Sonya O. Rose, 'Proto-industry, women's work and the household economy in the transition to industrial capitalism', *Journal of Family History*, vol. XIII, 1988, pp. 181–94; Jane Rendall, *Women in an Industrializing Society: England, 1750–1880* (Oxford, Blackwell, 1990).

141. Benita Eisler (ed.), *The Lowell Offering: Writings by New England mill women, 1840–1845* (New York, Harper Torchbooks, 1980), pp. 15–16, 18–24 (quotation from p. 15.)

142. Cott, *The Bonds of Womanhood*, p. 37.

Chapter 2 The forces that shaped the women's movements

1. On the consolidation of the middle class see Evans, *The Feminists*, pp. 28–9.

2. Gillis, *For Better, For Worse*, pp. 164 f.; Christine Stansell, *City of Women: Sex and class in New York* (New York, Alfred A. Knopf, 1986).

3. See Berg, *The Remembered Gate*, ch. 3, especially pp. 66–9; Cott, *The Bonds of Womanhood*, ch. 2.

4. See Christine Bolt, 'The American city: nightmare, dream or irreducible paradox?', in Graham Clarke (ed.), *The American City: Literary and cultural perspectives* (London and New York, Vision Press and St Martin's Press, 1988), pp. 13–35; Evans, *The Feminists*, pp. 29–30; and for an account which stresses the complexity of female reform endeavours, see Nancy A. Hewitt, *Women's Activism and Social Change: Rochester, New York, 1822–1872* (Ithaca, NY and London, Cornell University Press, 1984), pp. 21–3 and *passim*.

5. Berg, *The Remembered Gate*, p. 73, on the erosion of natural differences between men; Andrew Sinclair, *The Better Half: The emancipation of the American woman* (New York, Harper & Row, 1965), pp. 31–2, David Thomson, *England in the Nineteenth Century*, Harmondsworth, Penguin, 1983 edn), pp. 73–6 (quotation from p. 75); Shiman, *Women and Leadership*, pp. 40, 121–3.

6. Cott, *The Bonds of Womanhood*, pp. 63–4; Hall, 'The early formation of Victorian domestic ideology', pp. 30–1; Jeffrey Weeks, *Sex, Politics and Society: The regulation of sexuality since 1800* (London and New York, Longman, 1986 edn), p. 25; Margaret Bryant, *The Unexpected Revolution: A study in the history of the education of women and girls in the nineteenth century* (NFER Publishing Company, University of London, Institute of Education, 1979), pp. 26 ff.

7. Cott, *The Bonds of Womanhood*, ch. 2; Berg, *The Remembered Gate*, chs 4, 5; Davidoff and Hall, *Family Fortunes*.

8. Cott, *The Bonds of Womanhood*, ch. 2; Glenna Mathews, *'Just a Housewife': The rise and fall of domesticity in America* (New York, Oxford University Press, 1989); Colleen McDannell, *The Christian Home in Victorian America, 1840–1900* (Bloomington, Indiana University Press, 1986); J. Faragher and Christine Stansell, 'Women and their families on the overland trail to California and Oregon, 1842–1867', *Feminist Studies*, vol. 2, nos 2–3, 1975, pp. 150–66; Ann D. Gordon, Mari Jo Buhle and

Nancy E. Schrom, 'Women in American society – an historical contribution', *Radical America*, vol. 5, no. 4, 1971, pp. 3–66; Berg, *The Remembered Gate*, chs 4, 5; on female friendships see Caroll Smith-Rosenberg, 'The female world of love and ritual: relations between women in nineteenth-century America', in her collection of essays, *Disorderly Conduct: Visions of gender in Victorian America* (New York, Oxford University Press, 1985), pp. 53–76; Rendall, *The Origins of Modern Feminism, passim*; Levine, *Victorian Feminism*, 'Introduction'.

9. Leonore Davidoff, 'The separation of home and work?', in Burman (ed.), *Fit Work for Women*, p. 64; Linda K. Kerber, 'Separate spheres, female worlds, women's place: the rhetoric of women's history', *Journal of American History*, vol. 75, 1988, pp. 9–39; Ellen C. DuBois, Mari Jo Buhle, Temma Kaplan, Gerda Lerner and Caroll Smith-Rosenberg, 'Politics and culture in women's history: a symposium', *Feminist Studies*, vol. 6, 1980, pp. 26–64; John Mack Faragher, 'History from the inside-out: writing the history of women in rural America', *American Quarterly*, vol. 33, no. 1, Spring 1981, pp. 537–57, warns of confusing notions of Western woman as 'civilizer or helpmate' with reality; and while ackowledging male power, he stresses the importance of studying the 'histories of men, women and families in all their distinctive and critical variation'; Pamela Horn, *Victorian Countrywomen* (Oxford, Blackwell, 1991), pp. 4–5, notes that the cult of domesticity became stronger as the century progressed in country regions – elsewhere, it was coming under challenge; Frances B. Cogan, *All American Womanhood: The ideal of real womanhood in mid-century America* (Athens, University of Georgia Press, 1989) challenges the dominance of the true womanhood concept.

10. Alexis de Tocqueville, *Democracy in America* (New York, Vintage, 1945, originally published in English, 1838) vol. II, pp. 209, 212–14, 222–3; Sarah Josepha Hale, *Women's Record*, p. xlviii; Harriet Martineau, *Society in America* (New York, Saunders & Otley, 1837, 2 vols), vol. II, pp. 227, 245 f., 255–7; Frances Trollope, *Domestic Manners of the Americans* (New York, Whittaker, Treacher & Co., 1832), p. 75; Wright, *Views of Society and Manners in America* (London, Longman, 1822), p. 22; Charles Dickens, *American Notes* (London, Hazell, Watson & Viney, 1842), pp. 55, 119 on American courtesy towards women.

11. See Cott, *The Bonds of Womanhood*, p. 99; Boylan, 'Evangelical womanhood', p. 65.

12. See Sinclair, *The Better Half*, Part Four and *passim*; Berg, *The Remembered Gate*, pp. 96–9.

13. Anne Firor Scott, *The Southern Lady: From pedestal to politics, 1830–1930* (Chicago and London, University of Chicago Press, 1970), pp. 16–21.

14. Elizabeth Peabody to Maria Chase, Boston, 6 Oct. 1822, Folder 6, Rebecca Kinsman Munroe Collection, Sophia Smith Collection, Smith College, Northampton, Massachusetts (hereafter SSC).

15. Davidoff and Hall, *Family Fortunes*; Jeffrey Weeks, *Sex, Politics and Society*, pp. 24–33, especially p. 32; Elizabeth Fee, 'The sexual politics of Victorian social anthropology', in M.S. Hartman and L. Banner (eds), *Clio's Consciousness Raised* (New York, Harper & Row, 1974), p. 86; Martineau, *Society in America*, vol. II, p. 226.

16. See Jill Conway, 'Perspectives on the history of women's education in the United States', *History of Education Quarterly*, vol. xiv, 1974, pp. 1–12; Chambers-Schiller, *Liberty, A Better Husband*, pp. 77–82, 124–6, on the importance women attached to education (quotation from p. 124); and Peabody letters in Rebecca Kinsman Munroe

Collection, Folders 1–54, SSC, especially Elizabeth Peabody to Maria Chase, May 1821, Folder 4; *ibid.* to Gardiner, 31 May 1824, Folders 10–11; *ibid.* to Maria Chase, n.d., Folders 20–1; and *ibid.* to Maria Chase, 13 Nov., Folders 28–9.

17. Thomas Wood, *A History of Women's Education in the United States* (New York, Octagon Books, 1966), vol. II, pp. 228, 235, and ch. V generally.

18. Elizabeth Cady Stanton, *Eighty Years and More*, p. 37; Tyack and Hansot, *Learning Together*, chs 2–4.

19. For letters enthusiastic about teaching see Elizabeth Peabody, 18 March 1824, Folders 22–3, in SSC; and Clarissa Richmond to her sister Susanna, 2 June 1821, Folder 30, Hooker Collection, in SL. For cooler comments, see Eliza Perkins to Weltha Brown, 19 May 1819 (indicating the curriculum), Folder 10, Julia A.M. Pierce to her sister Sally Smith, 24 Nov. 1839 [?], letter of 6 May 1843 to 'Absent Friends', letters from Plainfield and Phoenix (n.d.) – source of the quotations – in Folder 45, letters of 14 June 1846 and 12 April 1851 from Aurelia M. Smith to her family, Folder 48, all in Hooker Collection, SL. For the complaint about there being no time to 'learn' the children, see Julia A. Porter to Clara Barton, 1854, Folder 31, Clara Barton Collection, SSC. Elizabeth Peabody enjoyed her teaching but took as much pleasure in her various other interests: see her letters from the 1820s in the Rebecca Kinsman Munroe Collection in SSC. On the liberating impact of literacy, see Joan M. Jensen, *Loosening the Bonds: Mid-Atlantic farm women, 1750–1850* (New Haven, CT and London, Yale University Press, 1986), pp. 182–3, and ch. 10 generally; Woody, *A History of Women's Education*, vol. I, p. 394, for the comparison of boys' and girls' schools; Degler, *At Odds*, p. 309; Solomon, *In the Company of Educated Women*, pp. 32–3, 40–1; Christine Bolt, *American Indian Policy and American Reform: Case studies of the campaign to assimilate the American Indians* (London and Boston, MA, Unwin Hyman, 1987), ch. 8, pp. 219–20, 267. On Sarah Douglass, see Sterling (ed.), *We Are Your Sisters*, pp. 127–3, 180 f.; Ida Husted Harper, *Life and Work of Susan B. Anthony* (Salem, NH, Ayer Co., 1983 reprint of 1898 edn), vol. I, pp. 45, 55, on Anthony's indignation that women teachers were paid less than men (often a quarter of the male salary) and her desire to take part in the wider world of reform after fifteen years of teaching. And see Richard M. Bernard and Maris Vinovskis, 'The female school teacher in ante-bellum Massachusetts', *Journal of Social History*, vol. X, 1977, pp. 332–45.

20. Solomon, *In the Company of Educated Women*, p. 21; Jensen, *Loosening the Bonds*, pp. 168–9 (quotation from p. 168); Helen G. Hole and Carol Stoneburner, 'The contribution of seven Quaker women to education', in Carole Stoneburner and John Stoneburner (eds), *The Influence of Quaker Women on American History: Biographical studies* (Lewiston, NY, Edwin Mellon Press, 1986), pp. 191–201.

21. Woody, *A History of Women's Education*, vol. I, pp. 380, 392–3.

22. Kathryn Kish Sklar, *Catharine Beecher: A study in American domesticity* (New Haven, CT and London, Yale University Press, 1973), p. 97; Woody, *A History of Women's Education*, vol. I, pp. 485–8.

23. Sklar, *Catharine Beecher*, pp. 97–8, Parts III and IV; Flexner, *Century of Struggle*, pp. 29, 31; and, on teacher training, Woody, *A History of Women's Education*, vol. I, pp. 467–83, 529–30; and Anne Firor Scott, 'The ever widening circle: the diffusion of feminist values from the Troy female seminary, 1822–72', *History of Education Quarterly*, vol. 19, Spring 1979, pp. 3–26.

24. Sklar, *Catharine Beecher*, pp. 97–8.

25. *Ibid.*, pp. xiii, 172–5, Parts II–IV; and on Emma Willard's belief in women's duty to educate children, see Willard, *History of the United States, or Republic of America* (Philadelphia, A.S. Barnes, 1843), p. 363; see also Jeanne Boydston, Mary Kelley and Anne Margolis, *The Limits of Sisterhood: The Beecher sisters on women's rights and women's sphere* (Chapel Hill, University of North Carolina Press, 1988).

26. *Proceedings of the Woman's Rights Conventions . . . 1848*, p. 6.

27. Woody, *A History of Women's Education*, vol. I, pp. 500–7; Kathryn Kish Sklar, 'The founding of Mount Holyoke College', in Carol R. Berkin and Mary B. Norton (eds), *Women of America: A history* (Boston, MA, Houghton Mifflin, 1979), pp. 177–201.

28. Flexner, *Century of Struggle*, pp. 29–30, quotation from p. 30.

29. Solomon, *In the Company of Educated Women*, p. 23, quoting Woody's findings.

30. Solomon, *In the Company of Educated Women*, p. 47; Woody, *A History of Women's Education*, vol. II, pp. 145–7, 160–78, 184.

31. See Solomon, *In the Company of Educated Women*, p. 43, for a disparaging comment by Lucy Stone on the 'numerous petty "female colleges" that have sprung into being': also p. 47; on the debate between those who urged special courses for women and those who thought they should do what men did, see Sara Delamont, 'The contradictions in ladies' education', in Sara Delamont and Lorna Duffin (eds), *The Nineteenth Century Woman: Her cultural and physical world* (London, Croom Helm, New York, Barnes & Noble, 1978), pp. 154–60; and for biographies of the three pioneers, see Elinor Rice Hays, *Morning Star: A biography of Lucy Stone, 1818–1893* (New York, Octagon Books, 1978 edn), especially Part One, and Hays, *Those Extraordinary Blackwells* (New York, Harcourt, Brace & World, 1967).

32. See Jane Purvis, *A History of Women's Education in England, 1800–1914* (Milton Keynes, Open University Press, 1991): Harriet Warm Schupf, 'Single women and social reform in mid-nineteenth-century England: the case of Mary Carpenter', *Victorian Studies*, vol. 17, March 1974, pp. 301–17; Ruby J. Saywell, *Mary Carpenter of Bristol* (Bristol, Historical Association, 1964); Douglas Charles Stange, *British Unitarians Against American Slavery, 1833–65* (Rutherford, Madison, Teaneck, Fairleigh Dickinson University Press; London and Toronto, Associated University Presses, 1984), p. 128; Patricia Hollis (ed.), *Women in Public: The women's movement, 1850–1900* (London, George Allen & Unwin, 1981 edn), pp. 224, 236–7; Bradley, *The Call to Seriousness*, pp. 46–7; P. Gardner, *The Lost Elementary Schools of Victorian England* (London, Croom Helm, 1984); Horn, *Victorian Countrywomen*, pp. 196–7; Jo Manton, *Mary Carpenter and the Children of the Streets* (London, Heinemann, 1976).

33. See Joyce Senders Pedersen, 'Schoolmistresses and headmistresses: elites and education in nineteenth-century England', *Journal of British Studies*, vol. XV, no. 1, November 1975, pp. 146–7; A. James Hammerton, *Emigrant Gentlewomen: Genteel poverty and female emigration, 1830–1914* (London and Totowa, NJ, Croom Helm, 1979), p. 40.

34. The last three paragraphs have drawn on Barry Turner, *Equality for Some: The story of girls' education* (London, Ward Lock Educational, 1974), pp. 61 (source of quotation), 66, 68, and see his ch. 3 generally; Josephine Kamm, *Hope Deferred*, ch. XI; Horn, *Victorian Countrywomen*, pp. 199–202.

35. On the Owenite Socialists, see Taylor, *Eve and the New Jerusalem*, pp. 230–7; Malmgreen, *Neither Bread Nor Roses*; on adult education, see Thistlethwaite, *America and the Atlantic Community*, pp. 137–8.

36. Kamm, *Hope Deferred*, pp. 166–72; Burstyn, *Victorian Education*, p. 23.

37. Kamm, *Hope Deferred*, pp. 173–4; Turner, *Equality for Some*, pp. 93–6.
38. Burstyn, *Victorian Edcuation*, pp. 23–4; Kamm, *Hope Deferred*, pp. 175–6.
39. Josephine Kamm, *How Different From Us: A biography of Miss Buss and Miss Beale* (London, Bodley Head, 1959 edn), chs I–VI; Kamm, *Hope Deferred*, pp. 177–8; Turner, *Equality for Some*, pp. 99–103; Bryant, *The Unexpected Revolution*, pp. 63–4, 72.
40. See Pedersen, 'Schoolmistresses and headmistresses', pp. 136–8, 147 ff.
41. Bessie R. Parkes, *Remarks on the Education of Girls* (London, Chapman, 1854), pp. 12, 14–15, 18–21; Burstyn, *Victorian Education*, p. 25; Sheila Fletcher, *Feminists and Bureaucrats: A study in the development of girls' education in the nineteenth century* (Cambridge, Cambridge University Press, 1980), pp. 14–16 (quotation from p. 16); Forster, *Significant Sisters*, pp. 140–4; Bryant, *The Unexpected Revolution*, pp. 76–80; Kamm, *Hope Deferred*, pp. 178–82; Candida Ann Lacey (ed.), *Barbara Leigh Smith and the Langham Place Group* (London, Routledge & Kegan Paul, 1987); see also the other useful volumes in this Women's Source Library series.
42. Deirdre David, *Intellectual Women and Victorian Patriarchy* (London, Macmillan, 1987); Martineau, *Society in America*, vol. II, p. 228; Dickens, *American Notes*, p. 50 (source of first quotation); Hale, *Woman's Record*, p. 564; *Harriet Martineau's Autobiography* (London, Smith, Elder & Co., 1877), vol. I, pp. 271 f., 311, 350; vol. II, p. 55 f.; Gaye Tuchman with Nina E. Fortin, *Edging Women Out: Victorian novelists, publishers and social change* (London, Routledge, 1989).
43. Hale, *Woman's Record*, p. 564; Eliza W. Farnham, *Woman and Her Era* (New York, A.J. Davis, 1864, 2 vols); Malmgreen (ed.), *Religion in the Lives of English Women*, 'Introduction', especially pp. 2, 6, 9–10; Nancy A. Hardesty, *Women Called to Witness: Evangelical feminism in the nineteenth century* (Nashville, TN, Abingdon Press, 1984), pp. 9–11 and *passim*; Hersh, *Slavery of Sex*, pp. 40–1; Carwardine, *Transatlantic Revivalism*, pp. 44, 56, 198; Banks, *Faces of Feminism*, pp. 14–17; Elizabeth Fox-Genovese, *Within the Plantation Household: Black and white women of the Old South* (Chapel Hill and London, University of North Carolina Press, 1988), pp. 231–5; Lebsock, *The Free Women of Petersburg*, ch. 7 and Epilogue; Rosemary Radford Reuther and Rosemary Skinner Keller, *Women and Religion in America: The nineteenth century* (San Francisco, Harper & Row, 1981), 'Introduction', chs 1, 3, 6; Winthrop S. Hudson, 'Evangelical religion and women's liberation in the nineteenth century', in Stoneburner and Stoneburner (eds), *The Influence of Quaker Women*, pp. 191–201.
44. See Kamm, *Hope Deferred*, pp. 176–7; Chambers-Schiller, *Liberty, A Better Husband*, ch. 6; Caroll Smith-Rosenberg, 'Women and religious revivals: anti-ritualism, liminality, and the emergence of the American bourgeois', in Leonard I. Sweet (ed.), *The Evangelical Tradition in America* (Macon, GA, Mercer University Press, 1984), pp. 199–231.
45. See diaries of Mrs Bardwell of Walpole, Vermont, 1855–1866, 3 vols, in Helen Temple Cooke Papers (pp. 59, Reel 966), SL – especially entries for 11 Nov. 1858, 25 Sept. 1859, 11 Jan. 1860, 19 May 1860, and 2 Sept. 1864; see also Barbara Welter, 'The feminization of American religion: 1800–1860', in Hartman and Banner (eds), *Clio's Consciousness Raised*, pp. 137–55.
46. Chambers-Schiller, *Liberty, A Better Husband*, pp. 1, 19–21, 62, 865 and *passim*; Lebsock, *The Free Women of Petersbury*, p. 216; Martha Vicinus, *Independent Women: Work and community for single women, 1850–1920*, (Chicago and London, University of Chicago and Virago, 1985), ch. 2; Nancy Hewitt, 'The parameters of women's power in American religion', in Sweet (ed.), *The Evangelical Tradition*, pp. 233–56; Harold E.

~

Raser, *Phoebe Palmer: Her life and thought* (Lewiston, NY, Edwin Mellon Press, 1987); Carwardine, *Transatlantic Revivalism*, pp. 182–4, 187–8, 191, 193; Hardesty, *Women Called to Witness*, p. 66, for quotation from Palmer; Shiman, *Women and Leadership*, ch. 7.

47. Hardesty, *Women Called to Witness*, ch. 5, especially p. 65; Ryan, 'A women's awakening', p. 604.

48. See, for instance, Bradley, *The Call to Seriousness*, pp. 40–1, on the influence of women in spreading evangelical religion in upper-class Victorian families.

49. See in Hale Family Papers, 1780–1967, Box 10, Folder 301, letters of 21 July 1816; Folder 302, 6 Feb. 1821; Folder 304, letter of 23 Feb. 1838 [?]; Box 11, Folder 312, letter of 1 April 1850: in SSC.

50. See Doreen M. Rosman's excellent account of *Evangelicals and Culture*, especially ch. 4; Wyatt-Brown, 'Conscience and career', pp. 186–90, in Bolt and Drescher (eds), *Anti-Slavery, Religion and Reform*, on the importance of evangelical mothers in 'conscience-building'; and Bradley, *The Call to Seriousness*, p. 191.

51. F.K. Prochaska, *Women and Philanthropy in Nineteenth-Century England*, p. 13; Margaret Maison, *Search Your Soul, Eustace: A survey of the religious novel in the Victorian age* (London, Sheed & Wells, 1961), Appendix; Nina Baym, *Women's Fiction: A guide to novels by and about women in America, 1820–1870* (Ithaca, NY, Cornell University Press, 1978); Douglas, *The Feminization of American Culture*; Elizabeth Jay, *The Religion of the Heart: Anglican evangelicalism and the nineteenth-century novel* (Oxford, Clarendon Press, 1979); Hardesty, *Women Called to Witness*, pp. 70–1; Sandra Sizer, *Gospel Hymns and Social Religion: The rhetoric of nineteenth-century revivalism* (Philadelphia, PA, Temple University Press, 1978); Shiman, *Women and Leadership*, pp. 45, 55.

52. Douglas, *The Feminization of American Culture*.

53. Prochaska, *Women and Philanthropy in Nineteenth-Century England*, pp. 13–14 (quotation from p. 14); Rosman, *Evangelicals and Culture*, p. 109.

54. Mary Kelley, *Private Woman, Public Stage: Literary domesticity in nineteenth century America* (New York and Oxford, Oxford University Press, 1984), pp. xi (source of quotation), 7–11, 334–5; Kelley, 'At war with herself: Harriet Beecher Stowe as woman in conflict within the home', in Kelley (ed.), *Woman's Being, Woman's Place: Identity and vocation in American history* (Boston, MA, G.K. Hall & Co., 1979), pp. 201–19; Susan K. Harris, *Nineteenth Century American Women's Novels* (Cambridge, Cambridge University Press, 1990); Judith Lowder Newton, *Women, Power and Subversion: Social strategies in British fiction, 1778–1860* (London, Methuen, 1985); H.B. Stowe to Mr Parton, 6 February 1868, Folder 29, Parton Papers, SSC.

55. Prochaska, *Women and Philanthropy in Nineteenth-Century England*, pp. 15–17; Berg, *The Remembered Gate*, pp. 199–200; Hall, 'Domestic ideology', pp. 21–32; Taylor, *Eve and the New Jerusalem*, pp. 125–6.

56. See letter of Lucretia P. Hale to Edward Hale, 25 March 1846, p. 3, Folder 388, and to Sarah Hale, 2 March 1849, Folder 391, Box 19, Hale Family Papers, SSC; Sarah Hale quoted in Baym, 'Onward Christian women', p. 255.

57. Prochaska, *Women and Philanthropy in Nineteenth-Century England*, pp. 38–9; Bradley, *The Call to Seriousness*, pp. 123–4, 137.

58. Prochaska, *Women and Philanthropy in Nineteenth-Century England*, p. 39.

59. Stange, *British Unitarians*, pp. 26 f.; Bradley, *The Call to Seriousness*, pp. 25, 30, 139–40.

60. Stange, *British Unitarians*, p. 27; Thistlethwaite, *America and the Atlantic Community*, p. 79–80; on American Quaker women and reform, see Margaret Hope Bacon, *Mothers of Feminism: The story of Quaker women in America* (San Francisco, Harper & Row, 1986), Stoneburner and Stoneburner (eds), *The Influence of Quaker Women*; Bradley, *The Call to Seriousness*, p. 138 on female inventiveness; see also Charles I. Foster, *An Errand of Mercy: The Evangelical United Front 1790–1837* (Chapel Hill, University of North Carolina Press, 1960), for early opposition to the work of British activists.

61. Cott, *The Bonds of Womanhood*, pp. 157 f.; an absorbing study of the kind of antebellum male reformer who did welcome the feminisation of religion is provided by Lewis Perry on Henry Clarke Wright, in *Childhood, Marriage and Reform* (Chicago, Chicago University Press, 1980); see Martineau's scathing comments on the American clergy at this time in *Society in America*, vol. II, pp. 353, 361: though her opinion of the British clergy (p. 364) was not flattering!

62. The American Female Moral Reform Association, established in 1834, soon had hundreds of chapters. Mary P. Ryan, *Womanhood in America*, pp. 85–9, 105–7, 110; Ryan, 'The power of women's networks', in Judith L. Newton, Mary P. Ryan and Judith R. Walkowitz (eds), *Sex and Class in Women's History*, (London, Routledge & Kegan Paul, 1983), pp. 167–86; Lori D. Ginzberg, *Women and the Work of Benevolence: Morality, politics and class in the nineteenth-century United States* (New Haven, CT and London, Yale University Press, 1990), chs 1 and 2; Hewitt, *Women's Activism*, pp. 39–46 and *passim*; Rendall, *Origins of Modern Feminism*, pp. 260–1; William McLoughlin, *Revivals, Awakenings, and Reforms: An essay on religion and social change in America, 1607–1977* (Chicago, University of Chicago Press, 1980); Berg, *The Remembered Gate*, especially ch. 8; Smith-Rosenberg, *Disorderly Conduct*, pp. 120 f.; Susan Porter Benson, 'Business heads and sympathizing hearts: the women of the Providence Employment Society, 1837–1858', *Journal of Social History*, vol. 12, Winter 1978, pp. 302–12; Boylan, 'Evangelical womanhood', p. 71; Prochaska, *Women and Philanthropy in Nineteenth-Century England*, pp. 184–9; Smith-Rosenberg, *Religion and the Rise of the American City: The New York City mission movement, 1812–1870* (Ithaca, NY, Cornell University Press, 1971); Timothy L. Smith, *Revivalism and Social Reform: American Protestantism on the eve of the Civil War* (Gloucester, MA, Peter Smith, 1976), pp. 123–4, 169–71, 211–12; Hardesty, *Women Called to Witness*, chs 8–11; Vicinus, *Independent Women*, pp. 77–80; Edward J. Bristow, *Vice and Vigilance: Purity movements in Britain since 1700* (Dublin, Gill & Macmillan and Totowa, NJ, Rowan & Littlefield, 1977), p. 62, notes that it was 'virtually impossible', in the 1840s, 'to attract women to a movement whose focus was prostitution': see also pp. 60–1, 68–71; Ellen DuBois, 'Women's rights and abolition: the nature of the connection', in Lewis Perry and Michael Fellman (eds), *Antislavery Reconsidered: New perspectives on the abolitionists* (Baton Rouge and London, Louisiana State University Press, 1979), p. 241; Stansell, *City of Women*, ch. 4, p. 250; Carolyn D. Gifford, 'Women in social reform movements', in Reuther and Keller (eds), *Women and Religion in America*, pp. 294–303; Anne Summers, 'A home from home: women's philanthropic work in the nineteenth century', in Burman (ed.), *Fit Work for Women*, pp. 33–63; Barbara Meil Hobson, *Uneasy Virtue: The politics of prostitution and the American reform tradition* (New York, Basic Books, 1987), ch. 3.

63. Blanche Glassman Hersh, *The Slavery of Sex: Feminist-abolitionists in America*

(Urbana, University of Illinois Press, 1978), pp. 136–52, 253–4 (quotation from pp. 136–7); Thistlethwaite, *America and the Atlantic Community*, pp. 129–30, suggests that American and English women followed a similar course, but Harriet Martineau is his only English example.

64. Taylor, *Eve and the New Jerusalem*, pp. 129–57; Malmgreen (ed.), *Religion in the Lives of English Women*, 'Introduction', p. 6.

65. See Susan P. Casteras, 'Virgin vows: the early Victorian artists' portrayal of nuns and novices', in Malmgreen (ed.), *Religion in the Lives of English Women*, pp. 129–60, especially pp. 132–3, 136–40 (quotation from p. 135), for some of the antipathies; also *English Woman's Review*, no. 1, October 1866, pp. 54 f.; Bristow, *Vice and Vigilance*, pp. 64, 68–9. On the work of the Orders, see Anna Jameson, *Sisters of Charity and the Communion of Labour: Two lectures on the social employment of women* (London, Longman, Brown, Green, Longmans and Roberts, 1859); Michael Hill, *The Religious Order: A study of virtuoso religion and its legitimation in the nineteenth-century Church of England* (London, Heineman Educational Books, 1973); Arthur A. Allchin, *The Silent Rebellion: Anglican religious communities, 1845–1900* (London, SCM Press, 1958). See also Vicinus, *Independent Women*, ch. 2.

66. See Chambers-Schiller, *Liberty, A Better Husband*, pp. 23–4.

67. See Catherine M. Prelinger, 'The female diaconate in the Anglican Church: what kind of ministry for women?', in Malmgreen (ed.), *Religion in the Lives of English Women*, pp. 161–92; Vicinus, *Independent Women*, ch. I, pp. 47, 60 f.

68. See Evans, *The Feminists*, and Rendall, *Origins of Modern Feminism*, on continental European feminism.

69. Chambers-Schiller, *Liberty, A Better Husband*, pp. 88–9; Bradley, *The Call to Seriousness*, p. 91; Solomon, *In the Company of Educated Women*, p. 34; Hardesty, *Women Called to Witness*, pp. 109–10; Jean Friedman, *The Enclosed Garden: Women and community in the evangelical South, 1830–1900* (Chapel Hill, University of North Carolina Press, 1985), p. 19, notes the limited involvement of southern women; Leonard A. Sweet, *The Minister's Wife: Her role in nineteenth-century American evangelicalism* (Philadelphia, PA, Temple University Press, 1983); Boylan, 'Evangelical womanhood', p. 72; Edna Healey, *Wives of Fame* (Hodder & Stoughton, 1988).

70. Taylor, *Eve and the New Jerusalem*, pp. 127–8, 133; Dews, 'Ann Carr and the female revivalists of Leeds', in Malmgreen (ed.), *Religion in the Lives of English Women*, pp. 76 f.; Jensen, *Loosening the Bonds*, pp. 145–6 and ch. 9 generally; and Hardesty, *Women Called to Witness*, ch. 7, on American women preachers, licensed and unlicensed; see also Smith, *Revivalism and Social Reform*, pp. 123–4, 144; Elaine J. Lawless, *Handmaidens of the Lord: Pentecostal women preachers and traditional religion* (Philadelphia, University of Pennsylvania Press, 1988); Barbara Zimkund, 'The struggle for the right to preach', in Reuther and Keller (eds), *Women and Religion in America*, pp. 193–205; Billington, 'Female labourers in the Church'; Deborah Valenze, *Prophetic Sons and Daughters: Popular religion in industrial England* (Princeton, NJ, Princeton University Press, 1985); Evans,. *Born to Liberty*, p. 111.

71. Taylor, *Eve and the New Jerusalem*, pp. 166–7, 172 f.

72. Anne C. Loveland, 'Domesticity and religion in the ante-bellum period: the career of Phoebe Palmer' *The Historian*, vol. 39, 1976–7, pp. 455–71; Alice Felt Tyler, *Freedom's Ferment*, p. 83; Hewitt, *Women's Activism*, p. 178; Raser, *Phoebe Palmer*; Keith J. Hardman, *Charles Grandison Finney, 1792–1895: Revivalist and reformer* (Syracuse, NY, Syracuse University Press, 1987).

73. Tyler, *Freedom's Ferment*, pp. 54–6; Margaret S. Fuller, *Woman in the Nineteenth Century* (Columbia, SC, University of Southern Carolina Press, Facsimile Reprint 1980); Susan P. Conrad, *Perish the Thought: Intellectual women in Romantic America, 1830–1860* (New York, Oxford University Press, 1976); Bell Gale Chevigny, *The Woman and the Myth: Margaret Fuller's life and writings* (Old Westbury, NY, The Feminist Press, 1976); Marie Mitchell Oleson Urbanski, *Margaret Fuller's 'Woman in the Nineteenth Century': A literary study of form and content, of sources and influence* (Westport, CT, Greenwood Press, 1980); Spender, *Women of Ideas*, pp. 144–55; *Harriet Martineau's Autobiography*, vol. II, p. 252, also pp. 70 f.: Fuller, it seems, thought Martineau commonplace.

74. See, for instance, Raymond Lee Muncy, *Sex and Marriage in Utopian Communities* (Bloomington, Indiana University Press, 1973); Gillis, *For Better, For Worse*, pp. 220–1; D'Ann Campbell, 'Women's life in utopia: the Shaker experiment in sexual equality reappraised – 1810 to 1860', *New England Quarterly*, vol. 5, 1978, pp. 23–38; Louis J. Kern, *An Ordered Love, Sex Roles and Sexuality in Victorian Utopias: The Shakers, Mormons, and the Oneida Community* (Chapel Hill, University of North Carolina Press, 1982); Sallie Te Selle (ed.), *The Family, Communes and Utopian Societies* (New York, Harper & Row, 1971).

75. Noyes quoted in Tyler, *Freedom's Ferment*, p. 194.

76. Taylor, *Eve and the New Jerusalem*, ch. VI.

77. O'Neill, *The Woman Movement*, pp. 18–20; and Garrison quoted in Clare Taylor, *British and American Abolitionists: An episode in transatlantic understanding* (Edinburgh, Edinburgh University Press, 1974), p. 93; see also p. 114.

78. See, for instance, Prochaska, *Women and Philanthropy in Nineteenth-century England*; Taylor, *Eve and the New Jerusalem*; and Thomis and Grimmett, *Women in Protest*, especially p. 58 on the way one good cause led to another. See also Keith E. Melder, *Beginnings of Sisterhood: The American woman's rights movement, 1800–1850* (New York, Schoken, 1977), p. 143 and *passim*, on American women reformers.

79. O'Neill, *The Woman Movement*, pp. 29–30; Taylor, *Eve and the New Jerusalem*, p. 275 (source of first quotation); Gail Malmgreen, *Neither Bread Nor Roses: Utopian feminists and the English working class, 1800–1850* (Brighton, Harvester, 1978); Friedman, *The Enclosed Garden*, pp. 6–7, 19–20; John W. Kuykendall, *Southern Enterprise: The work of national evangelical societies in the antebellum South* (Westport, CT, Greenwood Press, 1982); and Lebsock, *The Free Women of Petersburg*, ch. 7 and 'Epilogue', notes the important but changing role of women in reform, and the obstacles to feminism – including race prejudice – in the South.

80. O'Neill, *The Woman Movement*, p. 29; Evans, *The Feminists*, p. 64; Lori Ginzberg, ' "Moral suasion is moral balderdash": women, politics and social activism in the 1850s', *Journal of American History*, vol. 73, no. 3, December 1986, pp. 601–22, and *Women and the Work of Benevolence*, ch. 4.

81. On class complications in British reform, see Brian Harrison, 'A genealogy of reform in modern Britain', in Bolt and Drescher (eds), *Anti-Slavery, Religion and Reform*, pp. 131–3; on the bid for working-class support, see, in *ibid.*, Patricia Hollis, 'Anti-slavery and British working-class radicalism in the years of reform', pp. 294–5; and Prochaska, *Women and Philanthropy in Nineteenth-century England*, pp. 41, 84–5, 109, 136–7, 190–1. See also Paulson, *Women's Suffrage and Prohibition*, pp. 24–7; Thomis and Grimmett, *Women in Protest*, p. 135.

82. Thistlethwaite, *America and the Atlantic Community*, pp. 116–17; O'Neill, *The Woman*

Movement, pp. 29–30; Paulson, *Women's Suffrage and Prohibition*, p. 22, 27; Stansell, *City of Women*, emphasises the importance of class conflict among American women.

83. Paulson, *Women's Suffrage and Prohibition*, p. 29.
84. Thistlethwaite, *America and the Atlantic Community*, pp. 86, 109–10; Harrison, 'A genealogy of reform', pp. 122–3.
85. Hersh, *The Slavery of Sex*, p. 8.
86. See *ibid.*, pp. 190, 196–8; Ellen C. DuBois, in *Feminism and Suffrage*, p. 32, argues that 'What American women learned from abolitionism was less that they were oppressed than what to do with that perception.'
87. Jensen, *Loosening the Bonds*, pp. 186–9; J. William Frost, *The Quaker Origins of Antislavery* (Norwood, PA, Norwood Editions, 1980); Bacon, *Mothers of Feminism*; Nancy A. Hewitt, 'Feminist friends: agrarian Quakers and the emergence of women's rights in America', *Feminist Studies*, vol. 12, Spring 1986, pp. 27–50.
88. DuBois, 'Women's rights and abolition', p. 242.
89. On the Grimkés, see Gerda Lerner, *The Grimké Sisters From South Carolina* (Boston, MA, Houghton Mifflin, 1967); Katharine Du Pre Lumpkin, *The Emancipation of Angelina Grimké* (Chapel Hill, University of North Carolina Press, 1974); Elizabeth A. Bartlett (ed.), *Sarah Grimké: Letters on the equality of the sexes and other essays* (New Haven, CT and London, Yale University Press, 1988); Jean Fagan Yellin, *Women and Sisters: The antislavery feminists in American culture* (New Haven, CT and London, Yale University Press, 1989), ch. 2; and on the split of 1840, Aileen Kraditor, *Means and Ends in American Abolitionism* (New York, Pantheon, 1969), and Frederick B. Tolles (ed.), *Slavery and 'The Woman Question': Lucretia Mott's diary of her visit to Great Britain to attend the World's Antislavery Convention of 1840* (Haverford, PA, Friends Historical Association, 1952); on Maria Stewart, see Sterling (ed.), *We Are Your Sisters*, pp. 153–9; Marilyn Richardson, *Maria W. Stewart: America's first black woman political writer* (Bloomington, Indiana University Press, 1987); Yellin, *Women and Sisters*, pp. 46–8; and on Wright, see Eckhardt, *Frances Wright*, pp. 171 f.
90. See R.G. Walters, *The Antislavery Appeal* (Baltimore, MD, Johns Hopkins University Press, 1976), pp. 16 and *passim*; but see also Kraditor, *Means and Ends*.
91. Hersh, *The Slavery of Sex*, p. 30 and ch. 1 generally; Judith Wellman, 'Women and radical reform in antebellum upstate New York: a profile of grassroots female abolitionists', in Michael E. Dentrich and Virginia C. Purdy (eds), *Clio Was a Woman: Studies in the history of American women* (New York, Oxford University Press, 1979); Yellin, *Women and Sisters*, ch. 2.
92. See Ryan, *Womanhood in America*, p. 91 (source of quotation); Hersh, *The Slavery of Sex*, chs 4, 7; Margaret Hope Bacon, *I Speak For My Slave Sister: The life of Abby Kelley Foster* (New York, Thomas Crowell, 1974); Yellin, *Women and Sisters*, ch. 3; Milton Meltzer, *Tongue of Flame: The life of Lydia Maria Child* (New York, Thomas Crowell, 1965); Margaret H. Bacon, *Valiant Friend: The life of Lucretia Mott* (New York, Walker, 1980); Margaret H. Bacon, 'Lucretia Mott: holy obedience and human liberation', in Stoneburner and Stoneburner (eds), *The Influence of Quaker Women*, pp. 203–21; Jeffrey Kirk, 'Marriage, career and feminine ideology in nineteenth-century America: reconstructing the marital experience of Lydia Maria Child, 1828–1874', *Feminist Studies*, vol. 2, nos 2–3, 1975, pp. 113–17 especially.
93. See S.M. Grimké to Abby Kelley, 6/15/38; in Folder 2, Box 1, Abigail Kelley Foster Papers, American Antiquarian Society, Worcester, Massachusetts (hereafter

AAS). See Abby Kelley to Stephen S. Foster, Canterbury, NH, 1843; Kelley to Foster, 4 March 1843; Kelley to Foster, 28 March 1843; Kelley to Foster, 30 July 1843; Foster to Kelley, 10 Aug. 1843; Kelley to Foster, 13 Aug. 1843; in Folder 6, Box 1; Kelley to Foster, 28 March 1844, Folder 7, Box 1; Kelley to Foster, 2 Feb. 1845; 11 March 1845; and 25 March 1845; and C. Donaldson to Foster, 19 Jan. 1846: in Folder 8, Box 1; Galen Foster to Foster, 19 Jan. 1846, in Folder 9, Box 1; Foster to Kelley Foster, 9 Feb. 1847; Kelley Foster to Foster, 18 Aug. 1847; 9 Sept. 1847; 11 Sept. 1847: in Folder 1, Box 2; Kelley Foster to Foster, 3 April 1848; 3 Sept. 1847: in Folder 2, Box 2; Kelley Foster to Alla W. Foster, 1850s; Foster to Kelley Foster, 11 April 1850; Kelley Foster to Foster, 16 April 1850; 29 April 1850; Foster to Kelley Foster, 5 Aug. 1850; Foster to Kelley Foster, 26 Feb. 1850: in Folder 3, Box 2; Kelley Foster to Foster, 5 Aug. 1850; Foster to Kelley Foster, 27 July 1851; Foster to Kelley Foster, 3 Sept. 1851; Foster to Kelley Foster, 27 April 1852: in Folder 4, Box 2; Kelley Foster to Foster, 17 Jan. 1853; Foster to Kelley Foster, 6 April 1854: in Folder 5, Box 2; Foster to Kelley Foster, 2 March 1855; 31 Aug. 1855; 15 Sept. 1855; 27 Sept. 1855: in Folder 6, Box 2; Kelley Foster to Foster, Worcester, 1858 [?]: in Folder 7, Box 2; William Lloyd Garrison to Kelley Foster, 22 July 1859: in Folder 8, Box 2 – details of their quarrel are contained in this folder.

94. Degler, *At Odds*, p. 303.
95. Louis and Rosamund Billington, ‘ “A burning zeal for righteousness”: women in the British anti-slavery movement, 1820–1860’, in Jane Rendall (ed.), *Equal or Different: Women's politics, 1800–1914* (Oxford, Blackwell, 1987), pp. 82–111; Anthony J. Barker, *Captain Charles Stuart: Anglo-American abolitionist* (Baton Rouge and London, Louisiana State University Press, 1986), pp. 47, 52–3, 128–9, 149, 203, 210–11, 232, 248, 250–51 and *passim* on Stuart's links with female abolitionists and views on the 'woman question' in anti-slavery; Stange, *British Unitarians*, pp. 56–9, 82, 128–9, 147, 152–3, 195, 224–5, on Unitarian women, including Mary Carpenter and Harriet Martineau, and Unitarian sympathy for the Garrisonians' feminism; and Gail Malmgreen, 'Anne Knight and the radical sub-culture', *Quaker History*, vol. LXXI, Fall 1982, pp. 100–13.
96. Clare Midgley, 'Women anti-slavery campaigners in Britain, 1787–1868', (PhD dissertation, University of Kent, 1989) revised and published as *Women against Slavery: The British campaign, 1780–1870* (London and New York, Routledge, 1992).
97. See *ibid.*, chs II–V. For a tribute to the inspiration of British women abolitionists by Angelina Grimké, see Elizabeth Cady Stanton, Susan B. Anthony and Matilda Joslyn Gage (eds), *History of Woman Suffrage* (New York, Fowler & Wells, 1881–7), vol. I, p. 336.
98. See Hersh, *The Slavery of Sex*, pp. 129 f.; and on the black women abolitionists, Sterling (ed.), *We Are Your Sisters*, pp. 113 f., and 'Introduction' in Brenda Stevenson (ed.), *The Journals of Charlotte Foster Grimké* (New York and Oxford, Oxford University Press, 1988). On British women's family connections, see Midgley, 'Women anti-slavery campaigners', *passim*; Clare Taylor, *British and American Abolitionists*, *passim*.
99. On the connections between British and American women abolitionists, see Midgley, 'Women anti-slavery campaigners', ch. IV, section 4, and ch. V; Clare Taylor, *British and American Abolitionists*, pp. 4, 9, 10–11, 13 and *passim*; David Turley, *The Culture of English Antislavery, 1780–1860* (London and New York, Routledge, 1991).

100. See Hersh, *The Slavery of Sex*, pp. 121 f.; Bell Hooks, *Ain't I a Woman?*: *Black women and feminism* (London, Pluto Press, 1982 edn), pp. 124–6; Midgley, 'Women anti-slavery campaigners', pp. 394–5 and *passim*.

101. See, for instance, Hooks, *Ain't I a Woman?*, p. 141 (source of quotation); Rosalyn Terborg-Penn, 'Discrimination against Afro-American woman in the women's movement, 1830–1920', in Sharon Harley and Rosalyn Terborg-Penn, *The Afro-American Woman* (Port Washington, NY, Kennikat Press, 1978), pp. 17–27; Robert L. and Pamela P. Allen, *Reluctant Reformers* (Washington, DC, Howard University Press, 1974); John H. Bracey, Jr, August Meier and Elliot Rudwick (eds), *Blacks in the Abolitionist Movement* (Belmont, CA, Wadsworth Publishing Company, 1971), and especially William H. Pease and Jane H. Pease, 'Antislavery ambivalence: immediatism, expedience, race', pp. 95–107; Hersh, *The Slavery of Sex*, p. 129; L. and S.A. Burtis to Abby Kelley, 17 Jan. 1843, Folder 6, Box 1, Kelley Papers, AAS; Paulina S. Wright to Abby Kelley, August [?] 1843, in *ibid.*; Yellin, *Women and Sisters*, p. 59, and ch. 4.

102. Sterling (ed.), *We Are Your Sisters*, pp. 114 f.; Pease and Pease, 'Antislavery ambivalence', p. 102, for an instance of Angelina Grimké's tactlessness about race to Sarah Douglass; Gerda Lerner, 'The Grimké sisters and the struggle against race prejudice', *Journal of Negro History*, vol. XLVIII, 1936, pp. 277–91; Hersh, *The Slavery of Sex*, p. 128; Angelina Grimké to Abby Kelley, 15 April 1837, Folder 2, Box 1, Kelley Papers, AAS; Sarah Douglass to Abby Kelley, 18 May 1838, in *ibid.*; Sarah P. Remond to Abby Kelley, 21 Dec. 1858, in Folder 7, Box 2, in *ibid.*; Jean Fagan Yellin (ed.), *Incidents in the Life of a Slave Girl: Written by herself*, by Harriet A. Jacobs, ed. L. Maria Child, originally published Boston, MA, 1861 (Cambridge, MA and London, Harvard University Press, 1987), pp. xxii–xxiii, 255–6, on Child; Hewitt, *Women's Activism*, pp. 42, 95, 143, 190, 240, on Rochester 'ultraists' and blacks; Yellin, *Women and Sisters*, pp. 87–96.

103. D.A. Lorimer, *Colour, Class and the Victorians* (Leicester, Leicester University Press, 1978), ch. 2.

104. C. Peter Ripley (ed.), *The Black Abolitionist Papers*, vol. I, *The British Isles, 1830–1865* (Chapel Hill and London, University of North Carolina Press, 1985), p. 34 and 'Introduction' generally.

105. Ripley (ed.), *The Black Abolitionist Papers*, p. 33; Christine Bolt, *The Anti-Slavery Movement and Reconstruction* (London, Oxford University Press and Institute of Race Relations, 1969), pp. 34–5 and *passim*; Christine Bolt, *Victorian Attitudes to Race* (London, Routledge & Kegan Paul, 1971), especially 'Appendix'.

106. Ripley (ed.), *The Black Abolitionist Papers*, p. 23: quotation from Sarah Remond; see also pp. 243–4, 435–41; Sterling (ed.), *We Are Your Sisters*, pp. 146–7; Stanton, *Eighty Years and More*, p. 87; Benjamin Quarles, *Black Abolitionists* (New York, Oxford University Press, 1969).

107. See Thistlethwaite, *America and the Atlantic Community*, pp. 128–33.

108. Tolles (ed.), *Slavery and 'The Woman Question'*, in HWS, vol. I, p. 62, it is claimed that 'The movement for woman's suffrage, both in England and America, may be dated from this World's Anti-Slavery Convention', but proof is not offered; Taylor (ed.), *British and American Abolitionists*, pp. 91 f.; HWS, vol. I, ch. III; Stanton, *Eighty Years and More*, pp. 82–3 (and overall pp. 79–84); Otelia Cromwell, *Lucretia Mott* (New York, Russell & Russell, 1971 edn), pp. 76–87; Midgley, 'Women anti-slavery campaigners', ch. IV, section 4, ch. V, section 1.

109. Anne Knight to Abby Kelley Foster, 17 Aug. 1841, Folder 4, Box 1, Kelley Papers, AAS.
110. Thistlethwaite, *America and the Atlantic Community*, pp. 128–9; Taylor, *British and American Abolitionists*, pp. 86, 102, 104, 122, 125, 163–4; Midgley, 'Women anti-slavery campaigners', chs IV and V on British feminist abolitionists and ch. VI on the long-term implications of the American example; also Gail Malmgreen, 'Anne Knight'; Malmgreen, *Neither Bread nor Roses*; HWS, vol. I, p. 438; Midgley, *Women against Slavery*, pp. 168–9.
111. See, for instance, Stanton, *Eighty Years and More*, p. 79; HWS, vol. I, pp. 359–60, 433–6, where the lack of preparation and the religious conservatism of the organisers are noted.
112. Midgley, 'Women anti-slavery campaigners', ch. III, section 3, pp. 194–6, ch. V, p. 328. Though, of course, British feminists regularly made an analogy between female bondage and black slavery: see Taylor, *Eve and the New Jerusalem*, pp. 34–5. On the wide reform interests of abolitionists, see Turley, *The Culture of English Antislavery*, ch. 5. See also Yellin, *Women and Sisters, passim*.
113. This paragraph has drawn on Lilian Lewis Shiman,'"Changes are dangerous": women and temperance in Victorian England', in Malmgreen (ed.), *Religion in the Lives of English Women*, pp. 193–7; Brian Harrison, *Drink and the Victorians* (London, Faber & Faber, 1971), pp. 46–7, ch. 4, pp. 174–5, 192 and *passim*; Ian R. Tyrrell, *Sobering Up: From temperance to Prohibition in ante-bellum America, 1800–1860* (Westport, CT, Greenwood Press, 1979); William Rorabaugh, *The Alcoholic Republic* (New York, Oxford University Press, 1979), especially the last chapter; Epstein, *The Politics of Domesticity*, pp. 89–95, 100–7; Paulson, *Women's Suffrage and Prohibition*, ch. 3; Tyler, *Freedom's Ferment*, ch. 13; Hersh, *The Slavery of Sex*, pp. 167–70; Prochaska, *Women and Philanthropy in Nineteenth-Century England*, pp. 235, 238–9, 242, for data on women's involvement in temperance groups; Thistlethwaite, *America and the Atlantic Community*, pp. 93–6; Banks, *Faces of Feminism*, pp. 17–19; Thomis and Grimmett, *Women in Protest*, p. 116.
114. See Griffith, *In Her Own Right*, pp. 76–7; Mary Ryan, *Cradle of the Middle Class* (Cambridge, Cambridge University Press, 1981), pp. 135, 140, on women's numerical strength; Tyler, *Freedom's Ferment*, pp. 448–50; Jensen, *Loosening the Bonds*, pp. 196–8; Ian R. Tyrrell, 'Women and temperance in antebellum America', *Civil War History*, vol. 28, 1982, pp. 128–52; Stanton, *Eighty Years and More*, pp. 186–7; Friedman, *The Enclosed Garden*, p. 19, notes that in Georgia and Virginia, temperance groups were male, though women 'attended lectures and signed petitions'; Hewitt, *Women's Activism*, pp. 99 f., 109, 111–13, 163–5; Harper, *Life and Work of Susan B. Anthony*, vol. I, pp. 53, 64–71, 81–3, 87 f., 94–5; HWS, vol. I, pp. 152 f., 179–85, 344 f., 460, 845–8, 895.
115. Harrison, 'A genealogy of reform', pp. 132, 142 (quotation from p. 142); Garrison quoted in Taylor, *British and American Abolitionists*, p. 110.
116. Thomis and Grimmett, *Women in Protest*, p. 116; Shiman, ' "Changes are dangerous" ', p. 196.
117. Hersh, *The Slavery of Sex*, p. 166 (source of quotation); Thistlethwaite, *America and the Atlantic Community*, pp. 97–9.
118. Tyler, *Freedom's Ferment*, p. 428; for an indication of the international dimensions of the mature women's movement, see Stanton *et al.*, *History of Woman Suffrage*, vol. III, chs LV, LVI, LVII; vol. IV, chs LXXII, LXXIV, LXXV; vol. V, chs LI–LIV. By the

1850s, British women were organised in local Olive Leaf Circles which had strong Quaker backing and links with the anti-slavery movement: see Midgley, 'Women anti-slavery campaigners', ch. V, section 4.

119. Tyler, *Freedom's Ferment*, p. 413.

120. Thomis and Grimmett, *Women in Protest*, p. 135; Archibald Prentice, *History of the Anti-Corn Law League* (London, Frank Cass & Co., 1968; originally published 1853, 2 vols), vol. I, pp. 170–3; Judith Walkowitz, *Prostitution and Victorian Society: Women, class, and the state* (Cambridge, Cambridge University Press, 1980), ch. 6 and Table 1. See also Harrison, 'A genealogy of reform', pp. 126–7, on the League's long-term influence; and Shiman, *Women and Leadership*, pp. 50–3.

121. See Thomis and Grimmett, *Women in Protest*, p. 135.

122. *Ibid.*, ch. 3; Barry Reay, *The Last Rising of the Agricultural Labourers: Rural life and protest in nineteenth-century England* (Oxford, Clarendon Press, 1990), pp. 144–6.

123. Thomis and Grimmett, *Women in Protest*, ch. 4; quotation from p. 82.

124. This paragraph has drawn on Thomis and Grimmett, *Women in Protest*, *passim*; Alexander, 'Women, class and sexual differences'; Dorothy Thompson, 'Women and nineteenth century radical politics: a lost dimension', in Juliet Mitchell and Ann Oakley (eds), *The Rights and Wrongs of Women* (Harmondsworth, Penguin, 1976), pp. 112–38; and Taylor, *Eve and The New Jerusalem*, *passim*. Neil J. Smelser, *Social Change and the Industrial Revolution: An application of theory to the British cotton industry* (Chicago, University of Chicago Press, 1959) stresses the importance of declining opportunities for children at work in motivating labouring men to agitate against the employment of married women, needed to look after children at home.

125. Taylor, *Eve and the New Jerusalem*, p. xii.

126. *Ibid.*, especially chs III, VI–VIII; the reference to the Practical Moral Union is on pp. 73–4 (quotation from p. 73); Angus McLaren, *Birth Control in Nineteenth-Century England* (London, Croom Helm, 1978); Holton, *Feminism and Democracy*, p. 11.

127. See Celia Morris Eckhardt, *Fanny Wright: Rebel in America* (Cambridge, MA, Harvard University Press, 1984), chs 1–4, 7–8 (quotation from p. 171); also Stansell, *City of Women*, pp. 133–6, on Wright's influence in New York: as Stansell points out (p. 136), Wright 'never developed any sustained analysis of gender and did not speak explicitly about the problems of laboring women. She almost always addressed herself to men. But women did go to hear her.'

128. Eckhardt, chs 5–6; Tyler, *Freedom's Ferment*, chs 8, 9; and for criticism of British women abolitionists as foreign agitators, see Midgley, 'Women anti-slavery campaigners', ch. V, pp. 326–7. See also Campbell, 'Women's life in utopia', pp. 23–38.

129. On female reform networks see, for instance, Ryan, 'The power of women's networks'.

130. Degler, *At Odds*, pp. 368–9.

131. Eisler, *The Lowell Offering*, p. 15; see Dickens, *American Notes*, pp. 57–61, for a favourable comparison between Lowell and 'those great haunts of misery' at home.

132. Eisler, *The Lowell Offering*, 'Introduction' (quotation from p. 26); and see Thomas L. Dublin, 'Women, work and protest in the early Lowell mills', *Labor History*, vol. 16, no. 1, 1975, pp. 99–116; and Hannah Josephson, *The Golden Threads: New England's mill girls and magnates* (New York, Duell, Sloan & Pearce, 1949); Kennedy, *If All We Did*, p. 46.

133. See Kennedy, *If All We Did*, ch. 2; Matthaei, *An Economic History of Women in America*, pp. 145–6; Stansell, *City of Women*, ch. 7, quotation from p. 100.
134. Eisler, *The Lowell Offering*, p. 36; Evans, *Born for Liberty*, pp. 81–7, 99.
135. Kennedy, *If All We Did*, pp. 41–6; Eisler, *The Lowell Offering*, pp. 36, 189 (source of quotation).
136. See, for instance, Ryan, *Womanhood in America*, pp. 110–11; Stansell, *City of Women*, pp. 197 f, p. 219. See also, by Stansell, 'Women, children, and the uses of the streets: class and gender conflict in New York City, 1850–1860', *Feminist Studies*, vol. 8, 1982, pp. 309–35, on the attempts of middle-class women reformers to make over working-class family and street life according to their own vision of domesticity. But see, too, Smith-Rosenberg, *Disorderly Conduct*, p. 123, on the New York Female Moral Society's adoption of the cause of working women by the end of the 1840s. On Britain, see Taylor, *Eve and the New Jerusalem*, pp. 276–7: she notes, however, the growth of middle-class notions of women's sphere in the working class during the 1840s; see also sources cited in Note 81.
137. Ryan, *Womanhood in America*, p. 90; Taylor, *Eve and the New Jerusalem*, pp. 262–3.
138. Ryan, *Womanhood in America*, p. 90; see also Ginzberg, *Women and the Work of Benevolence*, ch. 5, on women's activism in the 1850s.
139. Jutta Schwarzkopf, *Women in the Chartist Movement* (London, Macmillan, 1991); F.C. Mather (ed.), *Chartism and Society: An anthology of documents* (London and New York, Bell & Hyman and Holmes & Meier, 1980), pp. 114–18, 165 (first and third quotations from p. 114); Dorothy Thompson, *The Early Chartists* (London, Macmillan, 1971), pp. 87–9, 115–30 (second quotation from p. 124); letter dated 21 Jan. 1851, to Mrs Rooke, from Miss Anne Knight in The Autograph Letter Collection (Women's Suffrage) of the Fawcett Library, London Guildhall University (hereafter FL), original in York City Library – source of fourth quotation; Rendall, *Origins of Modern Feminism*, pp. 235–8, 240–1; Thompson, 'Women and nineteenth century radical politics: a lost dimension', in J. Mitchell and A. Oakley (eds), *The Rights and Wrongs of Women*, pp. 112–38; Taylor, *Eve and the New Jerusalem*, pp. 265–75; Thomis and Grimmett, *Women in Protest*, ch. 6; Paulson, *Women's Suffrage and Prohibition*, p. 27; and Alexander, 'Women, class and sexual differences'; Dorothy Thompson, 'Women, work and politics in nineteenth-century England: the problem of authority', in Rendall (ed.), *Equal or Different*, pp. 57–81; Shiman, *Woman and Leadership*, pp. 40–1.
140. See Ginzberg, *Women and the Work of Benevolence*, chs 2, 3; and Prochaska, *Women and Philanthropy in Nineteenth-Century England*, Part One, ch. VI, pp. 227–8; also Anne F. Scott's *Natural Allies: Women's associations in American history* (Urbana, University of Illinois Press, 1992) for the best US overview.

Chapter 3   The women's movements take off

1. HWS, vol. I, p. 479; for a similar reflection on women's moral power in Britain, see Prentice, *History of the Anti-Corn Law League*, vol. I, pp. 171–3.
2. See HWS, vol. I, p. 72, for objectives expressed at Seneca Falls in 1848.
3. Evans, *The Feminists*, p. 66 (source of quotation); Ginzberg, *Women and the Work of Benevolence*, ch. 5.

4. HWS, vol. I, pp. 541, 823.

5. HWS, vol. I, ch. II, on women in newspapers; Jensen, *Loosening the Bonds*, p. 202; Hewitt, *Women's Activism*, pp. 255–6, 235; Ginzberg, *Women and the Work of Benevolence*, pp. 119 f.

6. Ginzberg, *Women and the Work of Benevolence*, pp. 112 (source of quotation), 99–100, 109–32; see Mrs Stanton's complaint that 'Men having separated themselves from woman in the business life, . . . now demand separate pleasures too': HWS, vol. I, p. 850. On the vital role in feminism of a dedicated few, see Harper, *Life and Work of Susan B. Anthony*, vol. I, p. 80. On women and anti-slavery in the 1840s, see Jensen, *Loosening the Bonds*, pp. 192–5.

7. On Anthony's progression to women's rights, see Harper, *Life and Work of Susan B. Anthony*, vol. I, especially chs V and VI, and p. 96. For such a progression generally, see comment in HWS, vol. I, pp. 349–50; and pp. 311–14, 677–8, for a sketch of some of the representative pioneers involved in women's rights.

8. See, in Garrison Family Collection, SSC, Martha Coffin Wright to Lucretia Mott, 1 Oct. 1848, Auburn, New York, Box 33, Folder 900; Wright to Elizabeth McClintock, 1850, Box 33, Folder 903; Wright from Cleveland, 25 Oct. 1855, Box 36, Folder 924; Wright from Cleveland, 25 Oct. 1855, Box 36, Folder 928; letter by Wright of 12 July 1860, Auburn, Box 36, Folder 940; Wright to LCM, 6 Jan. 1856, Auburn, Box 36, Folder 931. On Wright's part in the women's convention movement see HWS, vol. I, especially ch. XIV and pp. 462, 465; and for further information on Wright, see Margaret Hope Bacon, *Valiant Friend: The life of Lucretia Mott* (New York, Walker, 1980).

9. See, for instance, HWS, vol. I, pp. 802–5 (on Seneca Falls and Rochester Conventions); pp. 852–4 on 1852 Syracuse Convention.

10. See, for instance, *ibid.*, p. 463.

11. Hewitt, *Women's Activism*, pp. 134, 244–5.

12. DuBois, *Feminism and Suffrage*, pp. 51–2; Hersh, *The Slavery of Sex*, ch. 2, sees the reliance but does not stress its dangers; Griffith, *In Her Own Right*, p. 91, notes how the late-1850s sectional crisis distracted attention from the women's cause: especially that of abolitionists.

13. HWS., vol. I, p. 355 (quotation from Lucretia Mott), and pp. 102, 844.

14. Quotation from the call to the National Woman's Rights Convention at Syracuse, New York, 1852, in HWS, vol. I, p. 518.

15. Conclusion of the debate on the National Society proposal at the 1852 Syracuse convention: HWS, vol. I, pp. 540–2.

16. See *ibid.*, pp. 101–2, 193, 355, 632, 823–4.

17. *Ibid.*, pp. 619–20, 622, 625, 627–8; see also Harper, *Life and Work of Susan B. Anthony*, vol. I, chs VII–XII; and Hewitt, *Women's Activism*, p. 186, for the suggestion that Anthony's 'frequently curt orders and her relatively later conversion to the woman's rights cause' did not always endear her to local activists.

18. Elizabeth Fox-Genovese, *Within the Plantation Household*, pp. 96–8 and *passim*; Sterling (ed.), *We Are Your Sisters*, pp. 120, 176, 193, 220; Paula Giddings, *When and Where I Enter: The impact of black women on race and sex in America* (New York, William Morrow and Co., 1984); HWS, vol. I, pp. 115–17, for a speech by Truth at a women's rights meeting in 1851; on the lack of purpose to female activity in one Southern city (Lexington), see Jean H. Baker, *Mary Todd Lincoln: A biography* (New York, W.W. Norton, 1987), pp. 60–3.

19. See, for example, quoted in HWS, vol. I, p. 857, Anthony's view that 'we have only to take earnest hold of the work of disseminating its immutable truths' for the women's cause to enjoy 'a speedy triumph'.

20. See Rebecca M. Sanford's advice to 'Beware of *ultraisms*' in HWS, vol. I, p. 819.

21. See Hewitt, *Women's Activism*, pp. 237–9.

22. HWS, vol. I, pp. 836–44: Smith was especially dismayed that leading feminists were abandoning dress reform at this time, as an embarrassment to their movement. For the reference to 'interminable' resolutions, see *ibid.*, p. 114.

23. Anthony quoted in Harper, *Life and Work of Susan B. Anthony*, vol. I, p. 168; and see p. 150 on fund-raising difficulties in 1857, and pp. 165–6, 182, 257–8, on donations for the women's cause; and pp. 84, 258, on rich women's failure to join and give to the movement.

24. See Bessie Rayner Parkes, *Essays on Woman's Work* (London, Alexander Strahan, 1865), pp. 64–9; Diana Mary Worzala, 'The Langham Place circle: the beginnings of the organised women's movement in England, 1854–70', unpublished PhD thesis, University of Wisconsin at Madison, 1982; *English Woman's Journal*, vol. VI, September 1860, pp. 54–60; Lacey (ed.), *Barbara Leigh Smith Bodichon*, 'Introduction'.

25. On Bodichon, see Hester Burton, *Barbara Bodichon, 1827–1891* (London, John Murray, 1949); Sheila Herstein, *Mid-Victorian Feminist: Barbara Leigh-Smith Bodichon* (New Haven, CT and London, Yale University Press, 1985); Lacey (ed.), *Barbara Leigh Smith Bodichon*, 'Introduction'.

26. On Parkes, in addition to her own works, see references in Worzala; Herstein; Hammerton; Lee Holcombe, *Victorian Ladies at Work: Middle-class working women in England and Wales, 1850–1914* (Newton Abbot, David & Charles, 1973); Kamm, *Hope Deferred*; Bryant; Elizabeth K. Helsinger, Robin Lauterbach Sheets and William Veeder, *The Woman Question: Social issues, 1837–1883* (New York and London, Garland Publishing, 1983: vol. II of a trilogy).

27. On Boucherett, in addition to her own works, see references in Worzala; Herstein; Hammerton; Holcombe, *Victorian Ladies at Work*; Kamm, *Hope Deferred*; Bryant.

28. On Davies, see Barbara Stephen, *Emily Davies and Girton College* (London, Constable, 1927); Daphne Bennett, *Emily Davies and the Liberation of Women, 1830–1921* (London, André Deutsch, 1990), who also offers judgements on Davies's feminist contemporaries; Caine, *Victorian Feminists*, ch. 3.

29. See Herstein, *Mid-Victorian Feminist*, pp. 21, 84–5, 100, 104, 112–13, 115–16; Barbara Bodichon's *An American Diary* (London, Routledge & Kegan Paul, 1972, ed. Joseph W. Reed, Jr), p. 87, in which she takes pride in her simple dress.

30. On Norton see Alice Acland, *Caroline Norton* (London, Constable, 1948); and Forster, *Significant Sisters*, ch. 1; *English Woman's Journal*, vol. II, no. 8, October 1858, pp. 123–4; Herstein, *Mid-Victorian Feminist*, pp. 84–7, 133, 142; Shiman, *Women and Leadership*, p. 127.

31. See Liddington and Norris, *One Hand Tied Behind Us*, p. 11.

32. See Paulson, *Women's Suffrage and Prohibition*, pp. 32–7; Griffith, *In Her Own Right*, pp. 51–3.

33. HWS, vol. I, pp. 68–9.

34. Paulson, *Woman's Suffrage and Prohibition*, p. 36.

35. Griffith, *In Her Own Right*, pp. 50, 53.

36. *Ibid.*, pp. 45–50, 53; Lois Banner, *Elizabeth Cady Stanton: A radical for woman's rights*

(Boston, MA, Little, Brown, 1980), ch. 2. Stanton's hardening attitudes to race are noted below, p. 120.

37. Griffith, *In Her Own Right*, p. 54.
38. *Proceedings of the Woman's Rights Conventions . . . 1848*, pp. 4–7.
39. *Ibid.*; Griffith, *In Her Own Right*, pp. 53–4; on Mott's concern for women's economic oppression, see HWS, vol. I, p. 417; and J.R. Pole, *The Pursuit of Equality in American History* (Berkeley, University of California Press, 1978), p. 301, on women's analysis of 'the social and psychological processes . . . of subjugation'.
40. Griffith, *In Her Own Right*, p. 54; HWS, vol. I, p. 73; Paulson, *Women's Suffrage and Prohibition*, p. 39; Ginzberg, *Women and the Work of Benevolence*, p. 124.
41. HWS, vol. I, p. 173.
42. For comments comparing women's lot with slavery, see HWS, vol. I, p. 89, Emily Collin's reminiscences; Call for the 1850 National Women's Rights Convention in Worcester, *ibid.*, p. 22; Mrs Tracy Cutler, p. 384 – see also pp. 526, 599; and on this theme, Hersh, *The Slavery of Sex*, pp. 196–200 and *passim*. For an allusion to the influence of American freedom abroad, see speech of Ernestine Rose, 1851, HWS, vol. I, p. 237; and in *ibid.*, for an acknowledgement that some women agreed with men that they had all the rights they wanted, p. 165 (Lucy Stone in 1855).
43. See James C. Mohr, *Abortion in America: The origins and evolution of national policy, 1800–1900* (New York, Oxford University Press, 1978), chs 1, 4; Smith-Rosenberg, *Disorderly Conduct*, pp. 225 f.; Lucretia Mott, speech of late 1840s (second quotation) in HWS, vol. I, pp. 370, 372–3, 375; speech of Mrs Cutler, 1855, in *ibid.*, p. 164, and of Lucy Stone, 1850, in *ibid.* p. 166; speech of Ernestine Rose in 1851, *ibid.*, pp. 238–41. For the claim that women were morally superior to men – a claim rejected by Mott (p. 522) – see in *ibid.*, Eliza Farnham, speech of 1858, p. 669. For Stanton on the family and the need for easier divorce, see *ibid.*, pp. 718–22: see also pp. 723–37; Griffith, *In Her Own Right*, ch. 6.
44. Hersh, *The Slavery of Sex*, pp. 209–12; Smith-Rosenberg, *Disorderly Conduct*, pp. 183–4, 195–6.
45. Hersh, *The Slavery of Sex*, pp. 192–4; DuBois, *Feminism and Suffrage*, pp. 33–5; HWS, vol. I, pp. 81–2, 103, 146, 379–83, 415–16, 528, 523–40, 788, 850–51; Leach, *True Love and Perfect Union*, p. 7.
46. HWS, vol. I, pp. 376–7, Ernestine Rose, 1853; Leach, *True Love and Perfect Union*, pp. 6–7.
47. HWS, vol. I, p. 128.
48. *Ibid.*, Lucy Stone speaking in 1855, p. 165; see also *ibid.*, p. 577.
49. *Ibid.*, pp. 248, 260, 352, 362–3, 388, 581, 591; Jensen, *Loosening the Bonds*, pp. 203–4; Norma Basch, *In the Eyes of the Law: Women, marriage and property in nineteenth century New York* (Ithaca, NY, Cornell University Press, 1982), pp. 172 f.
50. HWS, vol. I, pp. 247–8, 258–9, 310, 318, 355–6, 522, 524, 530, 576, 582; Basch, *In the Eyes of the Law*, pp. 184 f. (especially p. 185).
51. For such accusations against feminists see, for instance, HWS, vol. I, pp. 307, 556, 604. For the acknowledgement of women's preference for practical matters rather than theoretical issues, see *ibid.*, p. 387.
52. See report on the 'Rights of Women in Wisconsin', 1856, in *ibid.*, pp. 316–17 (the writer is male).
53. See in *ibid.*, pp. 112, 1851, speech of Frances D. Gage; speech of Ernestine Rose, in *ibid.*, pp. 238, 241–2.

54. See the view of Lucretia Mott, speaking in the late 1840s, in *ibid.*, pp. 368–9; see also Esther Lukens, 1851, p. 311, in *ibid.*; and Eva Pugh, 1852, p. 357, in *ibid.* A favourite quotation was from Tennyson:

> The woman's cause is *man's*; they sink or rise
> Together, dwarfed or godlike, bold or free,
> If she be small, slight-natured, miserable,
> How shall man grow?
> The woman is not undeveloped man,
> But diverse.
> Yet in the long years, *liker* must they grow;
> The man be more of woman, she of man:
> *He* gain in sweetness and in moral height –
> *She* mental breadth, nor fail in childward care,
> Nor lose the childlike in the larger mind.

See *ibid.*, p. 263, quoted by Caroline Dall in 1859. For the attempt to emphasise equality yet deal with spheres (in Pennsylvania) see Jensen, *Loosening the Bonds*, p. 201.

55. Ernestine Rose's conviction – see *ibid.*, p. 242 – that women's intellectual capacity equalled that of men was unusual. See, for instance, the sympathetic Theodore Parker's belief, 1853, cited in *ibid.*, pp. 281–2, that 'men will always lead in affairs of intellect'; and the cautious comment: 'We came not here to argue the question of the relative strength of intellect in man and woman; for the reform which we advocate depends not upon its settlement': see *ibid.*, p. 361, Ann Preston in 1852.

56. See, in *ibid.*, debate containing various viewpoints on the debate about whether society or men should answer for women's subjugation: 1853, pp. 133–9, 144. For the view that women must fight for their own emancipation and throw off their customary timidity, see, in *ibid.* pp. 109, 110, 113, 272, 385, 524.

57. See, for instance, in *ibid.*, pp. 111, 219–20, 225.

58. See Levine, *Victorian Feminism*, pp. 14–24; Rendall, *Origins of Modern Feminism*, ch. 8; Bryant, *The Unexpected Revolution*, pp. 79, 82; Parkes, *Essays on Women's Work*, p. 4 (first quotation); see also p. 38; Miss Helen Taylor to Madame Barbara Bodichon, 7 Aug. 1869, in Autograph Letter Collection, Women's Movement, FL; see also in *ibid.*, Autograph Letter Collection, Women's Suffrage, Miss Philippa Strachey to Miss Aimée Fowler, 26 June 1909.

59. *The Times*, 21 May 1867, for the view that women should make their case with reference to expediency; see HWS, vol. I, p. 385, for instance, for the acknowledgement that the comfortably off woman did not treat her servant girl properly: 'Where are your philanthropic ladies who assist her? Where is she to go when her work is done? Does she sit in the same room with you? Does she eat at the same table? No, to your shame, she is confined to the basement and the garret.' Third quotation, HWS, vol I, p. 388; fourth quotation from Harper, *Life and Work of Susan B. Anthony*, vol. I, p. 140; Elie Halévy, *The Rule of Democracy* (London, Benn, 1952 edn), Book II, p. 491; Mary Lyndon Shanley, *Feminism, Marriage, and the Law in Victorian England, 1850–1895* (Princeton, NJ, Princeton University Press, 1989), p. 12; Caine, *Victorian Feminists*, ch. 2.

60. Jessie Boucherett, *Hints on Self-Help: A book for young women* (London, S.W. Partridge, 1863), p. 146.

61. Emily Davies, *Medicine as a Profession for Women* (London, Victoria Press, 1862), pp. 3–4; Barbara Bodichon, *Women and Work* (London, Bosworth and Harrison, 1857), pp. 12, 18.

62. Davies, *Medicine as a Profession for Women*, p. 4.

63. *Ibid.*, p. 8.

64. Boucherett, *Hints on Self-Help*, p. 136; HWS, vol. I, p. 385; Hill, *Women, Work, and Sexual Politics*, ch. 8; Rendall, *Women in an Industrializing Society*, pp. 98 f.

65. Parkes, *Essays on Woman's Work*, pp. 17, 38; *English Woman's Journal*, vol. I, no. 4, June 1858, p. 226 (source of quotation).

66. Parkes, *Essays on Woman's Work*, pp. 16–17.

67. See Holcombe, *Victorian Ladies at Work*, pp. 8–10; Parkes, *Essays on Woman's Work*, p. 140; Herstein, *Mid-Victorian Feminist*, ch. V; *English Woman's Journal*, vol. I, no. 3, May 1858, pp. 202–4.

68. See, for instance, the claim that Parliament did not neglect women's interests, used against British suffragists: Martin Pugh, *Women's Suffrage in Britain, 1867–1928* (London, Historical Association, 1980), p. 8. Also Lebsock, *The Free Women of Petersburg*, p. 240, who argues, *à propos* of that southern town, that 'Positive change in the status of women can occur when no organised feminism is present.' For a stimulating introduction to the subject of *Women in Public: Between banners and ballots*, see Mary P. Ryan's work (Baltimore, MD, Johns Hopkins University Press, 1990).

69. See also Basch, *In the Eyes of the Law*, pp. 22–4, 42–55.

70. Lebsock, *The Free Women of Petersburg*, p. 84; Basch, *In the Eyes of the Law*, pp. 27–8, 38–40, 68–70, 109–112, Chs 4, 7; Peggy A. Rabkin, *Fathers to Daughters: The legal foundations of female emancipation* (Westport, CT, Greenwood Press, 1980), pp. 22, 36, 40, 69, 89–91, 153–5; also Elizabeth B. Warbasse, 'The changing legal rights of married women, 1800–1861', PhD dissertation, Radcliffe College, 1960; and W. Leach, *True Love and Perfect Union*, pp. 174–81 (quotation from p. 178).

71. See Basch, *In the Eyes of the Law*, pp. 166–7 f.; Hersh, *The Slavery of Sex*, p. 55; Jensen, *Loosening the Bonds*, p. 195; and on the role of women in changing the law, see Richard Rapaport, 'Relationship of the women's movement to the passage of the Married Women's Property Acts in the mid-nineteenth century' (1973), cited in Rabkin, p. 10.

72. See Rose's reminiscences in HWS, vol. I, pp. 99–100.

73. Griffith, *In Her Own Right*, p. 43; HWS, vol. I, pp. 63–4 (p. 64 is the source of the first quotation); Basch, *In the Eyes of the Law*, chs 4–5, pp. 134–7 is the source of the other quotations; Rabkin, *Fathers to Daughters*, p. 89, ch. 11.

74. See HWS, vol. I, p. 256: though the law of Vermont in 1847 had shown the way.

75. See Basch, *In the Eyes of the Law*, p. 233, for the text of the 1848 Act (and pp. 233–7 for legislation through to 1862).

76. Rabkin, *Fathers to Daughters*, pp. 110–11; HWS, vol. 1, p. 64; Basch, *In the Eyes of the Law*, pp. 165–6 f.

77. Basch, *In the Eyes of the Law*, p. 159.

78. Harper, *Life and Work of Susan B. Anthony*, vol. I, pp. 105, 108–10 (quotation from p. 109); Stanton, *Eighty Years and More*, pp. 187–91; Rabkin, *Fathers to Daughters*, p. 113.

79. Harper, *Life and Work of Susan B. Anthony*, vol. I, pp. 189–90.

80. *Ibid.*, pp. 185–90; HWS, vol. I, pp. 676–88.

81. Harper, *Life and Work of Susan B. Anthony*, vol. I, p. 190.
82. *Ibid.*, pp. 219–20; Griffith, *In Her Own Right*, pp. 109–10; Basch, *In the Eyes of the Law*, pp. 236–7.
83. See Basch, *In the Eyes of the Law*, p. 225.
84. Here I have drawn heavily on Basch, *In the Eyes of the Law*, chs 7, 8; and Rabkin, *Fathers to Daughters*, pp. 123, 136–7, 139–45, 147, 153–7.
85. See Lee Holcombe, 'Victorian wives and property: reform of the Married Women's Property Law, 1857–1882', in Martha Vicinus (ed.), *A Widening Sphere: Changing roles of Victorian women* (London, Methuen, originally Indiana University Press, 1977), pp. 3–4; Holcombe, *Wives and Property: Reform of the Married Women's Property Law in nineteenth-century England* (Toronto, University of Toronto Press, 1983); Shanley, *Feminism, Marriage, and the Law*, pp. 15–6; Herstein, *Mid-Victorian Feminist*, p. 42.
86. Holcombe, 'Victorian wives', pp. 3–28; Levine, *Victorian Feminism*, pp. 135–41; Herstein, *Mid-Victorian Feminist*, pp. 36–42.
87. McGregor, *The History of Divorce in England*, p. 13; Susan Staves, *Married Women's Separate Property in England, 1660–1833* (Cambridge, MA, Harvard University Press, 1990).
88. Holcombe, 'Victorian wives', p. 9; Levine, *Victorian Feminism*, p. 135; Joan Perkin, *Women and Marriage in Nineteenth Century England* (London, Routledge, 1989), p. 294; Herstein, *Mid-Victorian Feminist*, pp. 70 f.; Holcombe, *Victorian Wives*, ch. IV.
89. *English Woman's Journal*, vol. I, no. 6, August 1858, p. 58; Shanley, *Feminism, Marriage, and the Law*, pp. 22–35.
90. Holcombe, 'Victorian wives', p. 12.
91. *Ibid.*, p. 11; Perkin, *Women and Marriage*, p. 301; Herstein, *Mid-Victorian Feminist*, pp. 90 f.; Shanley, *Feminism, Marriage, and the Law*, pp. 35 f.
92. Holcombe, 'Victorian wives', pp. 11, 15, 19–20; Perkin, *Women and Marriage*, pp. 301–2; Herstein, *Mid-Victorian Feminist*, pp. 79–80 f. (source of quotations).
93. Holcombe, 'Victorian wives', pp. 13, 16–17; *English Woman's Journal*, vol. I, no. 6, August 1858, 'The disputed question', p. 361, notes that when women argued for the right to develop their higher faculties they were accused, among other things, of 'Americanisation'.
94. Holcombe, 'Victorian wives', p. 13.
95. Levine, *Victorian Feminism*, pp. 137–8; Shanley, *Feminism, Marriage, and the Law*, pp. 50 f.
96. Holcombe, 'Victorian wives', p. 20; Perkin, *Women and Marriage*, p. 304; Shanley, *Feminism, Marriage, and the Law*, pp. 72–8.
97. Holcombe, 'Victorian wives', pp. 24–5; Levine, *Victorian Feminism*, p. 140; Perkin, *Women and Marriage*, pp. 305–6; Shanley, *Feminism, Marriage, and the Law*, p. 125.
98. *English Woman's Journal*, vol. I, no. 6, August 1858, p. 59; Shanley, *Feminism, Marriage, and the Law*, pp. 57 f., ch. 4.
99. Holcombe, 'Victorian wives', pp. 26–7; Levine, *Victorian Feminism*, pp. 139, 141; Shanley, *Feminism, Marriage, and the Law*, pp. 77–8, 103–4, 116 f.: the 1882 Bill was at last a government measure.
100. See Jensen, *Loosening the Bonds*, p. 200, on Pennsylvanian women; Griffith, *In Her Own Right*, p. 76.
101. See Hersh, *The Slavery of Sex*, pp. 49–50.

102. *Ibid.*, pp. 65–6; Griffith, *In Her Own Right*, pp. 101–2.

103. Griffith, *In Her Own Right*, pp. 92–101; Glenda Riley, *Divorce, An American Tradition* (New York, Oxford University Press, 1991), ch. 3; especially p. 81, source of third quotation; see also Stanton, *Eighty Years and More*, p. 215; Helsinger, Sheets and Veeder, *The Woman Question: Social issues*, pp. 27–9.

104. HWS, vol. 1, pp. 745–6.

105. Hersh, *The Slavery of Sex*, p. 67; Griffith, *In Her Own Right*, pp. 103–5; Stanton, *Eighty Years and More*, pp. 217–25; HWS, vol. I, pp. 718–841. On the press attitude to Stanton, see Martha Coffin Wright to Elizabeth Cady Stanton, 26 May 1860, Folder 940, Box 36, Garrison Family Collection, SSC.

106. Griffith, *In Her Own Right*, pp. 105, 159–60; Riley, *Divorce*, pp. 74 f.; Stanton, *Eighty Years and More*, pp. 225–7; Leach, *True Love and Perfect Union*, p. 5, on the 'divorce mania' of the late 1860s and early 1870s.

107. Stanton, *Eighty Years and More*, p. 216.

108. Quotation from Harper, *Life and Work of Susan B. Anthony*, vol. I, p. 194; Riley, *Divorce*, p. 83; Joseph M. Hawes, *Children in Urban Society: Juvenile delinquency in nineteenth-century America* (New York, Oxford University Press, 1971); Viviana Zelizer, *Pricing the Priceless Child: The changing social value of children* (New York, Basic Books, 1985); Leach, *True Love and Perfect Union*, pp. 179–80.

109. See Forster, *Significant Sisters*, pp. 15–52; Griffith, *In Her Own Right*, p. 163 and *passim*, emphasises Stanton's exploitation of her maternal image; Mary Poovey, *Uneven Developments: The ideological work of gender in mid-Victorian England* (Chicago, University of Chicago Press, 1988), ch. 3.

110. See Forster, *Significant Sisters*, pp. 33–40, 47–8; Perkin, *Women and Marriage*, pp. 26–7; Holcombe, *Wives and Property*; Poovey, *Uneven Developments*; Shanley, *Feminism, Marriage, and the Law*, pp. 25–9.

111. See Perkin, *Women and Marriage*, p. 302; Shanley, *Feminism, Marriage, and the Law*, pp. 36–44; Stone, *Road to Divorce*, pp. 353 f.

112. McGregor, *The History of Divorce in England*, p. 18; the *English Woman's Journal* reported the terms of the 'the new law of divorce' with very little comment: see vol. I, no. 3, May 1858, pp. 186–8; vol. I, no. 5, July 1858, pp. 339–41; vol. II, no. 7, September 1858, pp 56–62; vol. II, no. 8, October 1858, pp. 119–22; vol. II, no. 12, February 1859, pp. 415–17, 427.

113. Gillis, *For Better, For Worse*, pp. 209, 218; McGregor, *The History of Divorce in England*, p. 19.

114. See, for the concern to uphold respectability at the time of the debate on the 1857 Act, Allen Horstman, *Victorian Divorce* (New York, St Martin's Press, 1985); on the fear about the impact of easier divorce on older women, see the *English Woman's Journal*, vol. II, no. 12, February 1859, p. 427; and Stone, *Road to Divorce*, pp. 368 f., for a summary of the issues.

115. See P. Branca, *Silent Sisterhood: Middle-class women in the Victorian home* (London, Croom Helm, 1977 edn), p. 66; Sklar, *Catharine Beecher*.

116. Branca, *Silent Sisterhood*, p. 62.

117. *Ibid.*, ch. 4; and see J.G. Barker-Benfield, *The Horrors of the Half-Known Life: Male attitudes towards women and sexuality in nineteenth century America* (New York, Harper & Row, 1976).

118. Branca, *Silent Sisterhood*, pp. 65–8, 76; Tyler, *Freedom's Ferment*, pp. 440–1; Griffith, *In Her Own Right*, pp. 23, 69–70; John B. Blake, 'Mary Grove Nichols, prophetess of health', *Proceedings of the American Philosophical Society*, vol. 106, no. 3, June 1962, pp. 219–34; Jane B. Donegan's definitive *'Hydropathic Highway to Health': Women and water-cure in antebellum America* (New York, Greenwood Press, 1986); Judith W. Leavitt (ed.), *Women and Health in America: Historical readings* (Madison, University of Wisconsin Press, 1984); Stephen Nissenbaum, *Sex, Diet, and Debility in Jacksonian America: Sylvester Graham and health reform* (Westport, CT, Greenwood Press, 1980): health reform might, of course, appeal to men and women, feminists and non-feminists.

119. See Ann Douglas Wood, 'The fashionable diseases: women's complaints and their treatment in nineteenth century America', *Journal of Interdisciplinary History*, vol. 4, 1973, pp. 25–52; Joan Perkin, *Women and Marriage*, pp. 273–6; Brian Harrison, 'Women's health and the women's movement in Britain, 1840–1940'; Charles Webster (ed.), *Biology, Medicine and Society, 1840–1940* (Cambridge, Cambridge University Press, 1981), p. 26; Lorna Duffin, 'The conspicuous consumptive: woman as an invalid', in Delamont and Duffin (eds), *The Nineteenth Century Woman*, pp. 26–56.

120. See Berg, *The Remembered Gate*, p. 120; Caroll Smith-Rosenberg, 'The hysterical woman: sex roles and role conflict in nineteenth century America', *Social Research*, vol. 39, Winter 1972, pp. 652–78; Chambers-Schiller, *Liberty, A Better Husband*, pp. 163 f.

121. *English Woman's Journal*, vol. I, no. 3, 1 May 1858, pp. 145 f.; vol. II, no. 8, October 1858, p. 82; vol. II, no. 9, November 1858, pp. 209–10; Hersh, *The Slavery of Sex*, pp. 175–6, 179; Melder, *Beginnings of Sisterhood*, pp. 138–41, 154; Mary Roth Walsh, *Doctors Wanted. No Women Need Apply: Sexual barriers in the medical profession, 1835–1975* (New Haven, CT and London, Yale University Press, 1977), pp. 42–3; Harrison, 'Women's health and the women's movement', pp. 38–40; Leach, *True Love and Perfect Union*, ch. 9, especially pp. 243–60; Donegan, *'Hydropathic Highway'*; Nissenbaum, *Sex, Diet and Debility*.

122. See Prochaska, *Women and Philanthropy*, pp. 133 and ch. IV; Hollis (ed.), *Women in Public*, pp. 223–4, 239–43; Summers, 'A home from home'; *English Woman's Journal*, vol. I, no. 1, March 1858, pp. 13–27; vol. I, no. 6, August 1858, pp. 381–91, vol. II, no. 9, November 1858, pp. 145–59; vol. II, no. 11, January 1859, pp. 289–93; vol. III, no. 14, April 1859, pp. 73–85, vol. III, no. 16, June 1859, pp. 217–27; vol. III, no. 17, July 1859, pp. 316–24, vol. III, no. 18, August 1859, pp. 380–7, 421–4.

123. Regina Markell Morantz, 'Making women modern: middle class women and health reform in 19th-century America', *Journal of Social History*, vol. 10, June 1977, pp. 490–507.

124. Hersh, *The Slavery of Sex*, pp. 181–4; Jean L'Esperance, 'Doctors and women in nineteenth century society: sexuality and role', in John Woodward and David Richards (eds), *Health Care and Popular Medicine in Nineteenth Century England: Essays in the social history of medicine* (London, Croom Helm, 1977), pp. 107 f.; John S. Haller and Robin M. Haller, *The Physician and Sexuality in Victorian America* (Urbana, University of Illinois Press, 1974), pp. 100–2, chs IV, V.

125. First and second quotations from Stanton, *Eighty Years and More*, pp. 201–2; and see pp. 203–4; also Griffith, *In Her Own Right*, pp. 71–2, 92; Eckhardt, *Fanny Wright*;

Harrison, 'Women's health', p. 40; *English Woman's Journal*, vol. II, no. 11, January 1859, p. 353; vol. III, no. 13, March 1859, pp. 47–51; vol. III, no. 14, April 1859, p. 84 (source of third quotation); Leach, *True Love and Perfect Union*, pp. 284–6, 244 f.

126. See Walsh, *Doctors Wanted*, pp. 113–15; Harrison, 'Women's health', pp. 53–4; Weeks, *Sex, Politics and Society*, pp. 43–4; Davies, *Medicine as a Profession for Women*, p. 6.

127. Haller and Haller, *The Physician and Sexuality*, ch. II, pp. 29–30, 33–5, 37; L'Esperance, 'Doctors and women', pp. 118–20; Angus McLaren, 'The early birth control movement: an example of medical self-help', in Woodward and Richards (eds), *Health Care and Popular Medicine*, p. 96; E. Moberly Bell, *Storming the Citadel: The rise of the woman doctor* (London, Constable, 1953), p. 25 (source of the quotation); Walsh, *Doctors Wanted*, pp. 12, 55, 60, 80–1, 83, 98; Harrison, 'Women's health', pp. 18–19, 52 and *passim*; Caroll Smith-Rosenberg and Charles Rosenberg, 'The female animal: medical and biological views of woman and her role in nineteenth-century America', *Journal of American History*, vol. 60, no. 2, September 1973, pp. 332–56; Richard H. Shryock, *Medical Licensing in America, 1650–1965* (Baltimore, MD, Johns Hopkins University Press, 1972); Solomon, *In the Company of Educated Women*, pp. 118–22; Kent, *Sex and Suffrage in Britain*, ch. IV; Marina Benjamin (ed.), *Science and Sensibility: Gender and scientific inquiry, 1780–1945* (Oxford, Blackwell, 1991); Frank Mort, *Dangerous Sexualities: Medico-moral politics in England since 1830* (London, Routledge, 1987); Ludmilla Jordanova, *Sexual Visions: Images of gender in science and medicine between the eighteenth and twentieth centuries* (Hemel Hempstead, Harvester Wheatsheaf, 1989); Ornella Moscucci, *The Science of Woman: Gynaecology and gender in England, 1800–1921* (Cambridge, Cambridge University Press, 1990); Cynthia Eagle Russett, *Sexual Science: The Victorian construction of womanhood* (Cambridge, MA, Harvard University Press, 1989).

128. Walsh, *Doctors Wanted*, pp. 3 f. ((second) quotation from p. 15), pp. 80–1, 84, 104–5; Branca, *Silent Sisterhood*, pp. 78–81; Bell, *Storming the Citadel*, p. 61 (source of first quotation); Hollis (ed.), *Women in Public*, p. 49; Harrison, 'Women's health', p. 57; and Irvine Loudon, *Medical Care and the General Practitioner, 1750–1850* (Oxford, Clarendon Press, 1986), who emphasises the prosperity of general practice as a cause of the growth of male midwifery.

129. Hersh, *The Slavery of Sex*, pp. 177–9; Harriot K. Hunt, *Glances and Glimpses* (New York, Source Book Press, 1970, reprint of 1856 edn); Bell, *Storming the Citadel*, ch. 3, pp. 65–6; Forster, *Significant Sisters*, pp. 55–8; Walsh, *Doctors Wanted*, pp. 20–34, 60–1.

130. Herstein, *Mid-Victorian Feminist*, pp. 58–9, 138, 145–6; Forster, *Significant Sisters*, pp. 55–90; Dorothy Clarke Wilson, *Lone Woman: The story of Elizabeth Blackwell, the first woman doctor* (Boston, MA, Little, Brown, 1970); Bell, *Storming the Citadel*, pp. 35–6, 37–9, 44–5; Harrison, 'Women's health', p. 33; *English Woman's Journal*, vol. I, no. 2, April 1858, pp. 93–4 (source of quotation), and vol. III, no. 14, April 1859, pp. 142–3, on Blackwell: she in fact returned to England in 1869.

131. Walsh, *Doctors Wanted*, pp. 57–9, 64–6, ch. 3 (quotation from p. 78).

132. Elizabeth Garrett Anderson to Edith How-Martyn, 4 April 1908, in Autograph Letter Collection, Women's Suffrage, FL; Hollis (ed.), *Women in Public*, pp. 49–50; Bell, *Storming the Citadel*, chs 4–6; Davies, *Medicine as a Profession for Women*,

pp. 4–5, 7; and 'Female physicians' in *Thoughts on Some Questions Relating to Women, 1860–1908* (Cambridge, Bowes & Bowes, 1910), pp. 19–27; Jo Manton, *Elizabeth Garrett Anderson* (London, Methuen, 1965).

133. *English Woman's Journal*, vol. III, no. 13, March 1859, pp. 20–6 (source of first quotation); Matthaei, *An Economic History of Women*, pp. 182 (source of second quotation), 207; Philippa Levine, *Victorian Feminism, 1850–1900* (London, Hutchinson, 1987), p. 98; L'Esperance, 'Doctors and women', pp. 120–1, 127; Degler, *At Odds*, pp. 57–8; Harrison, 'Women's health', p. 32; Barker-Benfield, *The Horrors of the Half-Known Life*, Part 2; Jane B. Donegan, ' "Safe Delivered," but by whom? Midwives and men-midwives in early America', in Leavitt (ed.), *Women and Health*, pp. 302–17; Donegan, *Women and Men Midwives* (Westport, CT, Greenwood Press, 1978); J.B. Litoff, *American Midwives, 1860 to the Present* (Westport, CT, Greenwood Press, 1978); Vicinus, *Independent Women*, ch. 3; Jean Donnison, *Midwives and Medical Men* (London, Heinemann, 1977); Frances E. Kobrin, 'The American midwife controversy: a crisis of professionalization', *Bulletin of the History of Medicine*, vol. 40, July–August 1966, pp. 350–63; Rendall, *Women in an Industrializing Society*, p. 93; Susan M. Reverby, *Ordered to Care: The dilemmas of American nursing, 1850–1945* (Cambridge, Cambridge University Press, 1987); Barbara Melosh, *'The Physician's Hand': Work, culture and conflict in American history* (Philadelphia, Temple University Press, 1982); Darlene Clark Hine, *Racial Conflict and Cooperation in the Nursing Profession, 1890–1950* (Bloomington, Indiana University Press, 1989); Barbara Ehrenreich and Deirdre English, *Witches, Midwives, and Nurses: A history of women healers* (London, Compendium, 1972); Brian Abel-Smith, *A History of the Nursing Profession* (London, Heinemann, 1960); *English Woman's Journal*, vol. II, no. 7, September 1858, p. 17.

134. Forster, *Significant Sisters*, pp. 93–129; Miss Nancy Paul to Miss Alice Zimmern [?], 4 July 1906, in Autograph Letter Collection, Women's Movement, FL; and in *ibid.*, Florence Nightingale to Miss A.J. Clough, 26 May 1868; Lacey (ed.), *Barbara Leigh Smith*, pp. 9–10, 443–9; Monica E. Baly, *Florence Nightingale and the Nursing Legacy* (London, Routledge, 1988); Martha Vicinus and Bea Nergaard (eds), *Ever Yours, Florence Nightingale: Selected letters* (Cambridge, MA, Harvard University Press, 1990); Vicinus, *Independent Women*, ch. 3; Edward T. Cook, *The Life of Florence Nightingale* (London, Macmillan, 1913, 2 vols); Cecil Woodham-Smith, *Florence Nightingale, 1820–1910* (London, Constable, 1950); Davies, *Medicine as a Profession for Women*, pp. 5–6 (source of quotation); Holcombe, *Women at Work*, ch. IV.

135. Flexner, *Century of Struggle*, p. 107; George M. Frederickson, *The Inner Civil War: Northern intellectuals and the crisis of the Union* (New York, Harper & Row, 1965), and Ginzberg, *Women and the Work of Benevolence*, pp. 140 f., on the changing nature of American reform; Ann Douglas Wood, 'The war within a war: women nurses in the Union Army', *Civil War History*, vol. 18, no. 3, September 1972, pp. 197–211; Chambers-Schiller, *Liberty, A Better Husband*, pp. 97–9; Anne Firor Scott, *The Southern Lady: From pedestal to politics, 1830–1930* (Chicago, University of Chicago Press, 1970), pp. 83–6; Harper, *Life and Work of Susan B. Anthony*, vol. I, p. 239; Mary E. Massey, *Bonnet Brigades: American women and the Civil War* (New York, Alfred A. Knopf, 1966); Mary Livermore, *My Own Story of the War* (Hartford, CT, A.D. Worthington, 1889); Linus Brockett and Mary C. Vaughan, *Woman's Work in the Civil War: A record of heroism, patriotism and patience* (Philadelphia, PA, Zeigler, McCurdy, 1867).

136. The American Association for the Relief of the Misery of Battle Fields (New York, 1866), letter of Rev. Henry W. Bellows, DD, President, to M.J. Henri Durant, Secrétaire du 'Comité Internationale de Secours aux Militaires Blessés', p. 12, Clara Barton Collection, Folder 60, Box 3, in SSC.
137. Matthaei, *An Economic History of Women*, p. 207.
138. See Clara Barton to Rev. R. C. Stone, 5 Feb. 1876, Folder 20, Box 2; Barton to Marnie [Barton?], 16 July 1907, Folder 23, Box 2; Dr Edward B. Foote to Barton, 12 March 1875, Folder 37, Box 2; Lucy A. Frayer to Barton, 1 Nov. [1885?], Folder 38, Box 2; Joseph and Abby Sheldon to Barton, 25 March 1875, Folder 47, Box 25; Dr H.B. Storer (1875), Clairvoyant Examination of Miss C. Barton, File 49, Box 2; *The Philanthropic Results of the War in America. Collected from Official and Other Authentic Sources*, by an American Citizen (New York, Press of Wynkoop, Hallenbeck & Thomas, 1863), pp. 14–15, Folder 63, Box 3; *Report of the Red Cross. To the Hon. Committees of Foreign Relations and Foreign Affairs in the US Congress*, p. 14 (1890 report on the Red Cross by Barton), Folder 63, Box 3; *The Red Cross of the Geneva Convention. What It Is, Its Origin and History* (Danville, NY, 1881), pp. 55, 61, Folder 63, Box 3, Clara Barton Collection, in SSC. On Nightingale, see Forster, *Significant Sisters*, pp. 94–6, 110–11, 125. See also Harrison, 'Women's health', pp. 39–40.
139. Walsh, *Doctors Wanted*, ch. 6 and *passim*; Harrison, 'Women's health', pp. 50, 53; Leach, *True Love and Perfect Union*, p. 350 (source of quotation).
140. Holcombe, *Victorian Ladies at Work*, pp. 10–11, quoting Martineau.
141. *Ibid.*, p. 11; Helsinger, Sheets and Veeder, *The Women Question: Social issues*, pp. 134–5; Vicinus, *Independent Women*, ch. 1; *Transactions of the National Association for the Promotion of Social Science* (London, John Parker, 1862), for 1861, p. 687; Angela John (ed.), *Unequal Opportunities: Women's employment in England, 1800–1918* (Oxford, Blackwell, 1985).
142. Helsinger, Sheets and Veeder, *The Woman Question: Social issues*, ch. 3 (first and second quotations from pp. 115, 112); Emily Davies, *Thoughts on Some Questions Relating to Women, 1860–1808* (Cambridge, Bowes & Bowes, 1910), p. 18 (source of third and fourth quotations); Rendall, *Women in Industrializing Society*, pp. 60–2, 78; Burstyn, *Victorian Education*, ch. 3; Parkes, *Essays on Woman's Work*, pp. 76, 155–6, 185 f.; 219 f.; Bodichon, *Women and Work*, p. 51; *English Woman's Journal*, vol. III, no. 13, March 1859, p. 35, on the need for the sexes to do 'the work for which each is best fitted'; on the important part women could play in charitable institutions, see *ibid.*, vol. III, no. 15, May 1859, pp. 193–6; vol. I, no. 6, August 1858, p. 389; *Transactions of the National Association for the Promotion of Social Science* (London, John W. Parker, 1861), for 1860, pp. 815, 818.
143. Helsinger, Sheets and Veeder, *The Woman Question: Social issues*, p. 111; Bodichon, *Women and Work*, p. 14; Parkes, *Essays on Woman's Work*, pp. 221–2.
144. See, for instance, Hammerton, *Emigrant Gentlewomen*, ch. 1; letter from Frances Power Cobbe, 17 April 1867, to a woman who had asked her for help in obtaining work as a governess, in Autograph Letter Collection, Women's Movement, FL; *Transactions* of the NAPSS for 1861, p. 686; *ibid.*, for 1866 (London, Longman, 1867), pp. 420, 795.
145. Hammerton, *Emigrant Gentlewomen*, p. 126; *English Woman's Journal*, vol. I, no. 1, March 1858, pp. 1–2; *Englishwoman's Review*, vol. 1, October 1866, pp. 2, 31; Boucherett, *Hints on Self-Help*, pp. v, vii, 136–7; Parkes, *Essays on Woman's Work*,

pp. 87 f., 189–90 (quotation from p. 190); Alice Renton, *Tyrant or Victim? A History of the British Governess* (London, Weidenfeld & Nicolson, 1991), chs 3–7, 9–12.

146. Herstein, *Mid-Victorian Feminism*, p.136; Hammerton, *Emigrant Gentlewomen*, p. 126; Levine, *Victorian Feminism*, ch. 4, includes the SPEW in her discussion of *middle*-class women and work; *English Woman's Journal*, vol. I, no. 3, May 1858, pp. 203–4; *Transactions* of the NAPSS for 1860, p. 813.

147. Levine, *Victorian Feminism*, pp. 86 f.; Holcombe, *Victorian Ladies at Work*, p. 16; Hammerton, *Emigrant Gentlewomen*, p. 126; Herstein, *Mid-Victorian Feminist*, pp. 140–5; Boucherett, *Hints on Self-Help*, pp. v–vii, 150 f.; *Transactions* of the NAPSS for 1860, p. 820.

148. Levine, *Victorian Feminism*, p. 89; *Transactions* of the NAPSS for 1860, p. 819 (source of quotation).

149. Levine, p. 88 on SPEW's income; *Englishwoman's Review*, no. 10, July 1872, p. 216, noted that in the last year 100 women were helped to find temporary employment, 59 to find permanent employment, and 27 more provided with the means of learning useful trades.

150. *English Woman's Journal*, vol. II, no. 7, September 1858, p. 10: this reflection concluded a comprehensive article on the problems of women.

151. Boucherett, *Hints on Self-Help*, pp. 137, 139, 140–1, 143–5.

152. *English Woman's Journal*, vol. I, no. 5, July 1858, p. 292; vol. III, no. 13, March 1859, p. 46; vol. II, no. 8, October 1858, p. 142; vol. III, no. 18, August 1859, p. 428.

153. See, for instance, *ibid.*, vol. III, no. 13, March 1859, pp. 1–2, 6; vol. III, no. 15, May 1859, pp. 145–50; vol. III, no. 16, June 1859, pp. 283–4; *Englishwoman's Review*, vol. I, October 1886, pp. 12 f.; and for Greg's views, Helsinger, Sheets and Veeder, *The Woman Question: Social issues*, pp. 136–8; *Transactions* of the NAPSS, 1869, pp. 609–10, for a rare discussion in the 1860s of domestic service for middle-class women.

154. See, for example, Holcombe, *Victorian Ladies at Work*, pp. 18–20. And see Leonore Davidoff, 'Mastered for life: servant and wife in Victorian and Edwardian England', *Journal of Social History*, vol. 7, no. 4, Summer 1974.

155. Hammerton, *Emigrant Gentlewomen*, ch. 5 (quotation from p. 143); see also his 'Feminism and female emigration, 1861–1886', in Vicinus (ed.), *A Widening Sphere*, pp. 72–93; Maria Rye to Madame Bodichon, 7 Oct. 1862, in Autograph Letter Collection, Women's Movement, FL (source of first quotation); Herstein, *Mid-Victorian Feminist*, pp. 142–3. The NAPSS even hoped that convicted women and delinquent children could be sent to the colonies, with the help of the Prisoners' Aid Society and industrial or reformatory schools, combining the contemporary interest in the reformatory movement and female emigration in a single proposal: see *English Woman's Journal*, vol. II, no. 11, January 1859, pp. 291–2.

156. See, for instance, Caroline H. Dall, *Woman's Right to Labor* (Boston, MA, Walker, Wise, 1860), p. 104; *English Woman's Journal*, vol. I, no. 4, June 1858, p. 223; Leach, *True Love and Perfect Union*, pp. 158–60.

157. See Helsinger, Sheets and Veeder, *The Woman Question: Social Issues*, pp. 134–5; Chambers-Schiller, *Liberty, A Better Husband*, pp. 29–30; Stansell, *City of Women*, pp. 83 f.

158. Stansell, *City of Women*, pp. 147–54.

159. *Ibid.*; Faye E. Dudden, *Serving Women* (Middletown, CT, Wesleyan University Press, 1983), chs 3–5.

160. See, for instance, *Englishwoman's Review*, no. 4, July 1867, pp. 211, 217; HWS, vol. II (New York, Fowler & Wells, 1882), p. 904, Caroline Dall on the absence of a SPEW in America; Chambers-Schiller, *Liberty, A Better Husband*, pp. 97 f.; Hersh, *The Slavery of Sex*, pp. 124–5; Solomon, *In the Company of Educated Women*, p. 45.

161. *Englishwoman's Review*, no. 2, January 1867, pp. 165–7; Solomon, *In the Company of Educated Women*, p. 45; *Englishwoman's Journal*, vol. I, no. 4, June 1858, pp. 218–27; vol. II, no. 12, February 1859, pp. 361–74; Burstyn, *Victorian Education*, pp. 48–53 and *passim*.

162. Forster, *Significant Sisters*, p. 147.

163. *Ibid.*, p. 146. See letters in Autograph Letter Collection, FL, giving details of the campaign: Davies to Mr Dyke Acland, 12 and 19 Jan., 9 May, 2 and 14 Nov. 1863, circular of 28 Oct. 1863, Davies to Acland, 28 Dec. 1864, in which Davies is determined but reassuring about women's ambitions and abilities – mixed instruction or a 'neck and neck race between the sexes' was not proposed.

164. See, for instance, Helsinger, Sheets and Veeder, *The Woman Question: Social issues*, pp. 82 f.; Burstyn, *Victorian Education*, chs 4, 5; *English Woman's Journal*, vol. II, no. 11, January 1859, 'Are men naturally cleverer than women?', pp. 334–5; Davies thought some men in every field would 'do better than any woman', but felt that this was no reason 'for hindering women from doing their best': See Miss Emily Davies to Mr Dyke Acland, 28 Dec. 1864, Autograph Letter Collection, FL.

165. Herstein, *Mid-Victorian Feminist*, p. 174; Levine, *Victorian Feminism*, pp. 34–6; Burstyn, *Victorian Education*, p. 25; Forster, *Significant Sisters*, pp. 146–7, 149.

166. Joyce Senders Pedersen, 'The reform of women's secondary and higher education: institutional change and social values in mid and late Victorian England', *History of Education Quarterly*, Spring 1979, pp. 62–3, 71–3, 85–6; Herstein, *Mid-Victorian Feminist*, p. 174.

167. Holcombe, *Victorian Ladies at Work*, pp. 22–6; Herstein, *Mid-Victorian Feminist*, p. 175; Forster, *Significant Sisters*, p. 149.

168. Herstein, *Mid-Victorian Feminist*, pp. 176 f.; Forster, *Significant Sisters*, pp. 150 f.; Levine, *Victorian Feminism*, pp. 44–5; Burstyn, *Victorian Education*, pp. 26, 151–3, 155–6, 158–9; Sheldon Rothblatt, *The Revolution of the Dons: Cambridge and Society in Victorian England* (London, Faber & Faber, 1968); E.G.W. Bill, *University Reform in Nineteenth-Century Oxford: A study of Henry Halford Vaughan, 1811–1885* (Oxford, Oxford University Press, 1973), on reform in the other key centre on which feminists set their sights.

169. Burstyn, *Victorian Education*, p. 52.

170. Herstein, *Mid-Victorian Feminist*, pp. 176–7; Forster, *Significant Sisters*, p. 163.

171. See Delamont, 'The contradictions in ladies' education', p. 140, in Delamont and Duffin (eds), *The Nineteenth Century Woman*.

172. Herstein, *Mid-Victorian Feminist*, pp. 172–3.

173. *English Woman's Journal*, vol. I, no. 6, August 1858, pp. 364 (source of quotation), 361–7.

174. See DuBois, *Feminism and Suffrage*, p. 652, ch. 2; Stanton, *Eighty Years and More*, ch. XV; Harper, *Life and Work of Susan B. Anthony*, vol. I, chs XIII–XIV; Flexner, *Century of Struggle*, ch. X; Griffith, *In Her Own Right*, ch. 8; HWS, vol. II, ch. XVI; Kathleen Barry, *Susan B. Anthony: A biography* (New York, New York University Press, 1988), ch. 7.

175. DuBois, *Feminism and Suffrage*, ch. 2; Griffith, *In Her Own Right*, pp. 123–6 (source of

quotation p. 123); Harper, *Life and Work of Susan B. Anthony*, vol. I, pp. 248–74, 276–80; Philip S. Foner (ed.), *Frederick Douglass on Women's Rights* (Westport, CT, Greenwood Press, 1976); James M. McPherson, 'Abolitionism, woman suffrage and the Negro', *Mid-America*, vol. 47, 1965, pp. 40–7; HWS, vol. II, ch. XVII.

176. DuBois, *Feminism and Suffrage*, ch. 3; Griffith, *In Her Own Right*, pp. 127–33; Harper, *Life and Work of Susan B. Anthony*, vol. I, pp. 275–312; Stanton, *Eighty Years and More*, ch. XVI; HWS, vol. II, chs XIX–XX.

177. Griffith, *In Her Own Right*, pp. 133–43; DuBois, *Feminism and Suffrage*, ch. 6; Robert Riegel, 'Split of the feminist movement in 1869', *Mississippi Valley Historical Review*, vol. 49, 1962, pp. 485–96; O'Neill, *Everyone Was Brave*, pp. 18–21; HWS, vol. II, chs XXI–XXII; Harper, *Life and Work of Susan B. Anthony*, vol. I, pp. 305–7, 313–70; David Morgan, *Suffragists and Democrats: The politics of woman suffrage in America* (East Lansing, Michigan State University Press, 1972); Andolson, *Daughters of Jefferson, Daughters of Bootblacks*, pp. 5–10.

178. See DuBois, *Feminism and Suffrage*, pp. 63–71 and *passim*; Harper, *Life and Work of Susan B. Anthony*, vol. I, pp. 326–8; HWS, vol. II.

179. Reproduced in Rossi (ed.), *Essays on Sex Equality* (quotation from p. 96); see, generally, Barbara Caine, 'Feminism, suffrage and the nineteenth-century English women's movement', *Women's Studies International Forum*, vol. 5, no. 6, 1982, pp. 537–50; Shiman, *Women and Leadership*, p. 171.

180. *Englishwoman's Review*, no. 1, October 1866, pp. 26 f.; no. 2, January 1867, pp. 63–75; Herstein, *Mid-Victorian Feminist*, ch. VI; Barbara Bodichon, *Reasons for the Enfranchisement of Women* (London, Chambers of the Social Science Association, 1866), pp. 2–8, 10, 12 (quotation from p. 3).

181. *Englishwoman's Review*, no. 4, July 1867, pp. 199–208; no. 6, January 1868, p. 393; Herstein, *Mid-Victorian Feminist*, ch. VI (quotation from p. 163); Levine, *Victorian Feminism*, pp. 57–65; Fawcett, *Women's Suffrage*, ch. II; Helen Blackburn, *Women's Suffrage: A record of the women's suffrage movement in the British Isles* (London and Oxford, Williams & Norgate, 1902), Part 1; Constance Rover, *Women's Suffrage and Party Politics in Britain, 1866–1914* (London, Routledge & Kegan Paul, 1967), chs II, IV, VI; Ramelson, *The Petticoat Rebellion*, pp. 77–80, 84.

182. Harper, *Life and Times of Susan B. Anthony*, vol. I, pp. 423–54; David Morgan, *Suffragists and Liberals: The politics of woman suffrage in Britain* (Oxford, Blackwell, 1975), p. 12; Ramelson, *The Petticoat Rebellion*, p. 83; O'Neill, *Everyone Was Brave*, pp. 167–73; Helsinger, Sheets and Veeder, *The Woman Question: Social issues*, pp. 48–54; HWS, vol. II, pp. 586–755.

183. See, for instance, Herstein, *Mid-Victorian Feminist*, p. 150, for Bodichon's gloomy prediction in 1865; p. 123, on expectations of early progress in Massachusetts; Ramelson, *The Petticoat Rebellion*, p. 82, for optimistic British pronouncements; Griffith, *In Her Own Right*, pp. 122 f., on the change in Stanton's early optimism.

184. The first supporters of the women in America included Republican Senator Samuel Pomeroy of Kansas and Representative George W. Julian of Indiana; and in Britain, the Liberal MPs John Stuart Mill, Henry Fawcett and Henry Labouchere.

185. See Herstein, *Mid-Victorian Feminist*, pp. 165–6, on the British Liberal connection as early as 1867; and Harper, *Life and Work of Susan B. Anthony*, vol. I, pp. 365–6, for her view of the Republicans; Ginzberg, *Women and the Work of Benevolence*, pp. 184–5, on the suffragists' interest in partisan politics.

186. See letter from Martha Coffin Wright to Lucy Stone, 22 Aug. 1869, Folder 1001,

Box 39, Garrison Family Collection, SSC; and in *ibid.*, letter from Wright, 21 Dec. 1874; in *ibid.*, Folder 999, Wright to Henry Blackwell, 13 Nov. 1869; see also, in Folder 1005, Box 40, letters from Wright to Susan B. Anthony, 3 Sept. 1870, 31 Dec. 1870, in which she expresses suspicion of politicians and opposition to narrowing 'our platform'.

187. See DuBois, *Feminism and Suffrage*, chs 4–5 (quotation from p. 124); W. Leach, *True Love and Perfect Union*, pp. 164–5, on the Working Women's Protective Union of New York; also pp. 181–3.

188. See, for instance, Griffith, *In Her Own Right*, p. 137, but also p. 142; Herstein, *Mid-Victorian Feminist*, pp. 161–2.

189. See, for instance, Rover, *Women's Suffrage*, ch. III; Herstein, *Mid-Victorian Feminist*, pp. 160, 164.

190. See Paulson, *Women's Suffrage and Prohibition*, pp. 87–8.

191. *Ibid.*, p. 89; Griffith, *In Her Own Right*, p. 127; HWS, vol. I, pp. 229, 239; DuBois, *Feminism and Suffrage*, p. 104; Evelyn Pugh, 'John Stuart Mill, Harriet Taylor, and women's rights in America', *Canadian Journal of History*, vol. 13, 1978, pp. 428–9.

192. See Brian Harrison, *Separate Spheres*, p. 27 and *passim*; Sir Almroth E. Wright, *The Unexpurgated Case Against Women Suffrage* (London, Constable, 1913), pp. 2–6.

193. See the text of *The Subjection of Women* in Rossi (ed.), *Essays on Sex Equality*, pp. 125–242 (quotation from p. 125); Barbara Caine, 'John Stuart Mill and the English Women's Movement', *Historical Studies*, vol. 18, 1978, pp. 52–67; Lacey (ed.), *Barbara Leigh Smith Bodichon*, p. 4; Gail Tulloch, *Mill and Sexual Equality* (Brighton, Harvester, 1984); Caine, *Victorian Feminists*, pp. 33–8.

194. See *English Woman's Journal*, vol. III, no. 14, April 1859, p. 84, on the importance of provoking a discussion of ideas rather than 'particular items of practical reform'.

195. See, for instance, Margaret Oliphant, 'The great unrepresented', *Blackwood's Edinburgh Magazine*, vol. 100, September 1866, pp. 367–79; HWS, vol. II, p. 103.

196. These contacts are detailed in HWS, vol. I.

197. Catherine M. Sedgwick, 1859, quoted in Herstein, *Mid-Victorian Feminist*, p. 139.

198. See *English Woman's Journal*, vol. II, no. 11, January 1859, p. 342.

199. *Englishwoman's Review*, no. 6, January 1868, p. 393.

Chapter 4 The women's movements, 1870s–1880s

1. On women's negotiation of the difficult step from expected private life to controversial public roles, see Levine, *Feminist Lives*; Caine, *Victorian Feminists*; Julia Parker, *Ten Victorian Women in Public Social Service* (London, Macmillan, 1989); Jane Lewis, *Women and Social Action*. And see, on the fight for legal equality, Shanley, *Feminism, Marriage, and the Law*, ch. 3 (quotation from p. 81). On the changes in American reform, see Ginzberg, *Women and the Work of Benevolence*, chs 5, 6.

2. On the American feminists' opposition to regulation of prostitution, see Griffith, *In Her Own Right*, p. 160; David J. Pivar, *Purity Crusade, Sexual Morality and Social Control, 1868–1900* (Westport, CT, Greenwood Press, 1973), pp. 28–62, 97–9; HWS, vol. I, pp. 795–6; vol. III (Rochester, 1886; New York, Source Book Press, 1970), pp. 145, 397, 572, on events in Missouri, New York and Illinois; *A History of*

the National Woman's Rights Movement, pp. 70–1 (source of quotation). See also E.M. Sigsworth and T.J. Wyke, 'A study of Victorian prostitution and venereal disease', in Vicinus (ed.), *Suffer and Be Still*, pp. 77–91; Paul McHugh, *Prostitution and Victorian Social Reform* (London, Croom Helm, 1980); Kent, *Sex and Suffrage*, ch. II; Shanley, *Feminism, Marriage, and the Law*, pp. 82–6; Linda Mahood, *The Magdalenes: Prostitution in the nineteenth century* (London, Routledge, 1990), for a valuable recent study, whose focus is Glasgow; Judith Walkowitz, 'Male vice and feminist virtue: feminism and the politics of prostitution in nineteeth-century Britain', *History Workshop Journal*, vol. 13, Spring 1982, pp. 79–93; Levine, *Feminist Lives*, ch. 5; Weeks, *Sex, Politics and Society*, pp. 65, 84–5, 89–90 and *passim*; Ryan, *Women in Public*, ch. 3; Jeffreys, *The Spinster and Her Enemies*, *passim*; the important work of Frank Mort, *Dangerous Sexualities: Medico-moral politics in England since 1830* (London, Routledge, 1987), pp. 69 f.; Eric Trudgill, *Madonnas and Magdalens: The origin and development of Victorial sexual attitudes* (London, Heinemann, 1976); J.C. Burham, 'The medical inspection of prostitutes in America: the St. Louis experiment and its sequel', *Bulletin of the History of Medicine*, vol. 45, 1971, pp. 203–18; Ryan, *Women in Public*, ch. 3; Shiman, *Women and Leadership*, ch. 10.

3. Judith Walkowitz, *Prostitution and Victorian Society: Women, Class and the state* (Cambridge, Cambridge University Press, 1980), pp. 123–4.

4. See Christine Bolt, *The Anti-Slavery Movement and Reconstruction* (London, Oxford University Press and Institute of Race Relations, 1969), pp. 117–18 and *passim*; Clare Midgley, 'Women anti-slavery campaigners', ch. VI.

5. Walkowitz, *Prostitution and Victorian Society*, pp. 124 f.

6. *Ibid.*, pp. 113–14, 119–22, 133–5; Millicent G. Fawcett and E.M. Turner, *Josephine Butler: Her work and principles and their meaning for the twentieth century* (London, Association for Moral and Social Hygiene, 1927), pp. 76–7; Prochaska, *Women and Philanthropy in Nineteenth-Century England*, p. 206.

7. There are many accounts of Butler: see, for instance, Walkowitz, *Prostitution and Victorian Society*, pp. 115–19 and *passim*; E. Moberly Bell, *Josephine Butler: Flame of fire* (London, Constable, 1962); Forster, *Significant Sisters*, ch. 5; Fawcett and Turner, *Josephine Butler*; Nancy Boyd, *Josephine Butler, Octavia Hill, Florence Nightingale: Three Victorian women who changed their world* (London, Macmillan, 1982).

8. Walkowitz, *Prostitution and Victorian Society*, p. 115, stresses Butler's provincial outsider status; on the importance she attached to the vote see, for instance, Bell, *Josephine Butler*, pp. 83, 199; Walkowitz, *Prostitution and Victorian Society*, pp. 128–9.

9. *Sursum Corda: Annual address to the Ladies' National Association*, by Josephine E. Butler (Liverpool, J. Brakell, 1871), pp. 6, 33; HWS, vol. III, p. 942; see also Weeks, *Sex, Politics and Society*, pp. 86–7.

10. *Sursum Corda*, pp. 6, 8, 15 f.

11. *Ibid.*, pp. 20–1; Butler had, however, been a supporter of the North during the Civil War. See HWS, vol. III, pp. 145–6, for a letter from Butler to American suffragists which stresses the Anglo-Saxon heritage; and Hersh, *The Slavery of Sex*, pp. 125–6, on this theme in American feminist rhetoric.

12. On Butler's dauntlessness despite ill-health see, for instance, Bell, *Josephine Butler*, pp. 4–6, 251.

13. *Substance of the Speeches of the Rt. Hon. James Stansfield, M.P., on the Contagious Diseases Acts* (London, National Association for the Repeal of the Contagious Diseases Acts, 1875), pp. 28–9, 80, for an acknowledgement that the question was,

above all, one for women; see also *Sursum Corda*, p. 32; Walkowitz, *Prostitution and Victorian Society*, pp. 139–40.

14. See, for instance, *An Exposure of the False Statistics of the Contagious Diseases Acts (Women) Contained in Parliamentary Paper No. 149, on the Return of the Assistant Commissioner of Metropolitan Police*, By the Managers of Metropolitan Female Reformatories (London, W. Tweedie and F. Banks, 1873); *Speech of William Fowler, Esq., M.P., in the House of Commons, on May 24th, 1870, on the Contagious Diseases Acts, With Notes* (London, W. Tweedie, 1870), pp. 5, 7, 11–12, 17–19, 23, 25–8; *National Association for the Promotion of Social Purity* (1873), p. 10 (source of quotation); see also pp. 1–12; *The Contagious Diseases Acts and the Royal Commission. By A Necessarian. Published for the Ladies' National Association for the Repeal of Contagious Diseases Acts* (Manchester, Alexander Ireland, 1871), pp. 8, 12–14, 27, 29–30; Forster, *Significant Sisters*, p. 182.

15. *Sursum Corda*, p. 38.

16. *Ibid.*, p. 30.

17. See, for instance, Kent, *Sex and Suffrage*, pp. 74–5; Walkowitz, *Prostitution and Victorian Society*, pp. 136, 138–9 and *passim*. See, too, Gillis, *For Better, For Worse*, on the working-class attitudes to sexuality and pre-marital pregnancies that offended middle-class moralists; Françoise Barret-Ducrocq, *Love in the Time of Victoria* (London, Viking/Penguin, 1991) for unabashed working-class female comments on sexual matters and illegitimacy, of a kind that would have confirmed the worst fears of some middle-class moralists.

18. See, for instance, Walkowitz, *Prostitution and Victorian Society*, pp. 138–9; Fawcett and Turner, *Josephine Butler*, pp. 59–64, 73–4; Forster, *Significant Sisters*, pp. 186–7. However, not all the women campaigners were bold in their tactics; and Walkowitz, *Prostitution and Victorian Society*, p. 135, notes that 'Branches of the LNA often avoided holding mixed meetings with men in deference to local public opinion.'

19. *The Contagious Diseases Acts and The Royal Commission*, p. 27; *Vigilance Association for the Defence of Personal Rights. Speech Delivered by Mrs. Josephine Butler at the Fourth Annual Meeting of the 'Vigilance Association for the Defence of Personal Rights', held at Bristol, October 15th, 1874*, pp. 8–9; Walkowitz, *Prostitution and Victorian Society*, pp. 125, 129–30, 141, 256; Forster, *Significant Sisters*, pp. 170, 174, 189; Bell, *Josephine Butler*, p. 64; Fawcett and Turner, *Josephine Butler*, quotation on flyleaf; Shanley, *Feminism, Marriage, and the Law*, p. 86; Kent, *Sex and Suffrage*, pp. 65–6, 70; Myna Trustram, *Women of the Regiment: Marriage and the Victorian army* (Cambridge, Cambridge University Press, 1984), ch. 7.

20. Walkowitz, *Prostitution and Victorian Society* (p. 146 for the quotation), pp. 131–6, 143–5, 256; Forster, *Significant Sisters*, pp. 178–9; *The Contagious Diseases Acts and The Royal Commission*, p. 8; *Sursum Corda*, p. 33; Fawcett and Turner, *Josephine Butler*, p. 72. See James Beard Talbot, *The Miseries of Prostitution* (London, James Madden, 1844), p. 78, on the importance of establishing respectable houses to redeem prostitutes, and on the role 'discreet matronly females' could play in contacting and weaning prostitutes from their 'abandoned course'. See also Prochaska, *Women and Philanthropy in Nineteenth-Century England*, pp. 188–191, 206–7; Lewis, *Women in England*, p. 132; Walkowitz, *City of Dreadful Delight: Narratives of sexual danger in late-Victorian London* (London, Virago, 1992).

21. See, for instance, *Sursum Corda*, pp. 29–30.

22. Walkowitz, *Prostitution and Victorian Society*, pp. 141–3.

23. *Ibid.*, p. 143.
24. *Ibid.*
25. See Judith Walkowitz, 'The making of an outcast group: prostitutes and working women in nineteenth-century Plymouth and Southampton', in Vicinus (ed.), *A Widening Sphere*, pp. 72–93, especially 72–3, 93.
26. Walkowitz, *Prostitution and Victorian Society*, p. 131; Weeks, *Sex, Politics and Society*, p. 89 (source of quotation); Prochaska, *Women and Philanthropy in Nineteenth-Century England*, pp. 209 f., 220; Strachey, *The Cause*, p. 269. Elizabeth Blackwell, who was a member of the National Vigilance Association, saw herself as buffeting 'a black moral whirlwind': see Blackwell to Madame Bodichon, 9 Dec. 1886, Autograph Letter Collection, Women's Movement, FL.
27. Quoted in Fawcett and Turner, *Josephine Butler*, pp. 112–14.
28. *Vigilance Association*, pp. 5–7 (quotation from p. 6).
29. Fawcett and Turner, *Josephine Butler*, pp. 112–14.
30. See Walkowitz, *Prostitution and Victorian Society*, p. 140.
31. Weeks, *Sex, Politics and Society*, pp. 83–91 (quotation from p. 88); Lewis, *Women in England*, p. 140, Note 89; Mort, *Dangerous Sexualities*, Part Three, for a discussion of purity, feminism and the state, 1880–1914.
32. Weeks, *Sex, Politics and Society*, p. 83.
33. See Prochaska, *Women and Philanthropy in Nineteenth-Century England*, pp. 216–19; Sheila Jeffreys, *The Spinster and Her Enemies: Feminism and sexuality, 1880–1930* (London, Pandora, 1985), pp. 6–24; and opinions of Lucas and Hopkins quoted in *Opinions of Women on Women's Suffrage* (London, 1879), pp. 53, 57; Shiman, *Women and Leadership*, pp. 149–50.
34. Harper, *The Life and Work of Susan B. Anthony*, vol. I, pp. 469–70; Pivar, *Purity Crusade*, pp. 9, 64, 67, 79 f., 111, 118, 132, 146, 218 f. and chs 3–4 generally; Ryan, *Women in Public*, pp. 120–6.
35. Pivar, *Purity Crusade*, pp. 112, 116–17, 150–5; Patricia Hollis, *Ladies Elect: Women in English local government, 1865–1914* (Oxford, Clarendon Press, 1987), pp. 48–9, points out that the BWTA 'was not content with mere rescue work but from its inception ... tackled the problems which tempted men to drink'; Epstein, *The Politics of Domesticity*, p. 125; Shiman, ' "Changes are dangerous" ', pp. 204, 208–9.
36. Harper, *The Life and Work of Susan B. Anthony*, vol. II, p. 1007 (source of quotation), vol. I, p. 469; Epstein, *The Politics of Domesticity*, pp. 121, 136–7: Epstein, notes, however, that there was a tension between the WCTU's, commitment to female equality even as it upheld conventional morality: see pp. 128–36. See also *Women's Wages* (Rockford, IL, 1888), Parts II and III, by C.G.W. McCulloch, Folder 7, Box 1, Catharine Gouger Waugh McCulloch Papers, SL.
37. Linda Gordon, *Woman's Body, Woman's Right: A social history of birth control in America* (Harmondsworth, Penguin, 1976), p. 3, on these three factors in the regulation of birth control.
38. Perkin, *Women and Marriage in Nineteenth Century England*, pp. 276 f.; Branca, *Silent Sisterhood*, pp. 124 f.; Degler, *At Odds*, ch. XI; F. Barry Smith, 'Sexuality in Britain, 1800–1900: some suggested revisions', pp. 182–98, in Vicinus (ed.), *A Widening Sphere*; Weeks, *Sex, Politics and Society*, p. 23 and ch. 2 generally. Weeks notes that in England, despite the precedent of Scottish law and that existing in several American states, there was reluctance to move to punish incest: see pp. 31, 83.
39. Jeffreys, *The Spinster and Her Enemies*, pp. 31–3; Degler, *At Odds*, pp. 201, 203, 215

and *passim*; Weeks, *Sex, Politics and Society*, pp. 162–3; McLaren, *Birth Control in Nineteenth-Century England*, pp. 197 f.; Epstein, *The Politics of Domesticity*, pp. 126–8; Gordon, *Woman's Body, Woman's Right*, pp. 100, 109.

40. Gordon, *Woman's Body, Woman's Right*, chs 1, 3–5; Degler, *At Odds*, pp. 198 f.; Lucy Bland, 'Marriage laid bare: middle-class women and marital sex, 1880s–1914', in Jane Lewis (ed.), *Labour and Love: Women's experience of home and family, 1850–1940* (Oxford, Blackwell, 1986), p. 129; Weeks, *Sex, Politics and Society*, p. 163; J.A. and Olive Banks, *Feminism and Family Planning in Victorian England* (New York, Schocken Books, Liverpool, Liverpool University Press, 1964); Constance Rover, *Love, Morals and the Feminists* (London, Routledge & Kegan Paul, 1970); James Reed, *The Birth Control Movement in American Society: From private vice to public virtue* (Princeton, NJ, Princeton University Press, 1984 edn), pp. 39 f.; McLaren, *Birth Control in Nineteenth-Century England*, pp. 116 f., 190, 201 f.

41. Gordon, *Woman's Body, Woman's Right*, ch. 3; James C. Mohr, *Abortion in America: The origins and evolution of national policy, 1800–1900* (New York, Oxford University Press, 1975), chs 1–4, 6, pp. 195–6, ch. 8; Weeks, *Sex, Politics and Society*, pp. 71–2; J.A. Banks, *Prosperity and Parenthood: A study of family planning among the Victorian middle classes* (London, Routledge & Kegan Paul, 1954); McLaren, *Birth Control in Nineteenth-Century England*, pp. 123–5; Patricia Knight, 'Women and abortion in Victorian and Edwardian England', *History Workshop Journal*, no. 4, Autumn 1977, pp. 57–69; Smith-Rosenberg, 'The abortion movement and the AMA, 1850–1880', in *Disorderly Conduct*, pp. 217–44; Barbara Brookes, *Abortion in England, 1900–1967* (London, Croom Helm, 1988), pp. 1, 22–6, 42–3.

42. Reed, *The Birth Control Movement*, pp. 37, 391; Smith-Rosenberg, *Disorderly Conduct*, p. 222 (source of quotation); Mohr, *Abortion in America*, p. 196; Pivar, *Purity Crusade*, p. 146.

43. Smith-Rosenberg, *Disorderly Conduct*, pp. 243–4, 342; Leach, *True Love and Perfect Union*, pp. 62–3; Sheila Rothman, *Woman's Proper Place: A history of changing ideals and practices, 1870 to the present* (New York, Basic Books, 1978), pp. 81–5 for a view of social purists less sympathetic than mine.

44. Degler, *At Odds*, ch. VIII; Branca, *Silent Sisterhood*, p. 114; McLaren, *Birth Control in Nineteenth-Century England*, p. 197.

45. See Reed, *The Birth Control Movement*, chs 1–2; Banks, *Prosperity and Parenthood*, *passim*; Daniel Scott Smith, 'Family limitation, sexual control, and domestic feminism in Victorian America', *Feminist Studies*, vol. 1, nos 3–4, Winter/Spring 1973, pp. 40–57; Degler, *At Odds*, ch. IX, especially p. 220; Weeks, *Sex, Politics and Society*, pp. 45–6, 69; Branca, *Silent Sisterhood*, pp. 116 f.; McLaren, *Birth Control in Nineteenth-Century England*, ch. 12; Gordon, *Woman's Body, Woman's Right*, chs 3–4.

46. Mohr, *Abortion in America*, pp. 196–9; Reed, *The Birth Control Movement*, pp. 37–9; Smith-Rosenberg, *Disorderly Conduct*, p. 222; Epstein, *The Politics of Domesticity*, pp. 128–9.

47. McLaren, *Birth Control in Nineteenth-Century England*, pp. 178–9, 185; J.A. Banks and Olive Banks, 'The Bradlaugh–Besant trial and the English newspapers', *Population Studies*, vol. VIII, 1954–5, pp. 22–34.

48. Weeks, *Sex, Politics and Society*, p. 46; McLaren, *Birth Control in Nineteenth-Century England*, pp. 108–9.

49. McLaren, *Birth Control in Nineteenth-Century England*, pp. 112–13; Anne Taylor, *Annie Besant: A biography* (Oxford, Oxford University Press, 1992).

50. Weeks, *Sex, Politics and Society*, pp. 68–9; McLaren, *Birth Control in Nineteenth-Century England*, chs 3, 6, 8, pp. 158 f., and ch. 10 on Socialists who did favour birth control; Degler, *At Odds*, p. 314; Reed, *The Birth Control Movement*, pp. 40–5; Leach, *True Love and Perfect Union*, pp. 84–5; Carl Chinn, *They Worked All Their Lives* (Manchester, Manchester University Press, 1988), pp. 134 f.

51. See Weeks, *Sex, Politics and Society*, p. 162; the documentation on the CD campaign; McLaren, *Birth Control in Nineteenth-Century England*, p. 178, on Annie Besant's experience; Jeffreys, *The Spinster and Her Enemies*, p. 18, on the work of Ladies' Associations for the Care and Promotion of Friendless Girls.

52. Smith-Rosenberg, *Disorderly Conduct*, p. 243 (source of quotation).

53. Parkes, *Essays on Woman's Work*, p. 189.

54. Mrs Stanton quoted in Harper, *Life and Work of Susan B. Anthony*, vol. I, p. 379; and see *ibid.*, pp. 383–5, on reactions to Woodhull and the attempt to associate suffragists with free love; on feminists' preference for 'reformed legal marriage' to 'a non-marital relationship', while women's 'vulnerability and disadvantage prevailed', see Lucy Bland, 'Marriage laid bare', p. 128; but see also p. 129 on Annie Besant's views. On free love and Woodhull: Nelson Manfred Blake, *The Road to Reno: A history of divorce in the United States* (New York, Macmillan, 1962), pp. 100 f.; E. Sachs Arling, *The Terrible Siren: Victoria Woodhull, 1838–1927* (New York, Harper & Row, 1928); Leach, *True Love and Perfect Union*; Rover, *Love, Morals and the Feminists*; S. Ditzion, *Marriage, Morals and Sex in America: A history of ideas* (New York, Bookman Associates, 1953); H.D. Sears, *The Sex Radicals* (Lawrence, The Regents Press of Kansas, 1977); Riley, *Divorce*, pp. 76–7.

55. O'Neill, *Everyone Was Brave*, pp. 21–30; Degler, *At Odds*, p. 329; Leach, *True Love and Perfect Union*, p. 82.

56. Degler, *At Odds*, p. 166; Riley, *Divorce*, pp. 78–80; Carell D. Wright, *A Report on Marriage and Divorce in the United States, 1827 to 1886, etc.* (Washington, DC, Government Printing Office, 1889), pp. 127–64, especially p. 140.

57. HWS, vol. III, pp. 32–3; Wright, *A Report on Marriage and Divorce*, pp. 10, 207–12 on diversity of provision; children and alimony.

58. *A History of the National Woman's Rights Movement*, pp. 66–70 (quotation from p. 70).

59. Stanton in 1902 quoted in Blake, *The Road to Reno*, pp. 150–1; for a very similar statement by Stanton in 1869, see HWS, vol. III, p. 324.

60. Blake, *Road to Reno*, chs 9, 10 (to p. 136); Leach, *True Love and Perfect Union*, pp. 145, 284; Riley, *Divorce*, chs 4, 5; Jamil S. Zainaldin, 'The emergence of a modern American family law: child custody, adoption, and the courts, 1796–1851', *Northwestern University Law Review*, vol. 73, 1979, pp. 1038–89; Michael Grossberg. *Governing the Hearth: Law and family in nineteenth-century America* (Chapel Hill, University of North Carolina Press, 1985); Elizabeth Pleck, *Domestic Tyranny: The making of social policy against family violence from colonial times to the present* (New York, Oxford University Press, 1987).

61. Shanley, *Feminism, Marriage, and the Law*, chs 5, 6, and 'Epilogue' (p. 131 for second quotation): as Shanley points out, wife abuse was not confined to the working-classes, but since respectable Victorians were most likely to condemn it among other groups, feminists geared their arguments to Parliament accordingly (pp. 163, 167); Lewis (ed.), *Labour and Love*, p. 5; Levine, *Victorian Feminism*, pp. 132, 142–5; Jeffreys, *The Spinster and Her Enemies*, pp. 30–1; Perkin, *Women and Marriage in*

~

Nineteenth-Century England, pp. 116, 61; Forster, *Significant Sisters*, p. 51; McGregor, *Divorce in England*, pp. 23–4 (third quotation from p. 23); Hollis (ed.), *Women in Public*, pp. 168–6, 187–8, 192–3 (first quotation from p. 187); Cynthia Fansler Behrman, 'The annual blister: a sidelight on Victorian social and parliamentary history', *Victorian Studies*, vol. XI, no. 4, 1968, pp. 483–502; letter from the Earl of Dalhousie, 23 Feb. 1883, Autograph Letter Collection, Women's Movement, FL; Patricia Hollis, *Ladies Elect*, pp. 197, 238, 287–99, notes the opposition of women poor law guardians to outdoor relief, though see pp. 267–70 on their rather more sensitive treatment of unmarried mothers; Taylor, *Annie Besant*; Kent, *Sex and Suffrage*, ch. III; Wright, *A Report on Marriage and Divorce*, p. 146 on the small number and expensiveness of divorces in England and Wales; Riley, *Divorce*, p. 95. And see *Woman's Suffrage Journal*, vol. XV, no. 170, 1 February 1884, p. 33; no. 171, 1 March 1884, p. 41; no. 172, 1 April 1884, p. 79.

62. Chambers-Schiller, *Liberty, A Better Husband*, p. 207 (source of quotation), ch. 10 generally and 'Conclusion'; Weeks, *Sex, Politics and Society*, ch. 8 and pp. 165–7; Jeffreys, *The Spinster and Her Enemies*, ch. 5; Degler, *At Odds*, pp. 144–65; Solomon, *The Company of Educated Women*, pp. 98–100 on female friendships.

63. HWS, vol. III, p. 950.

64. See Hollis, *Ladies Elect*, pp. 139, 238, on the qualities of the often single women school board members and poor law guardians. On single women generally, see Vicinus, *Independent Women*; O'Neill, *Everyone Was Brave*, ch. 4, on leaders of the American women's movement who put their public lives before family claims; and Solomon, *In the Company of Educated Women*, pp. 118 f.

65. HWS, vol. III, pp. 726–7.

66. Rover, *Women's Suffrage*, pp. 24 (source of first quotation), 58–61, 170; Ramelson, *The Petticoat Rebellion*, pp. 83–4, 87–8, 90, 162; Blackburn, *Women's Suffrage*, pp. 102 (on early intensity and unity), 168–9 (source of second quotation).

67. Rover, *Women's Suffrage*, pp. 56–8, 60–1, 63; Ramelson, *The Petticoat Rebellion*, pp. 77–9, 84–5, 87, 93; Helen Blackburn, *Women's Suffrage*, ch. VI onwards (first quotation from p. 153, second from p. 126); Millicent Fawcett, 'The women's suffrage movement' in Theodore Stanton (ed.), *The Woman Question in Europe: A series of original essays* (New York, London and Paris, G. P. Putnam's Sons, 1884), pp. 12 f.; *Englishwoman's Review*, vol. IX, no. 44, 15 August, 1878, p. 337 (source of third quotation). See also vol. VIII, no. 52, 15 August 1877, p. 337 (source of fourth quotation); *Report of the Bristol and West of England Branch of the National Society for Women's Suffrage*, 1870, pp. 4–5; for 1871, pp. 3–4, 6–9 (pp. 8–9 on donors); for 1872, pp. 4, 7; for 1873, pp. 3–4, 7–9; for 1874, pp. 5, 7; for 1875, pp. 7–8; for 1876, pp. 3, 5–7; *First Annual Report of the Executive Committee of the Manchester National Society for Women's Suffrage*, 1868, pp. 15–20; *Fifth Annual Report*, 1872, p. 16 (source of last quotation); *Ninth Annual Report*, 1876, pp. 10–12, 17–32 (source of last quotation); on Mrs Fawcett, see Rubinstein, *A Different World for Women*; see tribute to Mrs Fawcett's leadership in letter from Miss Catherine E. Marshall to Mrs Fawcett, 7 Feb. 1917, Autograph Letter Collection, FL; on the demonstrations, not attempted by the agricultural labourers on their behalf, see *Women's Suffrage Journal*, vol. XV, no. 172, April 1884, pp. 60, 63–74.

68. Rover, *Women's Suffrage*, pp. 58–61; Ramelson, *The Petticoat Rebellion*, pp. 86, 93–4; *Report of the Bristol and West of England Branch of the National Society for Women's Suffrage*, 1872, p. 5; 1873, pp. 5–7; 1876, p. 5.

~

69. *Opinions of Women on Women's Suffrage*, (London, Central Committee of the National Society for Women's Suffrage, 1879), Preface (source of first quotation), pp. 9 f.; Quotations from pp. 9–10, 17–18; also, *Englishwoman's Review*, no. 11, October 1872, pp. 229–32; vol. IX, no. 67, Nov. 15, 1878, pp. 518–19.

70. *Opinions of Women on Women's Suffrage*, pp. 34, 35, 42; for the arguments of the suffrage movement, see also Rover, *Women's Suffrage*, ch. IV; Arabella Shore, 'Present aspect of women's suffrage considered', *Englishwoman's Review*, vol. VIII, no. 52, 15 August 1877, pp. 33, 7–47; no. 53, 15 September 1877, pp. 355–99, and *Report of the Bristol and West of England Branch of the National Society for Women's Suffrage*, 1872, p. 5; 1873, pp. 5–7; 1876, p. 5. See, however, Mrs Fawcett's assertion that 'The suffrage has not been claimed for women in England as an abstract and inalienable right, but it has been claimed upon the grounds of expediency; that is to say, on the ground that the good resulting from it would far outweigh any evils that might possibly attend it'; in Stanton (ed.), *The Woman Question in Europe*, pp. 4–5; see also p. xvi for a similar argument by Frances Power Cobbe.

71. Complaint of Emily A. E. Shirreff in *Opinions of Women on Women's Suffrage*, p. 43; Winifred Holt, *A Beacon for the Blind: Being a life of Henry Fawcett, the blind postmaster* (London, Constable, 1915), p. 290. The best treatment of British anti-suffragism is Brian H. Harrison, *Separate Spheres: The opposition to women's suffrage in Britain* (London, Croom Helm, 1978).

72. Harrison, *Separate Spheres*, ch. 2, especially pp. 41–2, and ch. 4; Fawcett, *Women's Suffrage*, ch. V; Rover, *Women's Suffrage*, chs V, VIII; on Gladstone, see pp. 118–20; Ramelson, *The Petticoat Rebellion*, p. 81; for Stanton's comments on anti-suffragism, HWS, vol. III, pp. 941–2; *Report of the Bristol and West of England Branch of the National Society for Women's Suffrage*, 1873, pp. 4–5, for an expression of sympathy for women's suffrage by Disraeli; *Women's Suffrage Journal*, vol. XV, no. 175, 1 July 1884, pp. 148–9, for Gladstone's views: he conceded that women were suited to local government duties.

73. *Opinions of Women's Suffrage*, pp. 13, 39.

74. Ramelson, *The Petticoat Rebellion*, p. 81 (source of quotation); Weeks, *Sex, Politics and Society*, pp. 169–70; Rover, *Women's Suffrage*, pp. 150–60; Liddington and Norris, *One Hand Tied Behind Us*, pp. 43–4; Harrison, *Separate Spheres*, pp. 47–8, 50–3.

75. Rover, *Women's Suffrage*, pp. 21–2; Ramelson, *The Petticoat Rebellion*, pp. 92–3; Harrison – in *Prudent Revolutionaries*, p. 23 – points out that Mrs Fawcett was willing to acquiesce in the exclusion of married women; see letter of Ursula Bright to Mr Henry Fawcett, 8 February 1884, acknowledging that to exclude qualified women from the suffrage cause would make suffragists and 'our cause ridiculous', Autograph Letter Collection, FL.

76. Blackburn, *Women's Suffrage*, pp. 135–8; HWS, vol. III, p. 889; and see also in *ibid.*, pp. 943–4; *Reminiscences* by ECS (Mrs Stanton).

77. Rover, *Women's Suffrage*, p. 53; Ramelson, *The Petticoat Rebellion*, ch. 8; Blackburn, *Women's Suffrage*, pp. 120–1. On the division over the CD acts among suffragists, see Caine, *Victorian Feminists*.

78. Hollis, *Ladies Elect*, pp. 53 f. (quotation from p. 54); Rover, *Women's Suffrage*, pp. 53, 112–13, 140–3; Fawcett, *Women's Suffrage*, pp. 30–1; Blackburn, *Women's Suffrage*, pp. 158–61, 170–2; Stanton, *Eighty Years and More*, pp. 397–8 (source of last quotation). See letter from Georgia Ferguson to Caroline Severance, 24 Oct.

1905, suggesting American women should 'organize – à la the English political societies of the Primrose League and the Liberal Association of Women', Caroline Severance Collection, Henry B. Huntington Library. See also Shiman, *Women and Leadership*, pp. 174 f.

79. Rover, *Women's Suffrage*, pp. 69, 111–12, 138; Ramelson, *The Petticoat Rebellion*, ch. 8.

80. Blackburn, *Women's Suffrage*, pp. 175–7 (quotation from p. 177).

81. *Ibid.*, pp. 178–9; *First Annual Report of the Executive Committee of the Manchester National Society for Women's Suffrage*, p. 15 (source of quotation).

82. *The Nineteenth Century*, June 1889; the *Fortnightly Review*, July 1889; Blackburn, *Women's Suffrage*, pp. 178–9. Compare with E. Lynn Linton, 'The modern revolt', *Macmillan's Magazine*, vol. 23, December 1870, pp. 142–9; quotation from letter of Mrs Lilias Ashworth Hallett to Mrs Henry Fawcett, July (1889), Autograph Letter Collection, FL.

83. See John Sutherland, *Mrs Humphrey Ward: Eminent Victorian, pre-eminent Edwardian* (Oxford, Clarendon Press, 1990), pp. 63–5, 198, 200, ch. 17, 21–9, 241, 264, 277–8, 295–30, ch. 25, 343–4, 365, 373.

84. Beatrice Webb recalled recanting swiftly and, though not publicising the fact, withdrawing from suffrage controversy: see on Webb, Lewis, *Women and Social Action*; and Sidney Webb to Mrs Cavendish Bentinck, 12 June 1912, in Autograph Letter Collection, FL, in which he claims to have converted his wife to suffragism when he married her.

85. Hollis, *Ladies Elect*, pp. 7–8, 31, 205–8; HWS, vol. III, pp. 851, 844–7, 871–2 (first quotation from p. 847).

86. Hollis, *Ladies Elect*, ch. 1 (quotations from pp. 10, 33), chs 2–5, especially pp. 185–92, 211–13, 238; *Report of the Bristol and West of England Branch of the National Society for Women's Suffrage*, 1870, p. 4; *Englishwoman's Review*, vol. VIII, no. 73, 15 May 1879, pp. 206 f.; no. 76, 15 August 1879, pp. 353 f.; no. 80, 15 December 1879, pp. 545 f.

87. Fawcett, *Women's Suffrage*, pp. 46–50; Fawcett in Stanton (ed.), *The Woman Question in Europe*, p. 20.

88. Fawcett in Stanton (ed.), *The Woman Question in Europe*, pp. 27–8; Blackburn, *Women's Suffrage*, pp. 155–8; HWS, vol. III, pp. 870–1.

89. Alan P. Grimes, *The Puritan Ethic and Woman Suffrage*, (New York, Oxford University Press, 1967), p. 76 (source of quotation) and ch. III generally; see also Sandra L. Myres, *Westering Women and the Frontier Experience, 1800–1915* (Albuquerque, University of New Mexico Press, 1982), pp. 220–1; Morgan, *Suffragists and Democrats*, p. 17; and articles by T.A. Larson: 'Emancipating the West's dolls, vassals and hopeless drudges: the origin of woman suffrage in the West', in Roger Daniels (ed.), *Essays in Western History in Honor of Professor T.A. Larson* (University of Wyoming Publications, 37, October 1971), pp. 1–16; and 'Woman suffrage in Wyoming', *Pacific Northwest Quarterly*, vol. 56, April 1965, pp. 57–66.

90. Morgan, *Suffragists and Democrats*, p. 17; Thomas Alexander, 'An experiment in progressive legislation: the granting of woman's suffrage in Utah in 1870', *Utah Historical Quarterly*, vol. 48, Winter 1970, pp. 20–30; Myres, *Westering Women*, pp. 221–3.

91. James Bryce, *The American Commonwealth* (London, Macmillan, 1893, 2 vols), vol.

II, p. 552 (source of quotation), p. 555; Grimes, *The Puritan Ethic and Woman Suffrage*, p. 46, and ch. II generally.

92. Grimes, *The Puritan Ethic and Woman Suffrage*, p. 27.

93. HWS, vol. III, p. 743 (source of quotation); but see Bryce, *The American Commonwealth*, pp. 555–6, for the view that Wyoming women seldom voted, made harsh jurors, and offered no lessons for the rest of America because they were a minority in the territory.

94. HWS, vol. III, pp. 776–8, 780–8; vol. IV, pp. 968–70; Paulson, *Women's Suffrage and Prohibition*, p. 90.

95. Grimes, *The Puritan Ethic and Woman Suffrage*, pp. 21–2 (quotation from p. 22); Flexner, *Century of Struggle*, p. 178; Myres, *Westering Women*, pp. 225–7. The official reasons for invalidating the 1883 law in 1887 and 1888 were that 'its nature has not been properly described in the title, . . . [and] that the Act of Congress organizing the Territorial Legislature did not empower it to extend the suffrage to women': see Bryce, *The American Commonwealth*, pp. 553, 556.

96. See DuBois, *Feminism and Suffrage*, p. 200; Harper, *The Life and Work of Susan B. Anthony*, vol. I, pp. 413–14 for a hostile view of the events of 1872; also Griffith, *In Her Own Right*, pp. 151–2.

97. Harper, *The Life and Work of Susan B. Anthony*, vol. I, p. 483.

98. See HWS, vol. II, pp. 545, 582.

99. HWS, vol. III, chs XXVIII–XXX; vol. IV, chs III, VI.

100. HWS, vol. III, chs XXVII–XXIX, especially p. 150; XXX; vol. IV, chs II, IV–V, VII, IX; Harper, *The Life and Work of Susan B. Anthony*, vol. I, chs XXVIII–XXIX; vol. II, chs XXXII–XXXIV.

101. Senator Vest of Missouri, January 1887, in discussions leading to the first vote on the Sixteenth Amendment, quoted in Harper, *The Life and Work of Susan B. Anthony*, vol. II, p. 620; HWS, vol. V, p. xxii.

102. Harper, *The Life and Work of Susan B. Anthony*, vol. II, p. 621.

103. *Ibid.*, p. 623; Morgan, *Suffragists and Democrats*, p. 18.

104. On the AWSA, see HWS, vol. IV, ch. XXII; Alice Stone Blackwell, *Lucy Stone, Pioneer of Woman's Rights* (Boston, MA, Little Brown, 1930); Hays, *Morning Star*; Flexner, *Century of Struggle*, p. 179.

105. Flexner, *Century of Struggle*, p. 305; HWS, vol. III, pp. 99–103 (first quotation from p. 99); pp. 275–6 (source of second quotation).

106. HWS, vol. III, p. 826 (source of quotation); Scott, *The Southern Lady*, pp. 172f.

107. HWS, vol. III, pp. iv–v; Harper, *The Life and Work of Susan B. Anthony*, vol. II, pp. 530–1, 542–3, 612–16. See Carolyn Stefanco, 'Networking on the frontier: the Colorado women's suffrage movement, 1873–1893', in Susan Armitage and Elizabeth Jameson (eds), *The Women's West* (Norman and London, University of Oklahoma Press, 1987), pp. 265–73: Stefanco believes that by 1893, when the vote was secured, Colorado women had 'created a social reform movement with characteristics unique for the period' (see p. 273); for a somewhat less positive picture of affairs in Colorado, see Myres, *Westering Women*, pp. 223–4.

108. Flexner, *Century of Struggle*, p. 179.

109. Paulson, *Women's Suffrage and Prohibition*, p. 155; HWS, vol. IV, pp. xv, xxi, xxix.

110. HWS, vol. III, pp. 701–2, 710: suffrage sentiment was also said to be encouraged by women's involvement in temperance, farmer, teacher, intellectual and other groups.

111. *Ibid.*, pp. 287–90 (quotation from p. 287).

112. See, for instance, *ibid.*, pp. 374–7, 394, 423–30, 530, 652 f., 675; Woody, *A History of Women's Education in the United States*, vol. II, pp. 441–4; Stefanco 'Networking on the frontier', pp. 271–2.

113. Rosalind Urbach Moss, 'The "girls" from Syracuse: sex role negotiations of Kansas women in politics, 1887–1890', in Armitage and Jameson (eds), *The Women's West*, pp. 253–61.

114. Ginzberg, *Women and the Work of Benevolence*, pp. 186–9; Flexner, *Century of Struggle*, pp. 179–80.

115. HWS, vol. III, p. 653.

116. Harper, *The Life and Work of Susan B. Anthony*, vol. II, pp. 578–9 (source of third quotation), 633, 636 (source of first and second quotations) f.; Stanton, *Eighty Years and More*, pp. 375, 412–14; Mari Jo Buhle, *Women and American Socialism, 1870–1920* (Urbana, Chicago and London, University of Illinois Press, 1981), pp. 66–9; HWS, vol. IV, pp. 124 f.

117. Sachs and Wilson, *Sexism and the Law*, p. 110; HWS, vol. III, ch. XXVII; Harper, *The Life and Work of Susan B. Anthony*, vol. I, pp. 474–80.

118. Flexner, *Century of Struggle*, pp. 222 f.

119. Steven N. Buechler, *The Transformation of the Woman Suffrage Movement: The case of Illinois, 1850–1920* (New Brunswick, NJ, Rutgers University Press, 1986), ch. 4 (quotation from p. 102); also pp. 50–1 and ch. 2 generally.

120. *Ibid.*, pp. 128–9; on the Illinois Women's Alliance, see also Buhle, *Women and American Socialism*, pp. 72–3.

121. Buechler, *The Transformation of the Woman Suffrage Movement*, pp. 121, 146.

122. On the efforts of working-class Denver women to obtain the vote 'through the auspices of labor politics' in the late 1880s, see Stefanco, 'Neworking on the frontier', pp. 270–1; Buhle, *Women and American Socialism*, ch. 1; and pp. 51 f. on the efforts of middle-class urban and rural women to defend the right to labour, and on their links with working-class women; see also ch. 1; Epstein, *The Politics of Domesticity*, pp. 137 f. on the WCTU and labour; Baker, 'The domestication of politics', pp. 636 f.

123. Paulson, *Women's Suffrage and Prohibition*, p. 137.

124. On women and social science, see Leach, *True Love and Perfect Union*, pp. 316–22, 324–46; Thomas L. Haskell, *The Emergence of Professional Social Science: The American Social Science Association and the nineteenth-century crisis of authority* (Urbana, Chicago and London, University of Illinois Press, 1977), pp. 99–100, 129; on the connection between British feminists and social scientific inquiry in the 1850s, see above, pp. 54, 84–6, 100, 113.

125. Buhle, *Women and American Socialism*, ch. 2, is especially useful on the nature and preoccupations of the women's movement in the Gilded Age.

126. *Englishwoman's Review*, no. 10, April 1872, 'Mixed education', pp. 153–62; no. 11, October 1872, 'Colonel Higginson on the Queen's Institute', p. 250; see also p. 266.

127. See, for instance, William Preston Vaughn, *Schools for All: The blacks and public education in the South, 1865–1877* (Lexington, University of Kentucky Press, 1974); Robert C. Morris, *Reading, 'Riting and Reconstruction: The education of freedmen in the South, 1861–1870* (Chicago, University of Chicago Press, 1981); David B. Tyack, *The One Best System: A history of American urban education* (Cambridge, MA, Harvard University Press, 1974); David Nasaw, *Schooled to Order. A social history of public schooling in the United States* (New York, Oxford University Press, 1979); Meyer

Weinberg, *A Chance to Learn: The history of race and education in the United States* (Cambridge, Cambridge University Press, 1977); Timothy L. Smith, 'Immigrant social aspirations and American education, 1880–1930', *American Quarterly*, vol. 21, 1969, pp. 523–43.

128. See the works by Tyack and Nasaw cited in Note 127; also Colin Greer, *The Great School Legend: A revisionist interpretation of American education* (New York, Viking Press, 1974); Michael Katz, *Class, Bureaucracy and Schools: The illusions of change in America* (New York Praeger, 1975 edn); Henry J. Parkinson, *The Imperfect Panacea* (New York, Wiley, 1968); and Patricia Albjerg Graham, *Community and Class in American Education, 1865–1918* (New York, Wiley, 1974).

129. See Woody, *A History of Women's Education in the United States*, vol. II, pp. 228–9.

130. *Ibid.*, p. 229; Tyack and Hansot, *Learning Together*, chs 5–6.

131. Woody, *A History of Women's Education in the United States*, vol. II, p. 470.

132. See Solomon, *In the Company of Educated Women*, pp. 46–7.

133. Woody, *A History of Women's Education in the United States*, vol. II, pp. 213 f., quotation from p. 245, citing Acting President Frieze of Michigan, statistics about co-education from p. 252; Solomon, *In the Company of Educated Women*, pp. 43 f.; Patricia Albjerg Graham, 'Expansion and exclusion: a history of women in American higher education', *Signs*, vol. 3, Summer 1978, pp. 759–73; Myres, *Westering Women*, p. 185; Leach, *True Love and Perfect Union*, pp. 9 f.

134. Solomons, *In the Company of Educated Women*, p. 47.

135. See *ibid.*, pp. 47–9, 80, 85 (source of quotation), 89–90 and ch. 6 generally; Woody, *A History of Women's Education in the United States*, vol. II, pp. 179–82; Lucille Addison Pollard, *Women on College and University Faculties: A historical survey and study of their present academic status* (New York, Arno Press, 1977); Mabel Newcomer, *A Century of Higher Education for Women* (New York, Harper, 1959), p. 82.

136. Catharine Clinton, 'Women and Harvard: the first 350 years; *Harvard Magazine*, September–October 1986, especially pp. 123–5; Woody, *A History of Women's Education in the United States*, vol. II, pp. 304–20; Solomon, *In the Company of Educated Women*, pp. 54–6; Elizabeth Cary Agassiz papers, Box 2, letters in Folder 9, SL.

137. Solomon, *In the Company of Educated Women*, pp. 46–7, 52, 55–6, 76 (source of statistic); Scott, *The Southern Lady*, pp. 110 f.; Woody, *A History of Women's Education in the United States*, vol. II, pp. 150, 183, 188, 252–5; Flexner, *Century of Struggle*, pp. 130–3.

138. Edward H. Clarke, *Sex in Education: Or, a fair chance for the girls* (Boston, MA, Osgood & Co., 1873); Rosalind Rosenberg, *Beyond Separate Spheres: Intellectual roots of modern feminism* (New Haven, CT and London, Yale University Press, 1982), pp. xv–xvi and ch. 1; Walsh, *Doctors Wanted*, pp. 119–32; Woody, *A History of Women's Education in the United States*, vol. II, pp. 109–35; Solomon, *In the Company of Educated Women*, pp. 103–4, 119–21, statistics from pp. 63–4.

139. Woody, *A History of Women's Education in the United States*, vol. II, pp. 189 f.; Solomon, *In the Company of Educated Women*, pp. 134 f.

140. Solomon, *In the Company of Educated Women*, ch. 8; National Association of University Women Archives, 1881–1976 (Microfilming Corporation of America, Film A319), Series I, Reel 1, the following: The Western Assocation of Collegiate

Alumnae, a short history; letter of 15 Feb. 1926, from Marion Talbot to Jane M. Bancroft; copy of letter to the Board of Directors of the American Association of University Women; Historical Facts Concerning the Western Association of Collegiate Alumnae, prepared by Marion Talbot and Bessie Bradwell Holmer; 'The Work that Awaits Us' (1887), paper by Lucy C. Andrews, quotation from p. 4, and see pp. 5–6.

141. See Mary Putnam Jacobi Papers, SL,: Folder 1, newspaper clipping, 'Woman as a Physician'; Folder 3, Autobiography, pp. 5–6, 8, 10, 12, 15, 16–71; addition by biographer, pp. 2, 4, 11, 16, 18–20; Folder 4, articles about Jacobi by Helen Johnston, pp. 119–21, and by Eugene P. Link, pp. 382–91; Folder 7, George Palmer Putnam by Mary Putnam, 13 Feb. 1861; Folder 11, Mary Jacobi to her mother, 23 July 1876; Folder 12, Alexander Agassiz to Mary Jacobi, 16 May 1878, 28 May 1878, 16 June 1879; Folder 19, Mary Jacobi to her sister Amy, 27 June 1904; Folder 20, letter from husband Abraham to Mary Jacobi; Folder 23, piece indicating Jacobi's early ambition; Folder 28, document commenting on Professor Munsterberg's comments on American women, pp. 5, 7, 10, 12, 14; Folder 31, The School of Medicine for Women of the New York Infirmary, paper at Laurel House, Lakewood, 3 March 1884, p. 16; Folder 32, 'The opening of the Johns Hopkins medical school' (1891); Folder 35, Case (documenting Mrs Jacobi's tumour), p. 1. See also, by Jacobi, *The Question of Rest During Menstruation* (New York, Putnam, 1876), pp. 168–9.

142. Levine, *Victorian Feminism*, p. 30; Lewis, *Women in England*, p. 91.

143. Fletcher, *Feminists and Bureaucrats*, especially pp. 3, 5, 16–19, 54 f., 68–75, 77 f., 88, 99, 102, 104 f., 111 f., 121 f., 129 f., 134 f., 151, 153, 155–6, 162, 166–72, 180 f. (quotation from p. 102). See also Bryant, *The Unexpected Revolution*, pp. 98–102.

144. Fletcher, *Feminists and Bureaucrats*, pp. 100–2, 154–6, 178–80; *A Guide to the Girls' Public Day School Trust* (London, The Trust's Head Office, n.d.), p. 1 (source of first quotation); Thomson, *England in the Nineteenth Century*, p. 135 (source of second quotation); Levine, *Victorian Feminism*, pp. 36–7; Bryant, *The Unexpected Revolution*, pp. 102–3 (fourth quotation from p. 103); article by Maria Grey on 'The women's educational movement', in Stanton (ed.), *The Woman Question in Europe*, pp. 46 f., (third quotation from p. 47); Josephine Kamm, *Indicative Past: A hundred years of the girls' Public Day School Trust* (London, Allen & Unwin, 1971); Edward W. Ellsworth, *Liberators of the Female Mind: The Shirreff sisters, educational reform and the women's movement* (Westport, CT, Greenwood Press, 1979); Carol Dyhouse, *Girls Growing Up in Late Victorian and Edwardian England* (London, Routledge & Kegan Paul, 1981), pp. 172–3.

145. Rita McWilliams-Tullberg, *Women at Cambridge: A men's university – though of a mixed type* (London, Victor Gollancz Ltd., 1975), Introduction, chs 4–6, p. 108 on developments at Oxford, and also p. 234; Annie M.A.H. Rogers, *Degrees by Degrees: The story of the admission of Oxford women students to membership of the university* (Oxford, Oxford University Press, 1938); Pedersen, 'The reform of women's secondary and higher education', p. 77 (source of statistic); see letter in Autograph Letter Collection, FL, of Miss Helene Stoehr to her sister Emily, 15 June 1890, on the brilliant result of Philippa Fawcett. Until 1882 a man resigned his fellowship on marriage, and only heads of colleges and professors were free to marry.

146. See R. D. Anderson, *Education and Opportunity in Victorian Scotland: Schools and universities* (Oxford, Clarendon Press, 1983) pp. 78, 253–7, 275–7; H. Hale Bellot,

~

University College London, 1826–1926 (London, University of London Press, 1929), pp. 369–71; F.M.L. Thompson (ed.), *The University of London and the World of Learning 1836–1986* (London and Ronceverte, Hambledon Press, 1990), article by Gillian Sutherland, 'The plainest principles of justice: The University of London and the higher education of women', pp. 35–56; Burstyn, *Victorian Education and the Ideal of Womanhood*, pp. 154 f.; Gillian Sutherland, 'The movement for the higher education of women: its social and intellectual context in England, *c*1849–1880', in P.J. Waller (ed.), *Political and Social Change in Modern Britain: Essays Presented to A.F. Thompson* (Brighton, Harvester, 1987), pp. 91–116; Caroline Bingham, *The History of Royal Holloway College 1886–1986* (London, Constable, 1987); Neville Marsh, *The History of Queen Elizabeth College* (London, King's College, 1986); Janet Sondheimer, *Castle Adamant in Hampstead: A history of Westfield College, 1882–1982* (London, Westfield College, 1988); Margaret J. Tuke, *A History of Bedford College for Women, 1849–1937* (London, Oxford University Press, 1939); Levine, *Victorian Feminism*, p. 46; Bryant, *The Unexpected Revolution*, pp. 88–9; J.W. Sherborne, *University College, Bristol, 1876–1909* (Historical Association, Bristol, 1977); Mabel Tylecote, *The Education of Women at Manchester University, 1883–1933* (Manchester, Manchester University Press, 1941).

147. Sutherland, 'The plainest principles of justice', p. 42; Solomon, *In the Company of Educated Women*, p. 49; Kamm, *How Different From Us*, ch. XV; Levine, *Victorian Feminism*, pp. 37–8; Pedersen, 'Schoolmistresses and headmistresses', pp. 149 f. and 'The reform of women's secondary and higher education', pp. 77–9, 81–2; Kathleen McCrone, *Sport and the Physical Emancipation of English Women, 1870–1914* (London, Routledge, 1988); J.A. Mangan and Roberta J. Park (eds), *From 'Fair Sex' to Feminism: Sport and the socialization of women in the industrial and post-industrial eras* (London, Frank Cass, 1987).

148. See Levine, *Victorian Feminism*, p. 40; Pedersen, 'Schoolmistresses and head-mistresses', pp. 152–4.

149. See, for instance, Fletcher, *Feminists and Bureaucrats*, pp. 100, 181–2; Kamm, *How Different From Us*, pp. 184–5; Pedersen, 'Schoolmistresses and headmistresses', pp. 1690–2.

150. Fletcher, *Feminists and Bureaucrats*, p. 180.

151. *Ibid.*, pp. 97, 180; Gray's article in Stanton (ed.), *The Woman Question in Europe*, pp. 47–8; Burstyn, *Victorian Education and the Ideal of Womanhood*, ch. 6.

152. Burstyn, *Victorian Education and the Ideal of Womanhood*, pp. 85–6, 150–1; see Solomon, *In the Company of Educated Women*, ch. 7, for a positive picture of 'The dimensions of the collegiate women's secondary and higher education', p. 81, 82–4. Also Pederson, 'Schoolmistresses and headmistresses', p. 155, and 'The reform of women's secondary and higher education', pp. 81, 83–4; Paul Atkinson, 'Fitness, feminism and schooling', in Delamont and Duffin (eds), *The Nineteenth-Century Woman*, pp. 105–8; and the heartening letters from Helen Wilson to her parents on life as a Bedford undergraduate, 1883–5, in Autograph Letter Collection, FL.

153. Quoted in Grey's Article in Stanton (ed.), *The Woman Question in Europe*, p. 62.

154. Flexner, *Century of Struggle*, p. 183; Scott, *The Southern Lady*, p. 152. The best contemporary introduction to the clubs is Jane Cunningham Croly's *History of the Woman's Club Movement in America* (New York, Henry G. Allen, 1898), a large study covering representative clubs, the General Federation, foreign clubs, and state and local work.

155. Scott, *The Southern Lady*, pp. 150–63, quotation from p. 162; and Nugent papers in Somerville–Howorth Family Papers, SL, Folder 54, vols. 19–22, on the work of the ladies of the Greenville First Methodist Episcopal Church, and the collection generally.

156. Armitage and Jameson (eds), *The Women's West*, pp. 167, 169, 268, 270–1; Myres, *Westering Women*, pp. 206–9 (quotation from p. 208).

157. Flexner, *Century of Struggle*, pp. 190–1; Stirling, *We Are Your Sisters*, pp. 429–30.

158. Flexner, *Century of Struggle*, p. 182; Karen J. Blair, *The Clubwoman as Feminist: True womanhood redefined, 1868–1914* (New York, Holmes & Meier, 1980), ch. 5; Buhle, *Women and American Socialism*, pp. 55–60, quotations from p. 59; Leach, *True Love and Perfect Union*, pp. 164–7, on employment, relief, and industrial education efforts among working-class women; Rothman, *Woman's Proper Place*, pp. 64 f.; Croly, *The History of the Woman's Club Movement*, pp. 15 f.

159. Flexner, *Century of Struggle*, pp. 210–11.

160. See Elizabeth Jane Clapp, 'The origins and development of juvenile courts in the United States during the Progressive era, *c.*1890–1910', PhD dissertation, University of London, 1991, pp. 90–5 (quotation from the club's historian p. 92); and Buechler, *The Transformation of the Woman Suffrage Movement*, pp. 125–7, on the Chicago Club. Dr Clapp's thesis is notably wide ranging.

161. See in the records of the New England Women's Club, SL, Box 3, vol. 11, account of the club's first meeting, 18 Feb. 1868; of 11 Jan. 1869; of 29 March 1869; of 12 April 1869; of 10 May 1869; of 29 May 1869; of 28 May 1869. Box 4, Folder 5, records of club meetings from May 1868 to June 1882: 1872–4 volume, meetings of 21 April 1873; of 9 June 1873; of 12 Jan. 1874; of 11 May 1874; 1874–6 volume, meeting of 22 March 1875; 1870–2 volume, meeting of 20 March 1871; 1877–82 volume, meeting of 15 Dec. 1879; meeting of 3 April 1882: Lucy Stone was now allowed to speak on the women's suffrage movement. Box 4, Folder 6, Club Journal, 1882–99: 1884–6, meeting of 25 Jan. 1886; meeting of 24 May 1886; 1886–7, meeting in Jan. 1887 on the Indian question; 1887, meeting of 23 April 1887; 1888–9, meeting of 10 Dec. 1888. Box 6, Folder 11, records of Committee on Work, meetings 1868–71: 1868–9 volume, meeting of 12 June 1869, meeting of 23 July 1869; 1869–71, meetings of 24 June 1870, 7 Oct. 1870, 23 Sept. 1871, 6 Oct. 1871; vol. 27, Records of the Dress Reform Committee, 1874–6, especially p. 20; Folder 13, the Annual Meeting of the New England Women's Club, for 1869; for 1873, especially p. 11. Box 8, Folder 14, Secretary's Annual Reports, 1885–98: 1885, pp. 11–12; 1886, pp. 6–9; 1887, pp. 3–4, 14–15; 1888, pp. 5, 13–14; 1890, pp. 2, 5; Folder 23, Committee on Work, 1868–99, 1868 report. See also Buhle, *Women and American Socialism*, p. 57; Solomon, *In the Company of Educated Women*, p. 51; HWS, vol. III, p. 287; Blair, *The Clubwoman*, pp. 32–6.

162. See Blair, *The Clubwoman*, ch. 1 and p. 27 on the boldness of American club women's commitment to cultural improvement; Croly, *The History of the Woman's Club Movement*, pp. 201–8 indicates how few and late-coming English clubs were; *Englishwoman's Review*, no. 10, April 1872, 'Letter from the New England Women's Club to the English Women's Association and gatherings', pp. 100–2, see also p. 145; no. 10, October 1872, p. 311; no. 7, July 1871, pp. 183–8; vol. VIII, no. l, 15 June 1877, article on 'Sorosis, the New York women's club', pp. 246–51; see also pp. 281, 507; HWS, vol. III, pp. 928, 942, 947 (source of second quotation); Harper, *Life and Work of Susan B. Anthony*, vol. II, pp. 564 (source of first quotation),

567; Liddington and Norris, *One Hand Tied Behind Us*, pp. 39–41; Estelle Freedman, 'Separation as strategy: female institution building and American feminism', *Feminist Studies*, vol. 5, no. 3, Fall 1979, pp. 51–2.

163. Epstein, *The Politics of Domesticity*, pp. 95–100, on the crusade of 1873–4; also Ruth Bordin, ' "A baptism of power and liberty": the women's crusade of 1873–1874', *Ohio History*, vol. 87, Autumn 1978, pp. 393–404; Jack Blocker, *'Give to the Winds Thy Fears'*: *The women's temperance crusade* (Westport, CT, Greenwood Press, 1985).

164. See Annie Wittenmyer, *History of the Woman's Temperance Crusade* (Boston, MA, James H. Earle, 1882); Mary Earhart, *Frances Willard: From prayer to politics* (Chicago, University of Chicago Press, 1944), chs IX–X; Blocker, *'Give to the Winds Thy Fears'*, 'Aftermath and Effects'.

165. I am indebted here to Epstein, *Politics of Domesticity*, ch. 5 (second quotation from p. 118); and Buhle, *Women and American Socialism*, pp. 60–9 (first quotation from p. 65). The figures about WCTU support are from Epstein, pp. 119–20, and from Lerner, *Teaching Women's History*, p. 49, which gives a useful brief summary of WCTU operations. See also Earhart, *Frances Willard*, chs XI–XVIII; Ruth Bordin, *Women and Temperance* (Philadelphia, PA, Temple University Press, 1981); Norman Clark, *Deliver Us From Evil* (New York, Norton, 1976); Frances E. Willard, *Glimpses of Fifty Years: The autobiography of an American woman* (Chicago, H.J. Smith & Co., 1889), pp. 370 f.; Willard, *My Happy Half-Century: The autobiography of an American woman* (London, Ward, Leck & Bourden, 1894), pp. 386, 388, 390; Willard, *Home Protection Manual* (New York, 1879), pp. 4, 26; Joseph Gusfield, *State Politics and the Temperance Movement* (Urbana, University of Illinois Press, 1966); Anna A. Gordon, *The Beautiful Life of Frances E. Willard* (London, Sampson, Low, Marston & Co., 1898), chs VIII–IX.

166. Epstein, *Politics of Domesticity*, pp. 132–7, 146 f.

167. Buechler, *The Transformation of the Woman Suffrage Movement*, pp. 117–21; Flexner, *Century of Struggle*, p. 189.

168. See Epstein, *Politics of Domesticity*, pp. 120, 124–5.

169. *Ibid.*, pp. 122, 137 f.; Buhle, *Women and American Socialism*, pp. 80–1.

170. Paulson, *Women's Suffrage and Prohibition*, pp. 114–15.

171. The information contained in this paragraph is largely drawn from Lillian Shiman, ' "Changes are dangerous": women and temperance in Victorian England', in Malmgreen (ed.), *Religion in the Lives of English Women*, pp. 200–11 (quotation from p. 206); and Shiman, *Crusade Against Drink in Victorian England* (London, Macmillan, 1988), pp. 105–6, 182–8; and Shiman, *Women and Leadership*, pp. 151–60.

172. Willard, *Glimpses of Fifty Years*, pp. 412, 433.

173. *Englishwoman's Review*, vol. VIII, no. 46, 15 February 1877, 'Influence of women on temperance', by H.B. Taylor, pp. 54–5, 57. Shiman, *Women and Leadership*, p. 160; Shiman, *Crusade against Drink*, pp. 208–9.

174. *Englishwoman's Review*, vol. VIII, no. 45, 15 January 1877, 'Dress for women, or women for dress', by Elizabeth P. Ramsey, pp. 1–9; Woody, *A History of Women's Education in the United States*, vol. II, pp. 98, 101 f., 116 f.; Leach, *True Love and Perfect Union*, pp. 256–7.

175. See Prochaska, *Women and Philanthropy in Nineteenth-Century England*, pp. 129–33, 175–81 on Hill and Twining; Hollis, *Ladies Elect*, pp. 8, 13–14, 20–5 on the Charity Organization Society; and on the Salvation Army, Hollis (ed.), *Women in Public*, pp. 223, 263–4; Shiman, *Woman and Leadership*, pp. 100–1.

176. S.J. Kleinberg, *Women in American Society* (BAAS pamphlet, 1990), p. 30; Alice Kessler-Harris, *Out to Work: A history of wage-earning women in the United States* (Oxford, Oxford University Press, 1982); Sarah Boston, *Women Workers and the Trade Union Movement* (London, Davis-Poynter, 1980); Norbert C. Soldon, *Women in British Trade Unions, 1874–1976* (Dublin, Gill & Macmillan, 1978); S. Lewenhak, *Women and Trade Unions* (London, Ernest Benn, 1977); Shelley Pennington and Belinda Westover, *A Hidden Workforce: Women homeworkers in Britain, 1850–1985* (London, Macmillan, 1985); Rendall, *Women in an Industrializing Society*, ch. 3; Eleanor Gordon, *Women and the Labour Market in Scotland, 1850–1914* (Oxford, Clarendon Press, 1991); Judy Lown, *With Free and Graceful Step?: Women and industrialization in nineteenth-century England* (Oxford, Polity, 1987).

177. Hollis, *Ladies Elect*, pp. 2, 6–7, 25–7; Levine, *Victorian Feminism*, pp. 90–1; I. Grant, *The National Council of Women: The first sixty years, 1895–1955* (London, 1955).

178. See Gladys Boone, *The Women's Trade Union League in Great Britain and the United States of America* (New York, Columbia University Press, 1942), p. 63; Harold Goldman, *Emma Paterson: She led women into a man's world* (London, Lawrence & Wishart, 1974).

179. Paterson, quoted in Hollis (ed.), *Women in Public*, p. 109.

180. *Ibid.*, pp. 50–1 (source of quotation); see also Lucy Middleton (ed.), *Women in the Labour Movement* (London, Croom Helm and Totowa, NJ, Rowman & Littlefield, 1977), article on 'Early years in the trade unions' by Dame Anne Godwin, pp. 94–5.

181. Godwin, 'Early years in the trade unions', p. 95.

182. Levine, *Victorian Feminism*, pp. 112–15; Godwin, 'Early years in the trade unions', pp. 96–7; Liddington and Norris, *One Hand Tied Behind Us*, p. 38.

183. Godwin, 'Early years in the trade unions', p. 96; A. Stafford, *A Match to Fire the Thames* (London, Hodder & Stoughton, 1961); Taylor, *Annie Besant*.

184. Levine, *Victorian Feminism*, pp. 118–23, and Shanley, *Feminism, Marriage, and the Law*, pp. 94–102, for a full discussion of this issue, to which I am indebted here; Hollis (ed.), *Women in Public*, pp. 46–8, 51–2; Jane M.E. Brownlow, *Women and Factory Legislation* (Congleton, Women's Emancipation Union, 1896); Angela John, *By the Sweat of Their Brow: Women workers at Victorian coal mines* (London, Routledge & Kegan Paul, 1984); Caine, *Victorian Feminists*, pp. 243–8.

185. See Catherine Webb, *The Woman with the Basket: The history of the Women's Co-operative Guild, 1883–1927* (Manchester, Co-operative Wholesale Printing Works, 1927); Jean Gaffin, 'Women and co-operation', in Middleton (ed.), *Women in the Labour Movement*, pp. 113–42; Margaret Llewelyn Davies, *Women's Co-operative Guild, 1883–1904* (Kirkby Lonsdale, Co-operative Women's Guild, 1904); Hollis (ed.), *Women in Public*, pp. 228–9; Levine, *Victorian Feminism*, p. 117; Lewis, *Women in England*, pp. 50–1 and *passim*; Liddington and Norris, *One Hand Tied Behind Us*, pp. 41–2; P.N. Blackstrom, *Christian Socialism and Cooperation in Victorian England* (London, Croom Helm, 1974); 'Co-operation as a substitute for Socialism', Box 5, vol. 18, New England Women's Club Records, SL; J. Gaffin and D. Thoms, *Caring and Sharing: The centenary history of the Co-operative Women's Guild* (Manchester, Co-operative Union, 1983).

186. Buhle, *Women and American Socialism*, p. 73.

187. *Ibid.*, ch. 1 and pp. 71–3 (quotations from p. 11).

188. *Ibid.*, pp. 73–82.

189. Flexner, *Century of Struggle*, pp. 198–205; Dolores Janiewski, *Sisterhood Denied: Race,*

gender and class in a New South community (Philadelphia, PA, Temple University Press, 1985), pp. 18–21, 69, 85.

190. Buhle, *Women and American Socialism*, pp. 82–4; Julie Roy Jeffrey, 'Women in the southern Farmers' Alliance: a reconsideration of the role and status of women in the late nineteenth-century South', *Feminist Studies*, vol. 3, Fall 1975, pp. 677–81; Janiewski, *Sisterhood Denied*, pp. 18–21.

191. See Frances Elizabeth Hoggan, 'Women in medicine', in Stanton (ed.), *The Woman Question in Europe*, p. 88; Blair, *The Clubwoman*, pp. 39 f.; Leach, *True Love and Perfect Union*, pp. 185–9, on the Association for the Advancement of American Women: and p. 167 on occupational gains by middle-class women; Boylan, 'Evangelical womanhood', pp. 73–5; Reuther and Keller (eds), *Women and Religion in America*, p. xii and chs 5 and 6 (by Barbara Brown Zikmund and Rosemary Skinner Keller respectively); Holcombe, *Women at Work*, pp. 18–19 and *passim*.

192. Harper, *Life and Work of Susan B. Anthony*, vol. II, p. 564; W.L. Twining, 'Laws', in Thompson (ed.), *The University of London*, p. 96; Prelinger, 'The female diaconate', in Malmgreen (ed.), *Religion in the Lives of English Women*, pp. 161–92; and Brian Heeney, *The Women's Movement in the Church of England, 1850–1930* (Oxford, Clarendon Press, 1988), Parts One and Two.

193. Levine, *Victorian Feminism*, pp. 91–2.

194. Jessie Boucherett, 'The industrial movement', in Stanton (ed.), *The Woman Question in Europe*, p. 104.

195. HWS, vol. III, p. 923; Harper, *The Life and Work of Susan B. Anthony*, vol. II, p. 577; Fawcett, 'The women's suffrage movement', in Stanton (ed.), *The Woman Question in Europe*, p. 6; 'Three decades of progress', *Englishwoman's Review*, vol. X, no. 44, 15 August 1878, p. 338.

196. 'Friends in America', in *Englishwoman's Review*, vol. XI, July 1872, p. 191.

197. Fawcett, 'The women's suffrage movement', pp. 23–4.

198. 'The thin end of the wedge', in *Englishwoman's Review*, vol. VIII, no. 55, 15 November 1877, p. 485; HWS, vol. III, p. 864 (source of second quotation).

199. See Levine, *Victorian Feminism*, pp. 66–9; Leach, *True Love and Perfect Union*, pp. 153–7 and *passim*, quotation from pp. 156–7. Caine in *Victorian Feminists*, pp. 46–9 notes how Victorian feminists criticised Comte and his leading English disciple, Frederick Harrison, but adapted 'the framework of their opponents and operated within it'.

Chapter 5　The women's movements in maturity

1. Rosenberg, *Beyond Separate Spheres*, p. 207 and *passim* (source of quotation); Cott, *Grounding*, ch. 1; on the need to give greater consideration to feminism and bureaucracy, see Vivien Hart's excellent article 'Feminism, and bureaucracy: the minimum wage experiment in the district of Columbia', *Journal of American Studies*, vol. 26, no. 1, April 1992, pp. 1–22, especially pp. 19–20.

2. On the belief that suffragism would make no real headway until it became a government question, see Lady Frances Balfour to Mrs Henry Fawcett, 7 Dec. 1891, Autograph Letter Collection, FL.

3. Document of 1894, headed 'Dr. Jacobi', in Folder 32, Mary Putman Jacobi

~

Papers, SL; article on 'The growth of women's suffrage in the United States', *Englishwoman's Review*, vol. XXVIII, no. 233, 15 April 1897, pp. 76–7, on American problems; Kraditor, *The Ideas of the Woman Suffrage Movement*, pp. 230–1.

4. Shiman, *Women and Leadership*, chs 12–13; Linda Walker, 'Party political women: a comparative study of Liberal women and the Primrose League, 1890–1914', in Rendall (ed.), *Equal or Different*, pp. 165–91; David Rubinstein, *Before the Suffragettes: Women's emancipation in the 1890's* (Brighton, Harvester, 1986), pp. 140–7.

5. Rubinstein, *Before the Suffragettes*, pp. 147–58 (quotation from p. 153).

6. *Ibid.*, ch. 10, especially p. 167; Hollis, *Ladies Elect*, p. 305 (source of quotation).

7. Rubinstein, *Before the Suffragettes*, p. 169.

8. Hollis, *Ladies Elect*, p. 391.

9. *Ibid.*, pp. 318 f. and *passim*.

10. *Ibid.*, p. 353.

11. Rubinstein, *Before the Suffragettes*, p. 177; and see letter of Lady Frances Balfour to Mrs Fawcett, June 1899, confiding that at the bottom of opposition to the London Government Bill including women was 'the deepest hostility to the suffrage'; see also Balfour to Fawcett, 7 July 1901: both in Autograph Letter Collection, Women's Movement Section, FL.

12. Martin Pugh, *Women's Suffrage in Britain, 1867–1928* (London, Historical Association, 1980), p. 13; letter to Miss Strachey from Mrs Isobel Abbott, 27 Oct. 1912, in Autograph Letter Collection, FL, on the connection between a good showing in local government and 'the suffrage cause'.

13. Rubinstein, *Before the Suffragettes*, p. 171 (source of quotation); Hollis, *Ladies Elect*, p. 471; Mary Drake McFeely, *Lady Inspector: The campaign for a better workplace, 1893–1921* (Oxford, Blackwell, 1988).

14. Rubinstein, *Before the Suffragettes*, p. 176.

15. Hollis, *Ladies Elect*, pp. 392, 398, 401 (source of quotation) and ch. 8 generally; pp. 422–3 and ch. 9 generally, p. 491; Fawcett, *Women's Suffrage*, pp. 49–50.

16. Hollis, *Ladies Elect*, ch. 10 (quotation from pp. 472–3).

17. Rover, *Women's Suffrage and Party Politics*, pp. 6, 21, 56; Middleton (ed.), *Women in the Labour Movement*, article by Margherita Rendel, p. 59; Les Garner, *Stepping Stones to Women's Liberty: Feminist ideas in the women's suffrage movement, 1900–1919* (London, Heinemann, 1984), chs 2–4, 6.

18. Rover, *Women's Suffrage and Party Politics*, pp. 65, 95, 194–5; Duncan Crow, *The Edwardian Woman* (London, George Allen & Unwin, 1978), ch. 13; Rubinstein, *Before the Suffragettes*, ch. 9; Brian Harrison, 'Women's suffrage at Westminster 1866–1928', in M. Bentley and J. Stevenson (eds), *High and Low Politics in Modern Britain* (Oxford, Clarendon, 1983), pp. 80–122.

19. Leslie P. Hume, *The National Union of Women's Suffrage Societies, 1897–1914* (New York and London, Garland Publishing Inc., 1982): see ch. 1; Diane Atkinson, *Votes for Women* (Cambridge, Cambridge University Press, 1988); Lisa Tickner, *Spectacle of Women: Images of the suffrage campaign* (London, Chatto & Windus, 1989); Sandra Holton, *Feminism and Democracy: Women's suffrage and reform politics in Britain, 1900–1918* (Cambridge, Cambridge University Press, 1986), pp. 6–7 (source of quotations); Garner, *Stepping Stones*, ch. 2; letter of Mrs Edith Zangwill to the NUWSS, 7 Nov. 1909, Autograph Letter Collection, FL, on the necessity for '*all* the suffrage societies'.

~

20. Hume, *The National Union*, 'Preface'.

21. *Ibid.*, pp. 16–17, 26–8, 36–7, 39, 40 and ch. VI; Holton, *Feminism and Democracy*, ch. 2 and *passim*; amended Constitution of the NUWSS, agreed 19 Mar. 1910, pp. 6–8, in Autograph Letter Collection, FL.

22. Hume, *The National Union*, pp. 7 f., 41–2, 59, 177–8; Strachey, *The Cause*, pp. 307–9; Brian Harrison, *Prudent Revolutionaries: Portraits of British feminists between the wars* (Oxford, Clarendon Press, 1987), ch. 1; David Rubinstein, *A Different World for Women: The life of Millicent Garrett Fawcett* (Hemel Hempstead, Harvester Wheatsheaf, 1991). Developments outside England had been reported in the *Women's Suffrage Journal*; see also Murphy, *The Woman's Suffrage Movement and Irish Society*; letter of 20 July [?] 1905, from Mrs Josephine Davies to Miss Palliser (on Wales) in Autograph Letter Collection, FL: and, in *ibid.*, letter from Lady Frances Balfour to Mrs Fawcett, 16 Dec. 1899; Lady Frances Balfour to Mrs Fawcett, 13 Nov. 1909, on Wales's 'rather stony soil'; Mrs A.M. Haslam to Miss P. Strachey, 21 Nov. 1909, on the work in Ireland; Dr Elsie Inglis of the Scottish Federation of Women's Suffrage Societies, to Miss Strachey, 10 Aug. 1913, in the Women's Suffrage section of the Collection. And see Tickner, *Spectacle of Women*, on the campaigns.

23. Hulme, *The National Union*, pp. 17–20, 141–2, 145 (source of quotation), 152, 155, 160, 195, 203–4, 210, 214; and M. Pugh, 'Labour and women's suffrage', in K.D. Brown (ed.), *The First Labour Party, 1906–14* (London, Croom Helm, 1985); Holton, *Feminism and Democracy*, ch. 3–4. The NUWSS drew the line, however, at advocating trade-union principles: see Miss P. Strachey to W. Rintoul, 19 July 1910, in Autograph Letter Collection, FL; and in the Women's Suffrage section of the collection, see letter of Miss K.D. Courtney, 6 Aug. 1913, carefully explaining the political stance of the NUWSS.

24. Hume, *The National Union*, pp. 18, 194; David Morgan, 'Women's suffrage in Britain and America in the early twentieth century', p. 282, in H.C. Allen and Roger Thompson (eds), *Contrast and Connection: Bicentennial essays in Anglo-American history* (London, Bell, 1976); Holton, *Feminism and Democracy*, ch. 1; Garner, *Stepping Stones*, p. 27.

25. Andrew Rosen, *Rise Up, Women! The militant campaign of the Women's Social and Political Union, 1903–1914* (London, Routledge & Kegan Paul, 1974), chs 2–3 (second quotation from p. 29); Strachey, *The Cause*, pp. 291–3; Sylvia Pankhurst, *The Suffragette Movement* (London, Virago, 1977, originally published 1931), Book IV, ch. 11, Book V, ch. 1; Harrison, *Prudent Revolutionaries*, ch. 1; David Mitchell, *The Fighting Pankhursts: A study in tenacity* (London, Jonathan Cape, 1967); letter of Christabel Pankhurst to Teresa Billington Greig, 4 Oct. 1956, Autograph Letter Collection, FL, for the equation with Mill.

26. Evans, *The Feminists*, p. 190; and for accounts by militants of their imprisonment, see in FL, Autograph Letter Collection, letters of and relating to Myra Sadd Brown and May Billinghurst. The term 'suffragette' was first used by the *Daily Mail* on 10 January 1906, distinguishing militants from moderate or constitutional suffragists.

27. Rosen, *Rise Up, Women!*, pp. 77 (source of second quotation), 53, 76–8, 94, 114–15, 209–12, and chs 4–16; Hume, *The National Union*, ch. II; Strachey, *The Cause*, pp. 293–303; as Strachey in *The Cause*, p. 311 points out, no regular membership records or full accounts were kept by the WSPU; Tickner, *Spectacle of Women*.

28. 'Why women want to vote' (WSPU pamphlet no. 27, London, The Woman's Press, n.d.); Garner, *Stepping Stones*, p. 312.

29. Holton, *Feminism and Democracy*, pp. 31 f., emphasises the symbiotic relationship between the WSPU and the NUWSS. Wright's letter is reprinted (quotation from pp. 77 and 86) in his *The Unexpurgated Case Against Woman Suffrage* (London, Constable, 1913); 'A reassurance', document in Folder 55, Box 9, Alice Morgan Wright Papers, SSC; and in *ibid.*, 'Mrs. Pankhurst talks on suffrage', *Times-Union*, 1 Dec. 1912; Letter from Sylvia Pankhurst to Miss Eleanor Garrison, Woman's Suffrage Union, Boston, 30 April 1912, Folder 1684, Box 57, Garrison Family Collection, SSC. For general assessments of militancy, see Ramelson, *The Petticoat Rebellion*, pp. 132 f.; Rosen, *Rise Up, Women!*, *passim*; Pugh, *Women's Suffrage in Britain*, pp. 23–5 and *passim*; Barbara Bliss, 'Militancy: the insurrection that failed', *Contemporary Review*, vol. 201, June 1962; Brian Harrison, 'The act of militancy: violence and the suffragettes, 1904–14', in his *Peaceable Kingdom: Stability and change in modern Britain* (Oxford, Clarendon, 1982), pp. 26–81.

30. 'Women as race builders' (WSPU pamphlet no. 32), by Emmeline Pethick Lawrence.

31. Emmeline Pankhurst to Miss E. Lloyd Garrison, 18 June 1914, Folder 1684, Box 57, Garrison Family Collection, SSC; Rosen, *Rise Up, Women!*, pp. 2203 f.; Bland, 'Marriage laid bare', pp. 135–8; Jeffreys, *The Spinster and Her Enemies*, pp. 45–6; McLaren, *Birth Control in Nineteenth-Century England*, pp. 198–200, 207; Crow, *The Edwardian Woman*, ch. 14; and in Autograph Letter Collection, FL, Mrs Fawcett to Lady Frances Balfour on the impossibility of a sex war 'as long as mothers have sons and fathers daughters': 5 March 1910.

32. Hume, *The National Union*, pp. 50–1, 59, 79–80; Strachey, *The Cause*, p. 313 (source of fourth quotation). For indications of the mixed responses to militant tactics from as early as 1906, and the problems caused by them, see in Autograph Letter Collection, FL, the following: Sarah Beard King to Miss Palliser, 5 Jan. 1906; G.M. Fullerton to Miss Palliser, 19 Jan. 1906; Helen B. Taylor to Mrs. [sic] Sterling, 15 Jan. 1906; Mrs Pollard to Miss Somerville, 6 June 1906 (source of first quotation); Mrs Edith Kerwood to Miss Stirling, 26 Oct. 1906 (source of second quotation); Laura S. Scott to Miss Palliser, 12 Jan. 1907, on men's superior physical force; Miss Edith Beck to Miss Strachey, 22 Nov. 1907; Miss Lily Redpath to Miss P. Strachey, 14 Nov. 1908, on Mrs Pankhurst's arrogance; Mrs Henry Fawcett to Lady Frances Balfour, 30 June 1909, on the militants' 'intensely moving' physical courage; Mrs Thomas Hardy to NUWSS, 28 Feb. and 9, 13, 14 March 1912, complaining of suffragette conduct and requesting the return of her subscription; Lady Frances Balfour to Mrs Henry Fawcett, 18 Oct. 1910; NUWSS circular letter of 29 June 1910, and report of 16 July 1910; Edith Dimock to Mrs Pethick Lawrence, 18 April 1910; circular to branch secretaries from Miss Marion Phillips, 24 Jan. 1910; Lady Frances Balfour to Mrs Henry Fawcett, 23 Oct. 1909; Philippa Strachey to Mrs A. Cliff, 6.7.14, declining to be drawn on the stance of its members towards such matters as tax resistance, in the Woman's Suffrage section of the Collection; letter from Miss I.O. Ford to Mrs Henry Fawcett, 14 April 1914, on Keir Hardie's alienation from the WSPU.

33. Liddington and Norris, *One Hand Tied Behind Us*, pp. 203–6, 209–10, 211, 218–19; Rosen, *Rise Up, Women!*, p. 70; Harrison, *Prudent Revolutionaries*, ch. 1; letter of Hannah Mitchell to Teresa Billington, 22 July 1856, on the North's importance.

34. Liddington and Norris, *One Hand Tied Behind Us*, p. 2209; Garner, *Stepping Stones*, chs 3–4, and p. 99; Rosen, *Rise Up, Women!*, chs 7, 14, pp. 217–20, 223–4; Harrison, *Prudent Revolutionaries*, pp. 41, 51–7.

35. Hume, *The National Union*, pp. 55, 149–52, 210, 214, 221 and *passim*; Pugh, *Women and the Women's Movement*, p. 5; Ramelson, *The Petticoat Rebellion*, ch. 14; letter of Bessie M. Stead of the Robert Browning Settlement to Miss Bompas, 15 May 1911, in Autograph Letter Collection, FL; and in *ibid.*, Industry Section, letters about getting working women to suffrage meetings, and reaching out to them. The Independent Labur Party (ILP) was formed in 1893; the Labour Representation Committee in 1900; the Labour Party in 1906.

36. James Bryce, *The American Commonwealth*, vol. II, pp. 550, 560–2; Morgan, 'Women suffrage in Britain and America', pp. 281–2, on the liquor and textile interests.

37. See Morgan, *Suffragists and Liberals*, ch. XI and *passim*; Morgan, 'Woman suffrage in Britain and America', p. 278 (source of quotation); Rover, *Woman's Suffrage and Party Politics*, pp. 143–6; Bliss, 'Militancy', suggests that militant tactics delayed the coming of the vote.

38. Harrison, *Separate Spheres*, pp. 71, 84, 93 and *passim*; Sutherland, *Mrs. Humphrey Ward*, pp. 299 f.; Jalland, *Women, Marriage and Politics*, p. 214 (source of first quotation: the others are from Harrison). See in Autograph Letter Collection, FL, Miss Philippa Strachey to Mrs Fawcett, 2 Nov. 1910, on the 'antis': their funds and trying arguments.

39. Evans, *The Feminists*, p. 198.

40. Blatch, *Challenging Years*, pp. 200–1, 204; Morgan, 'Woman suffrage in Britain and America', pp. 278–9.

41. See Susan B. Anthony to Mrs Elizabeth Hunt, 14 May 1900, Folder 1, Bisbee Hunt Collection, SSC.

42. Stefanco, 'Networking on the frontier', pp. 271–3 (quotation from p. 273); Flexner, *Century of Struggle*, pp. 228, 244; Myres, *Westering Women*, pp. 228–30; Paulson, *Women's Suffrage and Prohibition*, pp. 136–7; Mary Ray Peck, *Carrie Chapman Catt* (W.W. Wilson, 1944; reprint edition by Octagon, New York, 1975), pp. 70 f.; Robert Booth Fowler, *Carrie Catt, Feminist Politician* (Boston, MA, Northeastern University Press, 1986), ch. 1; HWS, vol. IV, ch. XXXVI, XXIX.

43. Letter of Carrie Chapman Catt to Catharine McCulloch, p. 6, complaining about Duniway, in Folder 21, Box 2, CGW McCulloch Papers, SL; see Duniway, *Path Breaking*, pp. 100–2, 201–7, 209–11, 228, in which she deplores the link between Prohibition and suffrage.

44. Article by Harriet Mills in the *Woman's Journal*, 5 December 1896.

45. *Woman's Journal*, 23 May 1896, p. 164; 26 September 1896, p. 308; 7 November 1896, p. 356 (source of quotations); see, on the California campaign of 1896, Christine Bolt, 'The less privileged half: women's suffrage, temperance and the women's movement – and the case of California', in Alec Barbrook and Christine Bolt, *Power and Protest in American Life* (Oxford and New York, Martin Robertson and St Martin's Press, 1980), pp. 178–86.

46. See, for instance, *Woman's Journal*, 7 November 1896, p. 356; 25 January 1896, p. 32. See also HWS, vol. IV, p. 493.

47. On Illinois, see Buechler, *The Transformation of the Woman Suffrage Movement*, p. 178 (source of quotation); HWS, vol. VI.

48. Flexner, *Century of Struggle*, pp. 270–1; Myres, *Westering Women*, p. 233.
49. On Illinois, see Buechler, *The Transformation of the Woman Suffrage Movement*, ch. 5; on Washington, see Flexner, *Century of Struggle*, p. 263; on Socialist support for suffrage in the West, see Buhle, *Women and American Socialism*, p. 230; see also document 'written at request of Senator Richard J. Barr', etc., pp. 2–5, Folder 36, Box 3, C.G.W. McCulloch Papers, SL; and Myres, *Westering Women*, p. 230.
50. See Bolt, 'The less privileged half', pp. 186–94; details of California campaign in Folder 105, Box 7, Harriet Wright Burton Laidlaw Papers, SL.
51. Myres, *Westering Women*, pp. 232–7; Buechler, *The Transformation of the Woman Suffrage Movement*, p. 223; and 'Autobiography', Catharine G. Waugh McCulloch, pp. 3–5 on work in Illinois: C.G.W. McCulloch Papers, SL, Box 2, Folder 17.
52. See, for instance, Griffith, *In Her Own Right*, pp. 193 f.
53. Flexner, *Century of Struggle*, pp. 226–8; Buechler, *The Transformation of the Woman Suffrage Movement*, pp. 224–5.
54. See Bolt, 'The less privileged half', p. 189; Myres, *Westering Women*, p. 237; Duniway, *Path Breaking*, pp. 209–11, for the view that 'every locality is its own best interpreter of its own plans to work'.
55. Flexner, *Century of Struggle*, pp. 244–7, 25, 6–7, 266; HWS, vol. V, pp. 678–9; Peck, *Carrie Chapman Catt*, pp. 95–102; Fowler, *Carrie Catt*, pp. 17–28 (quotations from pp. 25, 28). For concern about the 'antis', see for instance, four-page document headed 'Objections' in Folder 103, Box 7, Harriet W. Laidlaw Papers, SL; letters of 25 March and 17 April 1902 by Catharine McCulloch in Box 2, Folder 23, C.G.W. McCulloch Papers, SL.
56. Scott, *The Southern Lady*, pp. 176–84 (quotations from pp. 176, 177).
57. Aileen S. Kraditor, *The Ideas of the Woman Suffrage Movement, 1890–1920* (New York and London, W.W. Norton, 1981), pp. 165–6, on the 'states' rights' policy of NAWSA; see also p. 173.
58. The Shafroth–Palmer Amendment would have required any state to hold a referendum on women's suffrage once 8 per cent of its voters had signed an initiative proposal at an election requesting such a test: it was rejected by NAWSA after almost a year of uneasy support. See, in Somerville–Howorth Family Papers, SL, Folder 58, Report of the Organization of the Mississippi Woman Suffrage Association, Meridian, Mississippi, 5 May 1897 (source of first quotation); Minutes of the Second Annual Convention of the Mississippi Woman Suffrage Association (1899), pp. 13–14, 16–17, 20; Minutes of the Sixth Annual Report of the Mississippi Woman Suffrage Association (1910), pp. 13 (source of the second quotation), 20–22; Minutes of the Fifth Annual Report of the Mississippi Woman Suffrage Association (1909), pp. 19–20; Minutes of the Eighth Annual Report of the Mississippi Woman Suffrage Association (1912), pp. 18–19.
59. Minutes of the Ninth Annual Report of the Mississippi Woman Suffrage Association (1913), quoting Senator John Williams (source of the third quotation); Minutes of the Eleventh Annual Report of the Mississippi Woman Suffrage Association, p. 5, in *ibid*.
60. Scott, *The Southern Lady*, p. 182.
61. Kraditor, *The Ideas of the Woman Suffrage Movement*, p. 165, and see ch. 2 generally, where it is pointed out that this argument began in 1867 with Henry B. Blackwell, Massachusetts abolitionist husband of Lucy Stone.
62. McCulloch's letter to Laura Clay, 10 Dec. 1907, is in Folder 27, Box 2 of C.G.W.

McCulloch Papers, SL; Kraditor, *The Ideas of the Woman Suffrage Movement*, ch. 6; HWS, vol. IV, pp. 182–3, 246. See also Cott, *Grounding*, pp. 31–2.

63. *Woman's Journal*, 1 August 1896, p. 248.

64. Henry B. Blackwell to Catharine McCulloch, 18 Dec. 1906, Folder 26, Box 2, C.G.W. McCulloch Papers, SL; HWS, vol. IV, pp. 280–2, vol. V, p. 495: see also documents in Folders 25 and 26, Box 2, McCulloch Papers, on the work involved in a drive for municipal suffrage.

65. *Woman's Journal*, 1 August 1896, p. 248; for Blackwell, see Note 64; also Kraditor, *The Ideas of the Woman Suffrage Movement*, ch. 8.

66. HWS, vol. V, pp. 10, 18, 195–6, 207, 392, 551, 602, 632 on municipal suffrage; Peck, *Carrie Chapman Catt*, pp. 171–3; see Degler, *At Odds*, pp. 357, 359; HWS, vol. V, p. 46 (source of first quotation); Bryce, *The American Commonwealth*, vol. II, p. 556 (source of second quotation); and for favourable comments on women in equal suffrage states see, for instance, Duniway, *Path Breaking*, pp. 124–5; 'Status and future of the woman suffrage movement' (1902), p. 407, Folder 34, Mary Putnam Jacobi Papers, SL; Catharine McCulloch to Editor, *Record-Herald*, 17 April 1902, Folder 23, Box 2, C.G.W. McCulloch Papers, SL; a NAWSA leaflet on conditions in Arizona, California, Colorado, Idaho, Illinois, Kansas, Oregon, Utah, Washington and Wyoming, 1913, in Folder 117, Box 7, Harriet W. Laidlaw Papers, SL; an official document on Wyoming, 1901, on how women's suffrage had worked out, sent to the press and the legislatures in every state and territory, PK82, in Alice Locke Park Collection, Henry E. Huntington Library; and HWS, vol. IV, Appendix, 'Testimony from woman suffrage states'.

67. Jessie Ackerman, *What Women Have Done with the Vote* (New York, W.B. Feakins, 1913), looking at Australia, New Zealand, China, Finland and Norway, came to broadly optimistic conclusions, though noting (pp. 68–9, with qualifications) an increase in the numbers of insane females since women had the vote in Norway! See especially pp. 20, 31, 38, 52, 57, 71–2, 74, 85–6. The best brief account of the views of the 'antis' is by Kraditor, *The Ideas of the Woman Suffrage Movement*, ch. 2.

68. *Equal Suffrage: The results of an investigation in Colorado made for the Collegiate Equal Suffrage League of the New York State* (New York and London, Harper & Brothers, 1909), pp. ix, xiii; 258–9 (quotation from p. 259); letter from Miss M. Sheepshanks to Miss Alice Park, n.d., asking for details of how the vote was used in California, for use in *Jus Suffragii*, since it was always being cited by suffragists and antis, in Autograph Letter Collection, F.L.; Bolt, 'The less privileged half', p. 193 (source of second and third quotations).

69. O'Neill, *Everyone Was Brave*, pp. 47–8 and *passim*; Paulson, *Women's Suffrage and Prohibition*, pp. 141–2.

70. Buechler, *The Transformation of the Woman Suffrage Movement*, pp. 185–6, 202; Bolt, 'The less privileged half', pp. 189–90; Flexner, *Century of Struggle*, p. 223.

71. Kraditor, *The Ideas of the Woman Suffrage Movement*, pp. 44–5 and *passim*.

72. Buechler, *The Transformation of the Woman Suffrage Movement*, pp. 171, 196, 201.

73. Janet Giele, 'Social change in the feminine role: a comparison of woman's suffrage and woman's temperance, 1870–1920', PhD thesis, Radcliffe Collegiate, 1961, quoted in Degler, *At Odds*, p. 348.

74. See Buechler, *The Transformation of the Woman Suffrage Movement*, pp. 200, 226–7; Buhle, *Women and American Socialism*, p. 219, notes that appeals to America's natural rights tradition in arguing for female suffrage were popular 'Especially in the

Midwest ... well into the twentieth century', and were used by 'both mainstream suffragists and Socialists'; see also p. 229 on the opposition of Socialists to 'restrictive bills carrying literacy, property, or nativity requirements'. Bolt, 'The less privileged half', pp. 183–4, 190–1, 193–4, 347–8 on the efforts of suffragists in California, where non-whites and immigrants were an important factor, to surmount racism and elitism; and on the Progressive politics of some of them and the wide range of arguments they used for the vote see, for instance, 'Justice of the Negro', 1803 article in Box 14, Caroline Severance Collection, Henry E. Huntington Library; and in *ibid.*, Box 21, letter from Lucy Moore, 11 March 1900; and in Box 24, letter from Booker T. Washington, 5 March 1902, thanking Severance for 'expressing interest in our work and in the general cause of our people'.

75. Quoted in *Woman's Journal*, 3 June 1911, p. 175.

76. Jacobi, 'Status and future of the woman suffrage movement' (1902) Folder 34, Mary Putnam Jacobi Papers, SL; James P. Louis, 'Sue Shelton White and the woman suffrage movement', *Tennessee Historical Quarterly*, vol. XXIII, no. 2, June 1963, p. 177; 'Woman's wages' (1888), p. 54, Folder 7, Box 1, in C.G.W. McCulloch Papers, SL; and in *ibid.*, letter by McCulloch of the Illinois Equal Suffrage Association, 20 Nov. 1902, Box 2, Folder 23; Nathan quoted in Lagemann, *A Generation of Women*, p. 53; Duniway, *Path Breaking*, pp. 159–62, 164–6, 177–8. Fowler, *Carrie Catt*, p. 71 and ch. 4 generally.

77. See letter by Dewson from Chateau Frontenac, Quebec, Feb. 1912, Folder 1, Mary Williams Dewson Papers, SL.

78. See Elizabeth Fox-Genovese, *Feminism Without Illusions*; Buhle, *Women and American Socialism*, pp. 219–21; Cott, *Grounding*, pp. 30–2.

79. See Ruth Freeman Claus, 'Militancy: the English and American woman suffrage movements', PhD thesis, Yale University, 1975; Antonia Raeburn, *The Militant Suffragettes* (London, Michael Joseph, 1973), pp. 125–6, 216–17; Harriet Stanton Blatch and Alma Lutz, *Challenging Years: The memoirs of Harriet Stanton Blatch* (New York, G.P. Putnam's Sons, 1940), pp. 77, 92–3, 109, 113–15, 137–8, 198–9, 222–3, and 240; see also HWS, vol. V, p. xx; Peck, *Carrie Chapman Catt*, p. 170; and Strachey, *The Cause*, p. 333 (source of last quotation); and Robert Huff's interesting article, 'Anne Miller and the Geneva Political Equality Club, 1897–1912', *New York History*, vol. 65, no. 4, Oct. 1984, especially pp. 329–40; Tickner, *Spectacle of Women*, pp. 266–7.

80. Catt, quoted in Peck, *Carrie Chapman Catt*, pp. 152, 159, 210; see also pp. 162, 165–6, 168, 204, in which Catt says of the English militants: ' "Window-breaking is too much like hooliganism!" '

81. HWS, vol. IV, pp. 237–8, 280, 330–1 (quotation from p. 238).

82. *Ibid.*, pp. 377–8; Kraditor, *The Ideas of the Woman Suffrage Movement*, pp. 279–80.

83. Flexner, *Century of Struggle*, p. 274 (second quotation); Blatch, *Challenging Years*, p. 195 (first quotation).

84. HWS, vol. IV, p. 378.

85. Carrie Chapman Catt, *Woman Suffrage and Politics: The inner story of the suffrage movement* (New York, Charles Scribner's Sons, 1923), p. 245 (source of quotation); Flexner, *Century of Struggle*, pp. 272–6; HWS, vol. IV, pp. 3678–81; Stanton and Blatch, *Challenging Years*, pp. 196–7; Cott, *Grounding*, pp. 53 f.; E.C. DuBois, 'Working women, class relations and suffrage militance', in DuBois and Ruiz (eds), *Unequal Sisters*, pp. 176–94.

86. See 'Twenty-five answers to antis', p. 40, in Folder 4, Box 4, Ethel Eyer Valentine

~

Dreier Collection, SSC; HWS, vol. V, p. xv; Blatch, *Challenging Years*, pp. 137–8, 199–205; Halévy, *The Rule of Democracy*, Book II, p. 437, describes militancy as 'a distinctive form of anarchy specifically English'; see letter from Susan B. Anthony to Mrs Henry Fawcett, 14 May 1890, Autograph Letter Collection, FL, for expressions of affection for British suffragists, and vice versa; and in *ibid.*, E. Lyttelton [Hon. Mrs Alfred] to Miss Palliser, 15 June 1907, on happiness to use a visiting American as a speaker.

87. Elnora Monroe Babcock to Catharine McCulloch, 22 June 1906, Folder 25, Box 2, C.G.W. McCulloch Papers, SL; Alice Stone Blackwell speaking at the New England Women's Club, 22 April 1901, vol. 13 of the Recording Secretary, Box 4, New England Women's Club Records, SL; Peck, *Carrie Chapman Catt*, pp. 166–8.

88. *The Federation Bulletin*, vol. V, no. 9, June 1908, p. 280, comment by Helen M. Winslow; HWS, vol. V, p. 281; letter headed 'A reassurance' (second quotation), in Folder 55, Box 9, Alice Morgan Wright Papers, SSC; Raeburn, *The Militant Suffragettes*, p. 131.

89. 'To the Editor', draft letter by Morgan in Folder 73, Box 9, Alice Morgan Wright Papers, SSC; also in Folder 55 in *ibid.*, press clipping 'Miss Wright tells of British Jail'; and H.B. Stowe to S. and J. Parton, 1869, Folder 29, Parton Papers, SSC.

90. Bolt, 'The less privileged half', p. 192.

91. See undated fragment of the Illinois Equal Suffrage Association in Folder 36, Box 3, C.G.W. McCulloch Collection, SL, for a view from outside the West.

92. See S.L. Avery to C. Severance, 21 Feb., Box 14, Caroline Severance Collection, Henry E. Huntington Library; Georgia Ferguson to Caroline Severance, 16 Feb., 1912, Box 16, in *ibid*; Alice Lock Parke Biography, pp. 25–6, Box 8, Alice Park Collection, Henry E. Huntington Library.

93. *The Reply: An Anti-Suffrage Magazine*, May 1913, vol. 1, no. 1: Editorial; article on suffrage defeat in Michigan, p. 5; and another condemnation of English militancy, pp. 20–1.

94. See letter to Albert Boyden from Ida Tarbell, 23 Aug. 1912, Folder 5, Ida Tarbell Collection, SSC.

95. See Norbert C. Soldon, 'British women and trade unionism: the first hundred years', in Soldon (ed.) *The World of Women's Trade Unionism*, pp. 12–15; Sonya O. Rose, *Limited Livelihoods: Gender and class in nineteenth-century England* (London, Routledge, 1992); Eleanor Gordon and Esther Breitenbach (eds), *The World is Ill Divided: Women's work in Scotland in the nineteenth and early twentieth centuries* (Edinburgh, Edinburgh University Press, 1991); Lown, *With Free and Graceful Step*; Eleanor Gordon, *Women and the Labour Movement in Scotland, 1850–1914* (Oxford, Clarendon Press, 1991); Barbara Drake, *Women in Trade Unions* (London, Virago, 1984); (first quotation) Frances Power Cobbe, *The Duties of Women: A course of lectures* (London, Williams & Norgate, 1888), p. 188; (second quotation) Margaret Llewelyn Davies (ed.), *Life as We Have Known It: Co-operative women* (London, Virago, 1977; originally published 1931), p. 49.

96. Middleton (ed.), *Women in the Labour Movement*, article by Lucy Middleton, pp. 24–30; Gordon, *Women in the Labour Movement*, pp. 265–6.

97. Middleton (ed.), *Women in the Labour Movement*, p. 40; article by Sheila Ferguson.

98. Hollis, *Ladies Elect*, pp. 66–7; Middleton (ed.), *Women in the Labour Movement*, article by Lucy Middleton, pp. 28–9, 31; and pp. 40–55, article by Sheila Ferguson.

99. Middleton (ed.), *Women in the Labour Movement*, article by Margherita Rendel, pp. 57–82. See also Liddington and Norris, *One Hand Tied Behind Us*, p. 236.

100. Rubinstein, *Before the Suffragettes*, pp. 125, 129 (source of quotation), 118–22; Boone, *The Women's Trade Union Leagues in Great Britain and the United States* (New York, Columbia University Press, 1942), pp. 28 f.; Drake, *Women in Trade Unions*.

101. Middleton (ed.), *Women in the Labour Movement*, p. 98; Boone, *The Women's Trade Union Leagues*, p. 30, notes that in two years over 16,000 members joined the League; Rubinstein, *Before the Suffragettes*, pp. 123–7; Soldon, 'British women and trade unionism', p. 16; Gordon, *Women and the Labour Movement*, pp. 224–35.

102. Boone, *The Women's Trade Union Leagues*, pp. 167–8, 265.

103. Middleton (ed.), *Women in the Labour Movement*, article by Margherita Rendel, pp. 98–103, 108; Liddington and Norris, *One Hand Tied Behind Us*, pp. 240–1 (quotation from p. 240), 38, 79–80, 88–9; Boone, *The Women's Trade Union Leagues*, pp. 33–6.

104. See Boone, *The Women's Trade Union Leagues*, p. 68.

105. See article on 'The National Women's Trade Union League', from the Survey, 16 Oct. 1909, p. 105, in Folder 1, Box 1, National Women's Trade Union League of America Records, SL.

106. Rubinstein, *Before the Suffragettes*, pp. 110–18, 127; letter of Miss Marjory Lee to Miss Philippa Strachey, 9 July 1909, and Strachey's reply, 24 Aug. 1909, in Autograph Letter Collection, FL; and articles in the *Englishwoman's Review*, vol. XXX, no. 222, 16 July 1894, p. 193; vol. XXIV, no. 219, 16 October 1893, pp. 223–4; no. 215, 15 October 1892, pp. 217–18.

107. See Ellen Mappen, *Helping Women at Work*: *The Women's Industrial Council, 1889–1914* (London, Hutchinson, 1985).

108. Liddington and Norris, *One Hand Tied Behind Us*, p. 132.

109. Middleton (ed.), *Women in the Labour Movement*, article by Jean Gaffin, pp. 125–37; Liddington and Norris, *One Hand Tied Behind Us*, pp. 130–1, 136–42, 201–2, 243, 247 (first quotation from p. 141); Jane Lewis, *The Politics of Motherhood*: *Child and maternal welfare in England, 1900–1939* (London, Croom Helm and Montreal, McGill-Queen's University, 1980), pp. 167–8; Gordon, *Women and the Labour Movement*, pp. 266–70.

110. Boone, *The Women's Trade Union Leagues*, pp. 225–6; Jacoby, 'The Women's Trade Union League'; but also Virginia Woolf's 'Introduction letter' to Davies (ed.), *Life as We Have Known It*, on the danger of the middle-class woman being 'a benevolent spectator' (p. xxi) at the gatherings of working-class activists.

111. Buhle, *Women and American Socialism*, p. 184.

112. Alice Kessler-Harris 'Where are the organized women workers?', *Feminist Studies*, vol. 3, no. 1/2, Fall 1975, pp. 92–110; and *Out to Work: A history of wage-earning women in the United States* (New York, Oxford University Press, 1982). And see James T. Keneally, *Women and American Trade Unions* (St. Albans, VT, and Montreal, Quebec, Eden Press Women's Publications, 1978); press cutting, probably 26 April 1904, in Box 1, Folder 1, National Women's Trade Union League of America Records, SL, for second quotation.

113. Flexner, *Century of Struggle*, pp. 253–4; Mary T. Waggaman, 'National Women's Trade Union League of America', from the *Monthly Labor Review*, April 1919, of the Bureau of Labor Statistics, United States Department of Labor, pp. 237–8, Folder 1, Box 1, National Women's Trade Union League of America Records, SL; also in *ibid.*, Folder 12, Box 2, 'Outline of Work'; Wertheimer, *We Were There*, ch. 15; Allen F. Davis, 'The Women's Trade Union League: origins and organisation', *Labour*

History, vol. 5, 1964, pp. 3–17; Nancy Schrom Dye, *As Equals and as Sisters*: *Feminism, the labour movement and the Women's Trade Union League of New York* (Columbia, University of Missouri Press, 1980), especially chs 2–3, 5; Buhle, *Women and American Socialism*, pp. 188–90; O'Neill, *Everyone Was Brave*, pp. 153–6; Boone, *The Women's Trade Union Leagues*, pp. 43, 63, ch. IV.

114. *Souvenir History of the Strike of the Ladies Waist Makers' Union* (1910), pp. 6, 12, 25–6 (source of the quotations); article from *McClure's Magazine*, November 1910: 'Working girls' budgets: the shirtwaist-makers and their strike', by Sue Ainslie Clark and Edith Wyatt, pp. 85–6, both in Folder 62, Box 4, National Women's Trade Union League of America Records, SL; also Folder 57, 'The strike, 1910', pp. 54–5, reference to the 1909–10 strikers; Boone, *The Women's Trade Union Leagues*, pp. 77–83; Wertheimer, *We Were There*, pp. 293–309; on O'Reilly and Schneiderman, see Lagemann, *A Generation of Women*, chs 4–5; Meredith Tax, *The Rising of Women: Feminist solidarity and class conflict, 1880–1917* (New York, Monthly Review Press, 1979), generally, on cross-class efforts.

115. See, in Folder 58, of the League papers, 'The Strike, 1910', worker accounts of grievances; Folder 59, appeal 'To the women of Chicago' by Margaret Dreier Robins, President of the WTUL; Folder 59, Garment Workers' Strike; ' "On Strike": a collection of true stories', by Mary Field, Oct. 1911 (quotation from p. 744); Dye, *As Equals and as Sisters*, ch. 5; Boone, *The Women's Trade Union Leagues*, pp. 88–98.

116. See introduction to the Pauline Newman Papers, SL.

117. Letters from Newman to Rose Schneiderman of 20 Sept. 1910, 10 May 1911, 14 July 1911, 9 Aug. 1911, 12 Oct. 1911, 7 Nov. 1911, 21 Nov. 1911, 1 undated letter to her, 1 undated page about hopes of improving her English, letter of 26 March 1912, 14 April 1912, 9 June 1912 in Folder 77, Box 5, Pauline Newman Papers, SL.

118. See in *ibid.*, Newman to Schneiderman: 9 Aug. 1911, 5/7/11, letter with no details about Mrs Robins (p.4), 7 Nov. 1911, 3/5/12, 3/26/12, 9 Feb. 1912, 7/11/12, 26 July 1912, 9/-/11; Folder 109, article 'In the factory district'.

119. Kessler–Harris, 'Where are the organized women workers?', p. 92; Eisenstein, *Give Us Bread But Give Us Roses*, pp. 147–50; Buhle, *Women and American Socialism*, p. 196.

120. Buhle, *Women and American Socialism*, pp. 199–200, 212; on tensions between middle- and working-class women, see Robin Miller Jacoby, 'The Women's Trade Union League and American feminism', *Feminist Studies*, vol. 2, 1975, pp. 126–40: but also see Lagemann, *A Generation of Women*, p. 154 and *passim*.

121. Buhle, *Women and American Socialism*, pp. 190–6, 187–9, 179.

122. *Ibid.*, pp. 201–3; Boone, *The Women's Trade Union Leagues*, pp. 101–6; O'Neill, *Everyone Was Brave*, pp. 157–62.

123. Buhle, *Women and American Socialism*, pp. 83–9; ch. 3 (quotations from pp. 105–6); Lawrence Goodwyn, *The Populist Moment*.

124. Buhle, *Women and American Socialism*, pp. 107, 121 f., ch. 4 (quotation from p. 150).

125. *Ibid.*, p. 160.

126. *Ibid.*, chs 5–7.

127. *Ibid.*, p. 228.

128. Newman to Schneiderman, 4–14–12, in Folder 77, Box 5, Pauline Newman Papers, SL.

129. Sachs and Wilson, *Sexism and the Law*, p. 112 (also pp. 113–16); Kessler-Harris, *Out to Work*, ch. 7, especially p. 188; T. Scopkol, *Protecting Soldiers and Mothers* (Cambridge, MA, Belknap Press, 1992); Ronnie Steinberg, *Wages and Hours: Labor and reform in twentieth century America* (New Brunswick, NJ, Rutgers University Press, 1982); Susan Lehrer, *Origins of Protective Labor Legislation for Women, 1905–1925* (Albany, State University of New York Press, 1987); Claudia Goldin, 'Maximum hours legislation and female employment: a reassessment', *Journal of Political Economy*, vol. 96, 1988, pp. 189–205; Dye, *As Equals and as Sisters*, chs 6–7; V. Hart's forthcoming minimum wage study.

130. Linda K. Kerber and Jane De Hart-Mathews, *Women's America: Refocusing the past* (New York and Oxford, Oxford University Press, 1987), pp. 223–5 (quotation from p. 225); Wilson, *The American Woman in Transition*, ch. 5; Ellen Fitzpatrick, *Endless Crusade: Women social scientists and Progressive reform* (New York, Oxford University Press, 1990); O'Neill, *Everyone Was Brave*, ch. 3 and *passim*.

131. See M. Freeden, *The New Liberalism: An ideology of social reform* (Oxford, Clarendon Press, 1978); Derek Frazer, *The Evolution of the British Welfare State* (London, Macmillan, 1984 edn), pp. 131, 133, 138, 158–61; Lewis, *The Politics of Motherhood*, especially Part IV; Pat Thane, *The Foundations of the Welfare State* (London, Longman, 1983); Elizabeth Wilson, *Women and the Welfare State* (London, Longman Tavistock, 1977); Holton, *Feminism and Democracy*, pp. 15 f.; Gisela Bock and Pat Thane (eds), *Maternity and Gender Politics: Women and the rise of the European welfare states, 1880–1950* (London, Routledge, 1991); Carol Dyhouse, *Feminism and the Family in England, 1880–1939* (New York, Blackwell, 1989), pp. 88 f.; Linda Gordon (ed.), *Women, the State, and Welfare* (Madison, University of Wisconsin Press, 1991); Seth Roven and Sonia Michel, 'Womanly duties', *American Historical Review*, vol. 95, no. 4, Oct. 1990, pp. 1076–1108.

132. W. Reason, *University and Social Settlements* (London, Methuen, 1898), pp. 12–13.

133. *Ibid.*, p. 4.

134. *Ibid.*, p. 45.

135. *Ibid.*, pp. 90–1, and Directory of Settlements, pp. 179–90; Vicinus, *Independent Women*, pp. 211–14 (source of quotation).

136. See Hill, *The Religious Order*; Vicinus, *Independent Women*, ch. 6; Peter F. Anson and Allan Waller Campbell, *The Call of the Cloister* (London, SPCK, 1964); A.M. Allchin, *The Silent Rebellion: The Anglican religious communities, 1845–1900* (London, SCM Press, 1958).

137. Reason, *University and Social Settlements*, p. 92.

138. Hollis, *Ladies Elect*, pp. 14, 23–5 and *passim*; Summers, 'A home from home', pp. 53–7, on the Charity Organisation Society; letter of Mrs Mary Augusta Ward (Mrs Humphrey Ward) to Mr Matheson, 1 Nov. 1911, in Autograph Letter Collection (Women's Movement) FL about the need to think less about the 'machinery' and more about 'the actual doing of things' in settlement work: in her own Passmore Edwards Settlement she was forced to shift from a religious to a practical approach to the work (see Sutherland, *Mrs. Humphrey Ward*, ch. 18); Reason, *University and Social Settlements*, p. 93 (source of quotation); Vicinus, *Independent Women*, pp. 215, 244.

139. David Levine, *James Addams and the Liberal Tradition* (Madison, State Historical Society of Wisconsin, 1971), p. 40.

140. Reason, *University and Social Settlements*, pp. 136, 146–51; Allen F. Davis,

Spearheads for Reform: The social settlements and the Progressive movement (New York, Oxford University Press, 1967); Robert A. Woods and Alfred J. Kennedy (eds), *Handbook of Settlements* (New York Charities Publication Committee, 1911); Allen F. Davis, *American Heroine: The life and legend of Jane Addams* (New York, Oxford University Press, 1973).

141. Jane Addams, *Twenty Years at Hull House* (New York and Scarborough, ON, Signet Classic, New American Library, 1981 edn of 1910 original), p. 72; see also p. 64.
142. *Ibid.*, pp. 61–3, 70, 95 (source of quotation).
143. Reason, *University and Social Settlements*, p. 139.
144. Addams, *Twenty Years at Hull House*, pp. 42–3, 74, 145, 188–91, 207–9, 254–5; Levine, *Jane Addams*, p. 170; Robert Archey Woods, *English Social Movements* (London, Swan, Sonnenschein & Co., 1892), pp. vi, 11–12.
145. Reason, *University and Social Settlements*, p. 138.
146. *The Education of Henry Adams* (Boston, MA and New York, Houghton Mifflin, 1918), pp. 297–8, 353.
147. Blair, *The Clubwoman as Feminist*, pp. 27, 118 and *passim*.
148. Addams, *Twenty Years at Hull House*, p. 45; Kathryn Kish Sklar, 'Hull House in the 1890s: a community of women reformers', *Signs*, vol. 10, 1985, pp. 658–77.
149. Reason, *University and Social Settlements*, pp. 142–3, 145; Boone, *The Women's Trade Union Leagues*, pp. 57–8; Levine, *Jane Addams*, pp. 52 f., 138–9.
150. Mark H. Leff, 'Consensus for reform: the mothers' pension movement in the Progressive era', *Social Service Review*, vol. 47, September 1973, pp. 397–417; Levine, *Jane Addams*, p. 90, chs 7–9; Elizabeth Jane Clapp, 'The origin and development of juvenile courts', pp. 65 f., 141 and *passim*; Eisenstein, *Give Us Bread But Give Us Roses*, pp. 129–30; Davis, *American Heroine*; Levine, *Jane Addams*, pp. 52 f. 138–9; Boone, *The Women's Trade Union Leagues*, pp. 57, 63; Lagemann, *A Generation of Women*, ch. 3; Lillian D. Wald, *The House on Henry Street* (New York, Henry Holt, 1915), and R.L. Duffus, *Lillian Wald: Neighbor and Crusader* (New York, Macmillan, 1928); Sklar, 'Hull House in the 1890s'.
151. Robert H. Wiebe, *The Search for Order, 1877–1920* (New York, Hill & Wang, 1968 edn), pp. 122–3, 149–50, 171–2; also Lagemann, ch. 3; Davis and Levine, *passim*.
152. O'Neill, *Everyone Was Brave*, p. 162.
153. Addams, *Twenty Years at Hull House*, p. 76.
154. See, for instance, Levine, *Jane Addams*, ch. 9.
155. Rubinstein, *Before the Suffragettes*, p. 222.
156. *Ibid.*, pp. 222–6 (quotation from p. 225); *Englishwoman's Review*, vol. XXX, no. 240, 16 Jan. 1899, p. 61; as the *Review* pointed out (p. 68), club activity was strongest in New England and New York State; see also vol. XXV, no. 221, 16 April 1894, pp. 125–6; and Alfreda M. Duster (ed.), *Crusade for Justice: The autobiography of Ida B. Wells* (Chicago, University of Chicago Press, 1970), for a contemporary American view of the Pioneer Club.
157. Rubinstein, *Before the Suffragettes*, p. 226.
158. Blair, *The Clubwoman as Feminist*, ch. 3, especially pp. 15, 54–5; Leach, *True Love and Perfect Union*, pp. 185 f.; Croly, *The History of the Woman's Club Movement*, pp. 85 f.; B. Campbell, *The 'Liberated' Woman of 1914* (UMI Research Press, 1979), ch. VI.
159. Blair, *The Clubwoman as Feminist*, pp. 100–5; see also *The Federation Bulletin*, vol. II, no. 3, December 1904, p. 75; vol. VII, no. 6, March 1910, pp. 181–3; no. 6, April 1910, p. 213.

160. See, *The Club Woman*, vol. XI, no. 5, Jan. 1904, pp. 3–4; no. 8, April 1904, pp. 3–6; vol. XI, no. 12, Aug. 1904, pp. 3, 5; *The Federation Bulletin*, vol. I, no. 6, April 1904, pp. 69, 72–3, 75–6, 77–8; vol. II, no. 5, Feb. 1905, pp. 145, 154–9, 160–1; vol. II, no. 6, March 1905, Editorial Notes, pp. 186–9, 191–2; vol. II, no. 7, April 1905, pp. 219–29; vol. II, no. 8, May 1905, Editorial Notes, pp. 215, 252–3, 254–6; vol. IV, no. 5, Feb. 1907, pp. 178–84, 187–8, 201; vol. IV, no. 9, June 1907, Editorial Notes, pp. 326, 331–3, 334–5, 337–9; vol. VII, no. 7, April 1910, p. 213; vol. V, no. 2, Nov. 1907, articles by Florence Marshall, Anna Clark, Mrs Clarence Burns (p.52); vol. V, no. 9, June 1908, pp. 266, 279; vol. VII, no. 5, Feb. 1910, pp. 143–6, 146–7, 150–1, 154, 168; vol. VII, no. 6, March 1910, pp. 181–3. On the South's home mission societies, see Woman's Home Mission Society, Reports, 1898–1906, Folder 66, Somerville–Howorth Papers, SL: quotation from Minutes of the Eleventh Annual Meeting of the Woman's Missionary Society of the North Mississippi Conference (1890), The President's Address, p. 19; and see John Patrick McDowell, *The Social Gospel in the South: The Women's Home Mission movement in the Methodist Episcopal Church South, 1886–1939* (Baton Rouge, Louisiana State University Press, 1982). See also Margaret Gibbons Wilson, *The American Woman in Transition: The urban influence, 1870–1920* (Westport, CT, Greenwood Press, 1979), pp. 91 f.; Rothman, *Woman's Proper Place*, pp. 102 f.; and Marlene Stein Wortman, 'Domesticating the nineteenth-century American city', *Prospects: An Annual of American Cultural Studies*, vol. 3, 1977, pp. 531–72.
161. On these fears see, for instance, Club Journal of the NEWC, 1890–1, 30 March 1891; 1892–3, 9 Feb. 1893; 1895–6, 18 May 1896, Folder 6, Box 4, New England Women's Club Records, SL.
162. Blair, *The Clubwoman as Feminist*, pp. 106–14.
163. See volumes of the Recording Secretary, vol. 12 (1899–1900), meetings of 8 Jan, 12 Mar. 1900, vol. 13 (1900–2), meetings of 12 Nov., 1900, 4 Mar., 25 Nov., 9 Dec. 1901; vol. 16 (1907–10), meetings of 18, 25 Nov., 1907, 20 Jan., 10, 24 Feb., 9 Mar., 12 Apr., 21 Dec. 1908, 25 Jan. 1909, 1, 8 Mar., 15 Nov., 13 Dec. 1909; vol. 14 (1902–4), meetings of 16 Feb., 16 Mar., 20 Apr., 23 Nov. 1903, 14 Mar., 18 May, 7 Dec. 1904; vol. 15 (1904–7), meetings of 14 Nov. 1904, 16, 23 Jan., 6 Mar., 8 May, 6 Sept. 1905, 6 Mar. 1906, 13 May 1907 – all in Box 4, New England Women's Club Records, SL; and in *ibid.*, Folder 6, Club Journal for 1890–1, meeting of 23 Jan. 1899; in Box 5, volumes of the Recording Secretary, vol. 17 (1910–12), meeting of 11 Dec. 1911, 1 Apr., 25 Nov. 1912; vol. 18 (1913–15), meetings of 27 Jan., 14 Apr. 1913, in Box 5; in Box 8, Folder 14, Secretary's Annual Reports, 1885–98, report in 1892, 1894, 1897, pp. 7a–b, 1898, pp. 11–12; and in *ibid.*, Folder 23, Committee on Work reports, report for May 1896, p. 7; Box 9, Folder 28, Reports, 1908–22, 'The second quarter century', p. 2; Croly, *The History of the Women's Club Movement*, pp. 35 f.
164. See volumes of the Recording Secretary, vol. 13 (1900–2), meeting of 9 November 1903 on the need for women voters 'to overcome the evils of foreign unintelligent voters', in Box 4, New England Women's Club Records, SL; and in *ibid.*, Folder 6, Club Journal, meeting of 13 Mar. 1893 on the need for more rotation of club offices; Box 5, volumes of the Recording Secretary, vol. 17, meeting of 5 Feb. 1912 on Lawrence strike and current labour conditions; Box 6, Work Committee, vol. 26 for the struggle to secure speakers; Box 8, Folder 14, Secretary's Annual Reports, 1885–98, report for 1892 on the danger of the club lagging behind the times, report

for 1844–5, pp. 7, 9–10, on the difficulties of getting speakers and attentive audiences, for 1897, pp. 4–5, and for 1898; pp. 3–4; Box 9, Folder 28, Reports 1908–22, report for 1899 on problems in sustaining discussions. Mrs Josephine Ruffin, a well-educated black journalist and suffragist, whose black New Era Club sparked the debate in the Federation in 1900, was a member of the NEWC.

165. See, in the papers of Mary Church Terrell (microfilm edition consulted at Lamont Library, Harvard: originals in the Library of Congress): correspondence with husband Robert M. Terrell (1900–22 and undated) on her speaking engagements on race and social purity issues (especially 12 Aug. 1900, 5 Nov. 1911, 27 Oct. 1911, and Robert Terrell to Mary Terrell, 14 Nov. 1913); correspondence, 1886–1900, letter of 5 Sept. 1899; correspondence, 1901–3, letter of 17 Feb. 1901, clipping for the *New York Age*, 4 Jan. 1900; correspondence, 1904–5, letter of 26 Aug. 1904; correspondence, 1907, letter to the editor of the Charleston *News and Courier*; folder on the National Association of Colored Women (in subject files): manuscript of Program and Constitution, 1897. See also Tullia Hamilton, 'The National Association of Colored Women's Clubs', PhD thesis, Emory University, 1978; Sterling (ed.), *We Are Your Sisters*, pp. 398–9, 406, 422–3 (first quotation from p. 398); Wells – see Duster (ed.), *Crusade for Justice, passim* – notes the warm British response to her campaign; Terrell, *A Colored Woman in a White World*, chs 16–19, 23, 30; Elsa Barkley Brown, 'Womanist consciousness: Maggie Lena Walker and the Independent Order of Saint Luke', *Signs*, vol. 14, spring 1989.

166. See, for instance, the Ethel Eyer Valentine Dreier Papers in SSC (folders for 1909–10, 1911 in Box 1 and Box 5, Women's City Club folder); Sue S. White Papers, Box 1, Folder 10, SL; and Somerville–Howarth Collection, Folders 56, 58, 63, SL, for an indication of the role of club activities in the lives of busy women reformers. See also Duster (ed.), *Crusade in Justice*, ch. 39.

167. See Flexner, *Century of Struggle*, pp. 213–14; objects of the Consumers' League of Hartford, Connecticut Papers, SL. See also the rest of the papers of the Connecticut League in the collection, especially, in the context of this note, Consumers' League of Connecticut Constitution and report of meeting of April 1907, p. 76 (source of quotation), in Folder 7A, Box 1; and 'Twenty-five years of the Consumers' League movement' by Florence Kelley (1924), in Folder 24, Box 3.

168. Report of the General Secretary of the Consumers' League of Connecticut . . . 14 June 1913, p. 2, in *ibid.*, Folder 11, Box 2; Lagemann, *A Generation of Women*, p. 189, on 'exposure to human suffering' as a common stimulus to Progressives.

169. On Lowell, see William Rhinelander Stewart, *The Philanthropic Contribution of Josephine Shaw Lowell* (New York, Macmillan, 1911); on Nathan, see Lagemann, *A Generation of Women*, ch. 2, and Maud Nathan, *The Story of the Epoch Making Movement* (Garden City, NY, Doubleday Page, 1926); on Kelley, see Dorothy Rose Blumberg, *Florence Kelley: The making of a social pioneer* (New York, Augustus M. Kelley, 1966), and Florence Kelley, *Some Ethical Gains Through Legislation* (New York, Macmillan, 1905).

170. Davies, *Women's Co-operative Guild*, p. 57.

171. See, for instance, David Nasaw, *Schooled to Order*, pp. 120, 135, chs 8–9, though for the argument that immigrants did not oppose functional education, see Smith, 'Immigrant social aspirations and American education', pp. 527–8. See also James J. Kenneally, 'Women in the United States and trade unions', p. 66, in Soldon (ed.), *The World of Women's Trade Unionism*.

172. See, in Consumers' League of Connecticut Records, SL: Résumé of Minutes of Meetings of the Consumers' League of Hartford for years 1912–thro' part of 1918, Folder 1, Box 1; report of Annual Meeting of the CLC for 1909, pp. 7–8, Report of the Corresponding Secretary of the CLC in 1910, report of the Executive Secretary of the CLC for 1910, reports of the General Secretary of the CLC, 1914 and 1915, Folder 3, Box 1; Consumers' League of Connecticut, Hartford, bound volume of its meetings, 1902–11, especially pp. 53, 61, 76, 88–9, 107, 111, 125, 133, 141, Folder 7A, Box 1; the same for 1911–19, especially pp. 46, 63, Folder 7B, Box 1; Consumers' League of Connecticut, New Haven, records for 1907–14, especially pp. 37, 63, 75, 84, 151, 177–8, Folder 8, Box 2; Consumers' League of Connecticut, Convention and conference Reports, 1910–26, Report of Proceedings Upon a Conference on the Training of Children for Trades and Practical Life, Held at New Haven, Connecticut, 27 April 1910, especially pp. 36 f., 74 f., Folder 9, Box 2; Consumers' League of Connecticut Quarterly Meetings and Reports, 1908–12, including A Report of Some Efforts Being Made in Great Britain to induce Children of Fourteen Years to Enter the Skilled Trades and Industrial Schools, report of the CLC's Corresponding Secretary for 1910, of the General Secretary for 1911, especially p. 5, and for 1912, especially pp. 1–2, Report of the Committee on Vocational Guidance, 1 June 1912, Report of the Committee on Public Policy, 1 June 1912, Folder 10, Box 2; report of the General Secretary for 1913, especially pp. 2, 5, 6–7, 9, for 1913, p. 4, for 1914, Folder 11, Box 2.
173. Pivar, *Purity Crusade*, p. 25.
174. See Epstein, *The Politics of Domesticity*, pp. 122–3, 137–45; Buhle, *Women and American Socialism*, pp. 80–1, 90–1, 108–9.
175. See Epstein, *The Politics of Domesticity*, pp. 125, 129, 145.
176. *Ibid.*, p. 145; Peter G. Filene, 'An obituary for "The Progressive Movement"', *American Quarterly*, vol. 22, Spring 1970, pp. 20–34.
177. See Shiman, '"Changes are dangerous"', pp. 208–9; Earhart, *Frances Willard*, pp. 32 f.; Fitzpatrick, *Lady Henry Somerset*, pp. 159–74; Frances E. Willard, *Do Everything: A handbook for the world's white ribboners* (London, The White Ribbon Co., Chicago, The Woman's Temperance Publishing Association, 1895), p. 13 – also, p. 83 on the flexibility of the WCTU: 'The only binding rules are these: Pay your annual dues and never drink'; Gordon, *The Beautiful Life of Frances E. Willard*, pp. 210, 220–49; Isabel Somerset to Editor of the Transcript, February 1895, in Autograph Letter Collection, FL; Shiman, *Women and Leadership*, pp. 160 f.
178. See Hollis, *Ladies Elect*, pp. 48–9 (source of quotation); Shiman, '"Changes are dangerous"', p. 209.
179. Shiman, '"Changes are dangerous"', pp. 209–10 (quotation from p. 210); Earhart, *Frances Willard*, pp. 327–9, 335, 339.
180. Bell, *Josephine Butler*, pp. 233–5 (quotation from p. 234) and chapter on 'India 1888–1889' generally; Fawcett and Turner, *Josephine Butler*, p. 121; Pivar, *Purity Crusade*, pp. 218 f.; Fitzpatrick, *Lady Henry Somerset*, pp. 178–83; *A Good-Bye Message to Dominion White Ribboners* (Montreal, Lawrence and Cole, 1898), pp. 3, 6–8, 10–11; Gordon, *The Beautiful Life of Frances E. Willard*, pp. 182–7.
181. Weeks, *Sex, Politics and Society*, p. 90; Pivar, *Purity Crusade*, pp. 132 f.; Mort, *Dangerous Sexualities*, Part Three.
182. Weeks, *Sex, Politics and Society*, p. 92, ch. 7; Jeffreys, *The Spinster and Her Enemies*,

pp. 25–6; Crow, *The Edwardian Woman*, pp. 17–20; Buhle, *Women and American Socialism*, p. 252; McLaren, *Birth Control in Nineteenth-Century England*, p. 207; Anna Davin, 'Imperialism and motherhood', *History Workshop Journal*, no. 5, Spring 1978; Carol Dyhouse, *Feminism and the Family in England, 1880–1939* (New York, Blackwell, 1989), pp. 166 f.

183. Weeks, *Sex, Politics and Society*, p. 91; Pivar, *Purity Crusade, passim*; Mort, *Dangerous Sexualities*, Part Four.

184. Jeffreys, *The Spinster and Her Enemies*, pp. 20–52; Pivar, *Purity Crusade*, pp. 204, 246, 256–7; Linda Gordon, *Heroes of Their Own Lives: The politics and history of family violence* (New York, Viking, 1988).

185. Jeffreys, *The Spinster and Her Enemies*, p. 21; Pivar, *Purity Crusade*, pp. 105, 224, 231–2, 258 (source of quotation), 261, 246, 256–7; Mort, *Dangerous Sexualities*, pp. 179 f.

186. Weeks, *Sex, Politics and Society*, pp. 26, 31 (source of first and third quotations); Jeffreys, *The Spinster and Her Enemies*, pp. 74–9 (quotation from p. 78); Pivar, *Purity Crusade*, p. 146; and see Cunningham, *The Children of the Poor* and Lionel Rose, *The Erosion of Childhood* (London, Routledge, 1991) on the reasons why children were now differently regarded: the role of altruism is especially played down by Rose.

187. Weeks, *Sex, Politics and Society*, p. 92.

188. See, for instance, Jeffreys, *The Spinster and Her Enemies*, p. 19; Pivar, *Purity Crusade*, pp. 146, 153, 226 f., 259–60; Buhle, *Women and American Socialism*, p. 253.

189. Pivar, *Purity Crusade*, pp. 132–9, 272–3; Harriet Laidlaw, 'The A.B.C. of the question' [1912], quotation from p. 4, in Folder 149, Box 10, Harriet W. Laidlaw Papers, SL; Buhle, *Women and American Socialism*, pp. 253–7; John C. Burnham, 'The Progressive era revolution in American attitudes toward sex', *Journal of American History*, vol. 59, March 1973, pp. 885–908; Robert Riegel, 'Changing American attitudes toward prostitution, 1800–1920', *Journal of the History of Ideas*, vol. 39, July–September 1969, pp. 437–52; Reed, *The Birth Control Movement*, p. 58.

190. Pivar, *Purity Crusade*, pp. 139 f., 226 f., 275–6; Linda Gordon, *Heroes of Their Own Lives*; Gordon, 'Family violence, feminism and social control', in DuBois and Ruiz (eds) *Unequal Sisters*, pp. 141–56; Gordon, 'Single mothers and child neglect', *American Quarterly*, vol. 37, Summer 1985, pp. 173–92, especially pp. 185, 191–2; Viviana Zelizer, *Pricing the Priceless Child: The changing social value of children* (New York, Basic Books, 1985), Anthony M. Platt, *The Child Savers: The invention of delinquency* (Chicago, University of Chicago Press, 1969); Susan Tiffin, *In Whose Best Interests? Child welfare in the Progressive era* (Westport, CT, Greenwood Press, 1982); Roy Lubove, *The Struggle for Social Security, 1900–1935* (Cambridge, MA, Harvard University Press, 1968), p. 99; the mothers' pension laws were mainly awarded to widows, at the discretion of towns and counties; Clapp, 'The origins and development of juvenile courts'; Rothman, *Woman's Proper Place*, ch. 3; Thane, *The Foundations of the Welfare State*, pp. 117–18. The opposition to mothers' pensions of conservative child-care agencies was overborne by their popularity.

191. See Pivar, *Purity Crusade*, pp. 131; Summers, 'A home from home', pp. 41 f; Jane Lewis, 'The working-class wife and mother and state intervention, 1870–1918', in Lewis (ed.), *Labour and Love*, pp. 100 f. In the process, prostitutes' rights suffered.

192. Rosenberg, *Beyond Separate Spheres*, p. 54; quotation from Rheda Childe Dorr, a newspaperwoman; Jalland, *Women, Marriage and Politics*, pp. 280–7; Rubinstein, *Before the Suffragettes*, ch. 2 and pp. 217–19 on rational dress groups; Martha Banta,

Imaging American Women: Idea and ideals in cultural history (New York, Columbia University Press, 1987), ch. 1; Elaine Showalter, *Sexual Anarchy: Gender and culture at the fin de siècle* (London, Bloomsbury Press, 1991), pp. 1–18, ch. 3.

193. Rubinstein, *Before the Suffragettes*, ch. 3; Elaine Showalter, *A Literature of Their Own* (London, Virago, 1978); Elizabeth Ammons, *Conflicting Stories: American women writers at the turn into the twentieth century* (New York, Oxford University Press, 1991); Patricia Stubbs, *Women and Fiction: Feminism and the novel, 1880–1920* (London, Methuen, 1981); Showalter, *Sexual Anarchy*; Caine, *Victorian Feminists*, pp. 248–59.

194. See, for instance, Rubinstein, *Before the Suffragettes*, Section II; Patricia A. Vertinsky, *The Eternally Wounded Woman: Women, exercise and doctors in the late nineteenth century* (Manchester, Manchester University Press, 1990); Solomon, *In the Company of Educated Women*, ch. 8; Crow, *Edwardian Women*, ch. 6, 9; Kessler-Harris, *Out to Work*; Gluck, *From Parlor to Prison*, p. 216.

195. McWilliams-Tullberg, *Women at Cambridge*, ch. 8; Solomon, *In the Company of Educated Women*, pp. 58–61; Tyack and Hansot, *Learning Together*, chs 7–8.

196. See Report of the Southern Association of College Women. Together with the Constitution and By-Laws (1904); Seventh Report of the Southern Association of College Women (1910), pp. 21–2; Southern Association of College Women. Proceedings in Full of Tenth Annual Meeting (1913), pp. 11–12, 14, 17–28, 38, in National Association of University Women Archives, 1881–1976, read on microfilm at Lamont Library, Harvard University.

197. See Weeks, *Sex, Politics and Society*, ch. 8; Buhle, *Women and American Socialism*, pp. 253 f.; Chambers-Schiller, *Liberty, A Better Husband*, pp. 198–9.

198. See McLaren, *Birth Control in Nineteenth-Century England*, ch. 8; Weeks, *Sex, Politics and Society*, pp. 128–38.

199. Weeks, *Sex, Politics and Society*, pp. 126–8; Davin, 'Imperialism and motherhood'; Pivar, *Purity Crusade*, pp. 227 f.; Lewis, *The Politics of Motherhood*, 'Introduction', Part IV and *passim* (quotation from p. 20); and see Carol Smith (ed.), *Regulating Womanhood: Historical essays on marriage, motherhood and sexuality* (London, Routledge, 1992); Tyack and Hansot, *Learning Together*, ch. 8.

200. See Buhle, *Women and American Socialism*, p. 266; Rubinstein, *Before the Suffragettes*, pp. 45–7; Bland, 'Marriage laid bare', pp. 140–1; Cott, *Grounding*, pp. 41–4. Apart from the social stigma attached to free unions, the status of children born of such unions remained a problem. See also Garner, *Stepping Stones*, pp. 66–7.

201. Weeks, *Sex, Politics and Society*, pp. 99, 166; Chambers-Schiller, *Liberty, A Better Husband*, pp. 198–200; Jeffreys, *The Spinster and Her Enemies*, chs 5–6, pp. 134–7; Lillian Faderman, *Surpassing the Love of Men: Romantic friendship and love between women from the Renaissance to the present* (New York, William Murrow & Co., 1981); Cott, *Grounding*, pp. 44–5; Showalter, *Sexual Anarchy*, ch. 9.

202. See, for instance, Degler, *At Odds*, pp. 156, 160, 163–5; Bland, 'Marriage laid bare', pp. 124–5; Willard, *Glimpses of Fifty Years*, pp. 637, 641–2.

203. See Charlotte Perkins Gilman, *Women and Economics: The economic factor between men and women as a factor in evolution* (ed. Carl Degler, New York, Harper & Row, 1966; originally published 1898), 'Introduction' and pp. 157, chs IX, XI, pp. 277–8, 298, 314. Dolores Hayden, *The Grand Domestic Revolution* (Cambridge, MA, MIT Press, 1982); Joyce Berkman, *The Healing Imagination of Olive Schreiner* (Amherst, MA, University of Massachusetts Press, 1989), ch. 5; Mary A. Hill, *Charlotte Perkins*

~

Gilman: The making of a radical feminist, 1860–1896 (Philadelphia, PA, Temple University Press, 1980), pp. 234–5, 238 f. and *passim*; Garner, *Stepping Stones*, ch. 5 and *passim*; and Cott, *Grounding*, p. 41.

204. See Epstein, *The Politics of Domesticity*, p. 135.

205. See Pivar, *Purity Crusade*, p. 257; William O'Neill, *Divorce in the Progressive Era* (New Haven, CT, Yale University Press, 1967), pp. 140–51, on the dismay felt by some clerics and women's groups about the rising divorce rate.

206. Degler, *At Odds*, pp. 166–76; O'Neill, *Divorce in the Progressive Era*; Riley, *Divorce*, pp. 130 f.

207. Blake, *The Road to Reno*, pp. 145–50; Riley, *Divorce*, pp. 118–121, 125–6.

208. Reed, *The Birth Control Movement*, p. 56; Riley, *Divorce*, pp. 123, 128.

209. Rubinstein, *Before the Suffragettes*, pp. 42–5; 55; McGregor, *Divorce in England*, pp. 24–9; Bland, 'Marriage laid bare', pp. 138–9; Crow, *The Edwardian Woman*, pp. 14–16, ch. 11; Lady Frances Balfour to Mrs Fawcett, 16 Dec. 1909, Autograph Letter Collection, FL, on the problems of the poor under the existing divorce law.

210. McLaren, *Birth Control in Nineteenth-Century England*, pp. 179, 205 f., 221, 226, 240, 244; Lewis, *The Politics of Motherhood*, pp. 196, 198–201; Sheila Rowbotham, *A New World for Women. Stella Browne: Socialist feminist* (London, Pluto Press, 1977), Section 1; Browne also advocated abortion, from 1915 – see p. 34.

211. Mohr, *Abortion in America*, ch. 9; Gordon, *Woman's Body, Woman's Right*, pp. 213 f.

212. See Buhle, *Women and American Socialism*, pp. 271 f.; Margaret Sanger, *My Fight for Birth Control* (London, Faber & Faber, 1932); Reed, *The Birth Control Movement*, ch. 6; Gordon, *Woman's Body, Woman's Right*, pp. 216 f.; Elizabeth Fee and Michael Wallace, 'The history and politics of birth control: a review essay', *Feminist Studies*, vol. 5, no. 1, Spring 1979, pp. 201–15.

213. Reed, *The Birth Control Movement*, ch. 4 (quotation from p. 50); Richard Drinnon, *Rebel in Paradise: A biography of Emma Goldman* (Boston, MA, Beacon Press, 1970); Fee and Wallace, 'The history and politics of birth control', pp. 209–12; Gordon, *Woman's Body, Woman's Right*, pp. 225 f. (quotation from p. 243).

214. Rosaleen Love, '"Alice in eugenics land": feminism and eugenics in the scientific careers of Alice Lee and Ethel Elderton', *Annals of Science*, vol. 36, 1979, pp. 145–58.

215. Rosenberg, *Beyond Separate Spheres*, p. 53; Ellen Fitzpatrick, *Endless Crusade: Women social scientists and Progressive reform* (New York, Oxford University Press, 1990).

216. Rosenberg, *Beyond Separate Spheres*, pp. 55, 83–4, 107–13, 114–15, 139–46, 147, 174–7, 178–9, 203–8 and *passim*.

217. Baker, 'The domestication of politics', especially pp. 640–2; Wortman, 'Domesticating the nineteenth-century American city'; and for the period up to the 1880s, Ryan, *Women in Public*.

218. See, for a lesser-known American reformer interested in temperance and animal welfare, Selections from the Journal of Sarah Knowles Bolton, vol. II, 1902–11, Box 2, Sarah Bolton Papers, SL: see especially pp. 22, 23–4, 34, 48, 56, 101–2, 106–7; vol. III, pp. 26, 33; and American National Red Cross, Report of the President, Washington DC, 10 July 1900, p. 14, in Folder 63, Box 3, Clara Barton Collection, SSC (source of quotation).

219. See, for instance, Cobbe, *The Duties of Women*, p. 10; Harriet Martineau, *The Positive Philosophy of Auguste Comte* (London, George Bell, 1896), vol. 3, pp. 341–2, on Britain's retrograde and stationary system.

~

220. See, for instance, Gordon, *The Beautiful Life of Frances E. Willard*, pp. 24 f.
221. *Ibid.*, p. 232, for Willard's tribute to the political activism of British women.

Chapter 6   The War, the vote and after

1. Hume, *The National Union*, p. 221 (source of first quotation), *Feminism and Democracy*, ch. 5, on the importance of 'suffrage-labour campaigning' and its impact, actual and likely, on the pro-Liberal NUWSS rank and file: see also pp. 116–30, on the confident activism of the suffragists (the second, third and fourth quotations from pp. 117, 123 and 129); M.G. Fawcett, *The Women's Victory*, p. 85; Pankhurst, *The Suffrage Movement*, ch. VIII.
2. Hume, *The National Union*, pp. 222–3; Mrs Fawcett in HWS, vol. VI, p. 739; Fawcett, *The Women's Victory*, pp. 88–9.
3. Rosen, *Rise Up, Women!*, pp. 247–9 (quotation from p. 24); Arthur Marwick, *Women at War, 1914–1918* (London, Croom Helm, 1977), pp. 28–9: as Marwick points out, the war was not expected to last long and Mrs Pankhurst promised a return to the political arena 'at the first possible moment'. See also Martin Pugh, *Women and the Women's Movement in Britain, 1914–1959* (London, Macmillan, 1992), ch. 2.
4. Rosen, *Rise Up, Women!*, pp. 252–4.
5. Ramelson, *The Petticoat Rebellion*, p. 167; Holton, *Feminism and Democracy*, p. 132; Rosen, *Rise Up, Women!*, pp. 249–52, 268; Pugh, *Women's Suffrage in Britain*, pp. 29–32, 43–4, 54; Garner, *Stepping Stones*, pp. 55–9.
6. Morgan, *Suffragists and Liberals*, pp. 135–6; letter of Mrs Helen Auerbach to Mrs Fawcett, 9 Nov. 1914, hoping the NUWSS will concentrate on war work and avoid being drawn into contentious political issues, Autograph Letter Collection, FL; and in *ibid.*, letter from Mrs Fawcett on the split in the NUWSS over peace work, in letter to Miss K. Atkinson, 19 Feb. 1916; Mrs Israel Zangwill to Mrs Cavendish Bentinck, 19 Feb. 1915, in *ibid.*, on adult suffrage; Mrs Fawcett to Mrs Chapman Catt, 21 July 1915, on NUWSS divisions, which she plays down.
7. M.G. Fawcett in HWS, vol. VI, pp. 739–40; Garner, *Stepping Stones*, pp. 82–3; Ramelson, *The Petticoat Rebellion*, p. 168; Holton, *Feminism and Democracy*, pp. 131–2, 138; Marwick, *Women at War*, pp. 33–4, 44, 151 (source of quotation); Fawcett, *The Women's Victory*, pp. 91–105; Pankhurst, *The Suffragette Movement*, pp. 596–7; Jo Vellacott, 'Feminist consciousness and the First World War', in Ruth Roach Pierson (ed.), *Women and Peace: Theoretical, historical and practical perspectives* (London, Croom Helm, 1987).
8. Mrs Fawcett in HWS, vol. VI, p. 743. The best brief accounts of wartime activities are in Holton, *Feminism and Democracy*, pp. 145 f.; Alberti, *Beyond Suffrage*, ch. 3; Pugh, *Women and the Women's Movement*.
9. Rosen, *Rise Up, Women!*, pp. 256–7, 258, 260; letter of Asquith to Mrs Fawcett, 7 May 1916, Autograph Letter Collection, FL; and in *ibid.*, Mrs Fawcett to Mrs Catt, 21 July 1915; Lord Northcliffe to Lady Betty Belfour, 22 Dec. 1916, on the lack of movement for women's suffrage, in *ibid.*; Mrs Fawcett to Lord Northcliffe, 26 Dec. 1916, denying his finding, in *ibid.*; Mrs Fawcett to Miss P. Strachey, 23 Dec. 1916, on the need to renew suffrage work, in *ibid.*; and in *ibid.*, Mrs Fawcett to Lloyd George, March 1917; Mrs Fawcett in HWS, vol. VI, p. 743 (source of second

quotation); Morgan, *Suffragists and Liberals*, p. 139; Ramelson, *The Petticoat Rebellion*, pp. 168–9; Marwick, *Women at War*, pp. 153–4.

10. Mrs Fawcett in HWS, vol. VI, p. 744 (source of second quotation); Morgan, *Suffragists and Liberals*, pp. 127 f.; Rosen, *Rise up, Women!*, p. 259 (source of first quotation); Marwick, *Women at War*, pp. 154–5; Rover, *Women's Suffrage and Party Politics in Britain*, p. 207; women possessing the qualifications for graduation of a university refusing to admit women graduates (i.e. Oxford and Cambridge) were also enfranchised. See also Pankhurst, *The Suffragette Movement*, pp. 607–8, for the argument that memories of militancy and fears of its resumption were more important than women's war work in securing their enfranchisement; Pugh, *Women and the Women's Movement*, pp. 34–8; Garner, *Stepping Stones*, ch. 10; Fawcett in HWS, vol. VI, pp. 746–7.

11. Morgan, *Suffragists and Liberals*, pp. 137, 149; Rosen, *Rise Up, Women!*, pp. 258–61, 265.

12. Pugh, *Women's Suffrage in Britain*, pp. 33–4; Fawcett, *The Women's Victory*, p. 143; Holton, *Feminism and Democracy*, pp. 147–9; Pankhurst, *The Suffragette Movement*, p. 607 (source of quotation); Pugh, *Women and the Women's Movement*, pp. 12–18.

13. Marwick, *Women at War*, p. 157; Pugh, *Women's Suffrage in Britain*, p. 30 (source of statistic), and *Women and the Women's Movement*, pp. 18–21.

14. Marwick, *Women at War*, p. 157; Fawcett, *The Women's Victory*, pp. 143–4.

15. Fawcett, *The Women's Victory*, p. 106.

16. Fawcett in HWS, vol. VI, p. 741; Fawcett, *The Women's Victory*, pp. 121–4.

17. Pugh, *Women's Suffrage in Britain*, p. 31; Marwick, *Women at War*, p. 158, quoting E.S. Montague, who succeeded Lloyd George as Minister of Munitions.

18. Blatch, *Challenging Years*, pp. 253–5: she asked herself: 'What ails Englishmen – are they afraid of women?'

19. Pugh, *Women's Suffrage in Britain*, p. 31 (source of quotation); Mrs Fawcett in HWS, vol. VI, p. 741; Fawcett, *The Women's Victory*, pp. 115–17; Alberti, *Beyond Suffrage*, pp. 56–8; Pugh, *Women and the Women's Movement*, pp. 18–28.

20. Marwick, *Women at War*, p. 151; Pugh, *Women's Suffrage in Britain*, p. 31 (source of quotation); Gail Brabon, *Women Workers in the First World War* (London, Croom Helm, 1981).

21. Fawcett in HWS, vol. VI, p. 747 (source of quotation); Pankhurst, *The Suffragette Movement*, pp. 603–5; Pugh, *Women's Suffrage in Britain*, p. 34; Fawcett, *The Women's Victory*, pp. 148–52, for the Lords' Debate: Parliament was in fact aware of the American suffrage cause, on which its conference on the suffrage had collected information – see Miss M. Sheepshanks to Miss A. Park, 16 Oct. 1916, Autograph Letter Collection, FL.

22. The East London Federation of Suffragettes was renamed the Workers' Suffrage Federation in 1915. Mrs Fawcett to Lady Frances Balfour, 11 Jan. 1918, in Autograph Letter Collection, FL.

23. For works dealing with American militancy, see Notes 27–8, 31.

24. Peck, *Carrie Chapman Catt*, p. 213; see also Blatch, *Challenging Years*, pp. 251–2; and Mrs Fawcett to Mrs Chapman Catt, 15 Dec. 1914, Autograph Letter Collection, FL, on the difficulty of bringing women from the belligerent countries together.

25. See Levine, *Jane Addams and the Liberal Tradition*, ch. 14 (second quotation from pp. 203–4); and Blanche Wiesen Cook, 'Democracy in wartime: antimilitarism in England and the United States, 1914–18', in Charles Chatfield (ed.), *Peace*

Movements in America (New York, Schocken Books, 1973), pp. 39–57; Mrs Catt to Miss Alice Park, 13 April 1916, and circular letter from Catt, dated 11 May 1916, on IWSA finances, both in Autograph Letter Collection, FL, and in *ibid.*, Mary Sheepshanks to Alice Park, 10 May 1915.

26. See NAWSA letter of 5 January 1915, in Folder 19, Box 7, Harriet W. Laidlaw Papers, SL, for the association's attitudes to militancy, anti-democracy and rash peace demonstrations; Fowler, *Carrie Catt*, pp. 138–9; Carrie Chapman Catt and Nellie Rogers Shuler, *Woman Suffrage and Politics: The inner story of the suffrage movement* (New York, Charles Scribner's Sons, 1923), p. 249 (source of quotation); Barbara J. Steinson, *American Women's Activism in World War I* (New York, Garland, 1982).

27. Flexner, *Century of Struggle* pp. 276–7; Peck, *Carrie Chapman Catt*, pp. 240–1; Catt and Shuler, *Woman Suffrage and Politics*, pp. 246–7; Anne F. Scott and Andrew M. Scott, *One Half the People: The fight for woman suffrage* (Philadelphia, PA, B. Lippincott, 1975), ch. 3.

28. Flexner, *Century of Struggle*, pp. 277–9 (first quotation from p. 278); Catt and Shuler, *Woman Suffrage and Politics*, pp. 246, 248 (source of second quotation); Morgan, *Suffragists and Democrats*; Doris Stevens, *Jailed for Freedom* (Freeport, NY, Books for Libraries Press, 1971 edn, originally published 1920), pp. 22–38; Cott, *Grounding*, pp. 53 f.

29. Stevens, *Jailed for Freedom*, pp. 38–9.

30. Fowler, *Carrie Catt*, pp. 143–4 (quotation from p. 143); Flexner, *Century of Struggle*, pp. 281–2; Peck, *Carrie Chapman Catt*, pp. 221–37; Blatch, *Challenging Years*, pp. 207–9, ch. 5. For a tribute to Catt by one of the innumerable women she inspired, see Sherna Berger Gluck, *From Parlor to Prison: Five American suffragists talk about their lives* (New York, Monthly Review Press, 1985), pp. 107–8.

31. On the Woman's Party, see Inez Haynes Irwin, *The Story of the Woman's Party* (New York, Harcourt, Brace, 1971, first published 1921); and Loretta E. Zimmermann, 'Alice Paul and The National Woman's Party', PhD dissertation, Tulane University, 1964; Stevens, *Jailed for Freedom*, p. 42, ch. 3 (first quotation from p. 57); Peck, *Carrie Chapman Catt*, p. 253 (source of second quotation); Flexner, *Century of Struggle*, pp. 286–7; Blatch, *Challenging Years*, pp. 258–63, 279–2; Scott and Scott, *One Half the People*, ch. 3.

32. Stevens, *Jailed For Freedom*, pp. 59 (source of first quotation), 63–79, 84–5, 89–96, 99–121, 123–57, 174–228, 271–9 (second quotation from p. 190); Scott and Scott, *One Half the People*; Flexner, *Century of Struggle*, pp. 292–6; Blatch, *Challenging Years*, pp. 275–7 points out that the pickets contained women from all backgrounds and parties.

33. Stevens, *Jailed for Freedom*, pp. 227 (source of first quotation), 295 f. (third quotation from p. 302); S.S. White to C. Catt, 27 April 1918, Folder 21, Box 2, Sue S. White Papers, SL (source of second quotation); see also Ernestine Hara Kettler's account of her experiences as a militant in Gluck, *From Parlor to Prison*, pp. 254–64.

34. See Alice Paul to Kathryn Boyles, 18 June 1917, AF54, Anthony Family Collection, Henry E. Huntington Library.

35. Stevens, *Jailed for Freedom*, pp. 328, 337–40 and *passim*; ' "Militant" suffragists and how they won a hopeless cause', article by Sue Shelton White, in the *Montgomery Times*, August 1919, Folder 25, Box 2, Sue S. White Papers, SL; for the defence of militancy (source of quotation) see letter by Alice Locke Park Biography, PK.7, Box 8, Alice Locke Park Collection, Henry E. Huntington Library.

36. Stevens, *Jailed for Freedom*, chs 7–8, 15; Blatch, *Challenging Years*, pp. 280–1; see Sue Shelton White to Dr J.L. Weber, 17 Feb. 1919, on Wilson's insincerity, Folder 20, Box 2, Sue S. White Papers, SL.

37. Stevens, *Jailed for Freedom*, pp. 83, 290.

38. *Ibid.*, p. 241.

39. See Morgan, *Suffragists and Democrats*.

40. 'What "Militant" suffragists are and how they have won a case which seems hopeless', in Folder 25, Box 2, Sue S. White Papers, SL.

41. Anna Shaw to Alice Locke Park, 5 March 1909, PK.306, Alice Locke Park Collection, Henry E. Huntington Library; see also Cott, *Grounding*, p. 61.

42. Carrie Chapman Catt to Sue Shelton White, 6 May 1918, Folder 21, Box 2, Sue S. White Papers, SL. See also Peck, *Carrie Chapman Catt*, p. 271.

43. Catt to White, 6 May 1918.

44. Description of Harriet B. Laidlaw, NAWSA document of 11 July [1917?], Folder 140, Box 9, Harriet B. Laidlaw Papers, SL; for a more vigorous condemnation, see Dr J.L. Weber, in letter to Sue Shelton White, 2 Nov. 1919, Folder 20, Box 2, Sue S. White Papers, SL; Catt and Shuler, *Woman Suffrage and Politics*, p. 243; Fowler, *Carrie Catt*, pp. 145–53.

45. Flexner, *Century of Struggle*, p. 296.

46. Alice Locke Park to Carrie Chapman Catt, 17 Feb. 1917, in Alice Locke Park Biography, PK.7, Box 8, Alice Locke Park Collection, Henry E. Huntington Library.

47. Mrs. Blatch, though a Woman's Party supporter, believed that 'the effective use of woman-power would win the war', and published, in the spring of 1918, *Mobilizing Woman Power*, in which she 'told what women had done in Europe to win the war and called upon women in this country to do as much'. See Blatch, *Challenging Years*, pp. 283–4, 286. Also Peck, *Carrie Chapman Catt*, p. 258, for the reference to woman's hour; Scott and Scott, *One Half the People*, ch. 4.

48. Letter of 9 Dec. 1918, Folder 12, Box 2, Dewson Papers, SL, on Mary Dewson's Red Cross Work (source of quotation); J.S. Lemons, *The Woman Citizen: Social feminism in the 1920s* (Urbana, University of Illinois Press, 1973), ch. 1; Flexner, *Century of Struggle*, pp. 298–9; Steinson, *American Women's Activism in World War I*; HWS, vol. V, ch. XXIV; Catt and Shuler, *Woman Suffrage and Politics*, p. 338.

49. Wilson quoted in Stevens, *Jailed for Freedom*, p. 290.

50. Steinson, *American Women's Activism in World War I*, pp. 237 f., 308 f.; Peck, *Carrie Chapman Catt*, pp. 271–3; Blatch, *Challenging Years*, p. 390.

51. Fowler, *Carrie Catt*, pp. 140–2; Cott, *Grounding*, p. 60.

52. See, for instance, HWS, vol. V, p. 2: Catt was prepared to concede that neither NAWSA nor the Woman's Party 'deserved full credit for the adoption of the suffrage amendment': see Fowler, *Carrie Catt*, p. 153.

53. Carrie Chapman Catt to Sue Shelton White, 6 May 1918, Folder 21, Box 2, Sue S. White Papers, SL. On Mrs Catt's 'winning plan' see, for instance, Peck, *Carrie Chapman Catt*, pp. 256–7, 261–3; Scott and Scott, *One Half the People*.

54. Scott and Scott, *One Half the People* (quotation from ch. 4); Peck, *Carrie Chapman Catt*, p. 293; Catt and Shuler, *Woman Suffrage and Politics*, pp. 259–60; Flexner, *Century of Struggle*, pp. 288–9, 312, 386.

55. Peck, *Carrie Chapman Catt*, pp. 289, 298–9 (quotation from p. 298); Catt and Shuler, *Woman Suffrage and Politics*, ch. XIX; Flexner, *Century of Struggle*, pp. 300–1, 318.

56. Fowler, *Carrie Catt*, p. 150; Flexner, *Century of Struggle*, pp. 323–4.
57. Flexner, *Century of Struggle*, pp. 324–5, 327; Catt and Shuler, *Woman Suffrage and Politics*, ch. XX, pp. 339–40.
58. Catt and Shuler, *Woman Suffrage and Politics*, ch. XXI; Peck, *Carrie Chapman Catt*, pp. 313–14.
59. Catt and Shuler, *Woman Suffrage and Politics*, chs XXII–XXX; Peck, *Carrie Chapman Catt*, ch. 7; Flexner, *Century of Struggle*, pp. 328–37.
60. Stevens, *Jailed for Freedom*, pp. 255–8.
61. Catt and Shuler, *Woman Suffrage and Politics*, pp. 270–9, 446 (source of quotations); Flexner, *Century of Struggle*, pp. 306–12, 314–17, 327, 333.
62. Blatch, *Challenging Years*, p. 227; Scott and Scott, *One Half the People*, suggest that the passage of the Prohibition Amendment lessened the opposition of 'the interests' to women's suffrage.
63. Catt and Shuler, *Woman Suffrage and Politics*, p. 298; Sue S. White to Carrie C. Catt, 27 April 1918, Folder 21, Box 2, Sue S. White Papers, SL.
64. See article in *The Englishwoman's Review*, vol. XXVIII, no. 233, 15 April 1897, pp. 76–7, on 'The growth of women's suffrage in the United States'.
65. Flexner, *Century of Struggle*, pp. 330, 332–5.
66. *Ibid.*, p. 337.
67. See, for instance, Report of the Thirty-Fourth Annual Convention [of the Mississippi WCTU] Held in Columbus, Mississippi, 15–18 October, 1917, Folder 61, Somerville–Howorth Papers, SL, and in *ibid.*, Folder 67, on the work of Washington County Council of Defense Woman's Committee, and Folder 68, on the work of the Mississippi YWCA during the war; Harriet Laidlaw's war work for the United States Food Administration, Folders 76 and 77, Harriet W. Laidlaw Papers (SL); and in the New England Women's Club Papers, vol. 19, Box 5, entry for 21 May, 5 Nov., 12 Nov. and 10 Dec. 1917; 'Résumé of Minutes of meetings of the Consumers' League of Hartford for years 1912–thro' part of 1918', p. 12, Box 1, Folder 1, Consumers' League of Connecticut Records, SL.
68. Minutes of the Eleventh Biennial Convention of the National Association of Colored Women, 8–13 July (Denver, Colorado), pp. 19, 26 f., 50–1, 54, 56 (source of quotation), The Papers of Mary Church Terrell, read on microfilm at Lamont Library, Harvard University: reel 16.
69. See letter from Kate M. Gordon, Southern States Woman Suffrage Conference, 23 June 1915, to members of NAWSA's Official Board, and letter in reply by Nellie Somerville, 'Comment on letter to members of National Board', Folder 64, vol. 25, Somerville–Howorth Papers, SL, and Flexner, *Century of Struggle*, pp. 317–18. Also Cott, *Grounding*, pp. 68–71, on the NWP.
70. See items in Folder 121, Box 7, Harriet W. Laidlaw Papers, SL; Flexner, *Century of Struggle*, p. 318.
71. Kathy Peiss, *Cheap Amusements* (Philadelphia, Temple University Press, 1986), especially pp. 3–10, 185–8; Mrs Robins at the Fifth Biennial Convention of the National Women's Trade Union League of America (1915), p. 10, Folder 7, Box 1, National Women's Trade Union League of America Records, SL. See Estelle Freedman, 'The new woman: changing views of women in the 1920s', *Journal of American History*, vol. 61, September 1974, pp. 372–93; Pugh, *Women and the Women's Movement*, pp. 73–80.
72. Reed, *The Birth Control Movement and American Society*, ch. 5 (quotation from

pp. 60–1); Degler, *At Odds*, p. 410, notes 'over a million married women worked outside the home in non-agricultural jobs' in 1910 – see also pp. 412–15; Rosenberg, *Beyond Separate Spheres*, pp. 220–1; Cott, *Grounding*, ch. 5.

73. Reed, pp. 88, 90 (and ch. 7 generally); and Margaret Sanger, *My Fight for Birth Control* (London, Faber & Faber, 1932), chs V–VII, especially p. 97.

74. See Journal for 3 March 1914, Folder 217, Box 29, Margaret Sanger Collection, SSC; and, in *ibid.*, entry for 1924, pp. 191, 201–3, Folder 219; Stella Browne to Margaret Sanger, 9/17/15 and Bessie Drysdale to Margaret Sanger, 26 Oct. 1915, Folder for 1915, Box 37.

75. Margaret Sanger to Board of Directors, American Birth Control League, 8 June 1928, Folder 1339, Box 123, Margaret Sanger Collection, SSC.

76. Reed, *The Birth Control Movement and American Society*, ch. 8, pp. 106–10, 112–14, 117–20, 134–7; Reed discusses the hostility of eugenicists to birth control in the 1920s, when it still lacked respectability, and their conversion to the cause, in the 1930s, of directing birth control to the poor; Sanger, *My Fight for Birth Control*, p. 202 (source of quotation); see also pp. 307–9; David Kennedy, *Birth Control in America: The career of Margaret Sanger* (New Haven, CT, Yale University Press, 1970) is particularly useful on Sanger's struggles within the birth control movement.

77. Margaret Sanger to Mrs Joseph Wilshire, 25 Oct. 1929, correspondence folder for 1929, Box 37, Margaret Sanger Collection, SSC; Reed, *The Birth Control Movement and American Society*, pp. 122–3, 134–6.

78. Margaret Sanger to Mrs Joseph Wilshire, 25 Oct. 1929, correspondence folder for 1929, Box 37, Margaret Sanger Collection, SSC.

79. Margaret Sanger to Amelia Mitchell, 12 Nov. 1929, correspondence folder for 1929, Box 37, Margaret Sanger Collection, SSC; Sanger, *My Fight for Birth Control*, pp. 312–14.

80. Reed, *The Birth Control Movement and American Society*, p. 120.

81. *Ibid.*, pp. 109, 116–17; Sanger, *My Fight for Birth Control*, chs VIII, XIX–XXI and *passim*.

82. Margaret Sanger to Mrs F. Robertson Jones, 8 Dec. 1930, Folder 1342, Box 123, Margaret Sanger Collection, SSC; and in *ibid.*, Folder 1348, Box 123, Annual Report, Birth Control Clinical Research Bureau (1930), pp. 2–3 and social worker's report, September 1930.

83. Reed, *The Birth Control Movement and American Society*, ch. 10 (quotation from pp. 138–9); Smith-Rosenberg, *Disorderly Conduct*, p. 284; Gordon, *Woman's Body, Woman's Right*, Part III; Fowler, *Carrie Catt*, pp. 161–3; Linda Gordon, 'The politics of birth control, 1920–1940: the impact of professionals', in Elizabeth Fee (ed.), *Women and Health: The politics of sex in medicine* (Farmingdale, NY, Baywood Publishing Co., 1982), pp. 151–75; Cott, *Grounding*, ch. 5.

84. June Sochen, *Movers and Shakers: American women thinkers and activists, 1900–1970* (New York, Quadrangle, 1973), pp. 88, 104; Alberti, *Beyond Suffrage*, Appendix; Pugh, *Women and the Women's Movement*, pp. 260–1, notes that the dominance of older leaders may have inhibited growth.

85. Blatch, *Challenging Years*, p. 300 (source of first quotation), and for the second, Resolution adopted by the New England Women's Club, 15 Jan. 1921, Folder 7, Box 5, New England Women's Club Records, SL; Mrs Blatch – see *Challenging Years*, p. 313 – was disappointed that the Woman's Party concentrated on home affairs. See also Cott, *Grounding*, ch. 8.

86. See, in Fannie Fern Phillips Andrews Papers, SL, Box 6, Folder 43: 'A call to patriotic service' [1917], letter of 3 Jan. 1913 from Andrews to Mr Arthur Deering Call of the American Peace Society, and letter of 28 Dec. 1917 from Andrews to Mr Call; in Folder 44, letter of 18 Jan. 1915 from Andrews to Dr John Mez; in Folder 45; letter of 29 Oct. 1909 from Andrews to James L. Tryon about the American School Peace League; in Box 7, American School Peace League, Denver, Colorado, July 1909 on the work and aims of the organisation, Annual Report of the Executive Committee, July 1912, in Folder 56; also American School Peace League, Utah, July 1913 in Folder 62, and Annual Report of the Executive Committee, Read at the Annual Meeting, 10 July 1913, in *ibid.*; Box 8: Folder 68, Sixth Annual Convention, St. Paul, 4–11 July 1914, and American School Peace League, St. Paul, Minnesota, July 1914, and in Folder 74, American School Peace League, Oakland, California, August 1915; Box 9: Folder 80, Annual Meeting, 1916, in Folder 82, letters on the League's close relationship with the National Education Association, in Folder 86, letter from Andrews to Miss De Graff, about information from England about education during the war, and Annual Report of the Executive Committee, 1917, in Folder 90, Annual Report of the Executive Comittee, 1917–18, at the 1918 Annual Meeting in Pittsburgh, Pennsylvania, and in Folder 91, Annual Meeting, Milwaukee, Wisconsin, 1919; Box 10: Folder 93, Andrews to Mr William W. Andrew, 3 Feb. 1919, 27 Dec. 1918, 5 June, 17 April 1917; Box 11: Folder 98, 8 July 1920, Work in Foreign Countries, and Annual Report of the Executive Committee, July 1919 to July 1920, and Reports of the American School Citizenship League for 1923–24 and for 1924–25; Box 12: Folder 103, letter of 30 March 1915 indicating that funds were scarce, and in Folder 106 a résumé of her life by Mrs Fannie Fern Andrews, and in Folder 108, letter of 23 June, 1920 on the purpose of the League, and in Folder 109, teaching suggestions on how to link American history to the international peace movement; Box 15 on Andrews's suffrage connections, especially letter of 6 March 1915, in Folder 226, and on her connection with the League of Women Voters, in Folders 233–5; Box 20: Folder 272 on the International Congress of Women, The Hague, 28 April to 1 May 1915. And see Cott, *Grounding*, p. 257.

87. 'The sixth quinquennial of the International Council of Women, held in Washington, 4–14 May, 1925', by Fannie Fern Andrews, p. 1, Folder 175, Box 21, Fannie Fern Andrews Papers, SL. See also Peck, *Carrie Chapman Catt, passim*; Gertrude Bussey and Margaret Tims, *Women's International League for Peace and Freedom* (London, George Allen & Unwin, 1965).

88. Peck, *Carrie Chapman Catt*, p. 411.

89. 'The sixth quinquennial', pp. 4–8, especially 5–6; Peck, *Carrie Chapman Catt*, p. 415, notes the watering down of the disarmament resolution. See Richard J. Evans, *Comrades and Sisters: Feminism, Socialism and pacifism in Europe, 1870–1945* (Brighton, Harvester, 1987), pp. 121–2 and *passim*.

90. See in Folder 274, Box 20, Fannie Fern Andrews Papers, SL, press cuttings on the quinquennial, especially from the *Christian Science Monitor*, 14 May 1925.

91. Peck, *Carrie Chapman Catt*, pp. 410–13.

92. Blatch, *Challenging Years*, p. 310.

93. 'The sixth quinquennial', p. 1.

94. C.G.W. McCulloch to Mr C.B. Pallen, 17 July 1922, Folder 30, Box 2, C.G.W. McCulloch Papers, SL, pp. 5, 6.

95. See Peck, *Carrie Chapman Catt*, pp. 415–16, 418–32, 439–43, 449–51, 453

(quotations from pp. 427, 453); on Harriet Laidlaw's efforts for peace and the League of Nations, see Folders 79–83, 85 and 87 in Box 5, and Folder 88 in Box 6, Harriet W. Laidlaw Papers, SL: evidence of Anglo–American co-operation in the cause is considerable; its blacklist of offending organisations proved divisive within the DAR: see Peck, p. 429; letters on DAR controversy, Folder 30, Box 2, Eastman Collection, SSC. See also Folder 38, Box 3, C.G.W. McCulloch Papers, SL.

96. Southern Association of College Women. Proceedings of the Twelfth Annual Meeting (1915), pp. 11–13, 18, 35–6; Proceedings of the Thirteenth Annual Meeting (1916), pp. 12, 14; Proceedings of the Fourteenth Annual Meeting (1917), pp. 13, 49, 51–3; Proceedings of the Sixteenth Biennial Meeting (1921), pp. 22–3; 44; American Association of University Women, summary of past and present work, 1925; 'History of the A.A.U.F.', 1927, p. 1; Dr Kathryn McHale, 'The search for values by the American Association of University Women', pp. 1–2; Ruth W. Tyron, 'The N.A.U.W., 1881–1949' (1950), pp. 3, 5–6, 10–11, 17, 29–30; 'Fact sheet on the International Federation of University Women', p. 1: all in National Association of University Women Archives, 1881–1976, read on microfilm at Lamont Library, Harvard University; Mary Williams Dewson Papers, SL, Folder 3, booklet of the School of Housekeeping, Boston, pp. 3, 6, 7–8 (quotations from p. 3); (quotation from Gluck, *From Parlor to Prison*, p. 112); women's percentage of total college enrolments declined in the 1920s from 47.3 to 43.7: See Chafe, *The American Woman*, p. 58; Barbrook and Bolt, *Power and Protest in American Life*, p. 197; Cott, *Grounding*, ch. 3, p. 162, chs 6–7; Tyack and Hansot, *Learning Together*, pp. 218–20.

97. See, in National Association of University Women Archives, Programme for the Quinquennial Sessions of the International Council of Women to be held in . . . Washington . . . 1925, entry on the National Association of Colored Women, p. 64; National Association of Colored Women, Fifteenth Biennial Session . . . 1926, pp. 50 f., 78 (source of first quotation), 100; Meeting of the National Association of Colored Women . . . 1930, pp. 60–1 (source of second quotation), 67, 68 f., Mary Church Terrell Papers, read on microfilm at Lamont Library, Harvard University.

98. See letters from Mrs Terrell to her brother, 15 Jan. 1929, 26 March 1932, in *ibid.*; Catt, *Grounding*, pp. 92–3; Paula Giddings, *Where and When I Enter: The impact of black women on race and sex in America* (New York, William Morrow, 1984) *passim*; Terrell, *A Colored Woman in a White World*, ch. 31 onwards.

99. Scott, *The Southern Lady*, ch. 8.

100. Undated letter from Mrs Terrell to her husband, from the Chittenden, Columbus, Ohio, Mary Church Terrell Papers.

101. See Mary Williams Dewson Papers, SL, Folder 3, Bulletin of Women's City Club of New York, June 1925, 'From the President', pp. 3–4, 19, 21; and Women's City Club (of New York) clippings and speeches folders, Box 5, Ethel Eyer Valentine Dreier Papers, SSC: Dreier notes that the New York club had a very diverse membership and had made various influential studies – for example, on the licensing and policing of New York dance halls, improvements in city finances, and the working of the courts. Folders 156–63, Box 10, in the Harriet W. Laidlaw Papers, SL, testify to the continuing concern with prostitution. And see, in Somerville–Howorth Papers, SL, Folder 61, Mississippi Woman's Christian Temperance Union, Report of the Thirty-Fourth Annual Convention . . . 1917, especially pp. 26, 36 f.; Report of the Thirty-Fifth Annual Convention . . . 1922, especially p. 15;

Report of the Thirty-Ninth Annual Convention ... 1925, especially pp. 34–5; Report of the Fortieth Annual Convention ... 1926, especially pp. 25–6, 33, 35–6; also 'What is the WCTU?', WCTU pamphlet, n.d., p. 9; Paulson, *Women's Suffrage and Prohibition*, p. 173; also Lemons, *The Woman Citizen*, pp. 43–6, 92–3, 101, chs 3–5; Cott, *Grounding*, ch. 3.

102. Peck, *Carrie Chapman Catt*, pp. 306–7; Lemons, *The Woman Citizen*, ch. 2, on new associations.

103. June Sochen, *Movers and Shakers*, p. 116; Fowler, *Carrie Catt*, pp. 99–100.

104. William H. Chafe, *The American Woman: Her changing social, economic and political roles, 1920–1970* (London, Oxford and New York, Oxford University Press, 1974 edn), pp. 28–9; Cott, *Grounding*, pp. 67–75.

105. Sochen, *Movers and Shakers*, p. 114; Who's Who in New York ... No. 38: a tribute to Florence Kelley, in *New York Herald Tribune*, 9 Nov. 1924, Folder 24, Box 3, Consumers' League of Connecticut Records, SL; Cott, *Grounding*, pp. 97–8.

106. Fowler, *Carrie Catt*, pp. 100–3; Lemons, *The Woman Citizen*, pp. 49–50 and *passim*; Felix D. Gordon, *After Winning: The legacy of the New Jersey suffragists, 1920–1947* (New Brunswick, NJ, Rutgers University Press, 1986), ch. 2; quotation from leaflet on the League in Box 1, File 1 (General), League of Women Voters of Massachusetts Records, SL; see in *ibid.*, Box 11, Folder 158, 'Publications' reflecting the interests of the National NLWV in 1930; Louise M. Young, *In the Public Interest: The League of Women Voters, 1920–1970* (Westport, CT, Greenwood Press, 1989).

107. See, for instance, 'The Massachusetts League of Women Voters, organized 27 May, 1920. What it is *and* what it does', Box 1, Folder 1, League of Women Voters of Massachusetts Records, SL.

108. See literature on child labour in Folders 223 and 224, Box 17, in *ibid.*, for evidence of how League members studied an issue in depth and tried to reply to their critics.

109. Committee Newsletter (of the Committee on Women in Industry of the Massachusetts LWV), 'Unemployment legislation, 7 July, 1938', p. 3, in *ibid.*, Box 6, Folder 73, Box 12, Folder 166, Box 17, Folders 223–6.

110. See, in *ibid.*, Box 9, Folder 114: Legislation; and for details of other committees, Box 6, Folder 73, Box 12, Folder 166, Box 17, Folders 223–6.

111. See, in *ibid.*, Box 1, Folder 1: Massachusetts League of Women Voters, President's Speech, 1930 Convention. Mrs Mary Jenney Healy, pp. 3–4; Chafe, *The American Woman*, pp. 30–6.

112. Christine Bolt, *A History of the U.S.A.* (London, Macmillan, 1974), pp. 470–7, 474, 476–7; Boone, *The Women's Trade Union Leagues*, pp. 156–7; Chafe, *The American Woman*, pp. 52–3; Joseph G. Rayback, *A History of American Labor* (New York, Free Press, 1966), pp. 274 f.

113. Consumers' League of Connecticut Records, SL: Box 1, Folder 3, The Legislative Campaign of 1917, p. 1; Report of the General Secretary for the Year ending 31 Jan. 1919. The Women's Committee, pp. 1–2; Folder 4, Annual Meeting, Middletown, 16 Jan. 1924, Annual Meeting. Consumers' League of Connecticut, Town and Country Club, 15 Nov. 1927, Report of the Work of the Consumers' League of Connecticut for the Year Ending June 1918; vol. 5, Annual Meeting, Stamford, 25 Jan. 1926, Directors' Meeting, Program of the Industrial Conference, Hartford, Connecticut, 15 Oct. 1926, Meeting of 13 Feb. 1928, and Annual Meeting of Consumers' League of Connecticut, 5 Dec. 1932; Box 2, Folder 11, The Consumers' League of Connecticut. Report of the General Secretary for the

~

Period Ending 26 May 1915, p. 3; Folder 12, Report of the General Secretary . . . 31 Oct. 1918, pp. 1, 3; Box 3, Folder 24, Who's Who in New York . . . No. 38: a tribute to Florence Kelley, *New York Herald Tribune*, 9 Nov. 1924. And in Mary Williams Dewson Papers, SL, Box 2, Folder 17, 'How the Consumers' League works'.

114. Boone, *The Women's Trade Union Leagues*, chs V, VI (first two quotations from pp. 142, 172). And see, in National Women's Trade Union League of America Records, SL, Box 1, Folder 3, President's Report. To the Officers and Delegates to the Sixth Biennial Convention of the National Women's Trade Union League of America (1917); Folder 5 for report on the training school; Folder 4, Educational program, general, 1913–23, on the training school; Folder 7, clipping from *The Federation News*, 23 May, 1925, on the women trained by the League, and Fifth Biennial Convention of the National Women's Trade Union League of America (1915), pp. 59–61, 89 f., 101, 128, 143–5, 148 f., 207, 237–8, 253–5, 369, 373–4; Box 2, Folder 1 on the training school and other educational efforts, Folder 2 on conservative attacks on the League and other women's organisations, Folders 10 and 11 on the southern campaign, including in the latter, 'Women's place in industry in 10 southern states' by Mary Anderson, Director of the Women's Bureau (1931), Folder 13 on the women's auxiliaries; Box 3, Folder 43, letter of 23 June 1928 from the Chicago office of the WTUL on the League's legislative programme, Folder 44, letter of 12 March 1929 on the need for 'friendly understanding and cooperation between the business and professional women and the industrial woman'; Box 4, Folder 70, Strikes: Miscellaneous, 1911–29, on the cigarmakers' strike, 1929, and the valiant contributions of the organiser, Miss Sadie Reisch, Folder 71 on sweatshops; Box 6, 'Women in trade unions in the United States' (1920), Folder 78, articles in the *Christian Science Monitor*, March–April 1929, on women in the labour movements of Britain and America (source of third quotation), Folder 89, on efforts in New York which 'proved conclusively that there is nothing to the claims that women cannot be organized'. For statistics about the increase of the female workforce, see Chafe, *The American Woman*, pp. 50, 54.

115. See, in Pauline Newman Papers, SL, Box 5, Folder 78, letter from Rose Schneiderman to Pauline Newman, 11 Aug. 1917, 4 Feb. 1916; Folder 80, Leonora O'Reilly to Pauline Newman, 9 Nov. 1918, p. 5 (source of quotation), 9 May 1919, an undated fragment; Folder 101, John B. Andrews to Pauline Newman, 6 Dec. 1916; Folder 109, 'A unity center: "Women's garments and their makers" ' (1920s), pp. 5–11.

116. *Equal Rights*, 20 October 1923, p. 285; Susan D. Becker, *The Origins of the Equal Rights Amendment: American feminism between the wars* (Westport, CT, Greenwood Press, 1981), ch. 1; Nancy F. Cott, 'Feminist politics in the 1920s: The National Woman's Party', *Journal of American History*, vol. 71, June 1984, pp. 43–68.

117. *Equal Rights*, 2 June 1923, p. 124; Cott, *Grounding*, ch. 4.

118. *Equal Rights*, 28 July 1923, p. 188; 1 September 1923, 'Power is the best protection'; 20 October 1923, p. 286; and in Lillie Devereux Blake Papers, SSC, Folder 5, Address of President. Need of a Legislative League to give women equal rights in the states, and Folder 7, Equality in the United States, and the foremothers of the NWP and the need for the ERA. Becker, *Origins*, chs 4–5, on the NWP's work at home and abroad.

119. *Equal Rights*, 20 October 1923, p. 285; Becker, *Origins*, chs 6–7; Cott, *Grounding*, ch. 4.

120. See in Consumers' League of Connecticut Records, SL, vol. 5, Program of the Industrial Conference, Hartford, Conn., 15 October, 1926; Folder 13, Report of the Directors' Meeting, Center Church House, Hartford, 15 October 1926.

121. See in National Women's Trade Union League of America Records, SL, Box 3, Folder 41, Legislation: Equal rights pamphlets, *c.*1920–25: letter of Elizabeth Christman to Mary Anderson, 28 Nov. 1923; 'Protective legislation in danger' (November 1922), pp. 1–2; *New York Times*, 20 January 1924, 'Working women's case against "equal rights"'; editorial from Labor, 31 May 1924; article by Rose Schneiderman (no details) (source of first quotation); 'Why we should have labor laws for working women', by Maud Swartz, 1 April 1924, p. 4 (source of second quotation); Folder 40, Ethel M. Smith to Margaret Bondfield, 21 March 1926, pp. 1–2, and Maud Swartz and Elizabeth Christman to Belle Sherwin, 16 April 1926 (source of third quotation, p. 2). Also, in Consumers' League of Connecticut Records, SL, Box 2, Folder 9, Report of the Second Conference on Women in Industry, Called by the Chief of the Women's Bureau of the Federal Department of Labor, ... 1926, pp. 1–2. And see *Equal Rights*, 20 October 1923, article by Elizabeth G. Evans, p. 285; and letter to *New York Times* on the protective legislation question in Folder 12, Box 2, Mary Williams Dewson Papers, SL: see *ibid.*, Folder 19, Florence Kelley to Dewson, 2–17–24, for the view that the ERA would never be adopted. On the Woman's Party, see also Cott, *Grounding*, pp. 74 f.

122. See, for such a claim, *Equal Rights*, 28 July 1933, p. 188; Becker, *Origins*, p. 131.

123. Quoted in Barbrook and Bolt, *Power and Protest in American Life*, p. 200.

124. *Equal Rights*, 6 October 1923, leader on 'Why the argument' (source of first two quotations); 22 December 1923, p. 359; Blatch, *Challenging Years*, pp. 320–35 (third quotation from p. 327); 'The New Wisconsin Labor Code' by Professor J.M. Landis, Law School, Harvard University, pp. 3–4, on the way in which labour legislation was undermined (something he regretted), in Folder 40, Box 3, National Women's Trade Union of America Records, SL; Kessler-Harris, *Out to Work*, pp. 201 f.; Lemons, *The Woman Citizen*. IWSA was renamed the International Alliance of Women in 1926.

125. *Equal Rights*, 20 September 1922; Cott, *Grounding*, ch. 4, especially pp. 127, 135–6; Becker, *Origins*, pp. 40–1, ch. 3.

126. See Scott, *The Southern Lady*, p. 204; Chafe, *The American Woman*, pp. 29–30; see also Alberti, *Beyond Suffrage*, p. 101; Harrison, *Prudent Revolutionaries*, p. 1; Cott, *Grounding*, pp. 103–14.

127. See Elizabeth Israels Perry, *Belle Moskowitz: Feminine politics and the exercise of power in the age of Alfred E. Smith* (New York, Oxford University Press, 1987); in Sue S. White Papers, SL, 'Sue Shelton White by friends and associates' – letter from White to M. Dewson, 23 Nov. 1928, on women in southern politics; Box 2, Folder 18, clipping from the *Evening Star*, 8–21–31; Folder 22, letter of White to Mrs Howard, 8 Aug. 1924; Box 3, Folder 35, White to Mrs Jane Norman Smith, Chairman, National Woman's Party, NY, 15 Sept. 1928 (source of quotation), and letter from Eleanor Roosevelt to Governor Ross, Chairman of the Democratic National Committee, 28 March 1930; see also Folder 37; and Box 4, Folders 39 onwards, on White's work in the 1930s; Becker, *Origins*, pp. 99 f.

128. See in White Papers, 'Personal recollections', etc., letter from Mary Dewson, 11 Oct. 1858 (source of first and second quotations); and in Mary Williams Dewson Papers, SL: Box 1, Folder 1, letter of Feb. 1912 from Château Frontenac,

Quebec; Folder 3 on her career including 'An aid to the end', on her political activities, pp. 5–7, 11, 123–4 (source of the other quotations); and Box 2, Folders 11–12, 17 on her career. See also Susan Ware, *Partner and I: Molly Dewson, feminism, and New Deal politics* (New Haven, CT, Yale University Press, 1987).

129. See speech on the Women's City Club, Box 5, Speeches Folder, Ethel Eyer Valentine Dreier Papers, SSC.

130. Ida Tarbell, 'Is woman's suffrage a failure?', *Good Housekeeping*, October 1924, Folder 3, Ida Tarbell Collection, SSC.

131. Letter by Ethel Dreier, 6 March 1920, Box 1, Miscellaneous Folder, Ethel Eyer Valentine Dreier Papers, SSC.

132. Women in State Legislatures, report by Woman's Research Foundation, Folder 13, Box 1, Sue S. White Papers, SL; Chafe, *The American Woman*, p. 38.

133. Sochen, *Movers and Shakers*, pp. 106–12, 123–45, on radical feminists and feminist writers; Chafe, *The American Woman*, p. 58, on women in the professions.

134. See, for instance, W.E.B. DuBois, *The Education of Black People: Ten critiques, 1906–1960* (ed. Herbert Aptheker, Amherst, University of Massachusetts Press, 1973), pp. 66–7; Raymond Wolters, *The New Negro on Campus: Black college rebellions of the 1920s* (Princeton, NJ, Princeton University Press, 1975), p. 88.

135. Nancy Cox-McCormack Cushman to Margaret Grierson, 3 May 1963, Box 4, Cushman Papers, SSC.

136. 'Is woman's suffrage a failure?'

137. Cox-McCormack Cushman to Grierson.

138. Woman's National Convention for Law Enforcement, 1924, pp. 10, 25, 33, 76–9, in Folder 69, Somerville–Howorth Papers, SL.

139. Sochen, *Movers and Shakers*, p. 155, notes Eleanor Roosevelt's judgement that women's chief political contribution was social welfare; Lemons, *The Woman Citizen, passim*; Chafe, *The American Woman*, pp. 39–45; Cott, *Grounding*, 'Conclusion'; Gordon, *Winning*, ch. 10; Linda Gordon, 'Social insurance and Public Assistance', *American Historical Review*, vol. 97, no. 1, Feb. 1992, pp. 26–50.

140. Strachey, *The Cause*, pp. 370–4, on the economic impact on women of the war's end, and the pressure this put on the women's organisations; Pugh, *Women and the Women's Movement*, pp. 29–30, 43; Mrs H.M. Swanwick to Mrs Fawcett, 19 Dec. 1917, in Autograph Letter Collection, FL; and in *ibid.*, 'To the women electors of Great Britain and Ireland. A message from the Prime Minister', 28 Feb. 1918.

141. Jane Lewis, 'Beyond suffrage: English feminism in the 1920s', *The Maryland Historian*, vol. 7, Spring 1975, p. 3.

142. Rosanna Ledbetter, *A History of the Malthusian League, 1877–1927* (Columbus, Ohio State University Press, 1976), pp. 206–19; see Ruth Hall, *Marie Stopes: A biography* (London, Virago, 1978), p. 150, for the figure on the incidence of venereal disease; Cate Haste, *Rules of Desire: Sex in Britain: World War I to the present* (London, Chatto & Windus, 1992), ch. 3, on the complex wartime mixture of change and continuity; Dyhouse, *Feminism and the Family*, pp. 166 f.

143. Hall, *Marie Stopes*, chs 1–7; p. 185, on the two women's 'moments of vision'.

144. Hall, *Marie Stopes*, pp. 109–16.

145. Lewis, *The Politics of Motherhood*, p. 202; see also Haste, *Rules of Desire*, pp. 58 f.

146. Mary Breed and Edith How-Martyn (a suffragist and birth control activist), *The Birth Control Movement in England* (London, John Bale, Sons & Danielson, Ltd, 1930), p. 14, quoted in Ledbetter, *A History of the Malthusian League*, p. 219.

147. Hall, *Marie Stopes*, pp. 134–6; Stopes, though strongly attracted to women, had no sympathy for lesbianism: see pp. 37–9, 78–9, 187.

148. Hall, *Marie Stopes*, chs 8–9; on Stopes's idiosyncratic religious beliefs and battles with Catholic critics, see, for instance, pp. 199, 260–6; Ledbetter, *A History of the Malthusian League*, p. 220; Fryer, *The Birth Controllers*, pp. 226–7.

149. Lewis, *The Politics of Motherhood*, pp. 205–11; Hall, *Marie Stopes*, pp. 173–6, 180–2, 187 (Stopes, when setting up her clinic, guaranteed not to perform abortions – Sanger was rather more sympathetic: see Reed, *The Birth Control Movement*, pp. 118–19 – but neither could afford to encourage the suspicion that birth control facilities provided a cover for abortion), 189–90, 242, 268 (on Stopes's exaggerated claims for the diaphragm her clinic used: Hall points out that its follow-up procedures were inadequate); see Fryer, *The Birth Controllers*, pp. 230–2 on Catholic opposition to Stopes.

150. Ledbetter, *A History of the Malthusian League*, pp. 221–2 (source of quotations); Hall, *Marie Stopes*, pp. 267–8, 274; Strachey, *The Cause*, p. 391; Fryer, *The Birth Controllers*, p. 233, ch. 22 (figure regarding women treated from p. 256); Rowbotham, *A New World for Women*, Sections 2–4.

151. Fryer, *The Birth Controllers*, p. 230, see also ch. 21, pp. 256–69; David Doughan, *Lobbying for Liberation: British feminism, 1918–1968* (London, City of London Polytechnic, 1980), pp. 8–9.

152. Lewis, *The Politics of Motherhood*, p. 214; Haste, *Rules of Desire*, pp. 64–9; Hall, *Marie Stopes*, p. 269; Ledbetter, *A History of the Malthusian League*, pp. 228–9; Alberti, *Beyond Suffrage*, pp. 105–12, 119–25.

153. Gordon, *Woman's Body, Woman's Right*, p. 194; Weeks, *Sex, Politics and Society*, p. 116; for a discussion of the earlier importance of women's support networks, see Blanche Wiesen Cook, 'Female support networks and political activism: Lillian Wald, Chrystal Eastman, Emma Goldman', originally published in *Chrysalis*, 1977, reprinted in Linda K. Kerber and Jane De Hart Mathews (eds), *Women's America: Refocusing the past* (New York, Oxford University Press, 1987), pp. 273–94; Jeffreys, *The Spinster and Her Enemies*, pp. 121–7; Smith-Rosenberg, *Disorderly Conduct*, pp. 281, 287–94; Cott, *Grounding*, pp. 161–2; Susan J. Leonardi, *Dangerous by Degrees* (New Brunswick, NJ, Rutgers University Press, 1989).

154. Weeks, *Sex, Politics and Society*, pp. 105–6, 116–17 (quotation from p. 105); Jeffreys, *The Spinster and Her Enemies*, pp. 113–15; Haste, *Rules of Desire*, pp. 70–8, 84–8.

155. Weeks, *Sex, Politics and Society*, p. 116; Cook, 'Female support networks', pp. 279, 285; Alberti, *Beyond Suffrage*, pp. 112–16; Smith-Rosenberg, *Disorderly Conduct*.

156. Jeffreys, *The Spinster and Her Enemies*, p. 155, ch. 9; Smith-Rosenberg, *Disorderly Conduct*, pp. 275 f.

157. Lewis, 'Beyond suffrage'.

158. Doughan, *Lobbying for Liberation*, p. 5; Alberti, *Beyond Suffrage*, pp. 91–2, ch. 6; Pugh, *Women and the Women's Movement*, chs 3, 4; Harrison, *Prudent Revolutionaries*, *passim*; letter of Mrs Mary Ogilvie Gordon to Mrs M. Lees, 12 Jan. 1926, on the National Women Citizens' Association, Autograph Letter Collection, FL.

159. Rosen, *Rise Up, Women!*, pp. 266–9; article on the Women's Party in the *Daily Sketch*, 7 February 1919, in Autograph Letter Collection, FL; Pugh, *Women and the Women's Movement*, pp. 44–50, 66–71; Doughan, *Lobbying for Liberation*, pp. 4–5.

160. Lewis, 'Beyond suffrage', pp. 2–3; Pugh, *Women and the Women's Movement*, pp. 510–12; Mary Stocks, *Eleanor Rathbone* (London, Victor Gollancz, 1949); Alberti, *Beyond Suffrage*, ch. 6; Harrison, *Prudent Revolutionaries*, ch. 4.

161. Strachey, *The Cause*, pp. 375–85 (quotations from pp. 381, 384); Lewis, 'Beyond suffrage', p. 15; Alberti, *Beyond Suffrage*, ch. 8; Pugh, *Women and the Women's Movement*, pp. 66, 103–7; D. Stetson, *A Woman's Issue* (Westport, CT, Greenwood Press, 1982); C.A. Miller, 'Lobbying the Leagues, PhD, Oxford University, 1992.

162. Letter from Philippa Strachey to Mrs Fawcett, 11 Sept. 1920, on women MP's, Autograph Letter Collection, FL; Strachey, *The Cause*, pp. 384–5; Alberti, *Beyond Suffrage*, pp. 139, 147, 159–63, 184–5, 219; Harrison, *Prudent Revolutionaries*, pp. 306–7; Pugh, *Women and the Women's Movement*, pp. 52–66, 107 f.

163. Lewis, 'Beyond suffrage', pp. 5–6; Harrison, *Separate Spheres*, p. 244 (source of quotation); Banks, *Faces of Feminism*, pp. 163–79; Alberti, *Beyond Suffrage*, ch. 7; Harrison, *Prudent Revolutionaries*, p. 312; for Mrs Pethick Lawrence's encouragement at progress, see her letter of 21 March 1928 to Philippa Strachey, in Autograph Letter Collection, FL; Pugh, *Women and the Women's Movement*, pp. 236 f.

164. Jeffreys, *The Spinster and Her Enemies*, p. 134; Holton, *Feminism and Democracy*, p. 152; Dyhouse, *Feminism and the Family*, pp. 88 f.

165. Blatch, *Challenging Years*, pp. 333–4; Alberti, *Beyond Suffrage*, pp. 130–4, ch. 6; Harrison, *Prudent Revolutionaries*, pp. 104, 312 f.

166. Lewis, 'Beyond suffrage', pp. 8–12; Lewis, *The Politics of Motherhood, passim*; Alberti, *Beyond Suffrage*, pp. 125–30; on economic problems facing women, see speech by Miss P. Strachey, *c.*1920, Autograph Letter Collection, FL.

167. Lewis, 'Beyond suffrage', pp. 12–13; Alberti, *Beyond Suffrage*, pp. 84 f., 169, 174–80, 205–7, ch. 8; Becker, *Origins*, pp. 132–3.

168. Lewis, 'Beyond suffrage', p. 4; Jeffreys, *The Spinster and Her Enemies*, p. 162; Weeks, *Sex, Politics and Society*, p. 218; Alberti, *Beyond Suffrage*, pp. 116–20; Pugh, *Women and the Women's Movement*, pp. 247–8; Mort, *Dangerous Sexualities*, pp. 203 f.

169. Jeffreys, *The Spinster and Her Enemies*, p. 154.

170. Letter of Mary Dewson, 14 July 1958, Folder 19, Box 2, Mary Williams Dewson Papers, SL; Pugh, Preface.

171. Sheila Rowbotham, *Hidden From History* (London, Pluto Press, 1973), on postwar problems, especially relating to class. See Lewis, *The Politics of Motherhood*, ch. 6, on the efforts of labour women on behalf of women and children; Boone, *The Woman's Trade Union Leagues*, p. 402; Middleton (ed.), *Women in the Labour Movement*, pp. 84–93, 103–12, 137–45; Harrison, *Prudent Revolutionaries*, ch. 5; Alberti, *Beyond Suffrage*, pp. 90–6, 152, 159, 180 f., 219; Pugh, *Women and the Women's Movement*, Preface, and pp. 60, 64–6, 130–9.

172. Lewis, 'Beyond suffrage', p. 14; Harrison, *Prudent Revolutionaries*, quotation from p. 3; Pugh, *Women and the Women's Movement*, pp. 248 f.; Mary Stott, *Organisation Women: The story of the National Union of Townswomen's Guilds* (London, Heinemann, 1978); but see Susan Pederson, 'Gender, welfare, and citizenship in Britain during the Great War', *American Historical Review*, vol. 95, no. 4, Oct. 1990, pp. 1004–6.

Afterword

1. See, for instance, Mrs Fawcett's comment reported in *Women's Suffrage Journal*, 1 August 1884, p. 199; *The Reply: An Anti-Suffrage Magazine*, vol. 1, no. 1, May 1913,

Editorial; and Jane Marcus, 'Transatlantic sisterhood: labor and suffrage links in the letters of Elizabeth Robins and Emmeline Pankhurst', *Signs*, vol. 3, no. 3, Spring 1978, pp. 744–55.

2. A term used by Pugh, *Women and the Women's Movement*, p. 236.

3. Miss Grace E. Hadow to Miss P. Strachey, 5 May 1910, Autograph Letter Collection, FL; Gordon, *Women and the Labour Movement in Scotland*, pp. 235, 289.

4. See Olive Banks's *Becoming a Feminist: The social origins of 'first wave' feminism* (Hemel Hempstead, Harvester Wheatsheaf, 1990) for a profile of British feminist leaders during the nineteenth and early twentieth centuries.

5. See Griffith, *In Her Own Right*, pp. 210–13, on Mrs Stanton's difficulties with younger suffragists over her criticisms of Church authority in *The Woman's Bible* (1895).

6. See 'The new Wisconsin Labor Code', by Professor J.M. Landis, Dec. 1931, pp. 3–4, in Folder 40, Box 3, National Women's Trade Union League of America Records, SL; Gordon, *Women and the Labour Movement in Scotland*, p. 284.

7. See for instance, Thane, *The Foundations of the Welfare State*, pp. 98, 122–3; Jane Lewis, *Women's Welfare, Women's Rights* (London, Croom Helm, 1983).

8. Teresa Billington Greig to Christabel Pankhurst, 26.10.56, in Autograph Letter Collection, FL.

9. See, for instance, Phyllis Stock-Morton, 'Finding our own ways: different paths of women's history in the United States', in Offen, Pierson and Rendall (eds), *Writing Women's History*, pp. 65–8; Joan Scott, 'Deconstructing equality versus difference: or, the uses of poststructural theory for feminism', *Feminist Studies*, vol. 14, no. 1, 1988, pp. 33–50; Karen Offen, 'Defining feminism: a comparative historical approach', *Signs*, vol. 14, no. 1, 1988, pp. 119–57; Mary Poovey, 'Feminism and deconstruction', *Feminist Studies*, vol. 14, no. 1, 1988, pp. 51–65; Denise Riley, '*Am I That Name?': Feminism and the category of 'women' in history* (Basingstoke, Macmillan, 1988); Gisela Bock, 'Women's history and gender history: aspects of an international debate', *Gender and History*, vol. 1, no. 1, 1989, pp. 11–15; Marilyn Lake, 'The politics of respectability: identifying the masculinist context', *Historical Studies*, vol. 22, no. 86, 1986, pp. 116–31; David Morgan, 'Men made manifest: histories and masculinities', *Gender and History*, vol. 1, 1989, pp. 87–91; and the articles in Offen, Pierson and Rendall (eds), *Writing Women's History*, by Jane Rendall ' "Uneven developments": women's history, feminist history and gender history in Great Britain', pp. 48–54; and Gisela Bock, 'Challenging dichotomies: perspectives on women's history', pp. 1–23.

10. Harrison, *Prudent Revolutionaries*, p. 309, charts the coincidence of feminist booms and advances on the left, in Britain; see also his 'Women's suffrage at Westminister', pp. 87–91.

Index

KING ALFRED'S COLLEGE
LIBRARY